Materials purchased through a

"Clean Energy Choice Grant"

administered by the

"Renewable Energy Trust"

by local student Monica Morin

to achieve her

Girl Scout Gold Award

BERKSHIRE
ENCYCLOPEDIA OF SUSTAINABILITY
VOLUME 1

THE SPIRIT OF SUSTAINABILITY

Editor Willis Jenkins, *Assistant Editor* Whitney Bauman

Digital editions

Berkshire Encyclopedia of Sustainability is available through most major e-book and database services (please check with them for pricing).

For information, contact:
Berkshire Publishing Group LLC
120-122 Castle Street
Great Barrington, Massachusetts 01230-1506 U.S.A.
info@berkshirepublishing.com
Tel +1 413 528 0206
Fax +1 413 541 0076

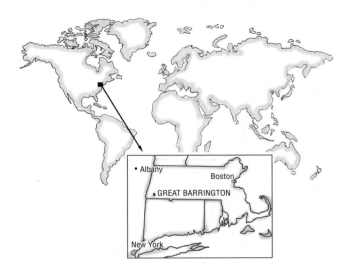

Library of Congress Cataloging-in-Publication Data
Berkshire encyclopedia of sustainability: the spirit of sustainability / edited by Willis Jenkins.
    p. cm.
  Includes bibliographical references and index.
  ISBN 978-1-933782-15-7 (v. 1 : alk. paper)
  1. Sustainable development.   2. Sustainable development—Moral and ethical aspects.
3. Sustainable development—Political aspects.   4. Sustainable development—Social aspects.   I. Jenkins, Willis.
  HC79.E5B4576 2010
  338.9'2703—dc22   2009035114

Editors

Editor
Willis Jenkins
Yale Divinity School

Assistant Editor
Whitney Bauman
Florida International University

A Project of the Forum on Religion and Ecology
The Spirit of Sustainability was developed under the auspices of the Forum on Religion and Ecology (FORE) at Yale University, the largest international multireligious project of its kind. We are especially indebted to Forum coordinators (and *Spirit of Sustainability* contributors) Mary Evelyn Tucker and John Grim.

Advisory Board
Ray Anderson, *Interface, Inc.*; Lester Brown, *Earth Policy Institute*; Robert Costanza, *University of Vermont*; Luis Gomez-Echeverri, *United Nations Development Programme*; Daniel Kammen, *University of California, Berkeley*; Ashok Khosla, *Development Alternatives Group*; and Christine Loh, *Civic Exchange, Hong Kong*.

Production Staff

Project Coordinator
Bill Siever

Senior Editor
Mary Bagg

Copyeditors
Wendell Anderson
Linda Aspen-Baxter
Kathy Brock

Editorial Assistants
Ashley Winseck
Echo Bergquist

Design
Anna Myers

Printers
Thomson-Shore, Inc.

Image Credits

Front cover photo by Carl Kurtz.

Photo used with the *Publisher's Note* and the *Introduction* by Carl Kurtz.

Photos used at the beginning of each section:

A. *Rock cairn*, Shuke Yixuan

B. *Rose mallow*, Carl Kurtz

C. *False white indigo*, Carl Kurtz

D. *Common blue violet*, Carl Kurtz

E. *Great blue herons*, Carl Kurtz

F. *Prairie Fire*, Carl Kurtz

G. *White pelicans feeding*, Carl Kurtz

H. *Sweet coneflowers*, Carl Kurtz

I. *Bobolink*, Carl Kurtz

J. *Reflected light*, Carl Kurtz

L. *Bindweed*, Carl Kurtz

M. *Prune orchard near Santa Clara, California*, Oregon State University

N. *Kildeer*, Carl Kurtz

O. *Hepatica leaves*, Carl Kurtz

P. *Distant Berkshire hills*, Berkshire Publishing staff

R. *Common yellowthroat warbler*, Carl Kurtz

S. *Great Barrington nestled in the Berkshires*, Berkshire Publishing staff

T. *Mountains in northern New Mexico*, Library of Congress

U. *Mount Everett*, Berkshire Publishing staff

V. *Praekestolen, Geiranger Fjord, Norway*, Library of Congress.

W. *Yellowthroat female*, Carl Kurtz

Beetle, dragonfly, moth, and ladybug illustrations by Lydia Umney. Other illustrations courtesy of the Library of Congress and the New York Public Library.

Contents

List of Entries

List of Contributors

A

Aderibigbe, Ibigbolade S.
University of Georgia
Indigenous Traditions—Africa

Ahmed, A. Karim
National Council for Science and the Environment
Precautionary Principle

Allison, Elizabeth A.
University of California, Berkeley
Biodiversity
Forests

Anderson, E. N.
University of California, Riverside
Indigenous Traditions—Asia

Azaransky, Sarah
University of San Diego
Liberationist Thought
Politics

B

Barnhill, David Landis
University of Wisconsin, Oshkosh
Ecology, Deep
Ecology, Social

Bassett, Luke H.
Yale Divinity School
Ecovillages

Baugh, Tom
Independent scholar, Hidden Springs, North
   Carolina
Conservation Biology

Bauman, Whitney
Florida International University
Ecocentrism (co-author: Jenkins, Willis)
Ecological Footprint
Sikhism
White's Thesis

Bendik-Keymer, Jeremy
LeMoyne College
Development—Concepts and Considerations

Benzoni, Francisco
U.S. Fourth Circuit Court of Appeals
Utilitarianism

Berkes, Fikret
University of Manitoba
Indigenous Traditions—The Arctic

Bohannon, Richard
College of St. Benedict and St. John's University
Architecture
Christianity—Evangelical and Pentecostal

Bratton, Susan Power
Baylor University
Stewardship (co-author: Cook-Lindsay,
   Austin)

Bromberg, Gidon
EcoPeace / Friends of the Earth Middle East
Jordan River Project

Brown, Donald A.
Pennsylvania State University
Climate Change
Ethics, Global

C

Cannon, Jonathan Z.
University of Virginia School of Law
Law

Carpenter, Carol
Yale University
Ecology, Cultural (co-author: Dove, Michael)

Chapple, Christopher Key
Loyola Marymount University
Hinduism
Jainism
Sacrifice

Chryssavgis, John
Greek Orthodox Archdiocese of America
Christianity—Eastern Orthodox

Clark, Meghan
Saint Anselm College
Community

Clingerman, Forrest
Ohio Northern University
Sacred Texts
Theocentrism
Values

Conradie, Ernst M.
University of the Western Cape
Christianity—Mainline Protestant

Cook-Lindsay, Austin
Baylor University
Stewardship (co-author: Bratton, Susan Power)

Curtin, Deane
Gustavus Adolphus College
Nonviolence

D

Davison, Aidan
University of Tasmania
Technology

De Gruchy, Steve
University of KwaZulu-Natal
Development, Sustainable

Deane-Drummond, Celia
University of Chester
Wisdom Traditions

Denny, Frederick Mathewson
University of Colorado at Boulder, emeritus
Islam

Dove, Michael
Yale University
Ecology, Cultural (co-author: Carpenter, Carol)

E

Eaton, Heather
Saint Paul University
Feminist Thought

Eisenbise, Kathryn S.
Manchester College
Christianity—Anabaptist

F

Fagg, Lawrence W.
Catholic University of America
Time

Figueroa, Robert Melchior
University of North Texas
Ecology, Political
Racism

Fredericks, Sarah E.
University of North Texas
Agenda 21
Energy
Millennium Development Goals

Freyfogle, Eric T.
University of Illinois College of Law
Conservation

G

Globus, Robin
University of Florida
New Age Spirituality

Gonzales, Tirso
University of British Columbia Okanagan
Indigenous Traditions—South America (co-author:
    Gonzalez, Maria E.)

Gonzalez, Maria E.
University of Michigan
Indigenous Traditions—South America (co-author:
    Gonzales, Tirso)

Gorman, Antonia
Humane Society of the United States
Creation
Eschatology

Gorringe, T. J.
University of Exeter
Culture

Gottlieb, Roger S.
Worcester Polytechnic Institute
Ecocide
Spirit and Spirituality

Grim, John A.
Yale University
Cosmology
Indigenous and Traditional Peoples

Gudmarsdottir, Sigridur
Reykjavik Academy
Pilgrimage

H

Haag, James
Suffolk University
Anthropic Principle

Haluza-DeLay, Randolph
The King's University College (Alberta)
Globalization
Place

Handley, George
Brigham Young University
Mormonism

Harrington, Eileen M.
University of San Francisco
Nonprofit Organizations, Environmental
Unitarianism and Unitarian Universalism

Harris, Adrian
Faith, Spirituality and Social Change Project
Paganism and Neopaganism

Hart, John
Boston University
Christianity—Roman Catholic
Cosmic Commons
Sacrament

Hartman, Laura M.
Augustana College (Illinois)
Council of All Beings
Creation Spirituality
Property and Possessions

Harvey, Graham
The Open University
Nature Religions and Animism

Higgins, Luke B.
Drew University
Process Thought

Hobgood-Oster, Laura
Southwestern University
Animals

Holthaus, Gary
Island Institute; The Atheneum School
Subsistence

I

Ives, Christopher
Stonehill College
Buddhism

J

James, George A.
University of North Texas
Chipko Movement

Jantzi, Terrence
Eastern Mennonite University
Peace (co-author: Kishbaugh, Aaron)

Jenkins, Willis
Yale Divinity School
Anthropocentrism
Ecocentrism (co-author: Bauman,
    Whitney)
Ethics, Environmental
Nature
Sustainability Theory
Volume Introduction

Johnston, Lucas F.
Wake Forest University
International Commissions and Summits

K

Karlberg, Michael
Western Washington University
Bahá'í

Kearns, Laurel D.
Drew Theological School and University
Christianity—Society of Friends / Quakers
Fundamentalism
*National Religious Partnership for the
    Environment*
Wise Use Movement

Kirk-Duggan, Cheryl A.
Shaw University Divinity School
African Diasporan Religions

Kishbaugh, Aaron
Independent scholar, Singers Glen, Virginia
Peace (co-author: Jantzi, Terrence)

Kover, T. R.
Katholieke Universiteit Leuven
Hybridity
Order and Harmony

M

MacDonald, Mary N.
Le Moyne College
Indigenous Traditions—Oceania

Manning, Robert E.
University of Vermont
Tragedy of the Commons, The

Martin-Schramm, James B.
Luther College
Population

Mathewes, Charles
University of Virginia
God (co-author: Wayner, Chad)

Mathews, Freya
La Trobe University
Dualism

McAnally, Elizabeth
California Institute of Integral Studies
Earth Day

McDaniel, Jay
Hendrix College
Beauty
Meditation and Prayer
Simplicity and Asceticism

Mickey, Sam
California Institute of Integral Studies
Individualism

Minteer, Ben
Arizona State University
Pragmatism

Miyamoto, Yotaro
Kansai University
Shinto

Muers, Rachel
University of Leeds
Future Generations

Mukonyora, Isabel
Western Kentucky University
Green Belt Movement

N

Nelson, Melissa
San Francisco State University
Indigenous Traditions—North America

Newman, Julie
Yale University
Education

Norgaard, Richard
University of California, Berkeley
Economics

O

O'Brien, Kevin J.
Pacific Lutheran University
Ecology
Ethics, Communicative

Oelschlaeger, Max
Northern Arizona University
Wilderness

Oestigaard, Terje
University of Bergen
Water

Oh, Irene
George Washington University
Justice

P

Pogge, Thomas
Yale University
Poverty

Primavesi, Anne
University of London
Gaia

R

Raskin, Paul
Tellus Institute
Future

Rigby, Kate
Monash University
Language

Rockefeller, Steven
Earth Charter International Council
Earth Charter

Rolston, Holmes, III
Colorado State University
Dominion
Science, Religion, and Ecology

Rose, Deborah Bird
Macquarie University
Indigenous Traditions—Australia

S

Sanford, A. Whitney
University of Florida
Vegetarianism

Scheid, Daniel
Duquesne University
Common Good

Schweiker, William
University of Chicago Divinity School
Responsibility

Sellmann, James D.
University of Guam
Daoism

Sideris, Lisa
Indiana University
Evolution

Simmons, Frederick
Yale Divinity School
Sin and Evil

Sims, Michael D.
Independent scholar, Eugene, Oregon
Waste

Smith, David H.
Yale University
Bioethics

Spretnak, Charlene
California Institute of Integral Studies
Green Parties

T

Thompson, Paul B.
Michigan State University
Agriculture

Troster, Lawrence
GreenFaith
Judaism

Tucker, Mary Evelyn
Yale University
Confucianism
World Religions and Ecology

Tyman, Shannon
University of Oregon
Anthroposophy
Biophilia

V

Van Horn, Gavin
Southwestern University
Biocentrism

Van Saanen, Marisa B.
Yale Law School
World Bank

Van Wensveen, Louke
Academia Vitae
Virtues and Vices

Van Wieren, Gretel
Yale University
Restoration

W

Wallis, Robert
Richmond the American International University in
   London
Shamanism

Wayner, Chad
University of Virginia
Ethics, Natural Law
God (co-author: Mathewes, Charles)

Winter, Miriam Therese
Hartford Seminary
The Universe Story

Wirzba, Norman
Duke Divinity School
Agrarianism

Wissenburg, Marcel
Radboud University Nijmegen
Libertarianism

Worthy, Kenneth
Independent scholar, Berkeley, California
Ecopsychology

Berkshire Encyclopedia of Sustainability

Publisher's Note:
Spirit Launches *Sustainability*

This volume, *The Spirit of Sustainability*, is the first of ten volumes making up the *Berkshire Encyclopedia of Sustainability*, an endeavor designed to bring together—in a format accessible to students and the general public—everything we need to know about environmental sustainability. The list of volume titles on the facing page reveals the broad scope of the project; expert contributors working in many academic and professional fields across the globe bring to the work a comparative, cross-cultural approach. In the introduction to this first volume its editor, Willis Jenkins, explores the religious, philosophical, and ethical dimensions of the environmental challenges we face as a global community. This preface by the publisher discusses how *The Spirit of Sustainability* came to be the first volume in the series, how we plan to cover topics in the encyclopedia at large, and why we at Berkshire Publishing happened to take on such an ambitious effort.

As well as being Berkshire's founder and publisher, I am an environmental author (with titles ranging from the 1989 *Home Ecology* to my recent *The Armchair Environmentalist*). One of my priorities as a publisher has been to include environmental topics in all Berkshire publications—discussions of e-waste (in *Human–Computer Interaction*, for instance); an article about the environmental challenges posed by the 2008 Beijing Games (in *China Gold*, a book primarily devoted to Olympic history and China's role in it, and to individual athletes and sporting events); and (in *Libraries We Love*), an article about a Seattle library with a "green roof" designed to grow grasses and sedum that help reduce rainwater runoff.

Our projects, which emphasize interdisciplinary scholarship and present subjects from diverse perspectives, commonly lead to synergistic new efforts. Through *The Encyclopedia of World Environmental History*, published by Berkshire in 2003, and by attending American Society for Environmental History conferences, we got to know a wide group of scholars whose focus on the environment often came from personal concern about the world today.

The idea to look at how religious and spiritual influence shaped attitudes and policies about the environment, both positive and negative, came to us early on. Many people in the Green movement speak of strong connections to the Earth as a single living organism; contemporary pagans' sense of Earth as sacred, as well as their animist belief ("all that exists lives"), support an ethics of sustainability; indigenous peoples from the Arctic to the Andes have innately deep-seated bonds to their place on the land and in the universe, with cosmologies and creation myths deriving from an Earth Mother or other deities of nature—this is just a small sampling of traditions worldwide we knew we'd cover in this *Spirit* volume. Conservative Christianity in the United States, however, had long been known for its anti-environmentalist position. Despite (and perhaps because of) the huge controversy sparked by Lynn White's 1967 declaration in "The Historical Origins of Our Environmental Crisis"—that Christianity not only established a dualism of man and nature but insisted that God wills man to exploit nature for his proper ends—the Christian Right's position seemed alarmingly unshakable. (See the articles on "Dominion" and "White's Thesis.") But when leaders within mainstream churches began to consider new interpretations of the biblical admonition of stewardship, another topic we explore in this volume, shifting values over the next decades attracted the increasing attention of journalists. From about 2000 to 2006, Berkshire partnered with Routledge to produce a Religion & Society series, and we thus were attuned to how religious traditions and practices have developed within the context of a wider planetary or natural community. By the end of our collaboration with Routledge we had *The Encyclopedia of Sustainability* on our independent drawing board.

We realized that a series on environmental challenges—one that included perspectives from the worlds of business, law, politics, resource management, and research and measurement tactics, for instance—would not be complete without a volume on spiritual and religious traditions.

We then began a conversation with Mary Evelyn Tucker and John Grim, co-founders of the Forum on Religion and Ecology (FORE). (FORE originated at Harvard's Center for the Study of World Religions; the United Nations officially announced its formation at a press conference in October 1998.) Located currently at Yale University, the Forum works with the faculties of the School of Forestry and Environmental Studies, the Divinity School, the Department of Religious Studies, and the Center for Bioethics. FORE's network of scholars has been essential to the creation of this volume, and we hope the volume will be of value to the network.

In 2007, Mary Evelyn kindly arranged a discussion about our plans for this volume at a meeting of the American Academy of Religion in San Francisco; she then recommended Willis Jenkins of Yale Divinity School as the editor, with Whitney Bauman, an associate professor at Florida International University (and the editor of the Forum's e-newsletter), as assistant editor. Working with them, and with the Forum, was gratifying; it taught us how scholars handling abstract topics can nonetheless be extremely down-to-earth about getting a job done, and done well.

Although we originally scheduled *The Spirit of Sustainability* as Volume 3, and later as Volume 2, in the end it took final shape more quickly than the others. Some might see this as providential. Functioning in many ways as an introduction to the whole project, it focuses not solely on religious beliefs and the environment, an important area of increasing influence in the real world, but on the underlying values and perspectives that shape how we approach environmental problems and search for solutions.

Our *Sustainability* Goals

In mapping out topics and organizing the volumes of the *Berkshire Encyclopedia of Sustainability*, our goals were straightforward. We set out to: (1) increase general knowledge of sustainability; (2) provide subject-specific coverage that is not readily accessible outside the scientific or academic community; and (3) connect current research with the political, professional, and personal opportunities available to individuals and organizations. Our goals are also revolutionary. We want to help individuals, policy makers, and businesses change the world. We are not making pronouncements about the right paths to follow, but bringing together the best thinking and using the toolkit of a global encyclopedia publisher to organize and integrate information from different areas of study (water conservation, alternative energy, ecosystems, consumer products, for instance) into an abundance of short-form material that will be widely useful.

In 2004 Berkshire Publishing distributed a survey among librarians; we asked them to tick off the subjects they'd most like see covered in newly published works. Our list was expansive—Asian studies; China/Chinese history and culture; environmental issues; international relations; Latino studies; personal relations and communications; primary text resources; religion and society; sports; technology and society; terrorism and global security; world history; world theater, dance, or music—and included a number of topics that coincided with Berkshire projects already or soon to be underway. Although the environment was not a "hot" topic at that point, the librarians put "environmental issues" at the top of list. I was surprised. A lot of reference material on environmental issues appeared to be quite good. Why then would librarians be asking for more?

I came to the conclusion that existing books often did a great job of explaining the problems—species loss, air pollution, climate change, toxic chemicals in our homes—but included very little about solutions. We needed to develop instead a project about solutions, about a green future.

But what to call it? Encyclopedias generally have boring titles, for good reason—titles should be solid, clear, unmistakable. An "Encyclopedia of Environmental Issues" would be the "right" title, it seemed. But that did not convey the spirit of the project.

The word "sustainability" came to mind. At first I dismissed it as too vague, too ephemeral, too much an insider term. But it shouldn't be, I thought. Sustainability ought to be a concept everyone can grasp.

When no other sufficient title came to mind, we made our early announcements using the *Berkshire Encyclopedia of Sustainability*, and somehow it stuck despite concerns, questions, and comments from our widening network. Dan Vasey, one of the editors now working on Volume 4, expressed a worry echoed by others, that sustainability seems to mean entirely different things to different people. Some people asked whether the term was itself sustainable—meaning that ideas and terms sometimes surge then fade, and an encyclopedia should not peg itself to an idea that is not well established. Is "sustainability" a flash in the pan, they asked, an idea that will be seen as "so 2009"? Or is it a major societal shift, like the Industrial Revolution, that needs to be documented?

Dan also pointed out a fundamental problem inherent in the encyclopedia format, which "by segregating interconnected subjects," he wrote, "makes sustainability look easier than it is. The concern extends to my own recent contribution, Agriculture. I tried to be holistic, and the word limits allowed me to consider population, urban sprawl, and phosphorus resources, but the best I could do on energy was to note reliance on fossil fuels and pressures from biofuel production. If I were to take full account of those and other trends and proposals—that we allocate metal and cement to wind, solar, and hydro; use the generated power to run tractors and fertilizer factories; grow the cloth that now comes from petroleum; achieve consumer equity—and then draw a flow chart of competing resource demands, the result would look and sound less sanguine."

Another editor, Peter Whitehouse, commented on the need to make connections from volume to volume: "In medicine there is a tendency to compartmentalize ethics and hence marginalize moral conversations. Business, like ethics, is a word signifying a set of concepts and practices. 'Natural capitalism,' for example, is only a start at looking how we account for the world's resources. Developing 'sustainable value' is a key approach but the values underlying that creation are key in my view."

Fortunately, our hundreds of authors seem now to agree that the term "sustainability" is sufficiently broad and inclusive, that it provides a way to measure change, and it makes connections between environmental issues and other global challenges.

By gathering the work of so many experts we also experienced something about how ideas go from being crazy to feasible, or from being farfetched to being commonly accepted. This shift is something blogs and newspaper articles can't capture, but an encyclopedia can. In effect we are taking a wide-angle snapshot here of something in an almost continual state of change, but the big picture—the panoply of ideas evolving to meet a complex, fast-changing, far-ranging set of global issues—is one we clearly need to see. Otherwise it's just too difficult

for those working in one part of an environmental field (whether ecosystems management, urban design, or bioremediation of toxic waste) to make broad connections and forge new collaborations. Our aim is to make it easier for a high school teacher, a small town financial manager, or a global executive, for example, to get a handle on the issues most relevant to their work and to the students, citizens, shareholders, and customers for whom they are responsible.

Designing *Sustainability*

Observation of the natural world has always informed and contributed to human design and aesthetics, even in cases where designers have chosen to create forms deliberately and sometimes aggressively "against" nature. In the modern world, human designs—and here a darker, more calculated meaning can underlie that term—impact the sustainability of our environment through a variety of areas and fields: product design, building design, town and regional planning, manufacturing and data management systems, and more.

Two "design challenges" confronted us with this project. Thoughts about our coverage came first: how should we ensure that design innovation and the ramifications of industrial and product design were fully explored in our different volumes? Our "appearance" came next: what should an *Encyclopedia of Sustainability* look like?

To our minds a print encyclopedia should be, in the words of William Morris, beautiful and useful. In other Berkshire encyclopedias we made photographs not only an essential element of the design but a supplementary teaching tool. For *Sustainability*, however, we were starting a series with one rather abstract subject, spirit, and two others, business and law, that don't easily lend themselves to visual enhancement. Although we used twenty-one different photographic images—one per letter group of entries—to enhance the title pages of the articles, photographs would not effectively add to the intellectual content of these first volumes. So we decided to use decorative elements with a "message." Our inspiration came from scientific illustration, which, in the days before photography became mainstream, conveyed to the general public an essential part of the discoveries being made about the natural word. Scientists were artists and artists were scientists—seeing the world afresh in a concerted effort to understand it and to organize knowledge about it. (This is similar to what happened in anatomical studies: drawing the human body was an essential part of understanding how it worked.)

For *The Spirit of Sustainability* we chose natural history as our theme: drawings (of a beetle, dragonfly, moth, and ladybug) by Lydia Umney, as well as other illustrations (creatures of the air and flora) from the archives of the Library of Congress and the New York Public Library. Subsequent volumes will feature other illustrations on relevant themes. In the science and regional volumes we'll turn to photographs more frequently, but readers can also access additional images and visual material online (www.thesustainabilityproject.com).

Our cover photograph by Carl Kurtz shows fireflies (*Pyractomena borealis*) on the Iowa prairie. We selected this image for the *Berkshire Encyclopedia of Sustainability* because it so vividly presents the beauty of a restored habitat and because it speaks volumes about the rich life that exists on our planet. It also has symbolic resonance. The myriad points of light remind us that a sustainable future depends on sparks of inspiration, innovation, and insight from people around the world.

Publishing Sustainably

At Berkshire we always ask ourselves how we can run our business in a way that will help preserve and even restore the planet. Publishing an encyclopedia devoted entirely to the idea (and the practice) of sustainability makes the challenge even more immediate. Using a "green" printer like Thomson-Shore and choosing the right paper, as we did for the *Berkshire Encyclopedia of China* (and are doing for the sustainability volumes), is only a first step. Submitting each volume for an Eco-Audit (on page xvi) sponsored by The Green Press Initiative, a nonprofit

organization with a mission to help those in the publishing industry conserve natural resources, is a second.

Many in the industry believe that depending more and more on the electronic world is a planet-friendly move. But reading and publishing online—as well as the virtually paperless editorial processes gradually adopted by sustainability-savvy publishers (Berkshire included)—are not carbon-free activities: data centers consume vast quantities of resources to keep the arrays of servers on which we depend running smoothly, twenty-four hours a day; e-waste and rare mineral extraction are other undesirable side effects of the paperless revolution. After chairing the first Green Data Centres conference in London in 2008, I came to realize that in some ways publishing on paper is a better choice than e-publishing. (We're doing both, trying to improve and streamline our digital and our "hardcopy" procedures.) Books that last, because of the paper they are printed on and the words they contain, fulfill an important concept of sustainability—the production of quality goods with a long life. Berkshire hopes to offset its carbon footprint (at least somewhat) by the knowledge that readers gain from the pages herein.

Other factors besides the physical printing of books contribute significantly to the carbon footprint industry-wide—for one, the supply chain and shipping methods by which books get to distributors, and finally to customers, are extremely inefficient and costly. (Volume 2, *The Business of Sustainability*, offers a substantial contribution to this discussion.) We are learning about our subject as we live it, and have the privilege of doing so with an extraordinary roster of sustainability experts and professionals.

Karen Christensen
Great Barrington, Massachusetts

Introduction:
The Spirit of Sustainability

Religions, philosophies, and ethics have shaped the cultural worlds in which we live, and continue to construct how we interpret and respond to social problems. The social and ecological imperatives of sustainability pose complex and comprehensive challenges to cultures and global society. Interpreting those challenges well requires understanding the moral traditions of the world, ancient and emerging. Building effective responses to those challenges requires learning how to engage with their moral resources, converse with their participants, and imagine new cultural possibilities. *The Spirit of Sustainability*, the first of ten volumes that will comprise the *Berkshire Encyclopedia of Sustainability*, intends to help readers identify and begin to explore the moral dimensions of sustainability.

Within these pages scholars from many disciplines introduce and explain key concepts, major traditions, and significant practices relevant to thinking about sustainability. The contributors cover topics that range widely across cultures and traditions, presenting readers with a lexicon of available and diverse vocabularies of sustainability. It is not, however, the lexicon of a shared discourse. Because these authors work from multiple academic fields and represent various traditions, they have differing and sometimes competing views; sustainability indeed absorbs disparate ideas, values, and projects, many of which vie for inclusion in contemporary thought and public conversation. This volume therefore offers a pluralist selection of articles related to one another by their significance for sustainability—a pluralist and contested concept in itself.

Rather than impose a master definition of the term "sustainability," we invited contributors to explain how their topic matters for making sense of sustainability's ambiguity and multiplicity. Some articles explore practices that may help interpret what sustainable living means; some enumerate goals that sustainability must include. Others introduce moral traditions or interpretive frameworks that can help us reason through the combined challenge of meeting those goals. A number of articles charge us with examining received notions of sustainability, or ask us to consider how sustainability challenges received notions of other social goals.

So while unavoidably partial, this volume represents the depth and breadth of the basic question at hand: what must we sustain? *The Spirit of Sustainability* invites students, general readers, scholars, and professionals to reflect on sustainability as a moral problem. Sometimes we avoid or truncate moral issues in sustainability discussions and—seeking the least controversial, most feasible steps forward—restrict ourselves to talk of market policies, political strategies, and technological possibilities. But deciding what we can and must sustain finally confronts the collective moral capacities of humanity. It tests what we might call the human spirit.

Sustainability as Moral Challenge

Encouraging contributors to reflect on morality and explore the realm of spirit may strike some as inviting trouble, more trouble than it is worth. Religion and ethics present perennial difficulties to public discussion—difficulties compounded when the public is global in extent. Debates over the good, let alone divine will or cosmic destiny, can easily divide pluralist cultures and frustrate collective responsibility. Indeed, liberal societies confront their social challenges first through existing market, political, and technological systems, in part because they want to avoid destabilizing moral debates.

But the challenge of sustainability begs for an evaluation of those systems. Consider again the basic question: what must we sustain? It arises because humanity's organization of economic, political, and technological systems has begun to threaten the ecological systems on which they rely. The root concept of sustainability refers to the ability of an activity to endure without undermining the conditions on which it depends. A related series of ecological and social problems—like biodiversity loss, demographic instability, toxic pollution, and climate change—indicate that the human endeavor may be undermining the conditions of its own endurance. Even a modest prudence suggests that we ask why, and what must be done to change things.

Sustainability presents an odd sort of challenge for global society, at once minimal and comprehensive. It asks us to consider the prospects for a merely decent survival of the human species, but by doing so it raises issues about the value of nonhuman life forms, the goals of economies, the form of humanity's presence on Earth, and the kind of futures we want to make possible. As we begin to consider what we should sustain, we are eventually forced to reflect on what sustains us. On what do human cultures and economies depend? How do human and ecological systems relate? What are the conditions for the human spirit?

There is a paradoxical depth to these questions. Although they inquire about the moral minimum of a decent survival, answering them invites reflection on the totality of our dependency and relations. As sustainability confronts political societies with decisions about how to protect what sustains us, it pushes sweeping moral questions into public visibility. Ethical frameworks and religious traditions can help foster civic debate about problems that call into question the trajectory of our economic, political, and technological systems.

Invoking morality and exploring religious traditions may in fact empower responses to overwhelming challenges. Faced with difficult choices about reform, societies may be tempted to embrace the easier supposition that history affords us no alternative—that markets are shaped by ungovernable forces, governments by inexorable tendencies of power, and cultures by inevitable technological progress. Globalization is sometimes presented this way. Perhaps the chief contribution we can make to "global ethics" is to refuse such suppositions, to insist that we can create some global institutions of governance based on shared values and commitments.

Presenting sustainability as a moral problem accomplishes something similar. It affirms the possibility that, through dialogue and deliberation, we can find alternatives to our present systems and that, doing so, we can resist reductionist interpretations of complex threats to our humanity. Treating sustainability as a moral problem

lets us consider the possibility that our economic, political, and technological systems might work differently and better, encouraging us to imagine how we can inclusively integrate several kinds of sustaining goods. What cultural commitments would it take to harmonize economic health, ecological integrity, social equity, and fairness to the future?

The Spirit of Sustainability provides resources for engaging those questions, understanding their context, and beginning to formulate workable answers. By introducing the question of sustainability in multiple moral perspectives, the volume also helps keep the concept of sustainability pragmatic: presenting the basic challenge sustainability poses to many cultures, traditions, and systems produces a common arena of discussion across many social worlds. This volume helps develop sustainability as a bridging or integrative rubric capable of describing shared moral jeopardy, of organizing social problems, and of gathering cultural resources for response. (For further discussion see Willis Jenkins's "Sustainability Theory" herein.)

Spirit: Exploring Religion, Culture, and Ecology

Any resource with encyclopedic ambitions will inevitably omit relevant topics; for just this one volume in a wider series on sustainability, we have had to select from an extensive range of possible articles. Our intention, however, was not to provide exhaustive coverage but to offer representative and introductory resources that will point readers to further connections and invite deeper examination of related topics. Many articles provide perspective for exploring other volumes of the *Berkshire Encyclopedia of Sustainability*. Most also suggest additional sources for study or contemplation.

The 147 articles here cover significant ground in philosophical, social, and environmental ethics, with emphasis on approaches to cultural critique and social change. Among these entries we have created (for several reasons) a special focus on religious traditions, practices, and concepts. First, interpreting our contemporary cultural context and its political possibilities requires an understanding of religious discourse; some of the obstacles to social change may have roots in religious values, while some of the paths to reform may involve spiritual dimensions. Second, for many people a full answer about sustenance must involve some reach toward depths typically described as religious—toward beauty, mystery, spirit, love, faith, or God.

Third, and most importantly, considering sustainability as a moral problem raises both basic and overarching questions; religious traditions have developed moral frameworks for thinking them through. A familiarity with religious, spiritual, and cultural traditions can help us engage the complexity and depth of sustainability challenges. This volume collects many of the most important resources for readers to consult as they begin exploring sustainability as a moral issue.

The burgeoning work in the field of Religion and Ecology, in which scholars have been exploring, evaluating, and revising the relationships of religion, culture, and environments, has provided an important arena for discussions of the spirit of sustainability. Indeed this volume was produced in collaboration with the Forum on Religion and Ecology (FORE), and its contributors include many participants from FORE events and publications. See, for example, Mary Evelyn Tucker's "Global Religious Traditions," and Frederick Mathewson Denny's "Islam," which expands his initial scope in a FORE publication to include issues of water management from the legal, economic, and ethical perspectives of the Islamic world. In addition, many of the quotations found throughout the volume have been made available by FORE.

This volume also moves beyond the usual discussions of religion and ecological change by considering the broader range of moral issues that must be raised in sustainability debates. Confronting sustainability requires not only ecological thinking but practical deliberations over such issues as the economic common good amidst global poverty, a stable international peace in the face of nuclear weapons, public health despite new anthropogenic risks, and social justice in fairness to future generations. Many contributors focus primarily on ecological dimensions of religious and ethical frameworks, likely because environmental commitments are the most underdeveloped topics or the arena in which the most significant change has been happening. But sustainability includes dimensions of exploration still more encompassing and interdisciplinary.

Not only must we investigate how religious and spiritual traditions think about their environments, or how nature provokes spirituality, but how we can meet the integrative, comprehensive challenges of sustainability with the civic and moral resources available to us.

There is no single definition of religion at work here, neither of culture, spirituality, or ethics. The variety of contributors and the diversity of topics encompass many notions of religion and culture. Several contributors on indigenous traditions make a point of not distinguishing between religion and culture, indicating that some Western categories of distinction may need rethinking. The normative orientation of this volume—relating cultural topics to sustainability as a moral problem—assumes broadly inclusive views of the relevant topics.

Finally, a word must be said about "spirit." The title of this volume employs a term now used within many notions of the religious, and yet also in order to escape from religious categories or institutions. In other contexts "spirit" may refer to the intelligence of humanity, the living force of animals, the vitality of life, the power of history, the breath of divinity, or the wisdom of the cosmos. Wildly variant, all those meanings converge in asserting that the global challenge of sustainability cannot be reduced to political calculation or market exercise. Facing sustainability as a moral problem requires a spirit of sustainability; it requires summoning our intelligence, acting with purpose, companioning with life and learning anew the economy of wisdom.

Absorptive and inclusive, "spirit" seems an apt metaphor to indicate the multi-disciplinary, pluralist, and many-cultured lexicon of moral resources the reader will find here. It also suggests liveliness, and the reader will find that—unlike staid reference works summarizing objective knowledge—many contributors explain their topics animated by a sense of common purpose. Pluralist and purposeful, multivalent and animated, spirit is a sustaining metaphor.

Willis Jenkins
New Haven, Connecticut

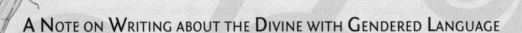

A Note on Writing about the Divine with Gendered Language

Referring to God is always a perilous linguistic activity—some monotheistic traditions in fact make that peril a key point. In a volume covering many vocabularies of the divine, mundane functions of language—like pronouns—can carry unwanted ideological baggage. They can make it seem like God is a man, *one English-speaking man* no less, which can raise objections for all sorts of reasons. In interfaith context, our language can lead us not only into gender trouble but number trouble.

Some scholars still use masculine pronouns as the default neutral, but for many readers that can make it seem as if the writing is emphasizing a masculine image of God. Other scholars might alternate between masculine pronouns in one paragraph and feminine ones in the next. Some even experiment with "hir" and "ze" as hybrids of his/her and she/he. In our view such contrivances start to trip up the reader, but they do show that talk about the divine stresses language, especially when cultural systems are under criticism for their complicity in sexism. Acknowledging what can be called a sexist patrimony (!)

of language, many scholars use feminine pronouns as the default, in order to interrupt the dominant gendered images they produce. We may not have any gender-appropriate language for God.

So in this volume we have encouraged authors to avoid using pronouns altogether. The effect can be clunky, for example, in a sentence like "God's got the whole world in God's hands," but one can take theological consolation in that it *should* be a little awkward to try to talk about the divine.

Beyond that encouragement, however, we have let the authors' prose stand as it appears, assuming that they are representing their tradition or subject with their language use. The divine in a tradition may be plural, immanent, transcendent, nonpersonal, specifically male, specifically female, androgynous, or any combination of those. Authors use the names and pronouns they think most appropriate to their topic or tradition.

WILLIS JENKINS

African Diasporan Religions

After West Africans were transported as enslaved persons across the Atlantic, African diasporan religions evolved in the Americas. Focusing on a Supreme Being recognized as the creator of all on Earth, and a community comprising all that is creation, the beliefs of these religions encourage practices of sustainable living. African American churches have been especially central to fostering a stewardship model to support God's provisions.

Traditional African worldviews are inherently religious, focusing on a Creator God, spirits, ruling powers, and human beings; some African indigenous religions have a pantheon of Gods. African religious thought is not monolithic, but varied, connecting the metaphysical and nonphysical sphere to the physical. Many Africans trafficked to the Americas practiced indigenous religion, Christianity, or Islam. When the African diaspora took place over nearly four centuries, transporting millions of West Africans in slave trade across the Atlantic to the Americas and the Caribbean islands, these scattered African populations managed to retain their customs, cultural identities, and belief systems as they struggled to adapt to new surroundings that were often hostile to (or derisive of) African philosophies and spirituality. African diasporan religions in these regions—while still drawing primarily on their indigenous traditions, a belief in a Supreme Being, and the importance of community—continued to be over the centuries influenced by Islam, Catholicism, Protestantism, and Pentecostalism, as well as traditions that emphasized divination and healing. In the twentieth century, Rastafarianism developed with a sociopolitical agenda. African Americans in the United States experienced a diaspora of their own after slavery was abolished and blacks were able to migrate to areas other than the South; a diaspora occurred to another extent after desegregation. How the philosophy and practices of African American faith communities and black churches—historically at the core of empowerment and political action—pertain to sustainable ways of living in the twenty-first century is the primary focus of this article.

Views of sustainability within African diasporan religions in general involve holistic, spirituality-based ecological strategies, processes, and attitudes concerning the viability, health, wellness, healing, and covenantal stewardship of God-given resources—humanity, natural resources, and all creation—in a world in which its adherents have been taunted by systemic racism, sexism, and class oppression. Stewardship, a model for a liberating, committed way of living, holds one accountable for the just, equitable, fiscally responsible, and loving use of God's provisions. Within this ethos, a heightened awareness of responsible use of resources prompts us to configure our human activity in a way that will ensure that life with complex diversity continues across all of our lived environments.

African Americans and the Environment

African American life and moral views—shaped by politics, social action, and spirituality—determine unique environmental concerns that often differ from European American views. Black churches, historically at the center of empowerment and political action, remain the major independent black institutions of influence for most African Americans. African philosophy (which lacks boundaries between sacred and secular), a legacy of racial injustice, and the historical, institutional black church contribute to the twenty-first-century black church "reality" as it functions today. Some faith communities or sects have been more separatist and not engaged in politics; some have a more otherworldly, apolitical, conservative stance. But by embracing a traditional African worldview of communalism and a social morality instilled by the minister and the church tenets themselves, faith community embody a sense of divine protection, empowerment, and hope.

Alienation from North American Land

Mark Stoll—the editor with Dianne G. Glave of *To Love the Wind and Rain* (Glave and Stoll, 2006), a work that displaces the old colonialist studies of African Americans and examines how these blacks have historically conceived, utilized, and managed to survive in their environmental space, both rural and urban—posits that enslavement helped alienate Africans from the land of North America. Even with the symbolic metaphorical Exodus motif and Promised Land, African Americans have not had mythic connections to land, as many European Americans have had with Plymouth Rock, Stone Mountain, or Yosemite Valley. Symbolic import has not fueled a commitment to veneration or preservation, making human beings, not nature, monumental in black sacred history, and signaling the wilderness Moses, not Adam and Eve in paradise. Moses and the children of Israel wandered through the wilderness and experienced enslavement, followed by divine liberation. Having been plucked from Africa, African diasporan peoples could not possibly experience a sense of paradise in the Americas, even though most African diasporan Christians see Adam and Eve as the first humans. With African American migration from the rural South to the North, Midwest, and West—from the post–Civil War period, during World War II, and then postdesegregation—came declining activism in some arenas, although blacks' beliefs in a system of social morality continued to exist.

Components essential to African Americans' perceptions and experiences of sustainability closely relate to class, ethnicity, gender, and race—the factors that have shaped where and how African Americans have been forced to live, work, and play: Blacks have had, for example, limited access to certain geographic areas; they have been subject to peonage (the use of laborers bound in servitude) and relegated to segregated public spaces. Thus environmental justice concerns the liberation of black people—a focus involving a relationship with the environment and depending on the sociopolitics surrounding it—where community is broadly cast, pursuit of collective rights important, and environment connected to production and work. Ironically, while often denied access to recreation in parks, forests, and the wilderness, many African Americans have appreciated the health and spiritual benefits of healing and wholesomeness from working and being out of doors.

Although the effect of desegregation has been far less detrimental to the environment than the larger movement of industrialization in the United States and globalization itself, the increasing migration of African American populations to so-called more liberal havens or neighborhoods has often resulted in ecological injustice, actions, beliefs, and other processes antithetical to sustainability. Heightened greed and use of the land without "giving anything back" have predominated in many instances of integration, especially in urban areas. With migration and superhighways moving populations of all classes and races in all directions, people have become disconnected from the land and prone to general disregard for the planet; the effect is exacerbated for most African Americans who were stolen from African and forced into enslavement, to have to be uprooted yet again when they already felt at odds with their new landscape. While many immigrant populations also relate to such estrangement, systemic, oppressive racism has historically stacked the deck (and continues to do so) against healthy, sustainable African diasporan communities. Detrimental to African diasporan environmental justice are the urban realities of middle-class flight, spiritual blight, industrial pollution, and alienation in neighborhoods where disconnectedness leads to self-absorption. Edicts like "No Child Left Behind," which force teachers to teach students to pass standardize exams, further dampen African diasporan children's capacity to learn and be competitive; such programs, along with cultural insensitivity, the belief that black children cannot perform well, and unfair sentencing that places more and more poor black youth in jail, ultimately create a pipe line from cradle to prison.

The Poverty Factor

A significant threat to sustainability within any group, particularly African peoples, is poverty. Some biblical proverbial traits and behaviors seen as the root causes of the poverty that threatens family and community include immoral sexual behavior, laziness, stinginess, wasting time and land, failure to change, injustice, idle talk, oppression, procrastination, inattentiveness, hastiness, lack of compassion, luxurious living, unwise borrowing, exploiting people, addictions and uncontrolled appetites, poor-on-poor oppression, corrupt government, greediness, pride, and disdain; often these characteristics are unfairly projected onto a poor population, especially one of color. Therefore, too often, a community's racial makeup can be the single variable that best predicts placing commercial hazardous waste facilities in their midst. Classism and racism ensure that too many poor and people of color experience greater environmental and health risks than the general population; they have less access for clean drinking water, clean air, parks, playgrounds, or safe working environments. The death to holistic life, especially in places like Cancer Alley on the Gulf Coast, where industry involving the use of toxins is rife, has resulted in deep losses of self, family, employment, space, place, communities, and land—a predicament often forged by spiritual dis-ease as well as physical sickness caused by pollution.

Sustainability, Harmony, Stewardship—and the Black Church

A tenet of African diasporan religion, as it has evolved into the institution of the black church, holds that as people focus on the right relationship with God, significantly they are to be in right relationship with the Earth. To affect sustainability requires engendering hope, making stewardship programs part of the black church, and partnering with civic agencies that can help work for ecologically friendly public policies. (The term "black church" is used here to embody the numerous sects and communities in which African Americans express their faith.) In the church's worldview, imbalance and injustice are fueled by heterosexism, classism, racism, sexism, and other phobias that encourage people to make someone who is different from them "other." Church members are encouraged to love themselves and love the planet that provides them living space, and to resist greed and systemic oppressions. "The Earth is the Lord's and the fullness thereof" becomes a rubric where one is continuously in God's presence, God's sanctuary. Thus nature and created order must not be abused or harmed. Sustainability involves living a harmonious, balanced life where people are one with God, themselves, and their neighbors, appreciating the planet for the abundant life it affords. According to Karen Baker-Fletcher, a professor of theology, a profound reason for this deep appreciation of the Earth is that we humans are dust (earth) and spirit, where our birth and our death connect us to everything that happens in, on, from, and around the Earth. As divine creative freedom shapes and exudes beauty through all creation, being stewards or holding the Earth in trust requires immense responsibility.

Robert E. Franklin, author of *Another Day's Journey: Black Churches Confronting the American Crisis*, (1997), envisions this responsibility amidst a unique African diasporan spiritual ecology that cultivates hope and endorses public activism—comprised of multisensory worship; intimate communal prayer; cathartic expressivism engaged, for instance, in therapeutic singing; sociopolitically framed religious education; and prophetic, imaginative preaching. Such practices galvanize congregants toward God's reign and commonwealth. Related to these are complex,

diverse spiritualities—from Evangelical, Holiness, and Charismatic movements to social justice, Afrocentric, contemplative, and new age philosophies—that shape the black church social witness: pragmatic accommodationism, prophetic radicalism, redemptive nationalism, grassroots revivalism, and positive-thought materialism. With twenty-first century changes, including decline in denominationalism, growth of Word churches, growth of Afrocentrism, and contemporary life and communal challenges, the traditional African American church institution might well need to assess how its ministries can effectively help to sustain the spiritual survival of its people as well the planet. Fundamental to sustainability is embracing a worldview that appreciates and connects God with all creation, environment, rituals, stewardship, community, and environmental justice, with a keen awareness of who we are and who God is.

African diasporan religions see the lack of awareness about who we are as a result of disconnecting from the land and ultimately from ourselves, each other, from spirit, and from God. Possessions and status become more important than relationships and the Earth. If our relationship with God dictates our lives, and if God is the generator of all creation, creation is to be revered. Just as farmers rotate crops so that the land can renew itself, people too need to renew their appreciation, connections, and commitment to the total healing of humanity and all creation. The noted author Alice Walker invites us to plant a tree when someone does great harm to one we love.

Sustainability and Activism

Dianne D. Glave, co-editor of *To Love the Wind and Rain*, notes that many activists have used a Christian framework to shape their endeavors, especially following Martin Luther King's nonviolent protest. Thus black environmental liberation theology, mentioned earlier in the context of freeing black people from environmental racism, can work to protect African diasporan peoples from exposure to toxic sewage plants, landfills, garbage dumps, and auto mechanics' shops. Glave notes that levels of environmental racism on people of color inequitably have caused birth defects, stillbirths, miscarriages, cancer, and autoimmune and stress-related illnesses (Stoll and Glave 2006). Skewed biblical interpretations of dominion implying stewardship *over* rather than *for* the Earth have allowed abuse, the abandonment of fiduciary (trusting) responsibilities involved in making a covenant with God, and thus the lack of care and displacement of many sentient beings. Preservation and conversation of resources and wildlife must include all human beings and creation. This work envisions engaging a sociocultural, moral geography, where destruction of creation is wrong. Working with the National Council of Churches (NCC), many African American church leaders have focused on quality of life and health issues in the African American community. Often ministers provide substantial help when communities want to protest, educate about, and negotiate with companies engaged in environmental racism in the effort to alter such detrimental practices.

With heightened technology, increased population, deforestation, extinction of thousands of species each year, lowering water tables, and depletion of other natural resources, sustainability is a global issue. The prison industrial complex, drug trafficking, and bankrupt educational practices that teach for tests and stifle creativity threaten and deplete many human resources, not just those of African Americans or people of color. If these trends continue, human beings are in danger of becoming extinct, for the Earth will no longer be able to maintain life as we know it. Human activity has caused huge ecological imbalances: record heat waves, related hurricanes, tsunamis, reduced grain harvests, droughts, and increased greenhouse gases.

While African American churches have inherited for a tradition of engaging in public policy, the levels of participation have varied. Most activism has focused on racial injustice and black economic development, while welfare reform, social services, health care and reproductive rights, education reform, and criminal justice receive far less attention. Commitment of time, energy, and resources to produce effective lobbying that would address these issues remains unfulfilled and yet significant for sustainability.

In nineteenth-century Brazilian Candomblé, a spirit-possession religion of the African diaspora in Brazil, leaders worked to address the imbalances within physical, spiritual, sociopolitical, and ecological systems due to oppressions, based upon their understandings of how to address causes and cures for illness. Candomblé posits a quest for right relationships among human beings—and among human beings, the natural world, and spirits. Via the Shona peoples' Mutopo principle, the worldview framing the mobilization of spirit mediums for environmental protection, the deity cares about ecological and human well-being. Candomblé, imbued with a sense of rejuvenation, provided an alternative awareness of identity and a way of thinking about reality for the enslaved, which parallels the African American enslaved experience of a God who allows one to know and take care of oneself. Both religious practices allow for joy amidst resistance, as believers cultivate individual and collective identity in opposition to the imposed subordinate status from dominant society.

African diasporan ecojustice, and thus sustainability, can be fostered when the community recognizes that its survival depends upon honoring rights of the most vulnerable, particularly the elderly, women, and children. This cosmology sees connections between God, humanity and all creation, the dead, and the yet-to-be born. Such Shona principles, together with Christianity practiced by African independent churches, create an engaging, activist response to contemporary environmental and social challenges brought on by colonialism. The church functions as a guardian for creation. For change to be affected any positions privileging power must shift to alternative value systems that do not dominate people or nature but encourage cooperative spirit of all existence. Change can be effected when the church and other faith communities challenge societal oppressions and abuses of class, race, gender, white supremacy, imperialism, and capitalism; when the desire for ecojustice presses us to work for balanced, healthy, sustainable environments and relationships; and when economic parity and development are central to ministry—all endeavoring to transform those poor in spirit and poor in material goods, honoring the world we hold in trust.

Cheryl A. KIRK-DUGGAN
Shaw University Divinity School

FURTHER READING

Amen, Ra. (2006). The role of feminism, traditional religion, and Christianity in addressing social and ecological problems in Zimbabwe. Unpublished paper. Berkeley, CA: Graduate Theological Union.

Baker-Fletcher, Karen. (1998). Sisters of dust, sisters of spirit: Womanist wordings on God and creation Minneapolis, MN: Augsburg Fortress.

Chapman, Audrey; Petersen, Rodney; & Smith-Moran, Barbara. (Eds.). (2000). Consumption, population, and sustainability: Perspectives from science and religion. Washington, DC: Island Press.

Fick, Gary W. (2008). Food, farming, and faith. Albany: State University of New York Press.

Franklin, Robert E. (1997). Another day's journey: Black churches confronting the American crisis. Minneapolis, MN: Augsburg Fortress.

Glave, Dianne, & Stoll, Mark. (Eds.) (2006). To love the wind and the rain: African Americans and environmental history. Pittsburgh: University of Pittsburgh Press.

Anderson-Stembridge, Matthew, & Radford, Phil. (2007). Bottom line ministries that matter: Congregational stewardship with energy efficiency and clean energy technologies. Washington, DC: Eco-Justice Program of the National Council of Churches.

Smith, R. Drew. (Ed.). (2004). Long march ahead: African American churches and public policy in post-civil rights America. Durham, NC: Duke University Press.

Agenda 21

Agenda for the Twenty-first Century (Agenda 21) is a plan for governmental and individual change for sustainable development created by the United Nations. It serves as a set of guidelines, implicitly based on ethical ideals, for national and local governments, nonprofit groups, science and education organizations, and even individuals for safeguarding the natural environment and humanity's place in it.

At the 1992 Earth Summit in Rio de Janeiro, representatives from more than 170 nations adopted Agenda for the 21st Century, commonly known as Agenda 21. The United Nations commissioned Agenda 21 to turn the dream and definition of sustainable development articulated in *Our Common Future*, the 1986 report of the World Commission on Environment and Development, into an action plan. Thus Agenda 21 outlined how the definition of sustainable development in *Our Common Future*—"meet[ing] the needs of the present without compromising the ability of future generations to meet their own needs," (WCED 1987, 8)—could be achieved through the cooperation of governments, nongovernmental organizations, businesses, scientists, educators, and the public. Agenda 21 particularly focused on social and economic issues, including poverty; the consumption and management of resources, including land, water, and waste; and the specific needs and talents of women, youth, and indigenous people.

Along with Agenda 21, the United Nations commissioned "The Earth Charter," a document on ethics identifying moral principles and values that could aid the quest for sustainable development.

Together these documents were intended to guide sustainable development at local, national, and international levels. "The Earth Charter," however, was not adopted in Rio. Consequently, even though grassroots movements have sought global support for the charter, the concrete actions of Agenda 21 have overshadowed ethical aspects of sustainable development in policy making. Yet a careful examination of Agenda 21 reveals that it too is influenced by ethics and values. Part of this influence is inevitable; all legal documents are shaped by their writers' ethical priorities. Part of the influence is intentional; Agenda 21's writers recognized that ethical values needed to be acknowledged because such values can function as challenges to and resources for achieving sustainable development.

Agenda 21 most explicitly discusses ethics when it acknowledges that its signatories may have diverse, even conflicting, ethical values; it subsequently charts a strategy for accommodating such differences. It assumes that the broad goals of sustainable development can be achieved in different ways, depending on the religious, social, and ethical values of particular peoples. For example, it acknowledges that decision makers deciding about reproductive rights and medical practices must consider local cultural and religious norms as well as a global vision of sustainable development. Agenda 21 also notes that promoting values (which it rarely names) that support sustainable development will be necessary to achieve its goals. Hima, traditional Islamic land sanctuaries, are one of the few such ethical concepts Agenda 21 identifies, in this case in its discussion of land sustainability.

Ethical reflection is not, however, delegated only to local communities implementing its action plan. Agenda 21 itself presupposes several ethical positions. For instance, it assumes that people have a moral responsibility to promote sustainable development. It particularly assigns this responsibility to governments, scientists, economists, nongovernmental organizations, educators, and individuals so they can protect present and future generations. This impulse could be rooted in a variety of religious and philosophical traditions that emphasize caring for others. As befits a secular legal document, Agenda 21 leaves such specification up to the reader.

The norm of equity also appears throughout Agenda 21. It emphasizes promoting equitable access to both physical resources and the political process during discussions of trade, economics, poverty, hunger, natural resources, and the diverse needs of developing and developed countries. Agenda 21 also directs special attention to many historically marginalized groups—including women, children, the poor, indigenous people, and people of developing nations—in its efforts to promote equity. Agenda 21 does not, however, examine race, a problem since people of color are more likely to suffer from environmental degradation than any other demographic, including the poor.

Though the ethics of Agenda 21 have limits, it is a significant step toward global consensus on the connection between sustainable development and morality, given its unprecedented number of signatories. Agenda 21 recognizes that religions and moral values shape belief and action, and that they can help attain the goal of sustainability. It also acknowledges the challenges of achieving widespread environmental goals in an ethically diverse world but aims for solutions that can resonate with multiple local beliefs. Finally, Agenda 21 embodies values, such as responsibility and equity, which are widely agreed upon components of a sustainable world. Thus Agenda 21 reveals a significant amount about the ethical priorities of its many signatories even though action rather than ethical reflection is its main goal.

Sarah E. FREDERICKS
University of North Texas

FURTHER READING

Agyeman, Julian; Bullard, Robert; & Evans, Bob. (Eds.). (2003). *Just sustainabilities: Development in an unequal world*. Cambridge, MA: The MIT Press.

Llewellyn, Othman Abd-ar-Rahman. (2003). The basis for a discipline of Islamic environmental law. In Richard C. Foltz, Frederick M. Denny, & Azizan Bahruddin (Eds.), *Islam and ecology: A bestowed trust* (pp. 185–247). Cambridge, MA: Harvard University Press.

Robinson, Nicholas; Hassan, Parvez; & Burhenne-Guilmin, Francoise, (Eds.). (1993). *Agenda 21 & the UNCED proceedings*. New York: Oceana Publications.

The Earth Charter Commission. (2000). The Earth charter. Retrieved April 24, 2009, from http://www.earthcharterinaction.org/content/

World Commission on Environment and Development (WCED). (1987). *Our common future: Report of the World Commission on Environment and Development*. New York: Oxford University Press.

Agrarianism

Agrarianism is more than a description of agricultural life. It outlines principles and practices that reflect a comprehensive understanding of nature and culture as a whole. Agrarianism affirms the sustaining value of the connection between land and bodies, the links between food production and consumption, a commitment to community, and the virtues of patience and care that have been lost in our modern culture.

For the first time in history more people now live in cities than in the country. This fact is of momentous significance because as urbanites and suburbanites insulated from any direct or meaningful contact with the land, it is more likely that we will forget or ignore that human health and vitality depend on the health and vitality of the many ecological memberships that constitute our environment. Failing to appreciate that we draw our nourishment from watersheds and fields, from forests and meadows, how many of us will really understand where food comes from and under what conditions it can be sustainably and safely produced? It is much more likely that we will abuse the very land and water upon which we all depend. Put simply, many of us are not in the position to see or know how the consumer decisions we make affect the natural and social communities beyond our immediate homes. Our ignorance tempts us to believe, falsely, that there is such a thing as a postagricultural society.

For ten thousand years the majority of people have lived an agricultural life. Moreover, those who were not farmers themselves lived in close, sympathetic proximity with agricultural realities and requirements. What agrarian life affords—though hardly guarantees—is the practical and intimate insight that insofar as we eat, breathe, and drink we also need to care for the geo-bio-chemical sources that feed us. To degrade, exhaust, or destroy one's land or livestock is also to put one's own life at risk. Agrarian life, which is not to be confused with the extractive and profiteering ethos of agribusiness, is an education that trains people in the arts of care and patience, attention and fidelity, humility and celebration—all with the aim of promoting our common life together. Perhaps it is for this reason that the early Middle English meaning of the word "culture" referred to a piece of land and the skills people need to work the land well. No matter how refined our sensibilities may become, a healthy and sustainable culture is always one that is built on healthy lands. As environmental historians have amply shown us—think of the Sumerian civilization between the Tigris and Euphrates rivers that came to an end when its soils became barren (the "Fertile Crescent" is now a desert)—the widespread destruction of a country's land will eventually lead to a culture's collapse.

Agrarianism represents a comprehensive philosophy and set of practices that holds together in one, synoptic vision the well-being of land and people together. It recognizes that human health and happiness cannot be secured at the expense of animal misery, degraded soil, polluted waterways, or synthetically propped-up plant life. All life forms a vast and indescribably complex set of memberships. The unique responsibility and opportunity of people is that we can know and celebrate our place within them. But to do this properly we must first appreciate that we are only one member, and that the memberships do not exist to serve our exclusive interests and desires. This is an inescapable law of sustainable life.

To adopt an agrarian worldview and set of responsibilities does not require that we all become farmers. What is necessary is that we learn to appreciate the vital connection between our lands and our bodies. We also need to develop the sensitivities and sympathies that follow from our committing to a specific community and region. Today's transient and consumer culture makes it less likely that we will work and shop responsibly. We live in global economies that make it very difficult, if not impossible, to appreciate the harmful and salutary effects of our daily decisions. For this reason one of our first priorities must be to develop and strengthen local economies in which the loop between production and consumption is as transparent as possible. We need to be able to see up close the effects of our decisions so we can then take the practical steps to correct our mistakes.

The most obvious and practical way for this to happen is for consumers to grow some of their own food—even a tiny garden will remind us that we draw our sustenance from land—or buy food tha is locally produced. Forming viable economic relationships with farmers and food producers is a first vital step on the way to making sure that we no longer (often unknowingly) contribute to the destruction or degradation of our life-giving habitats. Knowing that we eat in relation to a particular piece of land will make us less prone to destroy it.

A sustainable culture is one that honors the many sources and memberships of life. Agrarians have much to teach us because they appreciate our proximity with the plant and animal life that nourishes us. They can be a source of instruction to us because they have had to learn the lessons of patience and care. They can also be a source of hope because they safe-keep the land that is the literal ground of our life.

Norman WIRZBA
Duke Divinity School

FURTHER READING

Berry, Wendell. (2003). *The art of the commonplace: The agrarian essays of Wendell Berry*. Berkeley, CA: Counterpoint.

Freyfogle, Eric. (Ed.). (2001). *The new agrarianism: Land, culture, and the community of life*. Washington, DC: Island Press/Shearwater Books.

Holthaus, Gary. (2006). *From the farm to the table*. Lexington: University Press of Kentucky.

Institute for Agriculture and Trade Policy. (n.d.). Retrieved April 9, 2009, from http://www.iatp.org/

Jackson, Wes, & Vitek, Bill. (Eds.). (1996). *Rooted in the land: Essays on community and place*. New Haven, CT: Yale University Press.

Wirzba, Norman. (Ed.). (2003). *The essential agrarian reader*. Lexington: University Press of Kentucky.

Agriculture

The 1984 essays of Gordon K. Douglass proposed that advocates for sustainable agriculture were apt to focus on one of three aspects: producing food sufficient to support the human population, regardless of environmental costs; ecological integrity, or concern for minimizing resource depletion; and social sustainability, efforts to overcome industrial agriculture put forth by small, rural communities. All three remain part of sustainability discussions today.

While many discussions of sustainability are of comparatively recent origin, in 1984 the economist Gordon K. Douglass had already published a collection of essays entitled *Agricultural Sustainability in a Changing World Order.* Douglass proposed that advocates for sustainable agricultural tended to emphasize one of three discrete themes. First was an emphasis on food sufficiency: To be sustainable meant that an agricultural system could feed the human population, whatever the costs to the environment. Second was what Douglass called ecological integrity, or farming with an emphasis on minimizing the long-term depletion of the soil, water, and genetic resource base. Those focused on the third theme emphasized community, with a strong focus on rural social vibrancy. Douglass called this social sustainability.

A quarter century after Douglass wrote, the notion of sustainability has become more commonplace. Many people associate sustainable agriculture with fair trade (ensuring that poor farmers and farm labor get adequate compensation), localvores (people who prefer regionally-produced food), slow food (the international movement to resist globalization implied by chain restaurants and multinational food companies), and organic farming. Some activists would include humane animal production or vegetarianism on the list. All of these are seen in contrast to large-scale commodity production. Here, agricultural sustainability refers to a heterogeneous social movement that may not be easily grounded in any substantive conception of what sustainability entails. A full appreciation of how sustainability should be applied to food production needs to recover the themes at work in Douglass's early efforts.

Food Sufficiency

The idea that food availability is the key to sustainability may seem especially odd to consumers in industrialized nations who are attempting to reform their dietary habits. Yet throughout developing nations, simply having enough food remains a challenge. "Feeding the world" had long been a mantra for mainstream agricultural science, and in the 1970s it became an explicit ambition of large-scale commodity agriculture. During U.S. president Richard Nixon's administration, Secretary of Agriculture Earl Butz advocated using "food as a weapon," by which he meant that the West's capacity to produce prodigious amounts of grain could be used to political advantage through programs designed to meet the food needs of poor people in developing nations. He coupled this with an injunction for farmers themselves to "Get big, or get out," meaning that very large industrially organized farms would be the source of these food needs.

Although Butz himself was not one to use the word "sustainability" in the same sentence as "farming," his vision of agriculture's contribution to sustainability is one that dates back at least to the British political economist Thomas Malthus's notorious *Essay on the Principle of Population.* It is obvious enough that people must eat to live, so if any human society is to be sustainable, its people must be sustained by daily subsistence rations of food. Malthus (1766–1834) had prophesied that growth in human population would tend to outpace growth in agricultural production. If we reinterpret Malthus in light of sustainability, a sustainable human population would necessarily develop some means to check population growth or (more likely, in Malthus's view) achieve sustainable numbers at the price of perpetual misery in the form of starvation and wars fought over agricultural resources. In other words, forces that keep population growth in check become necessary for sustainability.

The food sufficiency view emphasizes a third way. Like the Malthusian viewpoint, it sees agriculture as necessary for the sustainability of human civilization, but contrary to Malthus, it emphasizes continuous increases in total food production so that a growing population can be fed. Advocates of this view often cite figures showing that agricultural productivity has indeed kept pace with global population growth over the two centuries since Malthus wrote. But in this view, the imperative of food sufficiency is also thought to be the overriding concern for agricultural sustainability. Food "trumps" or outranks the desire for "luxury goods," which may be thought to include environmental amenities as well as leisure consumption. Some who adopt the food sufficiency point of view may follow Malthus in thinking that elements of social justice, such as rights to healthcare or education and a fair distribution of life's opportunities, are also luxuries available only to those who have solved the hard problems of daily survival. Thus the Malthusian race between population and food sufficiency is viewed as the underlying tension in this view of sustainability. Many people who take this view, including many mainstream agricultural scientists, endorse an all-out campaign to use science and technology to increase and stabilize agricultural yields in order to keep winning that race.

There are, however, important skeptics among agricultural scientists, most notably the agricultural economist Lester Brown, who has devoted a lifetime to Malthusian calculations and who, in books such as *Who Will Feed China?*, questions whether agricultural science can continue to outpace population growth. Brown's questioning takes on many dimensions. One is that, as people become wealthier, per capita caloric consumption increases as people shift toward diets rich in animal protein. As such, the need for increasing agricultural productivity actually grows *faster* than human population. Furthermore, Brown notes that the putative success of agricultural science in sustaining the human population has actually been built on a number of resource-depleting production practices. Chemical fertilizers and pesticides accumulate in the environment with long-term effects on both human and environmental health that are only now being realized. Mechanized irrigation technologies often draw upon nonrenewable underground water supplies, and declines in soil fertility from intensive cropping amount to a form of mining.

Ecological Integrity

Brown's emphasis on broader environmental impacts reveals that that the ability to produce food depends upon maintaining the integrity of the natural resource base for doing so. A view of agriculture intent on increasing year-to-year yields in cereal crops or animal protein fails to recognize that a unilateral focus on feeding people day-to-day can actually result in farming methods that are not sustainable over the long run. In the ecological integrity view, it is agriculture *itself* that must be sustainable. It is not simply a matter of agriculture making society sustainable by ensuring that there is enough to eat. According to principles of ecological integrity, a truly sustainable agriculture is one that operates within the natural hydrologic cycle as well as the Earth's ability to regenerate fertile soils. Even subtler processes may be at work in the regeneration of genetic diversity.

Viewing agricultural sustainability in terms of ecological integrity, therefore, can be understood as a focus on whether agricultural practices can be sustained, without regard to whether these practices are productive enough to supply a growing population provisioned with food. Farming is done within soil, water, and climatic ecosystems, and the resilience of these ecosystems place limits on the kind of cultivation that can be done on a continuous basis. Although it is possible to exceed these limits for a period of time, agricultural ecosystems will eventually be stressed beyond their capacity to recover. At this point, productivity will decline precipitously and will not recover. What is more, the lag time for recovery of some ecosystem processes (such as soil fertility) may be quite long, allowing us to become complacent during decades of exploitative practice. A sustainable agriculture is thus one that does not stress agro-ecosystem processes beyond their ability to support continuous use.

Social Sustainability

Douglass's third paradigm—social sustainability—calls attention to the need for vibrant rural communities. It relied heavily on work done by the anthropologist Walter Goldschmidt, who studied two towns in California's San Joaquin Valley in the 1930s and 1940s. One was surrounded by many relatively small and diversified farms operated with family labor, while the other was set amidst a few very large monoculture operations typical of what we would today call industrial agriculture. Goldschmidt's study found that the community dominated by large commodity-oriented farms had difficulty maintaining basic infrastructure in the form of schools, public health, and municipal services, while the rural community consisting of small family-based operations had a thriving infrastructure and a rich communal life. Goldschmidt's research was published under the title *As You Sow* in 1947.

Douglass's 1984 book also came on the heels of a lawsuit over the University of California's participation in the development of a mechanical tomato harvester. The harvester was a large and expensive piece of equipment that could not be efficiently utilized by small growers. Along with some key legislation on migrant labor, the availability of the mechanized harvester precipitated rapid concentration in California's tomato industry. Hundreds of relatively small-scale farms were consolidated (through sale and bankruptcy) into a few dozen between 1968 and 1978. This concentration in the tomato industry led many to remember Goldschmidt's work and to conclude that the machine would indirectly cause decline in the rural communities where dozens of tomato farms had been replaced by one or two.

The scale-increasing effects of new technology and Goldschmidt's work led advocates of social sustainability to conclude that the industrial systems favored by advocates of food sufficiency were the opposite of a sustainable agriculture. Thus, social sustainability had a meaning tied to California in 1984, though the general phenomenon of larger and more specialized farms displacing smaller more diversified farms has been repeated in many places. The Irish writer and essayist Oliver Goldsmith (1730–1774) lamented a similar decline following the widespread adoption of enclosure methods in English farming with his poem "The Deserted Village" (1770):

> Ill fares the land, to hast'ning ills a prey,
> Where wealth accumulates, and men decay;
> Princes and Lords may flourish, or may fade:
> A breath can make them, as a breath has made;
> But a bold peasantry, their country's pride,
> When once destroy'd can never be supplied.

The point behind social sustainability suggests that a certain type of farm structure—small-scale and diversified family-operated farms—is more conducive to sustaining viable rural communities than is a farm structure consisting of industrially organized farms producing commodity crops. Here, as in the case of food availability, it is agriculture (though now a specific *kind* of agriculture) that is sustaining society, as opposed to being something that itself must be made sustainable.

Traditions of Agricultural Stewardship

These three ideas surveyed by Douglass in 1984 remain critical to any contemporary discussion of the values that define and support sustainable agriculture. Yet many environmental stewardship values in farming have older origins.

Popular appreciation of the environmental impact from agricultural chemicals can be traced to Rachel Carson's *Silent Spring* (1962). Carson (1907–1964) collected both scientific and anecdotal evidence for the impact that bioaccumulation of agricultural pesticides (especially DDT) was having upon wildlife. Some scholars cite her book as the beginning of the environmental movement. Yet within agriculture itself, there was a still older tradition of what we would today call ecological thinking. The horticulturist Liberty Hyde Bailey (1858–1954) had advocated a norm of "permanent" agriculture, by which he meant farming methods that maintained fertile soils and viable crops in perpetuity. Bailey was unarguably the most famous agricultural scientist of his era. He promoted outdoor "nature study" as a form of general education and developed a philosophy that saw the land itself as a locus of moral duty.

In the United States and Canada, Bailey's lessons on permanent agriculture were reinforced by the Dust Bowl, an episode of wind erosion that took on continental proportions between 1930 and 1936. The soil scientist Hugh Hammond Bennett (1881–1960) diagnosed the source of this environmental catastrophe in patterns of over-cultivation that depleted soils on the Great Plains, leaving them with weakened texture (e.g., tilth). When denuded of plant growth after harvest, these lands were vulnerable to the dry winds that blackened the skies of North America, depositing ruined soil in huge drifts and leaving lands totally unfit for farming. Bennett created extensive programs of soil conservation and worked with the popular author Louis Bromfield (1896–1956) to promote an approach to farming that anticipated many elements of what Douglass would refer to as the ecological integrity approach to sustainable agriculture.

Although Britain never suffered an agricultural environmental disaster on the scale of the Dust Bowl, parallel developments in the United Kingdom led to the founding of the Soil Association by Lady Eve Balfour (1899–1990). Drawing on the work of the botanist Sir Albert Howard (1873–1947), the Soil Association began to promote the extensive use of composting for developing soil tilth and eschewed the use of synthetic chemical fertilizers. Howard had argued that rhizomes (i.e., small, horizontal offshoots from the main root stem) engaged in a unique association with soil microorganisms. This "mycorrhizal association" was, in Howard's view, the ultimate source of plant health, but synthetic chemicals tended to destroy microorganisms and weaken tilth. Howard also believed that this health would be passed on to animals (including humans) who consumed healthy plants, and that returning animal manures to the soil through composting established a cycle that would make farming truly permanent. Thus the idea of systemic or holistic health was the driving value in the British organic movement.

On the European continent, a somewhat similar approach developed in connection with the philosophy of Rudolf Steiner (1861–1925). Steiner was an Austrian who emphasized the role of intuition and imagination in his thought. In 1924, Steiner gave a series of lectures on farming reputedly based on information he had gleaned from a particularly successful dairy farmer. The methods involved elaborate rituals for preparing composts, which were given intellectual support from Steiner's vitalist epistemology adapted from the thought of Johann Wolfgang von Goethe (1749–1842). Soil was conceived as a living organism. Healthy soils would support plant growth without artificial amendments, and healthy plants would resist pests and promote health in the animals that ate them. Thus, though different from Howard's approach in its philosophical underpinnings, Steiner's approach—called biodynamic farming—was similar in emphasizing soil health through composting, in foreswearing the use of chemicals, and in linking soil, plant, and animal health in a cyclic fashion.

Contemporary advocates of Bennett's ideas lament the decline of soil conservation practices in the half-century since his death, and continue to promote soil conservation as the key to sustainability in agriculture. Yet Bennett's approach to soil conservation was silent on chemical inputs. Indeed, by the 1980s North American approaches to soil conservation emphasized the use of herbicides in "no till" cultivation methods that did not expose soils to the eroding force of wind and rain. Although all of the movements mentioned above focus on soil tilth as the central concept, the elimination of chemicals in biodynamic farming and Howard's organic methods is more characteristic of what self-identified advocates of sustainable agriculture believe today. In fact, indigenous farming approaches from many nations have never used chemical inputs. What we now call "organic" is the result of networking and negotiation of many farmers and farm groups who had overlapping (but not always compatible) visions of what agriculture should be. The International Federation of Organic Agriculture Movements (IFOAM) was founded in 1972 to further this interaction and promote organic agriculture. This group continues to focus on elimination of chemical inputs. In the late 1990s, a similar ban on the use of genetic engineering was also included.

Implications for the Future

In conclusion, agricultural sustainability continues to find support from all three quarters noted by Gordon Douglass in 1984. Mainstream proponents of industrial commodity production continue to think that this model needs to be expanded worldwide in order to meet the needs of food sufficiency. Today, people taking this perspective believe that genetic engineering will be necessary to feed the world. The theme of ecological integrity has been taken up by various schools promoting organic approaches to production and who build on complex ecological relationships amongst plants, soils, and livestock. The theme of social sustainability may be foremost in the minds of those who advocate actions such as "fair trade," eating locally grown foods, and celebrating the conviviality and tradition that is characteristic of the slow-food movement. Here the emphasis is on the way that a particular type of agriculture (extending all the way up to food preparation) can create forms of social solidarity that make communities stronger and more vital. Recent trends have emphasized projects such as school and community gardens, or "urban agriculture," the idea of encouraging production of fruits and vegetables within the bounds of city limits. Like advocates of food sufficiency, those who focus on social sustainability see agriculture as making *society* sustainable, while those who emphasize ecological integrity are attempting to understand the underlying principles that make farming itself sustainable, or, to use the word preferred by Liberty Hyde Bailey, permanent. All of these notions have a place in the values that drive us toward a more sustainable future.

Paul B. THOMPSON
Michigan State University

FURTHER READING

Altieri, Miguel A. (1995). *Agroecology: The science of sustainable agriculture.* Boulder, CO: Westview Press.

Brown, Lester R. (1995). *Who will feed China?: Wake-up call for a small planet.* New York: W. W. Norton.

Carson, Rachel. (1962). *Silent spring.* Boston: Houghton Mifflin.

Douglass, Gordon K. (Ed.). (1984). *Agricultural sustainability in a changing world order.* Boulder, CO: Westview Press.

Feenstra, Gail. (1997). What is sustainable agriculture? Retrieved March 7, 2009, from http://www.sarep.ucdavis.edu/Concept.htm

Goldschmidt, Walter. (1947). *As you sow.* New York: Harcourt, Brace.

Jackson, Wes; Berry, Wendell; & Colman, Bruce. (Eds.). (1984). *Meeting the expectations of the land: Essays in sustainable agriculture and stewardship.* San Francisco: North Point Press.

Pretty, Jules. (Ed.). (2005). *The Earthscan reader in sustainable agriculture.* London: Earthscan.

Thompson, Paul B. (2009). *Sustainability and agrarian ideals.* Lexington: University Press of Kentucky.

Animals

Many world belief systems urge treating animals with compassion. But humans, feeling they have dominion over animals, often act in ways that use animals as resources. Practices such as over-hunting and habitat degradation contribute to an increased rate of species extinction. Factory farming inflicts suffering on animals. Such practices threaten not only animal survival, but sustainability of world ecosystems.

Definitions of sustainability, ethical considerations related to sustainable practices, and implementations of such practices are consistently anthropocentric, focusing almost exclusively on human survival. While other animals might be included in these systems or discussions, they are tangential or secondary at best to the consideration of the human animal. This dualism of the other-than-human animal (hereinafter "animal") and the human animal remains one of the most rigid hierarchical categories in the construction of ethical, religious, philosophical, political, and economic systems. While humans are one of the great ape species—along with chimpanzees, gorillas, bonobos, and orangutans—in recent history we have categorized ourselves based on our technological prowess, our philosophical and religious systems, our language, and the sheer size of our brains, among myriad things, as a species that is other than an animal or, at the very least, is unique and superior. In the meantime, ethologists and biologists continue

to dismantle the hierarchical imperative of human supremacy through discoveries about other animals and their lives even when such breakthroughs might not be their intention. Some of the most respected ethologists, such as Jane Goodall and Marc Bekoff, are breaking down these barriers in their careful observation of animals. They find other animals making tools, passing ideas to companions (thus they have "culture"), exhibiting emotions, displaying self-consciousness, communicating in complex ways, and suffering, a trait emphasized by the often-quoted English philosopher Jeremy Bentham (1748–1832).

It is important to address issues of animals in broader discussions of sustainability—first to examine general aspects of the survival of animals in the early twenty-first century, including species extinction, biodiversity, and land usage. After contextualizing the current state of discussions with a brief overview, this essay addresses in a very general way how some religious and philosophical systems take account of animals. Finally, it is imperative to ask whether or not and how animals are considered in the context of sustainability with the current state and the input of religious and/or philosophical systems in mind.

Species Depletion and Extinction

From honeybees to mussels to rhinos, animal extinctions caused by humans occur on an increasingly frequent basis. While specific extinction rates can only be estimated, primarily due to the fact that humans have not identified and categorized all animal species, global factors such as climate change suggest that the rate of extinction will continue to increase. Anthropogenic causes of species extinction include over-hunting, habitat degradation, introduction of environmental toxins and disease, to name only a few of the direct causes. One of the most pressing concerns is this rate of species extinction, which many scientists place at one hundred to one thousand times the background rate, with one plant or animal species disappearing every twenty minutes (Myers and Pimm 2003). Because of this, biodiversity declines significantly and the rate of species replacement is threatened. Biodiversity, the complex interaction of entire ecosystems of flora and fauna, is requisite for sustaining all life, not only human life. Therefore, in order to even consider the possibility of sustainability, a variety of animal life forms must be present on the planet.

Over-hunting and over-fishing are among the main causes of species depletion. Trawl nets, central to the commercial fishing industry, lead to degradation of the seafloor and the injury or death of countless sea animals not even part of the human food system. While most land animals eaten by humans are farmed in industrialized settings, hunting is still common in some cultures and for certain purposes. Whether or not hunting land animals or sea animals is ethical remains a topic of debate. In certain cultural settings, such as the United States, it is frequently deemed a more humane way of acquiring meat for food than industrialized factory farming. Indigenous cultures worldwide have practiced sustainable levels of hunting for thousands of years. But hunting is, at the very least, a questionable practice when the hunted is an endangered species. For example, the bushmeat industry (the killing and trading in primates), driven in many ways by the destruction of forests and the logging industries in Africa and Southeast Asia, is rapidly depleting primate populations. While there are approximately 6.5 billion human primates on the planet, a population that is rapidly increasing, there are decreasing numbers of other great apes: 600 Eastern mountain gorillas, 3,000 to 5,000 Eastern lowland gorillas, 45,000 Bornean orangutans, and 30,000 bonobos. Many estimates project that all great apes, except for humans, will be extinct in their natural habitats by the middle of the twenty-first century. The Great Ape Project, an international movement advocating the same basic rights afforded to humans for all other great apes, is one of many organizations attempting to reverse this trend.

Factory Farming of Animals

A major aspect of food production threatening sustainability is intensive factory farming, or confined animal feeding operation (CAFO). This method of farming, designed to provide inexpensive and plentiful supplies of meat, threatens sustainability on a number of levels while it invariably inflicts unimaginable amounts of suffering on domestic animal populations. The U.S. Department of Agriculture reported daily livestock slaughter figures for one day in June 2007: 126,000 cows, 3,000 calves, 386,000 hogs, and 10,000 sheep. Chickens are killed at the rate of 2.4 million per day in the United States alone. When producing this many animals for slaughter, the amount of land used to raise grains to feed them and the amount of land needed to process the waste products become particularly troubling environmental issues. Populations of these domesticated food animals are out of balance with their natural reproductive and survival rates. Thus, even if one does not take into account the level of suffering inflicted, the process of factory farming is generally deemed unsustainable because of its overall negative environmental impact.

Another area of human–animal tension connected to sustainability is the reintroduction of depleted species to their natural habitats. Often the loss of these species has led to environmental degradation. So, for example, when the top predator in an ecosystem is hunted to extinction, populations of other animals start to explode, starting a chain reaction of imbalance. The gray wolf in the United States is one of the most commonly considered depleted species because its near extinction raises the issue of reintroducing a former top carnivore to an ecosystem while also addressing how humans perceive and accept a predator species when domestic animals, such as cattle, are present in the same areas. Although most studies indicate that such fears are usually exaggerated, conflicts inevitably arise. What is obvious, however, is that the reintroduction of predator species actually increases biodiversity in any given ecosystem by returning a balance to the various carnivores, herbivores, and plants. In Yellowstone National Park alone, for instance, a population of approximately 1,500 wolves grew from reintroduction programs established during the late twentieth century; positive effects on biodiversity were recorded within only two years. In 2008, gray wolves lost protection under the Endangered Species Act, and hunting them has become lawful once again. Their population levels will be monitored, but conflicts with some ranchers have been immediately evident.

Implications for Sustainability

All of the issues concerning animals and sustainability revolve around the larger questions of whether or not other-than-human animal species need to be addressed in order to secure sustainable outcomes and whether or not other-than-human animals have intrinsic or inherent value regardless of the role they play in the sustainability of human life. Of course, these questions provoke the critical analysis of all systems of domination; the challenge of confronting these systems in order to enable sustainability remains imminent.

Obviously the depletion of animals through certain hunting or fishing practices directly impacts not only the survival of those species but of human life as well. If the oceans are fished to the extent that populations of sea animals plummet beyond recovery, then a major source of food for many humans will be destroyed. Other impacts of a significant decrease of biodiversity of animal life on complex ocean ecosystems are unknown, though projections are dire. But the unchecked growth of ocean plant life, particularly coastal algal blooms, will have repercussions including destroying some coral reef ecosystems and causing outbreaks of Pfiesteria (a tiny marine organism) resulting in the deaths of millions of fish. In addition, the mass population of domestic animals developed by humans for food and enabled by industrialized factory farming systems is not sustainable because of the environmental impacts of such systems. Whether from the release of methane gas (a major contributor to global warming) or from pollution of waterways from waste, confined-animal feeding operations cannot be maintained indefinitely. The level of antibiotic usage requisite to keep confined animals from dying of disease leads to drug-resistant forms of bacteria that impact humans as well as animals. Similarly, the reintroduction of top predator species is requisite for the survival of certain ecosystems and the maintenance of biodiversity. But the more complicated questions raised above, regarding the intrinsic value of animals and of animal rights, must also be addressed.

Role of Animals in Religion and Philosophy

While it seems apparent that, on a global scale, other-than-human animals are afforded little intrinsic value, most religious communities actually recognize animals as part of their ritual and belief systems. This is true for "world" religions (e.g., Islam, Judaism, Christianity, Hinduism, and Buddhism) and for the myriad indigenous traditions of the world. Briefly examining each of these traditions and the role of animals in them provides another perspective for the discussion of animals and sustainability. Each of these traditions is much more nuanced, complicated, and diverse than suggested by the brief overviews here. They offer just a glimpse into the inclusion or exclusion of animals into beliefs and practices that shape the attitudes and therefore actions of humans around the world.

The two major religions of South Asia are Hinduism and Buddhism, the latter of which spread through East Asia in the third century BCE and later into other parts of the global human population. Hinduism, the overarching designation for the complicated array of religious traditions and practices of India for over three thousand years, includes a variety of animals in both its practical and symbolic systems. For example, cows are often revered as sacred based on their relationship to Lord Krishna, and there are numerous cow sanctuaries throughout India. Also, the most devout Hindus, or more precisely those who are in the highest castes, practice a strict vegetarian diet. One need only see images of Ganesha, the elephant god, to witness the symbolic power of animals in Hinduism. Mohandas Gandhi (1869–1948) states in his book *The Moral Basis of Vegetarianism* that "the greatness of a nation and its moral progress can be judged by the way its animals are treated." Of course, not all Hindus are vegetarians, and not all animals live well in India. It is generally believed by Hindus that humans are more advanced in the process of the transmigration of souls than other animals, though all animals have been reincarnated as human and all humans have been animals. But in its imagery and practice, Hinduism does include myriad animals.

Buddhism appeared in northern India approximately 2,500 years ago, emerging from a predominantly Hindu context. There are some similarities, particularly the inclusion of animals in the process of the transmigration of souls, but there are also some unique aspects. The Jataka Tales, for instance, relate the stories of the former lives of the Buddha. In a number of these lives the Buddha is another animal, usually a quite compassionate one. Buddhism also pays special attention to *ahimsa*, the concept of non-harming, and extends this religious ideal outside of the human community to other animals. Again, in the Jataka Tales, compassionate ones encompass animals in their moral world, and animals are capable of achieving enlightened awareness.

The three Mediterranean-born religious traditions—Judaism, Christianity, and Islam—also include animals in their stories and rituals. The story of Noah's Ark, one of the most widely retold and visually portrayed sections of the sacred texts of Judaism, includes numerous animal actors. Divine punishment leads to a global flood, but Noah is instructed by God to preserve animal species as well as humans on his large boat. At another point in the Hebrew scriptures, an ass is wise enough to see an angel, even if the man riding on him did not. Balaam's Ass even speaks. Eating laws, popularly known as kosher, take animals into consideration in interesting ways. While vegetarianism is not mentioned, though it is in the creation stories at the beginning of the scriptures, humane ways of slaughtering animals are central to kosher practice. So, while they are rarely central to the creation story, animals are definitely part of the divine plan and of the everyday consideration of Judaism.

Christianity, which shares some sacred texts with Judaism, also includes a number of animals, often in relationship to particular saints. Jesus, the founding figure of the tradition, comments on God's love for the birds and, in apocryphal stories, condemns a person for abusing his mule. Stories of the holy men and women in the tradition are filled with animals who feed saints, provide them companionship, and instruct them in the ways to live. Saint Anthony Abbot, the patron saint for animals, was fed by ravens in the wilderness. His iconography includes a pig. Saint Francis of Assisi, the patron saint of ecology, communicated with wolves, crickets, and sheep. He held them up as examples of the true life of a Christian. Beginning in the late twentieth century increasing numbers of churches in the United States began holding services of blessing for animals on his feast day.

The Quran, the sacred text of Islam, includes six chapters named for animals (the Cow, the Cattle, the Bee, the Ant, the Spider, and the Elephant). It also emphasizes that animals praise God and that God cares for them. Many dietary laws are similar to those of Judaism, particularly the prohibition of eating pigs and the specification of ritual slaughter of animals for food. Numerous legal scholars of Islam, the primary interpreters of the texts who guide Muslims in their religious practice, address issues of the treatment of animals. In his groundbreaking work on animals in Islam, Richard Foltz, a scholar of comparative religions, points to the complexity of issues in Islam and in the varied Muslim cultures of the world. There is always a focus on treating animals with compassion while still acknowledging the supremacy of humans.

All of these traditions still favor humans, even recognize them as exceptional. In Hinduism and Buddhism, being born human is a blessed birth because it is the only birth that has the potential to achieve *moksha*, the end of the cycle of rebirth and suffering (*samsara*). Judaism, Christianity, and Islam all include creation stories that grant global dominion over all other animals to humans. Humans are described as closer to God, a likeness to God even, but at the least a vice-regent for God on Earth. But even with this undoubted anthropocentrism, each religion includes resources in scriptural texts, traditions, or practices that value animals.

Indigenous traditions vary so widely that it is impossible to summarize them. But a very general observation shows that the traditions that are tied more closely to specific places and lifeways in these ecosystems tend to incorporate animals and afford them inherent value in a more powerful way than the world religions listed above. Animals are sometimes understood as other nations or peoples with irreplaceable roles in the life of humans.

On another level, human life is often explained or understood through animals. As the renowned anthropologist Claude Lévi-Strauss (b. 1908) stated, "animals are good to think." We humans understand ourselves through the lenses of other animals. Without a variety of real animals on the planet, human cultural construction could become increasingly void of creativity; the metaphors and myths that explain human meaning would be empty.

Philosophical systems often address the question of the animals. Cartesian philosophy provides the foundation of modern discussions with its denial of moral standing of any kind for animals. Rather they are machines and respond as such to external stimuli. Immanuel Kant (1724–1804) continues in this trajectory suggesting that compassion to animals is only valuable in its connection to human compassion. And while most contemporary philosophers inheriting a Cartesian worldview would acknowledge that animals can feel pain, they still remove them from moral consideration.

Animal Rights Advocacy

Twentieth- and early-twenty-first-century animal rights discussions provide another framework for thinking about sustainability and animals. *Speciesism*, a word employed with increasing frequency, names the hierarchical bias of placing the human species above all other species. It is compared to sexism and racism as a way of enforcing systems of domination based on prejudicial dualisms. Arguably it is this elevation of the human as the only one worthy of moral consideration that fuels the massive human consumption patterns threatening the survival of all life. In other words, the same ideological systems that allow for the destruction of other animals, as individuals or species, are the foundation for the destruction of entire ecosystems and of the planet itself. Donna Haraway, a philosopher whose ideas have sparked debates in such diverse fields as primatology, developmental biology, and technoscience, addresses this

issue in a fascinating way, suggesting that humans are in complex webs or knots of species relationships, all with reciprocity at their core.

Positions among advocates of animal rights spread along a continuum. Some (often called liberationists) question the use of animals as resources for humans in any form whereas others limit the use of animals to essential human needs with the condition that suffering is minimized. While reaching their conclusions through different philosophical approaches, liberationists include thinkers such as Peter Singer, Carol Adams, Tom Regan, and Richard Ryder. Others, such as Steven Wise, argue for legal rights for other species. Often discussion of rights leads to discussion of responsibilities as well, further complicating the ideas of which actors are agents in discussions of moral and legal systems.

If even minimal rights are recognized for other animals (the right to live and be free of human-caused suffering), what impacts could be projected for sustainability? Their homes (forests, oceans, plains, deserts) would need to remain intact (habitat preservation), and humans could not inflict unnecessary suffering on them even for the most basic of human needs (food production would change significantly and become more humane). Many of the outcomes of increased sustainability would necessarily overlap—such as increased biodiversity, ecosystem preservation, and decreased greenhouse gas emissions. Input from or interpretations of many, though certainly not all, philosophical and religious systems supports these reconfigurations of human economic systems.

It seems apparent that discussions of sustainability necessarily must include discussions of animals both as an integral part of the ecosystem which sustains us and as a ubiquitous element of cultural and religious priorities worldwide.

Laura HOBGOOD-OSTER
Southwestern University

FURTHER READING

Bekoff, Mark. (Ed.). (2007). *Encyclopedia of human-animal relationships.* Vols. 1–4. Westport, CT: Greenwood Press.

Foltz, Richard. (2006). *Animals in Islamic traditions and Muslim cultures.* Oxford, U.K.: Oneworld Publications.

Gandhi, Mohandas K. (1969). *The moral basis of vegetarianism.* Compiled by R. K. Prabhu. Ahmedabad, India: Navajivan.

Haraway, Donna. (2008). *When species meet.* Minneapolis: University of Minnesota Press.

Hobgood-Oster, Laura. (2008). *Holy dogs and asses: Animals in the Christian tradition.* Urbana: University of Illinois Press.

Linzey, Andrew, & Clarke, Paul A. B. (Eds.). (1990). *Animal rights: A historical anthology.* New York: Columbia University Press.

Myers, Norman, & Pimm, Stuart. (March/April 2003). *The last extinction. Foreign Policy,* p. 28.

Peterson, Dale. (2003). *Eating apes.* Berkeley: University of California Press.

Regan, Tom. (2004). *The case for animal rights.* Berkeley: University of California Press.

Singer, Peter. (1975, Rev. 1990). *Animal liberation.* New York: Avon Books.

Spiegel, Marjorie. (1996). *The dreaded comparison.* New York: Mirror Books.

Sunstein, Cass R., & Nussbaum, Martha C. (Eds.). (2004). *Animal rights: Current debates and new directions.* Oxford, U.K.: Oxford University Press.

Torres, Bob. (2007). *Making a killing: The political economy of animal rights.* Edinburgh, U.K.: AK Press.

Waldau, Paul, & Patton, Kimberley. (Eds.). (2006). *A communion of subjects.* New York: Columbia University Press.

Zamir, Tzachi. (2007). *Ethics and the beast: A speciesist argument for animal liberation.* Princeton, NJ: Princeton University Press.

Anthropic Principle

The Anthropic Principle, first postulated in 1974 by Brandon Carter, states that certain features of the universe are essential for the development of intelligent life. In its "weak" form, the principle holds that humans interpret the universe because they can observe it. The "strong" form, which posits the inevitability of the universe and thus life, has been used to support the argument for intelligent design.

The human observer is struck by the immense complexity found in what may be described as "simple" phenomena: a cell, a drop of water, a neuron. Is there something special about the history of the universe? The expansion of scientific knowledge has informed us that very basic changes in the universe's history and makeup, for example, a shift of 1 percent in the gravitational force up or down—would result in a universe entirely different from the one we now inhabit. In fact, our presence would be impossible. We are entirely dependent upon the cosmic interactions and stabilities being "just right." The observation that certain features of the universe are absolutely necessary if human beings are going to a part of its history is known as the Anthropic Principle. Said differently, the universe appears to be "finely tuned" in certain respects that make it conducive to the appearance of intelligent life. Most agree that the Australian theoretical physicist Brandon Carter (b. 1942) articulated this theory in 1974 as a new cosmological explanation (Carter 1974). Typically, two versions of this principle are accepted: a "weak" version and a "strong" version.

The Weak Anthropic Principle posits that our status as intelligent living beings in the universe places us in a distinctive position. By observing those aspects of the universe that are necessary for us to be observing at all, we are able to claim that the universe had to be a certain way. That is, we only observe the universe because it is conducive to us playing this role. For some, this is a tautological statement. For others, this allows for important claims on what is necessary for life. For example, human beings are now living approximately 15 billion years after the Big Bang, and we now theorize that this is the length of time it took for stars to go supernova and then cool. Generally, there is nothing terribly controversial about the weak version of the Anthropic Principle.

The Strong Anthropic Principle adds the caveat that life inevitably evolved in the universe—life is a necessary aspect of the universe's evolution. It is not just that the universe had to be a certain way for life to emerge, but that the universe had to be the way it is. For instance, by postulating the possibility of many different universes (metaphorically varying the values in each universe), it becomes possible to determine whether another universe could produce life. Human beings are not just a coincidence. This version of the principle is much more controversial, primarily because it has been used to argue for an intelligent designer or some version of theism. Maybe God set the constants in the universe such that our appearance would be inevitable?

Another possible consequence of the strong version is that human beings are lifted to a place of preeminence. While not a necessary implication, this anthropocentric inkling in physics and cosmology has buttressed certain ecological viewpoints in devastating ways. If the universe is "set up" for the appearance of human beings, it is not far-fetched to propose a hierarchical system for life with *Homo sapiens* residing at the top.

For some scientists and theologians, the Anthropic Principle offers the solution to both the elevation of human beings and their contingency on God. For others, the claims of the Anthropic Principle are unhelpful and speculative. The value and application of this theory thus remain controversial.

James W. HAAG
Suffolk University

FURTHER READING

Barrow, John D., & Tipler, Frank J. (1986). The anthropic cosmological principle. New York: Oxford University Press.

Bostrom, Nick. (n.d.) Anthropic principle. Retrieved April 1, 2009, from http://www.anthropic-principle.com

Carter, Brandon. (1974). Large number coincidences and the anthropic principle in cosmology. In M. S. Longair (Ed.), *Confrontation of cosmological theories with observational data: Symposium no. 63 (Copernicus Symposium II) held in Cracow, Poland, 10–12 September, 1973* (pp. 291–298). Boston and Dordrecht, The Netherlands: D. Reidel.

Walker, Mark A., & Cirkovic, Milan, M. (2006). Astrophysical fine tuning, naturalism, and the contemporary design argument. *International Studies in the Philosophy of Science, 20,* 285–307.

WAP, SAP, AND FAP

With scientists, philosophers, and theologians debating about the many anthropic principles up for discussion—the Weak Anthropic Principle (WAP), the Strong Anthropic Principle (SAP), and the Final Anthropic Principle (FAP) among them—the terminology becomes ever more daunting for the layperson. The philosopher Nick Bostrom attempts to pinpoint the origin of this dilemma in his book Anthropic Bias: Observation Selection Effects in Science and Philosophy. *(Bostrom's website, www.nickbostrum.com, a good source for further reading on this and other macroquestions about the universe, keys the links it provides with several levity-inducing icons: a tasseled mortarboard for the scholarly, a propeller beanie for the general reader, and a bunch of cherries for recommended picks.)*

The term "anthropic" is a misnomer. Reasoning about [the phenomena of] observation selection effects has nothing in particular to do with homo sapiens, but rather with observers in general. [The theoretical physicist Brandon] Carter regrets not having chosen a better name, which would no doubt have prevented much of the confusion that has plagued the field. When John Barrow and Frank Tipler introduced anthropic reasoning to a wider audience in 1986 with the publication of *The Anthropic Cosmological Principle*, they compounded the terminological disorder by minting several new "anthropic principles," some of which have little if any connection to observation selection effects.

Source: Nick Bostrom. (2002). *Anthropic Bias: Observation Selection Effects in Science and Philosophy* (p. 6). New York: Routledge. Part of the series *Studies in Philosophy: Outstanding Dissertations*, edited by Robert Nozick.

Anthropocentrism

Controversies over sustainability often involve debate over whether and how anthropocentrism (human-centeredness) is appropriate. There are three major kinds of anthropocentric concepts: interest-based, epistemological, and cosomological. Each may be used differently for envisioning or debating the ethical obligations of sustainability.

Anthropocentrism means human-centeredness (from *anthropos* and *centrum*, a mixed Greek-Latin etymology). For many critics, ecological destruction traces to an anthropocentric moral logic—a failure to respect or care beyond the human world. Alternative views involve nonanthropocentric antonyms, like biocentrism, ecocentrism, or theocentrism. Others think that sustainability rather depends on an expanded, long-term or otherwise more satisfactory anthropocentrism.

Understanding debates over sustainability requires recognizing the various and sometimes conflicting conceptual uses of anthropocentrism. There are three major ways of understanding the claim that humanity lies at the center of the moral universe. Each can generate some kind of sustainability ethic, and each can resist nonanthropocentric alternatives.

Interest Anthropocentrism

First, in its most common sense, anthropocentrism designates ethical approaches that privilege human interests over the interests of nonhumans, including other organisms, other species, nature in general, and/or God. This may mean that *only* human interests count, or that among human and other-than-human interests, human interests are always the priority. The former view simply does not admit other-than-human interests as morally important; the latter view admits them but assigns them less significance than human interests.

Either claim can support an ethic of sustainability, perhaps even one with relatively strong commitments to ecological protection. It all depends on what counts as a genuine human interest. The botanist William H. Murdy writes that "our current ecological problems do not stem from an anthropocentric attitude per se, but from one too narrowly conceived" (Murdy 1975, 1172). From an ecological and long-term perspective, Murdy claims, a proper view of human interests must include protecting some degree of ecological integrity. This is sometimes called "weak anthropocentrism" to distinguish it from more exploitative views (see Bryan Norton's 2005 study *Sustainability: A Philosophy of Adaptive Ecosystem Management*). But the adjective "weak" misleads; this view might more accurately be described as a broadened or deepened sense of what objective human interests include.

Human interests, of course, extend beyond the minimum conditions for keeping the species alive; they are concerned with protecting the social, economic, and political conditions that sustain important cultural values. Valuing human dignity, for example, requires sustaining requisite environmental health, political freedom, and economic welfare. Valuing the experience of wilderness could justify preservationist environmental policies. A full account of human interest might therefore lead to measures protecting natural beauty, beloved animals, or symbolic landscapes; to precautions avoiding risks to cultural achievements; or maintenance of biodiversity for the sake of ongoing scientific exploration. Some even argue that human virtue, spirituality, or faith depends on intimate relations with the natural world, which makes sustaining the possibility of caring for the Earth a fundamental human interest (see John O'Neill's 1993 work *Ecology, Policy, and Politics: Human Well-Being and the Natural World*).

In each case, an anthropocentric ethic of sustainability involves putting *indirect* value on sustaining other-than-human creatures or ecological processes by *directly* valuing the ongoing realization of human interests. Some account of the character and context of human interest then determines what sustainability means (see Norton 2005).

Epistemological Anthropocentrism

In a second major kind of conceptual use, anthropocentrism refers to the claim that moral values always originate in human subjects. Or, in other words, moral values are anthropogenic: They are generated from human experience. This is an epistemological anthropocentrism because it claims that the values of other-than-human entities never come from beyond the human world, or at least that humans have no way of knowing any such values. Values come not from nature or from God, but from valuing human subjects.

The nonanthropocentric alternative to this view would be a realist claim that some other-than-human entities generate value for themselves and that we can recognize the claim this value makes on our moral regard for them. The environmental ethicist Holmes Rolston argues for this kind of epistemological nonanthropocentrism, claiming that all living organisms generate value as they defend the natural goods of their kind. An ethicist like J. Baird Callicott takes the anthropocentric side, arguing that humans can and should take into account the interests of nonhuman organisms and systems, but that the moral values at stake in doing so are entirely a cultural product, made from human sentiment.

Observe, then, that an ethical view may refuse anthropocentrism in the first sense while accepting it in the second sense. For example, one might value all sentient life equally (nonanthropocentric in the first sense), while admitting that one's notions about the value of sentience arise from human experience (anthropocentric in the second sense). Or a sustainability ethic might make biodiversity a more important objective than any competing human interests (nonanthropocentric in the first sense), while justifying that commitment with cultural notions about the goods of diversity (anthropocentric in the second sense).

Cosmological Anthropocentrism

In its third major use, anthropocentrism refers to a cosmological view that the human is the symbolic center for understanding Earth's history and future. In this hermeneutic (interpretive) use the human figure shapes how we make sense of the Earth, evolutionary history, or the cosmos. Any view supposing that humanity marks the apex of evolution is anthropocentric in this third sense. A view may also suppose that some human quality, if not the species itself, represents the ultimate end of nature. Perhaps humanity's subjective consciousness, however imperfect, reveals the teleological trajectory of nonhuman processes. In that case, the evolutionary Earth tends toward self-conscious complexity, currently represented in the human. Humanity might then have a very small ecological role in the story of the universe and yet provide a crucial interpretive key for making Earth's past and future into an intelligible narrative.

This third use also characterizes some religious worldviews. It is found, for example, in the Eastern Orthodox Christian view of the human as a "microcosm" of creation and creation as a "macrocosm" of the human. Here humanity's liturgical capacity to gather all creatures together in creative praise provides the image of the Earth's unity and center. A nonanthropocentric alternative would include a Gaian view, in which the self-regulatory capacities of the living organism provide the paradigm for interpreting the Earth. Any other view in which some process, logic, or randomness unrelated to humanity provides the intelligible key for making sense of the universe would also be nonanthropocentric in this third sense.

Debates over sustainability sometimes confuse these three different uses of anthropocentrism, so it is important to discriminate carefully how the concept works in various contexts.

Willis JENKINS
Yale Divinity School

FURTHER READING

Callicott, J. Baird. (1999). *Beyond the land ethic: More essays in environmental philosophy*. New York: SUNY Press.

Murdy, William H. (1975). Anthropocentrism: A modern view. *Science*, 187, 4182: 1168–1172.

Norton, Bryan. (2005). *Sustainability: A philosophy of adaptive ecosystem management*. Chicago: University of Chicago Press.

O'Neill, John. (1993). *Ecology, policy, and politics: Human well-being and the natural world*. London: Routledge.

Rolston, Holmes, III. (1994). *Conserving natural value*. New York: Columbia University Press.

Anthroposophy

The tenets of anthroposophy, a spiritual philosophy developed by Rudolf Steiner in the early twentieth century, give priority to balance, harmony, and natural rhythms among individuals, Earth, and cosmos. Biodynamic agriculture is an anthroposophical approach that emphasizes soil fertility and the health of both farm and community.

In 1923 the Austrian philosopher and educator Rudolf Steiner founded the Anthroposophical Society in Switzerland. He coined the term *anthroposophy* to describe his unique philosophical amalgam of science and religion. Steiner, who wrote almost thirty books on anthroposophy and related topics, was greatly influenced by hermeticism (the belief that a full understanding of humanity reveals the nature of the cosmos), by the thinking of Friedrich Nietzsche and Johann Wolfgang von Goethe, and by Christianity.

Anthroposophy is a material spirituality that seeks the cultivation of a physical and psychical Self in harmony with the greater universe. According to anthroposophical thought, earthly forces and cosmic forces act upon the world in a self-sustaining balance. Anthroposophy, meaning wisdom of the human being, has influenced movements in areas as diverse as medicine, agriculture, education, and art.

Anthroposophy encourages intuitive thinking and creativity. Its educational pedagogy led to the opening of Waldorf Schools, the first in Stuttgart, Germany, in 1919. Today there are more than nine hundred Waldorf Schools worldwide. Waldorf education is founded upon educational freedom and the rhythms of everyday life, and it fosters a sense of social responsibility.

From the perspective of environmental ecology, the most important offspring of Steiner's anthroposophical teachings is biodynamic, or "life forces" agriculture. According to the Biodynamic Association of the United States, biodynamic agriculture is a "unified approach to agriculture that relates the ecology of the earth-organism to that of the entire cosmos." In biodynamic farming the entire farm is considered a self-contained, evolving, integrated farm-organism. Soil fertility is given primary importance and is based on balance and natural rhythm. Biodynamics seeks to improve not only the health of the farm but also the community it feeds. Based on Steiner's anthroposophic concept of the producer–consumer relationship, biodynamics has helped support the movement for Community Supported Agriculture, a direct marketing relationship between farmer and customer whereupon the customer buys a share of the farm goods at the beginning of season and then shares in both the rewards and failures of the harvest.

Shannon TYMAN
University of Oregon

FURTHER READING

Davis, John. (Ed.). (1975). *Works arising from the life of Rudolf Steiner.* London: Rudolf Steiner.

Tummer, Lia, & Lato, Horatio. (2001). *Rudolf Steiner and anthroposophy for beginners.* New York: Writers and Readers.

What is biodynamic agriculture? (n.d.). Retrieved March 9, 2009, from http://www.biodynamics.com/biodynamics.html

Architecture

Architecture, a fine art that shapes the physical environment of a society, seems to be a natural sphere for sustainability. The use of renewable building materials, construction techniques that integrate buildings into the natural landscape, and people's innate spiritual connection to place help to make architecture one of the leading fields for the promotion of sustainable practices.

The base meaning of the Greek word *oikos*, from which stems the terms *ecology* and *economics*, is "house." It is no surprise, then, that sustainability has often focused on homes, both the buildings people inhabit as well as the larger-built environment—towns, farms, and cities—in which people conduct their daily lives.

In recent decades several prominent ethical bases for sustainable architecture have emerged. The American natural sciences writer Janine Benyus, for instance, has championed the idea of biomimicry, in which designers and engineers take their cues from nature to solve architectural problems. A building thus might mimic local landforms and vegetation to reduce energy consumption and work with the natural flow of wind and sunlight. The American social ecologist Stephen Kellert, among others, has made a complementary argument for biophilic design, which seeks to bring the affinity many people feel toward nature into the built environment, encouraging its inhabitants to value and protect the natural world. Another American, the architect and designer William McDonough, has taken a third approach—cradle-to-cradle design, which takes into account a product's full life cycle. Instead of the standard cradle-to-grave approach, which assumes products will eventually be discarded as waste, McDonough has argued that products themselves, when properly designed, can been seen as resources. This has been applied to architecture in the model of a living building, in which the built environment functions much like a tree, which produces no waste but replenishes its soil with its own leaves.

Christian theology, and religious social theory more broadly, have only occasionally elaborated on architectural questions, and most of this interest has come from Europe. The most significant theological treatments of the built environment have come from the British theologian T. J. Gorringe, who integrated a mainline Protestant concern for social justice with a concern for urban planning based on the work of the historian Lewis Mumford (1895–1990), and from the Finnish theologian Seppo Kjellberg, who argued for a holistic, nonanthropocentric model of urban life that conceives of humankind flourishing only within a larger context of the flourishing of all creation.

More interest has grown around theories and theologies of place. While these concepts often do not deal explicitly with architecture, in promoting the intrinsic value of particular places they provide a basis for envisioning architecture as interacting with local environments that are valued and respected. Such an ethic is perhaps most vividly embodied in the modern homesteading movement, which has often had either straightforward or implied spiritual underpinnings. Similarly, the study of sacred places, which has a long history in many religious traditions, imbues sites with a spiritual significance that can lead to a desire for sustainability.

Connections between valuing place and sustainability can take many practical directions. One of the most widely publicized examples comes from the development of Arcosanti, an alternative, self-sustaining community in the Arizona desert begun in the 1960s. Its founder, the Italian visionary architect Paolo Soleri, was heavily indebted to the theology of Teilhard de Chardin (1881–1955), who envisioned a new cosmology based on evolutionary science. Women's monastic communities (such as the Felician Sisters of Coraopolis, Pennsylvania, or Genesis Farm in New Jersey) have also been particularly active in green building in the United States. Several communities have connected a place-based ethic and stewardship of the land to innovative forms of sustainable architecture in their buildings, often drawing inspiration from the work of the American cultural historian Thomas Berry (1914–2009).

Architecture is also an arena of increasing engagement among a growing number of religious environmental organizations, as sustainable architecture becomes more established and more people are willing to make the substantial financial investments often required for building projects. Such activism has largely followed patterns established by the broader sustainable architecture movement, focusing most heavily on energy conservation and renewable energy. In this vein one of the earliest and largest organizational efforts has been Interfaith Power and Light (The Regeneration Project), which has concentrated heavily on energy concerns. Several religious organizations have also published green-building guidelines for synagogues or churches, including the National Council of Churches Eco-Justice Working Group, the Web of Creation, Shomrei Adamah of Greater Washington (D.C.), and a number of denominational bodies. In general, all of these green-building initiatives focus on energy consumption, and quite a few deal with additional issues, such as water conversation and landscaping. Less attention is devoted to more technically intimidating design problems, such as materials selection and construction practices. Other organizations, most notably the Evangelical Environmental Network, have focused more specifically on toxics reduction, connecting it to evangelical family values.

Architecture is a uniquely fruitful discipline for both activism and academic inquiry on sustainability and the values supporting it. By addressing the most basic aspects of how people live, reimagining the built environment provides a powerful tool for creating a more sustainable future.

Richard R. BOHANNON II
College of St. Benedict and St. John's University

FURTHER READING

Benyus, Janine. (1997). *Biomimicry: Innovation inspired by nature*. New York: William Morrow.

Bergmann, Sigurd. (Ed.). (2005). *Architecture, aesth/ethics and religion*. Frankfurt am Main, Germany: IKO.

Fox, Warwick. (Ed.). (2000). *Ethics and the built environment*. New York: Routledge.

Gorringe, Timothy J. (2002). *A theology of the built environment: Justice, empowerment, redemption*. New York: Cambridge University Press.

Kellert, Stephen; Heerwagen, Judith; & Mador, Martin. (Eds.). (2008). *Biophilic design: The theory, science, and practice of bringing buildings to life*. Hoboken, NJ: John Wiley & Sons.

Kilbert, Charles. (Ed.). (1999). *Reshaping the built environment: Ecology, ethics, and economics*. Washington, DC: Island Press.

Kjellberg, Seppo. (2000). *Urban ecotheology*. Utrecht, The Netherlands: International Books.

Lane, Belden. (2002). *Landscapes of the sacred: Geography and narrative in American spirituality* (Expanded ed.). Baltimore: Johns Hopkins University Press.

McDonough, William, & Braungart, Michael. (2002). *Cradle to cradle: Remaking the way we make things*. New York: North Point Press.

Soleri, Paolo. (2006). *Arcology: The city in the image of man* (4th ed.). Mayer, AZ: Cosanti Press.

Bahá'í

Founded in the nineteenth century, the Bahá'í Faith now has over 5 million members located throughout the world, representing a microcosm of humanity. Bahá'ís recognize nature as an expression of God's will, view science and religion as complementary approaches to truth, and strive to pursue processes of individual and community development that promote unity, interdependence, social justice, and ecological sustainability.

The Bahá'í Faith is an emerging world religion concerned with the spiritual, social, and ecological challenges facing humanity in an age of increasing global integration. The Persian founder of the Bahá'í Faith, Bahá'u'lláh (1817–1892), called for humanity to recognize a coming age of global interdependence and to implement principles and practices that could serve as the basis for a more just and sustainable world order. The nascent Bahá'í community has, until recently, been focused largely on processes of internal growth, which continue to occupy much of its attention. The worldwide expansion and consolidation of the community, however, has provided it with the human resources and administrative capacity to engage contemporary social and ecological problems in a direct and systematic manner, which it has begun to do.

For instance, in 1987 the Bahá'í Faith joined the World Wide Fund for Nature's Network on Conservation and Religion. Two years later a compilation of extracts from Bahá'í scriptures and other primary texts was published, entitled *Conservation of the Earth's Resources*. Study of this document within the Bahá'í community inspired a multitude of ecological stewardship and sustainable development initiatives around the planet, including environmental education programs, conservation projects, tree-planting activities, sustainable-technology innovations, awareness-raising campaigns employing the arts, and advocacy work in various policy arenas. This document has also inspired a growing body of scholarship exploring the social and ecological dimensions of sustainability from a Bahá'í perspective, and it has prompted the formation of Bahá'í-inspired professional organizations such as the International Environment Forum, which has members in over fifty countries.

Within the U.N. system, the Bahá'í Office of the Environment actively participated in planning processes leading up to the 1992 Earth Summit in Rio de Janeiro. Bahá'í offices at the United Nations also played an active role in most of the other global U.N. summits on social and environmental issues throughout the 1990s, and a Bahá'í representative cochaired the U.N. Millennium Forum of nongovernmental organizations at the end of the decade. Meanwhile, in 1995 Bahá'ís participated in the founding of the Alliance of Religions and Conservation, and in 1998 they became founding members of the World Faiths and Development Dialogue. Membership in these organizations brought Bahá'ís into direct dialogue with other faith communities regarding the spiritual dimension of environment stewardship and sustainable development. This involvement has stimulated a range of grassroots actions within the Bahá'í community. One example is the emergence of Bahá'í-inspired "community learning groups" among the indigenous Bribri and Cabecar peoples in Costa Rica, who are studying the relationship between moral leadership and environmental stewardship; initiating sustainable development projects such as school and family gardens, fish farms, and poultry raising; and collaborating with other local organizations to promote the conservation of natural resources.

Vision of Nature and Society

Underlying these examples of engagement is a sense of spiritual purpose derived from the Bahá'í teachings on nature and society. The Bahá'í Faith is founded on a belief in one unknowable Divine Essence—God. Bahá'u'lláh taught that although humans cannot comprehend God, the natural world is a reflection of God's attributes and an expression of God's will. Bahá'ís are thus urged to revere, contemplate, and unravel the mysteries of nature by drawing on the complementary methods and insights of both science and religion.

In this context, the Bahá'í teachings explain that while the universe is characterized by a great diversity of forms, it is nonetheless an organically integrated whole that is governed by relations of interconnection, mutuality, and balance. Likewise, humanity is understood as an organic whole that should be governed by these same characteristics. Religion, according to Bahá'u'lláh, is the one force capable of unifying humanity in this manner.

The Bahá'í teachings also liken human society to the human body, whose cells and organs, while diverse in form and function, are characterized by reciprocity and interdependence. Within the human body, the health and well-being of each part is inseparable from the health and well-being of the whole. Similarly, in the body of humanity, the interests of all individuals and groups are interdependent, and the well-being of the part is inseparable from the well-being of the whole.

This organic worldview informs the Bahá'í vision of nature and society. According to this worldview, unity and reciprocity are requisites of a just and sustainable social order. Bahá'ís thus believe that as long as human societies remain in states of conflict and competition, divided and indifferent to their organic interdependence, it will be impossible to address increasingly complex social and ecological problems in an effective and sustainable manner.

Evolutionary Perspective

According to the Bahá'í teachings, humanity has arrived at a critical historical juncture. Humanity's social evolution has led to unprecedented levels of interdependence and has dramatically increased our impact upon the ecological systems that sustain us. Yet inherited patterns of belief and behavior prevent humanity from addressing the challenges that we are now facing. As these inherited cultural codes prove maladaptive under contemporary conditions, Bahá'ís believe that the social and ecological crises facing us will continue to deepen and proliferate.

Bahá'ís hold that at this critical juncture in human history the question facing humanity is whether we will embrace our organic unity and interdependence as a species and self-consciously adapt to the new conditions of our existence, or whether we will cling to inherited patterns of belief and behavior and learn the lessons of interdependence the hard way, through the deepening social and ecological consequences of a failure to adapt. The goal of the Bahá'í community is, therefore, to effect those changes in human culture and consciousness that will hasten the construction of a more just and sustainable social order.

Likening human society again to an individual body, the Bahá'í writings teach that we have passed through the stages of our collective infancy and childhood and have now reached the turbulent transitional period of our collective adolescence, in which we are approaching our full physical capacity but our actions are not yet tempered by the wisdom and judgment that comes with maturity. Although this transitional stage will be difficult, Bahá'ís have confidence that the long-awaited age of maturity, alluded to in various ways by all of the major religious traditions of the past, will eventually be realized.

This process, according to the Bahá'í teachings, implies an organic change in the structure of society that will reflect the underlying principle, or truth, of the oneness of humanity. This principle entails the emergence of a consciousness of world citizenship, along with the eventual federation of all nations into an integrated system of governance that can coordinate and harmonize human affairs across the planet. The principle of oneness also entails: the establishment of the full equality of men and women in all arenas of human affairs; the elimination of all forms of prejudice and discrimination based on race, religion, or nationality; the establishment of a universal currency and other integrating mechanisms that promote global economic justice and shared prosperity; the adoption of an international auxiliary language that facilitates communication and mutual understanding; the demilitarization of the world and the redirection of massive military expenditures toward constructive social ends; and the emergence of an ethic of sustainable development that promotes the conservation and stewardship of the Earth's resources, along with the just and equitable distribution of the benefits that derive from them.

Dimensions of Change

In order to effect these changes, the Bahá'í Faith addresses itself to both individual and institutional dimensions of change. At the level of the individual, Bahá'ís engage in a number of spiritual disciplines, such as daily prayer and meditation, along with an annual period of fasting, as they strive to transcend the pull of their baser instincts and struggle to develop qualities of the spirit such as selflessness, moderation, purity of motive, and devotion to the common good—all of which they see not only as individual spiritual imperatives but as prerequisites for a just and sustainable collective future. To these ends, the Bahá'í community is also developing systematic approaches to the moral education of children, the spiritual and intellectual empowerment of adolescents, and the training of older youth and adults with skills and capacities for community service—as demonstrated by the Ruhi Institute, which has developed training materials and educational processes that are being used by tens of thousands of Bahá'ís and others around the world. In addition, Bahá'ís emphasize the education of individuals in the arts and sciences, which are recognized as powerful forces for social transformation and advancement. Examples of such an emphasis can be seen in Bahá'í-inspired projects such as the Mongolian Development Center in Ulaanbaatar, the Barli Development Institute for Rural Women in India, the Uganda Program of Literacy for Transformation, or the Foundation for the Application and Teaching of the Sciences in Colombia.

Difficult as these processes of individual education and development may be, Bahá'ís see them as necessary but insufficient conditions for the establishment of a more just and sustainable social order. Responsible and effective institutional forms are also needed. Toward this end, the Bahá'í community is constructing (at local, national, and international levels), institutional structures and practices it believes are suited to the age of maturity that humanity is entering.

For instance, the Bahá'í community, which has no clergy, employs a participatory system of governance with a unique electoral process that, while democratic in spirit, is entirely nonpartisan and noncompetitive. All adult community members are eligible for election, and every member has the reciprocal duty to serve if elected. Nominations, campaigning, and all forms of solicitation are prohibited. Voters are to be guided only by their own consciences as they exercise real freedom of choice in voting for those they believe best embody qualities such as trustworthiness, integrity, recognized ability, mature experience, and selfless service to others. Through a plurality count, the nine individuals that receive the most votes are called to serve as members of the governing assembly—even though they did not seek to be elected.

These assemblies, in turn, are guided by consultative principles that are intended to encourage decision making as a unifying rather than divisive process. These electoral and decision-making methods are used to govern the affairs of the Bahá'í community at the local, national, and international levels. With a current membership of over 5 million people drawn from over two thousand ethnic backgrounds and residing in every nation, these methods of governance are currently being learned and practiced in over ten thousand distinct communities around the globe. Based on decades of accumulated experience with these methods, Bahá'ís offer their administrative system as a model that others can learn from in their search for more just and sustainable institutional forms.

Science and Religion

As Bahá'ís focus on processes of individual and institutional transformation, they also emphasize the importance of applying scientific knowledge and methods in efforts to solve the mounting social and ecological problems facing humanity. But Bahá'ís believe only religion can inspire the vision, motivation, commitment, self-sacrifice, and unified action required to construct a just and sustainable social order that encompasses the planet.

Science and religion are thus understood by Bahá'ís as complementary systems of knowledge that can guide human development and channel humanity's intellectual and moral powers within processes of social evolution. According to this view, the methods of science have allowed humanity to construct a coherent understanding of the laws and processes governing physical reality. The insights of religion have, in turn, illuminated the deepest questions of human purpose and existence, clarified those shared values and essential principles that promote human well-being, and given constructive direction to individual and collective endeavors—including the enlightened application of scientific knowledge.

In this context, Bahá'ís interpret the purely materialistic interpretations of reality that are often advanced in the name of science as obstacles to dealing with the pressing challenges facing humanity. At the same time, they interpret the fanatical and divisive claims that are often advanced in the name of religion as equally problematic obstacles. According to the Bahá'í teachings, religion in its pure form is a single, universal, and transhistorical phenomenon that reflects humanity's ongoing response to expressions of a Divine will and purpose. Religious truth, Bahá'u'lláh taught, is revealed progressively over time according to the changing needs and capacities of ever-evolving human societies. At this stage in history, Bahá'ís believe, the purpose of religion is to renew and affirm the eternal spiritual truths that have been articulated within all past religious dispensations, while focusing humanity on the essential task of learning how to live together in a just and sustainable way, as an interdependent global community.

Future Prospects

The overarching purpose of the Bahá'í Faith is to effect the spiritual unification of the human family and establish a just and sustainable world order. To skeptics, this transformative project appears to be an expression of naïve idealism. To Bahá'ís, it appears to be the only realistic way forward at this critical juncture in history.

At this early stage in the development of the Bahá'í community, however, most Bahá'ís admit that they are still struggling to successfully apply many of their own teachings. In this regard, individual Bahá'ís vary significantly in their grasp of these teachings and in their commitments of time and energy to the work of the community. They also struggle to transcend cultural habits and inherited patterns of thought that often pull against or undermine their ideals. Bahá'í efforts to adopt more sustainable lifestyles—like the efforts of other people—are often compromised by limited understandings of the issues, or by the powerful pull of consumer culture, or by the unsustainable structures of contemporary society within which they currently live. Yet as the Bahá'í community grows, matures over time, and pursues its long-term project of spiritual and social transformation, the internal discourse of the community is increasingly focused on issues of sustainability; mechanisms are being established to deepen the community's grasp of, and commitment to, the principles and practices of sustainability.

In keeping with the spirit of openness, experimentation, and systematic learning that characterizes

THE BAHÁ'Í APPROACH TO SUSTAINABILITY

Today the Bahá'í Faith promotes the oneness of humanity, equality of the sexes, international justice, and world peace—all components in the striving toward sustainable life. The Persian founder of the faith, Bahá'u'lláh (1817–1892), urged humanity to put into practice such principles in light of a coming age of global interdependence; the following excerpt comes from one of thousands of scriptural "tablets" he wrote emphasizing nonliteral interpretations of the Bible and the Quran—this one a slim book of laws.

Verily, the Word of God is the Cause which hath preceded the contingent world—a world which is adorned with the splendours of the Ancient of Days, yet is being renewed and regenerated at all times. Immeasurably exalted is the God of Wisdom Who hath raised this sublime structure . . . Say: Nature in its essence is the embodiment of My Name, the Maker, the Creator. Its manifestations are diversified by varying causes, and in this diversity there are signs for men of discernment. Nature is God's Will and is its expression in and through the contingent world. It is a dispensation of Providence ordained by the Ordainer, the All-Wise.

Source: Tablets of Bahá'u'lláh revealed after the Kitáb-i-Aqdas, by Bahá'u'lláh (1892). Haifa, Israel: Bahá'í World Centre, 141–142.

the worldwide Bahá'í community, Bahá'ís offer their ongoing experience as a vast social experiment that is open for others to study. The long-term outcomes of this experiment, however, are still too distant to assess in an empirical manner. But the initial experience and accomplishments of the Bahá'í community raise thought-provoking questions about whether, or how, humanity might eventually adapt to conditions of heightened global interdependence.

Michael KARLBERG
Western Washington University

FURTHER READING

Arbab, Farzam. (2000). Promoting a discourse on science, religion, and development. In Sharon Harper (Ed.), *The lab, the temple and the market: Reflections on the intersection of science, religion and development* (pp. 149–210). Ottawa: International Development Research Centre.

Bahá'í International Community, United Nations Office. (n.d.). Statements and reports. Retrieved April 5, 2009, from www.bic-un.bahai.org

Bahá'í International Community. (2008). For the betterment of the world: The worldwide Bahá'í community's approach to social and economic development. New York: Office of Social and Economic Development, United Nations.

Bahá'i International Community. (1987). *Statement on nature.* New York: Bahá'í International Community Office of Public Information, United Nations.

Bahá'í International Community. (1992). *Sustainable development and the human spirit.* New York: Bahá'í International Community Office of Public Information, United Nations.

Bahá'í International Community. (1992). *The most vital challenge.* New York: Bahá'í International Community Office of Public Information, United Nations.

Bahá'í International Community. (1993). *World citizenship: Global ethic for sustainable development.* New York: Bahá'í International Community Office of Public Information, United Nations.

Bahá'í International Community. (1995). *Conservation and sustainable development in the Bahá'í Faith.* New York: Bahá'í International Community Office of Public Information, United Nations.

Bahá'í International Community. (1995). *The prosperity of humankind.* Haifa, Israel: Bahá'í International Community Office of Public Information.

Bahá'í International Community. (1996). *Sustainable communities in an integrating world.* New York: Bahá'í International Community Office of Public Information, United Nations.

Bahá'í International Community. (1998). *Valuing spirituality in development: Initial considerations regarding the creation of spiritually-based indicators for development.* New York: Bahá'í International Community Office of Public Information, United Nations.

Bahá'í International Community. (2001). *Sustainable development: The spiritual dimension.* New York: Bahá'í International Community Office of Public Information, United Nations.

Bahá'u'lláh. (1982). *Tablets of Bahá'u'lláh revealed after the Kitáb-i-Aqdas.* Haifa, Israel: Bahá'í World Centre.

Bahá'u'lláh; Abdu'l-Bahá; Shoghi Effendi; & Universal House of Justice. (1989). *Conservation of the Earth's resources: A compilation by the research department of the Universal House of Justice.* Haifa, Israel: Bahá'í World Centre.

Bushrui, Suheil. (2002). Environmental ethics: A Bahá'í perspective. In David Cadman and John Carey (Eds.), *A sacred trust: Ecology and spiritual vision* (pp. 77–102). London: The Temenos Academy and The Prince's Foundation.

Dahl, Arthur L. (1990). *Unless and until: A Bahá'í focus on the environment.* London: Bahá'í Publishing Trust.

Dahl, Arthur L. (1996). *The eco principle: Ecology and economics in symbiosis.* Oxford, U.K.: George Ronald; London: Zed Books.

Hatcher, William S., & Martin, J. Douglas. (1998). *The Bahá'í Faith: The emerging global religion.* Wilmette, IL: Bahá'í Publishing Trust.

Karlberg, Michael. (1994). Toward a new environmental stewardship. *World Order, 25,* 21–32.

Karlberg, Michael. (2004). *Beyond the culture of contest: From adversarialism to mutualism in an age of interdependence.* Oxford, U.K.: George Ronald.

Lalonde, Roxanne. (1994). Unity in diversity: A conceptual framework for a global ethic of environmental sustainability. *The Journal of Bahá'í Studies, 6*(3), 39–73.

White, Robert A. (1995). Spiritual foundations for an ecologically sustainable society. *The Journal of Bahá'í Studies, 7*(2), 47–74.

Universal House of Justice. (1985). *The promise of world peace.* Haifa, Israel: Bahá'í World Centre.

Vick, Holly Hanson. (1989). *Social and economic development: A Bahá'í approach.* Oxford, U.K.: George Ronald.

Beauty

The objective side of beauty is what most people consider first: the attractiveness of other people or things. But beauty's subjective side—the emotional and intellectual happiness humans gain as they interact with their world—is equally important for a sustainable planet. This aspect of beauty provides an inner sense of caring about and for the Earth and its inhabitants.

A sustainable community is creative, compassionate, equitable, participatory, ecologically wise, and spiritually satisfying, with no one left behind. The community at issue can be a household, workplace, classroom, village, city, province, or nation. It will be sustainable in two senses. It can *be sustained* into the indefinite future given the limits of its bioregions to supply resources and absorb wastes, and it will *offer sustenance*—material and spiritual—for people as they interact with one another and the surrounding world.

Beauty is part of the sustenance of a sustainable community. Beauty need not be limited to artistic or musical beauty. It consists of two qualities people often find in works of art and music, but which can be present in many other contexts: harmony and intensity. These qualities are fluid and dynamic as in music; often they come together as harmonious intensity and intense harmony.

Harmony and intensity are present in life in two ways. The first is the harmony and intensity that people see in other people, other animals, landscapes, events, and artifacts. Let us call this *beauty in the world*. The beauty of the natural world can be poignant or awesome, tender or frightening. In humanly made artifacts—buildings and cities, for example—the harmony will be of the more pleasant variety, and part of its beauty will be the way it combines two kinds of harmony that are part of a sustainable community: harmony with the Earth and harmony among people. Sustainable architecture can embody these two forms of harmony in their use of materials and energy from the surrounding bioregion and in the way they make space for human dwelling.

The second way that beauty is present in human life is through dwelling itself: how we live in the world, emotionally and intellectually, from a first-person perspective. Beauty is the harmony and intensity that people can experience emotionally and intellectually as they perceive, respond to, and interact with the surrounding world. This is the more subjective side of beauty. It is beauty as an *experience of the world*.

There are no subjects or selves who exist all by themselves, without a surrounding world with which they interact. This surrounding world consists of other people, animals, landscapes, soundscapes, the Earth itself. Consider a woman who feels at home in a certain landscape. She will experience the landscape of the region as beautiful in its own right through the palpable contrasts and textures of its flora and fauna. She may also experience aspects of the culture of the region as beautiful: the music, the food, the customs, and the buildings. And of course she will appreciate the people in the region. All will come together in what she calls her home. Her home in this context is not a building; it is a place where she feels at home.

And yet her feeling of being at home is not reducible to the objective dimensions of place. Her sense of home is an inner sense of being *with* the land and its people and caring about both. This is the subjective side of beauty. Accordingly, her sense of the spirit—that is, her spirituality—lies in this sense of communion, this sense of connection with wider harmonies and intensities.

Of course her capacities for appreciating beauty will be shaped by the social circumstances and cultural climates in which she lives. The world in which she finds herself is interpreted by the culture in which she lives. But her capacities are also being shaped by the natural world: landscapes and soundscapes, for example. Considerations of sustainability often include attention to wild animals, but the important role of domesticated animals ought not be forgotten. For some people, household pets are a primary instance of beauty in the nonhuman world. Imagine that her household includes a companion animal: a household cat. Her inner sense of well-being will be influenced by friends and family, to be sure; but it will also be influenced by the cat and its companionship. The cat has a world of her own, too. Not only humans, but also other animals, seek harmony and intensity in their interactions with the world. And of course other animals are beautiful, too.

To be sure, some might say that there is no beauty in the world—not even in cats—except as created or projected by human beings. This is anthropocentrism at its worst. It reduces beauty to a human contrivance. A healthy alternative is found in *Science and the Modern World* by Alfred North Whitehead (1861–1947), who critiques the idea of inert matter and offers a plausible argument that matter is energy, and that energy is inherently creative, bringing about its own harmonies and intensities quite apart from human projection. In this view, even if there were no humans, there would still be harmonies and intensities on Earth. They would lie in the experiences of animals and their worlds, and also in the harmonies and intensities of hills and rivers, mountains and trees.

The sustainability movement is premised on the hope that these two sides of beauty—one objective and one more subjective—can come together in human practices. Imagine that the woman is a gardener. The subjective side of beauty will include her knowledge of soil and plants and also the sense of rapport with the Earth brought about by working with these elements. And yet her sense of being with the Earth can include a respect for the objective harmonies of soil, sun, and plants as they exist independently of feelings and personal affinities. She can find it comforting, not depressing, that the land in which her garden resides can survive her death with its harmonies and intensities. All of these come together in her gardening. Her gardening is a spiritual practice and a sustainable practice.

Some people resist linking beauty and sustainability. They prefer to define sustainability in terms of moral obligation or ecological necessity. They say we ought to live in sustainable ways because our survival depends on it or because all living beings have a right to be protected from harm. Some might add that we are commanded by God to be good caretakers of the Earth and that the Earth belongs to God, not to human beings. Certainly there is wisdom in these more forceful and muscular ways of thinking. Nevertheless, an overemphasis on imperatives neglects a more joyful and spiritually meaningful way of looking at the world. If our categories are restricted to ideas concerning "right" and "wrong," we forget what the gardener knows. We forget that sustainable living must provide sustenance for human life and that a divine reality can be understood, not simply as a source of obligatory commands but as an indwelling lure toward beauty. We also neglect the fact that there can be a joyful side to sustainability: a side that includes laughter, play, merrymaking, rest, relaxation, dancing, and music. A sustainable world that lacks joy and merrymaking will be good but not happy. The need today is for sustainable communities that are good and happy, ethical and delightful, responsible and joyful. Martin Luther King Jr. called them beloved communities. We might also call them sustaining communities or beautiful communities.

Jay McDANIEL
Hendrix College

FURTHER READING

Baker-Fletcher, Karen. (1998). *Sisters of dust, sisters of spirit: Womanist wordings on God and creation.* Minneapolis, MN: Augsburg Fortress.

Berry, Thomas. (2009, forthcoming in September). *The sacred universe: Earth, spirituality, and religion in the twenty-first century.* New York: Columbia University Press.

Fox, Matthew. (2000). *Original blessing: A primer in creation spirituality.* New York: Jeremy P. Tarcher/Putnam.

Hope, Marjorie, & Young, James. (1994, Summer). Islam and ecology. *Cross Cultures, 44*(2), 180–192. Retrieved May 20, 2009, from http://www.crosscurrents.org/islamecology.htm

Whitehead, Alfred North. (1997). *Science and the modern world.* New York: The Free Press. (Originally published in 1925)

Whitehead, Alfred North. (1956). *Adventure of ideas.* New York: Penguin Group.

Biocentrism

Biocentrism, or "life-centeredness," defines a perspective that played an important part in the development of ecological theory and ethics throughout the twentieth century. Because biocentrism focuses on the flourishing of life, its interdependence, and the need to protect ongoing evolutionary possibilities for all creatures, it provides a way of framing the goals of sustainability discourse and practice.

The term "biocentrism" means "life-centeredness." It indicates a central concern for and prioritization of the biotic community as a locus of value, and is most closely associated with the fields of environmental ethics and environmental philosophy. When paired with the concept of sustainability, biocentrism offers a means for deliberating about what is likely to promote the well-being of future generations, not just for humans but for all Earthbound species.

In 1915 the horticulturalist Liberty Hyde Bailey (1858–1954) used the term "biocentric" in his book *The Holy Earth* to describe the "brotherhood relation" shared among all beings that "are parts in a living sensitive creation" (1919 [1915], 30). Bailey expressed his philosophy of "the oneness in nature and the unity of living things" throughout this work, but the title of the book alone indicated that he regarded the Earth and its life forms as sacred and worthy of reverent care. Biocentrism was thus early associated with responsibilities that went beyond material utilization of the Earth's resources.

During the twentieth century the science of ecology bolstered and provided content to the concept of biocentrism, highlighting the interdependence of natural systems and the importance of biotic diversity to their resilience. As the historian Roderick Nash put it, ecologists "were the scientists most likely to meet holistic-thinking theologians and philosophers half-way" (Nash 1989, 68). Beginning in the early 1970s, environmental philosophers who articulated what would become known as "deep ecology" drew attention to biocentrism as a critical facet of expanding ethical consideration to nonhuman species and the biosphere as a whole. The philosopher Arne Naess (1912–2009) is credited with naming "biocentric equality" (the right of all things to live and flourish) as one of deep ecology's most basic principles (Devall and Sessions 1985). Some have even promoted biocentrism as a religious alternative to human-focused "world" religions and secular humanism, arguing that biocentrism promotes "interspecies equality" and "a sense of planetary belonging" in which "the planet becomes its own church" (Watson 2005, 178).

Biocentrism is often contrasted with other terms that indicate the center of value (or the sacred center) for an individual or community. Anthropocentrism (human-centeredness) serves as the starkest contrast, and biocentrism is frequently paired with this term and used as a counterweight to suggest its ethical shortcomings. Terms like "ecocentrism" and "geocentrism" also highlight nonanthropocentric approaches to valuing the Earth and its living systems.

Critics of terms like "biocentrism" see them as overly abstract and unhelpful in offering unifying pragmatic solutions to environmental problems. But for some people this word continues to provide a shorthand way of articulating a larger philosophical vision in which all life is interconnected and which seeks to promote the interests of human and nonhuman life alike.

Biocentrism is one way of framing the goals of sustainability discourse and practice in that it focuses on the flourishing of life, its interdependence, and the need to protect ongoing evolutionary possibilities for all creatures. If sustainability is understood as a movement toward ensuring the local and planetary well-being of future generations, then biocentrism may be considered one method of rethinking the relationships between human communities and the natural world so that this vision might be approximated in practice.

Gavin VAN HORN
Southwestern University

FURTHER READING

Bailey, Liberty Hyde. (1919 [1915]). *The holy Earth*. New York: Scribner Press.

Devall, Bill, & Sessions, George. (1985). *Deep ecology: Living as if nature mattered*. Salt Lake City, UT: Gibbs Smith.

Lynn, William S. (1998). Contested moralities: Animals and moral value in the Dear/Symanski debate. *Ethics, Place, and Environment 1*(2), 223–242.

Nash, Roderick F. (1989). *The rights of nature: A history of environmental ethics*. Madison: The University of Wisconsin Press.

Norton, Bryan G. (1991). *Toward unity among environmentalists*. New York: Oxford University Press.

Rolston, Holmes, III. (1988). *Environmental ethics: Duties to and values in the natural world*. Philadelphia: Temple University Press.

Watson, Paul. (2005). Biocentric religion—a call for. In Bron Taylor (Ed.), *Encyclopedia of religion and nature* (pp. 176–179). London and New York: Continuum.

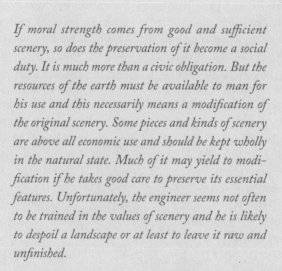

If moral strength comes from good and sufficient scenery, so does the preservation of it become a social duty. It is much more than a civic obligation. But the resources of the earth must be available to man for his use and this necessarily means a modification of the original scenery. Some pieces and kinds of scenery are above all economic use and should be kept wholly in the natural state. Much of it may yield to modification if he takes good care to preserve its essential features. Unfortunately, the engineer seems not often to be trained in the values of scenery and he is likely to despoil a landscape or at least to leave it raw and unfinished.

LIBERTY HYDE BAILEY

Source: Liberty Hyde Bailey. (1919 [1915]). *The Holy Earth*, pp. 116–117. New York: Scribner Press.

Biodiversity

The concept of biological diversity, or biodiversity, often focuses on the material impacts of species loss and on quantitative measures, such as the variety of species and number of individuals of a species in a given area. Enlarging the discourse to critically engage such qualitative values as morals, aesthetics, and symbolism, and to address social injustices, is essential for slowing the loss of biodiversity.

Human life depends, in ways that scientists do not yet fully understand, on other forms of life. Humans depend on intact ecosystems—the interdependent webs of living and nonliving things, including plants, animals, insects, microbes, and physical features of the landscape—to absorb pollution, maintain soil fertility and microclimates, and cleanse water. Without diverse and flourishing abundance in other forms of life, humans would have nothing to eat or wear, no clean water, no medicine, and no shelter or building materials.

Beyond these material concerns, without the diversity of life on Earth we would hear no bird song or crickets; we would see no colorful flowers; we would have no pollinators for our crops (we would have no crops); and we would have no pets, companion animals, or livestock. Scientists now believe that optimum human functioning relies on interactions with intact living biological diversity. This theory, known as the biophilia hypothesis, recognizes that the human species co-evolved with other forms of life, and, as such, is reliant on these interactions for well-being across a diversity of measures. People often find natural landscapes with open vistas, bright colors, and water sources to be soothing, in contrast with the noise and complexity of the urban environment. Hospital patients tend to heal faster and experience improved mood if they can see plants or trees outside their windows. Living nature—particularly

birds, insects, and flowering plants—ignites our aesthetic appreciation. Songbirds announce the arrival of spring with their melodious tunes. People experience awe and wonder upon observing large mammals, such as bears or whales. Conversely, snakes, spiders and some predatory carnivores such as wolves and hyenas can evoke strong emotions of fear and hatred. Symbolic thought is replete with animal images. Some scientists have suggested that the growth of human cognition was dependent on interactions with the natural world.

Three Levels of Biodiversity

Healthy ecosystems depend upon compositional, structural, and functional biodiversity at all scales, from microorganisms to landscape level. Three different levels of biodiversity are important for the maintenance of life functions: genetic diversity, population diversity, and species diversity. (A species is commonly defined, and most easily understood, as a group of organisms that interbreed in the wild, producing viable offspring. Scientists continue to debate the best definition of species, however, as different ways of defining species lead to different conservation outcomes. Viewing a species as a dynamic evolutionary unit contributes to the maintenance of evolutionary potential.)

Genetic Diversity

Maintaining the genetic diversity within a species—one dynamic evolutionary unit—means that the species maintains the ability to evolve and adapt to changing environmental conditions through random mutation among its genes. With reduced genetic diversity, the breeding individuals within a species have less genetic material to draw upon, and the offspring will have less variation; therefore, it is less likely that any one individual will have a random mutation that allows it to take advantage of new environmental conditions. Genetic diversity in agriculture, for example, provides an important guard against pests and diseases because with genetic variability some of the varieties of a crop are likely to have developed genetic resistance to a particular disease. But with increased cloning and narrowing of the varieties of crops, important genetic diversity within species is lost, putting the food supply at greater risk. Similarly, genetic diversity in the wild means that some individuals will likely be able to resist a disease outbreak, thus insulating a wild population against total loss.

Population Diversity

Population diversity within one species is also known as community diversity. Various populations of one species, living in different areas, will have phenotypic variability (observable differences) due to gene–environment interactions. That is, environmental and developmental conditions can cause differing expressions of the organism's genetic code, or genotype. Genotypes may be expressed differently, depending on the surrounding conditions, leading to variation within one species. This variation is both the result of and a contribution to plasticity, or environmental adaptability.

Species Diversity

When discussing biodiversity, it is usually species diversity to which people are referring, the number of distinct and different species of life. The eminent biologist Edward O. Wilson estimates species on the planet to number from 3.6 million to 100 million or more, depending on what method of delineating a species is used; only 1.5 to 1.8 million have been given scientific names (Wilson 2002, 14). Only a small proportion of the species that scientists have identified and named are represented by specimens in museums or written about in scientific journals.

Besides animals and plants—a small proportion of the huge diversity of life on Earth—there are numerous microorganisms and insects. More than half the species that have been described are insects; scientists believe that there are likely ten million different species of insects (with nearly 300,000 species of beetles alone) (Wilson 1992, 133–137). Of the millions of species on the planet, some 5 million to 15 million are eukaryotes, a group that includes animals, plants, fungi, and protists (protozoans and similar one-celled creatures), all organisms with a complex cell structure (Dirzo and Raven 2003, 142). However, the kingdom of Monera, single-celled prokaryotic organisms, has hardly been explored. As Wilson (1992, 145) points

out: "To plumb the depths of our ignorance, consider that there are millions of insect species still unstudied, most or all of which harbor specialized bacteria. There are millions of other invertebrate species, from corals to crustaceans to starfish, in [a] similar state."

Species-level diversity is necessary for maintaining the functioning of ecosystems. Because of the numerous interactions that occur in living systems, the whole system depends on the organisms occupying each niche. Resistance to external disturbances is correlated with species richness. For example, studies have shown that removing predators from food webs can cause trophic cascade (a condition in which certain prey species increase), resulting in imbalances throughout the ecosystem. Species diversity is decreasing as species become extinct—often due to human interference—and genetic diversity is decreasing, especially through monocropping in agriculture.

Species diversity rises and falls throughout time. Paleontologists have identified five major extinctions, including the Cretaceous-Tertiary extinction, which occurred 65 million years ago and killed the dinosaurs. Scientists believe that most of the previous extinctions were caused by the collision of asteroids with the Earth. These asteroids threw up huge clouds of dust and ash, temporarily changing the climate, slowing photosynthesis, and making it difficult for species that could not adapt to survive.

Biodiversity Loss

In *The Diversity of Life* Edward O. Wilson (1992, 254) wrote that he could not imagine a "scientific problem of greater immediate importance for humanity" than the ongoing loss of biological diversity. Species continue to disappear faster than biologists can identify and record them. Many ecologists believe that we are in the midst of a sixth great extinction because the current extinction rate of species is occurring at much greater than typical levels. Estimates of the current rate of extinction range from several hundred times greater than typical (Dirzo and Raven 2003, 154) to one thousand to ten thousand times the rate prior to the era of human influence (Wilson 2002, 99). Human-caused changes to conditions of the planet have made it less habitable for other species.

The major driver of biodiversity loss is the conversion of land for human uses, which leads to habitat degradation, destruction, and fragmentation that result in fewer habitats for other species. It is estimated that land-use change will have a large impact on terrestrial ecosystems through 2100, by which time more than 50 percent of current species could be lost. Land conversion happens through agriculture and aquaculture, human settlement, resource extraction, and transportation routes. Agriculture and grazing cause more degradation than any other use of the land. Large stretches of forested land may become fragmented through the extension of roads for commerce or logging. Many species depend on large stretches of contiguous intact forest for their survival. Roads subdivide forests into smaller fragments, each of which has a distinctive edge with different ecological qualities than the interior of the forest. Forest edges tend to be drier, warmer, brighter, windier, and less dense than forest interiors, creating inhospitable conditions for some species. In addition, roads open up threats from predators, invasive species, and humans.

More than 60 percent of ecosystems are degraded and unable to support their previous diversity of life. Wetlands and marshes are filled or drained for agricultural use or housing developments, destroying the habitat of wildlife and vegetation. The worst degradation and land conversion has occurred in the temperate grasslands, such as those of the Great Plains of the United States and the Argentine pampas, and in shrub lands and Mediterranean climates such as those found around the Mediterranean Sea, along the central and southern coasts of California, and around the tip of South Africa. Even if habitat loss were halted immediately, some species would still go extinct because of extinction debt, the delayed response to complex ecological factors already in motion.

Other factors influencing the decline of biodiversity, as the following examples describe, include the over-exploitation of species for human uses, the introduction of exotic species that outcompete native species, pollution, global climate change, and disease. Overexploitation of species has led to notable extinctions, such as that of the passenger pigeon. Once the most common bird in North America, the passenger pigeon suffered habitat loss from deforestation and, as a sought-after food source, became the victim of large-scale commercial hunting. The annual global loss of forestland converted for other use or harvested for timber is equivalent to an area the size of Texas and New Mexico combined. Introduced, or exotic, species such as zebra mussels, originally native to Russia, were accidentally introduced into North America, where they now outcompete local species, spread widely, and clog water-treatment plant valves. Industrial pollution of air, water, and soils damages plants and poisons animals. Global climate change is expected to cause modifications in the home ranges and life histories of wild species such that, for example, a species of leaf-eating caterpillar could hatch before the leaves it depends upon for food have appeared on the trees. Agricultural pests, weedy species, and disease carriers may all increase in a warmer climate. Local extinctions may occur as an area becomes too warm or too dry to support its historical species. Already some native grass habitats have experienced productivity declines of one-third for every 1°C of warming.

Preserving Biodiversity

Scientists and conservationists have developed a number of strategies for focusing attention and resources on those areas of high biodiversity facing the greatest threats. Conservation International (a nonprofit organization founded in 1987 and headquartered in Arlington, Virginia) has designated the world's thirty-four most biological rich regions facing the greatest threat of loss as biodiversity "hotspots." These are regions with 1,500 or more endemic plant species (representing 0.5 percent of the world's plant diversity), in which 70 percent of the original habitat has been lost. Hotspots are found in places as diverse as Madagascar, the Himalayas, Mexico, and California.

Because about two-thirds of the hotspots are found in forests, the World Wildlife Fund has established the Global 200 ecoregions, "a science-based global ranking of the Earth's most biologically outstanding terrestrial, freshwater, and marine habitats" (Activities of the WWF 2008). These 238 ecoregions represent the diversity of ecosystems and processes on Earth, including the full range of habitat types. (The World Wildlife Fund, founded in Switzerland in 1961, is an international nonprofit conservation organization. Its U.S. headquarters are in Washington, D.C.)

Directing attention to the level of threat, the "crisis ecoregions" approach compares the proportion of land converted to human use with the protected proportion. Crisis ecoregions are those places where the habitat condition and threats suggest that "substantial, irreversible, and irreplaceable losses of significant biodiversity are likely without successful conservation intervention," according to The Nature Conservancy's knowledge-sharing website (www.conserveonline.org).

Wilderness protection aims to keep some areas completely free of human influence so that natural processes can continue undisturbed. These areas, however, are frequently visited by people and, therefore, may not be completely undisturbed. But both recreation and nature tourism have been shown to have negative effects on wildlife.

Parks and protected areas have been established to protect and preserve endangered species. But particularly in developing countries, where the greatest species richness exists, parks are difficult to manage due to a lack of funding and human resources. In addition, some parks have been established in areas long used by local peoples who are understandably unwilling to cede access to lands they have traditionally used. National parks and even entire tourist-destination countries, such as Nepal, may be "loved to death." For example, in Yosemite National Park, Yosemite Valley, with its smog, gridlock, and trampled meadows, resembles Disneyland more than it resembles a pristine habitat for wildlife. Park officials concentrate visitor impact in one place so that the backcountry sustains much less user impact. Despite this overuse the park plays a critical role in engaging people in environmental issues and nurturing a love for other living beings.

In an international program of debt-for-nature swaps, a portion of a developing country's international debt is forgiven in exchange for its implementation of biodiversity conservation measures. A newer form of economic transfer in support of biodiversity is payment for environmental services. This system recognizes the myriad benefits that people receive from intact ecosystems, such as water purification and flood control by wetlands, and requires that those receiving the benefits contribute financially to their continuation. The payments may then support the preservation and maintenance of intact ecosystems.

Eco-agricultural systems seek to sustain rural livelihoods and protect biodiversity and ecosystem functioning through encouraging mosaics of wild and cultivated land in patterns, such as corridors and windbreaks. Integrated eco-agricultural systems create new protected areas that benefit farmers and work to raise the production of the farms to prevent land conversion. This system recognizes the dependence of many of the world's poor on rural livelihoods and endeavors to improve their livelihoods while protecting biodiversity.

Biodiversity as Human Context

The world's religions reflect human interactions with the rich diversity of life on Earth. The Old Testament of the Bible, the foundation for Jewish and Christian religions, situates humans in the context of life on Earth, placing them in the Garden of Eden, where they are instructed to be caretakers. Islam carries, at its heart, a charge to protect the natural world through following God-given codes (*al shariah*) of ethical and moral behavior that encompass all aspects of life. As a sign of God, nature is a means of communication from God to humanity and cannot be subject to human whims. In Hinduism, numerous gods take on aspects of various animals. Two of the most popular are the elephant-headed god Ganesh, who removes obstacles and presides over beginnings, and the monkey-faced Lord Hanuman, who reflects the divine Shiva. The Hindu and Buddhist precept of *ahimsa,* or nonharming, advises followers against killing other living beings. The historical Buddha reached enlightenment under a pipal tree (*Ficus religiousa),* and thus Buddhists revere this tree and, by extension, other trees.

In diverse non-Western cultures—including those of Indonesia, Brazil, Australia, India, Ghana, and the Himalayas—local people preserve species and forests through indigenous practices rooted in their religious beliefs. These people believe that gods or spirits inhabit natural elements of the landscape, and thus destruction or degradation of those elements will result in great harm to the individual or village. The power of this belief is manifest in its ability to protect an area of forest, even as food and other resources are harvested from the surrounding landscape.

Because human life evolved in tandem with other species, some scientists suggest that humans have an innate affinity for life and lifelike processes, a quality aptly termed *biophilia* (literally meaning "love of life"). According to the biophilia hypothesis, human well-being is nurtured and enhanced by diverse interactions with other forms of live, for it is from these sources that humans secure utilitarian material needs, along with aesthetic, intellectual, symbolic, religious, and spiritual needs. Many metaphors reflect connections to other forms of life: quick as a fox, social butterfly, wise old owl, beet red, carrot-top. The ecologist Stephen Kellert has created a descriptive nine-element classification to clarify, distinguish, and measure the values that humans attribute to nature. Kellert's classification includes those that are hierarchical, pragmatic, and quantifiable (such as utilitarian, ecological-scientific, and dominionistic values), as well as those that are less measurable and more emotional and qualitative, including moralistic, symbolic, and aesthetic values.

An Ethic of Biodiversity

Many environmental ethicists believe that without a dramatic shift in the dominant Western capitalist values people will be unable to slow the loss of biodiversity. According to this view, social and ecological justice are intrinsically interrelated. Overpopulation, poverty, corruption, inequities of power and wealth, and racial and gender discrimination all affect the preservation of biodiversity by creating perverse incentives and allowing for overuse of wild species and habitats. Social and economic policies that lead to greater human equality will decrease dependence on degraded ecosystems. Therefore, according to some environmental ethicists preservation of biodiversity requires social analysis and correction of injustices in local environments, along with scientific research on wild species and populations.

An ethic of biodiversity also holds that helping people cultivate a love and appreciation for wild species through outdoor activities is critically important. People will not protect what they do not care for, and they cannot care for that which they do not know. Just as conservation of biodiversity is critical to stable, resilient ecosystems, involvement of diverse viewpoints is essential in creating just and sustainable environmental policies. The conservation of human cultural diversity—displayed in language, religion, the arts, and cultural practices—is an important component of biodiversity conservation, according to some environmental ethicists. Enlarging the framework of discourse to critically engage such qualitative values as morals, aesthetics, and symbolism, and to address social injustices are essential for slowing the loss of biodiversity.

Elizabeth ALLISON
University of California, Berkeley

FURTHER READING

Activities of the WWF Japan: Ecoregions Programme. (2008). Retrieved July 14, 2009, from http://www.wwf.or.jp/eng/ecoregion/index.htm

Brandon, Katrina; Redford, Kent; & Sanderson, Steven. (Eds.). (1998). *Parks in peril: People, politics and protected areas.* Washington, DC: Island Press.

Cox, George. (1999). *Alien species in North America and Hawaii.* Washington, DC: Island Press.

Daily, Gretchen C. (2003). Win-win ecology: How the Earth's species can survive in the midst of human enterprise. *Science, 300*(5625), 1508–1509.

Daily, Gretchen C. (Ed.). (1997). *Nature's services.* Washington, DC: Island Press.

Dirzo, Rodolfo, & Raven, Peter. (2003). Global state of biodiversity and loss. *Annual Review of Environment and Resources, 28*, 137–167.

Gunderson, Lance Ho. (2000). Ecological resilience: In theory and application. *Annual Review of Ecology and Systematics, 31*, 425–439.

Kellert, Stephen. (1996). *The value of life.* Washington, DC: Island Press.

Perrings, C., et al, (Eds.). (1994). *Biodiversity conservation: Problems and policies.* Amsterdam: Kluwer Academic.

Pimentel, David; Wilson, Christa; McCullum, Christine; Huang, Rachel; Dwen, Paulette; Flack, Jessica; et al. (1997). Economic and environmental benefits of biodiversity. *BioScience, 47*(11), 747–757.

Raffaelli, David. (2004). How extinction patterns affect ecosystems. *Science, 306*(5699), 1141–1142.

Sala, Osvaldo; Chapin, F. Stuart, III; Armesto, Juan; Berlow, Eric; Bloomfield, Janine; et al. (2000). Global biodiversity scenarios for the year 2100. *Science, 287*(5459), 1770–1774.

Terbough, John. (1999). *Requiem for nature.* Washington, DC: Island Press.

Thorne-Miller, Boyce. (1999). *The living ocean.* Washington, DC: Island Press.

The Nature Conservancy. (n. d.). Retrieved June 5, 2009, from, http://conserveonline.org

Wilson, Edward O. (1992). *The diversity of life.* Cambridge, MA: Harvard University Press.

Wilson, Edward O. (2002). *The future of life.* New York: Alfred A. Knopf.

World Resources Institute. (1992). *Global biodiversity strategy.* Washington, DC: WRI, IUCN, UNEP.

World Wide Fund for Nature—India. (1999). *Religion and conservation.* Delhi: Full Circle.

Bioethics

Bioethics embodied all ethical considerations of life forms in modern scientific, technological, and medical contexts until the mid-twentieth century, when scholars began to define separately those issues concerning the environment and medicine. The current connection between public health and the environment suggests that biomedical and environmental ethics must reunite and expand their scope to enable the re-creation of sustainable civilizations.

When originally coined, the term *bioethics* referred to ethical issues raised for all life forms by modern science, technology, and medicine. What we now think of as ecology, environmental ethics, and biomedical ethics were subsumed under the rubric of *bioethics*. Few writers have effectively addressed anything like this range of issues, however. Ian Barbour, a scholar who focuses on the relationship between science and religion, Holmes Rolston III, a philosopher well-known for his contributions to environmental ethics, and (more recently) Bill McKibben, an environmentalist best known for his work on global warming, but who also has written on the dangers of human genetic engineering and the shortcomings of a growth economy, are important exceptions.

One reason the fields separated in the latter half of twentieth century is that practical ethicists dealing with real-world problems must spend an inordinate amount of time simply learning the facts in order to write or teach effectively about global warming, the fair treatment of animals, stem-cell research, or care for the dying. Moreover, the facts are constantly changing, and ethical theory is also a moving target.

Insofar as possible, however, it is important to hold together—intellectually if not as social movements—the breadth of bioethics. For one thing, there are common issues. One is whether the "natural" is normative. This matters for how we view everything from soil and vegetation to human reproduction and the end of life. The word *natural* has meant many things: the spontaneous, or that which is unaffected by technology, and even the rational. Appeals to the natural have been both passionately opposed and defended in biomedical ethics; they seem to have even more bite in the environmental area. Why is that? Should it be so? Environmental philosophers defend natural environments, although most of those now existing are consciously preserved human artifacts, and unfettered "natural selection" would eliminate others. Writers in biomedical ethics have challenged and defended notions of "natural" reproduction and a "natural" life span.

A second common issue is the role of religious institutions, myths, moral norms, and ideals of character. As with the problem of the natural, these symbolic considerations seem to sit more comfortably in the environmental arena than in the biomedical one, even though both often involve forms of utilitarianism that usually trouble religious ways of thinking. For example, arguments in favor of storing nuclear waste in Native American tribal lands, or insisting on the use of Western medicine in the same tribe, may be suggested by utilitarian criteria but are inconsistent and destructive to the group's mythology, worldview, or symbol system.

Because public health is not possible apart from a sustainable environment, and sustainability is not possible without major changes to widely held Western notions of the good life, length of life, and economic justice, the fields of biomedical and environmental ethics must reunite as a broad-gauged bioethics to enable the re-creation of sustainable civilizations. But they enable refreshing, intellectual cross-fertilization, as illustrated here. Siblings look at each other (and are looked at by third parties) as differing chips off the same old blocks. It can be helpful in understanding oneself and one's colleagues to engage in some comparative analysis and perhaps to discover unappreciated strengths in one's roots that can be built upon.

David H. SMITH
Yale University

FURTHER READING

Beauchamp, Tom, & Childress, James. (1994). *Principles of biomedical ethics.* New York: Oxford University Press.

Barbour, Ian. (1992). *Ethics in an age of technology: The Gifford lectures 1989–1991* (Vol. 2). New York: HarperOne.

Rolston, Holmes, III. (1999). *Genes, genesis and God: Values and their origins in natural and human history.* Cambridge, U.K.: Cambridge University Press.

McKibben, Bill. (2004). *Enough: Staying human in an engineered age.* New York: Holt Paperbacks.

Biophilia

The term biophilia *describes a biological and evolutionary basis for human connection with the natural environment. Because failure to sustain the biodiversity that characterizes our evolutionary past can have profound effects on the mental health of individuals and communities, biophilic practices are not only being adopted in psychology but in architecture and building.*

The psychologist Eric Fromm used *biophilia* (literally meaning "love of life"), in his 1964 book *The Heart of Man*, but the term has since been popularized by Harvard sociobiologist and entomologist Edward O. Wilson. Wilson first developed the term in his 1984 book of the same name to describe "an innate tendency to focus on life and life processes" at all levels.

Evolutionarily, Wilson argued, humans have been subconsciously compelled to appreciate nature because of our biological dependence upon the natural world. Our brains have developed in tandem with the environment around us, becoming more responsive as we are driven by the biological imperative to thrive within our environment. The result is that we still respond to our surroundings with those cognitive responses. We find certain natural elements pleasing or repulsive according to their role in our evolutionary history. For example, open space and grasslands with a view of water are often still considered pleasant places because they are reminiscent of African savannas where prey could be found and easily hunted, enemies seen, and water resources were available.

In *Biophilia*, as well as in *The Diversity of Life* (1992) and elsewhere, Wilson notes that the planet is experiencing an unprecedented rate of species extinction caused by human behavior. Wilson makes an argument for the intentional conservation of threatened flora and fauna in order to preserve the biodiversity that has shaped human biological and cultural evolution. By studying the world around us, he believes, we can learn more about ourselves and so become better equipped to solve the cultural problems that led to the current magnitude of environmental destruction. An ethic informed by biophilia may recognize the utilitarian, aesthetic, and spiritual benefits of nature for humans.

Wilson and Yale University Professor of Social Ecology Stephen R. Kellert edited a volume published in 1993 entitled *The Biophilia Hypothesis*. It was intended to illustrate the multidisciplinary repercussions of biophilia. The theory has been highly influential in circles that advocate an emotional affinity to the natural world, and this is evidenced in the diversity of fields, from health to architecture, that are represented in this volume.

In biophilia there are particularly profound implications for psychology. Ecopsychology, an emerging field of environmental study, takes as its premise the inextricable relationship of the individual mind and the individual's environment. It observes both the healing power of contact with nature and the personal crises that may be the result of a disconnection from nature. Biophilic psychologists, then, foster a holistic sense of mental, spiritual, and emotional health that, in turn, necessarily fosters a healthy environment.

There are important implications for sustainable design in the biophilia hypothesis. The historical presence of parks and other green spaces in cities is an example of the manifestation of biophilic needs in urban design. In 2008, Kellert co-edited a book entitled *Biophilic Design: The Theory, Science and Practice of Bringing Buildings to Life*. This collection of articles outlines specific principles of biophilic design and their repercussions on human health, performance, and well-being. Thus, sustaining the human connection to the natural environment requires both its conservation and inclusion in our communities.

Biophillia is ultimately a hopeful hypothesis. By illustrating deep, evolutionary relationships between humanity, other animals, and the rest of the biosphere, it argues that by conserving biodiversity (nonhuman nature), we conserve ecological relations that matter for our psychological, economic, and aesthetic interests (human nature). Biophilia assumes that humans can forge a healthier relationship with the ecosystem because it is in our best interest to do so.

Shannon TYMAN
University of Oregon

FURTHER READING

Fromm, Eric. (1964). *The heart of man: Its genius for good and evil*. New York: Harper & Row.

Kellert, Stephen R. (1997). *Kinship to master: Biophilia in human evolution and development*. Washington, DC: Island Press.

Kellert, Stephen R.; Heerwagen, Judith; & Mador, Martin. (2008). *Biophilic design: The theory, science, and practice of bringing buildings to life*. New York: John Wiley & Sons.

Kellert, Stephen, & Wilson, Edward O. (Eds.). (1993). *The biophilia hypothesis*. Washington, DC: Island Press.

Wilson, Edward O. (1984). *Biophilia: The human bond with other species*. Cambridge, MA: Harvard University Press.

EDWARD O. WILSON ON BIOPHILIA

In the nine essays comprising his popular book Biophilia: The Human Bond with Other Species, *Edward O. Wilson weaves his memories and observations of a life in the "field"—from his youth in the Florida panhandle to his eminence as an entomologist—with the history and philosophy of evolutionary biology. In the prologue Wilson writes of being stunned by the beauty of the South American landscape and describes his first experience with the concept of biophilia.*

On March 12, 1961, I stood in the Arawak village of Bernhardsdorp and looked south across the white-sand coastal forest of Surinam[e]. For reasons that were to take me twenty years to understand, that moment was fixed with uncommon urgency in my memory. The emotions I felt were to grow more poignant at each remembrance, and in the end they changed into rational conjectures about matters that had only a distant bearing on the original event.

The object of the reflection can be summarized by a single word, biophilia, which I will be so bold as to define as the innate tendency to focus on life and lifelike processes. Let me explain it very briefly here and then develop the larger theme as I go along.

From infancy we concentrate happily on ourselves and other organisms. We learn to distinguish life from the inanimate and move toward it like moths to a porch light. Novelty and diversity are particularly esteemed; the mere mention of the word *extraterrestrial* evokes reveries about still unexplored life, displacing the old and once potent *exotic* that drew earlier generations to remote islands and jungled interiors. That much is immediately clear, but a great deal more needs to be added. I will make the case that to explore and affiliate with life is a deep and complicated process in mental development. To an extent still undervalued in philosophy and religion, our existence depends on this propensity, our spirit is woven from it, hope rises on its currents.

There is more. Modern biology has produced a genuinely new way of looking at the world that is incidentally congenial to the inner direction of biophilia. In other words, instinct is in this rare instance aligned with reason. The conclusion I draw is optimistic: to the degree that we come to understand other organisms, we will place a greater value on them, and on ourselves.

Source: Edward O. Wilson. (1984). *Biophilia: The human bond with other species* (pp. 1–2). Cambridge, MA: Harvard University Press.

Buddhism

The basic tenets of traditional Buddhism—attaining wisdom; showing compassion; doing no harm to people, animals, and the Earth—seem to fit closely the concept and practice of sustainability. Modern Buddhism, particularly Western Buddhism, has gone even further in practice as Buddhists actively engage in movements and organizations that promote sustainability.

One of the biggest threats to sustainability is destructive human economic activity, much of which finds support from underlying feelings and ideas, whether fear, greed, notions of self and world, ideologies of economic growth, or beliefs in the ability of markets to generate technological fixes for environmental problems. Because Buddhism has for 2,500 years leveled much of its religious critique at mental states, it offers resources for understanding threats to sustainability and formulating responses to those threats.

Ethicists, economists, and policy makers have diverged in their conceptions of "sustainability" as it relates to the environment, economic systems, and communities. In general, however, sustainability has to do with "the optimal scale of the macro-economy relative to the ecosystem" and "justice extended to the future" (Daly and Cobb 1994, 145–146). In 1987 the World Commission on Environment and Development (now known as the Brundtland Commission) concluded that development is sustainable when it "meets the needs of the present without compromising the ability of future generations to meet their own needs." In large part, then, sustainability concerns the extent to which human practices—chiefly but not exclusively economic—maintain healthy ecosystems and communities over time. And what is clearly unsustainable are current levels of resource depletion and pollution, especially by more "advanced" economies that value endless expansion of production while ignoring limits to growth and the importance of community.

Depletion of nonrenewable resources and pollution at levels or in forms not absorbable by the environment are exacerbated by consumerism. Consumerism can be defined as both the belief that the ability to purchase and possess certain things will make a person happy and the actions based on that belief, including certain consumer behaviors and the assigning of high status to those who possess wealth or desired objects. The Buddhist thinker and Zen practitioner Ken Jones points out that, in contrast to that value system, many traditional societies have championed such status markers as "valued skills and knowledge, integrity and wisdom, as well as a rich and varied popular culture," and he criticizes "consumer culture in which this richness and diversity has been so diminished that the commodity market (which now packages experiences as well as things) comes to bear a disproportionate weight of the human need for meaning, significance, status, and belongingness" (Jones 1993, 22). Rita Gross, a scholar of Buddhism, writes that "the key question is what values and practices would convince people to consume and reproduce less when they have the technological ability to consume and reproduce more" (Gross 1997, 335). Buddhism provides such values and practices, as well as a view of self and world that contrasts with views that bolster destructive economic activity.

An Ethic of Restraint

Rather than specific rules or formulas, Buddhism presents a set of values that is helpful in fostering sustainability. Buddhism has traditionally emphasized restraint, generosity, simplicity, nonharming, and compassion. In an essay on Buddhist environmental ethics, Padmasiri de Silva

(b. 1933), author of many books on Buddhist psychology and ethics, writes, "Buddhism calls for a modest concept of living: simplicity, frugality, and an emphasis on what is essential—in short, a basic ethic of restraint" (de Silva 1990, 15).

Buddhism restrains, among other things, the mental states and dispositions that find expression in consumerism. Buddhism especially calls into question the "three poisons": ignorance, greed, and hatred. The historical Buddha taught that we suffer because we are ignorant of the fact of impermanence and we cling to ourselves and to things that give us a false sense of identity and security. When the objects of that clinging change or prove ultimately unsatisfactory, we feel anguish—we suffer. Buddhists have also noticed that when we are attached to certain things, we also feel anger toward whatever threatens those things. While feeling attraction to certain things, we feel aversion to other things. We succumb to greed and hatred.

Like others who have reflected on sustainability, Buddhists emphasize transforming our mindsets away from greed and acquisitiveness. They call for a focus on need, not greed, or as the Thai social activist and Buddhist Sulak Sivaraksa (b. 1933) has argued, more being rather than more having. Of course, some consumers in countries like the United States would argue that they do not get caught up in greed or believe that possessions are the key to happiness. But many middle- and upper-class Americans do in fact exhibit greed or clinging insofar as they are attached to their lifestyle and reluctant to simplify it to the extent necessary for global sustainability.

Buddhists have viewed hatred as an underlying cause of violence to other people, other species, and the environment in general. They have remedied it by cultivating loving-kindness (Pali, *mettā*), or compassion (Sanskrit, *karuṇā*), and avoiding unnecessary harming, as advocated by the first of the five Buddhist moral precepts. (The five precepts entail vows to restrain from taking life, taking what has not been given, engaging in improper sex, lying, and using intoxicants.) Hatred can be intensified in the economic arena, where the selfish pursuit of individual interests and pleasure, while in some cases making for profitable markets, can lead to conflict, if not violence, between people, or at least to a distrustful view of the other as a competitor. And in some cases people may come together in shared selfishness and thereby constitute a collective ego, what Zen teacher David Loy (b. 1947) has called the "*wego.*" When this happens, people may fail to recognize "our fear of insecurity, our nationalistic desire to 'win' at any cost, our desire to be number one, our culturally induced desire to find new frontiers to conquer" (Devall 2000, 391), all of which can lead to hatred and violence.

The economist Ernst Schumacher (1911–1977) expressed the Buddhist critique of greed and hatred in his book *Small Is Beautiful: Economics as if People Mattered* when he wrote, "The keynote of Buddhist economics . . . is simplicity and non-violence" and "the aim should be to obtain the maximum well-being with the minimum of consumption" (Schumacher 1973, 57). Richard Hayes (b. 1945), a professor of Buddhist philosophy, echoes Schumacher: "The Buddhist ideal of a life of simplicity, nonviolence towards all living beings, and non-acquisitiveness is one that human beings must learn to follow very soon if they have any interest in the continued survival of their own and countless other species" (Hayes 1990, 23). Simply put, Buddhism rejects unsustainable consumerism and materialism and offers instead a path of simplicity that, contrary to what one might expect, leads not to deprivation but to more fulfilling, nonmaterial forms of wealth and happiness.

Relational Awareness

Buddhist ethicists also argue that an underlying cause of the greed behind unsustainable economic practices is the poison of ignorance: the mistaken sense of existing as a separate individual with an unchanging essence, or soul, and only secondarily entering into relationships with other people and things. The ecophilosopher Joanna Macy (b. 1929) writes, "It is a delusion that the self is so separate and fragile that we must delineate and defend its boundaries, that it is so small and so needy that we must endlessly acquire and endlessly consume, and that it is so aloof that as individuals, corporations, nation-states, or species, we can be immune to what we do to other beings" (Macy 1990, 57). Buddhist meditation serves to uproot this ignorance and the false notion that one is a mind lording over mechanical nature.

Buddhism cultivates a relational way of knowing, a recognition that we are constituted through relationships with other things and exist thoroughly interconnected with those things. The individualistic, egotistical self is, according to Macy, "replaced by wider constructs of identity and self-interest—by what you might call the ecological self or the eco-self, co-extensive with other beings and the life of our planet. It is what I will call 'the greening of the self'" (Macy 1990, 57). Or as the professor of Environmental Studies and Zen practitioner Stephanie Kaza (b. 1947) terms it, we shift from a consumer identity to an "ecological identity." And in this way we can begin to release ourselves from ignorance, not only in the traditional Buddhist sense but also in at least five other senses:

1. Lack of knowledge about human impacts on the environment.
2. Incorrect knowledge or information.
3. Ignorance or denial of sustainability issues.

4. Ideas justifying the continuation of our destructive lifestyles or justifying passivity in the face of current challenges.
5. Unawareness of and disconnection from nature.

Interrelational Arising

The transformation of our way of knowing and our identity is backed by Buddhist metaphysics, especially in terms of *pratītya–samutpāda*, interrelational arising. This doctrine holds that all "things" should be seen as temporary events constituted through causal and logical interrelationship with other events in an ongoing process of change, and hence things do not exist independently or have any essence prior to or separate from this interactive shaping. Buddhist ethicists claim that insight into *pratītya–samutpāda* has ethical ramifications, several of which are relevant to sustainability. They contend that as this insight deepens we realize that we are indeed a part of a larger reality and that, as the Thai Buddhist nun Chatsumarn Kabilsingh (b. 1945) writes, "When we abuse nature we abuse ourselves." (Kabilsingh 1990, 8). Buddhist ethicists maintain that to the extent we realize interrelational arising, we also discern the pain of others, gain a greater sense of compassion, feel indebtedness to the countless things that nurture us, engage in fewer harmful acts, and, recognizing how our actions have countless effects on the world around us, acquire an enhanced sense of responsibility. Along these lines the writer and activist Allan Hunt Badiner argues, "With its emphasis on cooperation and interdependence, Buddhist practice can inspire the building of partnership societies with *need*-based, sustainable economies rather than *greed*-based, growth economics" (Badiner 1990, xvii).

Monastic Ideals

Some writers have championed Buddhist monasticism as a model for building such societies. The following list is adapted from the work of the educators Leslie Sponsel and Poranee Natadecha-Sponsel (1997, 49), who state that an ideal *sangha* (monastic community) embodies the following "ecologically appropriate attributes":

1. Population that is small and controlled.
2. Egalitarian communal life based on cooperation and mutual respect.
3. Limited resource consumption and the use of self-restraint in satisfying basic needs, wants, and desires—actions aimed at achieving sufficiency and sustainability.
4. An economy based on cooperation, reciprocity, and redistribution rather than competition.

5. Stewardship practices that limit environmental impact.
6. Holistic (systems), organic (ecology), and monisitc (regarding the unity of human nature) worldview that rejects accumulating material things in favor of enhancing the quality of life.
7. Values that promote harmony within the society and between society and nature, such as reverence (inherent worth), compassion or loving-kindness (*mettā*), and nonviolence (*ahiṃsā*) toward all life.
8. Self-examination, self-realization, and self-fulfillment—actions to nurture the "deep self."

Cognizant of these features of their tradition, Western Buddhists have emphasized the need to create *eco-sanghas* that are ecologically responsible and committed to their bioregions.

Practices and Activism

Buddhists around the world are engaging in practices and forms of activism that contribute to sustainability. Complementing a range of writings on Buddhist economics, the Bhutanese have adopted a novel economic indicator, Gross National Happiness, which takes into account just and sustainable social and economic development. The Sarvodaya movement in Sri Lanka has hammered out an alternative form of economic development aimed at sustaining the environment, village communities, and core moral and aesthetic values. In Thailand, conservation monks have protected forests by "ordaining" trees. Other Buddhists have expanded the precepts, as evidenced by the Vietnamese Zen Tiep Hien Order's fourteen mindfulness trainings, which include such guidelines as the eleventh, "Aware that great violence and injustice have been done to our environment and society, we are committed not to live with a vocation that is harmful to humans and nature," and the thirteenth, "Aware of the suffering caused by exploitation, social injustice, stealing, and oppression, we are committed to cultivating loving-kindness and learning ways to work for the well-being of people, animals, plants, and minerals" (Thich Nhat Hanh 1998, 20–21).

Cognizant of traditional *gathas* (short verses or hymns from the sutras), the Vietnamese Zen monk and peace activist Thich Nhat Hanh (b. 1926) has crafted "earth *gathas*" one of which reads,

> In this plate of food,
> I see the entire universe
> supporting my existence. (Thich Nhat Hanh
> 1990, 195)

Such Buddhist institutions as San Francisco Zen Center's Green Gulch Farm, Zen Mountain Monastery in the

Catskills, Zen Mountain Center in southern California, and Spirit Rock Meditation Center in northern California have taken steps to make themselves into green communities. Buddhists have also crafted new practices, including the "earth relief ceremony" performed by the Zen Center of Rochester; backpacking retreats, known as mountains and rivers *sesshins* (meditation sessions of several days), run by the Ring of Bone Zendo; retreats led by Thich Nhat Hanh for environmentalists; Joanna Macy's Nuclear Guardianship project as a way to deal with toxic nuclear waste; and the Council of All Beings, an exercise Macy started with Australian eco-activist John Seed, in which participants speak for animals, plants, and inorganic things affected by destructive human actions. In an overview of these practices the professor of Buddhist Studies Kenneth Kraft (b. 1949) writes, "An abiding faith in the fundamental interconnectedness of all existence provides many individual activists with the energy and focus to stay the course" (Kraft 1994, 178).

Questions and Challenges

Buddhism presents a vision of an alternative way of life that is more conducive to sustainability than are the ideologies and practices powering mainline economic systems and consumerism. And Buddhists have been drawing on their tradition to speak to issues of sustainability. But it is not clear how much of a practical effect this has had. Insofar as they continue to fly and enjoy modern creature comforts, even progressive Buddhists in the West leave large eco-footprints, and the majority of Buddhists in Asia are fully plugged into dominant economic models and live in highly consumerist societies.

Another challenge is the historical lack of Buddhist critical distance from rulers, merchants, and other powerful players in societies where the religion has flourished. Buddhism does not have a tradition of criticizing people in power, and it has never engaged in any sustained discussion of social justice and what constitutes just relations in a sustainable community, a lack that has been exacerbated at times by interpreting the doctrine of karma to mean that each person is getting exactly what he or she deserves in life. One area in particular that Buddhist thinkers have rarely addressed is distributive justice (the question of who reaps benefits and who shoulders burdens), which must be factored in to approaches to sustainability to ensure that the needs of the poor are not ignored by calls to simplify, reduce consumption, or preserve certain resources. The traditional emphasis on giving to others and thereby cultivating the virtue of generosity as the antidote to the poison of greed could prove helpful as Buddhist ethicists address this topic.

But even if the majority of Buddhists were to change their lifestyles in a more sustainable direction and, in a commitment to ecojustice, work to redistribute the consumption of resources in a way that alleviates poverty, we would still be left with the question of how much of an impact that would have on the overall crisis of sustainability. Some Buddhist thinkers have started to expand their reflection beyond individual thought and action, beyond the scope of monasteries and Sri Lankan villages, and to grapple with broader structures of economic, political, and military power. And they have started to link this critical analysis to constructive delineation of what, exactly, from the Buddhist perspective, is optimal existence, whether of humans, communities, or ecosystems, and how humanity might achieve that goal, or at least live along a sustainable path that leads in that direction.

The poet Gary Snyder, a Buddhist who has written extensively on ecological issues, provides a glimpse of what a Buddhist path of sustainability might entail: "Practically speaking, a life that is vowed to simplicity, appropriate boldness, good humor, gratitude, unstinting work and play, and lots of walking brings us close to the actually existing world and its wholeness. . . . No expectations, alert and sufficient, grateful and careful, generous and direct. A calm and clarity attend us in the moment we are wiping grease off our hands and glancing up at the passing clouds" (Snyder 1990, 23–24).

Christopher IVES
Stonehill College

FURTHER READING

Badiner, Allan Hunt. (Ed.). (1990). *Dharma Gaia: A harvest of essays in Buddhism and ecology.* Berkeley, CA: Parallax Press.

Bond, George D. (2004). *Buddhism at work: Community development, social empowerment, and the Sarvodaya movement.* Bloomfield, CT: Kumarian Press.

Daly, Herman E., & Cobb, John B., Jr. (1994). *For the common good: Redirecting the economy toward community, the environment, and a sustainable future* (2nd ed.). Boston: Beacon Press.

de Silva, Padmasiri. (1990). Buddhist environmental ethics. In Allan Hunt Badiner (Ed.), *Dharma Gaia: A harvest of essays in Buddhism and ecology* (pp. 14–19). Berkeley, CA: Parallax Press.

Devall, Bill. (2000). Deep ecology and political activism. In Stephanie Kaza & Kenneth Kraft, (Eds.), *Dharma rain: Sources of Buddhist environmentalism* (pp. 379–392). Boston: Shambhala.

Gross, Rita M. (1997). Toward a Buddhist environmental ethic. *Journal of the American Academy of Religion, 65*(2), 333–353.

Hayes, Richard P. (1990). Towards a Buddhist view of nature. *ARC,* XVIII, 11–24.

Ives, Christopher. (1992). *Zen awakening and society.* London and Honolulu: Macmillan and University of Hawai'i Press.

Jones, Ken H. (1993). *Beyond optimism: A Buddhist political economy.* Oxford, U.K.: Jon Carpenter Publishing.

Kabilsingh, Chatsumarn. (1990). Early Buddhist views of nature. In Allan Hunt Badiner (Ed.), *Dharma Gaia: A harvest of essays in Buddhism and ecology* (pp. 8–13). Berkeley, CA: Parallax Press.

Kaza, Stephanie, (Ed.). (2005). *Hooked: Buddhist writings on greed, desire, and the urge to consume.* Boston: Shambhala.

Kaza, Stephanie, & Kraft, Kenneth. (Eds.). (2000). *Dharma rain: Sources of Buddhist environmentalism.* Boston: Shambhala.

Kraft, Kenneth. (1994). The greening of Buddhist practice. *Cross Currents, 44*(2), 163–179.

Loy, David R. (2003). *The great awakening: A Buddhist social theory.* Boston: Wisdom Publications.

Macy, Joanna. (1985). *Dharma and development: Religion as resource in the Sarvodaya self-help movement* (Rev. ed.). West Hartford, CT: Kumarian Press.

Macy, Joanna. (1990). The greening of the self. In Allan Hunt Badiner (Ed.), *Dharma Gaia: A harvest of essays in Buddhism and ecology* (pp. 53–63). Berkeley, CA: Parallax Press.

Schumacher, Ernst F. (1973). *Small is beautiful: Economics as if people mattered.* New York: Harper & Row.

Snyder, Gary. (1990). *The practice of the wild: Essays by Gary Snyder.* San Francisco: North Point Press.

Sponsel, Leslie, & Natadecha-Sponsel, Poranee. (1997). A theoretical analysis of the potential contribution of the monastic community in promoting a green society in Thailand. In Mary Evelyn Tucker & Duncan Ryuken Williams (Eds.), *Buddhism and ecology: The interconnection of Dharma and deeds* (pp. 45–68). Cambridge, MA: Harvard University Press.

Thich Nhat Hanh. (1990). Earth Gathas. In Allan Hunt Badiner (Ed.), *Dharma Gaia: A harvest of essays in Buddhism and ecology* (pp. 195–196). Berkeley, CA: Parallax Press.

Thich Nhat Hanh. (1998). *Interbeing: Fourteen guidelines for engaged Buddhism* (3rd ed.). Berkeley, CA: Parallax Press.

Tucker, Mary Evelyn, & Williams, Duncan Ryuken. (Eds.). (1997). *Buddhism and ecology: The interconnection of Dharma and deeds.* Cambridge, MA: Harvard University Press.

World Commission on Environment and Development. (1987). *Our common future.* Oxford, U.K.: Oxford University Press.

Chipko Movement

The Chipko movement began in 1973 in India as an attempt by local people to assert their rights over local forest resources. Guided largely by Gandhian principles of nonviolence and active service, the movement was about village economics as well as ecology. The movement is noteworthy for the leadership and active roles of women.

Chipko was a successful and well-known grassroots movement for forest sustainability. It flourished in what is now the Indian state of Uttarakhand in the western Himalayas between 1973 and 1981. The name of the movement is derived from the resolution of the local people to embrace (*chipko*) the trees to stand in the way of the ax. The Chipko movement is considered one of the first so-called tree-hugging movements. The movement was part of a larger struggle by local people for access to forest biomass for their domestic economy. Since the nineteenth century, local access to forests had been gradually curtailed by the development of state-supported commercial forestry.

Scholars locate the catalyst of the movement in events that occurred in April 1973. The state forest department had refused to permit a local farm cooperative—the Dashauli Gram Swarajya Sangh, under the leadership of Chandi Prasad Bhatt (b. 1934)—to fell a limited number of ash trees for local needs. But it allowed a sporting goods manufacturer, the Symonds Company of Allahabad, to fell the entire nearby Mandel ash forest. This was especially repugnant to the women of the villages for whom ash trees were a source of fodder during scarce growing seasons.

In the 1960s the development of motor roads opened the region to more aggressive commercial exploitation. The state government auctioned forests to contractors from the plains that employed a labor force from outside the region. While ecological concerns had always been a part of the Chipko movement, its initial thrust was the protection of the forests from contract felling and the support of small, sustainable forest industries that could provide local employment. In April 1973, Chipko activists prevented the Symonds Company from felling the Mandal forest. In June, when the forest department allotted trees to the Symonds Company in another location, Chipko activists succeeded again.

When the annual government auction of forests continued in November 1973, women took a decisive role in the protest. In the absence of the men of the village, Gaura Devi (1925–1991), the head of the village women's organization, mobilized the women of the village. Confronting the contract workers in the forest they declared, as documented in field research by George Alfred James: "This forest is our mother's home; we will protect it with all our might." When it was clear that the women would not relent, the contractor's men departed.

Sunderlal Bahuguna (b. 1927), the most visible exponent of the movement, spread the Chipko message by *padyatras* (foot marches) to the most remote villages of the hills. The Garhwali folk singer Ghanshyam Sailani (1934–1997) accompanied Bahuguna on many of these journeys and composed songs that effectively expressed the ethos of the movement:

Embrace the Trees
Save them from felling
Don't let the hills
Be looted to the plains!

The successful protest against the felling of trees in the Advani forest is one of the most celebrated in the legacy of the Chipko movement. In October 1977, Sunderlal Bahuguna undertook a fast and appealed to forest contractors and district authorities not to carry out their intended work. Hundreds of women took a pledge to save the trees, even at the cost of their lives. They tied sacred threads around the trees, and for seven days guarded the forest while listening to discourses called Bhagavad Kathas from such ancient texts as the *Bhagavada Purana*. In these narrative traditions, the women found support in their struggle to save the forests they depended upon for their survival. Here the women gave voice, again documented in James's field research, to the most memorable slogan of the Chipko Movement: "What do the forests bear? Soil, water, and pure air! Soil, water, and pure air are the very basis of life."

While the government eventually made concessions to local forest-based industries, the ecological concerns of the movement came into sharper focus. In 1978 Sunderlal Bahuguna took a pledge to devote himself to the protection of the Himalayan environment in all its aspects. He argued that trees must be available to meet the needs of local people for food, fuel, fodder, fiber, and fertilizer. Gradually he came to hold that forest industries were not necessary to improve the economy of the people. Instead, he envisioned a self-sufficient rural community living in a sustainable relationship with its natural surroundings.

One of the most significant achievements of the movement was the ban imposed in 1981 on the felling of green trees for commercial purposes above the altitude of 1,000 meters (3,280 feet). That ban first imposed, in what was then the state of Uttar Pradesh, was followed by a similar measure in Himalachal Pradesh.

The influence of the Chipko movement is seen in numerous groups working in India and elsewhere to save the forest cover of the Earth. The most famous of these is the Appiko movement, whose ideals are similar to those of the Chipko movement, in the Western Ghats (mountain range) of south India.

George Alfred JAMES
University of North Texas

FURTHER READING

Guha, Ramachandra. (1991). *The unquiet woods: Ecological change and peasant resistance in the Himalayas.* New Delhi: Oxford University Press.
Rangan, Haripriya. (2000). *Of myths and movements: Rewriting Chipko into Himalayan history.* New York: Verso.
Shiva, Vandana, & Bandyopadhyay, J. (1986). *Chipko: India's civilisational response to the forest crisis.* New Delhi: Intach.
Weber, Thomas. (1987). *Hugging the trees: The story of the Chipko movement.* New Delhi: Viking Penguin.

Christianity—Anabaptist

The Amish and Mennonites, well known throughout the United States, belong to a wider branch of Christianity known as Anabaptism. Often persecuted in the past and misunderstood in the present, Anabaptists have a long history of simple living and stewardship of the land that can relate to modern ideas of sustainability.

Anabaptist Christianity in the United States is perhaps best characterized by diversity. Those descended from the Anabaptist tradition (including Mennonites, Amish, Hutterites, and multiple Brethren groups) may be urban dwellers with advanced academic degrees who are highly assimilated into American culture, or they may be rural members of distinct Old Order communities who travel by horse and buggy, eschew electricity, and end formal education in the eighth grade. Therefore it is not surprising to find a wide range of opinions regarding environmental sustainability across the Anabaptist spectrum.

The Anabaptist movement began in Europe during the Protestant Reformation. Most early Anabaptists were sympathetic to the reform movement, but they broke from the mainline reformers over the issue of baptism. The Anabaptists (meaning "re-baptizers") believed that only adults are capable of true faith, so they rejected the practice of infant baptism. They believed that Christian discipleship means following the teachings of Jesus in daily life, and they claimed that both faith and good works are necessary for salvation. Most Anabaptists were pacifists and refused to employ violent force or support their government's use of force. They suffered great persecution from both the Catholic and Protestant churches in Europe and eventually fled

to safety in rural areas. Many Anabaptists became farmers, and they continued in this occupation when they migrated to the United States in the second half of the nineteenth century. Until the 1950s most members of Anabaptist groups made a living in occupations related to agriculture. A concern for the land is a part of their religious and ethnic heritage.

Most Anabaptists focus their concern for the land through the lens of stewardship. They cite God's command to till and care for the land (Genesis 2:15, NRSV) as the foremost reason for responsibility for the natural world. Most believe that creation is a gift from God to be used by humanity, but deliberate misuse will eventually bring God's judgment. About half of Old Order Amish and Mennonites are still involved in farming as their primary profession, and many of them acknowledge that they feel closer to God when they are working in the soil. Their level of cooperation with conservation projects varies by group and area of the country, but most want to avoid any financial subsidies from the government, and some may be uninformed about effective methods. Some Old Order farmers, especially in Amish communities, are beginning to turn to grazing and organic farming but primarily for economic reasons. They are searching for an economically viable model that will sustain the small family farm.

Anabaptists not directly involved in agriculture address environmental concerns through their concern for the wider world, often characterized by simple living and concern for the least advantaged among us. Anabaptists emphasize right living (or radical discipleship) over right

doctrine, and they pattern that discipleship on the life and teachings of Jesus. They take seriously Jesus' depiction of "harsh judgment [that] fall[s] on those who build larger barns so that they can hoard their abundance (Luke 12:21) and those who feast sumptuously while their neighbors go hungry (Luke 16:19–31). Jesus calls the wealthy to sell what they own and give money to the poor so that they can come and follow Him (Matthew 10:17–30). And He proclaims ultimate blessedness to those who feed the hungry, give drink to the thirsty, welcome the stranger, clothe the naked, take care of the sick, and visit the imprisoned (Matthew 25:31–46)." For these reasons many Anabaptists seek to limit their own consumption of resources to make them available to others.

For most Old Order Anabaptists, concern for simple living is not based on environmental concern but on direct biblical commandments. But Anabaptists more assimilated to the wider culture are more likely to be aware of a global community and how their consumption choices impact that wider population. Their simple living and their concern for the global community is informed by the biblical commands, their concern for the least advantaged in the world, and their awareness of the impending worldwide ecological crisis.

Kathryn S. EISENBISE
Manchester College

FURTHER READING

Hostettler, John. (1993). *Amish society* (4th ed.). Baltimore: Johns Hopkins University Press.

Kauffman, J. Howard, & Harder, Leland. (1975). *Anabaptists four centuries later: A profile of five Mennonite and Brethren in Christ denominations.* Scottdale, PA: Herald Press.

Kanagy, Conrad. (2007). *Road signs for the journey: A profile of the Mennonite Church USA.* Scottdale, PA: Herald Press.

Redekop, Calvin. (Ed.). (2000). *Creation and the Environment: An Anabaptist Perspective on a Sustainable World.* Baltimore: Johns Hopkins University Press.

Weaver, Dorothy Jean. (2000). The New Testament and the environment: Toward a Christology for the cosmos. In *Creation and the environment: An Anabaptist perspective on a sustainable world.* Baltimore: Johns Hopkins University Press.

Christianity—Eastern Orthodox

Eastern Orthodox Christians believe that the predicament of the world's natural environment is not just ecological but spiritual, a problem that won't be solved unless natural resources are treated as the sacred creation and gift of God. Ascetic disciplines such as fasting—which involves learning to give rather than simply giving something up—are seen by Orthodox Christians as ways to connect to and preserve the natural world.

Orthodox Christianity retains—in its theology, liturgy, and spirituality alike—a profoundly sacred view of the natural environment, proposing a world richly imbued by God and proclaiming a God intimately involved with creation. To disconnect creation from the Creator, Orthodox Christians believe, is to desacralize both. For the way we relate to the world around us directly reflects the way we pray to "our Father in heaven." So we respond to the natural world with the same sensitivity with which we address God. All Christians understand that we must care for other human beings, as created "in the image of God." (Gen. 1:26 NRSV); it is time to appreciate the need to care for everything, as containing "the trace of God" (Tertullian, second century CE). Indeed, Orthodox Christians perceive the notion of sin as the stubborn refusal of humanity to regard the created world as a gift of communion—no less than a sacrament. In recent years, Ecumenical Patriarch Bartholomew (b. 1940), the spiritual leader of the Orthodox Church since 1991, has stigmatized environmental abuse as "sin."

In the seventh century CE, two mystics of the Eastern Christian Church eloquently described this relationship among nature, humanity, and God. Maximus the Confessor spoke of the world as a "cosmic liturgy," a magnificent altar on which human beings worship in thanksgiving and glory. The entire world comprises an integral part of this sacred song; God is praised by the sun and moon, worshipped by the trees and birds (Psalm 18:2). And Isaac the Syrian invited his spiritual disciples to "acquire a merciful heart, burning with love for all of creation: for humans, birds, and beasts." If today we are guilty of relentless waste in our world, it may be because we have lost the spirit of worship and the spirituality of compassion.

The predicament we face is not primarily ecological but in fact spiritual. It is a crisis regarding the way we imagine the world. We are treating the natural environment and its invaluable resources in an inhumane, godless manner precisely because we perceive it in this way. Unless we change the way we envisage creation, we are destined to deal with symptoms rather than with causes of the problem. One of the hymns of the Orthodox Church, chanted on the Feast of Epiphany (6 January) declares: "I have become the defilement of the air, the land, and the water."

The Orthodox Christian response to this urgent spiritual problem lies in its fundamental teaching concerning *ascesis* (or ascetic discipline). *Ascesis* is a technical term with much historical and theological baggage, whereas the word *discipline* has long been disassociated from its etymological meaning, implying the spiritual vision of a faithful disciple. Nevertheless, the intrinsic value of asceticism is discerned in the spirit of freedom and gratitude; its ultimate purpose is the rediscovery of wonder in the created world. The ascetic is one who is free, uncontrolled by attitudes that abuse the world, characterized by self-restraint and the ability to say "no" or "enough." The goal of asceticism is moderation, not repression; it looks to service and not selfishness. Without asceticism, none of us is authentically human.

An elementary example of asceticism in the Orthodox tradition is the discipline or rule of fasting. Orthodox Christians fast from dairy and meat products for half the

calendar year, in itself symbolic of reconciling one half of the year with the other—secular time with the time of the kingdom. This is because fasting entails learning to give, not simply to give up. Fasting is not to deny but to offer; it is learning to share with other human beings and to connect with the natural world. Fasting means breaking down barriers with one's neighbor and one's world: recognizing in others' faces, and in the Earth, the very face of God. Ultimately, to fast is to love; it is to see clearly, to restore the original beauty of the world. To fast is to move away from focusing on what we as individuals want and to consider first what the world needs. It is to liberate creation from control and compulsion. Fasting is to value everything for itself, and not simply for ourselves. It is to be filled with a sense of goodness, of Godliness. In the final analysis, it is a splendid summary of the Orthodox worldview and of Orthodox Christianity's approach to ecological issues because it encapsulates the effort to see all things in God and God in all things.

The ecological witness of the Orthodox tradition has been especially underscored by Ecumenical Patriarch Bartholomew, who has placed the ecological crisis at the forefront of his ministry. As spiritual leader of the Orthodox Church, which numbers over 300 million adherents, the ecumenical patriarch has been widely recognized for his pioneering work in confronting the theological and ethical imperative of environmental protection and declaring abuse of the natural environment as sinful: "To commit a crime against the natural world is a sin. For human beings to cause species to become extinct and to destroy the biological diversity of God's creation; for human beings to degrade the integrity of the Earth by causing changes in its climate, by stripping the Earth of its natural forests, or destroying its wetlands; for human beings to injure other human beings with disease and contaminate the Earth's waters, its land, its air, and its life, with poisonous substances . . . these are sins" (Chryssavgis, 2009).

Although its ecological initiatives date back to the mid-1980s, since 1989 the Ecumenical Patriarchate—located in the ancient Christian See of Constantinople (modern day Istanbul, Turkey)—has invited Orthodox Christians throughout the world to reserve 1 September, the official opening of the church calendar, as a day of prayer for environmental preservation. Numerous Christian communions have followed suit, encouraged by the World Council of Churches. In 1995, the ecumenical patriarch established the Religious and Scientific Committee, which to date has organized seven international, interfaith, and interdisciplinary symposia in the Aegean Sea (1995) and the Black Sea (1997), along the Danube River (1999) and in the Adriatic Sea (2002), in the Baltic Sea (2003) and on the Amazon River (2006), as well as in Greenland and the Arctic (2007). In 2002, Ecumenical Patriarch Bartholomew co-signed the "Venice Declaration" with Pope John Paul II, the first joint statement by the two world leaders; although the text of the declaration did not outline any binding action, it stated that protecting the environment is a moral and spiritual duty, and that Christians and other believers have a role to play in educating people about the ecological awareness—a responsibility toward self, toward others, and toward creation.

John CHRYSSAVGIS
Greek Orthodox Archdiocese of America

FURTHER READING

Bartholomew, Ecumenical Patriarch. (2008). *Encountering the Mystery.* New York: Doubleday Books.

Chryssavgis, John. (2009). *Cosmic grace, humble prayer: Ecological initiatives of the Green Patriarch Bartholomew*, 2nd rev. ed. Grand Rapids, MI: Eerdmans.

Kallistos of Diokleia. (1997). *Through the Creation to the Creator.* London: Friends of the Centre Papers.

Limouris, Gennadios. (Ed.). (1990). *Justice, peace, and the integrity of Creation: Insights from Orthodoxy.* Geneva: WCC Publications.

Sherrard, Philip. (1990). *Human image, world image.* Ipswich, U.K.: Golgonooza Press.

Zizioulas, John. (1989). Preserving God's Creation: Theology and ecology. *King's Theological Review* 12.

Christianity—Evangelical and Pentecostal

The concept of a faith-based sustainability has emerged from a number of Christian denominations, including Evangelicalism and Pentecostalism. Although still somewhat fragmented in theology and practice, an environmental movement based mainly on New Testament perspectives has begun to take shape among Evangelical and Pentecostal thinkers, leaders, and congregants.

Since the 1960s, Evangelicals and Pentecostals have become an increasingly diverse and politically significant voice in efforts to build a sustainable future. The terms *Evangelical* and *Pentecostal* are often contested and defined in a variety of ways. Evangelicals root their theology, ethics, and values in scripture, particularly the New Testament. Pentecostals do likewise but also place a heavy emphasis on the active role of the Holy Spirit. Both terms can also refer to particular denominations that identify themselves as Evangelical or Pentecostal—such as the Southern Baptist Convention or the Assemblies of God—but also can refer to congregations or individuals within Catholicism and mainline Protestantism.

There is strong debate on the relationship between Evangelicalism or Pentecostalism and sustainability, both from within and from without the churches. Most attention has been placed on Evangelicals, who, along with Pentecostals, have tended to show less environmental concern than other religious groups in the United States. With Pentecostals in particular, it is often assumed that an emphasis on the imminent return of Christ leads to a devaluation of the world and a license for unsustainable practices. But theological work is beginning to appear that connects the Pentecostal focus on the Holy Spirit and healing to environmental concerns. Within broader Evangelicalism, furthermore,

a robust environmental movement has emerged, bringing with it unique perspectives on sustainability.

History

Evangelical entry into environmental issues began with publications such as the conservative Protestant theologian Francis Schaeffer's (1912–1984) *Pollution and the Death of Man* (1970), accompanied by voiced concern from major Evangelical institutions. An early organizational backbone for Evangelical environmentalism later arose with the formation of the Au Sable Institute of Environmental Studies, which provides environmental science education for students in Christian colleges.

Evangelical environmentalism gained momentum in the 1990s with the formation of several organizations, including the Evangelical Environmental Network (EEN). In 1993 the EEN drafted the Evangelical Declaration on the Care of Creation, which argues that "biblical faith is essential to the solution of our ecological problems."

As a sign of the growing success of Evangelical environmentalism, several sharp critiques have emerged. Most notably, the Acton Institute, which promotes free-market capitalism and wise-use environmental ethics, helped to organize the Interfaith Council of Environmental Stewardship (ICES) in 2000 and produced the Cornwall Declaration on Environmental Stewardship, written in response to the EEN's Evangelical declaration and arguing that the Earth is a resource to be properly managed into fruitfulness. The Interfaith Stewardship Alliance emerged out of the ICES in 2005, and now is known as the Cornwall Alliance for the Stewardship of Creation.

Theological Contributions

At least three perspectives are distinctive to Evangelical understandings of sustainability. First, as Evangelical faiths are rooted in the biblical tradition, environmental sustainability is primarily understood through interpreting the Bible. This biblical emphasis also leads to a strong wariness about worshiping nature instead of God and an accompanying ambivalence toward mainstream environmentalism. Second, *stewardship* is the key Evangelical term for approaching sustainability issues. Stewardship ethics are commonly based in the first and second chapters of Genesis, whereby God gives humanity dominion over the rest of creation and, later, the responsibility of tending to the Garden of Eden. In the EEN's Evangelical declaration, stewardship is understood primarily in terms of caring for a creation in which all creatures are valued; it concludes by observing, "We are called to be faithful stewards of God's good garden, our earthly home." This caring for creation is, at its root, part of being a servant of God. The Cornwall declaration, on the other hand, understands stewardship in terms of the economic development of the Earth so that it is increasingly more productive for humanity. Third, recent Evangelical activism, especially as it has shifted toward climate change, has made sustainability into a matter of caring for the poor, an issue with a long history and much resonance among Evangelicals.

The contributions of Evangelicalism and Pentecostalism to sustainable practices are ambiguous, as there is no unified voice for these movements. Nonetheless, the work of organizations such as Au Sable and the EEN demonstrates that they carry unique strategies for grounding sustainability in a faith tradition.

Richard R. BOHANNON II
College of St. Benedict and St. John's University

FURTHER READING

DeWitt, Calvin. (1998). *Caring for creation: Responsible stewardship of God's handiwork*. Grand Rapids, MI: Baker Books.

Gabriel, Andrew. (2007). Pneumatological perspectives for a theology of nature: The Holy Spirit in relation to ecology and technology. *Journal of Pentecostal Theology*, *15*(2), 195–212.

Kearns, Laurel. (1997). Noah's Ark goes to Washington: A profile of evangelical environmentalism. *Social Compass*, *44*(3), 349–66.

Sharp, Kelly. (2006). Voices in the space between: Economy, ecology, and Pentecostalism on the US/Mexico Border. *Ecotheology*, *11*(4), 415–430.

Christianity—Mainline Protestant

Protestantism has obtained a reputation for promoting industrial growth, through the application of the Protestant ethic, with little regard for the effects on the environment. A closer look at Protestant theology, however, reveals a notion of societal transformation that may be crucial in order to adopt more sustainable practices.

In a famous essay titled "The Historical Roots of Our Ecological Crisis" (1967), the U.S. historian Lynn White Jr. (1907–1987) concluded that Christianity, particularly Protestantism, bears "a huge burden of guilt" in this regard. Although this essay has been widely criticized, those who agree with White's claim point out that those Western countries that are largely responsible for environmental problems—such as climate change, ozone depletion, toxic waste piling, and various forms of pollution—are also countries where Protestantism has historically been influential. This begs the question whether Protestantism provided religious legitimacy to industrialized economic growth and why it failed to confront unsustainable economic practices. It also sheds new light on how to assess the impact of what the German sociologist Max Weber (1864–1920) called the Protestant ethic (based on diligence and frugality) on the accumulation of capital.

The widespread sense of environmental crisis also provides Protestantism with an opportunity for renewal and reformation. As the Protestant axiom of *ecclesia reformata semper reformanda* (a reformed church is always reforming) indicates, such reformation is common to this tradition. This is perhaps the core Protestant intuition on sustainability; namely, it becomes possible not so much through conservation, preservation, or protection but through ongoing change, adaptability, and fruitfulness. At best, it stimulates not so much a sense of awe when confronted with the sacred and the untouchable but a spirit of protest over what is: the many faces of evil in society. But for ecosystems to be sustainable there is a need for both stability and adaptability. The Protestant tradition is engaged in an ongoing struggle to come to terms with this recognition. Ironically, it has been at its vigilant best when protesting against what is wrong in church and society, and at its worst when its calls for stability ended up in Protestant forms of orthodoxy, conservatism, and fundamentalism. Such an emphasis on stability is easily abused to defend a particular sociopolitical status quo and to reinforce forms of domination, including the ways in which humans have appointed themselves to "subdue" the Earth and to "rule" over it.

Although the ecological footprint of Protestant institutions remains by and large unsustainable and their commitment to issues of sustainability somewhat questionable, there has emerged since the 1960s numerous calls for an ecological reformation of Protestantism. While some have tried to defend their own traditions against accusations that they are anthropocentric (human centered), and that they promote human alienation from the Earth community and endorse unsustainable practices, many others have recognized that a Christian confession of guilt, and not a reiterated confession of faith, may be the more appropriate response.

Various levels of such calls for ecological transformation may be identified. Following are some examples:

1. Liturgical renewal: the production of sermons, guidelines, and interpretive material on environmental themes.
2. The inclusion of environmental concerns in Christian education.
3. Resolutions and declarations adopted by local church councils, synods, church leaders, and ecumenical bodies, such as the World Council of Churches, the

Lutheran World Federation, and the World Alliance of Reformed Churches.

4. Numerous local faith-based earth-keeping projects in the areas of sustainable agriculture, tree planting, water harvesting, organic vegetable gardening, recycling, indigenous church gardens, outdoor youth and family activities to promote the love of nature, nature conservation, and job creation in the field of applied technology.
5. The often neglected work of the laity wherever they live and wherever they are employed in various professions.
6. The cultivation of ecological virtues and forms of spirituality at home and through various youth movements, Bible study groups, and cell groups.
7. Theological reflection through the development of teaching material, conferences hosted, and the

production of a large corpus of academic publications.

Although the value of theological reflection may well be overestimated and its own ecological footprint underestimated, this is perhaps the most distinct and visible aspect of a Protestant response to environmental concerns. Individual theologians within particular confessional traditions in the wider Protestant world have made many contributions:

1. Günter Altner, Sigurd Bergmann, Ulrich Duchrow, Norman Habel, Phil Hefner, Gerard Liedke, Christian Link, Klaus Nürnberger, Larry Rasmussen, Paul Santmire, and Joseph Sittler in the Lutheran tradition.
2. T. J. Gorringe, Colin Gunton, Michael Northcott, and Peter Scott in the Anglican tradition.

World Council of Churches and Sustainable Dialogues

The World Council of Churches (WCC) was an early adopter of the vocabulary of sustainability. The concept was first discussed in its 1974 Bucharist consultation of theologians and scientists. Then at its Nairobi Assembly in 1975 it initiated a program unit entitled "Toward a Just, Participatory and Sustainable Society," which was meant to address three core issues on the social agenda of the church: economic injustice, political oppression, and ecological degradation. In 1983 at its Vancouver Assembly, the WCC redeveloped the program under the themes "Justice,

Peace and the Integrity of Creation." It used that motto to organize a series of conciliar dialogues for a process culminating in the World Convocation on Justice, Peace, and the Integrity of Creation, which met in Seoul in 1990. Discussions at the World Convocation debated priorities and connections among the three core social issues. Since then the WCC continues to pursue initiatives linking issues such as climate change, human rights, access to water, poverty, and international peace.

Willis Jenkins

3. Steven Bouma-Prediger, Martien Brinkman, Ernst Conradie, James Gustafson, Douglas John Hall, Dieter Hessel, Jürgen Moltmann, and Michael Welker in the reformed tradition.
4. John Cobb, Jay McDaniel, Sallie McFague, and James Nash within the Methodist tradition.
5. Sam Berry, Susan Bratton, Calvin DeWitt, Ron Sider, and Loren Wilkinson in an evangelical context.
6. Christian Redekop in the Anabaptist tradition.
7. Scholars such as Marthinus Daneel on indigenous churches in Africa and George Tinker on Native American Christianity.

Some of these scholars (especially in the case of the Anglican and Methodist traditions) are noted more for the theological schools to which they belong than for their confessional identity. Such a confessional point of departure also tends to obscure the reflective wisdom and the environmental theories and practice emerging from outside the Western world.

Such scholarly work may also help to retrieve the core insights on sustainability within a Protestant context. At first sight, theological concepts—such as covenant; divine election; God's sovereignty in church and society; justification through faith, law, and gospel; or *sola scriptura* ("scripture alone")—may hold little promise for ecological reformation. Perhaps the concept used most often is that of "covenanting," for example in the context of the World Convocation on Justice, Peace and the Integrity of Creation held in Seoul (1990). (See sidebar.) Despite the solemn language used here, it remains unclear what impact the dissemination and reception of this covenant had within the context of member churches.

Nevertheless, the transformative potential of the Protestant vision for the world should not be underestimated. The Lutheran notion of two kingdoms and the Calvinist vision on God's just rule in "every square inch" may harbor serious dangers, but they have also been employed to promote economic justice, peace, and a sustainable society. Ultimately such a vision becomes possible through seeing God's presence "in, with, and under" (as Martin Luther would say) the whole created world. If God's hand were to be withdrawn, the whole of creation would collapse. In terms of the Protestant vision, God's caring hand may be regarded as the ultimate source of sustainability.

Ernst M. CONRADIE
University of the Western Cape

FURTHER READING

Bouma-Prediger, Steven. (2001). *For the beauty of the Earth: A Christian vision for creation care*. Grand Rapids, MI: Baker Academic.

Conradie, Ernst M. (2006). *Christianity and ecological theology: Resources for further research. Study Guides in Religion and Theology 11*. Stellenbosch, South Africa: SUN Press.

Fowler, Robert B. (1995). *The greening of Protestant thought*. Chapel Hill: University of North Carolina Press.

Nash, James A. (1991). *Loving nature: Ecological integrity and Christian responsibility*. Nashville, TN: Abingdon Press.

Nash, James A. (1996). Towards the ecological reformation of Christianity. *Interpretation, 50*(1), 5–15.

Santmire, Paul. (1985). *The travail of nature*. Philadelphia: Fortress Press.

Christianity—Roman Catholic

From the first church statements on environmental deterioration and human deprivation by Pope John Paul II in 1979 to subsequent writings and teachings of Catholic clergy and laity about sustainability, care for all creation and concern for all people are evident. Catholic ecological teachings from diverse sources continue to promote the close relationship of social and economic justice to environmental concerns and care.

Sustainability in Catholic thought integrates care for all creation—Earth and the biotic community—with concern for all people, which includes a "preferential option for the poor," in the words of the Latin American bishops' Puebla Conference. Catholic thought includes official church pronouncements from sources such as the Vatican, national conferences of bishops, individual bishops, and organizations established by the preceding. It also includes unofficial statements and writings from the broader church community, including Catholic laity and clergy speaking either as representatives of some part of the community of believers, or as individual theologians, ethicists, scientists, or social scientists.

Teachings from the Institutional Church

Pope John Paul II issued the earliest global church statements on environmental deterioration and human deprivation. In his first papal journeys in 1979, he discussed themes for upcoming Jubilee year celebrations in 2000. In Cuilapán, Mexico, when he participated in the Latin American bishops' Puebla Conference, the pope declared that all private property has a "social mortgage" (it is, effectively, on loan from the broader community whose needs it should meet directly or indirectly), and that governments might expropriate unused lands from the wealthy, with

appropriate compensation, and redistribute them to landless peasant farmers so that they might provide food for their families and their communities. (The phrase "preferential option for the poor," which has become significant for Catholic social teaching, was first elaborated during this conference, as part of the Latin American bishops' "Puebla Document.") In Des Moines, Iowa, John Paul affirmed the efforts of heartland region bishops to conserve family farms. He urged farmers to conserve the land so that its agricultural productivity would be sustained to benefit future generations. Throughout his papacy, John Paul II continued to speak and write about environmental concerns, and the relationship of social justice to environmental stewardship; he made a significant contribution to Catholic thought in this regard. Perhaps his most influential statement was his World Day of Peace message, *The Ecological Crisis: A Common Responsibility* (1990), in which he declared that care for creation was an "essential part" of Christian faith. The latter phrase was highly significant: it elevated creation care to a requirement for Catholics, rather than leaving it as an option. This stimulated greater church involvement in environmental issues.

The wide dissemination of *The Ecological Crisis* had global impacts, including in the United States, where the Catholic bishops issued *Renewing the Earth* (1991). The bishops described creation as a "sacramental universe," revelatory of its Creator; they extended the Catholic understanding of sacraments beyond the traditional seven *ecclesial* sacraments, to include the *natural* sacraments of creation. The bishops declared, too, that they wanted to explore the relationship between concern for people and concern for Earth, and between natural ecology and social ecology.

National conferences of bishops in several countries addressed environmental concerns due to increased awareness of the unsustainable impact of human industrial, commercial, and economic practices. Among national bishops' statements, the Dominican Republic bishops promulgated the *Pastoral Letter on the Relationship of Human Beings to Nature* (1987), and the Guatemalan bishops issued *The Cry for Land* (1988), both released prior to John Paul II's message. The Australian bishops issued later *A New Earth: The Environmental Challenge* (2002).

In the United States, a series of regional bishops' pastoral letters, focused on area concerns, began when the bishops of Appalachia issued *This Land Is Home to Me* (1975). The document's particular focus was on the regional economic and ecological harm wrought by the coal industry. Subsequent regional documents included *Strangers and Guests: Toward Community in the Heartland* (Midwestern bishops 1980), which focused on saving the owner-operated family farm, preventing industrial harms to Earth and people, promoting land stewardship, safeguarding Native American treaty rights, and emphasizing that God's ownership of land takes precedence over private ownership.

The Columbia River Watershed bishops promulgated the first Catholic bioregional and international environmental document, *The Columbia River Watershed: Caring for Creation and the Common Good* (2001). Pressing regional issues addressed in this pastoral letter included salmon extinction; racism, particularly toward Native Americans; unemployment; and impacts of energy generation. The letter's ten "Considerations for Community Caretaking" illustrated developing Catholic sustainability proposals, including consideration of the common good; conservation of the watershed as a common good; conservation and protection of wildlife species; respect for indigenous peoples' traditions; promotion of justice for the poor, linking economic justice with ecological justice; and conservation of energy and construction of alternative energy generation facilities.

Perspectives from the Church Community

Several Catholic theologians and ethicists extended church teachings beyond their traditional expressions as they explored new exegetical (text-based) approaches to the Bible and analyzed Catholic doctrine. Pioneering works in the field offered distinct but complementary foci: John Hart, in *The Spirit of the Earth: A Theology of the Land* (1984), integrated biblical teachings, Catholic social thought, Native American spirituality, and the U.S. sociopolitical tradition, and their complementary roles in promoting care for Earth and human communities; Matthew Fox, in *Original Blessing: A Primer in Creation Spirituality* (1986), offered an innovative approach to humans' integration with their Earth context, focused on the implications of Yahweh's original blessing over the first humans, as described in Genesis; Thomas Berry, in *The Dream of the Earth* (1988), explored from Catholic and comparative religious perspectives human interaction with Earth, and offered a vision of a renewed Earth; Marcelo de Barros and José Luis Caravias, in *Teologia da Terra* (1988), described exploitation of indigenous peoples in Latin America from the colonial era to the present, linked ecological degradation to oppression of the poor, described the role of transnational capitalism and corporations in this oppression, and advocated new economic structures that would incorporate economic justice for the poor in general and for indigenous peoples in particular; Rosemary Radford Ruether, in *Gaia and God: An Ecofeminist Theology of Earth Healing* (1992), advocated an ecofeminist approach to environmental issues, noted links between male domination of women and human domination of nature, and urged conversion away from exploitation of both and toward the development of ecojustice, which would include new relationships among men and women, races, nations, and social classes; from Brazil, the liberation theologian Leonardo Boff, in *Ecology and Liberation* (1996) and *Cry of the Earth, Cry of the Poor* (1997), linked economic justice with ecological justice, and advocated new economic structures and new relationships among peoples and between people and Earth; and Ivone Gebara, in *Longing for Running Water: Ecofeminism and Liberation* (1999), offered an urban ecofeminist work which deplored, from that perspective, urban poverty, exploitation of the poor, and related ecological degradation, and offered a new ecological consciousness. Complementary works published soon thereafter included John Haught's *God After Darwin: A Theology of Evolution* (2000), which discussed the complementary relationships of theology and science to evolution, ecological responsibility, and responding to the needs of the biotic community and its Earth habitat; Rosemary Radford Ruether's *Integrating Ecofeminism, Globalization, and World Religions* (2005), which developed further social justice ideals; and Thomas Berry's *The Great Work* (2000), on ecological justice, human cosmic consciousness, and a human sense of cosmic place. John Hart's *Sacramental Commons: Christian Ecological Ethics* (2006) integrated appreciation of creation as revelation of divine immanence with advocacy of an equitable distribution of Earth commons goods; it proposed natural rights for all nature and provided principles for Christian ecological ethics. (See sidebar of Francis of Assisi's "Canticle of Creation" in the entry "Sacrament" on page 345.)

Intergenerational Implications of Catholic Teachings

Catholic ecological teachings, from diverse sources, promote ideas and ideals that relate ecological justice to economic justice. They argue for an equitable distribution and use of Earth's *commons goods* (earth, air, water, minerals) in order to meet the *common good* of humanity and of the community of all life, in the present and for the future. They integrate the well-being of creation and the well-being of community. The focus in most official church documents has shifted from human "dominion over" (which tended toward "domination of") to human "stewardship of" God's creation. "Stewardship," too, is somewhat problematic. While the term reminds people that, ultimately, they are caring for God's creation in trust from God, stewardship seems to imply a human managerial role over all creation. Several theologians and ethicists have replaced the constructs of dominion and stewardship with concepts of interrelationship and community: among people, between humans and other species, between biota and Earth, and between cosmos and Creator.

The impact of the human population on Earth's biosphere and available natural goods is rarely noted in institutional church documents, despite Earth's obvious limited carrying capacity—its ability to provide places for people to live and work, to produce food, to have potable water, and to acquire and use energy and minerals in sustainable ways. Institutional and community church writings do rightly note the impact of selfish human consumption and consumerism, in which natural goods are exploited to satisfy the wants of the human species (Earth's minority population), rather than to meet the needs of other biota (Earth's majority population).

People and planet can benefit, overall, from the theory and practice of Catholic socioeconomic-ecological teachings. While the tradition might lag behind in advocating responsible population numbers, it does foster reduced consumption, prioritizes needs over wants, advocates just and sustainable communities and care for creation, exhorts and exercises compassion for the poor, and, in all of this, helps to promote intergenerational responsibility and ecological sustainability.

John HART
Boston University

FURTHER READING

Berry, Thomas. (1988). *The dream of the Earth.* San Francisco: Sierra Club Books.

Berry, Thomas. (2000). *The great work: Our way into the future.* New York: Bell Tower.

Boff, Leonardo. (1996). *Ecology and liberation: A new paradigm.* Maryknoll, NY: Orbis Books.

Boff, Leonardo. (1997). *Cry of the Earth, cry of the poor.* Maryknoll, NY: Orbis Books.

Christiansen, Drew, & Grazer, Walter. (Eds.). (1996). *And God saw that it was good: Catholic theology and the environment.* Washington, DC: United States Catholic Conference.

de Barros, Marcelo, & Caravias, José Luis. (1988). *Teologia da terra.* Petrópolis, Brazil: Editora Vozes Ltda.

Ferro Medina, Alfredo. (1991). *A teologia se fez terra: Primeiro encontro Latino-Americano de teologia da terra.* [*Theology from the land: First Latin-American meeting on a theology of the land*]. São Leopoldo, Brazil: Editora Sinodal.

Fox, Matthew. (1986). *Original blessing: A primer in creation spirituality.* Santa Fe, NM: Bear & Co.

Gebara, Ivone. (1999). *Longing for running water: Ecofeminism and liberation.* Minneapolis, MN: Fortress Press.

Hart, John. (1984). *The spirit of the Earth: A theology of the land.* Mahwah, NJ: Paulist Press.

Hart, John. (2004). *What are they saying about environmental theology?* New York: Paulist Press.

Hart, John. (2006). *Sacramental commons: Christian ecological ethics.* Lanham, MD: Rowman & Littlefield.

Haught, John F. (2000). *God after Darwin: A theology of evolution.* Boulder, CO: Westview Press.

John Paul II. (1990). *The ecological crisis: A common responsibility.* Washington, DC: United States Catholic Conference.

Johnson, E. A. (1993). *Women, Earth, and creator spirit.* New York: Paulist Press.

Maguire, Daniel C., & Coward, Harold. (2000). *Visions of a new Earth: Religious perspectives on population, consumption, and ecology.* Albany: State University of New York Press.

Robb, Carol S., & Casebolt, Carl J. (1991). *Covenant for a new creation: Ethics, religion, and public policy.* Maryknoll, NY: Orbis Books.

Ruether, Rosemary Radford. (1992). *Gaia and God: An ecofeminist theology of Earth healing.* San Francisco: HarperSanFrancisco.

Ruether, Rosemary Radford. (Ed.). (1994). *Women healing Earth: Third world women on ecology, feminism, and religion.* Maryknoll, NY: Orbis Books.

Ruether, Rosemary Radford. (2005). *Integrating ecofeminism, globalization, and world religions.* Lanham, MD: Rowman & Littlefield.

Smith, P. (1997). *What are they saying about environmental ethics?* New York: Paulist Press.

U.S. Catholic Bishops. (1991). *Renewing the Earth: An invitation to reflection and action on environment in light of Catholic social teaching.* Washington, DC: United States Catholic Conference.

Christianity—Society of Friends / Quakers

The fact that two of the Society of Friends' shared beliefs (testimonies) are simplicity and integrity establishes its support of sustainability. Liberal and conservative Friends—or Quakers, as they are commonly known—have always resisted the distraction of material things to be closer to God and to sense more directly the presence of God in nature. This attitude is evident even in Quaker corporate endeavors.

Concern for sustainability and a range of environmental issues—in addition to peace, nuclear, population, and biotechnology concerns—is widespread across the Society of Friends, or Quakers as they are commonly known. Quakers trace their commitment to sustainability to the inclusion of simplicity and integrity, or right relationship, as "testimonies" (central guiding shared ethical beliefs and attitudes) that have been central to their faith from the Friends' beginnings in the Protestant reform movements of the mid-1600s in England. Other central testimonies include peace and equality/community, which have an ecological aspect in contemporary interpretation; some would add sustainability or Earth/environment to the list of testimonies that have evolved from the core testimonies (Helmuth 2007). Plainness was seen as a tool of both personal discipline and spiritual practice to cultivate an inner connection to the light of Christ in one's heart, and as a path of personal virtue to avoid the distractions of worldly things and the accumulation of wealth. George Fox (1624–1691), perhaps the most influential founder of the group, argued that the accumulation of wealth contributed to war and was a form of violence; he advocated the "right sharing" of economic resources, and integrity and honesty in economic transactions, in the interests of social justice. The testimony to simplicity meant plainness in dress, speech, buildings, and lifestyle. The commitment

to simplicity not only allows the individual to be less distracted and therefore closer to God, but also to sense the presence of God in nature. A common Quaker phrase is "There is that of God (or God's Light or Spirit) in everyone"; for many this becomes "There is that of God in everything." For more contemporary Friends, simplicity is valued as an approach to a lifestyle that is more connected to both nature and economic justice and less focused on consumption. This "sustainability" side of the commitment to the simplicity testimony reaches across the Quaker world, connecting theologically liberal and evangelical organizations of Friends.

The testimony of simplicity is not just followed by individuals in their spirituality, lifestyles, and consumption habits, but also by the Society of Friends in their various corporate expressions. Quaker meetinghouses have always been plain, unadorned, and lacking in religious symbolism, as Friends seek a place that does not detract from the inner experience of God's presence. In this same spirit, meetinghouses built in the last four decades have sought to include a predominance of natural lighting, and many feature floor-to-ceiling windows looking out onto natural settings. The incorporation of abundant natural light serves both to enhance energy stewardship, but it also has an obvious symbolic connection to the Light of God.

In the last decade, two key buildings that house Quaker organizations in the United States have been renovated with green-building and sustainability principles in mind. The newly renovated office of the Friends Committee on National Legislation (FCNL) was the first building in Washington, D.C., to be awarded a Leadership in Energy and Environmental Design (LEED) silver certification by the U.S. Green Building Council. The FCNL, founded in 1943, is the oldest registered ecumenical lobby in Washington, D.C. It represents a range of Quaker groups, and its motto (shared on the banner of its website, www.fcnl.org) is an apt summation of its vision of sustainability: "We seek a world free of war and the threat of war . . . a society with equity and justice for all . . . a community where every person's potential may be fulfilled . . . an earth restored." The renovated Friends Center, built in 1856 in Philadelphia—a historically central location for Quakers in the United States—is the first building in Pennsylvania to have a geothermal heating and cooling system. Like the FCNL building, it uses local or reused materials when possible, has a "green roof" (a roof covered with vegetation), uses geothermal energy, and has natural lighting and energy-efficient features throughout. But it is different in that it also has solar panels and uses a storm-water-runoff collection system for use in toilets and on the grounds. According to the Friends Center website (www.friendscentercorp. org), the building, scheduled for completed in July 2009, will be a "showcase for environmental sustainability."

A key organization of Friends' work on sustainability is Quaker Earthcare Witness (QEW), an outgrowth of the Friends Committee on Unity with Nature that began in 1987 in response to the work of the Quaker environmental activist Marshall Massey. QEW points out that the current concept of sustainability is already present in the Quaker understanding of "right relationship," which can be traced back to the preacher John Woolman (1720–1772): if humans are not in right relationship with the more-than-human natural world, then the Quaker dedication to a world without war and with just social relations cannot be achieved. As with FCNL, perhaps this larger Quaker vision is best summed up in the following statement (QEW 2003): "We are called to live in right relationship with all Creation, recognizing that the entire world is interconnected and is a manifestation of God . . . the Truth that God's Creation is to be respected, protected, and held in reverence in its own right, and the Truth that human aspirations for peace and justice depend upon restoring the Earth's ecological integrity."

Laurel D. KEARNS
Drew Theological School and University

FURTHER READING

Cox, Louis; Fabianson, Ingrid; Moon Farley, Sandra; & Swennerfelt, Ruah. (Eds.). (2004). *Earthcare for Friends: A study guide for individuals and faith communities*. Burlington, VT: Quaker Earthcare Witness.

Friends Committee on National Legislation (FCNL). (n.d.). Retrieved on June 5, 2009, from http://www.fcnl.org

Helmuth, Keith. (2007, December). Friends testimonies and ecological understanding. *Friends Journal*, 14–17.

Merkel, Jim. (2003). *Radical simplicity: Small footprints on a finite Earth*. Gabriola Island, Canada: New Society Publishers.

Environment: Quaker authors. (n.d.). Retrieved June 1, 2009, from http://www.pym.org/pm/lib_comments.php?id=499_0_108_0_C

QEW. (2003). Quaker Earthcare Witness's vision for the future. Retrieved June 4, 2009, from http://www.quakerearthcare.org/QEWPastandFuture/QEW_Future/QEW_Future.htm

Spring, Cindy, & Manousos, Anthony. (Eds). (2007). *EarthLight spiritual wisdom for an ecological age*. Philadelphia: Friends Bulletin.

Steere, Douglas. (1984). *Quaker spirituality: Selected writings*. Mahwah, NJ: Paulist Press.

Climate Change

Humans are understood to be causing climate change despite great natural variability of the climate system in the history of Earth. The consequences of human-caused climate change are likely to have devastating effects on our planet: precipitation that is excessive in some areas, inadequate in others; increased storm activity; change in sea levels; and potential loss of certain species and ecosystems.

Climate change is any long-term deviation in the expected patterns of the weather of a region or the entire Earth. Climate change can be distinguished from weather, which is usually understood to be short-term temperature, precipitation, wind, humidity, atmospheric pressure, and cloud events. The weather of a place often varies greatly day to day and season to season, but the climate of a place is usually more predictable because it is a description of longer-term average weather patterns (NCAR 2009).

The term *climate change* is often used interchangeably with the term *global warming*, but according to the National Academy of Sciences, "the phrase 'climate change' is growing in preferred use to 'global warming' because there are [other] changes in addition to rising temperatures." (EPA 2009).

Causes of Natural Climate Change

A report from the U.S. Global Change Research Program/Climate Change Science Program (2009) states that there are several causes of climate change: (1) natural factors, such as changes in the Sun's intensity or slow changes in the Earth's orbit around the Sun; (2) natural processes within the climate system, such as changes in ocean circulation; (3) human activities that change the atmosphere's composition (for example, and industrial and

agricultural- and food-production processes and the burning of fossil fuels emit greenhouse gases); and (4) land-use changes such as deforestation, reforestation, urbanization, and desertification.

Over the very long-term, regions on Earth and the entire Earth itself have gone through climate changes that are understood to constitute natural climate variability, that is, change not caused by human activities. The Earth's climate has changed many times during the planet's history, with events ranging from ice ages to long periods of warmth. From glacial periods (or ice ages) where ice covered significant portions of the Earth to interglacial periods where ice retreated to the poles or melted entirely, the climate has continuously changed (EPA 2009).

Natural climate change is believed to have been caused by several variations in Earth-Sun relationships; tectonic movement of the Earth's plates; volcanic emissions of gases and particles; changes in the cycling of carbon through the atmosphere, oceans, and biosphere; changes in naturally occurring greenhouse gases (GHGs), including carbon dioxide, methane, water vapor, and nitrous oxide; and occasional changes in the particulate matter in atmosphere due to Earth's bombardment by meteors and other space debris (U.S. Global Change 2009).

Scientists have been able to piece together a picture of the Earth's climate dating back decades to millions of years ago by analyzing a number of surrogate, or "proxy," measures of climate (such as ice cores, boreholes, tree rings, glacier lengths, pollen remains, and ocean sediments) and by studying changes in the Earth's orbit around the Sun.

For at least the last million years, our world has experienced cycles of warming and cooling that take approximately 100,000 years each to complete. Over the course of each cycle, global average temperatures have fallen and then risen again by about 5°C, each time taking Earth into an ice age and then warming it again (EPA 2009).

The greenhouse effect is a process by which certain gases (water vapor, carbon dioxide, methane, and nitrous oxide) trap heat within the Earth's atmosphere and thereby produce warmer air temperatures. These gases act like the glass of a greenhouse: they allow short (ultraviolet or UV) energy waves from the Sun to penetrate into the atmosphere, but absorb and reradiate long (infrared) energy waves that are emitted from the Earth's surface, thus warming the planet.

Causes of Human-Induced Climate Change

In addition to changes in the atmosphere's composition, changes in the land surface can have important effects on climate. For example, a change in land use and cover can affect temperature by affecting the amount of solar radiation the land reflects and absorbs. Processes such as deforestation, reforestation, desertification, and urbanization often contribute to changes in climate (including temperature, wind, and precipitation) in the places they occur. These effects may be significant regionally, but they are reduced when averaged over the entire globe.

Changes in land cover and land use can also affect the amount of carbon dioxide taken up (or sequestered) or released by the land surface. Since the Industrial Revolution (circa 1750), human activities have substantially added to the amount of heat-trapping greenhouse gases in the atmosphere. The burning of fossil fuels and biomass (living matter such as vegetation) has also resulted in emissions of aerosols that absorb and emit heat, and reflect light (EPA 2009).

Consequences of Human-Induced Climate Change

If greenhouse gases continue to increase, climate models predict that the average temperature at the Earth's surface could rise 1.8°C–4°C above the 1990 levels by the end of this century. Scientists are certain that human activities are changing the composition of the atmosphere and that increasing the concentration of greenhouse gases will change the planet's climate. But they are not sure by how much it will change, at what rate it will change, or what the exact effects will be (EPA 2009). In 1988, the Intergovernmental Panel on Climate Change (IPCC) was created by the World Meteorological Organization and the United Nations Environment Programme (UNEP). The IPCC issued a First Assessment Report in 1990 that reflected the views of four

hundred scientists. It stated that global warming was real and urged that something be done about it. Since its first report on the science of climate change, IPCC issued periodic analyses of the peer-reviewed science for 1995, 2001, and 2007.

IPCC has concluded with high levels of confidence that the Earth will experience warming in the years ahead because of human activities. Droughts, floods, and other forms of extreme weather will become more frequent and threaten food supplies. Plants and animals that cannot adjust will die out. Sea levels are rising and will continue to do so, forcing hundreds of thousands of people in coastal zones to migrate. According to IPCC, some of the poorest people in the world are the most vulnerable to climate change, although some of the richest countries are disproportionately responsible for causing climate change.

One of the main GHGs that humans are adding to the atmosphere, carbon dioxide (CO_2), is increasing rapidly. According to UNEP (2009), at the start of the Industrial Revolution in Europe, there were 280 parts per million (ppm) of carbon dioxide in the atmosphere. Today the overall amount of GHGs has topped 390 parts per million of carbon dioxide equivalent (all GHGs expressed as a common metric in relation to their warming potential) and the figure is rising by 1.5–2 ppm annually.

Some scientists believe it would be prudent to prevent the Earth's average temperature from rising more than 2°C over pre-industrialization levels to prevent dangerous climate change. Scientists believe there is a 50 percent chance of keeping the level to 2°C if the total GHG concentration remains below 450 ppm (UNEP 2009).

Observable Climate Change

Some consequences of global warming are already apparent. Numerous long-term changes in the climate have been observed, including extreme weather such as droughts, heavy precipitation, heat waves, and the intensity of tropical cyclones.

Trends towards more powerful storms and hotter, longer dry periods have been observed and are evaluated in the IPCC's Fourth Assessment Report, *Climate Change 2007: Synthesis Report* (2008). Warmer temperatures mean greater evaporation, and a warmer atmosphere is able to hold more moisture—hence there is more water aloft that can fall as precipitation. Similarly, if the weather is hotter, dry regions are apt to lose still more moisture, which exacerbates droughts and desertification.

The United Nations Framework on Climate Change—an international treaty produced at 1992's Earth Summit in Rio de Janeiro—has also documented several changes in climate patterns (UNFCC 2009). Drying has been observed over large regions including the African Sahel (the wide stretch of land reaching from the Atlantic to Africa's "Horn"), the Mediterranean, southern Africa, and parts of southern Asia. The frequency of heavy-precipitation events also has increased over many land areas. Significantly increased precipitation has been observed in eastern parts of North and South America, northern Europe, and northern and central Asia. There is also observational evidence for an increase of intense tropical cyclone activity in the North Atlantic since about 1970. The complexity of the climate system means predictions vary widely, but even the minimum changes forecast could mean frequently flooded coastlines, disruptions to food and water supplies, and the extinction of many species.

Extreme weather events are striking more often, and sea levels have already risen 10 to 20 centimeters over pre-industrialization averages. A rise in sea level will continue for centuries due to the time scales associated with climate processes and feedbacks. In its Fourth Assessment Report, the IPCC (2008) states that the contraction of the Greenland ice sheet is projected to continue to contribute to sea level rise after 2100. If this contraction is sustained for centuries, it would lead to the virtual complete elimination of the Greenland ice sheet and a resulting rise in sea level of about 7 meters (UNFCCC 2009).

Projections also point to continued snow-cover contraction, as well as widespread increases in thaw depth over most permafrost regions. (*Thaw depth* indicates the level to which the top active layer of permafrost soil—or permanently frozen ground—will thaw each summer.) A future of more severe storms and floods along the world's increasingly crowded coastlines is likely, and it will be a bad combination even under the minimum scenarios forecast. Furthermore, extra-tropical storm tracks are projected to move toward the Earth's poles, with consequent changes in wind, precipitation, and temperature patterns continuing the model observed over the last half century (UNFCCC 2009).

Climate Change Ethics

Climate change raises a host of ethical questions that challenge civilization (Brown et al. 2004):

- At what level should the international community agree to stabilize greenhouse gases in the atmosphere?
- How should global targets be allocated among nations?
- Who should pay for climate change damages or costs of climate change adaptation?
- Do nations have a right to delay reducing GHG emissions because new less costly reduction technologies may be invented in the future?

- Is scientific uncertainty about some climate change impacts an adequate justification for failing to take GHG reduction strategies?
- Are cost arguments against taking action to reduce GHG emissions made by some nations ethically justified?
- May any one nation refuse to reduce its GHG emissions to its fair share of safe global emissions on the basis that other nations have not agreed to reduce their emissions?

Climate change raises these questions for at least three reasons. First, those causing climate change are usually not those who are most vulnerable to its impact. Second, the harms to some victims of climate change are likely to be catastrophic. Third, national governments must set policy based upon global scale impacts, not on national interest alone.

Some developed nations have made commitments to reducing their climate change–causing emissions under the Kyoto Protocol, an amendment to the United Nations Framework Convention on Climate Change, and in some cases began to reduce emissions based upon their observations that other (developed) nations' emissions had continued to increase. Because the Kyoto Protocol will expire by its own terms, the nations of the world have begun to negotiate a replacement for the Kyoto Protocol, a process that will call for additional national commitments.

Donald BROWN
Pennsylvania State University

FURTHER READING

Brown, Donald; Tuana, Nancy; Averill Marilyn; Bear, Paul; Born, Rubens, et al. (2004). *White paper on ethical dimensions of climate change*. Retrieved May 18, 2009, from http://rockethics.psu.edu/climate/whitepaper/whitepaper-intro.shtml

Intergovernmental Panel on Climate Change (IPCC). (2008). *Climate change 2007: Synthesis report*. Retrieved May 24, 2009, from http://www.ipcc.ch/ipccreports/ar4-syr.htm

National Center for Atmospheric Research (NCAR). (2009). Retrieved April 27, 2009, from http://www.ncar.ucar.edu/

United Nations Environment Programme (UNEP). (n.d.). What is climate change? Retrieved April 27, 2009, from http://www.unep.org/themes/climatechange/whatis/index.asp

United Nations Framework Convention on Climate Change (UNFCCC). (n.d.). Retrieved April 27, 2009, from http://unfccc.int/essential_background/items/2877.php

United States Environmental Protection Agency (EPA). (2009). Climate change. Retrieved April 27, 2009 from http://www.epa.gov/climatechange/index.html

U.S. Global Change Research Program /Climate Change Science Program. (2009, March). *Climate literacy: The essential principles of climate sciences*. Retrieved April 27, 2009, from http://downloads.climate-science.gov/Literacy/Climate%20Literacy%20Booklet%20Low-Res.pdf

Common Good

The concept of the common good—something that benefits not just the individual but the larger community as a whole—is an ancient one also found in several religious traditions. Sustainability is the ultimate common good: doing what is right not only for the benefit of humans but for the whole of Earth and all its living and nonliving elements.

The "common good" is a key way to understand sustainability because it emphasizes the importance of a good shared in common that transcends but also includes the good of individuals. Traditionally it was a political notion, positing that the state seeks the well-being of the people by promoting a good that belongs to the community as a whole, that benefits everyone, and to which every citizen ought to contribute. The common good was not just one goal among many. As Aristotle explained, the common good was the aim of political life (Aristotle 2004). Christians adopted and expanded this concept by applying it to humanity's relationship to God. St. Augustine, for example, argued that all creatures, including human beings, are parts within the whole of the universe. For Augustine (1961, 66), humans sin when they set their hearts upon a limited good rather than the good of the whole, who is God, "the common good of all."

The medieval theologian Saint Thomas Aquinas elaborated on the common good, asserting that every part naturally seeks the good of the whole to which it belongs, "because every particular good of this or that thing is ordained thereto as its end" (Fathers of the English 1924). Since seeking the common good is not only a moral imperative but a natural inclination instilled by God, Thomas expects that every part is instinctively willing to sacrifice for the benefit of the whole. This is a far cry from totalitarian states, where the government may choose to sacrifice an individual on behalf of the rest. Rather, because every part inherently desires the good common to all, there is a natural tendency to risk oneself so that the whole may prosper. Indeed, there is something unnatural and wrong when one part refers the good of the whole to its own private good. This weakens the welfare of the whole, and it ultimately thwarts the individual's own well-being. Though Thomas thinks that the greatest aspect of creation is the unity and order among the various parts of the universe, he also presumes that God would take care of animals and plants, so he applies "common good" only to human communities. Thomas seems wrong on this limit now, and today Catholic bishops in the United States urge humanity to promote a broader, "planetary common good" (U.S. Catholic Bishops, 1996).

Viewing sustainability through the lens of the common good acknowledges that humans are only one part of a much larger planetary and cosmic whole and that human beings flourish only when they contribute to the good of the whole. Hence human beings need to recognize a planetary and cosmic common good that transcends them but also includes them. True sustainability for human beings will come when humans see themselves as only one part of the Earth and understand that human communities flourish when they act on behalf of the flourishing of the entire Earth community. When humanity takes something from the whole for its own private good, or humans set their hearts on the human good rather than the good of all creation, they undermine the Earth's capacity to sustain life and frustrate their own happiness. Humans violate the natural order when they fail to acknowledge that they belong intrinsically to the Earth as parts to a whole. Sustainability for the Earth's various ecosystems, which uphold the order and unity of the many parts that support life not only for humans but for all creatures, is the common good of all.

Other traditions present parallel conceptions of the common good, even though they might not use language exactly translatable as "common good." For instance, the Native American Lakota prayer *Mitakouye oyasin*—"all my relations"—reflects a visceral understanding of the common good. In praying these words, Lakota Sioux remind themselves to consider every creature in the universe as a family member, and they contain in ritual form the core of their spirituality: reciprocity with the rest of creation and balance within the universe.

Another prominent example is the Hindu notion of dharma. Based on a Sanskrit word, meaning "to support and sustain," dharma indicates both the cosmic and moral law that maintains the harmony and well-being of the universe and all creatures. Dharma recognizes that humans are parts of a cosmic whole, and that when any creature or species acts for its own selfish good, it invites personal, social, and even cosmic breakdown and suffering. Dharma reflects the Christian notion of the common good: humans live out their part in the universe and attain their greatest well-being when they refer any good that comes to them not to their own benefit but to the good of the whole, which is the cosmic common good. Concepts of the common good can be said to exist in other traditions as well. Strands of Buddhists, for example, and many indigenous

peoples would say that it resonates with their traditions in different ways.

Daniel P. SCHEID
Duquesne University

FURTHER READING

Aristotle (2004). *Nicomachean ethics*. (J. A. K. Thompson & Hugh Tredennick, Trans.). New York: Penguin Classics.

Augustine, St. (1961). *Confessions*. (R. S. Pine-Coffin, Trans.). New York: Penguin Classics.

Christiansen, Drew. (2000). Ecology and the common good: Catholic social teaching and environmental responsibility. In Drew Christiansen & Walter Glazer (Eds.), *And God saw that it was good: Catholic theology and the environment* (pp. 183–195). Washington, DC: Island Press.

Fathers of the English Dominican Province (Trans.). (1924). *Summa Contra Gentiles*. Chicago: Benziger Brothers.

French, William C. (1994). Catholicism and the common good of the biosphere. In Michael H. Barnes (Ed.), *An ecology of the spirit: Religious reflection and environmental consciousness* (pp. 177–194). Lanham, MD: University Press of America.

Hart, John. (2006). *Sacramental commons: Christian ecological ethics*. Lanham, MD: Rowman & Littlefield.

Longwood, Merle. (1973). The common good: An ethical framework for evaluating environmental issues. *Theological Studies, 34*, 468–480.

Schaefer, Jame. (2005). Valuing Earth intrinsically and instrumentally: A theological framework for environmental ethics. *Theological Studies, 66*, 783–814.

U.S. Catholic Bishops. (1996). Renewing the Earth. In Drew Christiansen and Walt Grazer (Eds.), *And God saw that it was good: Catholic theology and the environment*. Washington DC: United States Catholic Conference.

U.S. Conference of Catholic Bishops. (2001). *Global climate change: A plea for dialogue, prudence, and the common good*. Washington, DC: United States Catholic Conference.

Community

The importance of community to the pursuit of sustainability is critical to its achievement: any number of individuals cannot accomplish what can be done by the larger community. The participation of all forms of community—religious, national, cultural, global, etcetera—is essential if Earth and future generations are to prosper.

Community, as a moral category, has as many definitions as there are religious, cultural, and philosophical traditions. As a collection of individual persons linked by some commonality, community can be based upon family, locality, national or transnational identity, religious or cultural identity, common interest, mutual self-interest, and so on. Every human person is a member of numerous communities, and no individual is ever entirely without communal ties. Some of these communal ties are chosen. Many communities, however, are not based upon explicit choice. Every human being is a member of the global community of persons, the human family. Beyond the human family, all religious traditions seek to place humanity within the larger universe. Within the spirit of sustainability, current ecological crises mandate that approaches to community must extend from the human community to the Earth community. Crises like global climate change require a spirit of sustainability to include the natural world in community.

Sustainability, as a moral challenge, is both a problem *for* community and *of* community. Individual responsibility and participation are necessary but not sufficient for a program of sustainability. If purely a matter of individual choice and without an organized collective agenda, neither the viability of the community nor the Earth could be guaranteed. Six billion individual plans, even plans in the spirit of sustainability, cannot have adequate coordination and consistency to address communal and global concerns. Interdependence, globalization, and the current ecological crisis clearly highlight the need *for community* in order to achieve economic, developmental, and ecological sustainability. Similarly, governmental and international regulation and structures cannot succeed without individual agency. For example, greater funding of energy efficiency and environmentally friendly technology is only successful if consumers choose to buy energy-efficient products. Sustainability requires both a coordinated communal effort to develop energy-efficient automobiles and individual consumers to buy them.

A problem *of community*, the spirit of sustainability must focus attention on sustaining communities in themselves. In particular, the expansion of Western secular individualism has led to the need to renew focus on human community. Sustainable economic and ecological development requires participatory community and not simply assertion of individual liberties without any social support. Education, healthcare, economic opportunity, and resources are necessary for the sustainability of our local communities. Agency, participation, and strengthening social capital within local communities are necessary preconditions for addressing sustainability on larger levels.

Commitment to participation means that no community is exempt from the moral imperative to actively contribute to the project of sustainable development. Without an active local community, pragmatic, incremental change cannot occur. Without a sense of national, transnational, and global community, the systemic guiding of necessary development, energy policy, and ecological conservation cannot be implemented. Moreover, community, if understood exclusively and with firm boundaries can sabotage any program for sustainability. Environmental sustainability requires active participation of all communities and nations; should individual countries opt out it threatens to sabotage the entire program of environmental conservation. All sustainability initiatives, in order to succeed, require attention to the moral challenge *of* and *for* communities.

Community and sustainability intersect in a number of key ethical concepts: prudence, subsidiarity, the common good, solidarity, human rights, ecological responsibility, and a commitment to future generations. Prudence, or the virtue of right reason and judgment, requires that programs of sustainability take into account individual and communal participation in all areas of social, economic, and environmental commitments. Philosophically, the virtue of prudence guides the community's decisions concerning achievable sustainability goals. Subsidiarity mandates that programs of sustainability be enacted on every level of community from the individual family through the global with individual problems being addressed at the lowest level possible. This places the responsibility on the family for energy conservation in the home while recognizing the moral necessity of global energy policies in future sustainability. This is practically achieved through fostering a sense of solidarity among humans and with the natural world and through a broadening of the common good to account for the global common good.

A spirit of sustainability that includes economic, social, and ecological sustainability also must be one of human rights, which are central to developing individual agency and participatory community. In order to attend to ecological commitments and to future generations, sustainability must be understood as a moral imperative *of* and *for* community, all communities.

Meghan J. CLARK
Saint Anselm College

FURTHER READING

Dale, Ann, & Onyx, Jenny. (2006). *A dynamic balance: Social capital and sustainable community development.* Toronto: UBC Press.

The Global Development Research Center. (2008). Retrieved March 16, 2009, from http://www.gdrc.org/

Local Agenda 21. (n.d.). Retrieved March 16, 2009, from http://www.gdrc.org/uem/la21/la21.html

Meltzer, Graham. (2005). *Sustainable community: Learning from the cohousing model.* Victoria, Canada: Trafford.

Sustainable Communities Network. (2004). Retrieved March 16, 2009, from http://www.sustainable.org/

Wheeler, Stephen. (2004). *Planning for sustainability: Creating livable, equitable and ecological communities.* New York: Routledge.

United States Council of Catholic Bishops. (1991). Renewing the Earth: An invitation to reflection and action on environment in light of Catholic social teaching. Retrieved March 16, 2009, from http://www.usccb.org/sdwp/ejp/bishopsstatement.shtml

Confucianism

In Confucianism, one of the three major religions of China, the ultimate context for human life is found in the "10,000 things"—nature in all its variety and abundance. Confucian texts describe nature as the basis of a stable society and warn that imbalance results from not caring for it properly. Ecological dimensions of Confucianism are being explored in China and East Asia in a search for a sustainable future amidst rapid industrialization.

Confucianism conventionally has been described as a humanistic tradition focusing on the roles and responsibilities of humans to family, society, and government. Thus, Confucianism is identified primarily as an ethical or political system of thought with an anthropocentric focus. Upon further examination, however, and as more translations become available in Western languages, this narrow perspective needs to be reexamined.

Some of the most important results of this reexamination are the insights that have emerged in seeing Confucianism as not simply an ethical, political, or ideological system. Rather, Confucianism is being appreciated as a profoundly religious tradition in ways that are different from Western traditions. (This recognition may eventually result in expanding the idea of "religion" itself to include more than criteria adopted from Western traditions, such as notions of God, salvation, and redemption.) Confucianism is also being recognized for its affirmation of relationality, not only between and among humans but between humans and the natural world. The Confucian worldview might be described as a series of concentric circles where the human is the center, not as an isolated individual but as embedded in rings of family, society, and government. This is especially clear in the text of the *Great Learning* (*Daxue*), one of the four books of Confucianism. All of these circles are contained within the vast cosmos itself. Thus in

Confucian thought the ultimate context for the human is the "10,000 things," namely, nature in all its remarkable variety and abundance.

Historical Development

Four major periods of Confucian thought and practice can be identified. The first stage is that of classical Confucianism, which lasts from approximately the sixth century BCE to the second century before the Common Era. This is the era of the flourishing of the early Confucian thinkers, namely Confucius and Mencius. The second period is that of Han Confucianism, when the classical tradition was shaped into a political orthodoxy under the Han dynasty (206 BCE–220 CE) and began to spread to other parts of East Asia. The Han period saw the development of the theory that explained the correspondences of the microcosm of the human world with the macrocosm of the natural world—the relationship of the human to the seasons and the stars, for example. The third major period is the neo-Confucian era from the eleventh to the early twentieth century. This includes the comprehensive synthesis of Zhu Xi in the eleventh century and the distinctive contributions of Wang Yangming in the fifteenth and sixteenth centuries. The influence of both Confucianism and neo-Confucianism as an educational and philosophical system spread beyond China and shaped East Asian societies, especially Korea and Japan, along with Taiwan, Hong Kong, and Singapore.

In the twentieth century a fresh epoch of Confucian humanism, called "New Confucianism," has emerged. This represents a revival of the tradition under the influence of scholars who came to Taiwan and Hong Kong after Mao Zedong's ascendancy in 1949. Mao felt that Confucianism was essentially a feudal tradition, anchored in history, and, that for his own ideas to flourish, a radical break must be made with the past. The anti-Confucian campaigns during Mao's rule were virulent, especially in the Cultural Revolution of the 1960s and 1970s. But after Mao's death there was a resurgence of interest in Confucian values, in part encouraged by the government. Indeed, the International Confucian Society held two major conferences in Beijing and in Confucius's birthplace, Qufu, to explore the future of the Confucian tradition. These conferences were held to commemorate the 2,540th anniversary of Confucius's birth; they marked a renewed interest in Confucianism to balance the unsettling effects of the rapid industrialization and modernization of China. There is a growing movement in China and across East Asia to reevaluate Confucianism for a sustainable future. This has been encouraged by a number of leaders, including, as of 2009, the Chinese vice minister for the environment Pan Yue.

Models of Confucian Sustainability

Various Confucian and neo-Confucian thinkers have suggested ways for integrating spiritual practice or cultivation with action in the world and reciprocity with nature. Confucius, Mencius, Xunxi, and Zhu Xi have distinctive approaches described below.

Confucius: Moral Rectification Extending Outward

The acknowledged founder of the Confucian tradition was known as the sage-teacher Kongzi (551–479 BCE). His name was Latinized by the Jesuit missionaries as Confucius. Born into a time of rapid social change, Confucius was concerned with the goal of reestablishing political and social order through rectification of the individual and the state. The principal teachings of Confucius are contained in his conversations recorded in the *Analects*. Here he emphasized the cultivation of moral virtues, especially humaneness (*ren*) and the practice of civility or ritual decorum (*li*), which includes filiality (*xiao*). Virtue and civility were exemplified by the noble person's (*junzi*) behavior, particularly within the five relationships between ruler and minister, parent and child, husband and wife, older and younger siblings, and friend and friend. The essence of Confucian thinking was that to establish order in the society one had to begin with harmony, filial piety, and decorum in the family. Then, like concentric circles, the effects of virtue would reach outward to the society. Likewise, if the ruler was moral, it would have a ripple effect on the rest of the society and on nature itself, like a pebble dropped into a pond.

At the heart of this classical Confucian worldview was a profound commitment to humaneness and civility. These two virtues defined the means of human relatedness as a spiritual path. Through civility, beginning with filiality, one could repay the gifts of life both to one's parents and ancestors and to the whole natural world. Through humaneness one could extend this sensibility to other humans and to all living things. In doing so one became more fully human. The root of practicing humaneness was considered to lie in filial relations. The extension of these relations from one's family and ancestors to the human family and to the cosmic family of the natural world was the means whereby these primary biological ties provided a person with the roots, trunks, and branches of an interconnected spiritual path. Humans, nature, and the cosmos were joined in the stream of filiality. From the lineages of ancestors to future progeny, intergenerational connections and ethical bonding arose. Reverence and reciprocity were considered a natural response to this gift of life from parents and ancestors. Analogously, through reverence for heaven and Earth as the great parents of all life, one realized one's full cosmological being and one's place in the natural order. This can be considered a model for sustainability from the individual radiating outward.

Mencius: Botanical Cultivation of Self and Nature

Confucian thought was further developed in the writings of Mencius (371–289 BCE) and Xunzi (c. 310–219 BCE), who both debated whether human nature was intrinsically good or evil. Mencius's argument for the inherent goodness of human nature gained dominance among Confucian thinkers and gave an optimistic flavor to Confucian educational philosophy and political theory. This perspective influenced the spiritual aspects of the tradition as well because self-cultivation was seen as a means of uncovering this innate good nature. Mencius contributed an understanding of the process required for self-cultivation. He did this by identifying the innate seeds of virtues in the human and suggesting ways in which they could be cultivated toward their full realization as virtues. Analogies taken from the natural world extended the idea of self-cultivation of the individual for the sake of family and society to a wider frame of reference that also encompassed the natural environment. This can be described as a path of botanical cultivation. In addition to his teachings on personal cultivation, Mencius advocated humane government as a means to promote the flourishing of a larger common good. His political thought embraced appropriate agricultural practices and proper use of natural resources. In particular, he urged that the ruler attend to the basic needs of the people and follow the way of righteousness, not profit.

Xunzi: Ritual Relationship of Humans and Cosmos

Xunzi contributed a strong sense of the importance of ritual practice as a means of self-cultivation. He noted that human desires needed to be satisfied, and emotions such as joy and sorrow should be expressed in the appropriate degree. Rituals provided the form for such expression in daily human exchange as well as in rites of passage such as marriage and death. Moreover, because Xunzi saw human nature as innately flawed, he emphasized the need for education to shape human nature toward the good. Finally, he had a highly developed sense of the interdependent triad of heaven, Earth, and humanity that was emphasized also by many later Confucian thinkers. He writes: "Heaven has its seasons; earth has its riches; humans have their government" (deBary and Bloom 1999, 171). Heaven here is understood as the guiding force of the universe and Earth as the natural world within which humans lived and flourished.

Zhu Xi: Forming One Body with All Things

Confucianism blossomed during a neo-Confucian revival in the eleventh and twelfth centuries that resulted in a new synthesis of the earlier teachings. The major neo-Confucian thinker, Zhu Xi (1130–1200), designated four texts from the canon of historical writings as containing the central ideas of Confucian thought. These texts and Zhu Xi's commentaries on them became, in 1315, the basis of the Chinese civil service examination system, which endured for nearly six hundred years until 1905. Every prospective government official had to take the civil service exams based on Zhu Xi's commentaries on the Four Books. The idea was to provide educated, moral officials for the large government bureaucracy that ruled China. The influence, then, of neo-Confucian thought on government, education, agriculture, land, and social values was extensive. Views regarding nature, agriculture, and management of resources were derived from neo-Confucian understandings of the importance of humans' working to cultivate and care for nature as a means to fulfill their role in the triad of heaven and Earth.

Zhu Xi's synthesis of neo-Confucianism was recorded in his classic anthology, *Reflections on Things at Hand* (*Jinsilu*). In this work Zhu formulated a "this-worldly" spirituality based on a balance of cosmological orientation, ethical and ritual practices, scholarly reflection, and political participation. The aim was to balance inner spiritual cultivation with outward investigation of things in concert with the dynamic changes of the natural world. Zhu Xi affirmed these changes as the source of transformation in both the cosmos and the person. Thus neo-Confucian spiritual discipline involved cultivating one's moral nature so as to bring it into harmony with the larger pattern of change in the cosmos. Each moral virtue had its cosmological component. For example, the central virtue of humaneness was seen as the source of fecundity and growth in both the individual and the cosmos. By practicing humaneness, one could effect the transformation of things in oneself, in

society, and in the cosmos. In so doing, one's deeper identity with reality was recognized as forming one body with all things. As the *Doctrine of the Mean* stated: ". . . being able to assist in the transforming and nourishing powers of Heaven and Earth, one can form a triad with Heaven and Earth" (deBary and Bloom 1999, 333).

Confucian Relationality and Nature: Embodied Sustainability

From the classical texts to the later neo-Confucian writings there is a strong sense of nature as a relational whole in which human life and society flourishes. Indeed, Confucian thought recognizes that the rhythms of nature sustain life in both its biological needs and sociocultural expressions. For the Confucians, the biological dimensions of life are dependent on nature as a holistic, organic continuum. Everything in nature is interdependent and interrelated. Most importantly, for the Confucians nature is seen as dynamic and transformational. These ideas are evident in the *Book of Changes* (*I Ching* or *Yijing*) and are expressed in the Four Books, especially in *Mencius*, the *Doctrine of the Mean*, and the *Great Learning*. They come to full flowering in the neo-Confucian tradition of the Song (960–1279) and Ming (1368–1644) periods. Nature in this context has an inherent unity, namely, it has a primary ontological source (*T'ai ji*). It has patterned processes of transformation (yin–yang), and it is interrelated in the interaction of the five elements (water, metal, fire, earth, and wood) and nature's "10,000 things." Nature is dynamic and fluid with the movements of material force, or qi.

The Morality of Nature: Affirming Change

For the Confucians, humans are "anthropocosmic" beings, not anthropocentric individuals, meaning that the human is viewed as a microcosm in relation to the macrocosm of the universe. This is expressed most succinctly in the metaphor of humans as forming a triad with heaven and Earth. These relations were developed during the Han period with a complex synthesis of correlative correspondences involving the elements, directions, colors, seasons, and virtues. This need to consciously connect the patterns of nature with the rhythms of human society is very ancient in Confucian culture. It is at the basis of the anthropocosmic worldview where humans are seen as working together with heaven and Earth in correlative relationships to create harmonious societies. The mutually related resonances between self, society, and nature are constantly being described in the Confucian texts and are evident in art and architecture as well.

For Confucians nature is not only inherently valuable, it is morally good. Nature, thus, embodies the normative standard for all things; it is not judged from an anthropocentric perspective. There is not a fact/value division in the Confucian worldview, for nature is seen as an intrinsic source of value. In particular, value lies in the ongoing transformation and productivity of nature. A term repeated frequently in neo-Confucian sources is *sheng sheng*, reflecting the ever-renewing fecundity of life itself. In this sense, the dynamic transformation of life is seen as emerging in recurring cycles of growth, fruition, harvesting, and abundance. This reflects the natural processes of growth and decay in nature, human life, and human society. Change is thus seen as a dynamic force with which humans should harmonize and interact rather than withdraw.

In this context, the Confucians do not view hierarchy as leading inevitably to domination. Rather, they see that value rests in each thing but not in each thing equally. Everything in nature and society has its appropriate role and place and thus should be treated accordingly. The use of nature for human ends must recognize the intrinsic value of each element of nature, but also its value in relation to the larger context of the environment. Each entity is considered not simply equal to every other; rather, each interrelated part of nature has a particular value according to its nature and function. Thus there is a differentiated sense of appropriate roles for humans and for all other species. For Confucians, hierarchy is seen as a necessary way for each being to fulfill its function. In this context then, no individual being has exclusive privileged status in relation to nature. Rather, the processes of nature and its ongoing logic of transformation (yin–yang) is the norm that takes priority for the common good of the whole society.

Humane Society and Government: Grounds for Sustainability

Confucians were mindful that nature was the basis of a stable society, and that without carefully tending nature an imbalance would result. There are numerous passages in *Mencius* advocating humane government based on appropriate management of natural resources and family practices. Moreover, there are various passages in Confucian texts urging humans not to wantonly cut down trees or kill animals needlessly.

The establishment of humane society, government, and culture, however, inevitably results in the use of nature for housing, for production, and for governance. In this sense Confucians might be seen as pragmatic social ecologists who recognize that stable societies depend on both educational and political institutions, rather than as deep ecologists who largely focus the primacy of the natural world and the need to reduce human exploitation of nature. Nonetheless, it is clear that for Confucians human cultural values and practices are grounded in nature and part of its structure, and thus humans are dependent on its beneficence. In addition, the agricultural base of Confucian societies has always been recognized as essential to the political and social well-being of the country. Humans prosper by living within nature's boundaries and are refreshed by its beauty, restored by its seasons, and fulfilled by its rhythms. For Confucians, human flourishing is thus dependent on fostering nature in its variety and abundance; going against nature's processes is self-destructive. Human moral growth means cultivating one's desires not to interfere with nature but to be in accord with the great Dao of Nature. Thus the human mind expands in relation to the "Mind of the Way."

In short, harmony with nature is essential for Confucians, and human self-realization is achieved in relation to and in harmony with nature. The great triad of Confucianism—namely, heaven, Earth, and humans—signifies this understanding that humans can only attain their full humanity in relationship to both heaven and Earth. This became a foundation for a cosmological ethical system of relationality applicable to spheres of family, society, politics, and nature, itself. This is the relational basis for Confucian sustainability.

Mary Evelyn TUCKER
Yale University

FURTHER READING

de Bary, William Theodore, & Bloom, Irene. (Eds.). (1999). *Sources of Chinese tradition, vol. 1: From earliest times to 1600.* New York: Columbia University Press.

Tu Wei-ming, & Tucker, Mary Evelyn. (Eds.). (2003). *Confucian spirituality.* New York: Crossroads.

Tucker, Mary Evelyn, & Berthrong, John. (Eds.). (1998). *Confucianism and ecology: The interrelation of heaven, Earth, and humans.* Cambridge, MA: Harvard Center for the Study of World Religions.

Conservation

Conservation is a constellation of ideas and values reflecting a belief that people should take care of nature and other things of value. It encompasses wide-ranging critiques of less sensitive land-use approaches while prescribing various, sometimes conflicting steps needed to bring improvement. Usefully distinguished from both preservation and environmentalism, conservation increasingly promotes the maintenance of ecological systems, biological diversity, and sound land-use cultures.

In the broadest sense, conservation means protecting, maintaining, and preserving things of value over the long term, typically things that people find useful. Most often conservation refers to maintaining various parts and processes of nature, although the term is also used in settings unrelated to the natural world. Conservation expresses a desire to uphold and protect nature when beneficial to people. It is thus both a claim of normative value and a call for people to respect that value in their land uses and other activities.

Implicit in conservation is a critique of prevailing ways of using nature. Sometimes this critique is framed in moral rather than simply prudential terms, as an attack on crass materialism, individual selfishness, and short-sightedness. Sometimes the critique highlights instead our poor knowledge of nature's functioning and our alleged tendency, when managing nature, to fail to use sound science or economic reasoning; we charge ahead, manipulating nature,

without fully knowing what we are doing. In all instances conservation expresses a distinct call for reform. It variously proposes a move to new, allegedly better ways of living or a return to sounder resource practices that were embraced in the past.

Differing Perspectives

In many versions, conservation envisions the full, efficient management of nature to maximize human benefits on a sustained basis. This strand of conservation typically relies on the centralized management of nature by government or big business, using advanced scientific and economic expertise. This call for efficient management can stem from worries over resource shortages and resulting social conflict. It can reflect a belief that sound management can increase resource flows, not just maintain them.

An alternative strand of conservation questions the completeness of human knowledge and the ability of people to successfully manipulate nature so extensively, if not arrogantly. It sees need for greater caution, proposing that we work with nature, even mimicking it, so as to take advantage of the time-tested wisdom embedded in natural communities and ecological systems. While not ignoring scientific advances, this more humble strand of conservation honors and nurtures the local knowledge accumulated over time by generations of resource users.

A similar strand of conservation seeks to maintain particular natural conditions deemed essential to the preservation of national character, especially when national character has been forged in frontier conditions. This strand of nature conservation overlaps with related efforts to preserve historic buildings and neighborhoods that similarly provide reminders of a nation's history or culture.

In the United States early in the twentieth century, and in various parts of the world even today, conservation has included a claim that rights of access to nature, whether to land or to discrete resources, should be shared widely by all citizens. Nature should exist for the benefit of everyone, not just elites. This egalitarian strand of thought has at times featured sharp critiques of large-scale landholdings and natural-resource monopolies, as well as proposals to restore economic opportunities and to foster small-scale capitalism. It sometimes merges with a much older moral claim, based on biblical passages and natural-law reasoning, that humans share the Earth equally and possess inherent individual rights to gain direct sustenance from the Earth. Homestead laws reflect this conservation perspective, as do acreage limits on irrigation projects and government programs to help people enter farming.

In its varied calls for reform, conservation typically extends beyond sound resource practices to include the maintenance of social frameworks and cultural values that help sustain these resource practices. The underlying idea here—a central tenet of agrarian conservation—is that good land use can only arise out of a local culture that values it and makes it possible. Users of farms, forests, and grazing lands need to be embedded in social communities in which members expect one another to use land well and are willing to share their land-use wisdom. Practically speaking, good land use also must be economically feasible, which means that conservation should attend to the economics of land use to ensure that owners can afford to use land well. Further, according to this view, resource users must have intimate knowledge of and affection for their lands if they are to use the lands well. Put otherwise, the conservation of nature requires, and flows from, the conservation of sound, locally adapted, human cultures.

Contemporary conservation thought includes distinctly conflicting perspectives on several key points. In the view of some, for instance, conservation's goal of long-term productivity is best promoted by putting as much of nature as possible into private hands in the form of secure property rights, and by maintaining free markets. A contrary view agrees that resource users need secure, long-term rights but contends that market incentives are not strong enough to induce full conservation, particularly given ecological interconnections among land parcels. As for private property, this institution too often empowers private owners to exhaust or degrade what they own. In this view, the free market must be tempered by a socially supported ethic of care (a type of land ethic) and/or by legal requirements that push private owners to use nature responsibly.

Conservation also displays conflicting views on the chief source of the threats to sound resource-use practices. For generations, local communities have used conservation rhetoric to protect their resources—local wildlife, fish stocks, timber, and minerals—from exploitation by outsiders. Thus conservation is a tool to defend local land uses. At other times, outside groups, often led by scientific or intellectual elites, have used conservation arguments to challenge local resource-use practices that they view as destructive or based on unduly narrow senses of value. Similarly, conservation is used to resist market-driven changes in resource-use practices that benefit some users at the expense of other users, such as timber clear-cutting, the consolidation of farm fields, and the introduction of exotic species.

Conservation vs. Preservation or Environmentalism

Conservation is frequently defined in contrast to nature preservation, although the clash between these perspectives is also denied. When the two are presented as opposing ideologies, conservation typically entails the affirmative, full use of nature to supply flows of valuable resources while preservation entails setting nature aside and using it directly only for recreation. In practice, these two categories or ideologies are rarely distinct. Particularly when conservation is understood to foster a wide range of values and human needs, the conservation–preservation distinction fades if it does not disappear. In the view of some observers, preservation is better understood as a subset of conservation; it is the most appropriate ethic for managing lands that are ecologically sensitive, lands specially valued for recreation, and lands best used to perform ecological functions.

Conservation is also contrasted with environmentalism, a concept that largely dates from the 1960s. As commonly explained, environmentalism features a pronounced focus on protecting human health from polluted air and water, toxic contaminants, and tainted food. Environmentalism pays considerable attention to quality-of-life issues such as urban sprawl and traffic congestion while also pushing to preserve rare species and biotic communities. In contrast, conservation has centered on the productive use of farms, forests, fisheries, and mineral lands. It features greater stress on an ethic of stewardship, particularly in uses of private lands; on the economics of sound resource uses; and on rural culture's roles in sustaining good practices. Again, conflict is minimized by the many who believe conservation and environmentalism differ only in degrees of emphasis.

Outlooks

The most significant change in conservation over the past century has entailed broadening senses of value and a greater ecological orientation. More parts of nature are viewed as valuable, directly and indirectly, with corresponding efforts to protect them. Increasingly, conservationists conclude that resource management should focus less on flows of discrete resources (the dominant view a century ago) and more on the basic ecological processes that sustain all life. Except in the case of arable lands, conservationists today are prone to question radical manipulations of landscapes to promote one or a few resources. Thus, conservation now calls for ecologically healthy landscapes that supply multiple benefits, for affirmative ecological restoration, and for the protection of all species and samples of all biotic communities.

Eric T. FREYFOGLE
University of Illinois College of Law

FURTHER READINGS

Hays, Samuel P. (1959). *Conservation and the gospel of efficiency: The Progressive Era conservation movement, 1890–1920*. Cambridge, MA: Harvard University Press.

Hays, Samuel P. (2007). *Wars in the woods: The rise of ecological forestry in America*. Pittsburgh, PA: University of Pittsburgh Press.

Meine, Curt. (2004). *Correction lines: Essays on land, Leopold, and conservation*. Washington, DC: Island Press.

Newton, Julianne Lutz. (2006). *Aldo Leopold's odyssey*. Washington, DC: Island Press.

Phillips, Sarah T. (2007). *This land, this nation: Conservation, rural America, and the New Deal*. Cambridge, U.K.: Cambridge University Press.

Worster, Donald. (2008). *A passion for nature: The life of John Muir*. New York: Oxford University Press.

Conservation Biology

Conservation biology, a somewhat new field, is an interdisciplinary science that explores the relationships between religious beliefs and practices and conservation strategies and applications.

Conservation biology is an integrated, interdisciplinary response to the world's biodiversity crisis. This relatively new field draws from a wide range of scientific disciplines in order to document the extent of Earth's biodiversity and the impact of the human project on it, and to formulate and apply approaches to conserve and restore that biodiversity.

Religion matters to this discipline because conservation of habitat and biodiversity takes place in a social and cultural context; religion is frequently a major component of that context. Religions have played a substantial role in formulating views of nature and defining relationships of the roles of humanity in nature, thus linking religious life and practices with habitat and biodiversity. For this reason, religions can help make essential and substantial contributions to rethinking and responding to the conservation of species.

Religions also appear to be increasingly responsive to environmental issues, and the religious focus on the environment may well be a developing and continuing theme of theological inquiry and religious life. The principles, practices, and knowledge of conservation biology can contribute to those whose environmental perspective has, in the past, been primarily informed by religion and theology.

The converse is also true: an understanding of religious concepts and practices and how they are applied to governance and daily life is equally essential to the implementation of effective and lasting conservation management strategies. Recognition of this important link is obvious in the increasing number of specialists in conservation organizations whose primary mission is to explore the religious and theological links with natural systems and to help develop and implement culturally attuned conservation strategies.

Finally, the imposition of conservation strategies on cultures in the lesser-developed countries is giving way to the cooperative development of approaches to use and conserve habitat and biodiversity in a sustainable manner. In fact, it might be easier to develop cooperative relationships between religions and conservation science in the lesser-developed areas than in Western nations, where substantial tensions between various aspects of science and specific expressions of religion continue to exist and often obscure the critical nature of environmental issues. But despite these tensions, collaboration is increasingly evident.

Tom BAUGH

Independent scholar, Hidden Springs, North Carolina

FURTHER READING

Forum on Religion and Ecology. (n.d.). Retrieved May 8, 2009, from http://fore.research.yale.edu/religion

International Society for the Study of Religion, Nature & Culture. (2007). Retrieved May 8, 2009, from http://www.religionandnature.com/society

Gottlieb, Roger S. (Ed.). (2006). *The Oxford handbook of religion and ecology.* New York: Oxford University Press.

Kearns, Laurel, & Keller, Catherine. (2007). *Ecospirit.* New York: Fordham University Press.

Lodge, David M., & Hamlin, Christopher. (Eds.). (2006). *Religion and the new ecology.* Notre Dame, IN: University of Notre Dame Press.

Palmer, Martin, & Finlay, Victoria. (2003). *Faith in conservation: New approaches to religions and the environment.* Washington, DC: The World Bank.

Religion and Conservation Biology Working Group of the Society for Conservation Biology. (2009). Retrieved May 8, 2009, from http://www.conbio.org/workinggroups/Religion

Taylor, Bron R. (Ed.). (2005). *Encyclopedia of religion and nature.* London: Thoemmes Continuum.

Worldviews. Retrieved July 6, 2009, from http://fore.research.yale.edu/publications/journals/worldviews.html

Cosmic Commons

The Earth community's expanding exploration of space raises questions of how to prepare for contact with extraterrestrial life. The consequent disruption to human self-understanding and the danger that shared cosmic communities and resources will suffer from the ecological and social problems affecting Earth can be mitigated by a spiritual and ethical view of a "cosmic commons."

Twenty-first century space explorations and discoveries have the potential to diminish humans' self-understanding and sense of self-worth. In centuries past, Galileo Galilei (1564–1642) and Charles Darwin (1809–1882) profoundly disrupted human self-consciousness with their respective ideas that the Earth was not the center of the universe and that people were not a distinct, individual divine creation. These scientific discoveries of the heliocentric universe and biological evolution unnerved humans and provoked a sense of psychological and philosophical cosmic displacement.

Changes in religious perspectives would occur if contact were established with extraterrestrial intelligent life. People would come to realize that, in biblical terms, they are not the sole "image of God" in the cosmos, when that concept is understood to mean having intelligence, creativity, and responsibility. Humankind would realize that intelligent biota have evolved, diversified, and complexified elsewhere, and might even be more complex and have greater intelligence.

In the early twenty-first century humanity has begun to explore the near and distant heavens with more powerful telescopes and radio signals and more sophisticated all-terrain vehicles. Discoveries on Mars, among others, have altered previously accepted scientific views. The discovery of ice, for example, might signify the present or prior existence of some form of life, a possibility not generally accepted previously because of the apparently inhospitable environment of Mars. What follows theoretically is that if life has emerged on a planet so near to and yet so different from Earth, the likelihood is increased that there are other life forms, including even intelligent beings, elsewhere in the vast cosmos. It is noteworthy that soon after the discovery of water on Mars, Gabriel Funes, a highly regarded scientist who is Director of the Vatican Observatory, wrote in the Vatican newspaper *L'Osservatore Romano* that God might have created intelligent life elsewhere in the universe. Concurrently, scientists supported both by national governments and by private industry have embarked on a more dedicated search for intelligent life and a more intense exploration for extraterrestrial natural resources.

Contact with Extra-Terrestrial Intelligence (ETI) might affect not only the most profound human sense of displacement to date, it also has the potential to instigate an interplanetary conflict over available natural goods ("natural resources"). What is needed in preparation for such contact, along with the hope that other intelligent beings might be less bellicose than humans are, is a sense of existing in a dynamic cosmic commons.

One intellectual, political, and economic foundation for developing a cosmic commons consciousness has been provided by the United Nations document known as the Outer Space Treaty, ratified by member nations in 1966. This international document states in Article 1 that the exploration and use of outer space should be undertaken to benefit all nations, whatever might be the extent of their economic or scientific development; should be "the province of all [hu]mankind"; and should be open to all nations equally, in accordance with international laws (United Nations 2002, 4). If "all humankind" were amended to say "all intelligent species," Article 1 would have cosmic implications—at least for humanity.

Current terrestrial environmental and social conditions indicate that humans have yet to develop a responsible ecological–economic–ethical consciousness and practices on their home planet, let alone the ability to export them into the cosmos. In 2006, at Hong Kong University of Science and Technology, the scientist Stephen Hawking advocated a lunar base and a Mars colony because Earth might be destroyed by disasters such as "sudden global warming, nuclear war, a genetically engineered virus" ("Man must conquer other planets to survive, says Hawking" 2006). Since humans are a contributing or sole cause of such catastrophic events, the human consciousness and conduct carried into space cannot be the progeny of existing human thought and practices. If extraterrestrial exploration and economic and military development (which traditionally stimulate scientific explorations on such a scale) follow a "business as usual" mode, they may effect in new worlds degraded environmental conditions similar to what technology has wrought on Earth, and provoke conflict with other intelligent species. In order for Earth-originating colonists to avoid harming celestial bodies whose benefits they seek to utilize, for example, they must not use mining practices that blow off mountain tops, destroy forests and biota, and eliminate streams that provide habitat for biota and water for humans; and they must use energy production processes that do not cause or exacerbate climate change on other worlds, as carbon-based energy production has done on Earth. A significant conversion of consciousness is required for a fruitful conversation with another species that also is looking to enhance its well-being with natural goods available in a cosmic commons.

A corrective for human-related ecological and social problems, both on Earth and in the universe beyond, would be the integration of technology and ethics in a new cosmic consciousness, characterized by a cosmic concern for the well-being of the cosmic community and a commitment to concrete cosmic caretaking. Consciousness of the cosmos as an intercommunity commons would enable this to occur.

Religious thought, particularly in its doctrines and its ethical principles and practices that advocate care for creation (as in Judaism, Christianity, and Islam) or for Mother Earth (as in indigenous traditions), can have a positive impact on terrestrial/extraterrestrial ecological and commercial conduct in theory and in practice; complement scientific thought, research, and development; and promote interplanetary and intercultural sustainability as a corrective for ecologically harmful and politically unrestrained industrial, commercial, or military projects. If religions were to embody and promote their current and future prophetic perspectives on ecological responsibility, economic justice, and multiethnic respect in the Earth commons, for example, they could construct on this foundation the more far-reaching concept of a cosmic commons. If this were to occur prior to and in anticipation of contact with other intelligent species, it would provide a spiritual-ethical base that would invite all intelligent species to appreciate each other, engage in a new form of "interreligious dialogue," and share the collective goods of a livable, universal (in every sense of the word) commons.

John HART
Boston University

Further Reading

Berry, Thomas (2000). *The great work: Our way into the future.* New York: Bell Tower.

Hart, John (2006). *Sacramental commons: Christian ecological ethics.* Lanham, MD: Rowman and Littlefield.

Haught, John. (2007). *Christianity and science: Toward a theology of nature.* Maryknoll, NY: Orbis Books.

Man must conquer other planets to survive, says Hawking. (13 June, 2006). *The Daily Mail.* Retrieved May 28, 2009, from http://www.dailymail.co.uk/news/article-390524/Man-conquer-planets-survive-says-Hawking.html

McGrath, Alister (2002). *The reenchantment of nature: The denial of religion and the ecological crisis.* New York: Doubleday.

Michaud, Michael A. G. (2007). *Contact with alien civilizations: Our hopes and fears about encountering extraterrestrials.* New York; London: Springer.

Toolan, David. (2001). *At home in the cosmos.* Maryknoll, NY: Orbis Books.

Tumminia, Diana G. (2007). *Alien worlds: Social and religious dimensions of extraterrestrial contact.* Syracuse, NY: Syracuse University Press.

United Nations. (2002). *United Nations treaties and principles on outer space.* New York: United Nations.

Cosmology

Cosmology evolved from humans' efforts to describe their local natural worlds in relation to meaningful symbolic language. Ancient and indigenous cultures shaped narratives depicting the creation and continuum of life, and the challenge to sustain it. During the European Enlightenment a scientific view of cosmology emerged which would attempt to downplay mythic accounts of individual humans integrated into broader cosmic forces.

Cosmology is an ancient human impulse to describe the world. Typically, cosmologies arise from human efforts to narrate our fit in the seasonal change of the local natural world, as well as in the seemingly timeless movement of the transcendent heavens. Cosmology later emerged as a scientific concept and empirical description of the world beginning in the seventeenth-century European Enlightenment. In its earlier storied forms, cosmology was transmitted in mythic stories and narrative performances that had more affective and teleological agendas than Enlightenment empiricism and rational categorization. The dominant scientific mode of cosmological speculation for the past three centuries has been largely dismissive of ancient cosmological stories as subjective fantasies. In these earlier religious cosmological narratives humans explored their physical connections to local worlds and the larger cosmos. Symbolic language expressed these meaningful identifications between microcosm and macrocosm: namely, the human individual was understood as being integrated into broader cosmic forces.

Sustainability highlights the dependent character of these relationships: many cosmological stories advised that humans should take no more from the natural world than could be recycled, reused, and restored without harming the larger community of life. Extrapolating from these earlier insights as well as scientific knowledge, sustainable development would proceed not simply with human-centered objectives, but in consonance with a deeper understanding of the mutual character of desire for life among all beings-in-the-world. Thus, current human needs should be constrained by awareness of the requirements of future generations of life.

Sustainability requires humans to be responsible for the magnitude of their ecological footprint on the planet (i.e., how much land and water area is needed to regenerate used or depleted resources and to accommodate and absorb waste products), especially as human populations soar and biodiversity diminishes. Thus attention to the scale of desire is a crucial consideration in cosmological reflection. That is, all life desires to flourish, and this flourishing places all life in mutual relationships of sustainable desire. Rather than simply consider sustainable development for humans, then, we need to consider sustainable life.

In the indigenous cosmologies of the Axial ages (600–200 BCE) of Asia, Africa, and the Americas, diverse cultures transmitted stories that integrated ethical, empirical, and spiritual understandings linking the seasons, heavens, human behaviors, and local biodiversity. Yet these ideal scenarios could not prevent the collapse of many ancient societies due to environmental overuse and abuse. These older cosmologies were not simply *utopias*, but *heterotopias*, or alternative views that promoted values for sustaining life and calling normalcy into question. In

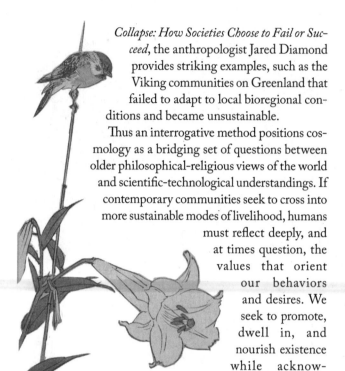

Collapse: How Societies Choose to Fail or Succeed, the anthropologist Jared Diamond provides striking examples, such as the Viking communities on Greenland that failed to adapt to local bioregional conditions and became unsustainable.

Thus an interrogative method positions cosmology as a bridging set of questions between older philosophical-religious views of the world and scientific-technological understandings. If contemporary communities seek to cross into more sustainable modes of livelihood, humans must reflect deeply, and at times question, the values that orient our behaviors and desires. We seek to promote, dwell in, and nourish existence while acknowledging that violence to plants and animals pervades the predator–prey relationships in life. We seek consciously to transform our behavior to sustain both human and natural communities.

Sustainable Cosmology

As narrative, cosmology brings the world, in which we live and have our experiences, into imaginative wonder and storied awareness. Just as the older cosmologies described how communities of life participated in their worlds through sensing, minding, and creating, so also contemporary cosmologies have begun to explore parallel modes in the life communities by which they have sustained themselves. Thus plant intelligence engages local environments from its own sense-making and cognition. While plant and animal cognition are strikingly different in relation to human intelligence, the continuity of cognition reaches across these differences. That is, contemporary cosmologies describe self-organizing and sustaining patterns of planetary emergence that organize both individual and communal forms of life. Humans, animals, and plants demonstrate intention, activity, and creative reaching out that suggest continuity and sustainable interdependence throughout life. An example of plant sentience and mentality traditionally denied in Western thought is that of both indigenous peoples' sense of relationality to plants as persons and Charles Darwin's work, especially *The Power of Movement in Plants.*

Rather than being bound by individual subjectivity, the reflective, narrative act of cosmology by humans flows from communal cognition of those spiritual and sustaining relationships with the other-than-human-life community. Cosmology not only grounds us in how we creatively know the world, but it also recognizes inherent differences, shared possibilities, and integral relationships throughout the world. Like a narrative thread woven imperceptibly through individual and community existence, cosmology becomes palpable in desire for the other. In current global acquisitive economies, humans sublimate integral desire in systematic narratives of analysis, commodification, and profit that distance the world for human management. In a sustainable or living cosmology, the mutual desires of life face one another in the givenness of the world. As limited beings now responsible for the continuity of life on the planet, we seek cosmological stories that balance personal desire and equity of need across the species and into the future.

Cosmology is an awareness, whether overt or hidden, of the anthropogenic weight on the world. Through the dynamics of natural selection and self-generation, humans have emerged as complex, individuated beings facing a world for which we are increasingly responsible. Cosmology, as both a narrating and engaging "other," increasingly provides a challenge to identity in a postcolonial world. Humans look out into billions of stars, a trillion galaxies with which we journey, but which we know only through our place in the local Earth-as-commodity. As one observer says, we humans suffer from a nature-deficit disorder that makes us autistic to matter in our home planet as well as in the stars (Berry, 1988). But not all peoples have seen matter as something separate from, and merely for, human use.

In East Asia since the beginning of the sixth century BCE, during which Confucianism and Daoism were articulated from indigenous traditions, there has not been one traditional cosmological narrative underpinning existence. Rather, worldviews in China have emerged that elaborate the character of qi (material-force) as the foundational basis for articulating the nature of the world and engaging in relational exchange. Likewise, *dao* in East Asia is a term that evokes profound, paradoxical inquiry into mutual desire as a flow of a singular reality. Thus the fourth-century BCE Daoist sage Zhuangzi could enter into simultaneous questioning and questing regarding butterfly and person, dream and relationship.

In Euro-Asia the ancient Mesopotamian icon of the garden has continuing cosmological resonance in Western civilization. The symbolic values embedded in both the term and the idea of "garden" evoke images of a paradisiacal civilization. The cosmological sense of the garden-as-paradise echoes throughout the Abrahamic traditions of Judaism, Christianity, and Islam. Gardens stand not only as multivalent icons of creation, nature, blessing, wilderness, and biodiversity, but also as heterotopias that challenge the failure of human communities to live their covenantal relationships. For example, water flowing through the Islamic gardens of Kashmir evokes the sustaining mercies of the divine *tawhid* uniting the diversity of creation. This *tawhid*, or unity, juxtaposes the divine sustaining mercy, flowing like water onto the ground of covenantal restoration, and trust. For Islam, this mercy not only secures *khalifah* stewardship, but it also challenges all Muslims to uphold that trust. As the aesthetic embodiment of sustainable flow, gardens manifest affective engagement with the larger-than-human creative act.

The icon of gardens may also be charged with ethical brokenness and fall that calls for restoration. The Garden of Paradise may be understood in relationship to the call (Genesis 1:28, Oxford Annotated Bible) authorizing the dominance of humans over all life. Historically this could be said to lead to a Western view of technology as the means to transcend even the limits of human aging and mortality. This paradisiacal dominance courses through contemporary forms of cosmology as a "progress-at-any-cost" mentality, and "technological fix" solution to any and all social and environmental problems. Such a cosmology drives us to the politics of "sixth extinction" (the notion that human activities are now annihilating vast numbers of species) because it denies human responsibility for climate change, biodiversity loss, and a world made toxic by a drive to produce and to consume endless products as an exclusively human right.

Cosmology sustains individuals and communities, then, not as some abstract ideal seducing isolated minds, but as awareness of a flow of mutual desire between places, peoples, and beings. The question facing us remains: is our desire for the journey with the community of life sufficiently strong to create a new story, a living cosmology?

John GRIM
Yale University

FURTHER READING

Bell, Diane. (1983). *Daughters of the dreaming.* Melbourne: McPhee Gribble.

Berry, Thomas. (1988). *The dream of the Earth.* San Francisco and Berkeley, CA: Sierra Club Books.

Foltz, Richard; Denny, Frederick; & Baharuddin, Azizan. (Eds.). (2003). *Islam and ecology: A bestowed trust.* Cambridge, MA: Harvard Divinity School Center for the Study of World Religions.

Forum on Religion and Ecology. Retrieved April 7, 2009, from http://fore.research.yale.edu/

Glacken, Clarence J. (1967). *Traces on the Rhodian shore: Nature and culture in Western thought from ancient times to the end of the eighteenth century.* Berkeley: University of California Press.

Grim, John. (Ed.). (2001). *Indigenous traditions and ecology: The interbeing of cosmology and community.* Cambridge, MA: Harvard Divinity School Center for the Study of World Religions.

Tucker, Mary Evelyn. (2002). *Worldly wonder: Religions enter their ecological phase.* Chicago: Open Court.

Council of All Beings

The Council of All Beings is a ritual designed by environmental activists to express grief over the degradation of the environment and to empower people to work to protect nature and improve the natural and cultural environment. It can be a brief exercise or a multiple-day event.

The Council of All Beings is a ritual designed to enhance environmental awareness. It was created in 1985 by the U.S. peace activist Joanna Macy (b. 1929) and the Australian rainforest activist John Seed (b. 1945). Macy had engaged in "despair and empowerment work" with antinuclear activists, and Seed recognized a similar need among environmental activists. In creating the Council of All Beings, Seed and Macy drew upon Macy's work and upon the ideas of deep ecology, as well as forms and symbols classic to many indigenous ritual systems. *Deep ecology*, a term coined by Norwegian philosopher Arne Naess (1912–2009), is a philosophy that rejects the human-centered view of the world in favor of a more intimate contact with nature; it depends upon a belief in the sacredness of nature as well as the support for biological and cultural diversity, and the need for direct action to protect nature and bring about fundamental change in society.

Macy's work posits that knowledge of environmental degradation causes emotional pain, which is often ignored or blocked out. The results, she contends, are disbelief, denial, and a double life. To reach a healthier state of being, Macy and Seed prescribe ritual action that allows for safe expression of this grief and its transformation into joy and power.

Drawing on deep ecology notions of the so-called ecological self, an enlarged sense of self that allows the individual to identify with the larger whole, the ritual offers an emotional and spiritual experience that goes beyond intellectual knowledge of environmental concerns. Because the ritual involves humans being silent and other creatures speaking, it is also seen as a tool to facilitate an ecocentric (viewing the entire environment as important and worthy of consideration), rather than an anthropocentric (viewing humans as the center of the world), perspective.

The ritual itself may be a brief exercise or a multiple-day experience shared among a small or large group of participants. Essential elements include mourning, a period of shared grief, often symbolized by found objects placed in the center of a circle; finding (often by means of a modified vision quest) a nonhuman entity (an ally) on whose behalf the participant will speak; creating a mask to represent this ally; and the council itself, which consists of an opening ritual, a time of solemn discussion in which participants speak as their allies (referring to humans as "they"), and a closing ritual. Frequently the masks are ceremonially burned at the closing of the ritual as a gesture of thanksgiving and release. Seed and Macy maintain that this experience of catharsis and changed identity gives environmental activists the spiritual and emotional renewal they need to continue their work.

Laura M. HARTMAN
Augustana College (Illinois)

FURTHER READING

Bragg, Elizabeth, & Rosenhek, Ruth. (2001). The Council of All Beings workshop manual: A step-by-step guide (Rev. ed.). Retrieved June 23, 2008, from http://www.rainforestinfo.org.au/deep-eco/cabcont.htm

Macy, Joanna. (1995). Working through environmental despair. In Allen D. Kanner, Theodore Roszak, & Mary E. Gomes (Eds.), *Ecopsychology: Restoring the earth, healing the mind* (pp. 240–259). San Francisco: Sierra Club Books.

Macy, Joanna. (1983). *Despair and personal power in the nuclear age.* Philadelphia: New Society Publishers.

Seed, John; Macy, Joanna; & Fleming, Pat. (1988). *Thinking like a mountain: Towards a Council of All Beings.* Philadelphia: New Society Publishers.

Creation

The biblical story of Creation often is referenced in support of two different perspectives on sustainability. One reading of the narrative gives humans domination over the world, allowing them to control and do as they wish; the other alludes to humanity's responsibility to protect and nurture all living and nonliving things.

Although stories concerning the origin of the universe and humanity's place within it exist in almost all traditional cultures, the term *Creation* usually refers to the originating actions of God as they are portrayed in the Hebrew Bible. Two competing Creation stories are preserved within the opening chapters of the Bible. The first, known as the Priestly (P) account, occurs in Genesis 1:1–2:4a and begins with the "spirit" or "breath" of God (in Hebrew: *ruach*) hovering over a primordial ocean. God speaks and a series of creative changes take place.

In this P narrative, human beings are said to be created in the divine image and given "dominion" over the world. The parameters of human dominion are not delineated in this narrative, although the textual pairing of dominion and humanity's possession of the divine image suggests that the human–world relationship is meant to mirror the God–world relationship. The characteristics of the God–world relationship, however, are open to interpretation.

Similarities between P and the Babylonian myth of Creation, the Enuma Elish, indicate that P may have been a reworking of the older legend. Intertextual comparisons between the Hebrew and Mesopotamian stories yield an image of God's creative acts as violent wrestings of order out of a threatening primal chaos. Through an overpowering series of divine commands, God imposes hierarchies and divisions upon the cosmos. The model for

human dominion, from this reading, is one of subjugation and control.

An alternate reading of the God–world relationship, however, is possible. Genesis 1:2a describes the primal state of the world as *tohu va-vohu*, a phrase that may indicate indeterminate potency rather than oppositional chaos. God's "hovering" over the primal waters, then, may signal divine protection and nurturance (see, for example, Deut. 32:11). If this interpretation is correct, God's creative process can be understood as tender and relational, and the divine speech can be heard as an invitation to an agential cosmos to enter into a cocreative partnership. The results of this partnership are celebrated by God, who declares each result to be good individually and very good collectively. From this reading, human dominion mirrors the divine when it is exercised through noncoercive cooperation with and appreciation for the Earth's individual creatures and collective processes.

The second Creation account, Genesis 2:4b–3, predates P and is known as the Jahwist (J) narrative. J begins with a desert landscape on which no rain has fallen nor vegetation appeared. God causes groundwater to surge up and cover the soil. From the resulting clay, God molds a human being. The dependency of humanity upon the Earth is accentuated by J through wordplay: the *adamah* (Earth) is used by God to make *adam* (Earth creature). After the creation of *adam*, God plants a garden of fruit trees and instructs the Earth creature to serve it (Hebrew: *'abad*) and protect it (Hebrew: *shamar*). Seeing that *adam* is lonely, God again turns to the soil, from which he makes animals. Although God perceives the animals to be appropriate partners for *adam*, the Earth creature is discontent with the choices. God then causes *adam* to sleep and removes a rib, fashioning it into another human. The original harmony within the garden is shattered when the human pair transgresses the boundaries set for them by God. Because of this transgression, the couple is expelled from the garden and harmony turns into discord: between human and divine, human and animal, human and soil, and human and human. Despite this discord, however, harmony between all beings remains the ideal.

Although neither P nor J represents Creation as taking place out of nothing, early Christian patriarchs worried that a co-eternal cosmos challenged God's omnipotence. In order to counter this challenge, the doctrine of *creatio ex nihilo* (Creation out of nothing) was developed. Contained within this doctrine is the assertion that God transcends the world but can be known through observations of the world. In this atmosphere, Western science developed as a form of piety: investigating the workings of nature as a way of understanding and admiring nature's craftsman. Through experiments and observations, a new scientific Creation narrative arose that began with a big bang and progressed through 15 billion years of evolutionary history. Like the biblical narrative, however, the scientific story is open to a variety of moral interpretations. On the one hand, the story of evolution can be read as a narrative of brutal competition in which humanity behaves naturally when it engages in domination and predation. On the other hand, the story can be read as an affirmation that all life has a common origin and that all species are mutually dependent. From this latter reading, all life can be seen as

worthy of moral concern, not only because all creatures exist in a kinship relationship but also because all life is dependent upon the well-being of the communal matrix in which it arose.

Antonia GORMAN
Humane Society of the United States

FURTHER READING

Berry, Thomas. (1999). *The great work: Our way into the future.* New York: Bell Tower.

Birch, Charles, & Cobb, John B., Jr. (1990). *The liberation of life: From the cell to the community.* Denton, TX: Environmental Ethics Books.

Cohn, Norman. (2001). *Cosmos, chaos, and the world to come.* New Haven, CT: Yale University Press.

Drees, Willem B. (2006). Religious naturalism and science. In Philip Clayton & Zachary Simpson, (Eds.), *The Oxford handbook of religion and science* (pp. 108–123). Oxford, U.K.: Oxford University Press.

Dryness, William. (1987). Stewardship of the Earth in the Old Testament. In Wesley Granberg-Michaelson (Ed.), *Tending the garden: Essays on the Gospel and the Earth* (pp. 52–66). Grand Rapids, MI: William B. Eerdmans.

Habel, Norman C., & Wurst, Shirley. (Eds.). (2000). *The Earth story in Genesis: The Earth Bible, Vol. 2.* Cleveland, OH: The Pilgrim Press.

Keller, Catherine. (2003). *Face of the deep: A theology of becoming.* London: Routledge.

Schloss, Jeffrey P. (2006). Evolutionary theory and religious belief. In Philip Clayton & Zachary Simpson (Eds.), *The Oxford handbook of religion and science* (pp. 187–206). Oxford, U.K.: Oxford University Press.

Swimme, Brian, & Berry, Thomas. (1992). *The universe story: From the primordial flaring forth to the ecozoic era—A celebration of the unfolding of the Cosmos.* San Francisco: HarperSanFrancisco.

Creation Spirituality

Creation Spirituality is an environmentally concerned spiritual movement drawing primarily on the work of the U.S. Episcopal priest Matthew Fox. With its focus on the goodness of creation and God's immanence in it, Creation Spirituality urges humans to affirm our cosmological origins and engage in sacred activism on behalf of the nonhuman world.

Creation Spirituality, or Creation-Centered Spirituality, is an environmentally concerned spiritual movement arising primarily from the work of Matthew Fox (b. 1940), a U.S. Episcopal (formerly Roman Catholic Dominican) priest. Unlike other forms of religion that may support human dominance over nature, Creation Spirituality explicitly enjoins an Earth-centered perspective and care for the environment. Practitioners of Creation Spirituality often lament human activity that destroys nonhuman nature, and promote feelings of connection with the natural world as a remedy for environmental destruction. Activism on behalf of nonhuman nature is viewed as holy work.

Fox began writing about Creation Spirituality in the 1970s and has formed a series of related educational institutions, including the Institute of Culture and Creation Spirituality (Holy Names College in Oakland, California) and the University of Creation Spirituality (also in Oakland, renamed Wisdom University in 2005). Fox split with the Roman Catholic Church in 1992 after having been commanded to a year of silence, from1988 to 1989, by the then-cardinal Joseph Ratzinger, later Pope Benedict XVI (b. 1927), for his unorthodox teachings. A worldwide affiliation of connectors (lay leaders) promotes Creation Spirituality and coordinates local, regional, and national gatherings.

Creation Spirituality focuses on the centrality of cosmology (the origin and nature of the universe) for religious life, arguing that the contemporary scientific story of the universe is a source of spiritual gifts and revelatory connectedness with creation. Creation Spirituality is explicitly panentheistic, arguing that God is neither removed from the created world nor equated with the created world, but rather dwells within and penetrates all aspects of the world. This panentheism justifies a view of creation as sacred and humans as capable of experiencing God firsthand. Creation, including humanity, is seen as good and blessed. Fox explicitly dismisses original sin and criticizes traditional Christianity's emphasis on human sin and human salvation, to the exclusion of creation and blessing.

Drawing in part from the Catholic tradition, Fox outlines four spiritual paths. The *via positiva* (positive path) gives value to awe, wonder, and joy, particularly in experiences of the natural world, often mediated by scientific understanding. The *via negativa* (negative path) affirms silence, meditation, emptiness, darkness, and pain as a source of closeness to God. The *via creativa* (creative path) names creativity as participation in divinity—as God is creator, so humans are creative. Artists are affirmed as holy practitioners, and all are encouraged to experience the divine through art as meditation. Finally, the *via transformativa* (path of transformation) promotes compassion and justice, exhorting sacred activism on behalf of the *anawim* (voiceless ones, including nonhuman nature) to encourage the growth of the Kingdom/Queendom of God.

Creation Spirituality has been criticized from a more traditional Christian perspective. Some condemn its rejection of original sin as ignorant or naïve about the presence of real human suffering and tragedy. Others criticize Fox's unorthodox readings of classic Christian texts. Still others reject its commitment to deep ecumenism, or a full acceptance of and participation in other religious traditions. From an environmentalist perspective, Creation Spirituality's major weakness could be perceived as its disconnection from orthodox Christianity, and thus its failure to persuade the majority of Christians to follow its mandate to care for the Earth.

Laura M. HARTMAN
Augustana College (Illinois)

FURTHER READING

Creation Spirituality Communities. (2008). Retrieved June 3, 2008, from http://www.creationspirituality.info/

Fox, Matthew. (1980). *Whee! we, wee all the way home: A guide to sensual prophetic spirituality.* Santa Fe, NM: Bear & Company.

Fox, Matthew. (1983). *Original blessing: A primer in Creation Spirituality presented in four paths, twenty-six themes, and two questions.* Santa Fe, NM: Bear & Company.

Fox, Matthew. (1988). *The coming of the cosmic Christ.* San Francisco: Harper San Francisco Publishers.

Ruether, Rosemary. (1990, July/August). Matthew Fox and creation spirituality: Strengths and weaknesses. *The Catholic World, 233*(1396), 169–172.

Culture

Culture is considered most commonly as either an ethos that shapes a way of life or the product of artistic and intellectual creativity—aspects of society that do not necessarily incorporate sustainability; today's postmodern consumer culture is a clear example of such preclusion. A global redefinition of "culture" must be considered and adopted if society and culture are to remain sustainable.

The two best known of the many senses of the word *culture* are, first, as a way of life and, second, as the product of human creativity, especially in the arts. Culture in the first, anthropological sense refers to "that most complex whole," the ethos of a particular group or region and includes everything—the way in which people relate, especially as this is structured by class, race, and gender; how people cook, build, and dress; the way they spend their leisure time; and so forth.

The word *culture* derives from the verb *to cultivate*, and this is recognized in "organic" notions of culture, which emphasize rootedness and the fact that cultures grow slowly over millennia. This relative permanence accounts for the fact that culture is about identity, the most important marker of which is language. The 3,500 languages currently in use all designate distinct patterns of human relating, behaving, and working. The loss of some languages, sometimes by outright proscription, rightly has been described as aiming at "culture death." Taking further the centrality of language, the anthropologist Clifford Geertz (1926–2006) defines culture in terms of historically transmitted patterns of meanings embodied in symbols, through which people communicate and develop their attitudes toward life. This is helpful, but does not emphasize sufficiently the way in which different economies and modes of production give rise to different cultures. There is

a constant and necessary dialectic between culture as signification and any given mode of production. The fact that cultural identities owe much to geography is part and parcel of this: mountain ranges and seas commonly mark different cultures, as do rivers and different soils. At the same time trade, migration, and conquest have always led to cultural cross-fertilization. All cultures "bleed at the edges," most obviously on the borders of different language uses.

Because cultures change with variations in the mode of production, culture is also about process. The decisive significance of how the experience of work and a way of life shape culture is reflected in the differences between peasant, industrial, working-class, managerial, and now postmodern cultures. Change may happen very slowly: the Bronze Age lasted for approximately two thousand years. Modes of agricultural production changed relatively little between 1000 BCE and 1000 CE (or even centuries later). Cultures have changed faster over the past 250 years than at any previous time in history. The pace of such change suggested to Enlightenment thinkers that there was a "foul wide gap" between the past and the present, which, for example, made the first century unintelligible to the eighteenth century. But Homo sapiens probably emerged a quarter of a million years ago. Ancient cultures, as we call those of Sumer or Babylon, are relatively recent in that time scheme. They are under the sand; only specialists know about them, and yet we still bear their imprint. This explains why contemporary writers can make powerful use of the ancient Sumerian text *Epic of Gilgamesh* (2500 BCE). The idea of redemptive violence that it describes is still with us today.

Because culture is about time and place, changing and belonging, the word is always qualified: we speak of peasant culture, nomadic culture, medieval culture, modern culture, Irish culture, Indian culture. As a noun it always evokes a snapshot, for culture is like the ancient philosopher

Heraclitus's river, always moving. Once we advance beyond hunter-gatherer society we have a situation where change, at varying paces, is part of the essence of culture. For urban cultures, not to change is to die. Places like Carcassonne, France, fossilized in the fourteenth century, are empty shells, devoid of life; places like Guangzhou (Canton), Rome, or London, on the other hand, have remained powerful living places for millennia but are essentially palimpsests. Culture is about process, which makes generalization difficult, but some propose that the issue of sustainability can be considered under three characteristics of culture: use of resources, structures of power, and values.

Use of Resources

It could plausibly be argued that the most sustainable cultures were those of the few remaining hunter-gatherer groups whose ecological footprint is probably the lightest of any human group. Their disadvantages are that, in the first place, hunting and gathering only supports ten people per acre; second, such cultures do little to harness the sun's energy; and third, they represent rather poorly the resources of human creativity. If culture as cultivation is about promoting "life in all its fullness" (John 10:10 NCV) rather than simply sustainability, hunter-gatherer groups do not go very far in this direction.

The agricultural revolution that marked the change from Paleolithic to Neolithic culture occurred between 12,000 BCE and 10,000 BCE, first in a hoe culture, which supported hamlets, and then in a plough culture that provided for much larger populations. This period marks the emergence of human settlement, and especially of the village, home to the majority of humans who have ever lived; only lately, since the year 2000, have more people around the world lived in cities than villages. The relatively primitive technology that supported the village until very recent times meant that this was necessarily a culture that was connected very closely to the seasons and respectful of natural forces. Patterns of work, of eating, and dressing, were all bound up with local materials, reuse, and recycling. Marx and Engels's jibe at the "idiocy of rural life" (2002 [1848]), however, points to the limitations of village life for most of human history. Witnesses from the end of the nineteenth century in Britain speak of laborers literally worked to death, too tired at the end of a day for study or any creative leisure. Such voices need to be set alongside the tendency to romanticize the village.

The date for the advent of towns is disputed, but we can say for certain that the growth of the city meant greater specialization, a more sophisticated division of labor, greater creativity, and therefore a more sophisticated culture in the sense of the arts and sciences. This is indicated in the Hebrew word for city, *ir*, which means "a place of stir."

Many vital inventions, including the potter's wheel and the emergence of writing, abstract mathematics, and astronomy, are bound up with increasing urban life about 3000 BCE. Tautologically, cities play a vital role in the emergence of "civilization." But they have always depended for food, water, and energy supplies on the surrounding region. Many cultures have disappeared as a result of profligate use of their resources, and this above all poses a threat to cities. The sustainability of megacities, of ten or twenty million or more, is in every sense moot.

Especially today, in the twenty-first century, sustainability is challenged by a consumer culture that lives on an endless use of resources and becomes a throwaway society. World population has more than doubled since 1960, and a finite planet lacks the resources to maintain such a culture, marked today by a global shortage of, for example, copper that is needed for electrical materials.

Structures of Power

Power, as the philosopher Michel Foucault reminds us, is everywhere. Any analysis of culture looks at how power is dispersed between genders, races, and classes. As the collaborators who developed communist theory, Marx and Engels considered that all history is the history of class struggle, and this has feminist and racial versions as well. Unbalanced power relations are inherently unstable. This can be considered a good thing, as the lack of balance is the key to the dialectical progress of history. Thus, it might be argued, hunter-gatherer societies appear to be egalitarian and relatively peaceful but lack the dynamic for progress. With the advent of the city, we have surplus appropriated by elite groups, and above all the king, a process at odds with the mutual help of the village. Force was needed to appropriate surplus and then to keep it. The U.S. historian Lewis Mumford (1895–1990) called the organization of power that began in the ancient civilizations of Babylon, Assyria, and Egypt—which from the start aimed at the exploitation and manipulation of the bulk of the citizenry— the "megamachine" (Mumford 1966). War, he argued, was one of the principal markers of city culture. Historically, social differentials and the violence that go with them were justified by ideologies of hierarchy; more recently they have been justified by the claim that competition is essential to the human good. Competition for scarce resources, which results in war from time to time, is the price paid for a lively and inventive culture and the technological progress of the past three centuries; advances in medicine, agriculture, and sanitation that make present population levels possible are evidence that war is worthwhile. On the other hand, it can be argued, the fact that nuclear and biological warfare is the apotheosis of this competitive progress indicates that it is ultimately unsustainable.

The idea that violence is primitive, an intrinsic part of human nature, is a key aspect of the justification for class and other differentials and the violence that follows from them. Mumford challenged this, arguing that violence is bound up with the rise of the city. He argued, and the many myths of a golden age seem to corroborate this, that cooperation came first and violence was the aberration (Mumford, 1991). Certainly it seems to be the case that when the gap between rich and poor exceeds a certain point, the bonds of society start to dissolve, a situation that burdened Israel's eighth-century prophets. This would seem to indicate that, rather than competition and aggression, it is egalitarianism, cooperation, and the search for peaceful relations that mark a sustainable society.

Values and Ideology

All cultures rest on values but these may be more or less sustainable. The failure of modernity, it has been argued, is a specifically cultural one, namely the inability to decide what people should value, believe in, and what sense they ought to make of their everyday lives.

Mumford (1991) spoke of the "life sustaining mores" of the village, in which communal solidarity took the forms of shared work and mutual care. For him, ethics took its roots there. The mutuality was a key part of its sustainability and may lie behind the emergence of words such as Hebrew *hesed*, meaning "kindness, loyalty, solidarity," and translated in Greek as *charis*, grace. These mores were, as we have seen, challenged by the rise of an aggressive and imperialist society, but it was only in the twentieth-century that an overt nihilism expressed itself in the death camps and the nuclear arms race and now consumerism. The imperatives of capital—short-term profit, market forces, and the cultivation of needs—are the driving force behind nihilism. Consumer capitalism, in its need for constant growth, subordinates meaning and value to profit. It defines human beings not as sinners in need of redemption (medieval and Reformation), or as citizens (Enlightenment), but as consumers. Getting and spending becomes the human project, and the allure of the commodity is the spiritual driver of the whole. Alan Durning (b. 1964), the author and founder of Sightline Institute (a not-for-profit research and communication center focused on sustainability), speaks of as this as the most fundamental change in the day-to-day existence of the human species in the whole of its history. Culture as a way of life organized around infinite growth is turned against culture as the nourishing of life in all its fullness. Limits that have been recognized as necessary by every previous human society are disavowed. The socially unstable gap between rich and poor is globally inscribed with obvious consequences for insecurity. "A private dwelling full of comforts necessarily confirms the whole worldwide infrastructure—including the need for armaments," wrote Rudolf Bahro (1994, 92), "because in [the] face of monstrous differences in standards it is a threatened luxury."

The growth of consumer society has been matched by the growth of a global entertainment industry that has, in the view of some cultural analysts, led to a situation where people are constantly distracted by trivia and where serious political discussion becomes difficult if not impossible. For such analysts, this indicates the possibility of culture death. The analysis is widely challenged, but the poverty and reactionary nature of democratic politics, the failure to respond to climate change, and the (related) complicity with free-market ideology lends it credence.

What this points to is that the recovery of a sustainable culture rests on the dialectic of signification and mode of production with which we began. Human beings need to turn from the cultivation of needs to renewed mutuality and cooperation, but they will only do this in conjunction with a new, probably steady state economy that emphasizes growth in depth over quantitative growth. Economics, we are coming to realize, is an expression of spirituality, and whether or not we survive depends on replacing infinite desires for consumable objects with infinite desires for understanding and for truth, beauty, and goodness, already in the fifth century Augustine's recipe for a sustainable culture: infinite desires for consumer goods cannot give us a sustainable culture; infinite desires centered on truth, beauty, and goodness might.

T. J. GORRINGE
University of Exeter

FURTHER READING

Bahro, Rudolf. (1994). *Avoiding social and ecological disaster: The politics of world transformation*. Bath, U.K.: Gateway Books.

Daly, Herman E., & Cobb, John B., Jr. (1990). *For the common good: Redirecting the economy toward community, the environment, and a sustainable future*. London: Green Print.

Geertz, Clifford. (1993). *The interpretation of cultures*. London: Fontana.

Gorringe, T. J. (2004). *Furthering humanity: A theology of culture*. Aldershot, U.K.:Ashgate.

Latouche, Serge. (1996). *The westernization of the world: Significance, scope and limits of the drive towards global uniformity*. Cambridge, U.K.: Polity.

Marx, Karl, & Engel, Friedrich (2002 [1848]). *The Communist manifesto*. London: Penguin Books.

Miles, Steven. (1998). *Consumerism as a way of life*. London: Sage.

Mumford, Lewis. (1966). *The myth of the machine: The pentagon of power*. Ann Arbor: University of Michigan.

Mumford, Lewis. (1991). *The city in history: Its origins, its transformations, and its prospects*. Harmondsworth, U.K.: Penguin.

Postman, Neil. (1986). *Amusing ourselves to death: Public discourse in the age of show business*. London: Methuen.

Tomlinson, John. (1991). *Cultural imperialism: A critical introduction*. London: Continuum.

Daoism

Of China's three major philosophies, Daoism may be the most environmentally oriented; its ultimate goal is that humans live in harmony and unity with nature. Daoism also celebrates the values of mercy, humility, and frugality, which support an environmental consciousness, and includes many teachings that seek to restrict human behaviors such as killing animals and damaging the environment.

Western philosophy has been criticized for perpetuating ideas, such as dualism and reductionism that promote distance from, if not outright antagonism toward, the environment. Chinese philosophy offers an alternative approach by advocating ideas, such as holism and nondualism, that encourage living in harmony with the environment. Chinese philosophy is commonly summarized in the expression *tianren heyi* ("nature and humanity unite as one"); *tian* is usually rendered as heaven, which represents the natural world in general. Nondualism is the philosophical concept that opposites are not independent dualities, but interrelated and interpenetrating, such that the universe and people form a united whole.

Confucianism, Daoism, and Buddhism are the three major philosophies of China. Confucianism advocates humans living in harmony with nature, but its main focus is social, moral, and political philosophy. Imported from India, Buddhism also promotes harmony with nature, but its primary concern is liberating people from suffering by means of meditation and enlightenment. Daoism has its own moral, social, and political philosophy and its own practices of meditation and interpretation of awakening, but Daoism goes beyond the other philosophies in its emphasis on living in harmony with the natural environment. In this sense, Daoism is China's foremost environmental philosophy in that it makes living in harmony and unity with the natural environment its ultimate goal.

Historical Background

Some Daoists claim that the ideas, masters, and texts of Daoism were originally generated by the *Dao* (meaning "Way," or the ordering and creative principle of the universe) in the primordial chaos of undifferentiated, pure potentiality of existence (*hundun*) from which all things are generated. Historians believe that Daoism had its conception in the ecstatic vision quests of the ancient shamans of southern China from about the tenth to fifth century BCE. Some see Daoism developing out of the individualistic thought of hermits like Yang Zhu (c. sixth–fifth century BCE), who believed the world formed an organic whole such that he would not remove one hair from his shin to benefit the world (that is, he thought that each and every thing was so interconnected that one could not save the whole world by destroying any part, even a tiny hair). Most commonly, however, the origin of Daoism is usually attributed to Laozi (or Lao-tzu, meaning literally "the old master" or "master Lao"). He is believed to have lived in the sixth to fifth century BCE and is the alleged author of the book that bears his name as its title, which is also known as the *Daodejing* (or *Tao Te Ching*; in English, Classic of the Way and its Power).

The second major figure in Daoism is Zhuang Zhou (or Zhuangzi, c. fourth–third century BCE, but also transliterated as Chuang Tzu), who is believed to have written the first seven, or inner, chapters of the text that bears his name as its title. The impact of the *Zhuangzi* on Daoist philosophy and religion cannot be overstated. Whether or not Zhuangzi advances the teaching of Laozi—as opposed to being simply an independent thinker in a similar vein—is currently under debate. The expression Lao-Zhuang, referring to the teachings of both thinkers, was first used in the preface to another Daoist work, the *Huainanzi* (139 BCE), and it was especially popular to discuss Lao-Zhuang teachings during the Wei Jin period of Chinese history (220–420 CE).

In the Later Han dynasty (25–220 CE), Laozi underwent a process of apotheosis and became a celestial god. By 165 CE he was deified as Taishang Laojun, the Most High Lord Lao. This led to the development of Daoism as a religion. Zhang Daoling, a small landowner, proclaimed a new order based on revelations that he said the god Laozi made to him in 142 CE. He advocated the rule of the Three Heavens, which would deliver the world from an age of decadence and establish a perfect state for the chosen "seed people." Zhang's movement began in Sichuan Province under the name of *Wudoumi dao* (Way of the Five Baskets of Rice, a name taken from the tax levied on followers) and later became known as *Tianshi dao* (Way of the Celestial Masters). The teachings and practices of this religion and related alchemical and meditative practices underwent a complex process of change and development during the ensuing centuries. Daoism is still practiced today both in and outside of China.

Daoist Ecology

Because the early Daoist texts criticize Confucian virtues and morality, some scholars wrongly assert that Daoism lacks a morality. The early Daoist texts do in fact advocate moral ideas, proposing that the best way to live is by modeling the forces of nature and living in harmony with it. Laozi encourages people to follow the Earth as a model the way the *dao* models its own spontaneity. Emulating forces of nature is a prominent part of Daoist practices. Laozi tells us that the best people are like water, and Daoists try to emulate the virtues of water. They celebrate its softness, flexibility, and frictionless traits, its ability to erode mountains, its murky and chaotic condition when agitated, and its depth and clarity when calm. To go with the flow, literally and metaphorically, is the Daoist key to proper living.

For Daoists, people are socialized to engage in purposeful action. People are taught to work hard and to impose their willpower to achieve results. Daoists advocate acting by nonpurposive action (*wei wuwei*). The Daoist concept of nonpurposive action is closely linked to being natural, not artificial, and being spontaneous, not contrived or forced. Acting in this way allows people to be creative and to self-realize, so they will be better equipped to live in harmony with others and the natural environment.

Zhuangzi develops Daoist environmental philosophy. Some scholars postulate that Zhuangzi may have been the warden of a forest reserve; he certainly was familiar with local flora and fauna. Zhuangzi advocates a type of perspectivism: He states that each creature is limited in its understanding by the perspective from which it experiences the world. He gives numerous examples of how different creatures find different habitats and foods pleasing. He maintains that there is no single correct or privileged perspective; rather, each perspective has its unique benefits and traits. Though Zhuangzi does not consider it the highest ideal, he proposes that a person should aspire to be "a companion of nature/heaven" (Watson 1968, 56–57). The ideal for Zhuangzi is to merge with nature in what can be called an experience of nature mysticism—becoming one with nature. Ultimately for Zhuangzi this mystical experience embraces death as a natural homecoming for the human spirit. An important aspect of Daoist environmental philosophy is the recognition that opposing forces of nature, such as light/dark, hot/cold, wet/dry, and life/death are interconnected, interpenetrating, and mutually dependent. Accepting the interplay between life and death changes the context in which humans exploit the natural environment. Our lives hang in a delicate balance along with each and every other creature.

One area in which Daoism can assist modern ecology and environmental ethics is in human transformation. Many people propose that humans must change how they think about the environment and especially how they behave toward it. Daoists have developed various ideas and methods to help people embrace natural and personal transformation. Embracing change as a natural fact allows one to think and act more profoundly than does simple conservation. Instead of conservation, Daoists seek to live in harmony in the face of rapid change. For example, selective burning or removal of dead trees would be allowed if it enhanced human harmony with the forest. People are also changing; we need to transform ourselves to become even more natural and to live in harmony with nature. Daoists advocate cutting loose (*jie*) from the restrictions of social custom, psychological feelings, and divisive ideas. Cutting loose helps Daoists break free from social conventions that encourage people to exploit natural resources. Another form of personal transformation advocated by Zhuangzi is the awakening (*jue*) experience. Daoists practiced breathing exercises, meditation, sitting in forgetfulness, and losing one's self-identity. Deep ecologists (who believe that the environmental crisis is motivated by people's superficial understanding of their relationship with nature) and ecofeminists (feminists who argue that the oppression of women is intimately tied to the degradation of the environment and vice versa) would agree with Daoism's emphasis on the role of personal transformation for living in harmony with nature.

In the development of religious Daoism, a number of precepts were created to restrain people's unnatural behaviors. Some of the precepts restrict humans from disturbing, harming, or killing animals, birds, eggs, and plants. They prohibit unnecessary damage to the environment, such as wantonly destroying trees, plants and herbs, digging holes, draining wetlands or creating lakes, burning grasslands, polluting wells, springs, rivers or oceans, and making, storing, and disposing of poisonous substances. The ancient Daoist ideal of traveling without leaving a footprint has positively influenced the low-impact outdoor-sports movement (popular in the western United States, the movement wants to curtail or remove the human "foot print" from the wilderness**)**.

Daoists celebrate mercy, humility, and frugality. From a Daoist perspective, human culture and industry are not sustainable without these three values. Human interpersonal relationships cannot be maintained without mercy and humility. Our positive interaction with the environment is enhanced and sustained through our expression of humility and frugality in exploiting resources. There is a story in the *Zhuangzi* that attempts to illustrate the Daoist ideal of frugality in working with nature. A Confucian sees a Daoist irrigating his fields with a bucket and so he tries to convince him to use a well sweep. The Daoist points out that employing machines causes people to worry about the mechanism, which in turn destroys the pure and simple life, replacing it with a mechanical one (Watson 1968, 134). Daoists are not opposed to using machines; they are opposed to the lack of humility and frugality expressed by most people who operate machinery. For Daoists, sustainable activities are those that entail mercy, humility, and frugality.

The ultimate goal for Daoists is to return to the primordial oneness of *dao*, or the way of nature. They employ a number of metaphors to express this union with nature. For example, Daoists talk about riding the wind, riding a dragon, entering water without getting wet or fire without getting burned, and living like a hermit in the mountains, only consuming dew drops. Zhuangzi expressed this union aptly: "Heaven and earth were born at the same time I was, and the ten thousand things are one with me" (Watson 1968, 43). Daoism can awaken us to a deeper understanding of and relationship with the environment.

The impact of Daoism continues in the modern era. The ratification of the constitution of the People's Republic of China in 1982 reinstated the peoples' right to religious freedom, and people returned to worship at Daoist temples. Communist Party members downplay the value of Daoism in particular and religion in general, but there is a growing number of practicing Daoists in mainland China. Because Daoist temples and monasteries are located in forests and on mountains, Daoists claim that they have been and continue to protect at least some of China's environment.

James D. SELLMANN
University of Guam

FURTHER READING

Addiss, Stephen, & Lombardo, Stanley. (1993). *Tao te ching (Lao Tzu)*. Indianapolis, IN: Hackett Publishing Co.

Ames, Roger T. (1989). Putting the *te* back into Taoism. In J. Baird Callicott & Roger T. Ames (Eds.), *Nature in Asian traditions of thought: Essays in environmental philosophy* (pp. 113–144). Albany: State University of New York Press.

Girardot, Norman J.; Miller, James; & Liu Xiaogan. (Eds.). (2001). *Daoism and ecology: Ways within a cosmic landscape*. Cambridge, MA: Harvard University Center for the Study of World Religions/ Harvard University Press.

Graham, Angus C. (Trans.). (1981). *Chuang-tzu: The inner chapters*. Channel Islands, U.K.: Guernsey Press Co.

Lau, D. C., & Ames, Roger T. (1998). *Yuan Dao: Tracing Dao to its source*. New York: Ballantine Books.

Rowe, Sharon, & Sellmann, James D. (2003). An uncommon alliance: Ecofeminism and classical Daoist philosophy. *Environmental Ethics*, *25*(2), 129–148.

Watson, Burton. (1968). *The complete works of Chuang Tzu*. New York: Columbia University Press.

Development—Concepts and Considerations

The environment complicates the concept of development. Until the twenty-first century, development focused on the quality of human life regarding wealth and, recently, our capabilities. But including the environment in these considerations raises difficult conceptual and ethical questions—about how to account for nonhuman life, include environmental conditions in our quality of life, and internalize the vast time-scale of most environmental processes.

As soon as the environment enters the discussion, the issue of development becomes complex. We associate development with human concerns, but what if the interests of nonhumans matter? It is also difficult to include all the indirect ways the environment matters to us and to figure out what time span is relevant when considering them. Finally, as if these problems weren't enough, the very concept of development is contested: What counts as development?

Before thinking about it, we must face the fact that development does not make sense from an ecological perspective. This is because life does not develop—it fluctuates by chance. One must make a distinction between the individual and the whole to see why. Individual organisms do develop, but one organism's development is often another one's doom. That is typically how the food chain works. There have been five mass extinctions since life began, and the last one—killing off the dinosaurs—allowed humans to evolve, free of being eaten by dinosaurs. From the perspective of life as a whole, all we see is chance—the chance of a meteor slamming into Earth and killing off the dinosaurs—and the fortune of not being eaten by a more powerful lifeform. This means that the very idea of progress does not make sense from an ecological perspective (Gould 1996). Accordingly, any talk about development on Earth must proceed with a maxim: Development happens within lives; between life-forms there is only chance.

What Counts?

A dictionary definition will tell you that the idea of development implies advancement, growth, even moving to a new stage in a process. Synonyms of *development* include *evolution*, even *formation*. What unifies all these notions and words is the idea of an ordered progression. Philosophers would say that development is teleological, from the Greek word *telos*, meaning a goal or an end. Development is goal directed. Almost always when we speak of development, there is a sense of what development goes toward. To say something is developing is to imply it has made progress. The question, of course, is progress in what? The development of an infant into a young child is progress in human life; the development of a thief is progress in illicit taking. Whenever we speak of development, we should have in mind the goal that gives development meaning.

The study of development has its roots in a natural science (biology) and in two social sciences (psychology and economics). When people speak of "sustainability" and "development," they are thinking primarily of the tradition deriving from economics, although both psychological and biological development are certainly relevant to this tradition. Economic development, since the time of the philosopher and economist Adam Smith (1723–1790), has been concerned with increasing the quality of human life. The question is, however, what counts as quality? What is its goal?

Much of the standard discourse of development tries to answer these questions. It is concerned principally with humans and only marginally with the environment. The question is how to measure quality of life for us, which makes sense since it is asking about only one form of life. Its answers make sense with our form of life, even if other life-forms—unfortunately—suffer.

There are two main approaches today to measuring the quality of human life and the extent to which humans develop from one point in time to the next, or do not. Both of these approaches have a tendency to speak of development as if it straddles a threshold between the developed and the underdeveloped. The first approach measures wealth, and the second measures capabilities. The first seems closely allied to economics, whereas the second is allied with human rights. It is also curious that the first approach does not have a clear goal, whereas the second does.

Development as Wealth

Before the nineteenth century, economics was a branch of moral philosophy because it is concerned with goods. When Adam Smith wrote *The Wealth of Nations* (2009 [1776])—now a foundational text for free-market theory—he thought he was filling out an account of the human good. The economy, he thought, can help or hinder humans from obtaining the things they need to have a good life. So if you are interested in helping people develop toward the human good, you should think about economics. As his book's title indicates, he focused on wealth—goods people own.

It took the rise of mathematical economics in the nineteenth century to make economics forget about moral philosophy. The twentieth century inherited a view of economics that studies a value-neutral set of patterns, devoid of any substantive conception of the good. For instance, economics might study capital flows, foreign direct investments, or currencies rates, but none of these weighed in on whether capital, investment, or currency will make one's life good. The assumption was that financial indicators reflect people's preferences: whatever people value, not what *is* valuable. Economics could then register how well people, businesses, market sectors, or nations can achieve their values, whether the values are good or not. Wealth became a purely abstract notion, a way of indicating how much ability someone has to achieve his or her values.

The abstraction from wealth as a set of goods to wealth as a sum of market value is an important transition in the history of wealth. By shearing value away from the human good, economic development becomes open ended and relative; in fact, it lacks a goal. If wealth is simply your ability to pursue your values in a market setting, there is no goal toward which you progress. You might say the goal is more wealth, but then what is the goal of that? As Aristotle (384–322 BCE) noted in *Nicomachean Ethics*, wealth is just a means. It cannot sensibly be the goal of life, because what

then is the goal of the means, or wealth? One of the problems of the standard discourse of development associated with economics is that it has lost the logic of development.

For much of the twentieth century, when people measured development, they measured such economic indicators as gross national product (GNP) or per capita income. The first measures the total value of goods and services produced in a given year by citizens of a nation or by businesses whose legal home is in that nation, and the second measures the average income of each citizen. The question was always relative: How does this figure in one country compare to that figure in another country? Which country is more developed? Or how does this year's figure compare to last year's numbers? Are we developing or receding? For such an approach to measure both wealth and development, the question of sustainability is: Can this growth continue over time? Can it be sustained? But we do not know what the growth is for, and we don't know what we are sustaining, since people have their own preferences.

It did not take long for critics to find problems with such an approach to development. By the last quarter of the twentieth century, a group of free-market economists and philosophers developed the largely Marxist insight into development that had been sidelined since the mid-nineteenth century in market-based economies, and they added a liberal twist. These development theorists, known as capability theorists, argued that we should look at individuals, not nations as a whole (a liberal idea), and at what those individuals can do and be, a Marxist idea (Sen 2000). This was an important moment. Even per capita income measurements won't tell whether an income can, say, buy a person health care in her or his country. And it will not tell about the nonresident aliens who work there.

Development as Capabilities

Remember that a goal is necessary to make sense of the logic of development. If one looks at GNP, one doesn't know what that goal is. Similarly, one doesn't know if one is on track toward it. Thus, for much of the twentieth century (and still often today), when economists and politicians speak of "developed" and "underdeveloped" countries, they promote conceptual confusion. If there is no clear goal toward which development moves, and no clear grasp of what stages are needed to reach it, then one cannot possibly lay claim to a measurement that a given country is developed while another is not. There's no structure for a comparison.

The advent of the capabilities approach by the economist Amyarta Sen and the philosopher Martha Nussbaum was therefore a boon, at least as far as the logic of development goes. Through Sen's collaboration with former United Nations advisor Mahbub ul Haq, the capabilities approach became, in 1990, the basis for the annual *Human Development Report*, which is considered the most fine-tuned assessment of development in the world and which acts as a basis for many discourses of development (all of them, however, still part of the standard discourse). These reports *do* give us a goal to development and a sense of what stages are needed to meet it.

The central insight in the capability approach is the idea that development means the development of our life-form (Nussbaum 2000). This is where the biological and psychological notions of development enter. The reasoning works like this: What could development for us be if it were not development of what lets us have a sound, human life? But what does let us? Our capabilities. Can we move around? Reproduce? Heal? (All biological notions.) Can we learn? Reason? Imagine? (All psychological notions.) By asking these questions and focusing on what people are able to do and to be, the capability approach brought back the idea of the human good that had been present in Smith and had been sidelined by free-market economics.

The *Human Development Report* looks at a set of central human capabilities to determine what each person in a country is able to do and to be. The capabilities are measured through indicators—for instance, children under height for their age (indicating nutrition) or the adult illiteracy rate (indicating education). Gender differences are studied closely; although the United States was most recently listed as having the number 2 GDP in the world, and the number 12 capabilities satisfaction, it is ranked number 107 when it comes to equality between genders (UNDP 2008). The result of this report is a fine-grained analysis of human flourishing in each country studied. Human development reports in general are useful for illuminating issues that standard GNP-based reports cannot. Under standard GNP-based approaches, there is no way of telling whether a country that has extremely high GNP—such as the Kingdom of Saudi Arabia (KSA)—distributes its wealth. But the capability approach, because it focuses on individuals, can tell: KSA has a huge concentration of wealth among a relatively small number of people, while the large mass of citizens and noncitizen guest-workers

exist with little. Similarly, approaches based on GNP and per capita income do not tell what people can do with their wealth, but the capability approach can. While there may be abject poverty in parts of India, people can vote, whereas in KSA they cannot. And although the United States of America seems wealthy, not everyone can afford such a basic thing as health care.

With the capability approach, development comes easy—at least as an idea. For instance, when we say that a country is "underdeveloped" we mean that it does not ensure basic capabilities—such as health—for a significant portion of its members. Moreover, the country is now underdeveloped in specific ways we can pinpoint. The United States is underdeveloped when it comes to the capability of universal physical health, but it is developed when it comes to the capability of freedom of expression. These are interesting and fairly specific conclusions compared to what we observe when measuring development by wealth. Moreover, the implied goal is clear: development reaches its target when and only when human beings are able to live sound lives—and when and only when they have all the capabilities underlying the indicators of the *Human Development Report*. We know what counts, and it admirably joins biological, psychological, and economic development.

Capabilities and Human Rights

Martha Nussbaum (2000) is clearest about the link between the capability approach and the human rights tradition: she claims that the capability approach is a form of human rights. The point is important, for over the second half of the twentieth century, human rights groups increasingly advocated rights as a measure of development, and in some contemporary political discourse, whether a country satisfies human rights or not determines whether it is developed. More importantly for our purposes, discourses of sustainability commonly appeal to human rights as a measure of basic social sustainability. They say that no community can truly be sustainable if it leaves human rights in disarray.

Nussbaum says that the capabilities approach covers the same set of entitlements as human rights and yet dispels the arbitrary appearance (2000, 284–285). Her point is convincing. Remember that the logic of development implies both a goal and a sense of the stages traversed in reaching that goal. Remember, too, that development draws on biological and psychological notions in some of its major forms. Keeping these things in mind, the problem with human rights as a measure of development is that they are not developmental notions; rather, they are legal ones.

Human rights are entitlements to certain kinds of goods, protections, or opportunities. The United Nations' *Universal Declaration of Human Rights* (1948), for instance, claims that we have a right to education (a good), freedom from torture (a protection), and a voice in our political process (an opportunity). These do seem to count when it comes to development, but the problem is that the source of these rights is vague and sometimes arbitrary. According to the political philosopher John Rawls (1993), when the Declaration was made, an "overlapping consensus" occurred among U.N. delegates. Few agreed on why we should have rights; they agreed only that we should have them. As a result, theorists have been at a loss to explain why, for instance, paid vacation appears as a fundamental right, as can be inferred from the Declaration's Article 24. Could Article 24 have been the result of political bargaining? But if so, that would increase the worry that human rights are arbitrary? Why should standards of development be up for political bargaining?

The capability approach has an advantage, since it begins with the idea of a sound, human life and tries to conceptualize the standards of development as a derivation of that. Rather than saying that the quality of life is measured by what powerful people say, the capability approach holds that quality of life depends on considering how human life develops. Development standards and development concepts go together.

That said, there are conceptually rigorous attempts to link human rights to human agency (i.e., the capacity to act), and these are similar to the capability approach. Commonly called "neo-Kantian" approaches due to their indebtedness to the eighteenth-century German philosopher Immanuel Kant, they differ from the capability approach only in taking the idea of the agent (or person) as primary, rather than the idea of the flourishing (or prospering) human being. The idea for neo-Kantian approaches is to derive what we *must* have from what we *need* in order to act (Gewirth 1996). Surprisingly, the rights generated are much the same as those generated by asking what a human needs to live a basically good life: freedom to act, an education to develop one's mind, health, and so on. Human rights in the neo-Kantian tradition are good measures of development because they begin by arguing that we need certain things to do what we want. The goal is clear: empowered human agency. And achieving each of the rights protecting our ability to

be fully active gives us a set of benchmarks for increasing or decreasing development. Focusing on our ability to act, too, we aren't far from the capability approach.

Once human rights are grounded in developmental concepts, they are good measures of development. Human rights are legal standards backed by moral authority. When one has a human right to X, it must be provided if at all possible. From a moral point of view, rights are nonnegotiable conditions. Thus, human rights provide us with a clear and powerful way to see if, from a moral point of view, states or non-state actors (such as corporations) are doing the minimum we expect. Human rights fold morality into quality of life. No reasonable human would say a quality life exists without moral conditions. Human rights spell out that idea. They underline the moral dimension of the quality of life.

The Interests of Nonhumans

Thinking about morality raises some difficult questions that make the idea of development hard to grasp and take us away from the standard discourse. At the limit, they make the idea of development seem absurd.

Suppose the moral point of view requires including the interests of nonhumans in our calculations. Suppose it is unfair to nonhumans, or just plain wrong, to act without heeding their interests. What, then, is development? Species develop by feeding on or outcompeting other species, or simply by being lucky. How can we conceptualize development across species?

Real problems arise when considering these questions. Many sustainability discussions want to include the interests of nonhumans in the idea of development. The global discussion surrounding the *Earth Charter* (2000), which presented principles for building an international, sustainable society in this century, is an example of the complex issues surrounding nonhuman interests. The Dalai Lama (Tenzin Gyatso) took part and so did many different groups from many different religions. For all of them, a sustainable world heeds the interests of nonhumans; sustaining means respecting. The problem is that one nonhuman's interests are another one's doom.

Morality goes where ecology does not. The philosopher James Rachels (2007) shows why. A moral person must honor all justified moral reasons. A justified moral reason is a consideration whereby any rational agent really should or should not do something, in view of a property's goodness or badness. Rachels presents the issue of suffering as an example. We have a moral reason to not cause suffering because suffering is bad. Suffering, though, does not honor the species barrier; all conscious creatures can suffer. So a moral person must respect that suffering is bad and avoid causing suffering to any sentient being. One interest of nonhumans must now be heeded. Following Rachels' thought, moral people won't eat meat, won't raze woods thoughtlessly in order to build houses, and won't contribute to global warming. There are many more things they will not do as well.

Would a moral person go so far as to stop an animal from making another animal suffer, as when wolves hunt down an elk? Does morality oppose the natural order? It all depends on whether there are reasons against preventing suffering. Perhaps starving is worse; perhaps letting elk overpopulate is, too. After all, both end in long, drawn-out suffering. Here morality re-approximates the order of nature, making sure everything is justified. And it hops over the species barrier, committing us in all sorts of ways to respect those properties of nonhumans that give us moral reasons. Just so, heeding nonhuman interests becomes a factor in our interests.

Should development be moral? It already is: even measuring wealth assumed that the ability to satisfy our preferences on a free market is valuable. One advantage of crossing the species barrier is that it shows us that development is a moral ideal. It is up to us to decide what matters when we conclude whether the world is getting better or worse. This is an interesting idea, but it leaves many unanswered questions and requires much future research. We have to figure out both what capabilities humans should have and what interests should be heeded in other species. If quality of life is essentially about living the good life, then here, the "good" in "good life" includes goodness toward other forms of life. And what does that entail, at a minimum? What are the stages of development? How do we measure them? And who decides what interests in which life-form matter? By what reasoning do we discover what would guide us to the right life-forms in the right situations? These are tough questions for anyone bent on sustainability.

Environmental Conditions

There is an easier way to involve the environment in discussions of human development, but only to a limited extent. Since we depend on the environment, aspects of the environment are human needs or things that have a lot of value. We depend on freshwater to live. Freshwater is a human need, and it is also worth a great deal to us whenever it can't be found. In much the same way, many aspects of the environment should be included in measures of human development. Think of our atmosphere. Think of the bees that pollinate plants and allow agriculture to flourish. The question is *how* to value them.

Wealth-based approaches have a harder time doing this than capability and neo-Kantian approaches. Market value may not reflect the importance of environmental goods. Water is such an example. Only recently has a global market for water sprung up. People have long assumed water is free and plentiful. But freshwater is limited, and the market will have to catch up with this fact. A different problem arises with goods in the future. Due to an idea called "discounting," the value of future freshwater is significantly less than we might think it should be. The reason why is that paying for some future good now expends value you could have invested and which would have grown in the meantime. As a result, some environmental good valued at, say, $1 now is *relatively* less valuable to you in the future, for the $1 you spend on it now could be invested in the meantime and become $2, thereby halving the relative cost of the future environmental good. You could afford twice as much of it in the future if you don't have to pay for it now. So we have difficulty valuing goods in the future based on their present worth. This problem is very serious for sustainability. One of the things sustainability discourses argue is that we have to preserve the environment for future generations, but discounting reduces the value of the environment in the future from the perspective of what you can spend or invest now. It doesn't pay to protect the future (Norhaus 2008). Some mainstream economists, like Nicholas Stern (2007), think this is unfair.

The capability approach has it easier, as do neo-Kantians. Since both depend on good environmental conditions, it's not hard to make aspects of the environment capabilities or to justify having rights to them. A capability theorist like Breena Holland (2008) can argue that water cycles form a metacapability that makes all other capabilities possible. Or a neo-Kantian can say that without freshwater, no human agent can act, so we have a right to freshwater. For these versions of the standard discourse, it isn't hard to include some of the environment.

Time Frame

There is one outstanding problem the environment poses to ideas of development: the problem of time frame, or what is called "temporal scale." Development is a time-based notion. It occurs over time, and our comparisons about development bring together a point now with a point from the past. The problem arises when we realize that the environment works on its own time. Our effects on it now are felt fully only in the future. We worry about what the effects of global warming will be by 2100, but the causes of those effects began in the early nineteenth century during the Industrial Revolution, and what we do in the next ten years will be decisive for the fate of our atmosphere. Any idea of development wanting to include the environment has thus to figure out how far ahead it should look (Norton 2008).

The United States can be used to illustrate this point. In 2008, it is considered one of the more developed nations in the world. But it is also the world's largest contributor to global warming, and the effects of that contribution are delayed. How should we measure the delayed effect in our assessment of development now?

All these questions surrounding development are genuine and worthwhile. Our flourishing (and maybe the moral order of life) is at stake.

Jeremy BENDIK-KEYMER
LeMoyne College

FURTHER READING

Aristotle. (1999). *Nicomachean ethics.* (Terence Irwin, Trans.). (2nd ed.). Indianapolis, IN: Hackett Publishing.

His Holiness the 14th Dalai Lama of Tibet. (n.d.). Retrieved September 30, 2008, from http://www.dalailama.com

Earth Charter. (2000). Retrieved September 30, 2008, from http://www.earthcharterinaction.org/content/pages/Read-the-Charter.html

Gewirth, Alan. (1996). *The community of rights.* Chicago: University of Chicago Press.

Gould, Stephen Jay. (1996). *Full house: The spread of excellence from Plato to Darwin.* New York: Three Rivers Press.

Holland, Breena. (2008, November). Ecology and the limits of justice: Establishing capability ceilings in Nussbaum's capability approach. *Journal of Human Development, 9*(3), 401–425.

Kant, Immanuel. (1996). Metaphysical principles of the doctrine of right. In (Mary J. Gregor, Ed. & Trans.) *Kant: The metaphysics of morals* (pp. 1–138). New York: Cambridge University Press.

Leopold, Aldo. (1968). *A Sand County almanac, and sketches here and there.* New York: Oxford University Press.

Morsink, Johannes. (1999). *The universal declaration of human rights: Origin, drafting, intent.* Philadelphia: University of Pennsylvania Press.

Norhaus, William D. (2008). *A question of balance: Weighing the options on global warming policies.* New Haven, CT: Yale University Press.

Norton, Bryan. (2008, September 6). Learning to think like a planet. In *Human Flourishing and Restoration in the Age of Global Warming.* Talk presented at a conference conducted at Clemson University, Clemson, SC.

Norton, Bryan G. (2005). *Sustainability: A philosophy of adaptive ecosystem management.* Chicago: University of Chicago Press.

Nussbaum, Martha. (2000). *Women and human development: The capability approach.* New York: Cambridge University Press.

Nussbaum, Martha. (2006). *The frontiers of justice: Disability, nationality, species membership.* Cambridge, MA: Harvard University Press.

O'Neill, John; Holland, Alan; & Light, Andrew. (2007). *Environmental values.* New York: Routledge.

Rachels, James. (2007). *The legacy of Socrates: Essays in moral philosophy* (Stuart Rachels, Ed.). New York: Columbia University Press.

Rawls, John. (1993). *Political liberalism.* New York: Columbia University Press.

Sen, Amartya. (2000). *Development as freedom.* New York: Anchor.

Smith, Adam. (2009 [1776]). *The wealth of nations: Books 1–3: Complete and unabridged.* New York: Classic House Books.

Smith, Adam. (2009 [1776]). *The wealth of nations: Books 4–5: Complete and unabridged.* New York: Classic House Books.

Stern, Nicholas. (2007). *The economics of climate change: The Stern review.* New York: Cambridge University Press.

United Nations Development Programme (UNDP). (2008). *Human Development Report 2007/2008.* Fighting climate change: Human solidarity in a divided world (highlights). Retrieved July 29, 2008, from http://hdrstats.undp.org/countries/country_fact_sheets/cty_fs_USA.html

United Nations General Assembly. (1948, December 10). *Universal declaration of human rights.* Retrieved May 17, 2009, from http://www.un.org/en/documents/udhr/

Development, Sustainable

During the last decades of the twentieth century, sustainable development emerged as a concept that links economic development and the needs of the world's poor with environmental sustainability. Despite criticisms of the concept, sustainable development points to the connections between issues of poverty, economic development, and the environment, which are also reflected in all the great religious teachings of the world.

The standard definition of sustainable development as "development that meets the needs of the present without compromising the ability of future generations to meet their own needs" comes from the World Commission on Environment and Development's (WCED) 1987 report, *Our Common Future.* This commission, sometimes called the Brundtland Commission (after the name of its chairperson), was established by the United Nations in 1983 to reflect on the growing deterioration of natural resources, and what this might mean for sustaining social development.

Historical Background

The Brundtland Commission was not the first high level gathering to consider this question. In 1968, a private group of economists, concerned about "the predicament of mankind" in the face of the carrying capacity of Earth, established themselves as the Club of Rome. They commissioned the Massachusetts Institute of Technology to study this matter, and in 1972 they published their hugely influential report, *The Limits to Growth*, arguing that "the strategy for dealing with the two key issues of development and environment must be conceived as

a joint one" (Meadows, Meadows, Randers, and Behrens 1972, 4).

The Limits to Growth was a key talking point at the United Nations Conference on the Human Environment in Stockholm in 1972, which produced the report, *Only One Earth.* This conference spoke of "ecodevelopment" and produced a range of recommendations on environmental matters. It led to the formation of the United Nations Environment Programme and encouraged national governments to establish environment ministries. There was very little impact on economic issues, however, and this created the context that led to the formation of the WCED in 1983.

The concept of sustainable development, promoted in the 1987 report of the WCED, shaped the United Nations Conference on Environment and Development held in Rio de Janeiro in 1992, known as the Earth Summit. Over one hundred heads of state and government adopted the Rio Declaration, Agenda 21, and a range of other conventions. More than 10,000 people attended the Global Forum on nongovernmental organizations (NGOs) which sought to promote sustainable development. The Commission on Sustainable Development (CSD) was created in December 1992 to monitor the decisions of the Summit, and it has continued to work within the United Nations system since then. This concern for sustainable development had an impact upon the Millennium Development Goals (MDGs), the seventh of which is to ensure environmental sustainability, with a concern to integrate the principles of sustainable development into the policies and programs of governments.

Ten years after the Rio Earth Summit, the nations of the world gathered again in 2002 for the World Summit on Sustainable Development (WSSD) in Johannesburg, South Africa. The hopes for sustainable development remained, but the hard reality of the economic policies of neo-liberal globalization, the conflicts surrounding the terrorist attacks of September 11, 2001, and strident voices from the global South (the term applies to the world's most poor and undeveloped nations, most of which are in the Southern Hemisphere), who demanded a focus on poverty and issues like HIV and AIDS, served to undermine the environmental concerns originally embedded in the term *sustainable development*.

Definition of the Concept

The opening section of *Our Common Future* (1987) contains a detailed discussion of the meaning of sustainable development. It points to two key concepts: the needs of the world's poor and the limitations of the ability of the environment to meet present and future needs. In terms of the first concept, sustainable development "requires meeting the basic needs of all and extending to all the opportunity to satisfy their aspirations for a better life" (WCED 1987, 4). This requires sustained economic growth, attention to equitable opportunities, limits to consumption, and the slowing of population growth.

In terms of the second concept, "at a minimum, sustainable development must not endanger the natural systems that support life on Earth: the atmosphere, the waters, the soils, and the living beings" (WCED 1987, 9). It must recognize the limits that exist to natural resource exploitation and the challenges to manage renewable resources, as well as to use nonrenewable resources slowly and carefully. The section concludes as follows: "In essence, sustainable development is a process of change in which the exploitation of resources, the direction of investments, the orientation of technological development, and institutional change are all in harmony and enhance both current and future potential to meet human needs and aspirations" (WCED 1987, 15).

The fundamental concern behind the concept of sustainable development, namely, the all-inclusive engagement of environmental concerns with human rights, global equity, and social justice, has been generally well received by religious people and faith communities across the spectrum. The teachings of all the great religions point to meeting the needs of the world's poor and respecting the limits of Earth. Over the past twenty years there have been many high-level meetings of religious communities to focus on the theme and to contribute to the wider global discussion.

Criticisms of the Concept

Three significant criticisms have been leveled at the concept of sustainable development. First, while recognizing the symbolic power of the term and its almost universal acceptance in global discussions, it has been noted that the two words themselves have no direct reference to the environment. This gives rise to two problems, the first of which is that there is no direct reference to Earth or ecology in the words *sustainable development*. Thus—once the history of the term is lost and its rootedness in environmental concerns is forgotten by a new generation of leaders, governments, and other key stakeholders—the term may come to be used as a slogan to cover a multitude of agendas, including some that work against the environment. Some suggest the term *ecojustice* to overcome this concern.

A further problem with the term is that the adjective *sustainable* can be overwhelmed by the noun *development* with its assumed focus on economic concerns. Thus, in many contexts, especially where English is not familiar, the term can come to mean *sustained* development, as opposed to stop-start development initiatives. In the New Partnership for Africa's Development (NEPAD), a continent-wide initiative, the term has been subtly changed to "sustainable growth and development."

Second, critics of the idea of "development" have argued that if development is a flawed concept, then sustainable development is hardly the goal to which the world should commit itself. There is a strong body of opinion that argues that "development" is synonymous with the imposition of Western modernity, along with capitalism and consumerism, upon the nations of the globe. Some argue that "development" is the child of colonialism, given that all the former colonial powers are considered "developed," whilst the colonies are "developing," and it therefore provides the moral grounds upon which certain nations have privileged status in global policy making. If this is the case, then promoting "sustainable development" is against the interests of many in the global South. A more radical critique suggests that it is precisely development, in the guise of such industrialization and consumerism, that is responsible for the environmental crisis; thus it is an oxymoron to speak of sustainable development.

The third criticism raises the fact that development should be a process or a means rather than a goal or an end. In this sense, the term *sustainable development* functions as a verb rather than a noun. Critics argue that people should not be trying to sustain development, but to sustain that to which development is striving. Development may be one means to that end, but given all the tensions about development theory and practice (so the argument goes), would it not be better to focus on the goal and allow different nations, communities, and cultures to figure out their own means to that goal? This is the thinking behind the emergence of two ideas that keep the notion of sustainability but focus on a different goal: sustainable livelihoods and sustainable communities.

Curiously enough, the concept of sustainable livelihoods was first used by the WCED in 1987, the same year it introduced the term *sustainable development*. Sustainable livelihoods is a way of integrating the macro concerns of public policy, laws, and structures with the micro concerns of household assets and livelihood strategies. It asks questions about what wider agencies need to put in place and what local actors can do, within the environmental constraints, to make livelihood outcomes sustainable. The second idea, sustainable communities, focuses on the goal of community, including the community of Earth and all living things. It asks questions about the strategies that need to be adopted to ensure that this community can be sustained through the generations.

Religious Engagement

For all the criticisms of the concept of sustainable development, the term points—insufficiently perhaps—to "an inconvenient truth" (Gore 2006). At the start of the twenty-first century, more and more scientists, social scientists, economists, politicians, and social activists are recognizing the indivisibility between issues of poverty and the environment, of economics and ecology. It has taken a long time, but the truth of the 1972 Stockholm report, *Only One Earth*, is now widely recognized: there is a fundamental connection between the way people organize their economies and the health of Earth, and humans carry a great deal of responsibility for the crisis they find themselves in. Yet this statement of judgment is also a statement of hope and opportunity.

These themes have lain dormant in the teachings of all the great religious traditions of the world, and they are now emerging with new clarity and conviction in many communities of faith around the world. At least five strong connections exist between religious ideas and beliefs, and the concerns embodied in the concept of sustainable development. In the first instance, religious beliefs focus on Earth, not as a cold meaningless object, but as the creation of a God who cares for the planet and for all living things. Furthermore, God or Spirit, or the life force, is understood to remain engaged in the ongoing life of the planet, giving human life a "telos," that is, a purpose. These beliefs provide the moral foundation for taking seriously the implications of the environmental crisis, a foundation which some scholars believe can *only* come from a religious perspective.

Secondly, religious thinking encourages a holistic understanding of Earth, nature, and humanity. Humans are seen as part of the wider fabric of "all living things," and so there is an ability to see the web of connections between human livelihoods and the environment. Some point to the fact that the Greek word *oikos*, meaning "home" or "household," is the root word in English for both "economics" (*oikos-nomos*, or "rules of the household") and "ecology" (*oikos-logos*, or "wisdom of the household"). Therefore the religious beliefs of Earth as the one home of humanity provide an intuitive connection to the concerns underlying sustainable development.

A third point of connection lies in the notion of the limits to human activity. Drawing on the idea of God's creation of all living things, religious beliefs stress the responsibility of human beings to live in balance with life, or to respect the limits to what they can do in pursuit of their own ends. This is also a theme that constantly emerges in discussions around sustainable livelihoods.

Perhaps the most significant engagement between religion and sustainable development centers on the fourth point of connection, namely, the issue of human culture and values, which is recognized even by nonbelievers. If it is scientifically true that humans are in a crisis created by their human inability to live within their limits, then as a global community humans need to "re-vision" how they structure their economy and livelihoods. These are human undertakings, and so people need to question their values, choices, and actions. According-ing to the Brundtland Commission, "perceived needs are socially and culturally determined, and sustainable development requires the promotion of values that encourage consumption standards that are within the bounds of the ecological possible and

to which all can reasonably aspire" (WCED 1987, 5)

Religious convictions are at their best when they can contribute to this "re-visioning" of human values so that they can best inform economic and political policies. Given that much of the crisis that sustainable development is trying to address is driven by the insatiable material demands of rich nations and people, there is a vital need for the affirmation of religious convictions that stress meaning and purpose in things other than consumer goods, and that speak to simplicity, shared resources, and respect for other life.

Finally, religious visions and religious communities enable the discussion about sustainable development to remain rooted in the vision of social and economic justice for the poor. Environmental debates often spin off into the conservation concerns of the wealthy, but the sheer numbers of religious believers in the global South, many of whom are not wealthy, means that religious perspectives will always highlight the relationship between environmental and economic justice.

In conclusion, sustainable development is a concept that emerged in the last decades of the twentieth century to deal with a fundamental crisis facing Earth as economic systems, policies, and activities clash with the carrying capacity of the natural environment. While a range of serious criticism has been leveled at the concept, these criticisms do not resolve the crisis. Religious visions and faith communities have a range of crucial insights and values that can and must contribute to the resolution of this crisis.

Steve DE GRUCHY
University of KwaZulu-Natal

FURTHER READING

The Earth Charter. Retrieved July 8, 2009, from www.earthcharter inaction.org/content/categories/Religion

Foltz, Richard C.; Denny, Frederick M.; & Baharuddin, Azizan. (Eds.) (2003). *Islam and ecology*. Cambridge, MA: Harvard University Press.

Gore, Albert. (2006). *An inconvenient truth: The planetary emergency of global warming and what we can do about it*. Emmaus, PA: Rodale Books.

Meadows, Donella H.; Meadows, Dennis L.; Randers, Jørgen; & Behrens, William W., III. (1972). *The limits to growth*. New York: Universe Books.

The Millennium Forum. Retrieved July 8, 2009, from www.un.org/millennium/declaration.htm

Niles, D. Preman. (2002). *Between the flood and the rainbow: Interpreting the conciliar process of mutual commitment*. Geneva: WCC.

Rasmussen, Larry L. (1996). *Earth community, earth ethics*. Maryknoll, NY: Orbis.

Ward, Barbara, & Dubos, Rene. (1972). *Only one earth: The care and maintenance of a small planet*. New York: W.W. Norton Company.

WCED (World Commission on Environment and Development). (1987). *Our common future*. Oxford, U.K.: Oxford University Press.

Dominion

That humans have dominion over the Earth, a claim of Abrahamic faiths, has been interpreted as the cause of the contemporary ecological crisis. Other interpretations emphasize that stewardship of the Earth is included in the idea of appropriate dominion. Humans may choose to be conquerors, gardeners, developers, trustees, or caretakers.

The Abrahamic religions affirm a special role for humans in creation. "So God created man in his own image; . . . male and female he created them. And God blessed them, and God said to them, 'Be fruitful and multiply, and fill the earth and subdue it; and have dominion . . .'" (Genesis 1:27–28, RSV). Famously, historian Lynn White Jr. (1907–1987) laid much of the blame for the ecological crisis on this Judeo-Christian belief in a 1967 article published in the magazine *Science.* The Genesis command had flowered in medieval Europe, licensed the exploitation of nature, and produced science and technology that have resulted in an ecological crisis. Islam has a similar concept: "I am setting on the earth a vicegerent [*khalifah*]" (Quran 2:30).

White's critics were quick to respond that there were two thousand years between the origins of such belief and these results. Other Biblical passages in Psalms and Job celebrated creation. Greek convictions were important: "Man is the measure of things" (Protagoras). Other factors played more immediate roles: the rise of capitalism, economies of growth, increasing populations, the rise of democracies, and increasing secularization. Liberal capitalist democracy arouses escalating aspirations in its citizen-consumers; by contrast Jesus hardly recommended maximizing consumption. Even White noticed that Eastern Orthodox Christianity did not develop such dominion attitudes, nor did Saint Francis within Western Christianity.

After the fall and disruption of the garden, nature too is corrupted and life becomes a struggle. Nature needs to be redeemed by human labor. Here theology, science, economics, and morality all joined to think that increasing development, thus relieving disease and poverty, is a good thing. For all of human history, humans have been pushing back limits. Life will get better; one should hope for abundance and work toward obtaining it. Humans have more genius at this (more capacity for dominion) than any other species.

These notions have been built into the Western concept of human rights: a right to self-development, to self-realization. Such an egalitarian ethic scales everybody up. When every individual seeks its own good, there is escalating consumption. When everybody seeks everybody else's good, there is, again, escalating consumption. White's article forced serious misgivings about the human dominion of classical and enlightenment Judaism and Christianity.

Theologians have replied that appropriate dominion requires caring for creation. True, there is a sense of dominion that means "Earth-tyrant," or humans subduing nature in a repressive sense, as a conqueror does his enemy. But there are more positive senses. Even keeping the military metaphor, an "Earth-commander" finds the interests of the commander and the commanded inseparably entwined, like a general and his infantry. Sometimes one encounters the metaphor of a pilot of spaceship Earth.

The couple was put in the garden "to till and keep it" (Genesis 2:15, RSV).

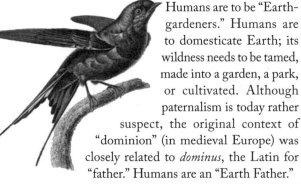

Humans are to be "Earth-gardeners." Humans are to domesticate Earth; its wildness needs to be tamed, made into a garden, a park, or cultivated. Although paternalism is today rather suspect, the original context of "dominion" (in medieval Europe) was closely related to *dominus*, the Latin for "father." Humans are an "Earth Father."

Perhaps the favored model is that of stewardship, although many prefer to speak of humans as Earth-trustees. A steward manages for the benefit of an owner; a trustee cares for that under his or her care. Environmental management appeals to scientists and developers. Hebrews have three different kinds of rulers: humans on Earth are and ought to be prophets, priests, and kings—roles unavailable to nonhumans. Humans should speak for God in natural history, reverence the sacred on Earth, and rule creation in freedom and in love.

The same Genesis stories teach about the human fall into sin. Humans covet and worship false gods; they corrupt their faiths and rationalize in self-deception. Faiths must be ever reformed; humans need their prophets and priests to constrain their kings. The righteous, humane life balances all three dimensions. Indeed, Christians have often been too anthropocentric. As the ethicist Larry Rasmussen explains, the need for repentance is perennial. Dominion on Earth is human destiny, but it is a fragile destiny.

Holmes ROLSTON III
Colorado State University

FURTHER READING

Berry, Robert J., (Ed.). (2006). *Environmental stewardship: Critical perspectives, past and present.* Edinburgh, U.K.: T & T Clark.

Birch, Charles; Eakin, William; & McDaniel, Jay B. (Eds.). (1990). *Liberating life: Contemporary approaches to ecological theology.* Maryknoll, NY: Orbis Books.

Cobb, John B., Jr. (1972). *Is it too late: A theology of ecology.* Beverly Hills, CA: Bruce.

DeWitt, Calvin B. (1998). *Caring for creation: Responsible stewardship of God's handiwork.* Grand Rapids, MI: Baker Books; Washington, DC: The Center for Public Justice.

Nash, James A. (1991). *Loving nature: Ecological integrity and Christian responsibility.* Nashville, TN: Abingdon Cokesbury.

Nasr, Sayyid Hossein. (1968). *Man and nature: The spiritual crisis of modern man.* London: George Allen and Unwin.

Rasmussen, Larry L. (1996). *Earth community earth ethics.* Maryknoll, NY: Orbis Books.

White, Lynn, Jr. (1967, March 10). The historical roots of our ecological crisis. *Science, 155,* 1203–1207.

Dualism

Dualism is a system of thought, characteristic of the West, which divides mind from matter then makes mind the exclusive preserve of humanity, leaving the rest of nature a realm of brute and blind materiality with no meaning or value for itself. Therefore, morally speaking, it can be used by people however they see fit. In order to become morally responsible to nature, dualism must restore mind to nature.

Dualism denotes a view commonly invoked by environmental thinkers to explain the anthropocentrism of Western attitudes to nature. Anthropocentrism has historically typified Western attitudes to nature, insofar as nature has been valued only as a resource for humanity rather than as a locus of moral significance and concern in its own right. From the prevailing viewpoint of Western civilization, plants, animals, and the nonhuman world generally have not been ascribed intrinsic value and, therefore, have not usually been granted moral standing and consideration. Many environmental thinkers see the current overexploitation of the natural environment and the resulting environmental crisis as an outcome of this deep-seated anthropocentrism of Western thought (Naess 1973; Routley and Routley 1982).

Dualism supports anthropocentrism by categorically separating mind from matter. From a dualistic perspective, mind and matter are not inherently inextricable aspects of reality but are distinct phenomena, such that mind cannot be fully explained in terms of matter nor matter in terms of mind. Historically, in the West, mind has been seen as exclusively and essentially the province of the human and matter the province of the rest of nature. This separation of the mental from the purely material has implications for value, since in order for a thing to be accorded value in its own right, rather than merely having value for people, it must matter to itself. It can only matter to itself if it has some kind of awareness of what happens to it, or possesses some kind of mental attribute. In separating mind from matter, and attributing mental attributes to humanity alone, while categorically denying them to the rest of nature, dualistic thinking represents nature as not mattering to itself and, hence, as lacking value in its own right. Since people cannot be morally responsible to things that lack value in their own right, they cannot be morally responsible to nature for the use they make of it. This is not to say that humans cannot be morally responsible to other people for the use they make of nature as a resource, since their use of that resource may either deprive others of it or make it available to them.

The moral hierarchy that dualism sets up between humanity and nature informs a whole cluster of core dichotomies or binary oppositions that have historically shaped Western thought: culture/nature, mind/body, spirit/matter, human/animal, reason/emotion, reason/instinct, subject/object, self/other, abstract/concrete, universal/particular, and theoretical/practical. Feminist thinkers have analyzed these foundational categories as intrinsically gendered: masculinity is defined in terms of the autonomy of mind and reason, femininity in terms of procreation and hence the body and nature

(Reuther 1975; Lloyd 1984; Plumwood 1993; Warren 2000). Against a background of poststructuralist thought, postcolonial theorists have shown that these categories are also characterized by race: Western identity defines itself in terms of reason and the correlates of reason, and the abstract, objective, and universal forms of thinking exemplified in science and "enlightened" Western modes of education, while non-Western identities are defined in terms of the irrational, the instinctual, the "superstitious," and "closeness to nature" (Memmi 1965; Plumwood 1993). From within a dualistic frame of reference, a "master identity" is constituted: men construct women; whites construct blacks; and colonizers construct the indigenous as subrational, ruled by instinct and the body, devoid of essential human consciousness, identified with nature rather than with civilization, and, as such, legitimate objects of domination (Plumwood 1993). Thus a whole system of domination, endemic to the West, rests on the prior, dualistic separation of reason from nature and consequent subordination of nature to reason. It follows that the key to dismantling the domination of nature, and all the groups that have come to be ideologically associated with it in Western thought, lies in the dismantling of dualism itself—restoring mind to nature, in some suitably expanded and plural sense, so that nature ceases to be the moral nullity it has been in the dualistic scheme of things. Whether or not such a dismantling of dualism requires only a political reorientation however, as feminist, postcolonialist and poststructuralist thinkers argue, or whether dualism is somehow built into the grain of theory itself, remains to be seen (Mathews 2008).

Freya MATHEWS
La Trobe University

FURTHER READING

Derrida, Jacques. (1976). *Of grammatology.* (Gayatri Chakravorty Spivak, Trans.). Baltimore and London: Johns Hopkins University Press.

Lloyd, Genevieve. (1984). *The man of reason.* London: Methuen.

Mathews, Freya. (2008). Why has the West failed to embrace panpsychism? In David Skrbina (Ed.), *Mind that abides: Panpsychism in the West.* Cambridge, MA: MIT Press

Memmi, Albert. (1965). *The coloniser and the colonised.* New York: Orion.

Naess, Arne. (1973). The shallow and the deep, long-range ecology movement. *Inquiry, 16,* 95–100.

Plumwood, Val. (1993). *Feminism and the mastery of nature.* London and New York: Routledge.

Reuther, Rosemary Radford. (1975). *New woman new Earth.* Minneapolis, MN: Seabury Press.

Routley, Richard, & Routley, Val. (1982). Human chauvinism and environmental ethics. In Don Mannison, Michael McRobbie, & Richard Routley (Eds.). *Environmental philosophy.* Canberra: Australian National University.

Warren, Karen. (2000). *Ecofeminist philosophy: A Western perspective on what it is and why it matters.* New York: Rowman & Littlefield.

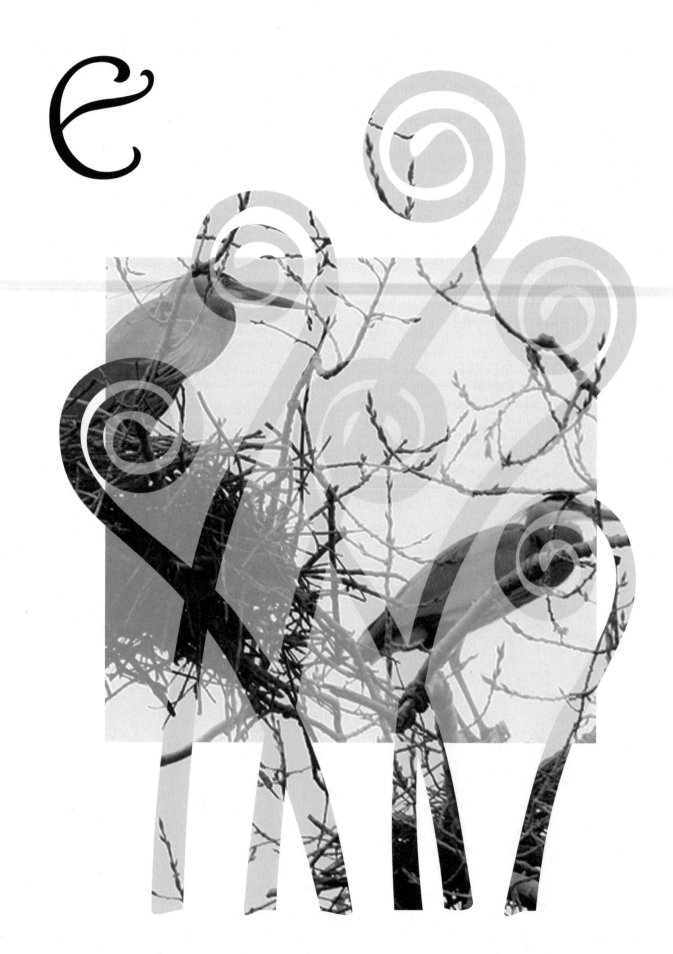

Earth Charter

The Earth Charter, finalized in 2000 after ten years of international collaboration and dialogue, asserts the responsibility of the peoples of Earth to create a sustainable global society. Its principles include respect for life and ecological integrity as well as social and economic justice and nonviolence. The Earth Charter Initiative, a global network of individuals, organizations, and institutions, acts to promote these principles.

The Earth Charter is a declaration of fundamental ethical principles for building a just, sustainable and peaceful global society in the twenty-first century. It seeks to inspire in all people a new sense of global interdependence and shared responsibility for the well-being of the whole human family, the greater community of life, and future generations. It is a vision of hope and a call to action.

The Earth Charter is centrally concerned with the transition to sustainable ways of living and sustainable human development. Ecological integrity is one major theme. The Earth Charter recognizes, however, that the goals of ecological protection, eradication of poverty, equitable economic development, respect for human rights, democracy, and peace are interdependent and indivisible. It provides, therefore, a new, inclusive, integrated ethical framework to guide the transition to a sustainable future.

The Earth Charter is a product of a decade-long, worldwide, cross-cultural dialogue on common goals and shared values. The Earth Charter project began as a United Nations initiative; it was carried forward and completed by a global civil society initiative, and was finalized and then launched as a people's charter in 2000 by the Earth Charter Commission, an independent international entity.

The drafting of the Earth Charter involved the most inclusive and participatory process ever associated with the creation of an international declaration. This process is the primary source of its legitimacy as a guiding ethical framework. The authority of the document has been further enhanced by endorsements from over 4,800 organizations as of 2009, including many governments and international organizations.

Origins

The proposal that led to the creation of the Earth Charter is found in *Our Common Future* (1987), the report of the U.N. World Commission on Environment and Development (WCED). Among its many recommendations, the Commission calls for the creation of a "Universal Declaration on Environmental Protection and Sustainable Development" in the form of "a new charter." With this idea in mind, Maurice Strong, a Canadian and secretary general of the 1992 Rio Earth Summit (United Nations Conference on Environmental Development), proposed that the summit draft an Earth Charter. The inclusion of the name "Earth" in the title of both summit and charter reflected the growing recognition in the 1980s that our planet is one, great, self-regulating ecosystem on which people are dependent in fundamental ways, and that Earth's ecosystem is being rapidly degraded by human patterns of production and consumption, thereby putting the human future at risk. During the preparatory process for the summit, some governments and a number of nongovernmental organizations submitted recommendations for the drafting of an Earth Charter, but the project lacked sufficient government support and was abandoned.

In 1994 Maurice Strong, acting as the chairman of the Earth Council, and Mikhail Gorbachev, acting in his capacity as president of Green Cross International, formed a partnership and restarted the Earth Charter consultation and drafting process as a civil society initiative. The formation of this partnership had the active support of Jim McNeill, the secretary general of the WCED, and of Queen Beatrix and Prime Minister Ruud Lubbers of the Netherlands. The Dutch government provided the initial financial support. The secretariat of the Earth Charter Initiative was based at the Earth Council in Costa Rica, and Ambassador Mohamed Sahnoun of Algeria became the first director of the project. The goal of the initiative was to draft a charter that would articulate the consensus taking form in the emerging global civil society on values and principles for sustainable development.

Hundreds of organizations and thousands of individuals participated. Forty-five Earth Charter national committees were formed, and these committees organized local dialogues. Earth Charter consultations were conducted on the Internet. Major regional conferences were held in Asia, Africa, Central and South America, North America, and Europe. In December 1996 the Earth Council and Green Cross International formed an Earth Charter Commission to oversee the drafting process. It was chaired by Strong and Gorbachev, and its membership consisted of eminent persons from around the world. The Commission invited Steven Rockefeller, a professor of religion and ethics from the United States, to chair and form an international drafting committee. The actual drafting process began in January 1997. Proposed and revised versions of the charter were issued during this process to generate comments and stimulate discussion. In March of 2000, the Commission finalized the text at a meeting at the United Nations Educational, Scientific, and Cultural Organization (UNESCO) headquarters in Paris, and the document was formally launched at the Peace Palace in The Hague three months later.

The Earth Charter is a product of the global ethics movement that inspired the Universal Declaration of Human Rights and that gained wide support in the 1990s. Driving this movement is the recognition that in an increasingly interdependent world, no nation acting alone can solve the major challenges it faces. Cooperation with other nations and peoples is essential, and building an effective global partnership requires common goals and shared values. The Earth Charter reflects the influence of both the new scientific worldview being shaped by physics, cosmology, and ecology and the wisdom of the world's religions, great philosophical traditions, and indigenous peoples. The drafting committee worked closely with the Commission on Environmental Law (CEL) of the World Conservation Union (formally called the International Union for Conservation of Nature, or IUCN), and the Charter builds on and extends international environmental and sustainable development law. The Earth Charter reflects the concerns and aspirations expressed at the seven U.N. summit meetings held during the 1990s on the environment, human rights, population, children, women, social development, and the city. Its inclusive vision is an expression of the growing awareness of the need for holistic thinking and inclusive, integrated problem solving.

Content

The Earth Charter contains a preamble, sixteen main principles, sixty-one supporting principles, and a conclusion entitled "The Way Forward." The preamble affirms that "we are one human family and one Earth community with a common destiny," and it provides an overview of the critical challenges and choices facing humanity (EIC 2000). It emphasizes that together with commitment to universal human rights there is needed a strong sense of universal responsibility. The Earth Charter seeks to expand humanity's ethical consciousness by recognizing that human beings are interdependent members of the greater community of human and nonhuman life on Earth; as members of this global community, people have significant ethical responsibilities that extend beyond their duties as members of a particular tribe, religion, or nation. The Earth Charter promotes a new sense of global citizenship that includes respect for cultural diversity and recognition that all life forms are worthy of respect and moral consideration regardless of their utilitarian value to people.

The principles of the Earth Charter are introduced "as a common standard by which the conduct of all individuals, organizations, businesses, governments, and transnational institutions is to be guided and assessed" (EIC 2000). The principles are divided into four sections whose titles indicate the inclusive nature of the Earth Charter's ethical vision: I. Respect and Care for the Community of Life; II. Ecological Integrity; III. Social and Economic Justice; and IV. Democracy, Non-Violence and Peace.

The Earth Charter states that "when basic needs have been met, human development is primarily about being more, not having more." The charter also affirms a number of universal spiritual values, including a sense of belonging to the larger evolving universe and "reverence for the mystery of being, gratitude for the gift of life, and humility regarding the human place in nature." The document culminates with a vision of peace and the joyful celebration of life. "Peace" is defined as "the wholeness created by right relationship with oneself, other persons, other cultures, other life, Earth, and the larger whole of which all are a part" (EIC 2000).

The Earth Charter Initiative, 2000–2009

Following the launch of the Earth Charter in 2000, the Earth Charter Commission assigned responsibility for oversight of the Earth Charter Secretariat and the larger

Earth Charter Initiative to a steering committee made up of members of the Commission and Drafting Committee. Over the next five years (2000–2005), the Earth Charter was translated into forty languages and widely disseminated around the world. Among the thousands of organizations that have endorsed the Earth Charter are UNESCO, ICLEI-Local Governments for Sustainability (founded as the International Council for Local Environmental Initiatives), and the World Conservation Union, the members of which include seventy-seven state governments and over eight hundred nongovernmental organizations from 142 countries. Efforts to secure recognition of the Earth Charter by the United Nations General Assembly are ongoing. Since the Earth Charter provides a valuable introduction to the subject of global ethics and to the meaning of sustainable development, it has been adopted as a teaching tool by many schools, colleges, and universities in all regions of the world.

In 2006 the Earth Charter Steering Committee and Secretariat were reorganized as Earth Charter International (ECI) with a new ECI Council made up of twenty-four members from nineteen countries and the major regions of the world. The ECI Council establishes policies and strategic guidelines for the Secretariat and larger Earth Charter Initiative, which is a worldwide network of individuals and organizations. The mission of the ECI and the Earth Charter initiative is to promote the transition to sustainable ways of living and a global society founded on the values and principles of the Earth Charter. ECI does not control the Earth Charter Initiative, and ECI strongly encourages the decentralized expansion of Earth Charter activities around the world. ECI does have over one hundred affiliates in fifty-seven countries with whom it actively collaborates. Six independent task forces operating in the fields of business, education, media, religion, youth, and the United Nations were formed in 2008 to advance decentralized engagement with the Earth Charter.

The Earth Charter is an expression of the widespread aspiration for a shared vision of a better world and social transformation. A growing number of individuals and organizations are finding that it can be used as a valuable guide to sustainable ways of living, an illuminating framework for education for sustainable development, a twenty-first-century moral compass for government and business policy making, a catalyst for cross-cultural and interreligious dialogue, and an instrument for assessing progress toward sustainability.

Steven ROCKEFELLER
Earth Charter International Council

FURTHER READING:

Corcoran, Peter B.; Vilela, Mirian; & Roerink, Alide. (Eds.). (2005). *The Earth Charter in action: Toward a sustainable world.* Amsterdam: KIT.

Corcoran, Peter B., & Wohlpart, A. James. (Eds.). (2008). *A voice for Earth: Writers respond to the Earth Charter.* Athens: University of Georgia Press.

EIC. (The Earth Charter Initiative). (2000). Retrieved August 3, 2009, from www.earthcharterinaction.org/content/pages/Read-the-Charter.html

Engel, J. Ronald. (2002). The Earth Charter as a new covenant for democracy. In Peter Miller & Laura Westra (Eds.), *Just ecological integrity: The ethics of maintaining planetary life* (pp. 37–52). Lanham, MD: Rowman & Littlefield.

Rockefeller, Steven. C. (2007). Ecological and social responsibility: The making of the Earth Charter. In Barbara Darling-Smith (Ed.), *Responsibility* (pp. 179–198). Lanham, MD: Lexington Books.

Soskolne, Colin L.; Westra, Laura.; Kotze, Louis. J.; Mackey, Brendan. G.; Rees, William. E.; & Westra, Richard. (Eds.). (2007). *Sustaining life on Earth: Environmental and human health through global governance.* Lanham, MD: Rowman & Littlefield.

Speth, James G. (2008). *The bridge at the edge of the world: Capitalism, the environment, and crossing from crisis to sustainability.* New Haven, CT and London: Yale University Press.

Speth, James G. (2004). *Red sky at morning: America and the crisis of the global environment.* New Haven, CT: Yale University Press.

World Commission on Environment and Development. (1987). *Our common future: From one earth to one world.* Oxford, U.K. and New York: Oxford University Press.

Earth Day

Earth Day is celebrated worldwide to promote environmental issues and sustainability. First observed in 1970, it has become the world's largest secular holiday.

Celebrations of Earth Day began in 1970 through the confluence of various efforts to raise awareness of pressing environmental issues and to work toward sustainable solutions. It is observed worldwide primarily on two days: the March equinox (around 19–21 March) and 22 April. The first ideas for Earth Day were developed by the peace activist John McConnell and Senator Gaylord Nelson (Democrat from Wisconsin, served 1963–1981).

McConnell founded Earth Day on the March equinox in 1970 to demonstrate engaged practices of peace and sustainability. The first celebration of Earth Day— 21 March 1970—was observed in San Francisco and several other cities in northern California. The following year, the United Nations first observed Earth Day, ringing the Japanese Peace Bell (a U.N. peace symbol from the Japanese people) at the exact moment of the equinox. The ringing of bells worldwide at the time of the March equinox is a continuing part of Earth Day celebrations.

Nelson founded Earth Day on 22 April 1970, as a national environmental teach-in, the goal of which was to promote grassroots environmental activism to bring environmental issues into the political arena. This celebration of Earth Day involved twenty million American participants, half of whom were public schoolchildren. Given the social and political momentum generated with the first Earth Day observances, numerous federal environmental initiatives were implemented, including the Environmental Protection Agency (1970), the Clean Air Act (1970), the Clean Water Act (1972), and the Endangered Species Act (1973).

Earth Day is celebrated in diverse ways, including rallies, speeches, advertising campaigns, and various activities for school children (e.g., arts and crafts, worksheets, games, field trips). Many of these celebrations also involve ecological restoration projects (e.g., tree planting, litter clean up). Earth Day has become a global event, celebrated in 2008 by over one billion people in approximately two hundred countries. Thus, Earth Day is often considered to be the world's largest secular holiday, bringing together people of different religious orientations, political alliances, ethnicities, and socioeconomic classes to work toward common goals of sustainability. Highlighting a sacred dimension of this holiday is Earth Day Sunday, or Ecumenical Earth Day, which is celebrated by Christian churches throughout the United States on the Sunday prior to Earth Day.

Earth Day has been criticized for various reasons, including its appropriation by corporations, media, and political organizations that celebrate the holiday nominally while failing to participate in sustainable practices; and the complacency that Earth Day fosters among those who adopt sustainable practices only during its celebrations. Although it has problems and limitations, Earth Day continues to have a positive impact, as can be seen by the inclusion of Earth Day events in the educational curriculum of schools worldwide.

Elizabeth McANALLY
California Institute of Integral Studies

FURTHER READING

Graham, Mary. (1999). *The Morning after Earth Day: Practical environmental politics.* Washington, DC: Governance Institute and Brookings Institution Press.

Hayes, Denis. (2000). *The official Earth Day guide to planet repair.* Washington, DC: Island Press.

History of Earth Day. (2009). Retrieved May 7, 2009, from http://www.earthday.net/node/77

McConnell, John. (n.d.). *What and when is Earth Day?* Retrieved May 7, 2009, from http://www.earthsite.org/day.htm

Nelson, Gaylord; Campbell, Susan; & Wozniak, Paul. (2002). *Beyond Earth Day: Fulfilling the promise.* Madison: University of Wisconsin Press.

Ecocentrism

Ecocentrism refers to an ethical perspective that privileges the integrity, health, or functioning of ecological systems. It usually stands in contrast to anthropocentric (human-centered) perspectives. Biocentrism represents another nonanthropocentric perspective, but it differs from ecocentrism in that it focuses on life or the life community rather than ecological systems.

Like anthropocentrism, the concept of ecocentrism functions in several different ways. It can refer to a principle or hierarchy of value, as in an argument that asserts ecological integrity as the most important moral good or that considers ecological systems as the bearer of ultimate value. In contrast, a second, weaker ecocentric argument may hold that ecological systems bear significance as the most basic context for human thought and action, or for the realization of transcendent goods (such as beauty or complexity). Those human or transcendent goods might have greater value, but because they depend on ecological systems, those systems accrue a final or genetic value of their own. In that case, ecocentrism refers to a contextual framework for ethics.

In a third way, ecocentric arguments may ask humans to imaginatively occupy a non-human perspective as they consider some course of action. In this way, ecocentrism functions to consider a policy, problem, or situation from the perspective of another species or the Earth itself, or as a moment in an unfolding evolutionary narrative. In this third way, the ecocentric component may form one aspect of a broader ethical system.

The author and environmentalist Aldo Leopold's "land ethic" is perhaps the greatest contribution to the formation of the ecocentric approach to ethics. Asking readers to include all the members and systems of the land in their sense of moral community, Leopold's *Sand County Almanac, and Sketches Here and There* includes all of the above functions: Sometimes he presents ecological systems and their creatures as bearing their own value, sometimes as valuable because of higher moral goods (beauty, integrity, and stability), and sometimes he asks readers to "think like a mountain." One of the great challenges to an ecocentric perspective is justifying nonanthropocentric knowledge, or the criteria by which one can assess the integrity, health, or functioning of complex evolutionary systems. Leopold did not offer a philosophical justification but seemed to suggest that humans can come into this wisdom through attentive participation in biotic communities and ecological systems.

While most ecocentric ethics usually focus on describing the moral importance of ecological systems, they must also resolve apparent conflicts between protecting or enhancing ecological systems and other moral values. Those who place moral value on individuals, whether human or nonhuman, worry that ecocentric approaches can lead to ignoring or suppressing the rights of individuals for the sake of systems or holisms. Animal advocates have pressed just this complaint to ecocentric environmental ethicists, as have ethicists concerned for the rights and dignity of human individuals. Ecocentrism does not necessarily suspend concern for individuals; animal rights and human rights may fit within an ecocentric approach so long as their protection accords with the healthy functioning of ecological systems.

Ecocentric perspectives may also be opposed by those who argue for a theocentric approach. A theocentric approach privileges the purposes, values, relations, or commands of God, as these are known by some religious traditions. Theocentric ethicists may worry that an ecocentric perspective places ultimate moral value on something other than God or divine law.

The same tension holds true for the relation between anthropocentric and theocentric approaches and is usually resolved by arguing that God's purposes align with the true purposes of humanity. Of course, ecocentric and theocentric perspectives could also converge in that way, as the Christian ethicist James Gustafson argues. Gustafson's *Ethics from a Theocentric Perspective* proposes that humans should relate to all things as they relate to God, which in Gustafson's system means that humans must respect ecological systems apart from any service they have for human benefit. When theocentric and ecocentric perspectives converge like that, it may produce moral attitudes of awe or reverence.

An ethicist might arrive at reverence from an ecocentric starting point as well. The environmental philosopher Holmes Rolston argues that an ecocentric ethic eventually leads one to reverence since it considers nature as a generative matrix of diverse values and as an unfolding evolutionary story. So perceived, nature teaches humans about their own marvelous contingency and complexity. As presented by the environmentalist Joanna Macy (1995), an ecocentric ethic may then begin to reconstruct anthropology, as it depicts selfhood according to its participation in the ecological systems upon which it depends.

Willis JENKINS
Yale Divinity School

Whitney BAUMAN
Florida International University

FURTHER READING

Callicott, J. Baird. (1999). *Beyond the land ethic: More essays in environmental philosophy.* Albany: State University of New York Press.

Gustafson, James. (1981). *Ethics from a theocentric perspective: Vol. 1. Theology and ethics.* Chicago: University of Chicago Press.

Leopold, Aldo. (1949). *A Sand County almanac, and sketches here and there.* New York: Oxford University Press.

Macy, Joanna. (1995). The ecological self: Postmodern ground for right action. In Mary Heather MacKinnon & Moni McIntyre (Eds.), *Readings in ecology and feminist theology* (pp. 259–269). Kansas City, MO: Sheed & Ward.

Rolston, Holmes, III. (2004). Caring for nature: From fact to value, from respect to reverence. *Zygon 39*(2), 277–302.

THINKING LIKE A MOUNTAIN

The pioneering U.S. environmentalist and writer Aldo Leopold (1887–1948) was perhaps the greatest contributor to the formation of the ecocentric, as opposed to the anthropocentric, approach to ethics. His 1949 book Sand County Almanac, and Sketches Here and There, *published posthumously and, on its fiftieth anniversary seemingly timeless in its message, begins with a rich depiction of life on his "farmed-out" land in central Wisconsin, expands to cover the natural beauty and rhythms of other locales, and culminates with a challenge for readers: to embrace his land ethic—or, as he writes elsewhere in the book, to "think like a mountain."*

The land ethic . . . enlarges the boundaries of the community to include soils, waters, plants, and animals, or collectively: the land.

This sounds simple: do we not already sing our love for and obligation to the land of the free and the home of the brave? Yes, but just what and whom do we love? Certainly not the soil, which we are sending helter-skelter downriver. Certainly not the waters, which we assume have no function except to turn turbines, float barges, and carry off sewage. Certainly not the plants, of which we exterminate whole communities without batting an eye. Certainly not the animals, of which we have already extirpated many of the largest and most beautiful species. A land ethic of course cannot prevent the alteration, management, and use of these 'resources,' but it does affirm their right to continued existence, and, at least in spots, their continued existence in a natural state.

In short, a land ethic changes the role of *Homo sapiens* from conqueror of the land-community to plain member and citizen of it. It implies respect for his fellow-members, and also respect for the community as such.

Source: Aldo Leopold. (1949). *A Sand County Almanac, and Sketches Here and There,* p. 204. New York: Oxford University Press.

Ecocide

Controversial for its allusion to genocide and specifically to the Holocaust, the term ecocide *emphasizes the urgency and gravity of the current ecological crisis. Ecocide also points to the contribution of modern technology and the role of modern society in allowing such devastation to occur; such issues parallel questions raised about Germany in the 1930s and 1940s.*

The term *ecocide* is used by a variety of authors and in a wide range of contexts, its essential force, for some, is to associate the environmental crisis with genocide in general and the Holocaust in particular. While there clearly are some drawbacks with this usage—especially surrounding the issue of sensitivity toward the victims of the Third Reich in World War II—there are also some benefits.

The first of these is that associating environmental destruction with, for example, the Holocaust immediately asserts the cataclysmic nature of the threat. If the environmental crisis is like the murder of Europe's Jews, it must be responded to with immediate and overpowering attention. This is not a matter of some slight technological miscalculation that can be remedied by improving gas mileage or eating more organic vegetables.

Second, and especially in its association with the Holocaust, the idea of ecocide calls into question the ultimate rationality of the technological and bureaucratic structures that define modernity. As the Nazis used their technical and bureaucratic competence to round up and deport Jews and to create efficiently rationalized forms of mass death, so today's transportation, energy, and manufacturing systems—each characterized by unprecedented sophistication—contribute to an enormously irrational and destructive overall consequence.

Third, and by implication, as nations that are capable of genocide must call into question every aspect of their culture, politics, economics, and religion, so a modern world culture that is committing ecocide must do the same. As intellectuals have asked about the full reality of German culture that allowed the Final Solution to be designed and to proceed with so little resistance, so we can ask about forms of knowledge, political authority, economic power, and self-awareness that allow us to produce atmosphere-altering chlorofluorocarbons (CFCs), tens of thousands of toxic chemicals, a commercial fishing industry that has decimated the world's fish stocks, and the widespread destruction of the rainforest.

Finally, some instances of environmental abuse are genocidal in that they actually do have focused and devastating effects on particular human communities. The generalized effects of, say, global warming or acid rain may be somewhat widespread and random, and even toxins in the water may affect by accident those with genetic vulnerabilities to chemical assault. Yet in other cases—for example, the consequences of uranium mining or other forms of mineral extraction on indigenous peoples—environmental damage rises to the level of physical and/or cultural destruction. The Ogoni of Nigeria have been devastated by oil drilling, and the native peoples of China, Canada, and India have been ravaged by the Three Gorges, James Bay, and Narmada River dam complexes respectively. For these peoples, ecocide simply *is* a kind of genocide: it is the ultimate conclusion of "environmental racism/injustice." The fate of the rivers, the land, the endangered species, and the endangered people are, as it were, pretty much the same.

Roger S. GOTTLIEB
Worcester Polytechnic Institute

FURTHER READING:

Bender, Frederic L. (2003). *The culture of extinction: Towards a philosophy of deep ecology.* Amherst, NY: Humanity Books.

Gottlieb, Roger S. (1999) *A spirituality of resistance: Finding a peaceful heart and protecting the Earth.* New York: Crossroad.

Katz, Eric. (1997). *Nature as subject: Human obligation and natural community.* Lanham, MD: Rowman & Littlefield.

Wenz, Peter. (1997). *Nature's keeper.* Philadelphia: Temple University Press.

THE DEATH OF AN EMPIRE

In the 75-year process of establishing itself as a superpower, the former Soviet Union proclaimed concern for public health and natural resources. Now the shrinking Aral Sea, doomed by errant irrigation schemes, has been drained to one-third its original volume, nearly half of all farmland is at risk of overcultivation and pesticide contamination, and air pollution in most major cities exceeds Soviet standards. Authors Murray Feshbach and Alfred Friendly discuss what went wrong.

When historians finally conduct an autopsy on the Soviet Union and Soviet Communism, they may reach the verdict of death by ecocide. For the modern era, indeed for any event except the mysterious collapse of the Mayan [E]mpire, it would be a unique but not an implausible conclusion. No other great industrial civilization so systematically and so long poisoned its land, air, water and people. None so loudly proclaiming its efforts to improve public health and protect nature so degraded both. And no advanced society faced such a bleak political and economic reckoning with so few resources to invest toward recovery.

In land area, the Soviet Union was the largest country in the world. In population in 1990 it ranked third after China and India. For decades it was the leading producer of oil and steel, the owner of a quarter of the planet's forest reserves and an equal portion of its fresh water. Yet it beggared itself by endangering the health of its population—especially its children and its labor force—the productivity of its soil and the purity of its air and water.

These threats, in turn, endanger prospects for economic recovery, even if sweeping systemic reforms take hold in the successor states. Aside from the time required to remedy decades of environmental abuse, the costs of cleaning up could drain staggering sums from all the resources needed to rebuild housing, roads, power plants and water systems and to modernize industry and agriculture.

The investments that former Soviets must make to combine ecological restoration with economic recovery can only be estimated. They will have to be enormous . . . to compensate for the long-term and continuing abuse of two essential resources, nature and human health.

Source: Murray Feshbach & Alfred Friendly Jr. (1992). *Ecocide in the USSR: Health and Nature Under Siege*, pp. 1–2. New York: Basic Books.

Ecological Footprint

The ecological footprint is a measure of how much land and water area a human population (or individual) requires to produce the resources it consumes and to absorb its wastes on an annual basis. The result of this assessment—a simple quiz—provides the number of Earths that would be necessary to support a given lifestyle.

The concept of the "ecological footprint" (EF) was developed in 1996 by Mathis Wackernagel and William Rees and outlined in *Our Ecological Footprint*. It suggests that in order to tread lightly on the Earth, we must measure our true footprint, which includes energy and resource consumption. A measurement tool—an online quiz—was soon developed to calculate the ecological footprint of individual humans and organizations (such as businesses, communities, cities, and countries). At the end of the assessment, one is told how many Earths would be needed if everyone on the planet lived a certain way. The concept of the ecological footprint depends upon the theory of limited resources or a limited carrying capacity (the limit to how much human consumption of resources is possible without some sort of ecosystemic collapse) of the Earth. The measurement is based upon the acres of biologically productive area it would take to sustain a population that uses *X* amount of resources.

Though there has been some controversy over what "carrying capacity" is, it has been used by many religious organizations such as GreenFaith and California Interfaith Power and Light to raise awareness about consumption patterns. Furthermore, it has aided in the development of methods for offsetting carbon emissions for activities such as flying and driving. Though there are environmental justice issues related to offsetting emissions (Cobb and Daly 2008), the tool is effective for use in many communities. (Carbon offsetting does not take into account the

distribution of environmental ills: one power plant that does not use all of its pollution credits could sell its credits to another plant so that it could pollute more than its alloted credits. Some communities would then have to deal with higher amounts of pollution than others.) Answering the question, "What constitutes a sustainable and/or good way of life?" (Cobb and Daly 1994) intersects with the topics of religion, spirituality, and ecology. In other words, the tool assumes a certain level of resource use, but the question remains whether or not that level of resource use is necessarily conducive to human and nonhuman progress and whether or not a specific level of resource use can or should be used for all 6-plus billion people on the planet. Does sustainability, according to the ecological footprint measure, smuggle in some normative assumptions about what "the good life" is that fails to take into account the diversity of peoples and environments on the planet? (Vanderheiden 2008).

On the one hand, the ecological footprint is a valuable yardstick for measuring the absurdity of the consumer lifestyle. On the other hand, the tool is rife with scientific and ethical lacunae. For example, there is no doubt that Vice President Al Gore has a huge footprint, given that he travels all over the world to deliver his message about global climate change. But is not this very message intended to change people's lives toward living in more sustainable ways? The EF does not take into account these complexities. As another example, would the very development of the EF by Wackernagel and Rees be within the "one planet" scenario of sustainability? Probably not, given that the idea and tool were developed over several conferences, and its very dissemination depends upon the energy necessary to run a computer with an Internet browser and connection. In a sense, the legacy of the EF still remains to be seen, but its message is clear: We must stop living as if there is more than the one planet upon which we live.

Whitney BAUMAN
Florida International University

FURTHER READING

Cobb, John B., & Daly, Herman E. (1994). *For the common good: Redirecting the economy toward community, the environment, and a sustainable future* (2nd ed.). Boston, MA: Beacon Press.

Cobb, John B., & Daly, Herman E. (2008, February 19). *The California Environmental Justice Movement's declaration on use of carbon trading schemes to address climate change.* Environmental Justice Matters. Retrieved December 19, 2008, from http://www.ejmatters.org/declaration.html

Ecological Footprint Quiz. (n.d.). Retrieved April 9, 2009, from http://www.myfootprint.org/en/visitor_information/

GreenFaith: Interfaith Partners for the Environment. (n.d.). Retrieved April 9, 2009, from http://www.greenfaith.org/

The Regeneration Project and Interfaith Power and Light. (n.d.). Retrieved April 9, 2009, from http://www.theregenerationproject.org/

Vanderheiden, Steve. (2008, June). Two conceptions of sustainability. *Political Studies, 56*(2), 435–455.

Wackernagel, Mathis, & Rees, William E. (1996). *Our ecological footprint: Reducing human impact on the Earth.* Gabriola Island, Canada: New Society Publishers.

HOW BIG IS *YOUR* FOOTPRINT?

Redefining Progress, a public policy think tank dedicated to finding economic solutions for a sustainable and equitable world, has partnered with the Center for Sustainable Economy to develop a measurement tool that calculates the "ecological footprint" of individuals and organizations. This Ecological Footprint Quiz, which determines how many Earths it would take to sustain life if everyone on the planet lived the same lifestyle as the test taker, estimates the area of land and ocean required to support consumption habits (of food, goods, services, housing, and energy) and to assimilate wastes.

According to the Redefining Progress website, the global population is overshooting the Earth's biological capacity by nearly 50 percent, meaning that at our current rate of consumption we need one and a half Earths. (Two Vancouver journalists quoted by Elizabeth Kolbert in her August 31, 2009, New Yorker article, "What's Wrong with Eco-stunts," commented on the shocking discovery that the typical number for "standard-issue North Americans" is nine.) Here are the results of author Whitney Bauman's test (retrieved from http://www.myfootprint.org/en/).

If everyone on the planet lived my lifestyle, we would need:

= 2.82 Earths

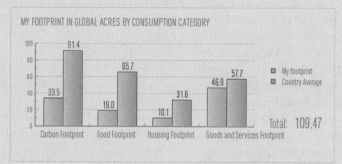

MY FOOTPRINT IN GLOBAL ACRES BY CONSUMPTION CATEGORY

□ My footprint
□ Country Average

Carbon Footprint: 33.5 / 91.4
Food Footprint: 19.0 / 65.7
Housing Footprint: 10.1 / 31.6
Goods and Services Footprint: 46.9 / 57.7

Total: 109.47

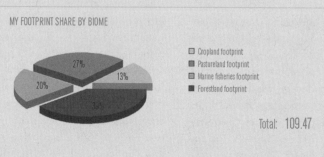

MY FOOTPRINT SHARE BY BIOME

□ Cropland footprint
■ Pastureland footprint
□ Marine fisheries footprint
■ Forestland footprint

27%
13%
20%

Total: 109.47

Ecology

As a subdiscipline of biology, ecology studies the relationship of organisms to their environments. Over 150 years of use, however, the term has evolved to signal the importance of relationships within and between natural and human systems, and to signify activism for a sustainable planet. By examining ecology in these contexts we can better understand how sustainability depends on scientific facts, worldviews, and practices that lead to social change.

The word *ecology* was neologized by the German biologist and public intellectual Ernst Haeckel (1834–1919), who, in 1860, proposed a new science based on the Darwinian idea of natural selection, a specialization within biology to study organisms in relationship with their living and nonliving environments. Haeckel derived the name for this science from the Greek word for household, *oikos*, which is also the root of "economics." This connection was intentional, and at one point, Haeckel defined ecology broadly as "the economy of nature."

Today, the term *ecology* continues to have multiple meanings, and while each emphasizes the importance of relationships and connections in our world, the differences between them are crucially important. Scientific ecology studies the relationships of organisms to their biotic and abiotic environments; a broader use of the word emphasizes the evolving character of relationships within all kinds of systems; and a more activist ecology signifies a movement emphasizing connections between human beings and the nonhuman world.

Ecology as a Science

In broadest terms, the science of ecology remains what Haeckel proposed: a subdiscipline of biology focused on how living systems and organisms survive and evolve through interaction with one another and their nonliving environments. However, contemporary ecologists concerned with presenting experimentally significant results tend to explain their work in more limited terms, subdividing the field by naming the particular questions and perspectives in which they specialize. Some ecologists articulate their focus by naming the object or region of their studies: disease ecologists, marine ecologists, animal ecologists, arctic ecologists. Another approach to classifying subspecialties focuses on the methods and scales of attention. At the smallest scales, physiological ecologists examine the chemical and biological factors shaping interactions between individual organisms and their environments, and behavioral ecologists examine the adaptations of organisms to their surroundings. Population ecologists study the changes and adaptations within a collection of organisms from the same species in a particular area, and community ecologists study patterns and processes among groups of organisms from different species. Ecosystem ecologists study the flows of energy and matter within a spatially explicit unit of organisms and abiotic material, and landscape ecologists study the broader scale patterns of environmental change across multiple ecosystems.

Some anthropologists and other social scientists also see their studies as a related subfield—human ecology—that studies the human species with special attention to its interrelationships and interactions with other living systems and environments. Such study of the human species adapts the basic assumption of all scientific ecology: no organism, species, or community can be studied without attention to the context and relationships that define it.

It is important to note, however, that the work of ecological scientists is not primarily about emphasizing or studying interconnectedness broadly construed; rather, it focuses on particular connections within a landscape, community, organism, or other system. Most contemporary ecologists seek to identify the particular relationships that are most central in their subject of study, building models of systems within the natural world rather than making grand and sweeping claims about it.

Many ecologists also work to dispel the romantic notions that all interrelationships are mutually advantageous and all ecosystems are fundamentally harmonious. Instead, the science depends upon a view of the natural world that includes predation and parasitism. Organisms do not only depend upon and relate to the world around them; they also consume and compete with one another and their environments. This means that ecology studies systems in which death and variation are inevitable. Furthermore, while earlier models of the natural world emphasized the stability of healthy functioning systems, contemporary ecology tends to emphasize that all communities are always in flux. Thus, any management of or interaction with a natural system must be adaptive and flexible, expecting unpredictable changes rather than seeking to create or preserve an unchanging status quo.

Ecology as a Characteristic of Systems

The science that Haeckel helped create grew substantially in the twentieth century, particularly expanding after the 1970s as its research program became associated with the environmental movement. This growth also led to a popularizing of the word *ecology*, which began to refer to much more than the research programs of ecologists. In the most general sense, ecology came to encompass not only the study of physical systems of the natural world but also the character of human institutions and metaphysical reality. In this sense, ecology is a way of talking about how the world and all its systems

are organized, calling particular attention to interconnectedness and organic development.

The emphasis in this use of *ecology* is on the importance of relationships on a broad scale, seeking less to model particular systems and more to make a declaration about the character of all structures, communities, and belief systems. This is demonstrated in the philosophical movement of deep ecology, which argues that a "deep" understanding of ecological systems teaches a metaphysical truth about the character of reality: Everything is always in flux; human beings are inseparable from the intricate interconnections of the nonhuman world; and all political and economic structures must be reexamined in light of this interconnectedness. Deep ecology moves beyond the data and analysis of scientific ecology to broader questions, arguing that the view of the world demonstrated in ecological research has moral and spiritual implications. In this context, ecology is a characteristic of systems—a truth about the way the world works and the ways human beings should work within it.

In a more casual sense, ecology can be used as a way to talk about the networks of relationship and change within any system. Any human community can be seen to have an ecology, and to note this is to identify and investigate the dynamic relationships between its influences, its context, and its participants. Human belief systems have an ecology as well because they are shaped by the environmental, traditional, and ideological factors that interact to form what and how people think. Just as an ecosystem evolves into complicated relationships of mutual dependence, consumption, and complementarity, this approach to ecology recognizes that any system or community develops over time based on the relationships within it and to other systems.

Ecology as an Activist Movement

Ecology has come to signify not just a scientific endeavor and a characteristic of systems, but also an integrated activist movement—a political and social campaign to change the ways people think and act in order to preserve the systems and living variety of the planet.

This type of ecology includes environmentalism and shares with that movement the goal of a sustainable future for the human race and other creatures. To label activism as "ecological" calls emphatic attention to interconnections: Humanity is not distinct from the environment that surrounds it, but rather fully part of, interdependent with, and inseparable from the world and its systems. Issues of social justice are not separable from the problems of climate change, pollution, and biodiversity degradation; instead, the ecology movement focuses on the ways in which degradation of the environment also degrades human lives, seeking political and practical responses that highlight the connections between both problems and solutions. Ecology responds to a singular challenge in which environmental degradation, human oppression, and unnecessary suffering all interrelate and develop together. Such a crisis can only be addressed by a united, adaptive, and interrelated activist movement.

This is the primary meaning of *ecology* in the philosophical and activist movement of ecofeminism, which argues that the marginalization of women is connected with, and cannot be fully addressed without attention to, the dismissal of the natural world. Similarly, the scholarly field of "religion and ecology" appeals primarily to this third definition, relating faith traditions and metaphysical truth claims to a unifying activist movement and thereby seeking to change human relationships to one another and the nonhuman world.

This use of *ecology* is also evident in popular culture, in which the prefixes *eco-* or *eco-friendly* are appended to ideas and products in order to suggest that they are produced and distributed by sustainable, just, and moral means. While these marketing tools may be casually applied and difficult to justify—and they certainly reflect less radical challenges to contemporary systems than movements like ecofeminism and deep ecology—they depend upon the public perception that *ecology* means an integrated, activist concern for the multiple challenges facing human societies in the contemporary world.

Ecology and Sustainability: Syntheses and Complexities

The rhetorical power of the word *ecology* comes from the fact that it encompasses all these different ideas, and so most uses of the word outside of a carefully defined scientific research program blur its meanings. For example, in one of the foundational essays of environmental ethics and religious environmentalism, "The Historic Roots of Our Ecologic Crisis," the historian Lynn White Jr. writes: "What people do about their ecology depends on what they think about themselves in relation to things around

them" (White 1967, 1205). In his title, White refers to ecology in the third sense, appealing to a unitary "crisis" to which activists must respond. In the quote, however, White appeals to ecology as a characteristic of systems, referring to the perennially adaptive interrelations between human beings and their nonhuman environments. Interestingly, White does not draw explicitly upon the science of ecology in his essay—somewhat ironic given that the essay was published in the journal *Science*—but his writing nonetheless gains credibility through linguistic association with that field.

As this example makes clear, there are rarely clean and absolute distinctions between different approaches to ecology, and many authors who use the term remain vague about exactly what they mean by it. It is therefore important to attend to what might be called the ecology of these ecologies: the network of changing relationships—of complementarity and competition—between these definitions. They might all be synthesized when the ecology movement embraces the dynamic interconnectedness of all systems with attention to how scientific models and research support this work. But the priorities between these types of ecology still matter. For instance, will statements about interconnectedness be narrowly defined and carefully justified, as in scientific ecology, or sweeping and universal, as in ecology as a characteristic of systems?

This attention to ecologies and their interactions is a necessary part of any study of sustainability. When advocates call for "ecological" sustainability, as many do, it is important to investigate whether they refer to rigorous scientific methods and principles, a worldview emphasizing interconnectedness, a broad-ranging activist movement, or some combination of all three.

Insofar as it is an activist movement responding to a crisis, sustainability often overlaps with, and is sometimes indistinguishable from, the movement of ecology. Both movements are based upon the claim that human lives and interests cannot be separated from the environments and natural systems with which humans live, and both offer a unified approach to moral challenges that are often seen as distinct and disparate. The broader idea that ecology is a characteristic of systems is a fundamental principle among advocates of sustainability, who increasingly recognize that any attempt to sustain a cultural or natural system must work in light of the interrelationships and adaptations within them. This is particularly the case in spiritual and religious discussions of sustainability, which frequently appeal to the interconnectedness of all reality as a foundational truth at the center of their belief system. Finally, activists, engineers, and managers who seek to achieve sustainability in practical terms frequently appeal to scientific ecology when developing management plans and predictive models for human interactions with the natural world.

Each definition of *ecology* can also be used to critique sustainability: Some research ecologists worry that the association of their work with an activist movement will detract from its scientific objectivity, and so they are cautious about attempts to draw direct connections between their work and sustainability. Some who emphasize that ecological systems are always in flux use this characteristic of systems to question the ideal of sustainability, asking if it is too static a goal in an adaptive world. Some who identify themselves as part of the ecology movement question the notion of sustainable "development," concerned that this term detracts from important critiques to be made of dominant and destructive economic systems.

Ecology emphasizes the importance of interconnectedness, but it also emphasizes the multiplicity of interconnections and ecologies. Understanding the complexity of this term therefore helps us to understand the complexity of sustainability as an idea, a reality, and a movement requiring attention to scientific facts, broad worldviews, and the ideals and practices that lead to social change.

Kevin J. O'BRIEN
Pacific Lutheran University

FURTHER READING

Allen, Timothy F. H., & Hoekstra, Thomas W. (1992). *Toward a unified ecology*. New York: Columbia University Press.

Botkin, Daniel B. (1990). *Discordant harmonies: A new ecology for the twenty-first century*. New York: Oxford University Press.

Fox, Warwick. (1984). Deep ecology: A new philosophy for our time? *Ecologist, 14*(5/6), 194–200.

Lodge, David M., & Hamlin, Christopher. (2006). *Religion and the new ecology: Environmental responsibility in a world in flux*. Notre Dame, IN: University of Notre Dame Press.

Merchant, Carolyn. (1992). *Radical ecology: The search for a livable world*. New York: Routledge.

Naess, Arne. (1973). The shallow and the deep, long-range ecology movement. A summary. *Inquiry, 16*, 95–100.

Peterson, Anna L. (2001). *Being human: Ethics, environment, and our place in the world*. Berkeley: University of California Press.

Rasmussen, Larry L. (1996). *Earth community, Earth ethics*. Maryknoll, NY: Orbis Books.

Sideris, Lisa H. (2003). *Environmental ethics, ecological theology, and natural selection*. New York: Columbia University Press.

Tucker, Mary E., & Grim, John A. (1994). *Worldviews and ecology: Religion, philosophy, and the environment*. Maryknoll, NY: Orbis Books.

Warren, Karen J., & Erkal, Nisvan. (1997). *Ecofeminism: Women, culture, nature*. Bloomington: Indiana University Press.

White, Lynn, Jr. (1967). The historical roots of our ecologic crisis. *Science, 155*(3767), 1203–1207.

Worster, Donald. (1994). *Nature's economy: A history of ecological ideas*. (2nd ed.). New York: Cambridge University Press.

Ecology, Cultural

With roots as ancient as Greco-Roman philosophy, cultural ecology examines questions of human relationship to the rest of nature. How does the environment shape society? How do ritual and identification of the sacred relate to economics and ecology? How does human transformation of nature create a sense of "place" and cultural identity? These questions and more remind us that human culture is part of the environment we hope to sustain.

The field of "cultural ecology"—which also may be called "human ecology," "ecological anthropology," or more recently "political ecology"—has ancient roots in the observation that differences in human society seem to correlate with differences in physical environment (see, e.g., Thucydides, Hippocrates, and Pliny). Modern interest in the relationship between human society and the environment was driven by the rise of environmentalism in the 1960s in North America and Western Europe. Contributors to this field have mostly come from anthropology and to a lesser extent from geography.

The Nature–Culture Dichotomy

Important cultural ecological research addresses the dichotomy between nature and culture, for example, by critiquing the conception of forests as quintessentially nonhuman. A pioneering, though controversial, contribution was the anthropologist and activist Darrell Posey's 1985 argument that the apparently "natural" forest islands in the Brazilian Amazon were actually created by the Kayapó Indians, whose land rights should thus be respected. More recent and very influential is James Fairhead and Melissa Leach's 1996 study in Guinea, West Africa, which demonstrates that what had been interpreted as forest remnants in an encroaching sea of human-created savanna was actually the expanding product of successful local community efforts to afforest the savanna.

Another body of research focuses on the rationality and functionality of human-livestock relations. In 1940, Edward Evans-Pritchard, for example, used detailed description of daily practices of animal husbandry to rebut earlier charges that African livestock systems irrationally valorized cattle. Irrationality was also the subject of Marvin Harris's famous though also controversial 1966 critique of popular views of the "sacred cow" of India. Using the detailed quantitative data on economics and ecology that came to define ecological anthropology in the 1960s, Harris showed that the sacred character of the cow served to protect vital economic and ecological functions of the livestock system.

Ecology and Social Organization

An enduring question has been the extent to which environment shapes society. An early contribution was Marcel Mauss's 1904 argument that although the winter concentration of seals made Inuit culture and society possible by allowing them to congregate, the environment does not account for Inuit religious, moral, or legal codes, or for the Inuit idea of the collective. This question is differently resolved in Julian H. Steward's influential 1938 study of the Shoshone, another foraging society. Focusing on the organization of human work in the pursuit of subsistence, he argues that the fact that pine nuts can best be harvested by individual families prevents the formation of a higher level of sociocultural integration.

Fredrik Barth broadened Steward's focus on the organization of work to include politics and ethnic relations. Borrowing the idea of the "niche" from animal ecology and applying it to ethnic groups in the Swat Valley, Northern

Pakistan, Barth (1956) showed, for example, that the political system of the Pathan group depended on a crop surplus to feed followers, and that this need for a crop surplus limited Pathan territory to altitudes low enough to support double cropping; the Gujar group graze livestock on hills inside Pathan territory, an ecological niche they are permitted to occupy because the Pathans look down on grazing. Clifford Geertz, in his 1972 comparative analysis of irrigation in Bali and Morocco, goes even further, arguing that the environment is an integral part of the text that is culture. Bali's generous rainfall shapes its highly collective irrigation societies and the complex ritual system that regulates them; in contrast, Morocco's dry and irregular climate shapes an irrigation system based on individual private ownership of water backed by law.

Studies of natural disasters have also been important. Whereas early work in this field focused on how to return the affected societies to equilibrium, cultural ecologists treat disasters as less "natural" and more "social" in origin and less abnormal and more "normal" in character. A seminal contribution was Raymond Firth's 1959 study of cyclones in Tikopia in the Solomon Islands, whose impact he measured in terms of the ability of society to adapt without altering fundamental mechanisms of social integration. Eric Waddell's 1975 study of the impact of severe frosts in highland New Guinea demonstrates, as did Firth's work, the existence of traditional, local means of coping with environmental perturbations.

Methodological Challenges and Debates

Cultural ecologists have borrowed heavily from the natural sciences to strengthen their defense of widely maligned smallholder practices, like swidden (slash-and-burn) agriculture. The most important defense of swidden agriculture in the twentieth century was Harold Conklin's 1957 study of the Hanunóo of Mindoro Island in the Philippines. This uniquely detailed analysis showed the rationality of swidden in local terms, just as other studies showed its lack of attraction, for political-economic reasons, to non-local state elites.

Conklin's initial (1954) research on the Hanunóo was a foundational contribution to ethnobotany, the cross-cultural study of botanical systems. His discovery that the Hanunóo recognized and classified 1,625 different plant types was compelling evidence of the existence of non-Western systems of knowledge and classification no less sophisticated than the Linnaean-based system of modern botanists. Other central works in ethnobotany include those by Brent Berlin et al. (1974) and Richard Ford (1978).

Some cultural ecologists forged powerful linkages with systems theory and cybernetics to defend non-Western environmental logic and critique that of modern industrialized nations. For example, Roy Rappaport's hugely influential 1968 work demonstrated that among Maring-speaking peoples in Papua New Guinea, ritual functioned to maintain biotic communities, redress population/land balances, limit the frequency of fighting, mobilize allies, redistribute pork surpluses, and make protein available to humans when most needed.

One of the criticisms leveled against these ecologically oriented analyses is that their units of analysis—whether "community" or "ecosystem"—are artificially bounded in space and time and ignore the wider political–economic context, especially the state. Repudiation of this bias is exemplified by the work of Robert Netting, who in 1990 critiqued his own earlier (1977) view of a Swiss alpine community as integrated, self-regulating, and self-sufficient.

Politics of Natural Resources and the Environment

The existence of indigenous knowledge of and rights to natural resources has become widely recognized in recent years, although the concept of indigeneity has itself been questioned. For example, in her 2000 work in Sulawesi, Indonesia, Tania Li argues that indigenous status is a narrow target, easily under-shot or over-shot, and thus excludes most people in the countryside. In addition, self-conscious indigenous status often develops only among people who have a history of engagement with, not estrangement from, the wider world. This also applies to the development of self-conscious environmentalism: in his research in Seram in Eastern Indonesia, Roy Ellen (1999) observes that the widening of political and ecological horizons has caused older, local, embedded forms of environmental knowledge to give way to a more explicit, conscious body of knowledge of higher order environmental processes.

The interaction of environmentalists with indigenous groups has drawn critical attention, as in J. Peter Brosius's 1999 study of international environmentalist support for the anti-logging protests of the Penan of Sarawak. The Malaysian government responded to these protests by adopting the international program of timber certification, thereby deflecting international criticism into a bureaucratic and economic discourse that obscured moral and political imperatives. More hopefully, Anna Tsing (1999) has written about the "collaboration" between urban environmentalists and tribal elders in Southeast Kalimantan, in which the latter try to counterbalance the former's disdain for the "primitive" with their simultaneous attraction to the "exotic."

Knowing the Environment

A final topic of cultural ecological study is the relationship between social identity and the sense of place, as exemplified by Charles Frake's 1996 study of East Anglia (U.K.), which reveals identity as linked to aspects of the contemporary landscape that evoke an imagined past. Another example is Maurice Bloch's 1995 study of the Zafimaniry of eastern Madagascar, whose sense of place is revealed through their enjoyment of the views, and the clarity, that is attained through clearing the forest. In both cases, human transformation of nature is essential to both the creation of place out of space and the creation of social identity.

The impact of cultural models on environmental perception is the subject of Tim Ingold's 1993 work on "global" vision, as epitomized by the iconic photo of Earth from space. Ingold argues, counter-intuitively, that this image reflects not the integration of modern society with Earth but its separation from the earth. Gregory Bateson (1904–1980) also carried out pioneering research on this dichotomy, arguing that the conscious human mind cannot comprehend the wider, systemic logic of the environment in which it is situated: "We are not outside the ecology for which we plan—we are always and inevitably part of it. Herein lies the charm and terror of ecology—that the ideas of this science are irreversibly becoming a part of our own ecological system" (1972a, 504).

Michael R. DOVE
Carol CARPENTER
Yale University

FURTHER READING

Barth, Fredrik. (1956). Ecologic relationships of ethnic groups in Swat, North Pakistan. *American Anthropologist, 58*, 1079–1089.

Bateson, Gregory. (1972a). Ecology and flexibility in urban civilization. In *Steps to an Ecology of Mind* (pp. 496–511). New York: Ballantine Books.

Bateson, Gregory. (1972b). Effects of conscious purpose on human adaptation. In *Steps to an Ecology of Mind* (pp. 440–447). New York: Ballantine Books.

Berlin, Brent; Breedlove, Dennis E.; & Raven, Peter H. (1974). *Principles of tzeltal plant classification; An introduction to the botanical ethnography of a Mayan-speaking people of highland Chiapas*. New York: Academic Press.

Bloch, Maurice. (1995). People into places: Zafimaniry concepts of clarity. In Eric Hirsch & Michael O'Hanlon (Eds.), *The Anthropology of Landscape: Perspectives on Place and Space* (pp. 63–77). Oxford, U.K.: Clarendon Press.

Brosius, J. Peter. (1999). Green dots, pink hearts: Displacing politics from the Malaysian rain forest. *American Anthropologist, 101*, 36–57.

Conklin, Harold C. (1954). *The relation of Hanunóo culture to the plant world*. Unpublished doctoral dissertation, Yale University, New Haven, CT.

Conklin, Harold C. (1957). *Hanunóo agriculture: A report on an integral system of shifting cultivation in the Philippines*. Rome: Food and Agriculture Organization of the United Nations.

Dove, Michael R. (1983). Theories of swidden agriculture and the political economy of ignorance. *Agroforestry Systems, 1*, 85–99.

Dove, Michael R. (2006). Equilibrium theory and inter-disciplinary borrowing: A comparison of old and new ecological anthropologies. In Aletta Biersack & James B. Greenberg (Eds.), *Reimagining political ecology* (pp. 43–69). Durham, NC: Duke University Press.

Dove, Michael R., & Carol Carpenter. (Eds.). (2007). *Environmental anthropology: A historical reader*. Boston: Blackwell.

Ellen, Roy. (1999). Forest knowledge, forest transformation: Political contingency, historical ecology and the renegotiation of nature in central Seram. In Tania M. Li (Ed.), *Transforming the Indonesian uplands* (pp. 131–157). Amsterdam: Harwood.

Evans-Pritchard, Edward Evan. (1940). *The Nuer: A description of the modes of livelihood and political institutions of a Nilotic people*. New York: Oxford University Press.

Fairhead, James, & Leach, Melissa. (1996). *Misreading the African landscape: Society and ecology in a forest-savanna mosaic*. Cambridge, U.K.: Cambridge University Press.

Firth, Raymond. (1959). *Social change in Tikopia: Re-study of a Polynesian community after a generation*. London: Allen & Unwin.

Ford, Richard I. (Ed.). (1978). *The nature and status of ethnobotany*. Ann Arbor: Museum of Anthropology, University of Michigan.

Frake, Charles O. (1996). Pleasant places, past times, and sheltered identity in rural East Anglia. In Steven Feld & Keith H. Basso (Eds.), *Senses of place* (pp. 229–257). Santa Fe, NM: School of American Research Press.

Geertz, Clifford. (1972). The wet and the dry: Traditional irrigation in Bali and Morocco. *Human Ecology, 1*, 23–39.

Harris, Marvin. (1966). The cultural ecology of India's sacred cattle. *Current Anthropology, 7*, 51–59.

Hewitt, Kenneth. (1983). The idea of calamity in a technocratic age. In Kenneth Hewitt (Ed.), *Interpretations of calamity from the viewpoint of human ecology* (pp. 3–32). Winchester, MA: Allen & Unwin.

Ingold, Tim. (1993). Globes and spheres: The topology of environmentalism. In Kay Milton (Ed.), *Environmentalism: The view from anthropology* (pp. 31–42). London: Routledge.

Li, Tania M. (2000). Articulating indigenous identity in Indonesia: Resource politics and the tribal slot. *Comparative Studies in Society and History, 42*, 149–179.

Mauss, Marcel, & Beuchat, Henri. (1979). *Seasonal variations of the Eskimo: A study in social morphology* (James J. Fox, Trans.). London: Routledge & Kegan Paul. (Original work published in 1950)

Netting, Robert McC. (1977). *Cultural ecology*. Menlo Park, CA: Cummings.

Netting, Robert McC. (1990). Links and boundaries: Reconsidering the alpine village as ecosystem. In Emilio F. Moran (Ed.), *The Ecosystem approach in anthropology* (pp. 229–245). Ann Arbor: University of Michigan Press.

Posey, Darrell A. (1985). Indigenous management of tropical forest ecosystems: The case of the Kayapó Indians of the Brazilian Amazon. *Agroforestry Systems, 3*, 139–158.

Rappaport, Roy A. (1968). *Pigs for the ancestors: Ritual in the ecology of a New Guinea people*. New Haven, CT: Yale University Press.

Steward, Julian H. (1955). The Great Basin Shoshonean Indians: An example of a family level of sociocultural integration. In *Theory of culture change: The methodology of multilinear evolution* (pp. 101–121). Urbana: University of Illinois Press.

Tsing, Anna L. (1999). Becoming a tribal elder, and other green development fantasies. In Tania Murray Li (Ed.), *Transforming the Indonesian uplands: Marginality, power and production* (pp. 159–202). London: Berg.

Waddell, Eric. (1975). How the Enga cope with frost: Responses to climatic perturbations in the central highlands of New Guinea. *Human Ecology, 3*, 249–273.

Ecology, Deep

First used in 1973 by Norwegian philosopher Arne Naess, the term "deep ecology" refers to a fundamental shift in values, in contrast to the "shallow ecology" of policy reform. Naess pointed the way for people with divergent worldviews to be able to agree on principles leading to concrete environmental activism, but critics of the movement charge that by favoring nature over society its ability to bring about true sustainability is compromised.

Deep ecology is one of the most important contemporary approaches to environmental philosophy. The term was first used in print in the 1973 article "The Shallow and the Deep, Long-Range Ecology Movement" by Arne Naess (1912–2009), a Norwegian philosopher. For Naess, the "shallow ecology" of resource conservation and policy reform was insufficient to deal with our deep-seated environmental problems. What is needed for true sustainability is a fundamental change in the way we conceive of and value the natural world, a change that at least implicitly involves religious values and assumptions. As such, deep ecology is radical in its critique and idealist in its emphasis on worldview rather than social structures.

Meanings and Characteristics

The relationship between deep ecology, sustainability, and spirituality is quite complex, in part because of the various meanings and associations of the terms. There have been, for instance, at least five primary ways the term "deep ecology" has been used. The first is a profound inquiry into the beliefs and values concerning nonhuman nature and our ontological and ethical relationship to

it. No specific views are detailed in this inclusive definition; any thoroughgoing questioning into nature and the human relationship to it would be considered deep ecology. Because of the fundamental character of the questioning, spiritual ideas and values would usually be involved. A second, similarly inclusive meaning derives from the assumption that any such deep questioning will result in one form or another of a philosophy that affirms the profound value of nature, our intimate relationship with it, and our responsibility to it. In some ways, these philosophies can be quite different, such as ecofeminism and social ecology, but whatever the specific goals and practices identified, the ideal is a far more sustainable way of living with nature.

The third meaning of deep ecology is far more pragmatic: a platform of eight principles first articulated by Naess and George Sessions in 1984 (Devall and Sessions 1985). The principles include the intrinsic value of nature and the value of biodiversity; a recognition of the ongoing ruination of the planet; the need to reduce human exploitation of nature; a call for major changes in policy and a decrease in human population; an appreciation of quality of life over material standard of living; and the responsibility to embody these principles by working for personal and social change. The focus on sustainability here is obvious, but the spiritual dimension is implicit in the fact that Naess formulated the platform in part as a way for people with divergent worldviews and spiritual values related to nature to come to agreement on principles that will lead to action. Naess illustrated this with the "apron" diagram, in which a diversity of religious ideas and intuitions at the top can logically support the deep ecology platform, and the platform can logically lead to divergent lifestyles, policies, and actions.

The fourth meaning of deep ecology, probably the most common, is a nature-affirming worldview (called "ecosophy" by Naess) with specific qualities: (1) a holistic view of nature as an interrelated system; (2) the equal intrinsic value of all of nature, often termed "biocentric egalitarianism"; (3) a rejection of anthropocentrism, the human-centeredness that focuses value and attention on humans to the detriment of nature; (4) an affirmation that humans are fully a part of nature with no "ontological divide" or essential difference dividing humans from the natural world; (5) an identification of the individual with the larger natural world, with the person not an autonomous individual but rather a "self-in-Self," a distinct individual who is also fully integrated into the whole of nature, which is our greater Self; and (6) an intuitive communion with nature rather than rational ethical obligations resulting in a spontaneous sense of care for the planet's suffering ("I am the rainforest defending itself," said the deep ecologist John Seed [Devall and Sessions, 1985]). Such ecosophies usually diverge from other approaches such as eco-feminism and social ecology in key points (i.e., that lead, unfortunately, to sectarian squabbles).

Deep ecology sometimes refers to the on-the-ground movement to enact deep ecology principles and values, providing a fifth meaning for the term. Here the focus is on a radically different lifestyle (sometimes in the form of primitivism) or on radical environmental activism—both based on the third and fourth meanings noted in the paragraph above. In this instance, the most famous example is the Earth First! organization. Their goal is not only sustainability or preservation but also the return to a state that existed before humans massively degraded the environment. Usually an Earth-based spirituality informs this movement.

Interest in spiritual attitudes toward nature in other cultures has been a common characteristic of deep ecology, particularly in the last two meanings of ecosophy and radical activism. Buddhist, Daoist, and Native American cultures have been a source of insight into the "new/old" view of nature—suggesting that, while deep ecology is new in terms of Western thought, it draws on long held views in non-Western cultures.

Another key characteristic of deep ecology is its focus on wilderness. Because anthropocentrism is the principal source of human degradation of the natural world, the ideal is often seen as pristine nature untrammeled by human manipulation. Many deep ecologists have considered personal experience of wilderness to be a spiritual encounter that leads to self-in-Self realization through the biocentric identification with nature. The protection of wilderness has also been emphasized by deep ecology, echoing the preservationism of the naturalist John Muir (1838–1914).

Deep Ecology and Sustainability

Given its acute interest in wilderness, deep ecology is profoundly interested in sustainability. But the term *sustainability* is also complex, and to make the analysis of the relationship between deep ecology and sustainability more precise, several distinctions can be made. First, some forms of sustainability are reductive and exploitive, such as a forestry practice that creates a one-crop tree farm where all other vegetation is killed by herbicides until the trees are clear-cut and replanted. Other forms of sustainability are ecological, seeking to conform to nature's processes and complexities and constraints. Deep ecology clearly supports the latter definition of ecological sustainability and offers a comprehensive critique both of the worldview and of the effects of exploitive sustainability.

Second, sustainability can be anthropocentric or biocentric. Most policies aimed at sustainability are focused on the goal of conserving resources for future human generations. Deep ecology rejects such a perspective, calling for the biocentric sustainability of the entire community of life.

A third distinction concerns the range of focus. Sustainability can be limited to environmental issues, dealing only with the preserving the nonhuman natural world. On the other hand, it can be ecosocial, involving social and economic dimensions as well as environmental ones. This "triple bottom line" approach (environmental, social, and economic) is increasingly common, particularly in sustainable development policies, in part because it includes attention to human well-being.

Criticisms

Some deep ecologists might object to this ecosocial perspective because they are worried about slipping into anthropocentrism. However, the ecosocial notion of sustainability can justifiably be used to critique deep ecology. As ecofeminists and social ecologists have argued, at least some versions of deep ecology reveal a multifaceted neglect of human society, crippling its ability to bring about true sustainability. One criticism censures deep ecology's emphasis on worldview as the source of the problem (anthropocentrism) and the ideal (an ecosophy). In this view, environmental problems involve the social dimension in various and essential ways. Some critics would argue, for instance, that political and economic structures, such as industrial capitalism and the nation-state, are principal agents of environmental pillage. Other causes of ecological devastation, some have claimed, are social ideologies (e.g., associating women with nature and devaluing both, or upholding an authoritarian social hierarchy) that enable the exploitation of both people and nature.

As such, critics contend, simply developing an ecocentric worldview and preserving wilderness ignores gross social injustice and will not halt the pillage of the planet. We need political and economic analysis, and we need a change in social ideology and social structures. Such a critique of deep ecology conforms to the ecosocial approach to sustainability, which includes social and economic dimensions as well as environmental.

Other criticisms of deep ecology are more philosophical or psychological. While deep ecology affirms that there is no ontological divide between humans and the rest of nature, it has tended to emphasize human degradation of the environment so much that humans can seem to be inevitably destructive, with no proper place in nature. Thus the responding emphasis on wilderness preservation emerges. Sustainability, however, calls for the sustainable use of the natural world and implies our interactive relationship with it. Deep ecology has praised hunter–gatherer cultures as a model for a sustainable society, but critics reject that ideal as inadequate for a world of over six billion people.

In addition, deep ecology's ideal of self-realization, of the identification with nature and loss of the individual ego, has been criticized by ecofeminists as a masculine ambition of psychological aggrandizement of the world. Similarly, some have argued that such a holistic ideal denies the reality and value of individuals, their relationships, and the community of different selves. Both of these limitations, it could be argued, are contrary to true sustainability.

Synthesis with Other Approaches

At this point it is useful to apply another distinction, between conventional deep ecology and critical deep ecology. *Conventional* deep ecology refers to the views and values that do not respond to the valid criticisms that have been made. It holds to the original principles without significant open-minded engagement with other views. *Critical* deep ecology, on the other hand, refers to a philosophy that adheres to the basic perspective of the philosophy while learning from and interacting with the substantial criticisms that have been made. There are perspectives (e.g., critical Marxism and critical utopianism) that remain within these traditions while at the same time reappraising certain aspects in light of new ideas or divergent views. Critical deep ecology joins self-criticism with the insights of social ecology, ecofeminism, and Christian stewardship.

The distinction between conventional deep ecology and critical deep ecology is certainly not absolute, but, rather, it marks a continuum upon which to locate different versions of deep ecology. The main point is that deep ecology need not be limited to the form that is so often criticized. By learning from other approaches, deep ecology can become even more significant to the notion of sustainability. A number of thinkers have shown how the basic perspective of deep ecology can be enriched by association with other views. Gary Snyder (b. 1930), author of *Turtle Island* and *Practice of the Wild*, for instance, is often heralded as a key deep ecology thinker. But he has always been intensely interested in social issues and has combined his radical environmental philosophy with anarchism. Snyder has criticized preservationists for attempting to freeze specific areas as pristine, in effect treating them like a commodity. Roger S. Gottlieb, who has written and edited a number of books on religion and the environment, has argued for the possibility of a reconciliation of spiritual deep ecology and leftist politics. The social ecologist John Clark has called for a dialectical engagement between deep ecology and social ecology, claiming that deep ecologists can support a social ecological perspective. In addition, it is also possible to show that deep ecology's holism can be articulated as relational rather than monistic, and thus in harmony with ecofeminism's insights about relationality. That is, while deep ecology stresses the unity of the natural world and the importance of thinking in terms of the whole of nature, it does not necessarily deny the distinctness of individuals or the reality and importance of relationships, as some have claimed.

A critical approach to deep ecology makes the methodology more sustainable in two senses. First, the inculcation of social concerns makes it resonant with the ecosocial version of sustainability, and second such a change can help make deep ecology remain a vibrant and enduring approach to environmental philosophy.

As a global community progresses toward a sustainable future, the work of researchers and philosophers in the field of deep ecology will provide an important foundation for the synthesis of environmental, social, and economic debates.

David Landis BARNHILL
University of Wisconsin, Oshkosh

FURTHER READING

Barnhill, David Landis. (2001). Relational holism: Huayan Buddhism and deep ecology. In David Landis Barnhill & Roger S. Gottlieb (Eds.), *Deep ecology and world religions* (pp. 77–106). Albany: State University of New York Press.

Barnhill, David Landis, & Gottlieb, Roger. S. (Eds.). (2001). *Deep ecology and world religion: New essays on sacred ground.* Albany: State University of New York Press.

Clark, John P. (1996). How wide is deep ecology? *Inquiry 39*, 189–201.

Clark, John P. (1998). A social ecology. In Michael Zimmerstein et al. (Eds.), *Environmental Philosophy: From Animal Rights to Radical Ecology* (2nd ed.) (pp. 416–440). Prentice-Hall.

Devall, Bill, & Sessions, George. (1985). *Deep ecology: Living as if nature mattered.* Salt Lake City, UT: Peregrine Smith.

Drengson, Alan, & Inoue, Yuichi. (Eds.). (1995). *The deep ecology movement: An introductory anthology.* Berkeley, CA: North Atlantic Books.

Fox, Warwick. (1990). *Toward a transpersonal ecology: Developing new foundations for environmentalism.* Boston: Shambhala.

Gottlieb, Roger S. (1995). Deep ecology and the left. *Capitalism, Nature, and Society, 6*(3), 1–20.

Gottlieb, Roger S. (1995). Reply to critics. *Capitalism, Nature, and Society, 6*(3), 41–45.

Katz, Eric; Light, Andrew; & Rothenberg, David. (Eds.). (2000). *Beneath the surface: Critical essays in the philosophy of deep ecology.* Cambridge, MA: M.I.T. Press.

Naess, Arne. (1973). The shallow and the deep, long-range ecology movement. A summary. *Inquiry, 16*, 95–100.

Naess, Arne. (1989). *Ecology, community and lifestyle: Outline of an ecosophy* (D. Rothenberg, Trans. and Ed.). Cambridge, U.K.: Cambridge University Press.

Sessions, George, (Ed.). (1995). *Deep ecology for the 21st century.* Boston: Shambhala.

Snyder, Gary. (1990). *The practice of the wild.* San Francisco: North Point Press.

Snyder, Gary. (1974). *Turtle Island.* New York: New Directions Press.

Ecology, Political

Originating in the 1970s from interaction among professionals in cross-disciplinary fields, and strengthened by research conducted from the 1980s to the present, political ecology has evolved to establish a "chain of explanation" that attempts to justify how environmental issues are impacted by political and economic factors in communities rather than by issues of overpopulation, technological introductions, or irrational land management.

Political ecology studies how political, economic, and social factors influence or explain environmental issues. The field originated during the 1970s with the overlapping interests of anthropology and geography; specifically, human ecology, cultural geography, cultural anthropology, and political economics. Important research reported in *Land Degradation and Society*, by Piers Blaikie and Harold Brookfield (1987), has focused on the land management activities of peasant communities in terms of history, economics, and interactions with governments and corporations, rather than on issues of overpopulation or irrational land management practices. The insights of Blaikie and Brookfield, a pioneer in multidisciplinary ecological studies and a development theorist, respectively, suggested that scholars and policy makers follow a "chain of explanation" across interacting scales of ecological and political economic relations.

Thomas Sheridan's *Where the Dove Calls* (1988), for example, examines how the interactions of a rural peasant community in Mexico depend largely upon sustenance farming for its immediate resources. At the local scale, sustenance farming is how individual households throughout the community feed their families and support the community. There are also cattle grazing practices that are subsidized by the state and regional agricultural and food resource agencies. In the years preceding political ecology studies, grazing cattle, as opposed to goat herding, would have been considered irrational, as it seemed too expensive for a localized sustenance economy and an inefficient use of local resources. But by understanding how local practices are influenced by national economic incentives connected to global corporations, political ecology can show that while grazing goats would be far more reasonable for local sustenance practices, grazing cattle brings the local community some revenue from the transnational corporations in the fast-food markets, the global cattle industry, and even the sustainable development policies of the World Bank. As a result, even the faintest subsidy that regional structures can provide the community for its contribution to the global food market is enough to shift the logic of local sustenance farming to the logic of the state and global cattle market.

Sustainability, social and environmental, is critically dependent upon understanding both the systems of resource use and the ways in which resource use determines human relationships across these scales. Issues of sustainability in political ecology grew significantly when the concept of *sustainable development* became central to international agencies like the World Bank, which has a responsibility to fund development and land management practices in many peasant communities and developing nations throughout the globe. The

international community, especially the United Nations focused upon sustainable development in documents, such as the Stockholm Report of 1972, the Brundtland Report of 1982, and the subsequent Earth Summits of Rio in 1992 and Johannesburg in 2002. Political ecologists use these documents and the debates surrounding them in order to discuss the global scale of political ecology as it relates to resource use across nations and local communities.

Critics of political ecology are concerned that the "chain of explanation" fails to explain the ways in which physical ecosystems impact the land management practice. Biodiversity, climate change, and the physical limitations of ecosystems have often been overlooked in political ecology. Other criticisms are concerned with the emphasis of peasant communities and developing nations, while failing to consider local actions of suburban land practices and the ways in which populations in the United States, the European Union, and other industrial nations have impacted the global economy and resource management. More recent applications of political ecology have attempted to meet these criticisms by considering suburbanites as land use managers too, and by including the discussions of climate change and ecological limitations as part of the newer versions of the "chain of explanation."

Robert Melchior FIGUEROA
University of North Texas

FURTHER READING

Biersack, Aletta, & Greenberg, James B. (Eds.). (2006). *Reimagining political ecology (New ecologies for the twenty-first century)*. Durham, NC: Duke University Press.

Blaikie, Piers M., & Brookfield, Harold C. (1987). *Land degradation and society*. London: Methuen.

Forsyth, Timothy. (2002). *Critical political ecology: The politics of environmental science*. New York: Routledge.

Paulson, Susan, & Gezon, Lisa L. (Eds.). (2004). *Political ecology across spaces, scales, and social groups*. Piscataway, NJ: Rutgers University Press.

Peet, Richard, & Watts, Michael. (Eds.). (2007). *Liberation ecologies*, second edition. New York: Routledge.

Robbins, Paul. (2004). *Political ecology: A critical introduction*. Hoboken, NJ: Wiley-Blackwell.

Sheridan, Thomas E. (1998). *Where the dove calls: The political ecology of a peasant corporate community in northwestern Mexico*. Tucson: University of Arizona Press.

Zimmerer, Karl S., & Bassett, Thomas J. (Eds.). (2003). *Political ecology: An integrative approach to geography and environment-development studies*. Lynton, U.K.: Guilford Press.

Ecology, Social

Social ecology is an approach that emphasizes the close linkage of environmental and social problems. A principal cause of both types of problems is political, social, and economic domination. The ideal is libertarian, egalitarian, and decentralized communities that work in harmony with the natural world. In such a view, sustainability must be comprehensive, including social justice and economic security for all.

The term *social ecology* is sometimes used for the general social scientific study of human-environment relationships (Guha 1995). But the term refers more narrowly to a school of radical ecophilosophy initiated in the 1960s by the writer and philosopher Murray Bookchin (1921–2006). The most fundamental insight of this approach is that environmental issues are inseparable from social ones. Social structures and ideologies cause environmental degradation, and environmental ruination harms people and affects different social groups unequally. Any serious examination of environmental issues or sustainability must consider social causes and effects.

Social ecology focuses on the millennia-long tradition of human domination as the principal cause of environmental exploitation as well as social inequities. Domination is found particularly in authoritarian, centralized governments (including ones that claim they are democratic and egalitarian); in a hierarchical society (with distinctions rooted in race, class, gender, or other variables); and in capitalism (which enables certain people to achieve wealth and power at the expense of others and the Earth).

The contrary ideal, then, is a libertarian, egalitarian, and decentralized society that recognizes its intimate and dependent relationship with the natural world. Only this type of society, social ecology would claim, can achieve anything approaching full sustainability.

The most important and distinctive influence in the development of social ecology—particularly as exemplified by the Russian anarchist Peter Kropotkin (1842–1921)—is communitarian anarchism that advocates for individual rights to be balanced with the needs of the community. This type of social ecology aims for a society of free and responsible individuals who recognize that their individual identity is deeply related to the local social group they belong to. Such an ideal can occur only in small social and political units, where a radical, direct democracy or consensus decision-making can take place. Broader issues, from regional to global, would be addressed through a confederation, in which the different communities retain their autonomy but cooperate in dealing with larger scale problems. How such bottom-up confederations can function effectively without ceding authority to a higher political organization is one of the challenges social ecology faces.

Social ecology's focus on decentralism and its goal of harmony with the natural world give it strong similarities to bioregionalism, which focuses on harmony and intimacy with the local ecosystem and emphasizes responsibility to the well-being of the whole community of life there. Both would say that sustainability can only be attained by small-scale societies closely tied to nature. Both emphasize (contrary to some preservationists and deep ecologists) the need for humans to use nature, while insisting any such use must conform to nature's processes and limits.

But social ecology's relationship with sustainability depends on how that term is used. Sustainability can mean a long-lasting system of exploitation of nature seen simply as a source of material wealth, something social ecology would oppose. The goal of sustainability could be (and too often is) that of making an essentially destructive and unjust system more tolerable and enduring, such as capitalism wedded to the nation-state or globalization. On the other hand, a strictly biocentric view of environmental sustainability would be criticized if it did not adequately consider the well-being of all humans. Social ecology insists on a "triple bottom line" approach that includes social justice and economic security for all as well as ecological sustainability. Indeed, the focus on both the social and the ecological makes this approach particularly congruent with the goal of sustainable development.

Social ecology's support for such an inclusive sustainability may or may not be religiously based. Bookchin, influenced by the tradition of Enlightenment rationalism, became a strident opponent of what he considered "irrationalism." In particular, he rejected the Asian and Earth-centered spiritualities common in deep ecology. But other social ecologists, such as John Clark, have recognized that spirituality, including traditions such as Buddhism and Daoism, can enrich social ecology and the type of comprehensive sustainability it champions. In fact, some spiritually based thinkers identified with deep ecology, such as Gary Snyder, display many of the essential values of social ecology. One of the most hopeful developments in social ecology is spiritually informed progressive politics that are open to dialogue with other approaches such as deep ecology, ecofeminism, and stewardship.

David Landis BARNHILL
University of Wisconsin, Oshkosh

FURTHER READING

Barnhill, David Landis. (2008). Gary Snyder's social ecology. *Indian Journal of Ecocriticism, 1*(1), 21–28.

Bookchin, Murray. (1982). *The ecology of freedom: The emergence and dissolution of hierarchy.* Palo Alto, CA: Cheshire Books.

Bookchin, Murray. (2007). *Social ecology and communalism.* Oakland, CA: AK Press.

Clark, John P. (1996, June). How wide is deep ecology? *Inquiry 39*(2), 189–201.

Clark, John P. (1998). A social ecology. In Michael Zimmerman, J. Baird Callicott, Karen J. Warren, Irene J. Klaver, & John Clark (Eds.), *Environmental philosophy: From animal rights to radical ecology* (2nd ed., pp. 416–440). Upper Saddle River, NJ: Prentice-Hall.

Clark, John P. (2005). Social ecology. In Bron Taylor (Ed.), *Encyclopedia of religion and nature* (pp.1569–1571). London: Continuum.

Guha, Ramachandra. (1994). *Social ecology.* Oxford, U.K.: Oxford University Press.

Kropotkin, Peter. (2002). *Anarchism: A collection of revolutionary writings.* Mineola, New York: Dover.

Light, Andrew. (Ed). (1998). *Social ecology after Bookchin.* New York: Guilford Press.

Economics

The beliefs and theories that drive current economic markets and stress the importance of economic growth evolved in an era when it seemed that industrialization and technology could overcome the limits of nature. To address today's environmental problems we need to develop an economic vision rooted in ecology and ethics to support how we democratically guide and individually work within a new economy that sustains our natural resources.

Economics, a formal disciplinary field within the social sciences, concerns the study and analysis of how goods and services are produced, distributed, and consumed. It explores the relationships between economic actors (i.e., sellers, consumers, workers, and investors) and the state and develops rationales for when public intervention in markets or direct public action is justified. As a variegated system of beliefs held by individuals, propagated by corporations, and invoked in political discourse, economics works very much like a religion. Economic beliefs rationalize individual and collective decisions that have important moral implications, give meaning to individual and corporate life, and explain how different people fit and relate to each other in a complex and highly differentiated world. Economics, however, evolved in a period when it appeared that technological change was overcoming the limits of nature. For this reason economic beliefs, as we have known them, neither fit nor work with recent ecological knowledge.

Historical Development

As the separation of church and state began to characterize the early modern era in Europe, there was also a gradual increase in material well-being. Exotic plants brought from the New World by global explorers increased agricultural productivity and improved nutrition; cottage industries arose, and commerce flourished. With states no longer tied to the Catholic Church, rulers began to search for new, secular reasoning to support their existence and actions. Economics as we now know it arose out of this context, augmenting medieval scholastic explanations of right market behavior with new rationales for the relationships among states, producers of goods, and emerging markets. By the eighteenth century, mercantilism became the dominant school of thought. Mercantilism sought to maximize revenues to the state, and ended up patterning the development of a global economy. The state gave trading rights to specific companies for particular areas in return for a share of the companies' monopoly profits. Domestically, too, government-mandated and -enforced market restrictions justified transfers from individuals and companies to sustain government.

Adam Smith, a secular moral philosopher, reasoned that trade between individuals allowed each to become better off. An individual's pursuit of self-interest can promote the public good, but trade restrictions reduce trade's potential benevolence. Thus was born *The Wealth of Nations* (1991 [1776]), in which Smith argues for free markets over state-sanctioned trade restrictions. Smith focused the rationale for state–market relations on the material good of the people and away from the power of the state. Complementing the historical shift toward democracy in general, while drawing on the religious metaphor of markets being guided as if by an invisible hand, the idea of a free-market economy steadily gained currency over the next century. It became the state's role to ensure favorable conditions for markets and do what markets could not do well. Thus states defined and defended property and, to a lesser extent, labor rights. States also assured the public safety and national defense, built roads and collaborated with the private companies in major projects like railroads, and provided for education, as an educated populace benefited all. With this shift toward supporting the private economy, the taxes that funded the activities of the state were seen as hurting the market economy. This led to the notion that perhaps the state should not undertake these collective activities.

Market economies facilitated entrepreneurship that encouraged the development and commoditization of new technologies. Markets and new technologies together dramatically accelerated the increase in material well-being, as well as the possible ways to increase it, for larger numbers of people during the nineteenth and twentieth centuries. During the twentieth century, global population more than tripled, but global economic activity through markets increased by a factor of fifty. The dramatic increases in population and market activity entailed systemic transformations of the ways in which people lived. Whereas most people had been engaged in a range of general activities associated with working the soil, now most were specialists—machinists, hair dressers, lawyers, truck drivers, and scientists, for example—who more and more often were drawn to living in ever-larger cities. Markets and new technologies transformed society and the land, how people related to each other and the environment, and how we understood nature and what it means to be human. Problems arose in communicating across special interests and from differing perspectives within the economic system. As market activity expanded, it became more difficult for individuals to be aware of how their market decisions affected other people and the environment at ever-greater distances. In some Christian denominations the God-fearing were once promised more bountiful crops in the fall and more lambs in the spring. Now, in adapting to the market economy constructed around Adam Smith's insight, some churches have begun to produce prosperity preachers who promise success on the job, better stock picks, and material happiness.

Ecological Impacts of a Market Economy

The social and ecological transformation facilitated by markets and technology has been fueled largely by the combustion of fossil hydrocarbons. Over millennia plants and trees removed carbon dioxide from the atmosphere, while inorganic deposits of carbon were stored in the earth as coal, oil, and natural gas. From the time of the Industrial Revolution this storehouse of energy was increasingly used to fuel transport, warm and cool buildings, and produce electricity for industry, lighting, and modern communications. In addition to depleting a stock resource for material gain, such practices have carelessly transformed environments, driven some species to extinction, and generally threatened life. Releasing carbon dioxide and other greenhouse gases back into the atmosphere is warming the globe faster than species can evolve and ecosystems can adjust. How we have rationalized and expanded the economic system must be addressed in any discussion of social and ecological sustainability.

Most agree that modifying our economy to conserve fossil fuel and explore new alternative technologies is absolutely central to achieving sustainability. Proposed modifications, however, run in opposite directions. The dominant argument of market economists, widely accepted by those who benefit most from the system currently in place, is that we simply need to "perfect" markets so that they balance environmental values with economic values. If we get prices right, they believe, we can shop our way to sustainability. By contrast, market critics argue that the overemphasis on markets in our lives is driving individualism and social fragmentation, materialism over spiritual meaning, and the destruction of nature. Nature, of course, is the book from which scientists learn, the very foundation of our economy, and the basis for much spirituality. In this sense, markets need to be subdued within a richer social organization based on these multiple ways of understanding people and their relations with each other and nature.

The "Shopping Our Way to Sustainability" View

As pro-market economists and their supporters see it, markets only transform the environment in undesirable ways because markets are imperfect. For example, we do not pay for the services of ecosystems, that is, for the benefits provided by healthy soil, forests, waterways, and oceans. If we paid the right price for what nature provides, we would sustain nature. In this view, we need to establish markets for the right to pollute the air and waterways, to use water kept clean and available by good watershed management, and to encourage people to remove carbon dioxide from the atmosphere by growing more trees. By capping the amount of carbon dioxide that can be emitted, distributing emission permits, and letting a carbon market arise, people will pick more efficient cars and wear sweaters when it is cold and shorts when it is hot. With markets for everything, individual choices would aggregate to the public good. Perfectly working markets, it would seem, should be the answer.

Another economic aspect that impacts the public good is the system of property rights. How rights should be established and distributed cannot be determined within the market framework of thinking. Rather, establishing the system of rights requires scientific and moral reasoning apart from the way in which economists read signals about values and scarcity through pricing. Thus, although economists acknowledge that limits need to be placed on the emission of carbon dioxide and other greenhouse gases, they can say nothing about the levels at which they should be set or how emission permits should be distributed. The course the economy follows will be affected by the scientific knowledge and distributive ethics underlying the system of rights.

Some economists, however, are avoiding all serious moral and scientific discussions, arguing that the key to sustainability is simply a matter of adjusting a few prices here and there, pricing ecosystem services, and using the "right" interest rate (the economists' lens on the future). But these economists are trying to determine "right" prices by looking at behavior and surveying preferences of people embedded in the current unsustainable economy. Critics of this approach consider it to be faulty as an economic theory and unwise in practice. In the meantime, advertisements promoting shopping our way to sustainability abound.

The Case for Subduing Markets

Those in favor of subduing markets believe the economy should be redesigned to promote the common good, and they see one way of achieving the common good through multiple forms of social organization. But with the dramatic expansion of markets over the last quarter century, many nonmarket social institutions have been weakened and thus need to be revived to envelope, substantially rebalance, and redirect the economy.

Another important critique made by those concerned with economic reform is that advertisers for market goods are increasingly defining the good life—the purpose of being here on Earth—in terms of material goods. The quantity of goods owned is no longer of primary importance. Rather, we find material-acquisition treadmills for every income, age, and interest group and constant pressure to be at the head of one's respective treadmill by purchasing the latest goods before others do. Such a system is in danger of privileging material consumption over being educated and intellectually curious, or pursuing one's interests in art, or helping the poor, or working for the common good. It will take more than critique to rebuild societies that prioritize nonmaterial and social goals. We need a reinvigorated social organization to define those goals and set the rules for markets so that the economy will help us work toward sustainability.

To some extent, we can see this social reinvigoration underway. Nongovernmental, noncommercial organizations are proliferating and are providing more outlets for working toward the common good. Religious institutions are beginning to address environmental destruction and raise new questions about the global economy. The rebuilding of society around nonmaterial ends, however, needs to be drastically accelerated.

The Problem of Economic Power

Although most people say they are willing to consider having the economy go in a new direction, it is unclear how many are willing to have their own well-being reduced, especially relative to others. For all people, regardless of income and wealth, uncertainty exists in economic reform, but the rich, having more material goods, take more risk in some ways than do the poor. Picking a sustainable path requires that we take into consideration the needs of future generations and assure that they have property rights; to provide them the current generation, rich and poor alike, must give up some, perhaps many, of what have been implicit rights to access nature's services beyond sustainable levels. Most ethical traditions support the notion that those with the most should give up the most to help those with the least.

The problem occurs when people with greater access to nature's services also have economic power that translates into political power. The same is true of corporations. Thus we see powerful public relations and advertising machines constantly delivering the message that the system is fine and that those who question current trajectories are just malcontents, ignorant of how the economic system works and has improved human well-being.

The Larger Economic Dilemma

For the vast majority of the 3 million years since humans became a separate line of primates, people lived in small groups and had shared experiences. Although in the past people did not know nearly as much about the world as we collectively know now, what people knew was common to nearly all; available knowledge could readily inform collective action. During the last one-half of 1 percent of human history, some fifteen thousand years ago, agriculture arose, a surplus developed, and a few people began to assume specialized tasks. Modern science and the modern state began to emerge some five hundred years ago. Yet throughout this time, a majority of the people worked the land and could easily share experiential knowledge.

About 150 years ago, a mere one two-hundredth of 1 percent of human history, natural philosophy began to break into the separate natural sciences and moral philosophy began to break into the separate social sciences. Around this time, the economic theory of markets began to widely influence our economic organization. We also began to formalize how science should inform democratic governance.

Fossil fuels and new combustion technologies became important economic drivers, but agricultural life was still widely shared at that time. The rise of industry and the coordination of production through markets that began in the mid-nineteenth century—a dramatic transformation discussed earlier—have divided people into increasingly specialized occupations with expertise in particular things. With specialization, our collective practical knowledge became widely dispersed among individuals. We have no formal process by which this dispersed knowledge is assembled into an understanding of the whole to inform collective action. Of course, science is now supposed to inform democratic decisions and bureaucratic action, to serve as our common enlightenment. But the same problems of specialization and dispersed knowledge simultaneously arose with the development of modern science.

Thus the modern human dilemma can be described as the challenge of collectively knowing and acting on the whole of our knowledge in a world in which our knowledge, both practical and scientific, is broken up and dispersed among different people. This dilemma is greatly aggravated by our large and growing population, our ability to exploit resources and transform ecosystems, and the multiple ways our actions interconnect with the environment through technologies and markets. The consequences of making mistakes have risen, keeping pace with the increasing dispersion of knowledge among individuals. At the same time, free market ideology has been deployed to shrink the role of government and collective action, whereas corporate interests have cast doubt on public science.

Getting a clear picture of the economy and its role in the current human trajectory is increasingly difficult. Half of the world's population is deeply immersed in the economic system, playing specialized roles and connecting through increasingly distant markets. Specialization in both scientific training and experiential knowledge gained through our economic roles makes it more and more difficult for a single individual to begin to see and understand the system as a whole. Furthermore, the economy is increasingly becoming people's lens on reality. Things are important in accordance with how people relate to them through the economy. Changing prices signal abundance or scarcity, telling people not only what to consume or conserve but in which areas to seek education, invest capital, and transform the land. In science, certainly among conservation biologists, market valuation techniques are becoming an essential way of expressing value to the public and aggregating environmental impacts in scientific analyses. The economy has become our window on nature.

Putting Economic Progress in Perspective

The dominant narratives underlying modern forms of consciousness have humankind proceeding along a path of progress. In some narratives, derived from some descriptions within the Judeo-Christian holy books, people are described as being above nature and are able to become even more God-like as they continue to progress morally. The philosopher and statesman Francis Bacon (1581–1626) augmented moral transcendence with knowledge transcendence, adding the narrative that through intentional advances in human understanding, people could attain a God's-eye view of how the world worked. They then could use this understanding to improve material well-being and, in essence, become more God-like in the process. Some futurists enthusiastically portray a time when genetically engineered, more God-like, genius-people will become entirely independent of ecological systems.

Economic progress, an ever-advancing gross domestic product, and the triumph of global markets and capitalism have become the most important carriers of transcendent messages feeding the modern consciousness in public discourse. The economic system, while numbing us to its socially and environmentally destructive forces, now sustains our transcendent narratives rooted in religious traditions. Thus, for some, to critique economic growth takes on the form of blasphemy. Yet following our current growth-at-all-costs economic path, which points to the depletion of natural resources and the extinction of many species, and perhaps of humans as well, can hardly be seen as transcendent narrative. This point needs to be refined and repeatedly communicated to policy makers and the public.

We need new economic ways of thinking and a fresh approach to organizing our social structure if we are to address environmental problems facilitated by past economic ways of thinking and organizing. An excessive focus on individual consumption of material goods and excessive specialization and globalized markets will prevent us from systemically understanding and responding to the human dilemma.

Richard B. NORGAARD
University of California, Berkeley

FURTHER READING

Costanza, Roberta; Cumberland, John; Daly, Herman; Goodland, Robert; & Norgaard, Richard. (1997). *An introduction to ecological economics.* Baton Rouge, FL: Saint Lucie Press.

Daly, Herman. E., & Cobb, John B. (1994). *For the common good: Redirecting the economy toward community, the environment, and a sustainable future.* Boston: Beacon Press.

Nelson, Robert Henry. (1991). *Reaching for heaven on Earth: The theological meaning of economics.* Savage, MD: Rowman and Littlefield.

Smith, Adam. (1991). *The wealth of nations* (3rd ed., unabridged). Amherst, NY: Prometheus Books. (Original publication date 1776)

Speth, James Gustave. (2008). *The bridge at the edge of the world: Capitalism, the environment, and crossing from crisis to sustainability.* New Haven, CT: Yale University Press.

Ecopsychology

A relatively new discipline, ecopsychology draws on psychology, ecology, and environmental philosophy to strengthen human relationships and connections with nature, with the goal of a healthier, more sustainable society.

Ecopsychology is an interdisciplinary field of thought and practice combining psychology, ecology, and environmental philosophy. Ecopsychologists apply ecological insights to psychotherapeutic practice, study human emotional bonds with Earth, search for an ecologically based standard of mental health, and develop radical critiques of modern culture and society based on insights gained from these activities. Inspired by the wisdom of ancient and modern non-Western cultures, ecopsychologists seek to build more intimate and spiritual relationships with nonhuman nature. Like transpersonal ecology, ecopsychology considers the human psyche or mind to be part of the natural world, even transcending individual bodies. Like deep ecology, ecopsychology fosters a sense of self that identifies with all of nature—the "ecological self"; thus, harm to nonhuman nature is harm to humans. Ecopsychology differs from environmental psychology by rejecting traditional empirical methods and their claim to scientific objectivity. Whereas environmental psychology is a subfield of conventional academic psychology, and deep ecology was developed primarily by academic philosophers (and transpersonal ecology builds on deep ecology with psychological theory), ecopsychology is inspired by a broader range of both academic and nonacademic sources from philosophy to psychotherapy and wilderness experiences, and more explicitly incorporates spirituality.

Modern human alienation from nature and the ensuing global environmental crisis harm modern people psychically, ecopsychologists say; such traumatic separations themselves in turn contribute to further environmental degradation. Practices that attempt to address alienation from nature and the pain, despair, and anger that result from knowledge and experience of environmental devastation include ecotherapy (ecologically attuned psychotherapy), deep ecology workshops, wilderness encounter sessions, and "councils of all beings." Deep ecology workshops, which aim to retrieve feelings of interconnectedness with the rest of nature through nature-encounter exercises, poetry, and music, can overlap significantly with the practice of "councils of all beings," in which participants temporarily set aside their human identities and speak on behalf of other life forms. These are examples of "re-Earthing" rituals that seek to foster joy, commitment, and inspiration through reconnection with Earth. Immediate nonverbal experiences with nature are seen as therapeutic for individuals and essential to ecologically respectful living and the development of new strands of environmental activism.

Ecopsychology is new. Although psychologist Robert Greenway advanced the notion of psycho-ecology as early as 1963, the field did not attract widespread attention until the social historian Theodore Roszak introduced the term ecopsychology in 1992 in *The Voice of the Earth*. The book turns on the idea of the "ecological unconscious"—the inherited "living record of cosmic evolution" that must be nurtured in childhood and the repression of which is "the deepest root of collusive madness in industrial society" (Roszak 1992, 320). More recently, the psychotherapist Andy Fisher has sought to build a radical ecopsychology that weaves together several currents: psychological theory that integrates the human psyche into nature; philosophy that counters human-nature dualism and calls for experiential knowledge of nature through phenomenology; therapeutic practice that recollects the human place in nature through experiences such as vision quests; and criticism that builds on socially radical views from both ecology and psychology (Fisher 2002). Although ecopsychology has yet to attain mainstream status even within the environmental movement, and its theorists and practitioners are limited mainly to Western Europe (predominantly Great Britain), North America, and Australia, Fisher

and other ecopsychologists are hopeful about the future of their movement; they continue to make progress in bringing coherence to this ambitiously broad field and in transforming human-nature relationships through their practices.

Kenneth WORTHY
Independent scholar, Berkeley, California

FURTHER READING

Fisher, Andy. (2002*). Radical ecopsychology: Psychology in the service of life*. Albany: State University of New York Press.

Kidner, David W. (2001). *Nature and psyche: Radical environmentalism and the politics of subjectivity*. Albany, NY: State University of New York Press.

Macy, Joanna. (1991). *World as lover, world as self*. Berkeley, CA: Parallax Press.

Roszak, Theodore. (1992). *The voice of the Earth: An exploration of ecopsychology*. New York: Simon & Schuster.

Roszak, Theodore; Gomes, Mary E.; & Kanner, Allen D. (Eds.). (1995). *Ecopsychology: Restoring the Earth, healing the mind*. San Francisco: Sierra Club Books.

Winter, Deborah DuNann. (1996). *Ecological psychology: Healing the split between planet and self*. New York: HarperCollins College Publishers.

Ecovillages

Developed during the late 1960s, ecovillages are envisioned as socially and environmentally sustainable communities. Often self-sufficient, these alternative settlements emphasize and support the close interconnection between humans and nature.

The inhabitants of an ecovillage generally set out to define and balance the needs of a human community with the ecological resources of their immediate environment and with an active integration of the community in that environment. Creating and maintaining conditions necessary for the social, economic, and spiritual functioning of a small village, ecovillages rely on small-scale interactions among individuals and between humans and their environment, and on large-scale networks to achieve sustainability and foster community. In a definitive article, Robert Gilman (1991) describes ecovillages as "human-scale, full-featured settlement[s] in which human activities are harmlessly integrated into the natural world in a way that is supportive of healthy human development and can be successfully continued into the indefinite future."

To achieve such social conditions, ecovillage inhabitants limit their numbers, often to populations between 150 and 500 people, so that members know one another and maintain direct political influence on the community. While ecovillages strive toward self-sufficiency, not all settlements are isolated and many participate in larger networks of communities, including resource and information-sharing networks like the Global Ecovillage Network and regional networks like Sarvodaya in Sri Lanka. Ecovillages integrate themselves into their environments by utilizing organic, noninvasive agricultural practices that use perennial systems (seasonal rotation of crop and land use) to maintain food supplies and ecosystem cycles throughout the year. By reducing their demand for goods outside the scope of the ecovillage, inhabitants further reduce environmental stress caused by the production and transport of those goods. The close relationship between an ecovillage and its ecosystem affects measures taken to support human development and community sustainability by linking the well-being of citizens to the village's agrarian economy and to the well-being of its natural and built surroundings.

Ecovillages arose from several models of intentional communities, religious and secular, combined with the increasing concern for and interest in the environment, beginning in the late 1960s with the establishment of The Farm in Summertown, Tennessee, and several similar alternative communities. The term "ecovillage," however, equally applies to both much older and much newer communities in which citizens combine intentionality (a commitment on the part of inhabitants to one another, the community, and the environment to collaborate in a responsive and respectful way) with environmental concern and action. While the ecovillage movement has ties to communes, religious communities, and other alternative communities, the diversity of settlements reflects the variety of methods used to engage the environment on a small, human scale while creating an equitable, spiritually fulfilling, and sustainable community. According to www.ecovillage.org, 440 ecovillages exist worldwide as of 4 June 2009. The communal nature of ecovillages tends to focus their efforts internally, but online networks like this website could facilitate more international collaboration.

Luke H. BASSETT
Yale Divinity School

FURTHER READING

Bang, Jan Martin. (2007). *Growing eco-communities: Practical ways to create sustainability.* Edinburgh, U.K.: Floris Books.

Dawson, Jonathan. (2006). *Ecovillages: New frontiers for sustainability.* Totnes, U.K.: Green Books.

Global Ecovillage Network. (2009). Retrieved on July 6, 2009, from gen.ecovillage.org

Gilman, Robert. (1991). The eco-village challenge. *Context*, 29, 10–14. Retrieved August 4, 2009, from http://www.context.org/ICLIB/IC29/Gilman1.htm

Miles, Malcolm. (2008). *Urban utopias: The built and social architectures of alternative settlements.* New York: Routledge.

Sarvodaya. (2009). Retrieved July 6, 2009, from www.sarvodaya.org

Education

Institutions of higher education, like all elements of contemporary society, must address the question of sustainability. But the issue for universities is greater than teaching about the environment; their commitment must also include research and policy formation for better solutions as well as improved, more sustainable operational systems, including energy consumption and waste reduction.

Scientific evidence suggests that at the turn of the millennium, Earth's ecosystems cannot sustain current levels of global economic activity and material consumption, let alone increased levels. The impact of a rapidly changing environment continues to force a reexamination of the paradigm in which society currently functions. Despite access to the continuous research that has lead to detailed knowledge of the complex ecological interdependencies and indicators of environmental degradation, society continues to act in ways that have a devastating impact on the ecological community and human health. The global economy increasingly is placing more and more pressure upon our natural resource base while the world population is projected to grow nearly two thirds by the year 2020. As of July 2009 the Earth sustained an estimated 6.79 billion people and population continues to rise; the size of the Earth obviously remains the same (CIA 2009).

Our educational system is designed to contribute to the well-being of society at the present and into the future through the creation and dissemination of knowledge and the education of its citizenry. The challenge at hand is to understand and determine how best to design our educational systems in a manner that both contributes to and, in essence, designs a sustainable future. One broad-level approach is shaped by the United Nations Educational, Scientific, and Cultural Organization (UNESCO), which proposes that the goal of the United Nations Decade of Education for Sustainable Development (2005–2014) is implement a process to:

> . . . make decisions that consider the long-term future of the economy, ecology and equity for all communities; to reorient education systems, policies and practices in order to empower everyone, young and old, [and] to make decisions and act in culturally appropriate and locally relevant ways to redress the problems that threaten our common future. (De Rebello, 2003)

This statement begs the question as to whether our educational systems are equipped and designed to achieve the goals outlined by UNESCO in 2005. Fifteen years prior to this proposed approach, the Talloires Declaration was written and endorsed in 1990 by an international group of twenty leading university presidents and administrators. Early on, the Talloires Declaration presented ten principles and actions to incorporate environmental sustainability into the academic missions and operational functions of colleges and universities alike; these principles still resonate with institutions twenty years later. With the endorsement of the Talloires Declaration by a collective of university leaders, higher education began the arduous yet now popular process of tackling these unprecedented environmental and sociopolitical circumstances. Higher education was challenged to find a voice and a place from which to contribute to the meaning and application of the principles of sustainable development via operational systems, educational models, and scholarship. For institutions of higher education to facilitate the transition to a more sustainable future, new institutional examples needed to be created and implemented in an effort to model for other organizations how to prioritize sustainability principles as a grounding framework for decision making and policy.

Higher education's commitment to sustainable development has a wide range of benefits spanning from the local to the global level. The movement among universities to become "sustainable" tends to manifest in the implementation of environmental concerns primarily through operational functions. Such initiatives have focused upon energy consumption, waste reduction strategies, procurement, land management, water use, and transportation. For example, campuses may now integrate renewable energy sources to power their buildings. Facilities may be cleaned with products certified by Green Seal (a nonprofit certification entity) and are less toxic to human and environmental health. Landscapes may be managed with low impact materials while buildings may be built to carbon-neutral standards.

Educational institutions that are taking on the challenge of developing a sustainable campus must raise numerous critical questions that call upon a multidisciplinary response. Some examples of these include:

• Can colleges and universities internalize the limitations and capacities of the Earth's natural life support systems, and if so, how?
• How ought the institutional systems and processes that lead to a sustainable system be shaped?
• How do we know when a campus is sustainable? What will it take?

These questions illustrate the complex nature of the challenge at hand and begin to frame the educational objectives that are necessary. Integrating sustainability into a university requires a process that reconciles a shared vision of a sustainable institution with the complexity, abstraction, depth, and moral and ethical implications that sustainability purports. The next set of questions is grounded in what it means to be a sustainable system. These are complex questions that require new knowledge, long-term thinking, and risk analysis:

• What ratio of renewable to non-renewable energy should a campus use?
• How do we define a sustainable food system for a campus?
• What parking/transit ratio should we strive for?
• How do we reduce our greenhouse gas emissions?
• How can integrated campus design advance sustainable development?

The combination of these two sets of questions begins to shape that which is called upon by education for sustainable development. Ultimately, a sustainable campus is one that not only focuses upon operational systems but recognizes the multidisciplinary educational opportunities implicit and essential in the process. The opportunity lies in embracing innovative operational systems that move

the university to becoming a "steward" capable of taking deliberate action and considering its impact on a scale that spans local to global and present to future. A university that integrates sustainability into curriculum, research, and operations requires more than just the implementation of education about sustainability to change behavior—it requires a transformed system that welcomes complexity, fosters integration, and rewards cross-disciplinary thinking.

Since the creation and signing of the Talloires Declaration in 1990, universities nationally and internationally have made great strides in laying the foundation for sustainable campuses. Beginning with their own sector-specific international declaration in 1990, colleges and universities became committed participants in the global push for sustainability. Since that time, higher education institutions have begun to establish a plan of action and have committed resources to fulfill their potentials as sustainability leaders over the past decade and predominantly since 2004. Examples of engaged campuses range from public and large private research institutions to small liberal arts colleges. As the training ground for leaders in business, policy, international affairs, and every other sector linked to issues of sustainability, higher education has the power to develop, study and implement scaleable models that can be adopted and shared by other sectors. The inherent role of research and intellectual capital give higher education a respected and far-reaching voice, a voice that can be used to drive ambitious sustainable change.

Julie NEWMAN
Yale University

FURTHER READING

Blewitt, John, & Cullingford, Cedric. (2004). *Sustainability curriculum: The challenge for higher education*. Sterling, VA: Earthscan.

Central Intelligence Agency (CIA). (2009). The world factbook. Retrieved August 17, 2009, from https://www.cia.gov/library/publications/the-world-factbook/geos/xx.html

Corcoran, Peter Blaze, & Wals, Arjen E. J. (Eds.). (2004). *Higher education and the challenge of sustainability: Problematics, promise, and practice*. Dordrecht, The Netherlands: Kluwer Academic Publishers.

De Rebello, Daphné. (2003). What is the role of higher education in the UN Decade of Education for Sustainable Development? Paper presented at the International Conference on Education for a Sustainable Future: Shaping the Practical Role of Higher Education for Sustainable Development. Retrieved May 27, 2009, from http://www.unesco.org/iau/sd/pdf/Rebello.pdf

Doppelt, Bob. (2003). *Leading change toward sustainability: A change-management guide for business, government and civil society*. Sheffield, U.K: Greenleaf Publishing.

Edwards, Andres R. (2005). *The sustainability revolution: Portrait of a paradigm shift*. Gabriola Island, Canada: New Society Publishers.

M'Gonigle, Michael, & Starke, Justine. (2006). *Planet U: Sustaining the world, reinventing the university*. Gabriola Island, Canada: New Society Publishers.

Energy

Energy use has been considered a moral and theological issue only since the 1970s. While many religious writers focus on the facts of energy use, many more are reviewing it not only technically but also from political, social, and ethical viewpoints. Most debated is the issue of nuclear energy; currently there is little consensus on its safety or ethical use.

Energy use is both a blessing and a curse. On the one hand, access to energy, especially high-quality energy sources such as fossil fuels and electricity (typically generated from fossil fuels, nuclear fuels, or moving water) enables higher levels of health care, education, and economic success. On the other hand, this same energy use causes environmental and social disruption in the form of mountaintop removal, smog, acid rain, climate change, cancers, and asthma. Yet it was only recently that energy use was recognized as a moral and theological issue. The advent of nuclear power sparked conversation about energy ethics, but it was not until the oil crisis and rising environmentalism of the 1970s that energy significantly entered religious and ethical literature. Religious people have shown their concern about energy use by investigating the technical details of energy production and consumption as well as the political and social ramifications of its use. Additionally, ethicists have developed moral positions on energy use, typically based on existing environmental and social ethics such as concern for the poor and powerless. From this work, many faith-based energy conservation movements have arisen. While religious environmentalists of all faiths are fairly unified in their support of conserving energy, decreasing the use of fossil fuels, and encouraging justice and widespread participation

in decision making about energy use, the ethics of nuclear energy are much more contentious.

Religious Education about Energy

Since the mid-1970s popular journals for a religious audience such as *Christian Social Action, Christianity and Crisis, Church and Society, Engage/Social Action, National Catholic Reporter, Sojourners, U.S. Catholic,* and *Witness* have devoted significant space to educating their readers about the basic facts of energy production and consumption. Common topics include statistics about energy use, available energy reserves, and comparisons of energy consumption by country or region. For example, the United States has approximately 5 percent of the world's population but uses about 25 percent of the world's energy. Fossil fuels accounted for approximately 82 percent of the world's marketed energy use as of 2002 and are highly disruptive to the environment and human health. The extraction, processing, and use of fossil fuels cause mountaintop removal, smog, and acid rain, as well as significant increases in rates of asthma, cancer, and other diseases. According to the Intergovernmental Panel on Climate Change, fossil fuel use accounts for 56.6 percent of the anthropogenic greenhouse effect driving climate change (Synthesis Report 2007, 36). Consequently, environmental and social disruption caused by energy use will only increase as climate change worsens. Popularizing facts such as these has been a major part of religious writings on energy; authors want their audience to recognize the negative ramifications of energy use.

Religious ethicists also educate their readers about alternatives to fossil fuels, especially conservation and renewable energy sources including wind and solar. Some also endorse nuclear power, though others vehemently oppose its use due to concerns about safety and justice. Finally, some endorse or critique existing energy legislation, although religious journals typically avoid explicit policy analysis.

Morality and Theology

While educating readers about the technical details of energy use has been a major focus of religious writings on energy, such texts also explore why energy should be a moral issue. To date, religious ethicists have treated energy as a subset of other environmental and social concerns such as biodiversity loss, water pollution, and hunger. Thus, existing theological ethics about energy tend to depend on what preexisting assumptions about the relationship of nature, people and God, gods, or the Ultimate imply for human responsibility—or how the extension of traditional concern for the poor and powerless can be extended to concern for those harmed by environmental degradation.

This article only addresses a few of the reasons why various religious traditions wish to sustain the environment and thus value sustainable energy. Concern for the environment may be rooted in the belief that God created the world good or that the world is ultimately God's, not humanity's. Religious environmental ethics may also be founded on the interdependence of all life, the flow of qi, or the Dao. Belief in sacred lands, the gods in the form of natural entities, and reincarnation may also inform the ecological sensitivities of religious believers. These sorts of beliefs ground the value of humanity and the environment, prompting an energy ethic since energy use can be so helpful and harmful.

Because religious traditions including Buddhism, Christianity, Confucianism, Daoism, Islam, and Judaism prioritize the needs of the poor in their ethics, discussions of energy use rooted in theological ethics may also revolve around concern for the poor and powerless. Thus some religious ethicists focus on the injustice of uneven distribution of affordable access to high-quality energy between countries or among the people within any one country. The use of high-quality energy sources such as electricity, natural gas, and oil enables cooked food and refrigeration, water sanitation, and the basic heating and cooling of homes. When women and children use high-quality energy and no longer have to spend hours a day gathering firewood or trash for fuel, they have more time for education and more time to work for money. Additionally, when high-quality fuels are used, organic matter remains in fields and forests to increase crop yields and decrease environmentally destructive runoff. Thus high-quality energy use enables people to have better nutrition, healthcare, incomes, and educational levels while preserving their local environment.

While increasing energy use can significantly benefit the poor and powerless, they are the first to suffer from the negative side effects of energy use, even if they are not the primary energy consumers. They are more likely to work in or live near environmentally disturbed areas such as mines, refineries, or highways as well as in areas most vulnerable to climate change. Unfortunately, their lack of information, money, time, or political power makes it difficult for many to fight such problems or to choose to work or live elsewhere. Consequently, those who use the least high-quality energy bear the burden of its use; as such justice (or injustice) with respect to the benefits and harms of energy use is a growing focus of religious energy ethics.

Action

For all of these reasons, and many others, religious people encourage action around energy issues. Individual or local activism is most popular and is often encouraged through lists of energy-saving tips: use compact fluorescent light bulbs; weatherize buildings; use energy-efficient appliances; walk or use public transportation; drive an energy-efficient vehicle.

While these activities have been encouraged since the oil crisis of the 1970s, Interfaith Power and Light, started in 1997 as Episcopal Power and Light by Sally Bingham and Steve McAusland, dramatically increased the number of religious organizations conserving energy. Interfaith Power and Light now includes twenty-eight state organizations comprised of over 4,000 congregations representing a cross section of religions in America: Buddhists; Muslims; Jews; evangelical, mainline, and liberal Protestants; and Roman Catholics. Interfaith Power and Light provides moral support, role models, and technical advice to help religious organizations conserve energy, buy renewable-generated electricity, or to advocate for energy and environmental legislation.

While the efforts of individuals or religious organizations to conserve energy are significant, some ethicists emphasize that individual changes are not enough; society as a whole also needs to be transformed. Theological ethicists such as James A. Nash, Ian G. Barbour, and others recognize that laws are necessary to encourage zoning friendly to mass transportation, incentives for conservation, renewable energy development, and recycling, and cap-and-trade systems in which businesses have financial incentives to reduce pollutants. These measures will be necessary to preserve energy and the planet for future generations while meeting the needs of the present.

Nuclear Controversy

While most religious environmentalists are united in their support of conservation and alternatives to fossil fuels, there has been and is much less agreement about the ethics of nuclear energy. Many popular articles illustrate this debate as does *Nuclear Energy and Ethics,* a compilation of views on nuclear energy sponsored by the World Council of Churches. The most common argument against nuclear energy centers on its safety. Radioactive material must be safely mined, refined, manufactured into fuel rods or pellets, and transported to power plants before any energy is harnessed. Power plants themselves must be well designed, maintained, and operated to prevent nuclear plant accidents. Additionally, the spent fuel and other contaminated wastes must be stored for tens of thousands of years to prevent air, water, and land contamination as well as harm to biota, including humans.

These technical challenges cause some ethicists to question whether it is possible to safely utilize nuclear energy and whether it is moral to saddle hundreds of future generations with the responsibility of managing our nuclear waste. The environmentalist and philosopher Kristin Shrader-Frechette observes that Egyptians have been unable to keep their tombs safe for three to four thousand years and thus wonders how humans could keep nuclear waste sites safe for tens of thousands of years amid wars, natural disasters, and social change (Shrader-Frechette 1991, 182).

Others, such as Gordon S. Linsley, a scientist at the International Atomic Energy Agency, argue that there are effective strategies for containing radioactive wastes. Linsley also maintains that the risk of harm from nuclear waste storage is often less than the risks from storing toxic chemicals and heavy metals. If society is willing to accept these risks, he argues, it should also be willing to accept the relatively lower risks of nuclear waste.

The marked difference in the risk assessment of nuclear energy stems in part from a tendency for the public to be more wary of risks that are involuntary, unfamiliar, and catastrophic, as a nuclear accident could be, while technical experts tend to focus on numerical assessments alone. Balancing these two perspectives is an enormous challenge.

The site-selection process for long-term nuclear waste storage facilities also raises moral questions. Should communities accept nuclear waste and the monetary compensation that comes with it to move their communities out of poverty?

The place of nuclear energy in developing countries is also a contentious issue. Some, such as the pathologist Carlos Araoz, the physicist Bena-Silu, and the nuclear physicist B. C. E. Nwosu, see nuclear energy as a sound way to increase the energy use of developing countries and subsequently increase their health, education, and economic power. Others, including environmental epidemiologist Rosalie Bertell and Achilles del Callar strongly oppose nuclear for safety reasons. They think that energy development in developing nations should follow a renewable, conservation-oriented path in order to avoid the problems of energy use in the developed world and the debt necessary for capital-intensive nuclear power. This debate ultimately hinges on the assessment of the risks of nuclear energy and questions of fairness between developing and developed nations, particularly whether the short-term needs of developing countries or the global, long-term environment should be prioritized if the two conflict.

Of course, energy carriers are not chosen in a vacuum; decisions are made between nuclear, fossil fuels, and renewables. In this milieu, nuclear energy gains supporters more concerned about imminent global warming from fossil fuels than long-term nuclear waste storage. Others are unwilling to accept the long-term risks of nuclear wastes. As yet there is no consensus among religious ethicists, environmentalists, or lay people about the safety and morality of nuclear energy, and none is expected soon.

Future Challenges

Despite the widespread controversy over nuclear energy, religious environmentalists generally agree about the necessity of conservation, of moving away from fossil fuels, and of focusing on justice. Future energy sustainability will require more thought about the morality of nuclear energy and the appropriate energy path for developing and developed countries. Attention must also be given to the theological and moral importance of individual *and* societal action. Finally, connecting energy sustainability

to theological issues beyond creation and justice will enable energy sustainability to be thoroughly integrated in the lives and beliefs of religious people.

Sarah E. FREDERICKS
University of North Texas

FURTHER READING

Araoz, Carlos. (1991). Setting the problem of nuclear energy in the developing world context. In Kristin Shrader-Fréchette, (Ed.), *Nuclear Energy and Ethics* (pp. 72–78). Geneva: WCC Publications.

Barbour, Ian G.; Brooks, Harvey; Lakoff, Sanford; & Opie, John. (1982). *Energy and the American values.* New York: Praeger.

Barbour, Ian G. (1993). *Ethics in an age of technology* (1st ed.). San Francisco: HarperSanFrancisco.

Bena-Silu. (1991). Nuclear technology today: Promises and menaces. In Kristin Shrader-Fréchette, (Ed.), *Nuclear Energy and Ethics* (pp. 55–65). Geneva: WCC Publications.

Bertell, Rosalie. (1991). Ethics of the nuclear option in the1990s. In Kristin Shrader-Fréchette, (Ed.), *Nuclear Energy and Ethics* (pp. 161–181). Geneva: WCC Publications.

Copeland, W. R. (1980). Ethical dimensions of the energy debate: The place of equity. *Soundings, 63*(2), 159–177.

del Callar, Achilles. (1991). The impact and safety of commercial nuclear energy: Perspectives from the Philippines. In Kristin Shrader-Fréchette, (Ed.), *Nuclear Energy and Ethics* (pp. 66–71). Geneva: WCC Publications.

Hessel, Dieter T. (1978). *Energy ethics: A Christian response.* New York: Friendship Press.

Hilton, F. G. Hank. (2001, May 28). Energy and morality 20 years later. *America, 184*(18), 18. Retrieved March 25, 2009, from http://americamagazine.org/content/article.cfm?article_id=930

Intergovernmental Panel on Climate Change. (2007). *Climate change 2007 synthesis report.* Retrieved May 25, 2009 from http://www.ipcc.ch/pdf/assessment-report/ar4/syr/ar4_syr.pdf

Linsley, Gordon. (1991). Radioactive wastes and their disposal. In Kristin Shrader-Fréchette, (Ed.), *Nuclear Energy and Ethics* (pp. 29–54). Geneva: WCC Publications.

Nwosu, B. C. E. (1991). Issues and experiences concerning nuclear energy and nuclear proliferation. In Kristin Shrader-Fréchette, (Ed.), *Nuclear Energy and Ethics* (pp. 79–88). Geneva: WCC Publications.

O'Neill, John, & Mariotte, Michael. (2006, June 16). Nuclear power: Promise or peril. *National Catholic Reporter*, 17–18.

Shrader-Fréchette, Kristin. (Ed.). (1991). *Nuclear energy and ethics.* Geneva: WCC Publications.

Smil, Vaclav. (2003). *Energy at the crossroads: Global perspectives and uncertainties.* Cambridge, MA: MIT Press.

Tester, Jefferson W.; Drake, Elisabeth M.; Driscoll, Michael J.; Golay, Michael W.; & Peters, William A. (2005). *Sustainable energy: Choosing among energy options.* Cambridge, MA: MIT Press.

United Nations Development Programme. (2005). *Energizing the millennium development goals.* New York.

Eschatology

Doctrines regarding eschatology—beliefs about the "end-times"—have been accused of denigrating the Earth in preference for a future paradise. In actuality, however, eschatological texts and traditions are more complex than this accusation would suggest and have provided inspiration for both the support and the subversion of sustainability.

The term "eschatology" (from the Greek *eschata*, meaning "last things") refers to religious and philosophical doctrines concerning the ultimate fate of the cosmos and the collective destiny of humanity. Although speculation concerning the interim fate of individual souls after death may be included within an eschatological doctrine, it is the corporate destiny of the world that forms eschatology's primary theme.

Origins in Holy Texts

While most religions contain some speculation about the future of the cosmos, in many cases these are "relative" eschatologies only, since no ultimate end of history is envisioned but only the relative end of one cosmic cycle followed by an endless repetition of successive cycles. In both Hinduism and Buddhism, for instance, cosmic epochs of growth and decay are said to come to a temporary end when the universe is annihilated. This annihilation is followed by a rebirth in which the epochal cycles of growth and decay begin again. In contrast, the Abrahamic religions (Judaism, Christianity, and Islam) present history as a linear progression in which the current age will come to a final end or edge (*eschaton*) beyond which something fundamentally new will occur.

Within Judaism, eschatological texts do not appear before the Second Temple period (536 BCE–70 CE). Biblical

texts written during the First Temple period (1006–587 BCE) make no mention of an "end-time" and say very little about an afterlife. Heaven, within these texts, is the exclusive abode of God and His angelic retinue, not a reward for the righteous (Psalms 115:16). Two possible exceptions to human exclusion from heaven exist: Enoch, who is ambiguously "taken" by God (Genesis 5:24), and Elijah, who is unambiguously lifted up to heaven in a whirlwind (2 Kings 2:11). These exceptions, however, are not presented as models that can be emulated by others. On the contrary, the rest of humanity is said to share a common home after death (Job 3:11–19). Most frequently, this home is located in Sheol, a place beneath the ground, which is pictured as dark, gloomy, and disordered but not as a location of distinctive punishment (Genesis 3:19; Psalms 6:5; Job 10:20–22). Instead, reward and punishment are meted out during life and are connected with such embodied concerns as long life, possession of property, and successful procreation. Time upon Earth is presented as precious, and humanity is encouraged to enjoy and appreciate our brief sojourn upon the planet, for each of us has a limited span of days before we vanish (Job 14; Psalms 90:10–17).

During the Second Temple period, Israelites came under first Persian and then Hellenistic imperial influences. Persian Zoroastrianism envisioned an eschatological battle between cosmic forces of good and evil, ending in a planetary conflagration and a physical resurrection of the dead upon a transformed Earth. Greek Platonism rejected notions of resurrected flesh and instead insisted on the immortality of the soul within the heavens. Over time, both of these ideas—separately and in various combinations—entered Jewish thought, perhaps because continuing foreign domination and domestic disappointments required the deferral of covenantal promises to a future date. Despite deferral to the end-time, however, these promises continued to be envisioned largely in Earthly terms, with their final fulfillment providing not only a renewal of the Jewish nation but also the material blessings of verdant pastures, abundant harvests, clean water teeming with fish, and justice between all people and among all creatures (Isaiah 11:3–9; Ezekiel 34:14, 27; 47:7–12).

Jesus' teachings on the Kingdom of God are consonant with other Jewish eschatological beliefs of the day, with perhaps a greater emphasis on the inauguration of the Kingdom within the present and its consummation in the immediate future. This sense of immediacy was reinforced when followers experienced their crucified Messiah as having been resurrected and raised to the right hand of God. This experience was interpreted by them as a signal that the *eschaton*, with its anticipated resurrection of the dead, had arrived—an arrival that they expected to be accompanied by a Second Coming (Parousia), the establishment of God's reign on Earth, a judgment on the living and the dead, an abolition of unjust social and political systems, and a renewal of the planet and its life-giving resources. As generations passed and the Parousia failed to occur, Christians changed their emphasis from an embodied resurrection upon a transformed Earth to a spiritual reward within heaven.

Islamic eschatology differs in specific details from Jewish and Christian variations, but there are broad similarities between the three arising out of cross-cultural fertilization during Islam's formative period. Similarities include an end-time appearance of a messianic figure, the resurrection of the dead, a final judgment, and the universal reign of God. In the Quran, eschatological fulfillment is pictured in physical but not in Earth-bound terms. The final reward is said to take place within an eternal Garden (al-Jannah) "the extensiveness of which is as the extensiveness of the heaven and the earth" (Surah 57:21). In the Garden, all the pleasures of Earth will be intensified and perfected, including cooling shade, flowing rivers, magnificent mansions, fine clothing and jewelry, banquets of fruit, fowl, and wine, and "pure" spouses of great beauty (Surah 18:30–31; 44:51–56; 56:1–38).

Modern Interpretations

In the current era, scholars have linked eschatological expectations with the ecological crisis. The historian Lynn White Jr., for instance, contended that "What people do about their ecology . . . is deeply conditioned by [religious] beliefs about our nature and destiny" (White 1968, 84). Whether our "destiny" is believed to be upon an Earthly paradise or within a heavenly paradise, Earth in its present form is devalued and rendered replaceable. This critique has sparked interest in recovering ecological wisdom within religious traditions. To date, however, sustained analysis of the specific eschatology-ecology connection has occurred predominantly within Christianity, perhaps because White identified Christian eschatology as the context within which the world-altering capabilities of modern science and technology arose. While many of the details of Christian analysis are inapplicable to other eschatological traditions, general assertions concerning the goodness of creation and the need for current human response in the face of future possibilities do occur elsewhere.

Within Christianity, attempts to negate ecologically destructive interpretations of eschatological doctrines have focused particularly on Jesus' conception of the Kingdom of God and on the Revelation of John (the final book of the New Testament). When analyzed using an ecological hermeneutic, Jesus' words and ministry can be seen to point toward a Kingdom characterized by natural verdancy, divine immanence, and human-divine-nonhuman reciprocity. For example, Jesus begins his ministry in the wilderness and repeatedly seeks divine connection, spiritual wisdom, and emotional comfort there (Matt. 4:1; Mark 6:31–32, 46; 9:2; Luke 9:28). He prays for God's reign to come to Earth and associates that reign with such mundane concerns as an adequate food supply and relief from indebtedness (Matt. 6:10–12). He assures his followers that God cares for both human and nonhuman creatures (Matt. 6:26a, 28b–29; 10:29; Luke 12:6, 24, 27); increases nature's abundance and restores its depleted resources (Matt. 14:16–21; Luke 5:4–6); uncovers the divine presence within corporeal matter (Mark 14:22–24); calls for peace between all creatures (Mark 4:37–39; 6:48–51; Luke 10:5); and reveals that his message is good news for the entirety of creation (Mark 16:15).

The Revelation of John provides a similar model of a just and relational future. Written within a generation of

Rome's destruction of the Second Jerusalem Temple, the book juxtaposes the "already" of oppressive political and economic systems with the "not yet" of an equitable society. Imperialism and economic greed are portrayed as bringing about war, slavery, and hunger for the masses while preserving luxury items for the wealthy (Rev. 6:6; 18). The text predicts that these injustices will result in the pollution of fresh water, the decimation of ocean life, and the destruction of previously fertile land (8:7–11). These ecological catastrophes are portrayed as the result of human choices, not as the inalterable will of God, when the text proclaims that a time will come "for destroying those who destroy the earth" (11:18). In contrast to the toxicity of this "old" way, a "new" way is anticipated—coming into existence only after the establishment of human-nature collaboration and cooperation (12:6, 14, 16). Revelation ends with a hopeful vision of God making a home on Earth (21:2–3) and of redemption and renewal bringing about a fertile planet where even urban centers abound in green-space and are replete with life-giving waters (22:1–2).

Antonia GORMAN
*Humane Society of the
United States*

FURTHER READING

Cragg, Kenneth. (Ed. and Trans). (1991). *Readings in the Qur'ān*. London: Collins Religious Publishing.

Keller, Catherine. (1996). *Apocalypse now and then: A feminist guide to the end of the world*. Boston: Beacon Press.

Maier, Harry O. (2002). There's a new world coming! Reading the Apocalypse in the shadow of the Canadian Rockies. In Norman C. Habel & Vicky Balabanski (Eds.), *The Earth story in the New Testament: The Earth Bible, Vol. 5* (pp. 166–179). Cleveland, OH: The Pilgrim Press.

Rossing, Barbara R. (2002). Alas for Earth! Lament and resistance in Revelation 12. In Norman C. Habel & Vicky Balabanski (Eds.), *The Earth story in the New Testament: The Earth Bible, Vol. 5* (pp. 180–192). Cleveland, OH: The Pilgrim Press.

Rossing, Barbara R. (2000). River of life in God's New Jerusalem: An eschatological vision for Earth's future. In Dieter T. Hessel & Rosemary Radford Ruether (Eds.), *Christianity and ecology: Seeking the well-being of Earth and humans* (pp. 205–224). Cambridge, MA: Harvard University Press.

Rowland, Christopher. (1982). *The open heaven: A study of Apocalyptic in Judaism and early Christianity*. New York: Crossroad.

Segal, Alan F. (2004). *Life after death: A history of the afterlife in Western religion*. New York: Doubleday.

Werblowsky, R. J. Zwi. (1987). Eschatology: Asian religions. In Mircea Eliade (Ed.), *The encyclopedia of religion* (p. 149). New York: MacMillan.

White, Lynn, Jr. (1968). *Machina ex deo: Essays in the dynamism of Western culture*. Cambridge: The Massachusetts Institute of Technology Press.

Wright, J. Edward. (2000). *The early history of heaven*. New York: Oxford University Press.

Ethics, Communicative

Communicative ethics developed from the work of the philosopher Jürgen Habermas, who argues that the most ethical approach to any moral challenge requires open communication from all involved parties capable of rational communication. Some environmentalists seek to expand this into an ethics of sustainability by incorporating voices of future generations and/or creatures of the natural world; it remains debatable whether such discourse can still be considered rational communication.

How should decisions about sustainability be made? Who should make these decisions, and to whom should they be accountable? Is there any place in such decision making for the interests and preferences of those who cannot speak for themselves—future generations of human beings, nonhuman animals and plants, ecosystems, and the Earth itself? These questions relate the issue of sustainability to communicative ethics, a contemporary approach to moral theory originating in the work of the German philosopher Jürgen Habermas (b. 1929).

Habermas argues that the basis of ethical decisions should be a discourse including all involved parties who are capable of rational communication. Influenced by the thinking of the eighteenth-century philosopher Immanuel Kant, Habermas works toward universal moral rules that do not depend upon theological or particularistic claims. Unlike Kant, however, Habermas stresses that individuals cannot be expected to develop or judge a valid moral norm on their own; instead, he finds the fundamental basis for ethics in interpersonal interaction and negotiation. His standard for ethics is based upon open and free communication, asserting that a norm or rule should be considered valid only if all who have a vested interest would agree to it with no

threat of domination or coercion. This is a radically democratic approach to ethics, and Habermas argues that while it may not be possible to achieve such inclusive communication in the real world, it is a vitally important ideal.

Regarding issues of sustainability, communicative ethics emphasizes that decisions about the futures of human communities and their interactions with environmental systems should ideally invite contributions and engagement from all persons who have a stake in the situation. This argues against any system of management in which experts or government leaders dictate solutions; instead, it declares open communication the most ethical procedure by which to respond to contemporary challenges. Along these lines, an environmentalist communicative ethics develops discourse between human beings who agree on the importance of reforming our relationships to the rest of the world and creating a sustainable society for future generations.

Some environmentalists see a serious limitation in Habermas's communicative ethics. By emphasizing that norms should be judged by the standard of rational communication, he limits moral consideration to those who are capable of such interaction. There is no room for future generations or nonrational creatures to have moral standing or the right to protection for their own sake, because they cannot communicate according to the standards Habermas has set.

A few thinkers have worked to adapt communicative ethics for this reason, arguing that it is possible to construct a communicative discourse that includes the natural world and future generations. John Dryzek and Joel Whitebook argue that biological sciences are a morally instructive form of communication with the nonhuman world. Taking a different approach, Robyn Eckersley argues that because communicative ethics is based on an ideal rather than a real discourse, it is entirely consistent to approximate what the interests of the natural world and future generations would be if they *could* rationally communicate.

These proposals offer a theoretical justification for a communicative ethics that includes future generations and the nonhuman world. Nevertheless, challenges remain: Can the interests of nonrational and non-present entities be fully voiced in human discourse? Scientists can understand many characteristics of natural systems through their research; some spiritual environmentalists believe that they can ritually commune with other species; and some imaginative voices attempt to speak for future generations. Whether these are accurate and legitimate representations, however, involves subjective judgment. Would a discourse that includes such judgments be recognizable as the rational communication for which Habermas calls?

Communicative ethics offers a powerful justification and procedure for a democratic and public approach to sustainable decision making, but it requires further refinement if one hopes to include voices outside of currently living, rational human beings.

Kevin J. O'BRIEN
Pacific Lutheran University

FURTHER READING

Benhabib, Seyla, & Dallmayr, Fred R. (Eds.). (1990). *The communicative ethics controversy.* Cambridge, MA: MIT Press.

Dryzek, John S. (1990). Green reason: Communicative ethics and the biosphere. *Environmental Ethics, 12*(3), 195–210.

Eckersley, Robyn. (1999). The discourse ethic and the problem of representing nature. *Environmental Politics, 8*(2), 24–49.

Habermas, Jürgen. (1990). *Moral consciousness and communicative action (Studies in contemporary German social thought).* (Christian Lenhardt & Shierry Weber Nicholsen, Trans.). Cambridge, MA: MIT Press.

Habermas, Jürgen. (1993). *Justification and application: Remarks on discourse ethics (Studies in contemporary German social thought).* (Ciaran P. Cronin, Trans.) Cambridge, MA: MIT Press.

Whitebook, Joel. (1996). The problem of nature in Habermas. In David Macauley (Ed.), *Minding nature: The philosophers of ecology* (pp. 283–317). New York: Guilford Press.

Ethics, Environmental

Environmental ethics, which examines humanity's responsibilities toward Earth and the nonhuman world, is a twentieth-century response to humanity's domination of nature and the current ecological crisis. Environmental ethics is distinct from traditional ethics because it considers obligations, benefits, and risks to ecosystems and nonhuman life as well as those to humanity, thus raising new questions about basic concepts and methods in our moral languages.

Environmental ethics considers how humans should interact with the rest of the world, how we should perceive the value of nonhuman existence, and how to understand problems and possibilities in the relation of cultural and ecological systems. A distinct academic field of environmental ethics developed in the twentieth century as ethicists, philosophers, religionists, scientists, and policy makers sought to respond to human-caused environmental problems. While anthropogenic ecological changes and theoretical reflection upon nature are as old as human history, treating environmental issues as a matter of practical ethics is a recent innovation. The development of a distinct area of ethical reflection corresponds to the recognition of humanity's unprecedented powers over nature and planetary impact, as well as the apparent difficulty that environmental problems pose to received ethical traditions and cultural patterns of action. Environmental ethics thus criticizes and cultivates the aptitude of received principles, concepts, metaphors, and frameworks for addressing environmental problems, and also attempts to construct new concepts and worldviews. The central task for the field is twofold: (1) to make environmental problems significant for the moral imagination and (2) to develop and criticize appropriate patterns of action for individuals and societies.

Environmental ethics typically does not address the full range of social topics relevant to discussions of sustainability. Issues of human rights, poverty, and economy relate peripherally to the field, but usually an environmental ethic does not directly address them, nor does it offer an integrative framework for considering social, economic, and ecological issues together. Meanwhile some questions that receive less attention in sustainability debates, such as the moral status of individual animals, are more prominent in environmental ethics. Nonetheless, the field has been crucial in raising questions that any sustainability framework must answer and in developing lines of moral reasoning that have helped shape visions of sustainability.

In recent decades the field has proliferated, supporting multiple journals, producing hundreds of publications, and creating cross-disciplinary collaborations with the environmental sciences, literature, anthropology, psychology, economics, law, history, sociology, and political theory, among others.

Basic Questions

Debate in environmental ethics often raises anew a number of meta-ethical questions (questions about basic concepts and methods in our moral languages): What is nature? In what way are humans part of the natural world, and is nature part of the human world? What is value, and can it be held by nonhumans? Should we recognize a morally significant difference between humans and other animals? Should we recognize moral

159

differences between ecological and cultural productions (expressed in distinctions such as wild/domestic and natural/artificial), or is it the case that our concepts for the more-than-human world have been produced by exploitative cultures and support unsustainable social systems?

Resolving meta-ethical questions may require appeals to a comprehensive worldview or new ontological proposals (theories of existence). Because of the fundamental character of those questions, the field hosts a lively exchange among religious scholars, cultural theorists, and philosophers that raises questions about the character of reality, the significance of life, and the purpose of humanity. Yet because these cosmological questions have been raised after reflecting on a series of urgent crises, others have argued that the field should not begin from such theoretical questions, but from practical problems.

Early efforts in the field concentrated on questions about value and anthropocentrism; they often criticized received traditions of ethics for focusing exclusively on human interactions and social benefit, thus ignoring the "moral considerability" of nonhuman life and ecological systems. Ethicists debated the possibility of nonanthropocentric alternatives to the received ethical traditions, or supplements and extensions to those traditions. A central project has thus been developing intrinsic value, some dignity possessed by nature that is independent of human interest yet demanding of human respect. If an entity holds intrinsic value, it does not mean it is inviolable, but it does condition human actions by requiring respect appropriate to its value. Intrinsic values contrast with instrumental values, or values that refer to the utility of something for human use. Anything that holds intrinsic value (persons, art, animals, ecosystems, and the like) requires that someone who would use it, affect it, or destroy it in pursuit of his or her own interests offer justified reasons for doing so. An account of nature's intrinsic value would therefore interrupt any assumptions that nature can be exploited indifferently, like so many resources for satisfying human interests, and it would require that personal and social projects conduct themselves in appropriate respect of nature's value.

Further questions in the debates over value ask what natural kinds and/or systems may possess intrinsic value (such as individuals, species, communities, and ecosystems), and why. Should we attribute intrinsic value to things in virtue of some quality such as beauty, complexity, or rareness, or is value basic and self-authenticating? How do nature's values relate to analogous cultural values of human creations, like art, cities, or spirituality? The philosopher Holmes Rolston has offered the most consistent and rigorous defense of intrinsic value, developing a naturalist ethic organized around self-valuing organisms, the value-generating evolutionary matrix that produces them, and the value-recognizing role of humans as moral agents.

Recognition of intrinsic values begins to decenter an absolute ethical anthropocentrism, which holds that only human interests matter. Many ethicists have developed nonanthropocentric proposals to expand the moral community so as to include other animals, all life, and/or ecological systems. Some propose rigorous ecocentric frameworks, in which ecological integrity takes precedence over some or all human interests. In the United States, a project of an expanded moral community and an ecocentric ethic often refers to the environmentalist Aldo Leopold's "land ethic," which recognizes the value of all members of "the biotic community" while privileging the "beauty, stability, and integrity" of the whole (Leopold 1949). In Europe, a project of an extended ecological ethics often refers to the "deep ecology" of the philosopher Arne Naess, which reframes human self-realization within ecological relations and interprets cultural forms within ecological systems.

Some ethicists think that pursuing the project of intrinsic value for nature and a nonanthropocentric ethic cannot be justified. They might argue that extensive ecological protections would be warranted by an enlightened anthropocentrism, which takes into account the environmental conditions of the full range of long-term human interests. Environmental exploitation degrades the common good of humanity, offending existing commitments to public health and political justice. An account of human flourishing might even justify strong ecological protections for the sake of spirituality, or the opportunity to live in harmony with natural beauty and wildness.

Other ethicists have criticized the organization of debate around value and anthropocentrism. Environmental pragmatists have argued that, rather than beginning from meta-ethics, which seems a complicated and roundabout way of approaching urgent problems, the field should begin from public policy dilemmas, working to create political consensus around them by appealing to moral values already held by the cultural mainstream. Pragmatists emphasize the range and diversity of relevant problems, which include land use (including resource management, development, agriculture, public parks, and wilderness); marine areas (including recreational and commercial fishing, water rights, undersea biodiversity); built environments (including urban areas); animals (wild, domesticated, exotic, endangered, and genetically modified, both as species and individuals); and ecological systems (from the microscopic to the planetary). Moreover, that geographical range is overlaid by temporal scope (including future generations and historical landscapes), growing populations, and changing technologies, especially around energy use. The variety seems to escape a unified theory of environmental ethics. Pragmatists argue that ethics should begin from specific issues, using theories and concepts as tools of understanding and working with the cultural values of the community most relevant to addressing the problem.

Three other major approaches also emphasize beginning from the political context of ecological problems, but they do so by challenging dominant ways of thinking about nature and humanity. First, human-rights approaches begin from the ecological mediation of social harms and social goods. Environmental-justice projects pursue this approach by documenting environmental harms (for example, toxic exposures, air pollution, disaster risks, and water scarcity) suffered disproportionately by some groups, usually the poor and racial/ethnic minorities. These projects often emphasize redress of environmental problems by realizing human rights of information, political participation, and livelihood. They may also argue for a substantive right to environmental goods, such as a right to clean water, biological diversity, a healthy habitat, or access to natural beauty.

Second, ecofeminist approaches trace a common logic of exploitation in female/male relations and in nature/human relations. That usually leads to critical suspicions that environmental concepts have been constructed for and by power relations in much the same way that gender concepts have been. In Western languages, nature concepts (including the Earth, soil, and the human body) take typologically feminine meanings, while cultural concepts (including rationality and technology) take typologically masculine meanings. In a context with hierarchical gender relations, then, technological powers will be privileged over Earthly integrity, and may even take on sexual metaphors. The semiotic differences of nature and culture and social construction of masculine and feminine can be used to organize and justify systems of exploitation, for example, in the assumption that humanity can exploit and dominate the Earth because of its higher purposes and rational powers. By contextualizing environmental problems within gendered conceptions of human personhood, ecofeminist analyses invite alternative constructions of humanity's ecological role and patterns of relational action with the more-than-human world.

The third approach derives from some indigenous peoples' initiatives, along with some environmentalisms of the global South (the poorest and "least-developed" countries, most of which are located in the Southern Hemisphere), which also have interrogated assumptions about a separate realm of "nature" marked off from the human and possessed of its own values. Like environmental justice projects, they may approach environmental problems as political conflicts over resources or as matters of public health, but they tend to emphasize how those ecological problems threaten their cultural survival. The traditional ways of life of their culture—including language and religion—may depend on ancient relations with a particular land or bioregion.

All three of these approaches begin to contest Western notions of human personhood and present to the moral imagination expanded notions of anthropology. All three elaborate the ecological vulnerability of human dignity, or how being human depends on healthy, life-giving, and meaning-producing relations with ecological worlds.

Normative Strategies

Those basic questions about a method and goal for environmental ethics determine what a successful environmental ethic must accomplish. There are three basic foci for ethical strategies in the field. One strategy focuses on nature's moral status, perhaps through an account of intrinsic value. Here an ethic orients environmental problems around the relative moral standing of nature. A second focuses on responsible forms of moral and political action. The pragmatist's problem solving is one example here; a stewardship ethic, in which environmental problems are occasion for right action in regard to a public or divine trust, represents another. A third strategy focuses on the ecological character of humanity. Here an ethic makes environmental problems matter for the ecological relationality of authentic personhood. Some ecofeminist and indigenous peoples' approaches represent this strategy, as well as many forms of deep ecology.

What an ethicist thinks about initial strategic questions in environmental ethics will shape how the challenges posed by environmental questions are interpreted. What responsibilities do we have to animals, species, ecosystems, the planet, the past, and to the future? Do we have obligations first to individuals (human persons, animals) or first to holisms (ecosystems, species)? What happens when individual interests conflict with those of a system or species?

The latter two questions have sparked particular debate in the field between those concerned primarily for the welfare or rights of animals and those interested primarily in the health or integrity of holistic ecological systems. The conflict comes into public view in debates over invasive species, culling overabundant populations, and reintroducing wild animals into areas where they will threaten domestic animals. Some theorists have suggested animal ethics and environmental ethics may be two separate fields, but most ethicists attempt to develop some scale or priority of values to keep both animal and ecological concerns together in context.

An ethicist's basic method or strategy involves organizing an approach to contextual questions, but how each ethicist reasons through those questions will be shaped by some tradition of moral reasoning. Consequentialism—the practice of maximizing the good—is one such tradition, and one of the most widely used, particularly through market-based approaches to environmental problems (in which the good is represented by human utility). The duty-based ethics of a deontological or Kantian tradition (the tradition of doing the right) is another, and is especially favored by ethicists emphasizing respect for intrinsic value or integrity. Aristotelian virtue traditions, Stoic cosmopolitanism, and natural law traditions are other major Western forms of moral reasoning, often mediated through Christian traditions. More recent Western traditions include phenomenological, process, and pragmatist forms of moral reasoning. Environmental theorists have shown great interest in non-Western traditions of reasoning, including indigenous and Eastern worldviews, as they seek moral traditions implicated less in the development of industrial exploitative powers.

Addressing environmental problems through any tradition, but especially the Western traditions that may be culpable of shaping a culture of exploitative powers, faces another crucial methodological decision: can received traditions of moral reasoning respond to the complexity and scale of environmental problems, or must ethics invent new values, frameworks, metaphors, and narratives? That question is especially important for religious communities, whose ancient traditions may be particularly stressed by unprecedented social problems. Environmental ethics has been influenced in this regard by theories that Western Christianity produced or supported modern ecological crises by shaping cultures with dualist and anthropocentric assumptions. Critics hold that a cosmology with a strong distinction between Creator and creation along with a story centered around human salvation has shaped Western culture into disregard for the natural world and a myopic concern for human benefit. Christian approaches, and any Western tradition that shares assumptions of its worldview, therefore must decide whether its tradition has the capacity to make environmental problems morally intelligible, and if so, which resources will be most helpful.

Any environmental ethic involves two kinds of cultural analysis. First, it must decide whether and to what degree a culture's inherited moral ideas require change, and whether ethics relates to a movement for social reforms. Second, deciding whether and how received ethical traditions meet the challenge of environmental problems depends in part on the assumed audience. Should environmental ethics be useful for policy makers, philosophers, land managers, environmentalists, or citizens? And what should it do for that audience: interpret a modern crisis, illuminate avenues of policy response, inspire social change, or guide personal behavior?

The planetary scale of environmental problems in relation to the scale of moral agency and social life creates interesting geographic dimensions for environmental ethics, as seen in the recent development of global ethics and place ethics. Because some environmental problems—like climate change—are both created by the combined technological agency of humans of many cultures and nations around the globe and produce a planetary effect, it seems that an adequate environmental ethic must also function as a global ethic: some framework supportable from most or all cultural standpoints and relevant to all the agents involved in creating or suffering the problem. Initiatives in global ethics, like the Earth Charter (an international declaration of fundamental ethical principles for building a just, sustainable, and peaceful twenty-first century), attempt to articulate the moral dimensions of global experience or the community of Earth.

Meanwhile, because environmental problems fundamentally involve the relation of human persons to their ecological context, it seems that an adequate environmental ethic should focus on communities as the nexus of personal, cultural, and ecological goods. Place ethics, including agrarian, bioregional, and environmental justice approaches, build an ethic from a community's interactive experience with the land or habitat in which it lives. Place ethics often employ narrative themes and nature writing, interpreting environmental issues within some better-or-worse story of a people's inhabitation in a place and by the measure of their attentiveness to its nonhuman residents.

The relation between ethics and social practice may also be shaped by four further views involving background social and political analysis. First, how do the environmental sciences relate to ethical inquiry, and which science in particular is most relevant? Second, what is the role of markets in creating and/or solving social problems? Third, how should ethics evaluate human technology in relation to ecological systems (is it generally threatening or promising)? Fourth, does environmental ethics require changed political structures (does it rely on or challenge political democracy)?

Given the variety of disciplinary perspectives and theoretical background it involves, environmental ethics might best be thought of as an interdisciplinary arena focused on practical problems that raise questions about our most important social institutions and cultural ideas, and even our ideas about the meaning of human life. As such, it is one of the most fertile and robust intellectual intersections in the contemporary academy.

Willis JENKINS
Yale Divinity School

FURTHER READING

Agyeman, Julian. (2005). *Sustainable communities and the challenge of environmental justice.* New York: New York University Press.

Armstrong, Susan J., & Botzler, Richard G. (2008). *The animal ethics reader.* New York: Routledge.

Curtin, Deane. (2005). *Environmental ethics for a postcolonial world.* Lanham, MD: Rowman & Littlefield.

Elliot, Robert. (Ed.). (1995). *Environmental ethics.* Oxford, U.K.: Oxford University Press.

Jenkins, Willis. (2008). *Ecologies of grace: Environmental ethics and Christian theology.* New York: Oxford University Press.

Hay, Peter. (2002). *Main currents in Western environmental thought.* Indianapolis: Indiana University Press.

Leopold, Aldo. (1949). *A Sand County almanac, and sketches here and there.* New York: Oxford University Press.

Light, Andrew, & de-Shalit, Avner. (Eds.). (2003). *Moral and political reasoning in environmental practice.* Cambridge, MA: MIT Press.

Light, Andrew, & Rolston, Holmes, III. (Eds.). (2003). *Environmental ethics: An anthology.* Oxford, U.K.: Blackwell.

Martínez-Alier, Juan. (2002). *The environmentalism of the poor: A study of ecological conflicts and valuation.* Cheltenham, U.K.: Edward Elgar Publishing.

Merchant, Carolyn. (1992). *Radical ecology: The search for a livable world.* New York: Routledge.

Minteer, Ben A. (2006). *The landscape of reform: Civic pragmatism and environmental thought in America.* Cambridge, MA: MIT Press.

Rolston, Holmes, III. (1994). *Conserving natural value.* New York: Columbia University Press.

Schlosberg, David. (1999). *Environmental justice and the new pluralism: The challenge of difference for environmentalism.* New York: Oxford University Press.

Schrader-Frechette, Kristin. (2002). *Environmental justice: Creating equality, reclaiming democracy.* New York: Oxford University Press.

Shiva, Vandana. (1988). *Staying alive: Women, ecology, and development.* London: Zed Books.

Wirzba, Norman. (Ed.). (2003). *The essential agrarian reader: The future of culture, community, and the land.* Lexington: University Press of Kentucky.

Ethics, Global

Global ethics examines claims about ethical obligations, responsibilities, and duties that apply to all humans without regard to where they live. Growing realization of how humans in one part of the world can dramatically affect life in other parts of the world has led to an increasing interest in global ethics, despite some disagreement about the scope of universal claims.

Whereas ethics can be understood as a domain of inquiry that examines claims about what is right or wrong, obligatory, or a matter of responsibility, global ethics refers to the field of inquiry examining ethical assertions that apply universally to all citizens of the Earth. Global ethics explores the nature and justification of ethical norms that would obligate all persons or humanity as a collective. Interest in global ethics has grown recently due to several factors: the increasing pressure of global problems requiring global solutions; the general phenomenon of globalization; and revived interest in global citizenship and cosmopolitanism (Dower 2003, 3–7).

New Interest

Many proponents of global ethics see new connections between people around the world as the basis for their interest in global ethics. For the first time in human history it is becoming obvious that people in one part of the world can harshly affect the health and environment of people in other parts of the world, even though separated from those who are causing the problem by both time and distance. Climate change is a strong example of this; so is the loss of upper-atmospheric ozone and overfishing by trawlers from developed countries at the expense of subsistence fishermen in poor developing countries. In addition, after witnessing the global monetary crises that arose in the latter part of

2008, it is now clear that irresponsible banking practices in one part of the world can devastate economies far away. Some toxic substances are known to put animals and people at risk; even at great distances from the place of emission, toxins travel long-range through air transport. Inadequate food inspection in one part of the world can make people sick thousands of miles away. Poorly secured nuclear materials on one continent can lead to terrorist destruction on another. In previous eras, responsibility to the distant poor might have been understood as a matter of charity; our era of globalized causal effects may create duties in regard to the basic needs of distant others.

Global ethics sometimes is discussed under the category of "cosmopolitanism," a term often used synonymously for global ethics. Cosmopolitanism is a social/political philosophy according to which all human beings belong to one domain—the domain of the world or cosmos (Dower 2003, 5). Cosmopolitanism usually holds that all humans have duties or responsibilities to each other because they share the Earth.

Global problems that have triggered an interest in global ethics recently include environmental problems such as climate change and loss of biodiversity, vulnerability to economic collapse, and new interdependency due to global trade, international terrorism, and international telecommunications. Topics investigated at institutions around the world, including the University of Birmingham (U.K.) Centre for Global Ethics, include the huge disparities between rich and poor, the nature of obligations between developed and developing countries, how to make trading arrangements fairer, the responsibilities of those causing global environmental problems to those who are most vulnerable to them, how military intervention might be better regulated, and the power of international institutions. Global ethics often is concerned with recognition and enforcement of human rights, the moral basis for a right to self-determination, the limits of nationalism and patriotism, and what response might be morally justified for such global problems as population growth and climate change. Another issue receiving increased attention in global ethics literature is migration and immigration (Santa Clara University 2008).

Criticism and Support

Two criticisms of global ethics are often discussed under the theories of relativism and communitarianism (Dower 2003, 123). According to relativism, moral values differ among cultures and societies and therefore cannot apply to all people around the world; it often is seen as the denial of the universality of values. In a similar way, communitarianism usually is understood to argue that ethical obligations only apply to the society or community to which one belongs because ethical and moral obligations originate among those who are in community with each other. In their strong forms, both relativism and communitarianism undermine claims to global ethics. If obligations exist only to the communities to which people belong, then no global ethical obligations can be claimed. Yet recently positions of relativism and communitarianism are rarely held in their stronger forms. A more frequently held notion is that some ethical obligations are acknowledged to be binding at the global scale while others are relevant only at the national, regional, or community scale.

As described by Nigel Dower in *An Introduction to Global Citizenship* (2003, 123–128), advocates of global ethical responsibilities respond to relativism and communitarianism by making several arguments:

- Although it may be true that not all people agree with global ethical principles, as a matter of ethics they ought to accept global obligations.
- Those who believe in relativism have no principled way of condemning atrocities of one group on another (such as the conquistadors' treatment of the Aztecs).
- Even though moral obligations may arise from social relations with others, there is no reason why ethical principles developed at a local scale should not be extended to a global scale.
- Because people are often members of more than one cultural group to which they acknowledge duties, there is no reason why they should not acknowledge obligations to the global community.

Other critics of global ethics argue that the values entailed by any global code are actually Western ethical ideas that proponents seek to impose on non-Western cultures. Those who make this argument sometimes charge that proponents of global ethics are guilty of cultural imperialism. In response, the proponents acknowledge that even when the adoption of tenets of global ethics would change the ethical principles of the more local culture, it does not mean that the group should not accept the more international principles. In other words, the fact that a local group does not acknowledge a global obligation within their moral code does not necessarily overcome the prescriptive argument that they should recognize a new moral obligation to others on the planet. Moreover, proponents of global ethical principles deny that all such claims are essentially Western and point to many examples of cross-cultural acceptance of the ethical principles they advocate.

Proponents of global ethics often are concerned with whether existing international institutions are sufficient to assure that global ethical obligations and goals will be complied with and achieved. For this reason, proponents of global ethics often question whether existing United Nations institutions are adequate for achieving the goals of the international human rights frameworks or whether nations should cede some sovereignty to international institutions. Opponents of world government often resist arguments made regarding the expansion of global ethical frameworks because they fear the loss of liberty. In response, proponents of global ethics often argue to improve international governance frameworks on those issues agreed to in democratic processes. If democratically elected governments agree to global international obligations no loss of liberty necessarily follows.

Donald BROWN
Pennsylvania State University

FURTHER READING

Dower, Nigel. (2003). *An introduction to global citizenship.* Edinburgh, U.K.: Edinburgh University Press.

Santa Clara University Markkulla Center for Applied Ethics. (2008). Global leadership and ethics. Retrieved April 27, 2009, from http://www.scu.edu/ethics/articles/articles.cfm?fam=IHRM

University of Birmingham Centre for Global Ethics. (n.d.). About global ethics. Retrieved April 27, 2009, from http://www.globalethics.bham.ac.uk/aboutglobalethics.shtml

Ethics, Natural Law

Natural law frameworks understand humans to be innately capable of pursuing natural goods and obligated to do so. Insofar as sustainability concerns cohere with these natural goods, natural law ethics could support sustainability. But natural law's concentration on human goods before those of nonhumans and the environment, as well as its inflexible, unchanging quality, may inhibit such connections.

Natural law ethics seek to uncover and understand moral norms by examining those human characteristics, capacities, and actions that are universally common and deeply enduring. Clearly then, natural law ethics—implicitly or explicitly—rely upon a theory of human nature. For most natural law theorists, human beings are taken to be both rational and capable of exercising the power of their will according to moral laws and norms. Hence natural law ethics often exhibit an account of practical rationality that highlights the capacity of individuals to purposively order their pursuits according to discernible moral laws. While many of these capabilities and priorities may cohere with sustainability practices, natural law's focus on human goods before those of nonhumans and the environment may prevent some from connecting it with the care of the ecosystem as a whole.

Natural law approaches in ethics have been employed at least since the Greek Sophists (c. fifth century BCE) and have been deployed in a wide variety of religious and philosophical traditions. Over the next 2,000-plus years, as varied a cast as Aristotle, Cicero, Augustine, Thomas Aquinas, William of Ockham, Hugo Grotius, Thomas Hobbes, Samuel von Pufendorf, and John Locke has been ascribed the title of "natural law thinker." Today, two relatively distinct natural law approaches are prominent. First, among contemporary legal theories, like that of John Finnis

(b. 1940), natural law approaches seek to designate those prescriptions that are more enduring and weighty than those in positive or common law (the laws created by humans), often with the aim of using these natural prescriptions to justify or critique positive law. Second, among Christian ethicists, particularly those working in the Roman Catholic tradition, the natural law is human beings' participation in God's eternal law. God has ordered Creation as a particular actualization of God's eternal reason. Humans participate in this actualization insofar as they live in accord with their nature, a nature given with an ability to recognize goods via reason and the inclination to pursue them.

In contemporary legal theory, Finnis is a representative figure who has defended and developed a natural law approach. For Finnis, reason directly perceives self-evident practical principles that indicate the basic forms of human values—namely, self-preservation, knowledge, play, aesthetic experience, friendship, "practical reasonableness" (the ability to intentionally orient particular actions to ends conceived as good), and religion. In addition to pursuing these values, reason can perceive a basic set of methodological requirements of practical reasonableness, which help to distinguish sound and unsound practical thinking, as well as judge acts as reasonable or unreasonable. Taken together, according to Finnis, these self-evident principles and methodological requirements compose the natural law.

In Christian ethics, natural law approaches often orient themselves in relation to what many consider the paradigmatic account of natural law found in Saint Thomas Aquinas's *Summa Theologiae*. For Thomas (c. 1225–1274), a law is a rule or measure of action. All acts, insofar as they are human, pursue an end and require deliberation and reasoning. The ultimate end of all human acts is twofold: on the one hand, God, the uncreated good; on the other, happiness, a created good, which is the attainment or enjoyment of the ultimate end. Laws guide and direct human activity toward happiness; natural laws, more particularly, guide toward activity fitting for a human's nature. For Thomas, fitting and natural human activity includes the inclination to pursue the good, to preserve one's life, to reproduce, to educate one's offspring, to know the truth about God, and to live in society.

Each of these approaches in natural law ethics raises difficult conceptual and moral questions. First, particularly for those working in contemporary legal theory, the source or origin of the natural law is unclear. Though legal theorists may attempt to ground the natural law upon the structure of reason or upon evolutionary history, neither basis is generally accepted as an obligating authority for a human agent. That is, even if humans are inclined to pursue goods according to their nature, the natural law theorist needs to show why they are obligated to do so.

A second difficulty for natural law approaches is that they need to give an adequate description of how one comes to know or apprehend the content of the natural law as well as explore the extent to which one's apprehension may be limited or volition misshapen. In particular, some ethicists have challenged natural law approaches for assuming that human rationality is suitably disposed to perceiving the fullness of the natural law.

These difficulties aside, natural law ethics could fit well with a concern for sustainability, as they hold that humans are by nature suited to pursue worthwhile goods and ends. Yet, some tendencies should be kept in mind. For one, a natural law ethic—with its dependence on a theory of human nature—concentrates its view on anthropocentric concerns. Historically, natural law theories have not highlighted the moral significance of human relationships with other creatures and their environs. Though natural law ethics may provide abundant resources for thinking about how to sustain the natural goods of humans, fewer resources are available to defend the goods of other natures—animals, plants, mountains, ecosystems, and the like. A second important tendency is that natural law ethics see natural laws as fixed in reality and unchangeable. Insofar as problems related to sustainability are "new" moral problems, natural law ethics may have to reinterpret its conception of human goods to properly address them.

Chad WAYNER
University of Virginia

FURTHER READING

Benzoni, Francisco J. (2008). *Ecological ethics and the human soul: Aquinas, Whitehead, and the metaphysics of value*. Notre Dame, IN: University of Notre Dame Press.

Crowe, Michael. (1977). *The changing profile of the natural law*. The Hague, The Netherlands: Martinus Nijhoff.

Finnis, John. (1980). *Natural law and natural rights*. Oxford, U.K.: Clarendon Press.

Haakonssen, Knud. (1996). *Natural law and moral philosophy: From Grotius to the Scottish Enlightenment*. New York: Cambridge University Press.

Porter, Jean. (1999). *Divine and natural law: Reclaiming the tradition for Christian ethics*. Grand Rapids, MI: Eerdmans.

Santmire, H. Paul. (1985). *The travail of nature: The ambitious ecological promise of Christian theology*. Minneapolis, MN: Augsburg Fortress Press.

Evolution

Although competitive evolutionary processes and Darwin's theory as evolutionary science may pose complications for relating evolution to sustainability, an evolutionary ethic of sustainability might suggest an obligation to safeguard natural processes, even when they appear to conflict with cherished human values. A new movement called the Epic of Evolution seeks to infuse the scientific account of our universe and our planet with beauty, meaning, and purpose.

Evolution has a complex relationship to questions of sustainability. Knowledge of evolutionary and ecological science is essential for evaluating human impacts on the environment, but arriving at normative guidelines for human conduct in light of evolutionary science may be problematic. Negative associations of Darwin's theory as applied in the social realm must be considered, as well as the broader philosophical problem of deriving an "ought" for human behavior from nature's "is." Moreover, evolutionary theory evokes a long view of Earth's past and future that may suggest there is little humans can ultimately do, either to preserve or destroy the ancient and ever-changing natural world of which we are a tiny part.

But the relationship of evolution to sustainability need not be seen as negative. Although it is true that evolutionary processes reveal a harsh and competitive side of nature, for example, we need not model human communities and social ethics on natural communities. Rather, an evolutionary ethic of sustainability might suggest an obligation to safeguard natural processes, even when they appear to conflict with cherished human values such as cooperation, compassion for the sick, or respect for the inherent worth of each individual. Accepting that humans are a minuscule part of a vast and dynamic natural world does not necessarily entail abandoning efforts to sustain nature that seem ultimately futile or ephemeral.

An environmental movement quickly gaining momentum, the Epic of Evolution, seeks to infuse the scientific account of our universe and our planet with beauty, meaning, and purpose. In contrast to notions of science as value-neutral and of the natural world as coldly mechanistic or devoid of meaning and mystery, the Epic of Evolution translates science into a common creation myth for all of Earth's inhabitants. Its proponents, including the astrophysicist and science educator Eric Chaisson, the late ecotheologian Thomas Berry, and Michael Dowd, an inspirational speaker and former pastor, hope to reignite passionate concern for a natural world whose story is our own story. This "New Story" tells of a universe charged with consciousness of many varieties. Humans exist on a continuum with other conscious entities (as evolution suggests), but our particular form of consciousness entails unique moral obligations to ensure that the unfolding cosmogenesis continues. In this sweeping evolutionary perspective, it makes little sense to think of ourselves, or any animal, as having dominion over Earth. Realizing this should not demean humans; it should instead inspire wonder and a commitment to allowing nature's story to continue by caring deeply for the world around us.

Lisa SIDERIS
Indiana University

FURTHER READING

Epic of Evolution homepage. (2009). Retrieved July 17, 2009 from http://epicofevolution.com/abouttheEpic.html

Berry, Thomas, & Brian Swimme. (1992). *The universe story: From the primordial flaring forth to the ecozoic era—A celebration of the unfolding of the cosmos.* New York: HarperCollins.

Chaisson, Eric. (2006). *The epic of evolution: Seven ages of the cosmos.* New York: Columbia University Press.

Dowd, Michael. (2007). *Thank God for evolution: How the marriage of science and religion will transform your life and our world.* New York: Viking.

Sideris, Lisa H. (2003). *Environmental ethics, ecological theology, and natural selection.* New York: Columbia University Press.

THE EARTH AS *TITANIC*

The eco-theologian Thomas Berry (1914–2009), who referred to himself as a "geologian," wrote prodigiously of the need for humans to accept responsibility for their actions and to become better stewards of the Earth. Here he discusses the evolving role of humanity's relationship with the Earth, comparing the planet's current state (and our lack of care for it) to the sinking of the Titanic.

In April of the year 1912 the *Titanic*, on her maiden voyage across the Atlantic, struck an iceberg and went down at sea. Long before the collision those in command had abundant evidence that icebergs lay ahead. The course had been set, however, and no one wished to alter its direction. Confidence in the survival capacities of the ship was unbounded.... What happened to that "unsinkable" ship is a kind of parable for us, since only in the most dire situations do we have the psychic energy needed to examine our way of acting on the scale that is now required. The daily concerns over the care of the ship and its passengers needed to be set aside for a more urgent concern, the well-being of the ship itself....

Now our concerns for the human community can only be fulfilled by a concern for the integrity of the natural world. The planet cannot support its human presence unless there is a reciprocal human support for the life systems of the planet. This more comprehensive perspective we might identify as macrophase ethics. This is something far beyond our ordinary ethical judgments involving individual actions, the actions of communities, or even of nations. We are presently concerned with ethical judgments on an entirely different order of magnitude. Indeed, the human community has never previously been forced to ethical judgments on this scale because we never before had the capacity for deleterious action with such consequences.

As indicated by Brian Swimme in *The Hidden Heart of the Cosmos* [Orbis Books, 1999], humans, through our scientific insight and our technological skills, have become a macrophase power, something on the level of the glaciations or the forces that caused the great extinctions of the past. Yet we have only a microphase sense of responsibility or ethical judgment. We need to develop a completely different range of responsibility.

Source: Thomas Berry. (1999). *The Great Work: Our Way Into the Future*, pp. 100–101. New York: Bell Tower.

F

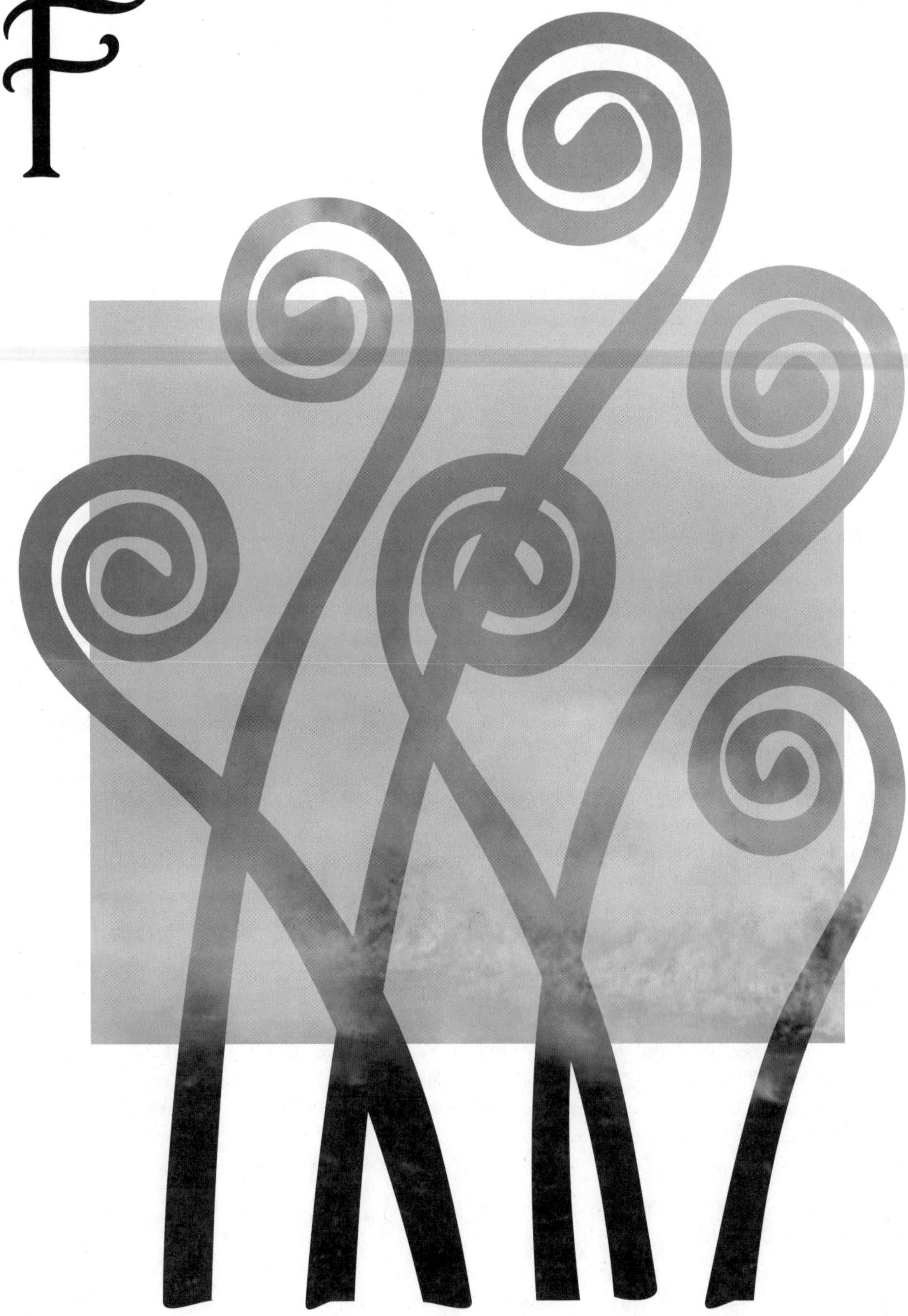

Feminist Thought

Feminism and environmentalism emerged in the latter twentieth century; by the 1980s a connection between the two was made. In some cultures, women and nature are associated symbolically. Organizations, conferences, and studies around the world have declared that sustainability is not possible without equity, justice, and economic and political growth for women. The result is a global awareness of various connections between women and ecology, some using the term ecofeminism.

Feminist views on sustainability are broad and deep, covering hundreds of topics from thousands of women and organizations, which, in turn, represent hundreds of thousands of women. There is agreement on some issues and a range of views, approaches, and strategies on others. Some put a greater emphasis on women's equity and rights as a road to sustainability, while others emphasize ecological integrity as foundational. Given the diversity of peoples, cultures, and worldviews and the complexity of issues, this is to be expected.

Historically, feminist views on sustainability come from two different directions: "women in development" (WID) approaches, and what came to be called ecofeminism. In the early twenty-first century these converge, and together they represent a complex overlay of concerns, analyses, approaches, and strategies. This was not always the case.

Women in Development (WID)

This term came on the international scene in the early 1980s from those assessing the impact of development on women. After three decades of a development agenda for less industrialized countries—then termed the "third world"—it was evident that in many places women were not benefiting; oftentimes the programs made their lives more difficult.

Organizations, such as Development Alternatives with Women for a New Era (DAWN) or Association for Women's Rights in Development (AWID), assessed that many of the difficulties for women were rooted in a basic lack of equity, in the ideas and processes of development, and in capitalist and macroeconomic systems. The United Nations (U.N.) Decade for Women: Equity, Development and Peace (1976–1985) culminated in a pivotal conference in Nairobi, Kenya, which recognized that the development agenda had failed women; as a result, the United Nations Development Fund for Women (UNIFEM) was established. The conference's final document, *The Nairobi Forward-looking Strategies for the Advancement of Women*, became a benchmark of and launch pad for systematic gender analysis, critiques, collective visions, and strategies for a sustainable life and livelihood for women, especially for poor women.

Enlarging Feminist Visions

This vision of feminism was born of the experiences of activists and analysts who desired a process of economic and social development that was geared to human needs rather than financial gains. This also meant that development based on equity required access to economic and political power. If there was to be equality, peace, and development by and for the poor and oppressed, it was inextricably linked to the same objectives by and for women. As the WID efforts increased, it was evident that multiple issues intersected. The term WID changed to "gender and development" (GAD), expanding the focus to be able to tackle the social and ideological causes of women's subordination and the uneven power relations between women and men: women's rights were human rights. Practically, this enabled violence against women to be treated as a public-policy issue rather than a private domestic problem, insisting that there can be no development in situations of women's oppression. Sustainability had to address economic, cultural, and physical violence against women.

The women and development agenda soon enlarged again. GAD became WED—"women, environment, and development"—which later changed its emphasis to sustainable development. Environmental issues surfaced on global, development, and economic agendas, evidenced with the United Nations World Commission on Environment and Development and the publication of *Our Common Future*, or the Brundtland Report, in 1987. This report placed sustainable development—"development that meets the needs of the present generation without compromising the ability of future generations to meet their own needs"—on the political landscape. It activated a global search for alternative models and strategies to development. The call for sustainable development opened the door for cooperation and consultation between global, national, and local partners, bridging governmental and civic society. Women assumed it would include them.

Over these years, women's organizations sprang up all over the world. In addition to those mentioned, there were many more, including the African Women's Development and Communication Network (FEMNET, 1988); Women's Environment & Development Organization (WEDO, 1990); Women and Environments Education and Development Foundation (WEED, 1991); and Women in Development Europe (WIDE). Currently there are thousands of nongovernmental organizations addressing aspects of gender and feminism, development, environment, and sustainability.

The quantity of activities, research, conferences, and publications coming forth from these interconnecting national and international agenda was astonishing. The establishment of women's voices, networks, and collaboration represents colossal efforts of thousands of women, who also represent thousands of women's voices and views on sustainability. Many women from all over the globe—such as Peggy Antrobus, Gita Sen, Rosi Braidotti, Filomina Chioma Steady, Wangari Maathai, Chief Bisi Ogunleye, and Vandana Shiva—spent years working on these issues.

At the same time, environmental issues were becoming more serious around the world. The United Nations launched a call to deliberate "environment and development." In consultation with a vast array of citizen's groups, experts, and national leaders, the U.N. proposed an agenda for sustainable development for the twenty-first century called Agenda 21. In 1991, as the world prepared for the 1992 United Nations Conference on Environment and Development (UNCED) in Rio de Janeiro, over one thousand women came from eighty-three countries to discuss and present an alternative and progressive feminist and ecological agenda. They held the World Women's Congress for a Healthy Planet in Miami, Florida, and produced the Women's Action Agenda 21, a document about the interrelated issues of women, development, sustainability, and environmental stability. It focuses on a critique of the forces underpinning the problems and offers solutions. The preamble, from which the following points are extracted, is candid about the intent and analysis.

- We speak on behalf of . . . the millions of women who experience daily the violence of environmental degradation.
- As long as Nature and women are abused by a so-called free-market ideology and wrong concepts of "economic growth," there can be no environmental security.
- We are outraged by the inequities.
- We will no longer tolerate the enormous role played by the military establishments.
- We . . . pledge our commitment to the empowerment of women, the central and powerful force in the search for equity.
- We demand our right, as half the world's population, to bring our perspectives, values, skills, and experiences into policy making.
- We equate lack of political and individual will among world leaders with a lack of basic morality and spiritual values and an absence of responsibility towards future generations.

The text covers a wide range of related topics, and is divided into eleven sections that give concrete evidence of the problems, as well as reactions, concerns, and actions that will be taken. The topics covered—each with six to ten separate commitments to action—include: democratic rights; environmental ethics and accountability; militarism and the environment; debt and trade; poverty, land rights, food security, and credit; population policies and health; biotechnology and biodiversity; nuclear power and alternative energy; science and technology; women's consumer power; and information and education.

The Women's Action Agenda 21 represents the first international feminist manifesto on sustainability, providing a useful representation of what was occurring in feminism and sustainability, predominantly from the developing countries. Although intended to influence UNCED and its outcomes, these enormous collaborative efforts, incisive analyses, strategies of sustainability, global scope, and actions plans were barely noticed. UNCED went ahead without much interest in the comprehensive analysis of the gendered dimensions of these issues. A comprehensive blueprint of action to be accepted globally, nationally, and locally, the official report of UNCED was a nine-hundred-page document entitled *Agenda 21*. Although the document included Chapter 24, "Global Action for Women Towards Sustainable and Equitable Development," and several additional references to women, most of the women's work from Women in Development (WID) to UNCED was omitted. Since then, much has changed; of 2009, most development or environmental institutions have specific areas of gender research and actions. The Women's Action Agenda 21 has been enormously useful and is regularly updated, most recently in 2002. It is now called the Women's Action Agenda for a Healthy and Peaceful Planet 2015, and represents diverse experiences of thousands of women striving to bring the UNCED agreements to life. Generally, activists and academics from political science, international development, sociology, and feminism or gender studies inhabited this feminist path toward sustainability. The presence of religion, if mentioned, was secondary at best. If there were religious teachings or reasons that motivated these women to work for justice, peace, or equity, they were not made explicit. From the other side, most feminist scholars of religion did not pay attention to this work. Much of feminist religious scholarship was focused on retrieving the voices of women from the past, reinterpreting texts, reclaiming justice for women, and confronting and resisting the male control of religious texts, institutions, and interpretations. The road to feminism and sustainability that explicitly included religion was a different one, most often associated with ecofeminism.

Origins of Ecofeminism

During the same time period, from the 1970s onward, another set of voices and views on feminism and sustainability were bringing forth a new set of concerns with the term *ecofeminism*. Ecofeminism has activist and academic roots with women working in toxic waste, health, media, antiwar movements, spirituality, art, theater, energy, urban ecology, or conservation; its supporters took the stance of theorist, activist, educator, dreamer, or social critic. Ecofeminism, a term first used in 1974 by the French feminist Francoise d'Eaubonne (1920–2005), sees connections between the domination of nature and the exploitation of women. Some hailed the movement as a new wave of feminism.

Women were observing critical links between militarism, gender, classism, racism, and environmental destruction. In the 1970s and early 1980s, several books became influential to ecofeminism: Susan Griffin's *Woman and Nature*, Mary Daly's *Gyn/Ecology*, Rosemary Radford Ruether's *New Woman/New Earth*, and Carolyn Merchant's *The Death of Nature: Women, Ecology, and the Scientific Revolution*. These were precursors to a burgeoning of ecofeminist work in academia, especially in the fields of philosophy, theology, and religious studies. These and other books—such as Charlene Spretnak's *The Politics of Women's Spirituality: Essays on the Rise of Spiritual Power Within the Feminist Movement*, Starhawk's *Dreaming the Dark*, and essays by Ynestra King—were important texts for women trying to integrate and interconnect their personal, ecological, and political concerns.

Conferences and publications allowed for creative imaging at what this alliance between ecology and feminism could bring. Conferences, such as "Women and Life on Earth: Ecofeminism in the Eighties" (1980), and "Ecofeminist Perspectives: Culture, Nature, Theory" (1987), were followed by publications of anthologies that articulated ecofeminist perspectives: *Reweaving the World: The Emergence of Ecofeminism* (edited by Irene Diamond and Gloria Orenstein); Stephanie Leland and Leonie Caldecott's volume, *Reclaim the Earth: Women Speak Out for Life on Earth*; and *Healing the Wounds: The Promise of Ecofeminism* (Judith Plant, editor).

Because it was such a flexible term, ecofeminism spawned countless projects in many fields. Women began to develop ecofeminist theories and ecofeminist political philosophies. Ecofeminism began to shift from a large set of interconnections to both in-depth historical critiques of the past, and cultural and intellectual analyses of a viable and sustainable future for women and the Earth. Ecofeminists began to focus their gaze on more theoretical examinations of the problems. Specific people worked and published on ecofeminism in specific ways: in philosophy (Karen Warren, Val Plumwood), animal rights (Carol Adams), ethics (Cris Cuomo), feminist politics (Greta Gaard, Ariel Sellah, Noel Sturgeon), sociology (Mary Mellor), and religion (Anne Primavesi, Rosemary R. Ruether, Ivone Gebara, Carol Christ), to name a few.

During the 1980s and early 1990s, ecofeminist vitality and visions were evident. The activist groups, conferences, academics, and socially engaged citizens formed a base from which, over time, one could refer to ecofeminism in many contexts. The feminist and ecological connections were becoming obvious. It was not a world of ideas and ideals, but a set of convergences that congealed over time. Eventually, links were forged with those working on women, environment, and development.

Ecofeminism can be imaged as resembling a traffic roundabout: many roads go in and out and not all intersect. The entry points into the ecofeminism intersection could be activism and social movements, academia, religion, women and development, or global feminism. Although ecofeminism represents a range of women/nature interconnections, there are three main roadways into the intersection: empirical evidence, conceptual/ideological or cultural/symbolic relationship to women and nature, and epistemological connections between women and nature.

Empirical Evidence: Women, Environment, and Development

There is empirical evidence that environmental problems disproportionately affect women in most parts of the world. By 1989, the U.N. noted that women are the worst victims of environmental destruction. The poorer she is, the greater is her burden. But the increased burdens women face result not only from environmental deterioration: there is a sexual division of labor found in most societies that considers family sustenance to be women's work, and women, as primary caregivers, generally bear primary responsibility for the food and the health of family members. Providing fuel, food, and water for families becomes increasingly difficult with environmental degradation. To make matters worse, economic resources, property, or financial independence are inaccessible to most women.

Ecofeminists examine the sociopolitical and economic structures that restrict many women's lives to poverty, ecological deprivation, and economic powerlessness. This type of ecofeminism resonates with the general thrust of years of connecting women, environmental, and development work. Thus the path to sustainability involves equity, justice, and economic and political power for women.

Conceptual/Symbolic Connections: Women and Nature

A second ecofeminist avenue is the study of the conceptual and symbolic connection between women and nature, mainly in Western worldviews. Such cultures developed ideas about a world divided hierarchically and dualistically. Dualistic conceptual structures identify women with femininity, the body, sexuality, Earth or nature, and materiality; men are associated with masculinity, the mind, heaven, the supernatural, and a disembodied spirit. Dualisms such as reason/emotion, mind/body, culture/nature, heaven/Earth, and man/woman give priority to the first over the second. Ecofeminists refer to these pairings as hierarchical dualisms and claim they foster the domination that is entrenched in Western history, worldviews, and social structures. Religion, philosophy, science, and cultural symbols reinforce this worldview, making male power over both women and nature appear natural and thus justified. Social patterns, including sexual norms, education, governance, and economic control reflect this logic of domination. Religions, in particular, are powerful forces in influencing these worldviews and fortify these social norms. The path to sustainability is to analyze and reconstruct the cultural and religious worldviews regarding women and nature.

Epistemological Connections: The Nature of Women

The third ecofeminist roadway involves two kinds of epistemological connections between women and nature: that is, two ways to understand the closeness between women and knowledge of nature. Since environmental problems affect women more directly, it may be possible that women possess greater knowledge and expertise in finding solutions to pressing environmental problems. For example, in many parts of the world, women are the land's custodians

and have greater agricultural knowledge than men. Thus, according to some ecofeminists, these women are in a good position to develop new practical and intellectual ecological paradigms and to address local environmental problems.

Others make a different epistemological connection. They see women as "closer" to nature and the Earth than men and as possessing innate traits of caring, community building, nonviolence, and Earth sensitivity. This type of women–nature essentialism is found in some cultures and contexts. Most ecofeminists consider the connections between women and nature to be based in cultural ideologies rather than in essence. Where women have expertise in agriculture and ecological systems, it is not due to their essential nature but to their life experiences.

Ecofeminists differ on foundational assumptions, on the nature of the relationship between women and the natural world, on ecological paradigms, on feminist approaches, on the roots of environmental crises, and on goals and the means of achieving them. Their goals can range from radical to moderate change. They may use social tools, such as Marxist analysis that considers class to be the foundational problem. They could be part of a black, Hispanic, or indigenous context where race and ethnicity are the key tools for understanding. They may be drawn to liberal or postmodern approaches. They may advocate environmental resource management, deep ecology, social ecology, or new cosmologies in their ecological frameworks. Buddhist, Native American, Wiccan, Goddess-worshiping, Hindu, Muslim, Christian, Jewish, and thoroughly secular versions of ecofeminism exist. Ecofeminist thought and activism occur globally—in India, Asia, Africa, and Latin America as well as Europe and North America. Ecofeminism represents countless combinations of the distinct strands of feminism and different ecological viewpoints. From the beginning, those who accepted that feminist theory and practice must include an ecological perspective and others who believed that solutions to ecological problems must include feminist analyses disagreed as to the nature of these connections.

Women, Environment, and Development (WED) or Ecofeminism?

By the 1990s several specific tensions had emerged. In-depth ecofeminist research revealed the extent to which Western cultures were rooted in ideologies of domination, a central one being the interconnected domination of women and nature. While this work exposed the ideological substructure of the problem, it did not describe in a straightforward manner how to change it. A tension existed between those who developed ecofeminist theories, usually from affluent countries, and those working for political change in social movements, usually from developing countries. Some ecofeminists seemed to be more interested in the historical and symbolic connections between women and nature or sophisticated theories of how the world should be rather than the actual suffering of women and ecosystems. Others perceived the greatest need to be in addressing economic and material realities and in concrete issues of women's poverty and ecological stress. How was there to be a relationship between those providing historical and theoretical analysis and those addressing violence against women, resisting pollution, loss of agricultural land, militarism, or global capitalism?

The whole arena of WED and ecofeminism was inconsistent. The discomfort became an explicit focus of conversation. Women reflected differently on the relationships between women and the natural world, and misogyny and the ecological crisis. Many from the WED side concentrated more on women's issues than environmental problems, and others the reverse. Spirituality or religion was central to some, and for others they were irrelevant or aroused suspicion. Some found the diversity unmanageable, and others rejoiced in the multitude of voices. Some kept the ecology–feminist connection but changed the words, using phrases such as *feminist ecology*, *feminist social ecology*, *feminist green socialism*, *feminist environmentalism*, and *feminist analyses of the environmental crisis* and WED.

It took time and effort for activists and academics to work together and to comprehend the complex relationships between the ideological analysis of the cultural-symbolic levels and the social, economic, political, and material difficulties. Yet throughout it all there was a mutual willingness to collaborate and to challenge. The issues are too difficult and complex for any one approach to be sufficient. All share the desire for a sustainable future.

Sustainability and Feminism

Today there are countless projects linking women, development, environment, and sustainability. They come in all shapes and sizes, and the diversity is manifold. They deal with agriculture, biotechnology, fisheries, water, forests, or biodiversity. Other groups confront violence, global capitalism, militarism, and water piracy. Some are analytic, others activist. Some examine the dynamics of environmental ruin while others create local sustainable projects. They may deal with the theoretical or practical dimensions, or both. Thousands of organizations dedicate time, money, and effort toward sustainable analyses and practices that are more gender conscious. Small local groups exist everywhere. Larger organizations like the United Nations, the World Bank, the Worldwatch Institute, and most development organizations are addressing issues at the intersection of feminism and sustainability.

Feminist thoughts about sustainability represent social, political, spiritual, economic, and ecological transformation. It is analysis, critique, vision, and action that transform the forms and patterns of relationships between women and men, between diverse cultures, between people and animals, and between humans and the larger Earth community. Lively debates continue on every topic: among transcultural or context-specific approaches, theory and social transformation, and in international conversations about democracy, globalization, and the meaning of sustainability. In general, the link between feminism and sustainability is about a desire to heal the wounds caused by the splits between nature and culture, mind and body, women and men, reason and emotion, spirit and matter, theory and action, and ultimately between humans and the Earth.

Heather EATON
Saint Paul University

FURTHER READING

Adams, Carol. (2005). *Ecofeminism and the eating of animals: Feminism and the defence of animals.* Sacramento, CA: Black Powder Press.

Association for Women's Rights in Development (AWID). (n.d.) Retrieved April 29, 2009, from http://www.awid.org/

Cuomo, Chris J. (1998). *Feminism and ecological communities: An ethic of flourishing.* London: Routledge.

Development Alternatives with Women for a New Era (DAWN). (n.d.). Retrieved April 29, 2009, from http://www.dawnnet.org/

Eaton, Heather. (2005). *Introducing ecofeminist theologies.* London: T&T Clark International.

Eaton, Heather, & Lorentzen, Lois Ann. (Eds.). (2003). *Ecofeminism and globalization: Exploring religion, culture and context.* Lanham, MD: Rowman & Littlefield.

Gaard, Greta. (1998). *Ecofeminist politics: Ecofeminists and the greens.* Philadelphia: Temple University Press.

Gebara, Ivone. (1999). *Longing for running water: Ecofeminism and liberation.* Minneapolis, MN: Fortress Press.

Kheel, Marti. (2008). *Nature ethics: An ecofeminist perspective.* Lanham, MD: Rowman & Littlefield.

Mies, Maria, & Shiva, Vandana. (1993). *Ecofeminism.* London: Zed.

Nairobi forward-looking strategies for the advancement of women. (1985, July 26). Retrieved on May 9, 2009, from http://www.un-documents.net/nflsaw.htm

Ress, Mary Judith. (2006). *Ecofeminism in Latin America: Women from the margins.* Maryknoll, NY: Orbis Books.

Ruether, Rosemary Radford. (Ed.). (2005). *Integrating ecofeminism, globalization, and world religions.* Lanham, MD: Rowman & Littlefield.

United Nations Development Fund for Women (UNIFEM). (n.d.). Retrieved April 29, 2009, from http://www.unifem.org/

Warren, Karen. (2000). *Ecofeminist philosophies.* Lanham, MD: Rowman & Littlefield.

Women's Action Agenda 21. (n.d.). Retrieved April 29, 2009, from www.iisd.org/women/action21.htm

Women's Environment and Development Organization (WEDO). (n.d.). Retrieved April 29, 2009, from http://www.wedo.org/

Forests

Forests contribute to the Earth's habitable conditions through maintenance of oxygen and carbon levels, water filtration, and nutrient cycling, among many other functions. Yet human harvesting of forest products and clearing of forests for roads, agriculture, and human settlements threaten the ecological services that forests provide.

Forests, which cover about one-third of the land area of the planet, hold an ambivalent place in the human imagination. People are dependent on intact forests for diverse ecosystem services, yet we clear forests for economic gain. In stories and legends, forests are depicted both as welcoming promised lands, rich in all varieties of natural resources, and as wild and untamed homes to dangerous beasts and threatening calamities. Reflecting these polyvalent attitudes, the U.S. philosopher Henry David Thoreau (1817–1862) wrote, "The West of which I speak is but another name for the Wild; and what I have been preparing to say is, that in Wildness is the preservation of the world. Every tree sends its fibers forth in search of the Wild. Cities import it at any price. Men plough and sail for it. From forest and wilderness come the tonics and barks that brace mankind" (Thoreau 1851 in Nash 1990, 38).

Benefits of Forests

People use forests as sources of raw materials for manufacturing processes or subsistence livelihoods. Forests are logged for timber and for wood pulp to make paper (more than 40 percent of all trees logged are turned into paper). Many human populations rely on forests for hunting, non-timber forest products (e.g., fruits, nuts, vegetables, spices, meats, oils, saps, dyes, rubber, medicines, and raw materials for traditional arts and crafts), and forage for livestock. In addition to their material benefits, forests often serve as sites of inspiration, rejuvenation, and epiphany.

While forests are home to uncounted wild species (only a small percentage of the world's tropical rain forest species have been identified), they also provide a diverse array of benefits to humans. Known as "the lungs of the world" because of their essential functions in producing oxygen and moderating the water and carbon cycles, forests provide a diverse array of ecosystem services, including water catchment and filtration, nutrient cycling, soil formation, biodiversity preservation, biomass generation and decomposition, and carbon sequestration that create and maintain habitable conditions on Earth.

With increasing concerns about climate change due to anthropogenic carbon emissions, the essential activity of forests as carbon sinks, which take up atmospheric carbon in their growing processes, has come to be seen as very important. Through the Clean Development Mechanism of the Kyoto Protocol (1997), developing countries are paid to plant and maintain forests in order to capture atmospheric carbon and offset the carbon emissions of the wealthier countries that have made commitments to reduce greenhouse gases.

Dangers of Forest Loss

Recognizing the importance of forests to human and planetary well-being, scientists have warned of the dangers of forest loss. In 1996, the World Resources Institute estimated that just over half (53.4 percent) of the original forest area (meaning the forest area on the Earth as it is estimated to have existed 8,000 years ago, assuming current climactic conditions) remained (WRI 1996). During the 1990s, the U.N. Food and Agriculture Organization reported a global loss of 0.22 percent of forest cover annually, with the most significant losses in the tropics. Forests are cleared for the economic value of their timber, to create agricultural fields, and to expand human settlements. In addition, selective harvesting of timber or wild species, cattle grazing, and water diversion can degrade forests, decreasing soil fertility and biodiversity and lowering their productivity. Selective harvesting of timber that removes trees at the same pace at which they regenerate may be sustainable, and may, in some cases, enhance species diversity within forests by creating a wider variety of ecological niches. Such harvesting must be carefully monitored, through either scientific forest management or traditional taboos, to ensure that the pace of removal does not exceed the pace of regeneration.

Decreased quality or outright loss of forests causes a loss of the ecological goods and services that forests provide. Forest destruction is also a spiritual loss, as the richness of the living world is decreased and humans lose the opportunity to commune with various wild species. Meaningful relationships with the natural world may be necessary for optimum human functioning, according to the biophilia hypothesis proposed by the biologist Edward O. Wilson and the ecologist Stephen R. Kellert. Human wellbeing depends on the wholeness and coherence of living systems. The human species evolved in conjunction with natural processes that shaped human facilities and cognition. Only relatively recently, in evolutionary time, have humans begun living indoors. Because of our long co-evolution with other species, human beings are intrinsically dependent upon close relations with nature and natural processes for individual and general well-being.

In cultures throughout the world, forests have been places of refuge, contemplation and solace, where people could escape the hurly-burly of daily life to contemplate transcendent truths or interact with deities, spirits, and supranormal forces. The loss of forests reduces these opportunities, as well as opportunities for the aesthetic and uplifting appreciation of nature. In traditional and indigenous cultures, healing practices, spirituality, and worldview are often intertwined in systems that view illness as a spiritual imbalance or disruption. Forest loss also affects the ability to engage in these spiritual and traditional healing practices, as the necessary herbs for such practices are often only to be found in forests.

Scientists and policymakers in the developed countries have primarily been concerned with the loss of biological diversity, the loss of undeveloped wilderness, and the loss of recreational opportunities, while activists in the developing countries have been more concerned with the maintenance of rural livelihoods that depend on the extraction of timber and non-timber forest products for their subsistence, as well as preventing neocolonialist bio-prospecting and bio-piracy that would unfairly extract resources from the forests.

North America, South America, and Russia are home to the largest swaths of forests. Tropical rain forests, found in warm, low-elevation areas such as the Amazonian basin

of South America, are richest in biological diversity. The soil is relatively nutrient-poor, making it difficult to grow crops on the bare soil if the forest is cut down. If clearing the tropical rain forest continues at current rates, these forests will be gone by the end of the twenty-first century. Temperate forests are found in eastern North America and northeastern Asia. Because these forests are extremely productive, turning out 1,800 tons of vegetation per acre (as compared with 185 tons per acre in a tropical forest), most of the original temperate forest has long since been cleared. At the highest latitudes and altitudes of North America and Eurasia, the alpine and boreal forests are found, and they represent the largest terrestrial biome. Precipitation occurs mainly in the form of snow. Boreal forests are extensively logged and may vanish unless logging is limited. The boreal forests, circling the subarctic zone around the Northern Hemisphere, are estimated to constitute 25 percent of the world's remaining forest. Thus, although forested areas continue to exist in many climate zones of the Earth, forest resources are being depleted for human use, threatening overall sustainability of life on the planet.

Elizabeth A. ALLISON
University of California, Berkeley

FURTHER READING

Eisenberg, Sheryl. (2004, February). Taking trees personally. *This Green Life*. Retrieved March 29, 2009, from http://www.nrdc.org/thisgreenlife/0402.asp

Food and Agriculture Organization of the United Nations. (2003). *State of the world's forests, 2003*. Rome: United Nations. Retrieved March 29, 2009, from http://www.fao.org/DOCREP/005/Y7581E/Y7581E00.HTM

Kyoto Protocol: Mechanisms: Clean development mechanism. Retrieved May 22, 2009, from http://unfccc.int/kyoto_protocol/mechanisms/clean_development_mechanism/items/2718.php

National Aeronautics and Space Administration (NASA). (1998). Tropical deforestation. *The Earth Science Enterprise Series:* FS-1998-11-120-GSFC. Retrieved March 29, 2009, from http://www.iwokrama.org/library/pdfdownload/NASAdeforestation.pdf

Rosenzweig, M. L., & Daily, G. C. (2003, June 6). Win-win ecology: How the Earth's species can survive in the midst of human enterprise. *Science 300*(5625): 1508–1509.

Thoreau, Henry David. (1851). Walking. Reprinted in Roderick F. Nash, (Ed.) (1990), *American environmentalism: Readings in conservation history* (3rd ed.),p. 38. New York: McGraw Hill.

United Nations Framework Convention on Climate Change: Kyoto Protocol, Clean Development Mechanism. (Adopted 1997; entered into force 2005). Retrieved May 22, 2009, from http://cdm.unfccc.int/index.html

Wilson, Edward O., & Kellert, Stephen R. (Eds.). (1993). *The biophilia hypothesis*. Washington, DC: Island Press.

World Resources Institute. (2009). Earthtrends: Environmental information. Retrieved May 27, 2009, from http://earthtrends.wri.org/

World Resources Institute. (1996). Forests, grasslands and drylands—Forest extent: Forest area (current) as a percent of original forest area. Retrieved August 6, 2009, from http://earthtrends.wri.org/searchable_db/index.php?theme=9&variable_ID=313&action=select_countries

Fundamentalism

Fundamentalists adhere to foundational truth that is often grounded in literalist interpretations of sacred texts. Some religious fundamentalists may oppose environmentalism because it challenges God's supremacy or God's plan for the Earth, or because worldly care detracts from faith. Some combine anti-environmentalism with support for free-market capitalism. There are, however, fundamentalist groups whose cultural practices reflect ecological and social sustainability.

Fundamentalism is a term loaded with connotations, but it is basically used to describe groups that demand a strict adherence to a basic set of principles and are to some degree aggressive in their defense. The term is usually used in reference to religious groups, but sometimes it may describe nonreligious groups or social movements. There is no definitive type of fundamentalism that can be applied to all of the various manifestations of twentieth-century religious movements that respond to modernization (or the incursion of certain forms of Westernization), secularization (or the declining influence of religion and religious truth claims), and religious pluralism—all of which challenge the validity and hold of traditional religious forms in a wide variety of faiths. Fundamentalists see or perceive a threat to their way of life and their claims of foundational truth, which are often grounded in literalist or rigid readings of sacred texts or practices. Fundamentalist stances can be related to conservative or orthodox beliefs but exceed them both in the intensity or rigidity.

Because fundamentalist groups focus on defending the past and achieving a triumphant future, they often do not address contemporary concerns for sustainability, and they may be opposed to such movements. Because of the centrality of non-negotiable truth claims in their belief structures, fundamentalists are often less interested in any kind of interfaith or ecumenical cooperative work with those judged more liberal in their faith or with those who have allegiance to other ideologies. Since many religious efforts toward sustainability embrace interfaith efforts, fundamentalists within the Abrahamic, sacred-text-based religions—Judaism, Islam, and Christianity—are far less likely to be involved in such efforts.

Whereas fundamentalist groups reject some aspects of modernity and modernization, they are not entirely anti-modern, and they may adeptly use technological, financial, and political instruments of modernity. Their critique of the modern embrace of science and natural knowledge over religious revealed knowledge pertains to sustainability. Ironically, in their critique of modernization—its disenchantment of the world and resulting spiritual alienation, the dominance of an often destructive technological orientation, and the erasure of particularity—along with a nostalgia for a lost or threatened way of life, religious fundamentalists can appear to have common cause with what might be termed "green fundamentalism."

Great political differences color the relations between religious fundamentalists and religious environmentalists on many issues such as the family, the place of women, the role of the religion in the state, the economic system, or the truth claims of science and the need for environmental concern. Significant differences among religious fundamentalists in general in the rejection or embrace of the global economic market may also affect these views. Indeed, many Christian fundamentalists find more of a common cause with what might be termed a certain "market fundamentalism," in which neoclassical ways of organizing the economy are seen as almost sacred practices that cannot be changed in the face of the planetary demand for a more sustainable economy.

Yet even within any one religious tradition in any given locale, it is often hard to discern who might be termed fundamentalist, other than those who claim the term. For example, in Judaism, some would assert that the ultra-orthodox (Haredi) and the Lubavitch-Chabad Chassidim could be viewed as fundamentalist (although the attitude toward scripture is not the same as Christian literalism) and that many Orthodox Jews have fundamentalist views about science. But this becomes less clear in Israel, where the Heschel Center for Environmental Learning and Leadership works with "the ultra-religious, religious and secular" and where there is growing environmental concern within the Chabad. Similarly, what part of the spectrum of conservative Christianity in the United States is fundamentalist versus evangelical? The general public and media tend to confuse these terms; even scholars differ, and many scholars consider fundamentalism to be a subset of evangelicalism. Christian fundamentalists tend, however, to be more literal in their reading of scripture and more inclined toward a premillennial dispensational theology (the belief that Jesus will return before his one-thousand-year reign).

Like fundamentalists, most evangelicals tend to be political and social conservatives. Those referred to as the Christian Right in the United States are more fundamentalist than evangelical and often are not members of evangelical associations such as the National Association of Evangelicals (NAE). Although there has been a surge of interest and commitment to a variety of environmental issues among evangelicals, this is harder to find within the world of Christian fundamentalism, and what is there often aims to counter the influence of "green evangelicalism" and its embrace by high profile evangelical leaders such as the Reverends Joel Hunter, Tri Robinson, or Richard Cizik, the former vice president of governmental affairs for the National Association of Evangelicals.

Fundamentalist Views on Environmentalism and Evolution

Examples of Christian fundamentalist interest in environmental issues illustrate another viewpoint. One of the earliest fundamentalist/evangelical Christian voices on the environment was Francis Schaeffer, whose prescient voice was very influential on green evangelicals through his 1970 book *Pollution and the Death of Man*. Perhaps the most well-known Christian fundamentalist to champion an environmental cause is Pat Robertson with his 2006 "conversion" to accepting the reality of global warming, but that was not necessarily an embrace of larger sustainability issues. Other significant indicators of a shift within some sectors of the U.S. Christian fundamentalist world are the recent statements by leading Southern Baptists (but not the Southern

Baptist Convention) on the need to respond to global climate change, and the nascent greening of the Salvation Army (which may or may not be considered fundamentalist). Still, Christian fundamentalism strongly tends toward anti-environmental positions, sometimes vehemently so, and for a variety of reasons.

Religious fundamentalists may be wary of environmentalism as a new paganism or as a competing religion. In more fundamentalist Christian circles, it may even be associated with the Antichrist and a one-world government (as indicated by treaties such as Kyoto and other international governmental environmental efforts), all of which may be taken as signs of the end-times. Other reasons for the frequent anti-environmental stance of fundamentalists include the perception that the central task of most religious fundamentalists is the advancement and protection of the faith, from which too much care for this world, or for worldly things, detracts. Christian fundamentalists intensify this with an otherworldly focus, which can range from a primary regard for the rewards of salvation and the afterlife and/or heaven (and thus a disregard for this world) to a theology of imminent eschatology, or the end of this world and the return of Christ. If this world is going to end soon, then there is often no perceived need for environmental concern and, in fact, the environmental deterioration of the planet fits into some dramatic interpretations of the last book of the Christian scriptures, Revelation. Such views may be supported by a hard (as opposed to soft) interpretation of dominion in the book of Genesis. In this reading, the bounty and resources of the Earth were put here by God for human thriving and to help humans "be fruitful and multiply." To question either population growth or resource consumption out of concern for the sustainability of the planet, then, would doubt God's will and commands.

Furthermore, within the Abrahamic religions, the wide scientific conversation regarding evolution is seen by some as a direct challenge to the literalist readings of Genesis and of a creator God who directs all Earthly processes. Whereas this is especially true within Christianity, the embrace of creationism has a similar effect within Orthodox Judaism, especially within the ultra-Orthodox, where a major split has developed over whether the world is several thousands of years old rather than millions or billions of years old. Within Islam, for example, some parts of the Gulen movement in Turkey embrace creationism and work with creationists in the United States.

Views of the age of the Earth and how it came into being relate to fundamentalist understandings of the omnipotence of God and the uniqueness of humanity. To worry about something like the sustainability of the oceans or global warming may doubt that God is in charge and that God will right things according to a grand plan. Further, from a fundamentalist perspective, science often is accused of viewing humans as another animal (as opposed to being distinct from the rest of creation and in the image of God) by pointing out the biological similarities with other species and the biological underpinnings of our thoughts and actions (Acton 2007, 22). Due to these tensions with science, however, there is vehement opposition by some to the scientific consensus on global warming. It is, however, worth noting that fundamentalists do not reject all science, and often go out of their way to promote science that is seen to agree with their worldview, such as in their dispute with climate change science. (The "Global Warming Petition" of the Oregon Institute for Science and Medicine [www. oism.org/pproject], lists thousands of scientists who challenge climate change science, but who are often in unrelated fields or medicine or engineering, are high school biology teachers, or use fraudulent names).

Religious Fundamentalism and Capitalism

Contrary to what one might expect from movements that respond to modernization, another central motivation of opposition to environmentalism within fundamentalist (and more moderate) Christians comes not from explicit religious and theological doctrines, but from their implicit belief in the supremacy of free-market capitalism, often viewed as a system that rewards those who are blessed by God. Critics point out that this "health and wealth" Gospel is seen by many to promote consumerism. For these religious and economic conservatives, anything that is seen to thwart the workings of the invisible hand of the market, as most regulation concerned with sustainability is viewed, is a threat (Acton 2007, 60 and 71–110). This view is also embraced by many Jews, such as the influential Rabbi Daniel Lapin, whose group, the American Alliance of Jews & Christians, lists "Environmental Stewardship Consistent with Free Markets and Property Rights" as one of its priorities on its website (www.rabbidaniellapin.com).

The Acton Institute for the Study of Religion and Liberty, and the related Interfaith Council on Environmental Stewardship (ICES), now the Cornwall Alliance, are prominent examples of the well funded, religiously based, free-market-oriented, counter-environmentalist "green" movement. These groups particularly take aim at the "green" evangelicals that make the headlines, such as the aforementioned Richard Cizik. They have clear ties with the "Wise Use" movement and its anti-environmental regulation agenda, as well as with well-known fundamentalist U.S. Christian-right activists such as James Dobson of Focus on the Family (FOF) and Donald Holdel, a past president of FOF who was secretary of energy and then secretary of the interior under former president Ronald

Reagan. Holdel is listed as one of the environment advisers of the "Effective Stewardship" video curriculum produced and distributed by Acton and the Cornwall Alliance. Publications and activist campaigns of these groups demonstrate the connection between a firm belief in free-market capitalism and a critical or dismissive stance toward many key sustainability issues: for instance, the booklet that accompanies the Effective Stewardship curriculum asserts that "the world is not experiencing overpopulation or destructive, manmade global warming or rampant species loss" (Acton 2007, 100). A central figure for these groups is E. Calvin Beisner, listed as the national spokesman for the Cornwall Alliance and author of *Where Garden Meets Wilderness: Evangelical Entry into the Environmental Debate*, which criticizes well-known green evangelicals such as Calvin DeWitt and the Evangelical Environmental Network. Among documents Beisner has written for the Cornwall Alliance that challenge key green evangelical documents is "The Cornwall Declaration" (2007) written in response to "The Evangelical Declaration on the Care of Creation." The Cornwall Declaration, sent to 37,000 religious leaders, affirms private property ownership and market economies, while the Evangelical Declaration (2000) promotes "lifestyle choices that express humility, forbearance, self-restraint, and frugality" and "godly, just, and sustainable choices." Another example of the contrast between the two groups is seen in an "open letter" to the signers of the Evangelical Climate Initiative's "Call to Action," arguing "against the extent, the significance, and perhaps the existence of the much touted scientific consensus on catastrophic, human-induced global warming" (An open letter 2009). In addition to being skeptical of anthropogenic climate change, the open letter also demonstrates the complex logic related to their clear allegiance to free-market capitalism: "we believe it is far wiser to promote economic growth, partly through keeping energy inexpensive, than to fight against potential global warming and thus slow economic growth. And there is a side benefit, too: wealthier societies are better able and more willing to spend to protect and improve the natural environment than poorer societies. Our policy, therefore, is better not only for humanity but also for the rest of the planet" (An open letter 2009). This quote illustrates how any "market fundamentalism" can hinder efforts to achieve sustainability or even to begin to understand what a sustainable economic system might look like.

Fundamentalist Groups and Sustainable Living

Skepticism and opposition to the idea that human actions create potentially disastrous climate change, as in the "We Get It" campaign's concern to protect the poor from environmental policies that "further oppress the poor" and prevent them from fulfilling "their God-given potential as producers and stewards" (The WeGetIt.org Declaration [n.d.]), are rallying points for more conservative Christian environmentalism. There is, however, a broader spectrum of conservative Christian sustainability activity that refrains from involvement in the heated debate over climate change. Many point to some Amish and Mennonites as examples of more sustainable living, although few would term them fundamentalists. Organizations that explicitly link addressing poverty and furthering sustainability around the globe include Floresta, which aims to educate, assist, and develop programs to combat the problems caused by deforestation in third world countries that have been, and Target Earth International, whose mission is to serve the Earth and serve the Poor." Both organizations work in the Caribbean and Central America. Within ultra-Orthodox and Orthodox Judaism, Rabbi Natan Slifkin, creator of the concept and organization Zoo Torah, develops programs to show conservative Jews in Israel the importance of all animals. (Slifkin's books were banned in 2005 by a coalition of about twenty prominent Haredi rabbis in Israel and the United States because he suggested that the Talmud needed to be read in light of scientific evidence over the age of the Earth.) There is growing concern for sustainability within the more moderate segments of Jewish Orthodoxy.

Many local Christian environmental movements in the developing world would fit much of the theological profile of fundamentalism such as the Association of African Earthkeeping Churches in Zimbabwe, whose members are primarily Zionists and Apostles, and the Baptist Brackenhurst Environmental Program in Kenya. Both of these organizations have worked to plant millions of trees and to establish more sustainable agricultural practices, while the Khanya Programme in South Africa emphasizes permaculture techniques. Although this article has focused on many of the U.S.-based, politically activist Christian fundamentalists who are the most ardent in opposing environmentalism and sustainability, there are many in the broad spectrum of fundamentalist belief across the globe who neither care for nor militate against sustainability. Others work on local sustainability issues but remain silent in the global debate. And many use cultural practices that

are already far more sustainable than those of the United States.

Laurel D. KEARNS
Drew Theological School and University

FURTHER READINGS

Acton Institute. (2007). *Environmental stewardship in the Judeo-Christian tradition.* Grand Rapids, MI: Acton Institute.

An open letter to the signers of climate change: An evangelical call to action and others concerned about global warming. (2009). Retrieved June 2, 2009, from http://www.cornwallalliance.org/docs/an-open-letter-to-the-signers-of-climate-change-an-evangelical-call-to-action-and-others-concerned-about-global-warming.pdf

Beisner, E. Calvin. (1997). *Where garden meets wilderness: Evangelical entry into the environmental debate.* Acton Institute for the Study of Religion and Liberty. Grand Rapids, MI: W. B. Eerdmans.

Bliese, John R. E. (2002). *The greening of conservative America.* Boulder, CO: Westview End Press.

Beisner, E. Calvin. (2006, July 27). A call to truth, prudence, and the protection of the poor. Retrieved April 26, 2009, from http://erlc.com/article/a-call-to-truth-prudence-and-protection/

The Cornwall Declaration on Environmental Stewardship. (2007). In *Environmental stewardship in the Judeo-Christian Tradition* (pp. 7–11). Grand Rapids, MI: Acton Institute. (Also retrieved June 4, 2009, from http://www.cornwallalliance.org/articles/read/call-to-truth/)

Climate change: An evangelical call to action. (n.d.). Retrieved July 13, 2009, from http://christiansandclimate.org/learn/call-to-action/

Cromartie, Michael & Derr, Thomas Sieger. (1995) *Creation at risk? Religion, science, and environmentalism.* Wilmington, DE: ISI Books.

Daneel, Marthinus L. (2001). *African Earthkeepers: Wholistic interfaith mission.* Maryknoll, NY: Orbis Books.

Evangelical declaration on the care of Creation. (2000). In R. J. Berry (Ed.), *The Care of Creation: Focusing Concern and Action* (pp. 17–22). Downer's Grove, IL: Intervarsity Press. (Also retrieved June 4, 2009, from http://www.creationcare.org/resources/declaration.php)

Kearns, Laurel & Keller, Catherine. (Eds.). (2007). *EcoSpirit: Religions and philosophies for the Earth.* New York: Fordham Press.

Martin, Marty & Appleby, R. Scott. (Eds.). (1993–2004) *The fundamentalism project* (Vols. 1–5). Chicago: University of Chicago Press.

Peterson, Anna L. (2005). *Seeds of the kingdom: Utopian communities in the Americas.* New York: Oxford University Press.

Schaefer, Francis A. (1970). *Pollution and the death of man: The Christian view of ecology.* London: Hodder & Stoughton.

Slifkin, Natan. (2006). *The challenge of creation: Judaism's encounter with science, cosmology and evolution.* Brooklyn, NY: Yashar Books.

The WeGetIt.org Declaration. (n.d.). Retrieved June 4, 2009, from www.wegetit.org/declaration

Wright, Richard T. (1995, June). Tearing down the green: Environmental backlash in the Evangelical sub-culture. *Perspectives on Science and the Christian Faith 47,* 80–91. Retrieved June 4, 2009, from, http://www.asa3.org/aSA/PSCF/1995/PSCF6-95Wright.html

Future

All cultures are infused with myths and prophecies that express humankind's expectations and fears for the future. By the latter decades of the twentieth century, however, realization spread that without sustainable practices the human enterprise more and more compromised the ecosphere's capacity to support future life.

The advent of sustainability as a development ideal opens a new chapter in the relationship between culture and the future. The growing awareness that shortsighted collective behavior today imperils human well-being tomorrow brings unprecedented urgency to the challenge of understanding and shaping the future. At the core of the notion of sustainability lies a riveting moral imperative: the responsibility of the living to bequeath an undiminished world to the unborn. This obligation requires present generations to adopt an integrated perspective that weighs the long-term implications of contemporary practices and adjusts them accordingly. By highlighting the interdependence of society and planet, this systemic framework extends the ambit of ethical concern to other people distant in space, generations distant in time, and creatures distant in kinship.

We live, however, in the eternal now, poised at the moving boundary between completed and uncompleted time. From the vantage point of today, we cast a double-faced Janus gaze both back toward yesterday and ahead toward tomorrow, reflecting on where we have been and imagining where we are heading. Past permeates present, leaving its imprint on the tangible world of nature and society and, also, on the world of ideas through our varying interpretations of the content and meaning of history. The future does not directly affect the flow of events, for, according to a basic tenet of modern science, the direction of causality points only forward in time.

Imagining the Future, Affecting the Present

But images of the future do affect the present through their influence on human values and action, thus introducing a teleological element into the dynamic of social evolution. All cultures are infused with myths, prophecies, dreams, and nightmares that express collective expectations, hopes, and fears; they circumscribe the limits of the possible, the desirable, and the horrific. Prevailing images of the future reinforce existing norms and societal structures in times of political quietism and cultural hegemony; dissident visions of the future energize and legitimize oppositional groups in times of social and cultural change.

In premodern cultures with a fatalistic mind-set, individual and collective destinies were linked to the higher dictates of suprahuman forces. Oracles, seers, and priests divined the workings and providence of the universe and offered guidance on how to propitiate the gods but proposed little hope for worldly salvation. Then, the great cultural shift that began with the Renaissance and reached an apotheosis in the Enlightenment brought heightened faith in human reason, science, and progress. By ascribing agency to human actors, anointing them as authors of their own historical narrative, theological formulations of collective destiny began giving way to pragmatic and ethical formulations for guiding social evolution.

Alongside this philosophical upheaval, modernity released a powerful set of world-changing forces—rapid technological innovation, market economies, democracy, and law-governed institutions—that set population, production, and consumption on exponential growth curves. With human impacts on nature growing apace, unbounded demographic and economic expansion set a collision course with the limits of a finite planet. By the latter decades of the twentieth century, concern spread that the human enterprise more and more compromised the ecosphere's capacity to support life, thereby threatening the long-term prospects for human development. The age of sustainability had arrived.

Sustainability invites us to collectively and self-consciously construct the future: to generate plausible images of the world decades from now, establish collective goals, and adapt current choices and behaviors for the journey. Envisioning global futures poses new challenges to both science and the popular imagination. Of the immense web of possibilities opening into the future, only one strand will crystallize into history through the interplay of unfolding patterns, chance, serendipity, and human choice. The most sophisticated computer models remain far too imperfect to simulate accurately the breathtaking intricacy of the nested social and ecological systems that comprise the integral Earth. Better models can reduce epistemological uncertainty, but not the inherent uncertainty of complex systems—bifurcations at critical thresholds and emergent properties. Most profoundly, human systems carry the additional uncertainty of volition: the global future depends on human choices that have not yet been made. Coming full circle, those choices will be influenced by the ways we think about the future.

Scenarios for a Sustainable Future

In light of this indeterminacy, sustainability analysts are developing new approaches to explore the future and inform current decisions. The evolving field of scenario analysis is employed widely to develop a range of coherent stories consistent with historical conditions, driving forces, scientific knowledge, and historical insight. State-of-the-art scenarios of the global future combine quantitative simulation and qualitative analysis to track current trends as they branch into an array of possible outcomes. The aim is to stimulate the imagination, better grasp forthcoming risks and opportunities, provoke discussion, and guide decision making.

Broadly, scenarios fall into three archetypal categories: evolutionary, degenerative, and transformative. Evolutionary futures unfold gradually from incremental changes in

technology, environment, and society. The evolutionary approach to sustainability relies on government-led policies to promote environmentally friendly technology and poverty alleviation, but it faces the practical and political challenge of mounting a sustained campaign sufficient to counter the effects of an expanding world economy. If the evolutionary strategy fails, global development could degenerate, veering toward a more fragmented, authoritarian, or chaotic world. Environmental controls might eventually be imposed, but not without great conflict and misery.

Transformative futures envision fundamental institutional and cultural changes to redirect development from catastrophe to sustainability. These scenarios are rooted in a shift in human consciousness and aspirations away from consumerism and individualism and toward qualitative aspects of human well-being: personal relationships, community engagement, creative endeavors, and appreciation of nature. An inclusive sense of solidarity would become the foundation for more effective and just governance from local to global levels. In calling attention to such visions, the sustainability project rekindles age-old hopes for an organic and interdependent global civilization, no longer as abstract hope, but as necessity for a resilient and livable future.

Paul D. RASKIN
Tellus Institute

FURTHER READING

Carpenter, Steve R.; Pingali, Prabhu L.; Bennett, Elena M.; & Zurek, Monika B. (Eds.). (2005). *Ecosystems and human well-being. Volume 2: Scenarios* (Millennium Ecosystem Assessment). Washington, DC: Island Press.

Heilbroner, Robert. (1995). *Visions of the future: The distant past, yesterday, today, and tomorrow.* New York: Oxford University Press.

Raskin, Paul; Banuri, Tariq; Gallopín, Gilberto; Gutman, Pablo; Hammond, Al; et al. (2002). *Great transition: The promise and the lure of the times ahead.* Boston: Tellus Institute.

Swart, Rob; Raskin, Paul; & Robinson, John. (2004). The problem of the future: Sustainability science and scenario analysis. *Global Environmental Change, 14*(2), 137–146.

World Commission on Environment and Development (WCED). (1987). *Our common future.* Oxford, U.K.: Oxford University Press.

Future Generations

Concern for future generations figures significantly in discussions about sustainability. While some contemporary philosophers believe that future generations may be discounted in such debates because future existence cannot be guaranteed, others emphasize the commonality of present and future peoples as inhabitants of the Earth who will inherit a value system, as well as the natural environment.

A relationship to future generations is implicitly central to many of today's most public controversies—not only over environmental protection, but also over genetic research, welfare systems, and the purpose of education, to name but a few. Questions about sustainability and about future generations have been closely linked from the early days of "sustainable development," as the definition from the Brundtland Report, *Our Common Future*, shows: "Sustainable development is development that meets the needs of the present without compromising the ability of future generations to meet their own needs" (World Commission on Environment and Development 1987).

Modern paradigms of ethical thought have, in various ways, failed to consider adequately the temporal dimension of ethics. The question of the ethical relation to future generations, as it is known and discussed in contemporary philosophy, is in the strict sense a modern problem. Histories of the question often begin in the eighteenth century with the debates between Edmund Burke, Thomas Paine, and others about the significance of the French Revolution (1789–1799). Our relationship with future generations becomes a problem once it lies within the power of humanity to redetermine the conditions of human existence.

Many modern arguments against taking future generations seriously in ethical debate rest on the fact that future generations are, by definition, not "present"; they are not present to express preferences, enter into contracts, or assert rights. Their very existence, let alone their behavior or their needs, is in doubt. Economic practices of time-related "discounting" of benefits and harms are explained, to some extent, by the level of uncertainty attached to anything related to future generations. There are, furthermore, the well-known philosophical conundrums articulated by the British ethicist Derek Parfit (b. 1942). If we take a "person-affecting" view of ethics (if we say that an action or situation is only ethically relevant if it is good or bad, beneficial or harmful, *for someone*), and if we also concede that what we do now will, or might, affect *which persons come into existence* in the future, it seems that we cannot relate ethically to future persons at all—since our actions do not benefit or harm anybody in particular (different people come into existence than would have existed had we acted differently). Parfit and others have negotiated this problem in various ways, notably (in Parfit's case) by adopting a non–person-affecting approach.

Considering future generations in the context of thought about sustainability makes it hard to maintain their ethical irrelevance on the grounds that we "do not know" their wants or needs. Future generations are, as the political philosopher Onora O'Neill and others have pointed out, in many ways no more different from us than are distant strangers about whom we can reliably say have need for or are entitled to sufficient food, livable environments, freedom from the threat of violence, and so forth.

Thinking about sustainability means, for many environmental ethicists, recognizing the limits on our ability to reinvent humanity—and hence recognizing future generations, as Avner de-Shalit has argued, as members of a community with us. Nurturing a sense of commonality with future generations—not merely common humanity, but common inhabitation of the Earth—has been one of the aims of the Future Generations Program at the Foundation for International Studies, University of Malta. Significant for its work are the preambles to numerous United Nations documents that refer to aspects of the natural environment, or in one case to the human genome, as the "common heritage of humanity." Taking "humanity" here to have temporal as well as spatial extension, some have called for specific advocates for future generations to participate in international deliberations about the environment.

Concern for future generations, in debates about sustainability, may be criticized on the one hand as excessively anthropocentric, and on the other hand as insufficiently attentive to present injustices. Do we value nonhuman nature only as "resources" we can pass on to "our children," rather than as having intrinsic value of its own? And what is the relationship between preserving resources for "our children" and distributing them justly in the present? One way to address these issues may be to consider the "sustainability" of ways of life and value systems, rather than only of patterns of resource consumption. Future generations are the inheritors, not only of our resources but also of our values, and the significance of this aspect of responsibility toward them should not be overlooked.

Rachel MUERS
University of Leeds

FURTHER READING

Agius, Emmanuel, & Chircop, Lionel (Eds.). (1998). *Caring for future generations: Jewish, Christian and Islamic perspectives.* London: Adamantine Press.

Auerbach, Bruce. (1995). *Unto the thousandth generation: Conceptualising intergenerational justice.* New York: Peter Lang.

De-Shalit, Avner. (1995). *Why posterity matters.* London: Routledge.

Kim, Tae-Chang, & Harrison, Ross. (Eds.). (1999). *Self and future generations: An intercultural conversation between East and West.* Cambridge, U.K.: White Horse Press.

O'Neill, Onora. (1994). Distant strangers and future generations. In Tae-Chang Kim and James A. Dator, (Eds.) *Creating a New History for Future Generations.* Kyoto, Japan: Institute for the Integrated Study of Future Generations.

Parfit, Derek. (1984). *Reasons and persons.* Oxford, U.K.: Oxford University Press.

Tremmel, Joerg C. (Ed.). (2006). *Handbook of intergenerational justice.* Cheltenham, U.K.: Edward Elgar.

World Commission on Environment and Development. (1987). *Our common future.* Oxford, U.K.; New York: Oxford University Press.

Gaia

The name Gaia, Earth goddess of the Greeks, refers today to the scientific theory first proposed and developed by James Lovelock in the 1970s. It views the Earth as a superorganism—a single, dynamic, self-regulating system. To sustain this self-regulation we must stop using and depleting natural resources as if they exist solely for human use.

The English scientist James Lovelock (b. 1919) first developed Gaia theory, the theory that the Earth is a self-regulating superorganism in which life is intricately entwined with everything else on the surface of the Earth, in the 1970s. Despite criticism from scientific colleagues Lovelock has continued to use the name Gaia for his theory because it conveys the image of a living Earth. According to the Greek creation myth *Theogony*—related and compiled by the eighth-century BCE poet Hesiod—Gaia, the primal Earth goddess, brought forth the world out of Chaos. Alone she gave birth, first to Uranos (the Sky) so that he might cover and surround her and provide a home for the "blessed gods." Then she brought forth the Mountains and Pontos (the Sea). Although Earth goddesses abound in creation myths of numerous cultures as diverse as the Sumerian and Maori, Gaia's name has become the ubiquitous symbol of Earth as a living, divine body. Some, however, see Gaia as a pagan cult and enemy of Christianity (especially those defensive of the view that monotheism has set humans apart from nature and stripped nature of its sacredness). Others, notably Al Gore in his book *Earth in the Balance*, see a return to the spiritual sense of our place in nature (and a pan-religious perspective) as an integral part of our global civilization's responsibility for the Earth.

Gaia Theory

With the growth of climate change awareness, Gaia is now a recognized scientific term, a theory based on the concept of Earth as a superorganism composed of all life tightly entwined with the air, the oceans, and the surface rocks. James Lovelock developed Gaia theory to describe how and why, as life appeared on the planet and grew abundant, its evolution and the Earth's evolution merged into a single dynamic system. At the suggestion of his friend and neighbor William Golding, author of *Lord of the Flies*, Lovelock named the system *Gaia* after the primordial cosmic goddess of Greek myth.

Gaia theory describes how Earth's ability to sustain life results from the following properties of living organisms, three of them being intrinsic and one extrinsic. First, all organisms alter their environment by taking in free energy and excreting high-entropy waste products in order to maintain a low level of internal entropy. (Entropy is the technical term for energy still existing but unavailable for work purposes.) Second, organisms grow and multiply, thus providing an intrinsic positive feedback to life (the more life there is, the more life it can beget). Third, for each environmental variable there is a maximum level or range for the growth of a particular organism. The important extrinsic (fourth) factor is that organisms both alter and are constrained by their environments.

Together these factors ensure feedback between life and its environment, such that organic life is sustained through a dynamic disequilibrium between its component parts. Therefore changes within organisms and in organisms' relationships with the environment are built into the system. The properties that make the system sustainable alter and constrain the environment of each organism—to the point where any organism may lose the ability to sustain life and become extinct. That being so, accounts of sustainability based on use of global environmental resources must presuppose that what is sustainable at one period in Earth's history is not so forever.

The greatest value of Gaia theory in regard to sustainability is its insistence that we focus on our essential status as organic members of the entire community of life on Earth. This view offers a comprehensive interpretive framework for thinking through the challenges of sustainability by considering human life as part of a single, self-regulating system comprising physical, chemical, biological, and human components. So it follows that the ability of the planet to sustain human life is constrained by the functioning of common environmental resources, climatic variables, and the limits of the ecosystem. A primary Gaian insight is that as an emergent phenomenon, human life is neither external to nor independent of the planetary system's self-regulatory whole and cannot be analyzed reductively by separating it or by cutting it off from the processes or the flow of evolution. Gaia theory's cohesive approach to sustainability embodies goals that pertain to all aspects of the planetary system, not just human life alone.

Implications of Gaian Insight

Adhering to Gaian views of Earth as a single self-regulating system means renouncing our species' claim to absolute privilege regarding use of the Earth's material resources. The very factors that make such resources sustainable for any species constrain their use: overuse or abuse lead to extinctions. Practically, this means that we cannot assume that the Earth and its resources evolved and now exist solely for human use and benefit. The effects of such claims to human exceptionalism are now evident in the reduction of biodiversity and the shrinkage of the Earth's resources through our exploitation, over-industrialization, and technologization. The scale of this exploitation far outstrips that of natural resource replacement or disposal. The Gaian vision of human interaction with the environment—and of human rights constrained by those of our planetary partners—finds far-reaching implications of this imbalance for both ecological integrity and social justice.

Such implications are of particular concern to four classes of people singled out in the proceedings from the 1992 United Nations Conference on Environment and Development as being most at risk from environmental degradation, most vulnerable to its effects, and most powerless to do anything about them: women, children, indigenous peoples, and the poor. Yet the dominant free-market model of development and continuing growth presupposes that the resources needed to sustain such a model are and will be available. Relying on science, technology, and the spread and improvement of education, we expect to pass on a better, more prosperous global situation than the one we inherited. The presupposition behind this expectation is that the global biophysical environment will sustain such growth. In the light of Gaia theory, that expectation is itself unsustainable.

As a religious moral focus rather than a scientific term, Gaia offers a vision of the world and a possibility of speaking about it as a sacred totality. That means that supporters of the Gaian vision see human participation in the system as ultimately sustained by the power of the whole: human life cannot be separated from our understanding of the whole of existence. Therefore, those who relate to Gaia as sacred consider it a religious duty to sustain all aspects of her life.

Anne PRIMAVESI
University of London

FURTHER READING

Lovelock, James. (1991). *Gaia, the practical science of planetary medicine.* London: Gaia Books.

Lovelock, James. (1995). *Gaia: A new look at life on Earth* (rev. ed.). Oxford, U.K.: Oxford University Press.

Lovelock, James. (1995). *The ages of Gaia: A biography of our living Earth* (2nd ed.). Oxford, U.K.: Oxford University Press.

Lovelock, James. (2003, December 18). The living earth. *Nature, 426,* 769–770.

Lovelock, James, (2009). *The vanishing face of Gaia.* London: Allen Lane.

Primavesi, Anne. (2000). *Sacred Gaia: Holistic theology and earth system science.* London: Routledge.

Primavesi, Anne. (2009). *Gaia and climate change: A theology of gift events.* London: Routledge.

United Nations Conference on Environment and Development, 1992. (1997, May 23). Retrieved May 26, 2009, from http://www.un.org/geninfo/bp/enviro.html

Globalization

Although the rise of globalization is hard to deny, different opinions as to its benefits exist. It is a controversial issue; many worry about the potential negative consequences—especially a loss of cultural diversity and accelerating environmental degradation from global trade—but globalization also offers the possibility of increased awareness of worldwide environmental issues.

Globalization is a highly contested concept. In common parlance the term usually means the increasing economic and cultural integration of the world. However, there are other understandings of globalization, such as the development of "global citizenship" or the spread of political and economic freedom. However conceived, observers debate whether globalization is beneficial or not, and for whom. Increasing awareness of environmental change as a worldwide phenomenon has intensified debates over the consequences and concept of globalization.

To say that globalization means increasing economic integration means that more and more national and regional economies have been pulled into production for the world economic system. During the colonial era that lasted roughly from the 1500s into the 1900s, the industrializing countries relied on raw materials from their colonies. This world system generated a dynamic of core and periphery countries that form the general pattern of "developed" and "developing" nations today. So while globalization is often touted as a phenomenon of the latter decades of the twentieth century, economic analyses show that the world's economic flows were a larger part of global production in the period from 1880 to 1914.

Nevertheless, while internationalization processes predate today, the term *globalization* is used to describe a new social condition. The sociologist Roland Robertson (1992, 8) defines globalization as "both the compression of the world and the intensification of consciousness of the world as a whole." Thus the characteristic of contemporary globalization is that of awareness and magnitude, as more distant localities are more tightly and extensively linked in terms of the flow and interaction of people, ideas, consumer goods, material resources, travel, media, diseases, hazardous wastes, and so on. A wider range of people are more aware of their worldwide links, and these links have become more significant for more peoples, regions, and nations.

Globalization also refers to the development of a number of transnational institutions, such as global trade agreements, the United Nations, and corporations not tied to any single country. Some analyses, such as Saskia Sassen's *Globalization and Its Discontents* (1998), suggest that the nation-state is becoming less relevant. At the same time, core countries have continued to wield a great deal of political and economic power over the global world system. While more places are pulled into the world economic system, rates of production and consumption are markedly unequal, which highlights the fragmentation and unevenness of global processes. In part, this is supported by an ideological campaign that espouses freer global trade as the mechanism of increasing standards of living for all peoples of the planet.

It is this version of globalization that has generated anti-globalization social movements. In their analyses, developing countries are trying to navigate "a world where winners and losers are already set" and a system that seems to favor the existing global structure (Hossay 2006, 130). Leslie Sklair (2000, 348), Professor Emeritus at the London School of Economics, echoes this assessment and suggests that only religious counter-cultures and environmentalism have any potential to counter the dominance of "global capitalist consumerism."

But lest globalization be seen as merely an economic phenomenon, other aspects of globalization refer to cultural and political processes. The exchange of consumer goods, media images, and ideas in this unequal environment has raised fears of global cultural homogenization. American culture (e.g., the ubiquitous blue jeans, Coca-Cola, U.S. television, and capitalist individualism) is known and desired around the world; Western (meaning European-derived) institutional forms and ideas are widely dispersed. Thus globalization may lead to loss of human cultural diversity. But Western ideals such as representative democracy and human rights are potentially positive contributions of global exchange, and transnational migration has caused both strains and interaction. Furthermore, cultures are always in flux and locales engage the same things differently, which may result in hybridization rather than homogenization. Global communication has also intensified awareness of the plurality of human cultures, and their diverse and contrasting models of human relations, nature, social institutions, and so on. Global communications also quickly alert distant others to political events and natural disasters, sometimes resulting in quick response, such as the reaction to the Indian Ocean tsunami in December 2004.

Global awareness and the increasingly tight weave of global institutions is a process that also has environmental consequences. The lengthened distances but shortened time between resource extraction, production, consumption, and disposal of goods and services increase environmental effects. Climate change is only one of the environmental effects that have planetary-scale effects. The brunt of effects will be felt by those not responsible for the production of climate change gases, leading to issues of "climate justice," the concept of dissolving and alleviating unequal burdens created changes in climate (Roberts and Parks 2007). Long-distance pollution or chemical transport is another vector of globalization, affecting places far from the site of production. Region-wide ecosystem degradation is not just the cumulative result of many smaller local effects. Some argue that globalization weakens the knowledge and attachment to local places that may be necessary to live in less environmentally damaging ways or to effectively protect local environments. Loss of such cultural diversity may mean loss of alternative ways of living with and on the earth. But global awareness and intensification may also produce "global citizens" aware of the increasingly global environmental impact of human action. In the final analysis, globalization is a highly contested concept with effects that are not yet known.

Randolph HALUZA-DeLAY
The King's University College (Alberta)

FURTHER READING

Bunker, Stephen G., & Ciccantell, Paul S. (2005). *Globalization and the race for resources.* Baltimore: Johns Hopkins University Press.

della Porta, Donatella; Andretta, Massimiliano; Mosca, Lorenzo; & Reiter, Herbert. (2006). *Globalization from below: Transnational activists and protest networks.* Minneapolis: University of Minnesota Press.

Hossay, Patrick. (2006). *Unsustainable: A primer for global environmental and social justice.* London: Zed Books.

Millennium Ecosystem Assessment. (2005). *Synthesis report.* Retrieved August 9, 2008, from http://www.millenniumassessment.org/en/index.aspx

Roberts, J. Timmons, & Parks, Bradley C. (2007). *A Climate of injustice: Global inequality, north-south politics, and climate policy.* Cambridge, MA: MIT Press.

Robertson, Roland. (1992). *Globalization: Social theory and global culture.* London: Sage.

Sassen, Saskia. (1998). *Globalization and its discontents: Essays on the new mobility of people and money.* New York: New Press.

Sklair, Leslie. (2000). Social movements and global capitalism. In J. Timmons Roberts & Anne Hite (Eds.), *From modernization to globalization: Perspectives on development and social change* (pp. 340–352). London: Blackwell.

God

The Western perception of God's transcendence has implications for human action in promoting a sustainable world. Faith that God will sustain the Earth may limit human will to advance sustainability; conviction that all value exists in God may lead to a devaluation of creation; and attempts to know the world as God does, without self-interest, may result in an uncritical approach to future planning.

In most Western religions and for many Western philosophers, God is typically understood to be the transcendent reality that exists in relationship to the created order as being "other." These religions (and most of these philosophers) have traditionally represented the main issue of concern vis-à-vis God to be humanity's relationship with the divine, with the rest of the cosmos playing a decidedly secondary role.

The two sentences above point to some difficulties and contradictions. As seen from the first sentence, it is very hard, if not impossible, to define "God" without reference to what God is understood to stand for or against, and without mentioning that to which God is supposed to relate. Thus one decisive characteristic of God is that God, being wholly other and not "here" in some locally constraining way, is *not creation*. Yet God is also understood to have some relationship with creation, typically one of governance over it. As for the second sentence, the priority of the God–humanity relationship means that, in general, persons have tended to want to organize their existence around God, perhaps downplaying the importance of their relationship to the rest of the cosmos.

The concept of God's transcendence poses some complications for practicing sustainability ethics. On one hand, God's existence above and apart from the material world may bolster the ambitions of those who purport to have a "God's eye view" of the nature of reality, a view that is legitimated by its radical escape from parochial perspectives. In this way conceptions of God often function to reinforce our confidence in our apprehension of reality. Perhaps this is necessary for genuine objectivity, and insofar as we seek a knowledge untainted by narrow self-interest, it is well and good. But at times a provisional understanding of the world (e.g., its meaning, significance, and direction) may be elevated to an ultimate view. The self then sprints to facilitate the unfolding of the world and its future, drawing exuberant confidence from its ability to know the world as a transcendent (and omniscient) God knows the self. When confronted with questions about sustainability, this confidence may uncritically hasten provisional plans and pridefully exalt one's ability to advance history. Epistemologically, then, "God" may symbolize both the human intellect's most noble ambitions and one of its most dangerous predilections.

On the other hand, God's transcendence can also produce in believers a sense that the true value of the created order is wholly derivative from elsewhere, and thus has no genuine value in itself. In short, that is, all real value exists "altogether elsewhere," namely, in God. Those who come to believe this may well be tempted toward a thoroughgoing instrumentalization of the world, in which everything in the world is valuable only insofar as it is of use for us and our own projects, projects which may be decidedly "otherworldly" in their aims. So God can provoke in us a hyperactive structural hostility to the givens of nature and creation.

Alternatively, such believers may be tempted toward an attitude of quietist escapism from the world, whereby all worldly things are seen merely as impediments to our true end, which is fundamentally elsewhere. Since, on this view, God as creator and governor is master of creation, the narrative of history should feature God as the prime actor and agent. When confronted with questions of sustainability, one's relatively diminutive capacity to act should not be inordinately elevated. God will direct the course of history, sustaining the world until it comes to its close. When one meets the intermediate questions of sustainability, the most fitting response may be for one to wait for God's answer, thus perhaps too hastily surrendering the capacities to sustain that one may have. Ethically, then, "God" may present deep and profound challenges to any moral system of sustainability.

For all this, however, God is not simply a difficulty to be overcome. Indeed, the basic concerns about sustainability have come to grip many believers who affirm a transcendent deity. To strengthen and broaden these convictions, "God" should probably be understood in a way that implies divine responsibility for the world without also implying exclusive (i.e., humanity-paralyzing) agency for directing the course and setting the end of history.

Many other theological avenues may provide one understanding of God sufficient to elicit the need to take up sustainability questions, as well as the responsibility necessary to answer them well. But for many, the understanding of a transcendent God will be a temptation toward provisional answers or will dull the need to provide any answer at all.

Charles MATHEWES
Chad WAYNER
University of Virginia

FURTHER READING

Bouma-Prediger, Steven. (1995). *The greening of theology: The ecological models of Rosemary Radford Ruether, Joseph Sittler, and Jürgen Moltmann.* American Academy of Religion Academy Series. Atlanta: Scholars Press.

Jenkins, Willis. (2008). *Ecologies of grace.* New York: Oxford University Press.

McFague, Sallie. (1987). *Models of God: Theology for an ecological, nuclear age.* Philadelphia: Fortress Press.

Tanner, Kathryn. (2006). *God and creation in Christian theology.* Philadelphia: Fortress Press.

 Berkshire's authors and editors welcome questions, comments, and corrections: sustainability.updates@berkshirepublishing.com

Green Belt Movement

The Green Belt Movement focuses on tree planting in Africa and elsewhere, but also, through education and advocacy, strives for the empowerment of women in African society. Some have linked Christianity and indigenous African religions to the ecology movement, but the Green Belt Movement, led by Wangari Muta Maathai, is primarily concerned with the practice of planting trees.

The 2004 Nobel Peace Prize winner, Wangari Muta Maathai, is widely known for her leadership of the Green Belt Movement, through which she encourages women to plants trees in the effort to stabilize the ecosystem of her native Kenya. By planting trees to counter soil erosion, water problems, and the loss of tree resources, the Green Belt Movement (founded in 1977) addresses several dimensions of empowering women.

Maathai's resolve to address questions about the environment alongside those of social justice is striking to scholars of religion and ecology who are aware of environmental degradation in Africa. For example, she uses the transformative act of planting trees in Kenya to draw attention to women as victims of oppression. In *African Earthkeepers*, Marthinus Daneel similarly ties African adaptations of Christianity to the rise of ecotheology in a group of African Initiated Churches (AIC) in patriarchal rural Zimbabwe, where women help the male church leaders plant trees to reduce damage to their environment. Daneel, in his analysis, incorporates Shona religious ideas that often draw on nature imagery to express truths about the divine. This heightens people's awareness of the sacredness of life on Earth. But in Maathai's case, women who are the mothers and crop producers of Mother Earth come first.

Today people continue to follow Maathi's lead, successfully planting trees in Tanzania, Uganda, Malawi, Lesotho, Ethiopia, and Zimbabwe. In these countries where adherents of both Christianity and Islam are to be found, indigenous religious ideas persist, and new religious movements are being developed. The religious pluralism in Africa raises questions about the spiritual dimension of the Green Belt Movement. Maathai does not provide any religious blueprint or conceptual system that might be used to explain the involvement of religious communities in her movement. Maathai focuses on a path of action, and, without saying so, challenges scholars of religion familiar with Africa to address the predicament of humanity in religious terms. Given the spread of Christianity in postcolonial Kenya, it is time for a rigorous ecofriendly critique of this world religion closely tied to a civilization whose capitalist economy has contributed to the destruction of the environment since the colonial era.

Isabel MUKONYORA
Western Kentucky University

FURTHER READING

Daneel, Marthinus. (1998). *African earthkeepers*. Pretoria: University of South Africa Press.

Hodge, Joseph Morgan. (2007). *Triumph of the expert: Agrarian doctrines of development and the legacies of British colonialism*. Athens: Ohio University Press.

McDonald, David A. (Ed.). (2002). *Environmental justice in South Africa*. Athens: Ohio University Press.

Mukonyora, Isabel. (1999). Women and ecology in Shona religion. *Word and World Journal, 19*, 276–284.

Green Parties

Green parties formed, beginning in the 1970s, as alternatives to traditional political parties to put forth an ecosocial analysis and vision. Green parties are active in over seventy countries and have been in the political forefront regarding policy informed by nonviolence, community-based economics, and ecological sustainability. Regional organizations of Green parties exist in the Americas, Europe, the Asia-Pacific region, and Africa.

Green politics emerged in the 1970s as a comprehensive political analysis and vision that brings together ecological and social concerns as an interrelated central focus, and were the first to present an ecosocial politics and the first political champion of the orientation known as "sustainability." The seeds of ecological awareness in what became a grassroots movement had already been planted in the 1960s as the counterculture initiated a demand for organic food and nontoxic products and began to honor nature as a moral and spiritual practice. During the 1970s the need for a profound reorientation of political options became increasingly compelling as the traditional parties and governments on both sides of the liberal–conservative spectrum proved incapable of addressing the mounting environmental crises, such as the growing pollution of the air, soil, and water. It was clear to proto-Greens in several countries simultaneously that the policies and guiding ideologies of the existing parties were skewed by their belief in unqualified economic growth as a panacea for societal ills, at the expense of the natural world and all life on Earth.

During the last quarter of the twentieth century, the Green analyses and their proposed solutions to a range of problems were largely marginalized by the larger parties, but as the planetary crises (global climate disruption, and damage to communities from the new "free trade" laws enforced by the World Trade Organization) deepened after the mid-1990s, many of the Green solutions (such as farmers markets

and other aspects of community-based economics, energy-efficiency, and pedestrian-friendly city planning) began to move quickly into mainstream acceptance. Since the 1970s, Green-party platforms (also known as programs) have advocated the following: community-based economics, local food security, and regional trade; nonviolence; revitalized democracy; personal and social responsibility; respect for diversity; and a planetary perspective.

The overarching framework of Green political thought seeks to present a coherent analysis of what is needed to achieve a sustainable society while also meeting the needs of healthy humans embedded in healthy processes and cycles of nature. As such, Green political thought presented the first integrative politics, breaking through the dominant position of both the socialist and capitalist political economies by declaring that nature is not a "mere externality," as economists have asserted for so long. In response to the socialist cry, "Labor is the source of all wealth!" Greens replied, "Nature is the source of all wealth!" Green platforms are attentive to both, not as isolated issue areas but as interrelated, dynamic elements; these platforms recognized nature as the ground of our being, not a store of "raw materials." At the heart of the Green perspective is a moral commitment to nonviolence and a refusal to accept as "human nature" the massive destruction of recurring wars (and the lucrative arms trade that fuels them) or domestic violence. Greens encourage education in the rich history of nonviolence and its many ramifications so that we can progress to wiser ways of interacting: peace on Earth, peace with the Earth.

Origins and Growth

The first proto-Green party with an ecosocial program was the Values Party in New Zealand, which attracted adherents throughout the first half of the 1970s and won 5 percent of

a national vote in 1975, but then splintered and disbanded. The group that became the Green Party of Tasmania began meeting in 1972, initially in opposition to the flooding of a large lake for a hydroelectric project. The group that became the Ecology Party (later the Green Party) in Great Britain began meeting in 1973. Switzerland saw the first Green Party member elected to a national parliament in 1979.

In 1981, seats were won in both national legislative bodies of Belgium by each of the two Belgian Green Parties: Agalev (representing the Flemish, Dutch-speaking area) and Ecolo (representing the French-speaking Walloons). The largest electoral success to date at the national level was the German Green Party's winning 28 of the 497 seats in their federal parliament in 1983 (Spretnak and Capra 1984). The oldest regional coordination of Green Parties is the Federation of European Green Parties (the EuroGreens); its thirty-two member parties united to form the European Green Party in 2004 in Rome to further their influence in the European Parliament. Other regional coordinations include the Federation of Green Parties of the Americas (formed in 1997 in Mexico City), the Asia Pacific Green Network (formed in Brisbane in 2000), and the African Green Network. The first networking of global Greens occurred in 1992 in Rio de Janeiro; the Global Greens Network had over seventy member parties by 2009.

Electoral success for the Greens has depended largely on whether their country's electoral system is based on proportional representation (as in Germany, Belgium, and many European states) or winner-take-all elections (as in the United States, the United Kingdom, and elsewhere). With the former, winning 5 percent of the vote results in that party's winning 5 percent of the seats in the legislative body; with the latter, winning 5 percent of the vote amounts to nothing. In the European Union from the 1980s on, some countries that did not use proportional representation in their own elections allowed it for electing their parliamentarians to the European Union Parliament (EP); that opening allowed several Greens to be elected to the EP from various countries. By the twenty-first century, all member nations of the European Union were using proportional representation to elect their representatives to the EP. The size of the Green delegation, which formed an alliance in the EP with the European Free Alliance, had grown by the time of the 2007–2009 session to 42 seats out of 785. Greens have proven to be substantively effective in many ways in the European Parliament, especially by introducing environmental legislation on a wide range of issues.

In the United States, a national Green founding meeting in 1984 followed within a few months the publication of a U.S. book on the new Green parties in Europe, *Green Politics: The Global Promise*. It was decided at that gathering to establish a pre-party national network of local Green politics groups seeding Green ideas throughout the country. Beginning in 1990 the energy shifted to establishing state-level Green parties. In 1996 those Green parties united to become the Green Party of the United States, which is a confederation of the state-level parties. As of May 2009, there were 158 Green elected officials in the United States. Greens have also been central in achieving electoral reforms in local elections, such as ranked-choice voting (instant run-off voting), district elections for city council, and unrestricted opportunities for registering to vote.

Charlene SPRETNAK
California Institute of Integral Studies

FURTHER READING

Federation of Green Parties of the Americas. (2009). Retrieved April 2, 2009, from http://fpva.org.mx/docs/english.htm

Global Greens Charter. (2001). Retrieved April 2, 2009, from http://www.globalgreens.org/globalcharter

Green Party of Canada. (2009). Retrieved April 2, 2009, from http://www.greenparty.ca/

Green Party of the United States 2008 election database. (2008). Retrieved November 5, 2008 from http://www.gp.org/elections/candidates/index.php

Spretnak, Charlene, & Capra, Fritjof. (1984). *Green Politics: The Global Promise*. New York: Dutton.

Zelko, Frank, & Brinkmann, Carolin. (Eds.). (2006). *Green parties: Reflections on the first three decades*. Washington, DC: Heinrich Böll Foundation North America.

Hinduism

Many of the fundamental concepts and applications of Hinduism have served as a model for sustainability for the people of India. Belief in the interconnectedness of humans and the cosmos; the moral precepts of yoga; and everyday practices, many inspired by Mohandas Gandhi's view of self-sacrifice and active compassion, have guided Hindus' way of life and hold promise for India's future in the global economy.

Hinduism offers many conceptual and applied models for maintaining a sustainable lifestyle. Most Hindus live in India, a relative newcomer to the world economic stage. Most live close to the land in a self-sustaining village-based economic system. Some may regard this lifestyle to be backward and out of date, but the agricultural methods developed by small-scale farmers have proven effective and currently support more than half of India's population. Although the drive to globalization has created a growing urban class that has lost touch with its village roots, virtually all Indians are familiar with the founding values of the Indian Republic as articulated by Mohandas Gandhi (1869–1948), who believed that a life of self-sacrifice and active compassion for others would cultivate social harmony. Gandhi asserted that only true "self-rule," the result of self-control and a disciplined will, can foster economic and political self-determination.

The values required for a sustainable economic system can be seen within the traditional worldview of India. The Indic model encourages people to recognize the web of relations among humans, nature, and animals, and to develop sensitivity to the need for the protection of the Earth. The traditional Hindu emphasis on the connections between the structures of the human body and human cultures with the broader realms of creation provides a conceptual foundation for the enactment of sustainable values.

Sacrifice and Sustainability

Hinduism, like many religions, recognizes the need to perform sacrifice for the sake of the community's greater good. In the Sanskrit language, the word for sacrifice, *yajna*, derives from the root *yaj*, which means "to worship, adore, honor, consecrate, offer" (Monier-Williams 1899, 838). Hindu models for sacrifice have influenced the cultures of South Asia, and can be understood by examining three narratives: the sacrifice of the primal person (*purusa*) in the Rig-Veda; the *asva medha* (horse sacrifice) in the Brhadaranyaka Upanishad; and a twin tale of sacrificial cosmogony and anthropogeny in the Aitareya Upanishad, Each of these demonstrates a connection between human order and the larger cosmos, providing a foundational philosophy for sustainability.

In the sacrifice of the primal person in the Rig-Veda (one of Hinduism's oldest and most revered scriptures), the human person, divided up, comprises both the social order and the various constituents of the cosmos. This Vedic hymn poses a question: "When they divided Purusha, how many pieces did they prepare? What was his mouth? What are his arms, thighs, and feet called?" (Lincoln 1991, 7). The response makes direct correlations between the body parts and the now infamous Hindu caste system: "The priest was his mouth, the warrior was made from his arms; his thighs were the commoner, and the servant was born from

197

his feet." In this social order the higher tasks performed by priests, physicians, lawyers, and teachers require a sound head. The ownership of land and the maintenance of political order require strong arms. Merchants and shopkeepers and other business folk move goods, as referred to through the extended metaphor of the legs. Servants, the "salt of the earth," perform the sort of labor required for agricultural production and construction projects. This hierarchy reflects human physiology and gives sacrificial sanction to human occupations. Civil duty (dharma) assumes religious significance.

The second part of the hymn correlates the human body with the far-flung regions of the universe:

> The moon was born of his mind;
> of his eye, the sun was born;
> From his mouth, Indra and fire;
> from his breath, wind was born;
> From his navel there was the atmosphere;
> From his head, heaven was rolled together;
> From his feet, the earth; from his ears, the directions.

By identifying body parts with heavenly bodies, the heavens and the earth, and the elements of fire and wind, sanctity is given to both self and cosmos. Like the moon, our mind reflects and changes. Without the light of the sun, we cannot see. Our mouth proclaims our intentions and desires, and like the God of War, Indra, allows us to stake our claim in the world. Each breath we take generates and relies on the circulation of air. Our head pulls us upward; our belly gathers us toward the center and allows us to expand; our feet anchor us to the earth. Our ears orient and stabilize us within the space of the four directions. Through this sacrificial vision, each human being finds a place of importance within the cosmos. This sacrifice signals continuity between the human person, her place in society and within nature.

The horse sacrifice was performed in the twelfth year of the reign of powerful kings in India. For a full year the king would pursue a horse that had been released to the northeast of his kingdom; leaving his hair uncut, his beard unshaven, and remaining celibate for the duration of one year, he would follow wherever the horse wandered and eventually claim this territory as his own. At the end of the year, the horse would be captured and butchered in what undoubtedly was a deeply emotional ceremony. Just as in the sacrifice of the

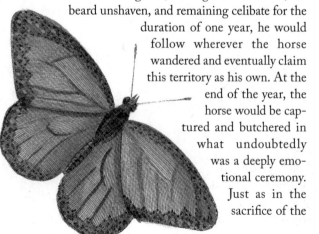

primal person, where human body parts were matched with larger realms, so were the various portions of the sacrificial horse:

> Om! Verily, the dawn is the head of the sacrificial horse;
> the sun, his eye; the wind, his breath; universal fire, his open mouth.
> The year is the body of the sacrificial horse; the sky, his back;
> the atmosphere, his belly; the earth, the underpart of his belly;
> the quarters, his flanks; the intermediate quarters, his ribs;
> the seasons, his flanks; the month and half months, his joints;
> days and night, his feet; the stars, his bones; the clouds, his flesh.
> Sand is the food in the stomach; rivers are his entrails.
> His liver and lungs are the mountains; plants and trees, his hair.
> The east is his fore part; the west, his hind part.
> When he yawns, then it lightens.
> When he shakes himself, then it thunders.
> When he urinates, then it rains.
> Voice, indeed, is his voice. (Hume 1931, 73)

This description of sacrifice in the Brhadaranyaka Upanishad adds the passing of time to a description of the physical aspects of the universe, correlating the steps of the horse to day and night and the year to its whole body. In a later section of the same text, the parts of the horse are aligned with human body parts, as in the Purusa Sukta of the Rig-Veda.

Another variation on this process of worldly creation can be found in the Aitareya Upanishad. The performance of sacrificial ritual generates a form of interior, spiritual, creative heat known as *tapas*. This heat explodes the body of the primal person, creating the various parts of the universe. After the pieces of the universe have been created, they again gather, re-forming the human body.

> When the man was heated, his mouth broke off, like an egg. From the mouth there was speech; from speech, fire. His nostrils broke off. From the nostrils there was breath; from breath, wind. His eyes broke off. From the eyes was vision; from vision, the sun. His ears broke off. From the ears there was hearing; from hearing, the four quarters. His skin broke off. From the skin there were hairs; from the hairs, plants and trees. His heart broke off. From the heart there was mind; from mind, the moon. His navel broke off. From the navel there was the downward breath; from the downward breath, death. His penis broke off. From the penis there was semen; from semen, the waters. (Lincoln 1991, 9)

The scattering of body parts into the elements and heavenly bodies signals an intimacy between human physiology and the larger order and operation of the cosmos. As noted by Bruce Lincoln, author of *Death, War, and Sacrifice: Studies in Ideology and Practice* (1991, 10), this outward movement also has a moment of contraction in an endless pattern of expansion and contraction: "Each breath thus alternately de-creates the body while creating the world, then de-creates the world in order to re-create the body." The re-creation of the body proceeds as follows:

> Fire, having become speech, entered into the mouth. Wind, having
> become the breath, entered into the nostrils. The sun, having become
> vision, entered into the eyes. The four quarters, having become hearing,
> entered into the ears. The plants and trees, having become hairs, entered
> into the skin. The moon, having become the mind, entered into the heart.
> Death, having become the downward breath, entered into the navel. The
> waters, having become semen, entered the penis.
> (Lincoln 1991, 9)

The sacrifice of (or sacrificial, meditative attention to) the body results in the formation of or instantiation within the cosmos. The sacrifice of the cosmos results in the creation of the human body. Our body parts all eventually return and disappear into the air and earth. By recognizing these connections, one sees a common origin and a common end, body and universe.

The early sacrifices of India were dramatic and bloody, especially the horse sacrifice. Sacrifice of goats, water buffalo, and chickens still takes place in certain parts of India, particularly Bengal, Orissa, and Assam. Pressure from the Buddhists and Jainas, and more recently the British, has reduced the incidence of animal sacrifice, replacing it with ceremonies known as *pujas* that involve offerings of fruits and grains and flowers, as well as extensive cycles of prayer and chanting.

Indicating a continuity with the earlier processes documented above from the Vedas and Upanishads, a modern-day priest, Kumar Panda, described that in the process of readying himself to sacrifice a goat to the goddess Durga in a ritual conducted at Chandi Temple in Cuttack, Orissa, he transformed his body into a microcosm of the universe by correlating it to nature: *earth* is equated with parts of the body below the waist; *water* is symbolized by the stomach region; *fire* is represented by the heart; *wind* is equivalent to the throat, nose and lungs; *sky* corresponds to the brain. Kumar Panda reported a change of consciousness and the dissolution of his identity into the personage of Durga. After several hours immersed in mediation and ritual he saw lightning flashes; he then became one with the goddess, and the differences among water, fire, and sun's rays disappeared (Preston 1985, 51, 53). By becoming the goddess, his body expanded beyond the confines of ego and moved into a trance (*samadhi*) of cosmic consciousness. The feeling of deep connection in such rituals resides not only with the attendant priest but also with the tens of thousands who participate in this annual sacrifice.

Sacrifice expressed in simple ritual can be found in India in numerous ways, from the daily lighting of the kitchen fire to the creation of threshold art to the observance of a fast based on the phases of the moon. Veneration of animals can be found in the presence of cows, goats, camels, and elephants on city streets as well as in the household ritual of feeding the birds on one's windowsill before starting one's own meal. In India the excitement of large ritual moments, such as the Kumba Mela, where millions gather at the confluence of the Yamuna and Ganges rivers in Allahabad, serve to cement the religious identity of social groups. The constancy of small ritual moments, such as prayer and the maintenance of one's household shrine, serve to stabilize the family and the individual, establishing connections with the larger natural order.

The correlation of the cosmic person and the sacrificial horse to the broader forces of the universe and the ritual dismemberment of a goat in the contemporary sacrifice to the goddess Durga described above provide a different sacrificial mode. Rather than focus on loss, this approach emphasizes connectivity. These rituals do not provoke recollections of a broken past or advocate social change or tweak an individual's conscience. The exuberant rituals of India proclaim that the human person stands in solidarity with and in celebration of the great forces that drive the universe. By seeing the changing nature of the human mind in the phases of the moon, by seeing the warmth of the heart reflected in the household heart, sacrifice and ritual bring an individual to a place of identification with and empathy for the natural order.

Rituals in India evoke a primal connection between one's sensorial body and the broader powers of the universe. Much of India continues to thrive through a village-based, subsistence economy. Emotional, cultural, and physical sustainability have been achieved through a cycle of rituals and sacrifices within one's religiously sanctioned social duty (dharma). Although this system has been seen as oppressive by some, it has provided an adequate method for the sustainability of Indian culture even in the face of interkingdom conflict, waves of migration, and periods of foreign rule, including the lineage of Mughal rulers from Afghanistan who dominated northern India for centuries, and the era of the British Raj, which extended its colonial administration throughout much of the subcontinent.

As globalization extends into India and the rest of Asia, modernity threatens the rhythms of ritual and sacrificial life. India now boasts the largest middle class in the world and more than a hundred cities with populations exceeding 1 million people. Private home ownership and private automobile ownership are on the rise, but an awareness of pollution has spawned numerous environmental advocacy groups throughout India.

Mohandas Gandhi suggested that by returning to the bare necessities of life, one could disentangle oneself from the damaging effects of the British colonial system. He spun his own thread and wove his own clothing. He led "salt marches," targeted at the British Salt Tax that made it illegal for Indians to produce or sell their own salt, and thus helped to spare people from unfair taxation and reliance on imported goods. India's response to the difficulties of an enmeshed global economy might well take inspiration from Gandhi's well-known creed: "There is enough in this world for every person's need, but not enough for every person's greed."

Yoga and Sustainability

Aside from the ritual-bound traditions of India, the theories and practice of yoga offer a way to reflect on the human condition and sustainable values. Patanjali, a scholar who most likely lived circa 300 CE, codified this tradition. Yoga begins with a series of ethical values adhered to by Buddhists and Jainas as well as Hindus: nonviolence, truthfulness, not stealing, sexual restraint, and nonpossession. Gandhi advocated these as well, reinterpreting them in response to the ills of colonial occupation. In the practice of sustainability, nonviolence might be employed to help slow the pace of habitat destruction and the endangerment of species around the planet. Truthfulness might encourage the better dissemination of knowledge about the harmful effects of resource exploitation, such as deforestation, monoculture agriculture, and global warming. By recognizing how the cutting of forests, the pumping of oil, and the waste of water rob the bounty of the Earth, persons might refrain from such damaging activities. By controlling sexual impulses, the rate of population growth might be slowed. Through the minimization of possessions, people might grow accustomed to living on the bare necessities of life, a requisite step toward sustainability.

Other aspects of yoga similarly can help cultivate a sustainable lifestyle. The observances of purity, contentment, austerity, study, and devotion can help move a person from being outwardly focused and acquisitive to a place of inner stability. Refined movements of the body (*asana*) can bring one into a place of communion with nature. Control of the breath (*pranayama*) helps promote good health. Control of the senses brings an ability to concentrate, meditate, and move into a sense of deep connection with one's place in the nature. For the person established in yoga, needs are few and delights are many.

Contemporary Environmentalism in India

Environmentalists such as M. C. Mehta have acknowledged that India's traditional environmental wisdom can provide a valuable resource for moving the public to support the steps necessary to improve air quality, deal with water pollution, and slow global warming. He has commented:

> The elements of nature such as air and water are being overtaken by greed. Greed has overtaken us, leaving us under the cloak of greed. For people wearing that cloak of greed, it is very hard to come out and see real life. With correct understanding they will be in a position to respect law, and enforce it. Then we can have sustainable elements. (Personal interview with M. C. Mehta, 11 December 2006)

Hinduism's sacrificial model calls for a reconnection with the elements that have been celebrated since the Vedic period, an acknowledgment of the real connection between the human order and the cosmic order. Vandana Shiva, an ecologist and physicist, has become one of the world's most outspoken critics of globalization and has provided a critique of the "patenting" of traditional ways of knowledge for economic gain by corporations. Her activism in the realm of seed production has helped expose the excesses of the human attempt to manipulate nature. She takes a broad historical view in developing her analysis of "enclosure," or the marking off of what once held in common, to be commoditized and controlled by industrial and commercial forces.

> The "enclosure" of biodiversity and knowledge is the final step in a series of enclosures that began with the rise of colonialism. Land and forests were the first resources to be "enclosed" and converted from commons to commodities. Later, water resources were "enclosed" through dams, groundwater mining and privatization schemes. . . . The destruction of the commons was essential for the industrial revolution, to provide a supply of raw material to industry. (Shiva 2001, 44–45)

Shiva, much inspired by Gandhi, advocates what she calls living economies. One such example is Mumbai's magnificent lunch distribution system, the Mumbai Tiffin Box Suppliers Association, which delivers 175,000 lunches each day "with no documentation, no order, no bosses" and yet manages to make only one mistake every 16 million deliveries (Shiva 2005, 70). This organization has been studied by Harvard Business School as a model for human and social ingenuity. For Shiva this exemplifies the sort of people-based economy required for sustainability, joining self-determination with interdependence. Her advocacy of sustenance economy would require a shift from a corporate model to one in balance with nature, valuing partnerships, mutuality, and reciprocity.

Hinduism offers many approaches to a sustainable lifestyle. The village model still prevails throughout India, where the food is grown locally, manufactured goods are rare, and even clothing tends to be homespun. For the growing number of urbanites who have entered into the more complex, globalized economy, some visionary pieces of legislation, particularly the use of compressed natural gas for buses and auto-rickshaws, have helped mitigate some of the deleterious effects of modernization.

To become truly sustainable, India will need to look backward to its tradition that emphasizes the interconnection between the human and the cosmic and forward to the increased generation of clean fuels, local production of food, and further innovations on the Gandhian model of self sufficiency.

Christopher Key CHAPPLE
Loyola Marymount University

FURTHER READING

Chapple, Christopher K. (1993). *Nonviolence to animals, Earth, and self in Asian traditions.* Albany: State University of New York Press.

Chapple, Christopher K. (2001). Hinduism and deep ecology. In David Barnhill & Roger Gottlieb (Eds.), *Deep ecology and the world religions* (pp. 59–76). Albany: State University of New York Press.

Chapple, Christopher K. (2008). Sacrifice and sustainability. *Worldviews: Global Religions, Culture, and Ecology, 12*(2/3), 221–236.

Chapple, Christopher K., & Tucker, Mary Evelyn. (2000). *Hinduism and ecology: The intersection of Earth, sky, and water.* Cambridge, MA: Center for the Study of World Religions and Harvard University Press.

Fuchs, Stephen. (1996). *The Vedic horse sacrifice in its culture-historical relations.* New Delhi: Inter-India Publications.

Hume, Robert E. (Trans.). (1931). *The thirteen principal Upanisads* (2nd ed.). London: Oxford University Press.

Lincoln, Bruce. (1991). *Death, war, and sacrifice: Studies in ideology and practice.* Chicago: University of Chicago Press.

Monier-Williams, Monier. (1899). *A Sanskrit–English dictionary.* Oxford, U.K.: Clarendon Press. (Available online at http://acharya.iitm.ac.in/sanskrit/dictionary/dict.php)

Preston, James. J. (1985). *Cult of the Goddess: Social and religious change in a Hindu temple.* Prospect Heights, IL: Waveland Press.

Shiva, Vandana. (2001). *Protect or plunder: Understanding intellectual property rights.* London: Zed Books.

Shiva, Vandana. (2005). *Earth democracy: Justice, sustainability and peace.* Cambridge, MA: South End Press.

Hybridity

The concept of hybridity involves the amalgamation or combination of previously distinct elements into a new variation. In terms of sustainability, this involves the artificial combination or fusion of naturally distinct kinds of being, such as species or ecosystems, into new forms not found in nature. Thus it fuels the debate over whether the natural world should remain as it is or be altered by humans and technology.

Hybridity refers in its most basic sense to the blending or fusion of previously distinct forms or categories—be these different species, races, linguistic varieties, cultures, or traditions—into a new variation. The discourse of hybridity has appeared in postmodern, postcolonial, and feminist theory, where such blending or fusion of categories and typologies has been seen as a way of overcoming previous ironclad social classificatory schema that reinforced noxious forms of social oppression and dominance.

In the context of environmentalism and sustainability, the issue of hybridity involves the artificial combination or fusion of naturally distinct kinds of being, such as species or ecosystems, into new forms not found in nature. Indeed some have suggested that such hybridization may be the only way to preserve what little biodiversity we have left. For instance, due to global warming for the last decade, the forests of British Columbia have been ravaged by the infestation of mountain pine beetles. As of March 2008, the British Columbian

government officials announced that the beetle will soon run out of food, leaving the difficult question of restoration: if the forests were to be repopulated by the old flora the beetle is likely to make a reappearance. This has lead some scientists to suggest that we should introduce new non-native and possibly genetically modified species that would be better able to cope with these new climatic conditions (Oosthoek 2008). Of course, while few may debate the need for hybridization on a pragmatic level, many environmentalists, concerned with issues of wilderness conservation and preservation, are wary of introducing the postmodern discourse and rhetoric of hybridity into the debate on sustainability. For in some sense the question of sustainability, particularly as it pertains to wilderness conservation, involves preserving as much as possible the original integrity of wild, nature forms and ecosystems—an integrity some fear would be completely undermined by the discourse of hybridity, with its celebration of fusion and blending.

Origins

The term *hybridity* originated in biology to refer to the selective breeding of plants but rose to prominence in racist, colonial discourses of the nineteenth century, where, in association with doctrines of racial purity, it was pejoratively used as a stigma to highlight the supposed perilous effects of racial intermixing. According to pseudoscientific theories of race, hybrids (or the offspring of mixed-race couples) were held to be diseased monstrosities and aberrations, far inferior to even the lowest races, as they were the result of the unnatural transgression of the "natural" boundaries of race. Despite its past historic usage as a means of social exclusion and oppression, in recent years the discourse of hybridity and the trope of the hybrid have become widely celebrated by postmodernist theorists precisely because they transgress such fixed categories and boundaries, thereby undermining the legitimacy of these and revealing new possibilities.

An important aspect of postmodern criticism attempts to critique and overcome what is seen as a fundamental trend within Western metaphysics towards totalizing essentialism. Influenced by the French philosopher Jacques Derrida's post-structuralist reading of the Western tradition, postmodernists argue that Western thought, starting with the ancient Greeks, attempts to conceptualize and articulate the heterogeneity of reality in terms of binary categories, such as nature/culture, male/female, and mind/body, in which the former is seen as superior and dominant over the latter, thereby naturalizing and reinforcing certain hierarchical social relations and forms of dominance. Consequently, a truly liberational form of politics, Derrida argues, consists in unsettling or destabilizing these binaries by demonstrating their contingency and bringing to light previously repressed meanings that lie outside or between such categories, a technique he termed "deconstruction."

Derrida's strategy of deconstruction would fundamentality influence postcolonial theory, particularly the work of one of its main theorists, Homi K. Bhabha. In his book *The Location of Culture*, Bhabha argues that the various forms of cultural and linguistic hybridity, such as Creole, that emerged during the colonial period served to undermine and unsettle certain hierarchical binary oppositional categories of their European colonial masters and forge new emancipatory forms of cultural expression and identity.

Environmental Debates

The introduction of the discourse of hybridity into the environmental debate, however, is generally credited to Donna Haraway, a feminist theorist and professor of technoscience, and her well-known metaphor or trope of the cyborg. In her paper "The Cyborg Manifesto," Haraway argues for the cyborg as a "cybernetic organism, a hybrid of machine and organism, a product as much of social reality as well as a creature of fiction" (Haraway 1991, 149). The cyborg would overcome and confuse rigid boundaries and dichotomy between the natural and artificial, thus serving to subvert the essentialist discourse of Western metaphysics and providing the means of allowing us to rearticulate and realize human potentialities.

Initially Haraway intended her trope of the cyborg to be a critique of what she saw as certain essentialist

tendencies within radical feminist thought, which identified women with the biological and organic rather than the mechanical and artificial. Some theorists have used Haraway's metaphor to argue for "cyborg environmentalism," a way of thinking promoted by Ursula K Heise. This new theory would overcome similar essentialist assumptions of a fundamental binary oppositional dichotomy between the natural and artificial held by many conservationists and deep ecologists, and it would open new enriching technological possibilities for the benefit of both the human and nonhuman world. Heise, for instance, suggests using new biotechnologies to resurrect previously extinct species, while proponents of the hedonistic imperative argue that we should use all available technology to eliminate pain and suffering among all natural species (Heise, 2003).

Critics, however, argue that that by blurring the boundaries between the natural and artificial, cyborg environmentalists seem to leave the natural world open for the unhindered technological appropriation of nature. Could not a genetically engineered forest, for example, be celebrated and lionized as a liberatory symbol of hybridity? Similarly, given the ability to re-engineer previously extinct species, could not humans push on with their industrial appropriation of nature, regardless of its cost to the natural species, secure in the knowledge that they could genetically resurrect these species at a more "convenient" date. Moreover, framed in terms of an ethical imperative to "improve" the natural world, as do advocates of the hedonistic imperative, it would seem that the value of the natural itself is understood in terms of a lack or deficiency. This would seem to render the question of preservation largely meaningless, for why preserve the natural world when it is so obviously in need of improvement. Yet, many advocates of environmental preservation argue that the value of the nonhuman natural world lies precisely in its alterity and otherness to the human world. In other words, it consists in respecting certain boundaries, not in overcoming and obscuring them. Furthermore, critics charge cyborg environmentalists with having a romantic and naïvely uncritical understanding of technology and being woefully unaware of the way in which, as the German philosopher Martin Heidegger (1977) has argued, technology intrinsically manifests humanity's will of power, control, and domination over the natural world. In Haraway's defense, she has noted that she is fully cognizant of the historical and potentially oppressive and violent uses of technology and argues that the introduction of an appropriate socialist-feminist political discourse because women, due to their historically marginal position in such culturally constituted hierarchies, would be suitably sensitive to such abuses of power and develop technology in suitably liberatory ways. Nevertheless, critics argue that she seems to ignore Heidegger's observations that technology itself is not simply a neutral instrument, but enframes, structures, and limits the way in which humans understand and engage with the world and each other.

Consequently, the inclusion of the postmodern rhetoric of hybridity into the discourse of sustainability fundamentally brings into focus the very question of what we understand to be the "crisis" of the environmental crisis and what we take the goals of sustainability to be. If the environmental crisis is understood largely in terms of the threat it poses to our current standard of existence and well-being, then the environmental crisis is seen as simply a technological problem, with the issue of sustainability being solely a matter of devising new technology that allows us to live within our means—the human development of new biological hybrids would be yet one more possible way in which we use our technical arsenal to combat environmental destruction. If, however, we understand the environmental crisis to consist of the loss of the nonhuman natural world (or the world not directly created by us to service our needs) and see sustainability as a matter of seeking to live in ways which will allow its continued existence, then the issue of hybridity, far from being the solution, lies at the very root of the problem we seek to address.

T. R. KOVER
Katholieke Universiteit Leuven

FURTHER READING

Bhabha, Homi K. (1994). *The location of culture.* London: Routledge.

Derrida, Jacques. (1973). *Speech and phenomena: And other essays concerning Husserl's theory of signs.* David B. Allison (Trans.). Evanston, IL: Northwestern University Press.

Haraway, Donna J. (1991). *Simians, cyborgs and women: The reinvention of nature.* New York: Routledge.

Heidegger, Martin. (1977). *The question concerning technology and other essays.* William Lovitt (Trans.). New York: Harper and Row.

Heise, Ursula K. (2003). From extinction to electronics: Dead frogs, live dinosaurs, and electric sheep. In Cary Wolfe (Ed.). *Zoontologies: The Question of the Animal.* Minneapolis: University of Minnesota.

Oosthoek, Sharon. (2008, July 7). Nature 2.0: Redefining conservation. *New Scientist.* Retrieved June 12, 2009, from http://www.newscientist.com/article/mg19926631.400-nature-20-redefining-conservation.html

The Hedonistic Imperative (n.d.). Retrieved June 12, 2009, from http://www.hedweb.com

chat Berkshire's authors and editors welcome questions, comments, and corrections: sustainability.updates@berkshirepublishing.com

I

Indigenous and Traditional Peoples

Indigenous people—who understand themselves as having emerged or formed as a people in relation to a particular place—tend to be more environmentally aware than non-natives who seek to supplant them. The lifeway of native peoples brings together knowledge of local ecosystems with land and biodiversity management routines, cultural institutions that affirm and activate identity with in-spirited persons in that place, and cosmologies that celebrate native identity with natural processes.

The term *indigenous* refers to that which is native, original, and resident to a place. While often thought of as remote minorities, indigenous peoples are a significant global population of over 500 million in Africa, South Asia, Southeast Asia, Central Asia, Australia, the Pacific region, Northern Eurasia, and the Americas. Having been used in international settings, the term *indigenous* has been claimed by these diverse local, tribal, and traditional peoples as they struggle for their right to exist. The term is not without its ambiguities as, for example, in India where mainstream, dominant Indo-Aryan peoples claim native status and refer to local, tribal societies as *adivasi*, or "first peoples." Yet, the very ambiguity of the term carries insight into the single most demanding challenge faced by all of these traditional peoples, namely, their sustainability as distinct peoples in relation to their homelands. *Indigenous*, thus, refers to small-scale societies around the planet who share and preserve ways of knowing the world embedded in particular languages, story-cycles, kinship systems, worldview dispositions, and integrated relationships with the land on which they live.

Indigenous spokespeople have described their traditional ecological knowledge as interwoven into their social fabric of their existence as a people. The term *lifeway* refers to this dynamic, integrated, and living knowledge. The lifeways of contemporary indigenous societies and the ecosystems in which they reside are vital, interactive wholes. The close connections between territory and society, religion and politics, and cultural and economic life are the means whereby indigenous peoples have maintained, and are reviving, their knowledge systems. Indigenous lifeways are descriptive of enduring modes of sustainable livelihood that marshal knowledge about particular animals, plants and minerals so as to conserve them even as the people use them for food, healing, shelter, clothing, and ritual activities. Indigenous knowledge also is prescriptive of ecological imaginaries or deep attractors between place and people that activate sustaining relationships with the community of life. Thus, this knowledge often constitutes an environmental ethics that may not be systematized, but which places definite limits on behavior through ritual prohibitions, taboos, gender regulations, and age-grade restrictions.

Traditional environmental knowledge (TEK) has been appropriated for use in non-native settings in the pharmaceutical industry, for instance, but less is known about the biopiracy of unscrupulous outsiders who prey upon indigenous knowledge of local life (*bios*). Indigenous ways of knowing, however, are not simply expressions of instrumental rationality, or a functional knowledge for accomplishing specific tasks. Indigenous, or native, science knows the world as something other than as the inanimate objects it comprises, yet, indigenous knowledge is certainly capable of objective understanding and of recognizing utilitarian relationships.

Just as indigenous knowledge is inextricably tied to engagement with local place as social identity, so also individuals actively pursue relationships with the natural world as spiritual persons. Indigenous ways of knowing are not primarily characterized by techniques of quantification and measurement or through experimental method, though each of these techniques should not be understood as absent from native knowledge. For example, indigenous fishing peoples clearly observe over time the seasonal runs of fish and calculate appropriate techniques for assuring food supplies. But their knowledge is often connected with experiential learning, personal accomplishments, mythic stories regarding the spawning grounds of fish, ritual activities, and personal dream or visionary relationships with fish. While indigenous knowledge can be labeled a *scientia*, or knowing, it is actually quite different than Western science and is closer to *philosophia*, or a love of wisdom. Rather than simply a system of pragmatic subsistence techniques, then, indigenous ecological knowledge is a wisdom path that emphasizes integral relationships with place and local biodiversity as the means for sustainability.

Because indigenous knowledge is often located in or transmitted during rituals, some have described it as simply liminal or marginal, arcane knowledge that has no practical meaning. Indigenous knowledge embedded within complex ceremonials is not exclusively liminal, that is, an entry into extraordinary space and time outside of that which is ordinary. In fact the opposite is often the case; namely, indigenous knowledge manifested at these peak ceremonial moments has deep and abiding connections with both extraordinary presences such as ancestors and spirit-powers, as well as with ordinary events such as canoe making, gardening, gender roles, and healing practices. Time as adjustment to seasonal placement is central to an interpretation of indigenous lifeways. In seasonal time, space, authority, and spirit-presences resonate with one another in the ceremonial and symbol-making contexts of indigenous knowledge.

This is not an attempt to romanticize indigenous knowing as mystical narratives or to lift it into a purely spiritual realm in which nature is divinized in a turn toward an idealized pantheism. Rather, indigenous knowledge is a form of responsible life in a living, empowered world. Responsibility results from both a conscious act and a sense of deeply felt response to something unconscious, mysterious, gratuitous, and powerful. Therefore, indigenous knowledge honors individual reflective behavior. This individual act, however, is not that of an isolated mentality, but always understood as a communal act responsibly undertaken with spiritual humility in the face of cosmological unknowing. Indigenous

elders still hope for all peoples to awaken to that spiritual enlightenment illuminating responsible life.

As the indigenous educator Gregory Cajete, from Santa Clara Pueblo in the North American Southwest, says, native science is "a metaphor for a wide range of tribal processes of perceiving, thinking, acting, and coming to know that have evolved through human experience with the natural world. Native science is born of a lived and storied participation with the natural landscape. In its core experience, Native science is based on the perception gained from using the entire body of our senses in direct participation with the natural world" (Cajete 2004, 5). Embodiment is a key to understanding the integral character of sustainable relationships established in indigenous ecological knowledge. The interrelationships of embodiment may be evident in one's personal body and social body, as well as modes of ecological body in landscapes and cosmological body that manifest in dreams and songs.

Discussions of "dreaming" in Australian Aboriginal traditions interface knowledge, land, time, and lifeway. Dreaming is known in over two hundred languages of indigenous peoples of Australia by many terms such as *jukurrpa* among the Walpiri, and *altjirra* in Aranda. Dreaming named not only the creative time of the origins of everything, but it also named places of significance, the responsible relationships of humans to those places, animals, plants, and all natural phenomena of those places. Ngarrindjeri peoples of southern Australia spoke of their governmental system, or *tendi*, as a council of elders who transmitted a certain form of knowledge that came to the people from the Dreamtime. Dreaming, then, conveys some ideas among Aboriginal peoples of traditional ownership. April Bright of the MakMak (Sea Eagle) peoples, of the Marranunggu language group in Northern Territory, Australia, gives expression to lifeway when describing what "traditional ownership" meant to her mother. She said: "Traditional ownership to country for my Mum was everything—everything. It was the songs, the ceremony, the land, themselves, their family—everything that life was all about. This place here was her heart. That's what she lived for, and that's what she died for" (Rose et al. 2002, 15). Embedded within "ownership," then, for this MakMak elder as transmitted to her daughter, was not simply individual control of private property or separate knowledge systems of collected data. Rather, ownership appears to be interwoven with diverse forms of indigenous knowledge as affective and embodied wisdom. The land and knowledge of the land are centered in one's personal body and interwoven with the social body, the ecological body, and the cosmological body.

These shared ways of knowing, attention to the world, and abiding in the individual and communal bodies underlie the wisdom and the specificity of indigenous knowledge. Thus, the Maori scholar Linda Tuhiwai Te Rina Smith observes, "*Whakapapa* is a [Maori] way of thinking, a way of learning, a way of storing knowledge, and a way of debating. . . . *Whakapapa* also relates us to all other things that exist in the world. We are linked through our *whakapapa* to insects, fishes, trees, stones, and other life forms" (Smith 2000, 234–235). The wisdom transmitted here seems to speak across its specific Maori context, but only the Maori can determine if that wisdom is transferable as more than environmental poetry. What is evident is that indigenous peoples shares ecological wisdom despite incredible cultural differences between these many distinct language groups. Indigenous knowledge manifests a unity, a lived experience in which beliefs, practices, and ethics are a participatory whole.

What this sacred knowledge reveals today is not simply the ashes of an extinct, fossilized way of knowing, but the embers that indigenous elders are rekindling to guide their peoples with awareness of deeper purpose. The metaphor of embers evokes that frank understanding that indigenous ecological knowledge was "tossed away" by the industrial-technological worldview. Still, embers calls to mind the flame of commitment that all humans need to recover for ecological ways of knowing. We face challenges to find again—in our multiple ways of knowing—wise and sustainable ways forward.

John GRIM
Yale University

FURTHER READING

Bell, Diane. (1993). *Daughters of the Dreaming* (2nd ed.). Minneapolis: University of Minnesota Press.

Berkes, Fikret. (2008). *Sacred Ecology*. (2nd ed.). London: Routledge.

Cajete, Gregory. (2004). *Native science: Natural laws of interdependence*. Santa Fe, NM: Clear Light Publishers.

Grim, John. (Ed.). (2001). *Indigenous Traditions and Ecology: The Interbeing of Cosmology and Community*. Cambridge, MA: Harvard Divinity School, Center for the Study of World Religions.

Rose, Deborah Bird; D'Amico, Sharon; Daiyi, Nancy; Deveraux, Kathy; Daiyi, Margaret; et al. (Eds.). (2002). *Country of the heart: An indigenous Australian homeland*. Canberra, Australia: Aboriginal Studies Press for the Australian Institute of Aboriginal and Torres Strait Islander Studies.

Smith, Linda Tuhiwai. (2000). Kaupapa Maori Research. In Marie Battiste (Ed.), *Reclaiming indigenous voice and vision* (pp.225–247). Vancouver, Canada: UBC Press.

I looked ahead and saw the mountains there with rocks and forests on them, and from the mountains flashed all colors upward to the heavens. Then I was standing on the highest mountain of them all, and round about beneath me was the whole hoop of the world. And while I stood there I saw more than I can tell and I understood more than I saw; for I was seeing in a sacred manner the shapes of all things in the spirit, and the shape of all shapes as they must live together like one being.

Black elk

Source: John G. Neihardy (2008). *Black Elk Speaks: Being the Life Story of a Holy Man of the Oglala Sioux, the Premier Edition*, p. 33. Albany: State University of New York Press.

Indigenous Traditions—Africa

African peoples face the challenge of sustaining a unique identity in an increasingly globalized and Westernized society. Their indigenous traditions of proverb, festival, and divination involve values that carry an ethic of respect and celebration for ancestors and the divine from the past to the future, and reflect a general concern for sustaining all life on Earth.

Indigenous religious traditions in Africa universally hold that a life lived in harmony with the environment fosters spiritual and physical health. The question of sustainability as it applies to these traditions and values is twofold: how can indigenous African traditions survive in an increasingly modernized world, and how can these traditions, especially proverb, festival, and divination, help their practitioners face the challenges of sustainable living.

Differences and Shared Values

Due to the expansiveness of the African continent, indigenous religious traditions of Africa are rooted in diverse customs and practices. (While there is no African word equivalent to *religion*, many African terms convey the sense of practice and thought that reflect the meaning of the word in the West.) Most indigenous African traditions, however, share a common reverence for a Supreme Being, and all consider a life lived in harmony with their environment, both social and physical, a key to maintaining spiritual and physical health. Despite considerable differences in the language, the mode of worship, and the ritual used to express the existence and qualities of a Supreme Being, most African indigenous traditions subscribe to a common structure in their

belief system. This belief system is usually divided into major and the minor beliefs. The major beliefs, listed here hierarchically, include beliefs in the Supreme Being and in divinities, spirits, ancestors, and magic and medicine. The minor beliefs, which are essentially derived from the major ones, include, among others, beliefs in morality, life after death, reincarnation, and a last day of judgment.

Indigenous African traditions are characteristically monotheistic. Many casual observers, based on the expansive devotion of Africans to the divinities, have unfortunately labeled the these traditions polytheistic. A deeper examination of the African concept of the Supreme Being contradicts this view. As the religious studies scholar Bolaji Idowu (1973, 23) insists, indigenous traditions in Africa subscribe to a "diffused monotheism," whereby Africans gain access to the Supreme Being through the divinities; the divinities are not ends in themselves. The indigenous African concept of the Supreme Being is therefore not in tandem with the essential nature of polytheism, in which all the gods are "equal" but in which one god is conceded to be the "leader." Indigenous African traditions do not consider the divinities equal in any way to the Supreme Being. In fact, the Supreme Being is their creator, and the divinities are mere representatives or messengers.

Indigenous African traditions pervade every aspect of the everyday lives of their practitioners. Thus, as the religious philosopher John Mbiti (1982, 5) writes, "Africans are notoriously religious." It is therefore quite understandable that, even in contemporary societies, with many Africans following other religions such as Christianity and Islam, Africans still return to the "confines" of their indigenous traditions to find solutions in difficult moments of life, when the "foreign religions" seem to fail them.

One crucial and common characteristic of these traditions has not only shaped but has actually enhanced the sustainability of indigenous African values and worldviews. Lacking the complement of written scriptural documents afforded other religions such as Christianity, Islam, and Judaism, indigenous African traditions have almost exclusively depended on oral sources to disseminate their vales and views through proverbs, festivals, and divination—dynamic forms of communication that have played vital roles in sustaining the much-cherished African heritage from the past to the present.

Proverbs

African proverbs are highly regarded and existentially employed as "wise sayings." Proverbs, derived from the timeless wisdom of ancestors, are used to drive home points during discussions and to explain figurative contexts for events and situations. In some African traditions there are proverbs about proverbs. The Yoruba people of Nigeria say, "A proverb is a horse that can carry one swiftly to ideas," while the Zulus say, "Without proverbs language would be but a skeleton without flesh, a body without a soul."

Through proverbs Africans express beliefs about the Supreme Being, impart theological and moral teachings, and illustrate the metaphysical dimensions of human existence. There are numerous proverbs on different attributes of the Supreme Being. The Yoruba denote that God is the ultimate custodian of justice by saying, "Leave your fight to Olodumare and look on; he is the defender of the defenseless." The Akan people of Ghana and Côte d'Ivoire express their belief in the omnipresence of God in the proverb that instructs, "If you want to tell it to God, tell it to the wind." But the celebration of proverbs as a means of fostering societal sustainability cannot be undertaken blindly. Proverbs must be approached with discerning minds to ensure that they address the transitory and new challenges of the modern world. This should not, however prevent us from recognizing proverbs as a foundation from the past upon which we can build both the present and the future.

In *The West and the Rest of Us*, Chinweizu, a Nigerian writer and critic of African literature, cautioned against treating ancestral knowledge as "absolute" at a time when Africans are beset by so many societal challenges and the culture itself often discourages adopting new strategies and change—and yet he stressed the importance of maintaining reverence and respect for such wisdom. Chinweizu (1975, 1) included in his book the following version of a well-known passage, attributed by John of Salisbury to Bernard of Chartres, the twelfth-century French philosopher who observed intellectuals of his time relying on the great thinkers of ancient Greece and Rome:

> We are like dwarfs sitting on the shoulders of giants, we see more things and more far off than they did, not because our sight is better, nor because we are taller, but because they raise us up and add to our height by their gigantic loftiness.

This metaphoric saying, a proverb in itself, extends across cultures and eras, but it has a special resonance for indigenous African peoples whose traditions and beliefs have been passed from generation to generation without a formal or scriptural text. In proverbs, concepts of sustainability derive from humbly and patiently listening to the African ancestors and learning from their wisdom, so as to seek guidance not only for the present but for the future. Proverbs have also been extensively used to elevate the relevance of nonhumans in sustainability. For example, many African proverbs use animals as impersonators of humans to teach and pass on the messages of traditional wisdom and the tenacity of purpose in the community. In the forefront of such proverbs are those associated with the cunning of the hare, the mischievous intelligence of the tortoise, the shrewdness of the monkey, and the opportunism of the chameleon.

Festivals

Festivals in African traditional settings are associated with different aspects of communal life. They celebrate milestones such as birth, initiation, marriages, and funerals, and they solemnize community veneration of divinities. John Mbiti points out that festivals create a dynamic for community renewal, unity, and cohesion. Sometimes they serve as the bond that links ancestors (and also the divine) with the living. This bond is central to the survival and sustainability of the community from one generation to the next.

The significance of festivals is demonstrated by the role they play in the day-to-day lives of twenty-first-century African communities and nations. Governments in many African countries have risen to the challenge of not only identifying the values of traditional festivals but actually giving strong support to their celebration as state events. The traditional Intawasa festival in Zimbabwe, for example, has become an annual national celebration of Zimbabwe's heritage with multidisciplinary offerings of theater, music, literary performance, and dance.

In Swaziland, the traditional Umhlanga festival and Reed Dance is no longer held just to honor the king's mother by gathering reeds to repair her house; it also celebrates the people's belief in "purity" as a moral societal value (a trait symbolized by the fact that young women must remain virgins until they marry). Such purity satisfies a requirement of the gods, through which the people of the land are said to be blessed with prosperity and an abundant harvest for the preservation and continuation of the community. Ironically the focus on puberty, and the festival itself, also calls attention to the fragility of human life in this polygamous country, where the HIV/AIDS epidemic is rampant (with over 40 percent of the population believed to be infected), and the life expectancy, according to the CIA World Factbook (available through www.cia.gov), averages 31.88 years.

In West Africa the Osun Osogbo Festival in Nigeria has become the epitome of traditional festivals, one to which participants flock from all parts of the world. The original festival dated to the early eighteenth century, when the town of Osogbo was founded by a group of hunters. In return for venerating the goddess of the Osun River as the protector and harbinger of fertility, the goddess protected the townspeople from invasion by Fulani warriors. These festivals, like others across Africa, help to sustain national identity by preserving the norms and values of the people, but they also bolster economic sustainability. The Zimbabwean Intawasa festivals, for instance, promote the city of Bulawayo as a tourist destination, create employment, and provide a viable market for artists' wares.

In festivals the dynamics of sustainability surface in the rhythm and the resonance of age-old celebrations in dance, song, and other works of art, all of which bind the present with the past in order to protect the future. This protection is enforced through the Kpalevorgu festival in Ghana, whose degraded forestlands have also been the focus of many promising international partnerships to support sustainable living. Through various festivals celebrated by the Yoruba people of western Africa, groves such as oke-Ibadan, Osun, Olumo, and Orosun have been ritualized and preserved, a practice that increasingly calls attention to their threatened biodiversity.

Divination

Laura Grillo, a researcher who has conducted much fieldwork in urban West African divination, defines *divination* as a technique used to determine the future and make authoritative pronouncement about it. Grillo notes, however, that this definition does not give full credit to the African functional use of divination. For Africans, divination may include prediction but is not by any means limited to it. The practice of divination is essentially considered a diagnosing process to determine the causes of all kinds of life crises, including childbirth, disease, death, economic misfortune, and natural disaster. After the diagnosis, divination prescribes the remedy for the crisis. The ultimate objective—after ensuring favorable dispositions of divine forces, usually through prescribed sacrifice—is to re-engineer a return to well-being of either the individual or the community.

Divination has become central to contemporary African society as a way of implementing sustainability strategies for different sectors of community life or for the environment. Examples of this abound in all parts of Africa. Grillo highlights the use of divination in two urban West African communities: the Dogon people of Mali use divination as a vehicle for bringing about favorable divine responses about the future; the Yoruba people use the process of divination to foster moral uprightness and order in society by assigning individual and communal responsibilities. Nicola Robins, a sustainability strategist, has described the transformation of Sangoma divination in South Africa as it moved from dealing with agro-pastoral related challenges of the traditional community to resolving modern-day challenges on spiritual, social, economic, educational, and even political level, both for the individual and the society.

In the traditional practice of divination, ritual objects have been derived from natural elements, and devotees have always been reminded of their sacredness and the importance of protecting and preserving them. The sacralizing of hills, mountains, forests, and rivers has protected such natural objects from degradation and abuse. Through divination we are able to listen to what is important, determine how to interpret different forms of intuition, and perform sacrifices, not necessarily the physical ones, in order to affect a holistic sustainability of human well-being.

Toward a Sustainable Future

Indigenous African peoples—whose beliefs embrace what Jacob Olupona (2006, 260), a scholar of indigenous African traditions, has called a "reutilization of the environment"— contribute to sustainability through the modern-day practice of their traditions.

Proverbs, festivals, and divination continue to play central roles in different aspects of fostering economic, ecological, political, moral, social, and spiritual sustainability in the twenty-first-century world. These indigenous traditions can help to ensure the survival of the African identity, and, more importantly, engage in the challenges of propelling the growth and development of the African continent and its people.

Ibigbolade S. ADERIBIGBE
University of Georgia

FURTHER READING

Chinweizu, Onwuchekwa Jemie. (1975). *The West and the rest of us.* London: NOK Publishers.

Dorm-Adzobu, Clement; Ampadu-Agyei, Okkyearne; & Veit, Peter G. (1991). *Religious beliefs and environmental protection: The Malshegu Grove in Northern Ghana.* African Centre for Technology Studies World Resources Institute from the Ground Up Case Study Series 4.

Grillo, Laura. (2005). Trajectories in African ethics. In William Schweiker (Ed.), *Blackwell companion to religious ethics* (pp. 438–448). Oxford, U.K.: Blackwell.

Malunga, Chiku, & Banda, Charles. (2006). *Understanding organizational sustainability through African proverbs: Insights for leaders.* Rugby, U.K.: Practical Action Publishers.

Mbeki, Thabo. (1988). *The African renaissance: South Africa and the world.* Tokyo: UNU Press.

Mbiti, John S. (1988). *Introduction to African religion.* Oxford, U.K.: Heinemann Educational Publishers.

Mbiti, John S. (1994). *African religions and philosophy.* Oxford, U.K: Heinemann Educational Publishers.

Munoz, Louis J. (2001). *The roots of the West: An introduction to the European cultural tradition.* Ibadan, Nigeria: Book Craft.

Olupona, Jacob. (2006). Religion and ecology in African culture and society. In Rogers S. Gottieb (Ed.), *The Oxford handbook of religion and ecology.* New York: Oxford University Press.

Robins, Nicola. (n.d.). The African spirit of sustainability. Retrieved April 11, 2009, from http://www.enviropaedia.com/topic/default.php?topic_id=258

PROBLEMS WITH CONSERVATION IN AFRICA . . . AND SOME SOLUTIONS

Land conservation practices, generally thought of as beneficial, can have a negative impact on those most in need—of either the land's resources or the livelihood they provide. Author Yaa Ntiamoa-Baidu explains the African perspective in this chapter from African Rain Forest Ecology and Conservation: An Interdisciplinary Perspective.

In the Western world, resources conserved are mainly those for which people have no immediate need. In Africa, people are being asked to conserve resources that they depend on for their everyday needs. Protective efforts are purported to be in the interest of the people, but who really benefits from forest and wildlife reserves? Is it the local person who has lost his land to conservation and has neither access to the resources of his land to support his traditional way of life nor access to modern developments to improve his quality of life? Is it the forestry or wildlife officer whose livelihood depends on the maintenance of conservation departments? Is it the government, which requires foreign exchange earnings to provide amenities, most of which is consumed by the city or town dweller? Or is it the Western world, where natural resources have been destroyed in the process of development, and where forest products are required to maintain the overconsumptive way of life, but also where conservation of tropical forest in the interest of global environmental health and biodiversity conservation are vehemently advocated?

Protected areas in Ghana and Africa as a whole will survive only if they provide benefits that are substantial enough for the local communities. There is, therefore, an urgent need to address the question of equitable distribution of the benefits from protected areas. Alternatives for the local communities and development options that will increase protected area benefits must be found. These might include development of appropriate agricultural technologies and facilities to increase productivity through increasing yield per unit area rather than increasing acreage of arable land; promotion of agricultural practices that encourage forest conservation; and farming of favorite or useful wild animals or plant species, such as grasscutters (*Thryonomys swindetianus*) and chewing sticks.

Source: Yaa Ntiamoa-Baidu. (2001). Indigenous Versus Introduced Biodiversity Conservations Strategies: The Case of Protected Area Systems in Ghana. In William Weber, Lee J. T. White, Amy Vedder, and Lisa Naughton-Treves (Eds.), *African Rain Forest Ecology and Conservation: An Interdisciplinary Perspective*, p. 392. New Haven, CT: Yale University Press.

Indigenous Traditions—
The Arctic

Indigenous peoples of the Arctic recognize the spirit of beings other than humans and practice ritual respect for all beings. From their beliefs and values emerge two key ideas of interest to environmental scientists and related to sustainability: humans as an integral part of ecosystems, and the importance of continuing to use resources to maintain respectful relationships and stewardship traditions.

There is no single accepted definition of the Arctic. The *Arctic Human Development Report* (AHDR) defines the Arctic as: all of Alaska; Canada north of the sixtieth parallel, plus northern Quebec and Labrador; Greenland; Iceland; the northernmost counties of Norway, Sweden, and Finland; and the northern parts of Russian Siberia. The AHDR Arctic covers an area of 40 million square kilometers or about 8 percent of the surface of Earth, with a population of about 4 million people, almost half of them in the Russian Arctic.

People of the Arctic

Humans have occupied large parts of the Arctic at least since the Ice Age, and from as early as 40,000 years ago in the European Arctic. Contemporary residents of the Arctic include indigenous populations and recent arrivals. Some countries such as Iceland have no indigenous populations; others such as Greenland have a majority; the Canadian Arctic has an equal split; and all others (United States/Alaska, Russia, Norway, Sweden, and Finland) have a minority of indigenous peoples. Indigenous peoples are those who show one or more of the following characteristics: they identify themselves as indigenous; they speak a language different from that of the dominant society; their cultures are different from that of the dominant society;

and they often diverge from the mainstream society by being hunters, nomads, or pastoralists.

Prior to World War II, many Arctic societies led a relatively self-sufficient way of life based on extended families or kinship groups, and in some cases, small communities. Livelihoods were based mostly on hunting, trapping, fishing, gathering, and herding, and the trading of products from these pursuits. These activities provided a strong connection to the environment, and this connection was important for two reasons. First, it was a matter of survival; animals were important for food and for the local economy. Second, traditional pursuits were important for maintaining social relationships and cultural identity. For example, seal hunting not only provided food for sharing; it was a way of life and a symbolic part of Inuit culture.

After World War II, most indigenous societies were impacted in a variety of ways. The introduction of mandatory education and establishment of permanent villages made it difficult to pursue the seasonal round of activities on the land. Transportation and communications changed at an increased pace after World War II. Motor boats, snowmobiles, and four-wheel all terrain vehicles (ATVs) became common. Television became available in most Arctic households and provided exposure to new lifestyles and role models.

Culture and Religion

Arctic indigenous societies have been in a rapid social and economic transition since World War II, but religious transition started even earlier. The vast majority of Arctic indigenous people are affiliated with some form of Christianity. The major periods of religious conversion were the eighteenth and nineteenth centuries. In many cases, the adoption of Christianity did not mean the complete replacement of one religion with another. Rather, in most indigenous societies, elements of old and new beliefs were mixed together, and the resulting system still retained some traditional values and beliefs. But generalizations are difficult to make because there are large differences from region to region, and in some cases, even between adjacent communities.

The Arctic indigenous world is diverse. The mixing of indigenous groups with one another and with the more recent European immigrants has produced a melting pot of cultures. Despite this mixing, indigenous Arctic values and beliefs vary by area. Most indigenous pre-Christian beliefs were characterized by animism, the idea that humans, animals and plants, in addition to other natural phenomena that Westerners consider inanimate, such as mountains, springs, rivers, and glaciers, all share a spirit that energizes them; belief in spiritual beings; and more broadly with pantheism, the doctrine that identifies the universe with the Creator.

With animism at the core of their belief systems, most indigenous peoples believed that humans were not the only beings capable of independent action. For example, the Tlingit in the area of St. Elias Mountains, a glacier field that straddles Alaska, Yukon, and British Columbia, tell stories in which glaciers are sentient and responsive. Many Arctic and other Northern peoples consider animals to be capable of deciding to make (or not to make) themselves available for the hunt. Since survival depended on the ability to hunt wildlife and marine mammals, it was rather important for hunters to maintain the cooperation of their prey. The belief among some indigenous groups such as the Dene and the Cree of Canada was to maintain a reciprocal relationship between humans and animals. Animals gave themselves willingly to hunters, but for their part, humans needed to maintain a relationship of respect and to observe certain rituals to take care of the spirits of the animals.

In many parts of the Arctic, people observe rituals signifying respect—rituals in which the remains of animals are returned to the environment to ensure the continuation of the spiritual cycle of life. For example, in Barrow, Alaska, a proper practice is to return the lower jawbone of a hunted bowhead whale to the sea. The Dene and the Cree hang beaver bones on trees or return them to the lakes and rivers they came from. Other practices of ritual respect include talking to the animals to ask for their permission for the hunt, and making offerings at the time of the hunt or during consumption of the animal. Some animal parts are taboo for certain people, but this practice varies widely.

In addition to animals, certain areas of the land also receive respect because traditional beliefs and practices are often tied to the land. Some mountains, springs, or parts of the land where certain ceremonies take place may be considered sacred. Sacred sites are found in many regions and cultural groups, almost universally across the Arctic. For example, 263 sacred sites were identified in one district alone in the Yamal-Nenets area in Russia. Such sacred sites have been receiving attention from the International Conservation Union as potential additions to national and international conservation networks.

Sustainability Principles

The recognition of the spirit of beings other than humans and practices of ritual respect for beings may be considered two principles of Arctic indigenous traditions. They give rise to two further key ideas or insights regarding sustainability. The first is the notion that humans are integral part of ecosystems, sharing the land with other beings as their kin. Many indigenous groups, and not only the ones in the Arctic, hold a community-of-beings worldview in which animals and other beings are related to humans. They are nonhuman persons but persons nonetheless and kin. Many indigenous cultures see humans and nature, not in an adversarial relationship involving domination and control, but in a symbiotic relationship with mutual obligations involving respect. This is a very different worldview from the Western concept of an external environment separate from human society, which leads to the dualism of nature/culture, mind/matter, and eventually to the idea of human domination and control of nature.

The wisdom of indigenous cultures is consistent with scientific ecology on the interrelatedness of all life forms and their biophysical environment. Many of the words in Northern indigenous languages that usually get translated as "land" (*ashkii* in Cree, *aski* in Ojibwa/Anishinaabe, *ndeh* in Dene) carry a meaning that goes well beyond land as physical landscape to encompass the living environment including humans. The literature on ecosystem-based management and social-ecological systems embraces a view of ecology similar to indigenous worldviews that considers humans as part of an integrated, interdependent entity in which the natural world and the human world sustain one another over time.

The second idea or insight suggested by Arctic indigenous environmental ethics is the importance of continuity of resource use to maintain respectful relationships and stewardship traditions. Using the environment and resources is important not only for obtaining food and maintaining culture, but also as a way of building ecological knowledge and relationships. Such practical engagement with the environment may be the basis for putting humans back into the ecosystem. It involves the knowledge, skills, and sensitivities that developed through long experience in a particular environment.

Many indigenous people have remarked that they have to use a resource to respect it. This is the basis of an indigenous conservation ethic for sustainable use. Loss of indigenous traditions or the imposition of a preservationist ethic can break the link between use and respect. From an indigenous viewpoint, non-use preservation only serves to alienate people from the land and, thus, from their stewardship responsibilities. The lesson from Arctic indigenous people is that the relationships of respect and reciprocity are essential for the stewardship of the environment and for sustainability.

Outlook for the Twenty-First Century

Arctic societies are increasingly tied to national policies and to the global economy. Rapid economic, political, and demographic changes; resource development; trade barriers; and animal rights campaigns have all produced shocks and stresses. For example, ocean pollution in the Arctic, mainly from long-range atmospheric transport of pollutants, threatens food sources through the accumulation of toxic substances in the food web. Hunting, fishing, and herding are threatened by climate change that is affecting animal distributions and interfering with the ability of people to predict the weather and seasonal animal distributions.

Globalization and the volatility of world markets for raw materials such as oil and gas result in boom-and-bust cycles that have come to characterize Arctic economies. The narrow economic base of most Arctic communities has made them vulnerable to political and economic decisions made elsewhere. The rapid shrinking of the pack ice of the Arctic Ocean has stimulated shipping activity, which, in turn, may further stimulate oil and gas development. Such amplifying relationships between global environmental change (such as climate change) and globalization (the "shrinking" of the world) have produced a "double exposure" to vulnerabilities affecting human security.

Against this backdrop, indigenous peoples throughout the Arctic have been adapting to change in a number of ways. They are pursuing land claims, resource rights, and regional government powers. Arctic indigenous people have become world leaders in the struggle for indigenous rights, co-management of resources, and the recognition of the importance of indigenous knowledge. They are revitalizing their languages and traditional practices to help maintain their connection to the environment.

These efforts often involve the pursuit of political autonomy as a first step. Greenland has home rule. Native land claims in Alaska and the Canadian Arctic have been settled. The Norwegian Saami have regional government powers. Assimilation pressures in the post-Soviet Chukotka (and elsewhere) have declined. With these changes, many Arctic indigenous cultures are undergoing revitalization. Cultural reaffirmation is not simply a reactivation of old customs but a rediscovery of cultural roots to anchor people in a rapidly changing world. Adapting to the contemporary Arctic lifestyle means a blurring of the opposition between tradition and change, indigenous culture and Western culture, and town living and harvesting the land.

Fikret BERKES
University of Manitoba

FURTHER READING

Arctic climate impact assessment. (2005). Cambridge, U.K.: Cambridge University Press. (Also retrieved September 24, 2008, from http://www.acia.uaf.edu)

Arctic human development report. (2004). Akureyri, Iceland: Stefansson Arctic Institute.

Berkes, Fikret. (2001). Religious traditions and biodiversity. In *Encyclopedia of biodiversity, Vol. 5,* pp. 109–120. San Diego, CA: Academic Press.

Berkes, Fikret. (2008). *Sacred ecology.* (2nd ed.). New York: Routledge.

Berkes, Fikret; Huebert, Rob; Fast, Helen; Manseau, Micheline; & Diduck, Alan. (Eds.). (2005). *Breaking ice: Renewable resource and ocean management in the Canadian North.* Calgary, Canada: University of Calgary Press.

Brightman, Robert A. (1993). *Grateful prey: Rock Cree human-animal relationships.* Berkeley: University of California Press.

Cruikshank, Julie. (2005). *Do glaciers listen? Local knowledge, colonial encounters and social imagination.* Seattle: University of Washington Press and Vancouver: University of British Columbia Press.

Csonka, Yvon, & Schweitzer, Peter. (2004). Societies and cultures: Change and persistence. In *Arctic human development report* (Chapter 3). Akureyri, Iceland: Stefansson Arctic Institute.

Fienup-Riordan, Ann. (1990). *Eskimo essays: Yup'ik lives and how we see them.* New Brunswick, NJ: Rutgers University Press.

Freeman, Milton M. R. (Ed.). (2000). *Endangered peoples of the Arctic: Struggles to survive and thrive.* Westport, CT: Greenwood Press.

Krupnik, Igor, & Jolly, Dyanna. (Eds.). (2002). *The earth is faster now: Indigenous observations of Arctic environmental change.* Fairbanks, AK: Arctic Research Consortium of the United States.

Nuttall, Mark, & Callaghan, Terry V. (Eds.). (2000). *The Arctic: Environment, people, policy.* Newark NJ: Harwood Academic Publishers.

Oozeva, Conrad; Noongwook, Chester; Noongwook, George; Alowa, Christina; & Krupnik, Igor. (2004). *Watching ice and weather our way.* Washington, DC: Arctic Studies Center, Smithsonian Institution.

Turner, Nancy J. (2005). *The earth's blanket: Traditional teachings for sustainable living.* Seattle: University of Washington Press.

Indigenous Traditions—Asia

Asia is the largest, most populous continent, and its peoples are as diverse as its landscapes. Nevertheless, traditions of the indigenous people do share some characteristics: connection to the land and a belief in spirits, particularly ones dwelling in animals and nature. Because of these factors, conservation and protection of resources is reinforced and strengthened by the native religions.

Few generalizations can be made about Asia's vast number of indigenous minority groups. Those few, however, are important, especially for the ways in which these groups connect to the natural world and thus encourage the practice of ecological conservation and preservation. All groups are closely tied to their local landscapes, and have been (except for recently migrated groups) for a very long time. All see the landscape as full of spirits. Edward Tylor (1832–1917), recognized as one of the founders in the field of social anthropology, introduced the word *animist* to describe these societies (Harvey 2006); the term refers to the belief that all of reality is pervaded by spirits or souls, and that all reality is in some sense animate. Spirits dwell in mountains, trees, animals, and other entities. They need worship, care, and concern. Such spirits may be human-like in consciousness—other-than-human persons—or quite alien. They act on humans in ways that go beyond the everyday and direct. They are like wind or breath: invisible and intangible, yet active and felt.

Nearly universal in Asia are beliefs in powerful tree spirits. Trees and groves are worshiped from the Europe–Asia border to Tibet and Thailand. Field research conducted by the sociologists Barbara Anderson and E. N. Anderson, as well as the work of other scholars, reveals that these "tree beliefs" have influenced majority religions, especially Buddhism, in which reverence for tree spirits is often used to promote conservation of trees (Darlington 1998).

The more powerful predatory animals are also considered to be bearers of particularly powerful spirits. Wolves, bears, tigers, eagles, and similar animals are widely respected and revered. Most societies believe in "shape changing": animals can take different forms including human form, and humans with special powers can take the form of animals.

Spirits of departed humans are usually important in Asian minority groups. Many groups also worship gods—remote, powerful beings that do not reside in local tangible objects—in addition to spirits. Spirits and gods are "supramundane" rather than "supernatural." Most of these societies distinguish human and nonhuman realms, but conceptualize this differently from the "human versus nature" dichotomy of European thought.

All groups have local informal religious practitioners who contact gods and spirits, including the dead, and communicate with them. Communication often involves an altered state of consciousness—a trance (in a very broad sense) or something similar—and it requires special rituals, different from and more elaborate than communication with living humans. In many societies, the religious person is a shaman, one who sends his or her soul to the realms of the supramundane beings. In others, the spirits enter the religious practitioner—a spirit medium—in a "possession trance." Many societies have both shamans and spirit mediums; occasionally the same individual will serve as both. Some indigenous societies have priests: formal, organized officiants who intercede, hold ceremonies, and worship without the need to enter an altered mental state.

In these societies, conservation or protection of resources is motivated or strengthened by religion. This ranges in importance. Small, low-density groups in Malaysia and Indonesia may be minimally motivated to conserve. Some do not practice obvious conservation. Many small-scale traditional societies around the world do not protect biotic resources, at least not effectively (Hames 2007). In Asia, however, almost all groups at least make the effort. Many groups effectively protect whole sacred mountains and forests. No Asian minority religions maintain that destroying plant and animal environments is a positive good, as do many developers and political regimes in Asia and elsewhere.

Beyond these generalizations, Asia's indigenous minorities are as varied a set of peoples as the world affords. They speak hundreds of very different languages. They live in environments ranging from arctic coasts to tropical mountains. Some live in scattered hunting-gathering bands, others are densely populated societies practicing intensive agriculture. Some are completely nonliterate, while others retain ancient literary traditions. Some have religions based largely on remote gods, others are purely concerned with local spirits.

All are culturally closer to neighboring or nearby majority cultures than to distant minorities. There was never a barrier to contact between neighboring groups, and religious ideas and practices have always flowed from local minority to majority groups and vice versa. Old ideas of cultural isolation or cultural dependence have long been abandoned. So has the belief that the minorities retained ancient forms of majority beliefs. Research has shown that both majority and minority groups in a given region often developed their religion from similar origins, and both have thus influenced each other.

Asia's minorities can be broadly classified into three great geographical assemblages: North Asia (north of central China and of the Islamic world of central Asia); Southeast Asia; and the Indian subcontinent. Outliers include remote groups in Indonesia and the Philippines.

North Asia and Shamanism

North Asia is the home of shamanism: for years the classic source on the subject has been Mircea Eliade's 1964 book *Shamanism: Archaic Techniques of Ecstasy*, but more recent sources are to be preferred for Asian research. The word, which has its origin in Tungus, a language spoken from far north China to the Arctic, has been loosely used for any folk religious practitioner who goes into trance, and thus for all manner of disparate people worldwide, but careful scholarship reserves it for North and East Asian soul-senders and their Native North American counterparts. The remote Turkic groups of southern Siberia are also shamanistic. Mongush B. Kenin-Lopsan's *Shamanic Songs and Myths of Tuva* (1997) presents a particularly good "insider's" account with details on environmental thought.

Societies that have practiced shamanism in recent times are largely hunting-gathering, fishing, or herding peoples, though many societies with long-established agriculture share the system. Historical evidence suggests that China, Japan, Korea, and Tibet were dominantly shamanistic in very early times. In China the ancient word *wu*, originally meaning a shaman, now means a spirit medium, implying a rather dramatic change in religion (Waley 1955). Shamanism survives today in Japan (Blacker 1986) and is the ultimate source of many of the widespread shape-changing stories about the fox and the *tanuki* ("raccoon dog," often mistranslated as "badger"). Shamanism also survives in minority religions in China (the Hmong and Mian, for example) and Tibet. It is often absorbed into majority religions, as in bön, the oldest spiritual tradition of Tibet (Snellgrove 1967). Spirit-mediumship in Korea is so obviously closely related to Tungus and Mongol shamanism that the spirit mediums (*mudang*) are almost always called shamans in Western-language literature (Kendall 1988). At these points the distinction between shaman and spirit medium becomes blurred. After extreme repression under Communism, shamanism has experienced a huge revival in Russia, where many dubiously qualified persons, if not to say outright frauds, have capitalized on its new popularity (Balzer 1990).

Shamans are usually healers. They visit the otherworld to find causes of illness. If the causes are seen to be violations of social and ritual rules, social harmony is served; the cause may also be witchcraft, in which case identifying the witch may cause social conflict. The shamanic journey is long and hard (Humphrey 1996), especially if a whole tribe suffers sickness or ill luck. Real environmental landmarks and scenes are incorporated into journey narratives, which may become celebrations of the group's territory and regular travels. Widespread is a belief in a "world tree" at the center of the cosmos—its roots in the underworld, its trunk in this (middle) world, and its crown in the sky-world or heaven. Shamans often climb up or down this tree on spirit journeys.

Shamans are often shape changers, able to take the form of bears, eagles, or other "power animals" as needed. Stories of shape changing abound: all humans and nonhumans are persons, all interact and can often change into each other. The unity of humans with the rest of the world is assured, and society includes both human and nonhuman persons.

Conservation and Sacrifice

Throughout the shamanistic world, religion serves the cause of conservation. Respect is shown by proper ceremonies and by taking no more from nature than is necessary for immediate personal and family needs. Religion often protects lands and especially waters from pollution, because purity is a major ritual requirement of respect for spirits.

On the other hand, sacrifice is often important and may involve the sacred wild species. Sacrifice of wild creatures teaches respect and reverence for them, and probably leads to some conservation in the end. The Mongols sacrifice sheep and other animals, leaving the hide suspended from a pole. The Koryak of northwest Siberia sacrifice dogs suspend them on similar poles. In early historic times, human sacrifice occurred in central Asia; a leader's retainers were sacrificed to accompany him or (rarely) her in the other world.

Mongols and Shamanism

The Mongols are not really a minority since they have their own independent country, Mongolia, but they are so typical in their shamanism that they should be discussed. They speak several closely related languages within the Altaic family, which also includes the Turkic and Tungus languages. Most were traditionally herders (largely of sheep, goats, and horses, and also of yaks) but many practiced some agriculture and all hunted when possible. Like many East Asian peoples the Mongols trace their descent from powerful animals—in the Mongol case, the union of a gray wolf and a beautiful doe (de Rachewiltz 2004). The Mongols recognize a remote and impersonal sky god, Tengri, as the highest power and most revered entity, but direct more of their religious activity at more immediate spirits of good and ill. Some groups have multiple sky gods. Evil spirits of disease and ill luck cause many problems, and the shaman sends his soul—shamans in this tradition are usually male—to the other world to find what has gone wrong. (*Shamans and Elders: Experience, Knowledge, and Power among the Daur Mongols*, by Caroline Humphrey and shaman Urgunge Onon, 1996, documents such practice.)

The Mongols have always protected local forests, mountains, and waters (see the historical notes in de Rachewiltz 2004). Their concern for ritual and practical purity of water has been instrumental in conserving Siberia's Lake Baikal (Metzo 2005). Buddhism has been widely adopted by many Mongols. It has not deeply changed shamanistic practice, but it has added a new dimension of respect for life. The Mongols have not given up hunting or butchering animals, but Buddhism has strengthened traditional prohibitions against unnecessary taking of life.

The Ainu of Japan

Less typically shamanic, and unique in language and culture, are the Ainu, the indigenous minority of northern Japan living primarily on the island of Hokkaido. Until Japanese intrusion changed their lives in the nineteenth century, they supplemented a fishing lifestyle with hunting and small-scale agriculture. Their lives were tightly bound to local animal and plant life, and their religion was devoted to animal powers. They traditionally sacrificed bears in a major festival (the *iyomante*) and also sacrificed eagles, eagle owls, foxes, wolves, and other creatures whose predatory power indicated great spiritual strength (Brett L. Walker 2001). The fishing-owl was a guardian bird. The salmon, a sacred fish, offered itself to humans for food. Such divine creatures were *kamuy*, "gods" (the Ainu word is derived from—or perhaps possibly the source of-the Japanese equivalent, *kami*). Small sticks (*inau*), shaved in patterns, were ritually set up for spirits. Long and beautiful ritual songs informed people of the histories and needs of wolf, owl, and bear gods, killer whales, sharks, and other powerful animals (Philippi 1982). Healing was the most important role of Ainu religious officiants. These shamans—often or usually female—were in Japan and Korea usually spirit-mediums in actual practice. Male elders who took on priestly function presided over other rituals.

Indigenous Traditions in Southeast Asia

Southward, shamanism grades into a vast complex of spirit-based religions found throughout mainland Southeast Asia and most of the island world east of it. Here, trance is more usually spirit-mediumistic than shamanic. (China's southern minorities retain both, and share a fondness for epic and mythic chants used in rituals for curing, fertility, and life-passage rites.) Many of these chants draw heavily on parallels between natural and cultural themes—or, more accurately, between the wider society (animals, plants, spirits, geographic phenomena) and the narrower human one.

The Akha and Cultivation Practices

A particularly well-studied group is the Akha, a Tibeto-Burman people (Sturgeon 2005). They live at middle elevations in the mountainous regions where China, Burma, Thailand, and Laos come together; they are divided between the four countries. They live by shifting cultivation and, increasingly, settled agriculture and tree cropping. (Shifting cultivation is a system in which land is cleared, burned, used to grow a mixture of agricultural crops for a few years, and then abandoned for a fallow period; tree cropping refers to growing trees that produce food.) The forests of the Ahka were preserved carefully until recently; they still hold a few elephants, tigers, and other "charismatic megafauna" (large creatures whose popular appeal makes them the convenient focus of environmental activists and conservation campaigns wishing to raise funds or draw attention to more humble endangered species), as well as hundreds of species of birds and small mammals. The forests are the abode of the spirits. Some are highly sacred, others less so. Certain trees are particularly revered. Origin and migration stories link the Akha closely to their homelands. Until recently the Akha maintained high population densities while preserving their landscape, through ritually regulated wise use; today, political pressures in these borderlands have had a devastating effect. This is one the clearest cases of an extremely sophisticated traditional ecological system eroded by outside pressures. The culturally related Sani, Lahu, and Yi have broadly comparable beliefs about nature, forests, and conservation, and they too have suffered heavy environmental losses in recent years. A wide range of the plants and animals living today in southwest China are mentioned in the Lahu creation myth (Arthur R. Walker 1995).

In south China and Southeast Asia most minority groups live by shifting cultivation. With this practice of cutting down small areas of forest, burning them, and planting crops in the ash, fertility is exhausted in a few years, and a new area is cut. Usually the rotation period is long-term, with a field re-cut every twenty to fifty years. This practice, as well as the more drastic slash-and-burn cultivation, has been blamed for deforestation, but most groups have religious rules against overcutting. In fact, deforestation has been done largely by majority cultures, especially by large-scale logging and agribusiness interests. Only a few minority groups with high populations and fewer ties to the land have overcut forests. In fact, the existence until modern times of magnificent forests, in spite of high population densities of shifting cultivators, is a tribute to the religiously coded management practices of both minority and majority peoples. Until the last two generations, Southeast Asia was unique in supporting huge, densely populated, ancient civilizations, as along with the small societies considered here, and yet maintaining 90 percent forest cover with high biodiversity.

Spiritual Practices

Throughout Southeast Asia, nature spirits are all-important, with tree spirits often taking pride of place. Sacred trees and groves get varying degrees of protection. Some are absolutely protected, others cropped for fuel, construction timber, fruit, rattan, and other goods. Sacred status keeps them from being leveled for agriculture or clear-cut logging, and thus protects local wood supplies. In most areas certain kinds of trees—often wild fig trees (*Ficus* spp.)—are sacred wherever found and also protected to varying degrees. (Sacred groves were also important in Africa and Europe, but links with Southeast Asia are tenuous.) Mountains are central presences, and in Indonesia, where volcanoes abound, these fire-peaks have major religious significance.

Animals are less revered but generally respected, and, as usual, powerful predators have varying degrees of taboo or respected status. In northern Southeast Asia, animal ancestor myths are common; many groups trace their descent to a dog or similar being. "Merit feasts" involving sacrifice of buffaloes or cattle exist among many minority peoples, and those who host such feasts get social and religious recognition. The worshipers share the sacrificial meat according to kinship; often, each category of kin gets a particular cut of the animal.

Concerns with growth and fertility, especially the all-important rice, are almost universal, and much art and ceremony is dedicated to rice and other staple crops. Along with environmental phenomena, ancestors are revered, especially in Indonesia, and marriage is widely important, not just to unite two individuals but to unite whole descent groups (see Tannenbaum and Kammerer 2003). Kinship is complex and all-important and is routinely projected on nature through cosmology and symbolism.

Many of Southeast Asia's minority religions are highly dualistic, with strong contrasts established between humans and spirits, men and women, wife-giving and wife-taking groups within the kinship network, and other social categories. Complex cosmological symbolism projects these on the universe; they may be represented by sacred geography, sacred biology, classes of gods, clothing designs, ritual usages, and points in the house, for example. Ethnic groups differ dramatically, making this region one of the most religiously and cosmologically rich and diverse in the world (Schiller 1997).

The Indian Subcontinent

The religions of the so-called tribal peoples of the Indian subcontinent are, if anything, even more diverse. India has the largest "tribal" population in the world, but the only real defining feature of a "tribe" is that it did not have fully literate state-level society when the British colonial regime defined them as such. There are hundreds of groups, from tiny hunting-gathering bands to ethnic groups numbering in the millions that, like the Santal, have complex societies and large towns with hierarchic political systems (Archer 1974).

The Indian subcontinent is a meeting ground of all Asian traditions. In the north, Tibetan-related groups often have shamanic religions (Snellgrove 1967). In the east, the "tribals" of eastern India and northern Bangladesh are culturally Southeast Asian, grading westward into more typical Indian cultures. In the southern mountains of India are groups who worship gods associated with cattle herding, hunting, and farming. In general, the "tribals" share varying degrees of belief in gods and sacred animals with the majority caste Hindus. For at least 2,500 years sages have equated tribal gods with the major Indian trinity of Brahma, Vishnu, and Shiva; tribal gods are seen as incarnations of these. Goddesses embody the feminine aspects of the trinity.

Some specialized indigenous groups in India focus their spiritual practices on particular concerns or aspects of their daily lives. The very small Toda group of far southern India, a specialized dairying group, has made milking their special breed of water buffaloes and processing the milk in dairies an integral part of their religion. The dairies serve as temples of varying degrees of sanctity (Arthur R. Walker 1986).

Afghanistan–Pakistan Borderlands

The "Kafirs" (Arabic for "pagans") of the Afghanistan–Pakistan borderland are the sole group in west Asia to have preserved a non-Abrahamic, non-Iranic religion. (They were the subject of the renowned 1896 study *The Kafirs of the Hindu-Kush*, by George Scott Robertson, a British soldier-surgeon attached to the Indian Foreign Service who made a year-long expedition to the remote area of what was then called Kafirstan; since Robertson wrote, the groups in Afghanistan have converted to Islam, but about 4,000 Kalasha maintain the old religion in northwest Pakistan.

The religion centered on a pantheon of gods and goddesses, including a high god Imra, a very important war god, Gish, and a goddess of cultivation and fertility, Disani or Dizne (Jettmar 1986). The Kalasha are deeply concerned with purity. Female life events, including menstruation, involve complex rituals. They share some veneration for trees and lakes (which are gates to the realm of gods), and the widespread use of the house as cosmological symbol. They sacrifice animals, including goats and cattle, often for merit feasts. Singing and dancing are very important in rituals and the many festivals. Divisions of labor—men herding and plowing, women cultivating—are religiously maintained. Relations with animals and the landscape are ritually regulated, but the Kalasha appear not to be as intensely involved with the wider natural world as are most East Asian groups. This has not spared them from being shamelessly romanticized by tourist agencies and similar interested parties, and (partly in consequence) subjected to "development" at its least sensitive level. Peter Parkes's (2000) excellent account of this could be applied, all other things being equal, to many Asian minority groups.

Challenges to Indigenous Traditions

Only one minority religious tradition (the Kafirs) survives in western Eurasia, where the Abrahamic religions—specifically Christianity and Islam (and one might add Communism, sometimes called "a Judeo-Christian heresy")—promote conversion and do not tend to accept local traditions. In sharp contrast, Hinduism, Buddhism, and East Asian majority religions such as Daoism, Confucianism, and Shinto, have generally been highly tolerant, either leaving local peoples alone or allowing them to maintain their faiths as local manifestations of the majority ones. Thus in East and South Asia, thousands of local groups retain their own religions.

Unfortunately, many indigenous groups in the Indian subcontinent are extremely poorly known to scholarship, and the area is now in the grips of rapid religious change. Conversion to world religions has been rapid. In Indonesia, forced conversions under the dictatorship of Suharto, who was in power from 1967 to 1998, devastated local religions. Extreme forms of Islam, alien to the region until the 1970s, have propagated in Muslim areas of Indonesia and in Malaysia, presenting risks to "pagan" minorities.

As the freedom to practice indigenous traditions in these regions is endangered, so is the handing down of spiritual beliefs that long upheld conservation of the Earth's resources and the preservation of its species.

E. N. ANDERSON
University of California, Riverside

FURTHER READING

Agrawal, Arun. (2005). *Environmentality: Technologies of government and the making of subjects*. Durham, NC: Duke University Press.

Anderson, Danica; Salick, Jan; Moseley, Robert; & Xiaokun, Ou. (2005). Conserving the sacred medicine mountains: A vegetation analysis of Tibetan sacred sites in Northwest Yunnan. *Biodiversity and Conservation 14*, 3065–3091.

Archer, W. G. (1974). *The hill of flutes: Life, love and poetry in tribal India: A portrait of the Santals*. Pittsburgh, PA: University of Pittsburgh Press.

Balzer, Marjorie Mandelstam. (Ed.). (1990). *Shamanism: Soviet studies of traditional religion in Siberia and Central Asia*. Armonk, NY: M. E. Sharpe.

Balzer, Marjorie Mandelstam. (1997). *Shamanic worlds: Ritual and lore of Siberia and Central Asia*. Armonk, NY: M. E. Sharpe.

Batchelor, John. (1901). *The Ainu and their folk-lore*. London: The Religious Tract Society.

Beyer, Stephen. (1978). *The cult of Tara: Magic and ritual in Tibet*. Berkeley: University of California Press.

Blacker, Carmen. (1986). *The catalpa bow: A study of shamanistic practices in Japan* (2nd ed.). London: George Allen & Unwin.

Bogoras, Waldemar. (1904–1909). *The Chukchee* (2 vols.). American Museum of Natural History, Memoirs, 11. Leiden, The Netherlands: E. J. Brill.

Bogoras, Waldemar. (1917). *Koryak texts*. Leiden, The Netherlands: E. J. Brill.

Bogoras, Waldemar. (1918). *Tales of the Yukaghir, Lamut, and Russianized Natives of East Siberia*. AMNH Papers XX:1. New York: American Museum of Natural History.

Buijs, Kees. (2006). *Power of blessing from the wilderness and from heaven: Structure and transformations in the religion of the Toraja in the Mamasa area of South Sulawesi*. Leiden, The Netherlands: KITLV.

Chindarsi, Nusit. (1975). *The religion of the Hmong Njua*. Bangkok: Siam Society.

Darlington, Susan M. (1998, Winter). The ordination of a tree: The Buddhist ecology movement in Thailand. *Ethnology 37*(1), 1–15. Retrieved May 27, 2009, from http://ccbs.ntu.edu.tw/FULLTEXT/JR-ADM/susan.htm

de Rachewiltz, Igor. (2006). *The secret history of the Mongols: A Mongolian epic chronicle of the thirteenth century* (Vols. 1–2). Leiden, The Netherlands: Brill.

Eliade, Mircea. (1964). *Shamanism: Archaic techniques of ecstasy* (Rev. ed.). London: Routledge & Kegan Paul.

Elwin, Verrier. (1991). *The Muria and their ghotul*. Oxford: Oxford University Press.

Fitzhugh, William, & Chisako Dubreuil. (Eds.). (1999). *Ainu: Spirit of a northern people*. Washington, DC: Smithsonian Institution, National Museum of Natural History, Arctic Studies Center, with University of Washington Press.

Goullart, Peter. (1955). *Forgotten kingdom*. London: John Murray.

Guha, Ramachandra. (1993). *Social ecology*. Delhi: Oxford University Press in India.

Hames, Raymond. (2007). The ecologically noble savage debate. *Annual Review of Anthropology, 36*, 177–190. Retrieved in May 27, 2009. from http://www.unl.edu/rhames/ms/savage-prepub.pdf

Hamilton, Roy W. (2003). *The art of rice: Spirit and sustenance in Asia*. Los Angeles: UCLA Fowler Museum of Cultural History.

Harrell, Stevan. (2001). *Ways of being ethnic in southwest China*. Seattle: University of Washington.

Harrell, Stevan. (Ed.). (1995). *Cultural encounters on China's ethnic frontiers*. Seattle: University of Washington Press.

Harrell, Stevan. (Ed.) (2001). *Perspectives on the Yi of southwest China*. Berkeley and Los Angeles: University of California Press.

Harvey, Graham. (2006). *Animism: Respecting the living world*. New York: Columbia University Press.

Huber, Toni. (1999). *The cult of pure crystal mountain*. New York: Oxford University Press.

Humphrey, Caroline, with Onon, Urgunge. (1996). *Shamans and elders: Experience, knowledge, and power among the Daur Mongols*. Oxford, U.K.: Oxford University Press.

Jettmar, Karl. (1986). *Religions of the Hindukush: The religions of the Kafirs, Vol.1* (Adam Nayyar, Trans.). Warminster, U.K.: Aris and Phillips.

Jochelson, Waldemar. (1908). *The Koryak. American museum of natural history, Memoir 10*. Leiden, The Netherlands: E. J. Brill.

Kendall, Laurel. (1988). *The life and hard times of a Korean shaman: Of tales and the telling of tales*. Honolulu: University of Hawaii Press.

Kenin-Lopsan, Mongush B. (1997). *Shamanic songs and myths of Tuva*. Mihály Hoppál (Ed., Trans.). Budapest: Akadémiai Kiadó.

Lopatin, Ivan A. (1960). *The cult of the dead among the natives of the Amur Basin*. The Hague: Mouton.

Maggi, Wynne. (2001). *Our women are free: Gender and ethnicity in the Hindukush*. Ann Arbor: University of Michigan Press.

Maskarinec, Gregory. (1995). *The rulings of the night: An ethnography of Nepalese Shamas oral texts*. Madison: University of Wisconsin Press.

Maskarinec, Gregory. (1998). *Nepalese Shaman oral texts*. Cambridge, MA: Harvard Oriental Studies 35.

Metzo, Katherine R. (2005, June). Articulating a Baikal environmental ethic. *Anthropology and Humanism, 30*(1), 39–54.

Müller-Ebeling, Claudia; Christian Rätsch; & Surendra Bahadur Shahi. (2007). *Shamanism and Tantra in the Himalayas*. Rochester, VT: Inner Traditions.

Nowak, Margaret, & Stephen Durrant. (1977). *The tale of the Nišan Shamaness: A Manchu folk epic*. Seattle: University of Washington Press.

Ohnuki-Tierney, Emiko. (1981). *Illness and healing among the Sakhalin Ainu: A symbolic interpretation*. Cambridge: Cambridge University Press.

Ohnuki-Tierney, Emiko. (1999). Ainu sociality. In William Fitzhugh and Chisako Dubreuil (Eds.), *Ainu: Spirit of a northern people* (pp. 240–245). Washington, DC: Smithsonian Institution, National Museum of Natural History, Arctic Studies Center, with University of Washington Press.

Orans, Martin. (1965). *The Santal: A tribe in search of a great tradition*. Detroit: Wayne State University Press.

Parkes, Peter. (2000). Enclaved knowledge: Indigent and indignant representations of environmental management and development among the Kalasha of Pakistan. In Roy Ellen, Peter Parkes, & Alan Bicker (Eds.), *Indigenous environmental knowledge and its transformations: Critical anthropological perspectives* (pp. 253–292). Amsterdam: Harwood Academic.

Philippi, Donald. (1982). *Songs of gods, songs of humans: The epic tradition of the Ainu*. San Francisco: North Point Press.

Rangan, Haripraya. (2000). *Of myths and movements: Rewriting Chipko into Himalayan history*. London: Verso.

Rivers, W. H. R. (1906). *The Todas*. London: MacMillan and Co.

Robertson, George Scott. (1896). *The Kafirs of the Hindu-Kush*. London: Lawrence and Bullen.

Rouget, Gilbert. (1985). *Music and Trance*. Chicago: University of Chicago Press.

Roux, Jean. (1966). *Faune et flore sacrées dans les sociétés altaïques*. Paris: A. Maisonneuve.

Roux, Jean. (1984). *Religion des Turcs et des Mongoles*. [Turkish and Mongol Religion]. Paris: Payot.

Schiller, Anne. (1997). *Small sacrifices: Religious change and cultural identity among the Ngaju of Indonesia*. New York: Oxford University Press.

Snellgrove, David L. (Ed. & Trans.). (1967). *The nine ways of Bon: Excerpts from gZi-brjid*. London: University of London, London Oriental Series.

Shapiro, Judith. (2001). *Mao's war against nature: Politics and the environment in revolutionary China*. Cambridge, U.K.: Cambridge University Press.

Shutova, Nadezhda. (2006). Trees in Udmurt religion. *Antiquity 80*, 318–327.

Sturgeon, Janet. (2005). *Border landscapes: The politics of Akha land use in China and Thailand*. Seattle: University of Washington Press.

Tannenbaum, Nicola, & Kammerer, Cornelia Ann. (2003). *Founders' cults in Southeast Asia: Ancestors, polity, and identity*. New Haven, CT: Yale University Press.

Tylor, Edward. (1871*). Primitive culture*. London: John Murray.

Vainstein, Sevyan. (1980). *Nomads of south Siberia: The pastoral economies of Tuva*. Cambridge, Studies in Social Anthropology, 25. Caroline Humphrey (Ed.), Michael Colenso (Trans.). (Original work published in Russian in 1972)

van Wouden, F. A. E. (1968). *Types of social structure in eastern Indonesia*. Rodney Needham (Trans.). The Hague: Martinus Nijhoff.

Waley, Arthur. (1955). *The nine songs: A study of shamanism in ancient China*. London: G. Allen and Unwin.

Walker, Anthony R. (1986). *The Toda of south India: A new look*. Delhi: Hindustan.

Walker, Anthony R. (Ed.) (1995). *Mvuh Hpa Mi Hpa: Creating heaven, creating Earth: An Epic myth of the Lahu people in Yunnan* (Shi Kun, Trans.). Chiang Mai, Thailand: Silkworm Books.

Walker, Brett L. (2001). *The conquest of Ainu lands: Ecology and culture in Japanese expansion, 1590–1800*. Berkeley: University of California Press.

Indigenous Traditions—Australia

The spirit of sustainability is prominent within the religion and philosophy of the Australian Aboriginal people. It emphasizes the preeminence of the land and configures humankind as part of the larger whole through a world-view referred to in English as Dreaming. *Indigenous religion requires attentiveness to the needs of all things and proposes that those who destroy what has been created ultimately destroy themselves.*

The Australian Aboriginal words for the concepts at the center of their traditions and worldview have no single equivalent in English, but many indigenous people have been using the word *Dreaming* for about a hundred years, primarily as a noun, to express how the world, its features, and all of its beings came to take their shapes and connectivities. The meanings of Dreaming include creation, continuity, religious action, and ecological connectivity. A spirit of sustainability is beautifully articulated in the concept of Dreaming, although not in those English words of course. The Aboriginal philosopher Mary Graham distills Aboriginal religious philosophy into two main precepts: the land is the law, and you are not alone in the world. These two principles can be understood as an indigenous ethic and practice of connectivity. The second precept—you are not alone— situates humanity as a participant in a larger living system. The first requires that humans submit to the workings of the world; it offers joy and celebration within a mode of participation. Graham develops this precept with the further explanation that "all meaning comes from land"

(Graham 2008, 181–182). Sustainability is an outcome of the practices of care that reflect these two precepts.

Dreaming

Creation stories vary across the Australian continent, yet at the same time they are connected through the travels and actions of Dreamings—the great shape-shifting creators who walked this Earth. All across the land, Dreamings made a world of form and difference; they brought into being and organized the different countries, languages, peoples, species, cultures, plant communities, and sources of fresh water.

One side of Dreaming is that which endures. Dreamings created *countries*—not as political entities in the way they are often considered today but as homes for human groups and for distinctive plants and animals and the unique landforms that sustain their lives. The landscape itself is sacred geography. The other side of this created world is ephemeral: the living things, the relationships between and among them, the waters that support their lives, the cultural forms of action and knowledge that sustain the created world. Through actions of knowledgeable living things (a category that is not exclusively human), Dreaming is actualized in present time. The enduring life of the creation is carried through contemporary time and space by ephemeral life forms.

Caring for Country

The term *caring for country* is another indigenous contribution to contemporary English. *Care* concerns relationship and responsibility. People care for their own home country, so that each country is ideally a matrix of ongoing life, moral action, and ultimate meaning. Since colonization by Europeans in the nineteenth and twentieth centuries, Aboriginal peoples' capacity to care for country has been radically diminished in many regions. As people were dispossessed and either killed or taken away from their homes, and as country was converted to private property and to industrial agriculture and pastoralism, the losses have been extreme. Ecosystems may collapse rapidly, as has happened in central Australia, where the rate of mammalian extinctions is the highest in the world (Johnson 2006, vii). They may also (or alternatively) collapse slowly, as appears to be happening in many other areas. It is difficult to sort out the variables, but in many parts of Australia the loss of Aboriginal care is causally linked to major changes in ecosystems.

Yet all over Australia, Aboriginal people continue to care for country as best they can. In areas of former reserves, where ecosystems remain relatively intact, that care continues to be expressed in daily life, ritual action, and in an underlying religious philosophy of relationship and responsibility. Caring for country is communicative. Aboriginal people say that their country calls them into action: it relays messages; they listen, smell, see, understand, and respond. The "call of country" is communicated by all the senses, and the people who are away from their home country experience sensory deprivation that feels like loss, banality, and inertness of spirit. Kathy Deveraux, an elder of the Mak Mak clan whose home is in the swamps and floodplains near the northern city of Darwin, described the experience of coming home: "You see the birds, you see the country, and your senses come back to you. You know what to do and where to go" (Rose et al. 2002, 1).

Caring for country is founded in knowledge. Many people have an encyclopedic knowledge of the plants and animals of their country, of the habitat requirements of plants, of the food and other habitat requirements of the animals, of how to interpret the tracks and other traces of life in the land. Old people, in particular, hold deep knowledge of the histories of disasters and refuges and of the communities of symbiosis that enable all the forms of life to flourish through the generations.

Care and the nurturance of ecosystems express two major ethical propositions concerning the flourishing of life in this created world. These propositions give rise to sustainable ecosystems and, in the view of many Aboriginal people, are applicable to all people in all times and places (Neidjie, Davis, and Fox 1985). The first is that a country and its people take care of each other. This proposition emphasizes place and proximity in the organization of care and asserts that relationships of care are reciprocal. To take care of one's country is to take care of the conditions whereby country can continue to provide sustenance for living things, including the people who belong to (and take care of) the place. The second proposition is that those who destroy their country ultimately destroy themselves. This proposition follows directly from the first; attentiveness to the needs of other living things pervades this whole ethic of care.

Mutuality

Ecological knowledge is coded into iconography, song, and story; a great deal of myth and ritual articulates ecological knowledge for a given country. The more complex ritual performances include not only song, dance, and designs applied directly to the body, but sacred objects that bear designs, some of which are permanently inscribed and some of which are painted. Iconographic representation of a plant or animal species speaks to relationships between a group of people and that species. At the same time, images of plant or animal species also concern that species quite directly: the image speaks to a site that is part of the creation story for that species and to care that ensures the flourishing of that species.

Aboriginal fire ecology is one of the best examples of caring for country. Mandated by Dreaming action and stories, Aboriginal people's use of fire aims to produce a mosaic effect of patches of country at various stages of regrowth after fire. The effect is to increase habitat diversity and thus to facilitate biodiversity. The burning of vegetation is carried out country by country in accordance with local knowledge. Because fire ecology is linked to local conditions, the timing, frequency, and organization of fires varies across the continent. People's explanations for why they burn vary, but hunting is an important component. There is a mutuality to burning: it improves the lives of other creatures by increasing habitat diversity and removing desiccated vegetation to make way for nutritional green growth. At the same time, it also improves the lives of humans, not only by improving the health of animals which will be hunted, but also by making the country easier to travel through. An aesthetic of "clean" country refers to country that has been properly burnt: cleared up but not wiped out.

April Bright, a Mak Mak clan Elder whose home country has experienced continuous Aboriginal burning through the era of colonization, explains: "'Burn grass' takes place after the wet season when the grass starts drying off. This takes place every year. The country tells you when and where to burn. To carry out this task you must know your country. You wouldn't, you just would not attempt to burn someone else's country. One of the reasons for burning is saving country. If we don't burn our country every year, we are not looking after our country" (Rose et al. 2002, 25).

Respect

For over 40,000 years, indigenous people in Australia have lived in and cared for the driest inhabited continent on Earth. During the time of human inhabitation there were periods that were more arid and periods that were wetter; the seas pulled back and then came in again. In a few regions in the far south, ice sheets pushed people out, but most of the continent has been continuously inhabited through many ecological changes. In the course of millennia, people developed a philosophical-religious ecology that is located in country, in ecosystems, and in ongoing creation. Dreaming is all about this living world—how it came into being and how it continues to come into being. People's religious life, as much as their economic life, celebrates the joy and plenitude of life in country.

Since colonization, Aboriginal people and Australian ecosystems have suffered enormously. And yet even in the most devastated areas, the spirit of responsibility remains. Phil Sullivan, an Aboriginal man whose home is on the Darling River in a region of drought and failing irrigation ventures, speaks of his experience of trying to sustain relationships between people and country: "We may lose our . . . language, even the rock art may fade, but we will never lose what's inside our hearts—our spiritual connection to country. The outward things may pass but the respect, the thing inside, will last. We respect our animals and our land. That's what I call our last line of defence. The last line of defence is respect" (Rose, Watson, and James 2003, 102).

Deborah Bird ROSE
Macquarie University

FURTHER READING

Graham, Mary. (2008, November). Some thoughts on the philosophical underpinnings of Aboriginal worldviews. *Australian Humanities Review, 45*, 181–194. Retrieved January 19, 2009, from http://www.australianhumanitiesreview.org/archive/Issue-November-2008/graham.html

Johnson, Chris. (2006) *Australia's Mammal Extinctions: A 50,000-year history*. Melbourne: Cambridge University Press.

Neidjie, Bill; Davis, Stephen; & Fox, Allan. (1985). *Kakadu man: Bill Neidjie*. Queanbeyan, New South Wales, Australia: Mybrood.

Rose, Deborah. (1996). *Nourishing terrains: Australian Aboriginal views of landscape and wilderness*. Canberra, Australia: Australian Heritage Commission. Retrieved March 30, 2009, from http://www.environment.gov.au/heritage/ahc/publications/commission/books/pubs/nourishing-terrains.pdf

Rose, Deborah; D'Amico, Sharon; Daiyi, Nancy; Deveraux, Kathy; Daiyi, Margaret; Ford, Linda; et al. (2002). *Country of the heart: An indigenous Australian homeland*. Canberra, Australia: Aboriginal Studies Press.

Rose, Deborah; Watson, Christine; & James, Diana. (2003). *Indigenous kinship with the natural world*. Sydney: National Parks and Wildlife Service, New South Wales. Retrieved March 30, 2009, from http://www.environment.nsw.gov.au/resources/cultureheritage/IndigenousKinship.pdf

ABORIGINAL CONCEPTS OF COUNTRY

While studying the peoples in Western Australia and New South Wales, Deborah Bird Rose was inspired by the twentieth-century philosopher Emmanuel Levitas's term "nourished terrain." She developed her own definition of how Aboriginals experience "country" as a place that gives and receives life. "Not just imagined or represented," she writes, "it is lived in and lived with."

Country in Aboriginal English is not only a common noun but also a proper noun. People talk about country in the same way that they would talk about a person: they speak to country, sing to country, visit country, worry about country, feel sorry for country, and long for country. People say that country knows, hears, smells, takes notice, takes care, is sorry or happy. Country is not a generalised or undifferentiated type of place, such as one might indicate with terms like 'spending a day in the country' or 'going up the country.' Rather, country is a living entity with a yesterday, today and tomorrow, with a consciousness, and a will toward life. Because of this richness, country is home, and peace; nourishment for body, mind, and spirit; heart's ease.

Source: Deborah Bird Rose. (1996). *Nourishing Terrains: Australian Aboriginal Views of Landscape and Wilderness*, pp. 7. Canberra, Australia: Australian Heritage Commission. Retrieved October 1, 2009, from http://www.environment.gov.au/heritage/ahc/publications/commission/books/pubs/nourishing-terrains.pdf

Indigenous Traditions— North America

A common belief among indigenous peoples of North America is that everything on Earth and in the universe has a soul and is animated by spirit—although with over 560 recognized tribes in the United States alone, there is considerable variation to the theme. Many peoples consider land and water and everything that lives on it and in it to be sacred, a belief that often—but not always—lends itself to a sustainable lifestyle.

Native Americans today practice a wide variety of religious traditions, from their original indigenous ways to Christianity and combinations of the two in unique forms of syncretism. It is important to note that most North American tribal spiritual leaders do not refer to their practices as "religion"; instead, they refer to "spiritual traditions," "sacred ways," and "spiritual ways of life." The term *religion* is often associated with European, Middle Eastern, and European-American institutions based on holy texts, prophets, and monotheism. This differs significantly from the sacred ways of native peoples who have site-specific, Earth-centered, spiritual ethics and practices based on intergenerational oral teachings often referred to as "traditional knowledge," "natural laws," or "original instructions."

With 4 million reported American Indians and 562 recognized American Indian and Alaskan native nations in the United States, the range and diversity of spiritual traditions is immense. In Canada, there are 1,172,790 reported aboriginal people living in more than six hundred First Nation, Métis, and Inuit bands and off-reserve communities. In Mexico, there are approximately sixty distinct indigenous groups that speak over sixty unique languages. The indigenous cultural diversity within and between these three North American nation-states is vast and complex— vast because of inherent cultural diversity (ethnic, linguistic, philosophical, and artistic) and complex because of the severe changes in traditional practices due to numerous waves of colonialism which tribes responded to, accommodated, and resisted in numerous resilient ways.

There is an almost unfathomable variety of indigenous religious and spiritual expressions in North America— from Inuit traditional shamans in northern Canada to Mormon Paiutes in the U.S. Great Basin; from Yaqui syncretic Catholics in the southwestern United States and Mexico to Lakota Sun Dancers in the plains of the United States; from Native American Church worshippers to urban mixed-blood (Métis, Mestizo, Creole) pan-spiritualists in major North American cities. From this vast diversity, the major Native American spiritual practices can be grouped into four main categories: (1) traditional, (2) Christian or other major religion, (3) syncretic—a unique combination of Christian and traditional spiritual practices, and (4) pan-tribal—an intertribal blend of varied spiritual beliefs, practices, and ceremonies. This article will focus on the first category, the traditional spiritual teachings of North America—the precolonial spiritual philosophies, ethics, and ceremonies.

Key Concepts

Given all of the geographic, ethnic, cultural, and linguistic diversity of Native American spiritual traditions, some consistent key concepts can be generalized and summarized.

These teachings originate in the oral tradition and can now be found in published forms. In terms of philosophy and belief, most native spiritual traditions are considered holistic and animistic. They originate in ideas that the spiritual and material worlds are intimately entwined and that nature is an embodiment of sacred and spiritual energies. Therefore, everything on Earth and in the universe—plants, animals, clouds, humans, rocks, and so forth—has a soul and is animated by spirit. This belief is also often called pantheistic, meaning that the source of the universe, the universe itself, and nature (including humans) are all merged as part of one sacred, spiritual creation. These teachings support the idea that the divine or sacred is both immanent and transcendent, with the emphasis on immanent, prioritizing a more personal and intimate relationship with the sacred in daily life.

Native Americans often refer to their teachings as the "original instructions" because, according to their cosmologies and cosmogonies, they were the first spiritual teachings given to them, in their own languages, by their Creator or Creators in the Creation Time. Each native language serves as the foundation and medium for distinct philosophical, psychological, and intellectual perspectives that are often impossible to interpret within a Western worldview and the English language. These original, oral instructions are like the holy texts of other religions except they are more spoken, personal, and dynamic. Within these oral instructions are specific ethics, values, lessons, and worldviews that explain how to live a spiritually healthy, balanced, and good life in harmony with other humans and the Earth. These spiritual values are infused with practical science and observation to support the survival and regeneration of the people and all that the people need to survive—food, water, shelter, clothing, and medicine. To support this regeneration, many Native nations, like the Yurok Tribe of northern California, practice world renewal ceremonies to literally "keep the Earth in balance." These values and practices could also be called an embodied sustainability in the sense that they help a particular group of people sustain themselves within a specific ecosystem and traditional homeland.

A common spiritual instruction that Native Americans share is the perception and understanding that a Great Power and Great Mystery exists in the universe that is ultimately unknowable to the human mind. This power reminds humans to be humble and grateful for the gifts of life. In dreams, visions, death, darkness, and the unknown, there is a Great Mystery that must be revered and placated. This value in, and respect for, Mystery helps humans

realize that they are part of a larger universal cycle of life and death, creation and destruction, and that reverence, humility, and humor are aids for peaceful living.

Two other interrelated concepts central to Native American spiritual traditions are kinship and reciprocity. Native peoples understand that they are intimately and personally connected, as if in a family, to the extended family of the natural world. Through food, water, breath, and other needs, humans depend on the plants, animals, soils, climate, and sun for their nourishment and continuance. Therefore, they are holistically interrelated to all that lives, especially to the "kin" in their local environment. The Raramuri ethnoecologist Enrique Salmon has called this "kincentric ecology": "Indigenous people view both themselves and nature as part of an extended ecological family that shares ancestry and origin. It is an awareness that life in any environment is viable only when humans view that life surrounding them as kin" (Salmon 2000, 1327). Since humans depend on nature for survival, they must treat it with care, respect, and honor, and make offerings and sacrifices to these other life forms and their spirits. For example, when a Cree hunter prepares to hunt, he makes special prayers and offerings to the Moose Spirit so that it will give up its life to sustain the hunter and his family. After he kills the moose, he sings a song to it to help its spirit be at peace and offers a sacred herb such as tobacco, sweetgrass, or sage to symbolically and literally thank the moose and reciprocate for the gift of its life. This emphasis and practice of reciprocity is extremely important and exhibited in numerous ways when gathering, collecting, or hunting food or medicine. It is also expressed when exchanging gifts or trading with friends, family, or folks at traditional gatherings, ceremonies, or powwows. This spirit of kinship and reciprocity is also encouraged with all peoples, including strangers and people from different backgrounds. In this sense, Native American spiritual traditions teach about the importance of cultural pluralism, intercultural respect, and the gift economy.

Traditional Rituals and Ceremonies

According to Carl Waldman's *Atlas of the North American Indian*, the North American religious traditions "can be seen as a diffusion and cross-fertilization of two distinct cultural traditions: the Northern Hunting tradition and the Southern Agrarian tradition" (Waldman, 67). Animal worship, shamanism, ritual healing, and interspecies communication characterize the Northern Hunting tradition. The Southern Agrarian tradition is part of elaborate seasonal and agricultural cycles of planting, growing, and harvesting foods at certain times. In these tribal systems, priesthoods and religious institutions are more formalized and hierarchical with secretive and esoteric forms of worship.

Many of the ceremonies and rituals practiced by Native Americans from both of these generalized traditions involve sacrifice, the quest of a vision, and use of music, dance, art, and plant and animal medicines to shift one's consciousness from the ordinary to the supernatural. Sacrifice is emphasized in the Lakota sweat lodge and Sun Dance ceremonies where fasting is required and one is purified through intense heat, sweating, dancing, and prayer. Fasting is very common in many tribal traditions where a young person enters a rite of passage and seeks a vision through fasting alone in nature for a specific period of time, often for four days and nights. This practice is often called a vision quest. Other ceremonies involve group activities where the four elements (air, fire, water, earth) are used with particular songs and dances to make offerings to ancestors, plants, and animals, or Earth spirits. The Pueblo Corn Dances of the American and Mexican Southwest are examples of these group rituals of giving thanks to the Corn Mother through elaborate group songs, dances, and offerings. The Huichol of Mexico use their sacramental plant peyote as a medicine to induce altered states of consciousness and communication with unseen spirits and energies.

All of these rituals and ceremonies require an intimate understanding of the local ecology and web of relationships. Therefore, land and water and the life that lives on and within them are considered sacred and personal. The landscape must be cared for and tended in a familial and regenerative way. The Hopi of Arizona use certain clays and dyes in their ceremonies and sacred arts; thus, they must have a practical and scientific understanding of geology, soils, and geography for sustainably harvesting these clays over thousands of years. Likewise, Midé priests, Ojibwe traditional healers, use the oil from bear and sturgeon, two totem animals, in special healing ceremonies. They must have a detailed knowledge of the life cycles, physiological stages, anatomy, and behavior of those animals to harvest, extract, and utilize those oils in healing ways. In this sense, native religion, science, and art merge as a holistic way of living.

All of these rituals occur in sacred places in specific native lands and waters. Therefore, the concept of holy lands and sacred places is central to all Native American traditions.

Kinship Ecology and the Ecological Indian

For food, medicine, clothing, shelter, sacred practices, and daily nourishment, Native Americans historically practiced extensive and intensive land management that was guided by ethics of restraint, sacrifice, moderation, reciprocity, gratitude, and celebration. Due to their elaborate belief systems revolving around kinship and reciprocity and practical expressions and behaviors involving offerings to the natural world, Native Americans have often been called the "first ecologists" or "original environmentalists." The label of the "ecological Indian" is met with both approval and disdain by native peoples of North America. On one hand, indigenous peoples throughout the world are the only groups of humans who have demonstrated living sustainably within their local ecosystems for thousands of years before colonialism radically disrupted their ways of life. On the other hand, some native groups have also overexploited natural resources and either moved or disappeared due to that overexploitation. Regardless of which position one takes, it is still considered a stereotype to label Native Americans as ecologists rather than getting to know who they are as individual modern people with diverse views, opinions, and practices. Even though many native peoples have expressed highly complex and sophisticated ecological philosophies and practices, to say "all Native Americans are ecological" is overly romantic, essentialistic, and problematic.

Religious Freedom Struggles and Controversies

Native Americans today face ongoing threats to their sacred ways as many tribes struggle to maintain relationships with their sacred places and have access to their traditional medicines and ancestral lands. Religious freedom is still difficult and controversial for Native Americans as many non-natives misunderstand, stereotype, and discriminate against native peoples and their spiritual beliefs and practices. For example, the people of the Winnemem Wintu nation of northern California struggle to protect their sacred sites from being again flooded by the expansion of a river dam. Another threat to Native American spiritual traditions is the New Age Movement where "white shamans" and "plastic medicine men" fake Native American traditions and charge non-natives large amounts of money to participate in so-called ceremonies. Extractive industries such as mining, logging, damming, and military uses continue to threaten and destroy Native American shrines, burials, emergence places, and origin sites at an alarming rate. Industrial land uses, New Age commercialism, cultural stereotypes and ignorance, and governmental restrictions are some of the main factors that threaten the religious freedom of today's Native Americans.

Despite these and other major challenges to Native American religious freedom and spiritual expression, today's Native Americans continue to practice traditional sacred ways. As the Ojibwe activist Winona LaDuke has stated, these time-tested spiritual traditions illustrate a worldview not based on conquest. They demonstrate a much needed philosophy, ethics, and embodied practice of ecological kinship and intergenerational responsibility.

Melissa K. NELSON
San Francisco State University

FURTHER READING

Beck, Peggy V., & Walters, Anna L. (1988). *The sacred: Ways of knowledge, sources of life.* Tsaile, AZ: Navajo Community College Press.

Caldicott, J. Baird, & Nelson, Michael R. (2004). *American Indian environmental ethics: An Ojibwa case study.* Upper Saddle River, NJ: Pearson Education.

Deloria, Vine, Jr. (1994). *God is red: A native view of religion.* Golden, CO: Fulcrum Publishing.

Deloria, Vine, Jr. (2006). *The world we used to live in: Remembering the powers of the medicine men.* Golden, CO: Fulcrum Publishing.

Graham, Harvey. (2006). *Animism: Respecting the living world.* New York: Columbia University Press.

Grim, John. (1998). *Indigenous traditions and ecology: The interbeing of cosmology and community.* Cambridge, MA: Harvard University Press.

Kelley, Dennis F., & Crawford, Suzanne J. (2005). *American Indian religious traditions: An encyclopedia.* Oxford, U.K.: ABC-CLIO.

Kidwell, Clara Sue. (2001). *A Native American theology.* Maryknoll, NY: Orbis Books.

Martin, Joel. (2001). *The land looks after us: A history of Native American religion.* New York: Oxford University Press.

Nabokov, Pete. (2007). *Where the lightning strikes: The lives of American Indian sacred places.* New York: Penguin.

Nelson, Melissa K. (2008). *Original instructions: Indigenous teachings for a sustainable future.* Rochester, VT: Bear & Company/Inner Traditions.

Niezen, Ronald. (2000). *Spirit wars: Native North American religions in the age of nation building.* Berkeley: University of California Press.

Salmon, Enrique. (2000). Kincentric ecology: Indigenous perceptions of the human–nature relationship. *Ecological Applications, 10*(5), 1327–1332.

Smith, Huston. (2007). *A seat at the table: Conversations with American Indian leaders on religious freedom.* Berkeley: University of California Press.

Sullivan, Lawrence. (1989). *Native American religions: North America.* New York: Macmillan Publishing Company.

Treat, James. (1996). *Native and Christian: Indigenous voices on religious identity in the United States and Canada.* New York and London: Routledge.

Vecsey, Christopher. (1991). *Handbook of American Indian religious freedom.* New York: Crossroad Publishing Company.

Waldman, Carl. (2000). *Atlas of the North American Indian.* New York: Checkmark Books.

Wessendorf, Kathrin. (2008). *The indigenous world 2008.* Copenhagen: International Work Group for Indigenous Affairs.

Indigenous Traditions—Oceania

In Oceania indigenous beliefs and practices reflect an awareness of the interdependence of all life. Ritual (such as the Hawaiian hula) and dynamic concepts (such as the Dreaming of Australia) celebrate habitats and engage the individual and community in life-giving power. Western resource exploitation and rising seawaters that threaten to submerge some island homelands are among the dangers to ecological and cultural sustainability in the area.

The indigenous peoples of Oceania follow both the ways of their ancestors and the Christianities brought to them by missionaries. In some places indigenous lifeways and introduced faith are well integrated while in others they constitute separate and competing ways of living in the world. Overall, styles of religion in the Pacific emphasize social and ecological relationships. Traditional environmental knowledge among indigenous peoples in Oceania and elsewhere emphasizes a reciprocity between people and other life-forms; this give-and-take structures traditional myth and ritual and influences Pacific appropriations of Christianity. The region of Oceania, extending from the large island of New Guinea in the west to Hawaii and Rapa Nui (Easter Island) in the east, includes the islands of the Pacific Ocean and the landmass of Australia. Indigenous ways of life in the region are conditioned by its diverse environments, from the deserts of central Australia to the rainforests of New Guinea to the coral atolls of the central Pacific. In ritual practices people seek their own well-being and that of their land, crops, and animals, and in mythic narratives they tell of how the land was shaped, how people came to dwell in their particular territory, and how social institutions arose. Sustaining fertility and well-being in the present and maintaining the cosmic order handed down from the ancestors is of ultimate concern both individually and socially. The physical diversity of the region is echoed in the social diversity, which includes societies led by chieftains and more egalitarian communities with a variety of kinship patterns. These intersect with modern political systems introduced in the colonial era. Throughout Oceania spirit beings of various kinds—ancestral ghosts, creator gods, and spirits dwelling in trees and pools and features of the landscape—are understood as active players in the social world. With the introduction of Christianity the triune Christian God and Christian saints have been incorporated into that world.

Religion from an Ecological Point of View

Classic Western definitions of religion emphasize relationship to God or gods and speak of beliefs, practices, values, and symbols. These approaches to religion can be used in exploring the ways of life of the peoples of Oceania. But an ecological orientation toward religion—an orientation that construes religion as the linking and empowerment of the many domains of experience—is preferable. Rather than negating other perspectives it suggests that religion is awareness of the interdependence of all of life. Actions to sustain life and to tap into life-giving power flow from such awareness. While the term "religion" has no exact equivalent in traditional Oceania there are indigenous notions that share in its significance. Among them are the "Dreaming" in indigenous Australia and *mana* and *tapu* in Polynesia and parts of Melanesia. All three terms have ecological import and, as a consequence of colonial and missionary incursion into the Pacific, all three have had an influence on how contemporary scholars of religion think about their subject.

The "Dreaming" is an English term adopted by Australian indigenous peoples to represent ideas about origins and the ongoing empowerment of the world. It refers at one level to an epoch in which beings with extraordinary powers, such as the Rainbow Snake, appeared from below the ground or from the sky or from over the horizon. These powerful beings shaped the earth, distributed plants and animals and water, and established human cultures. They are themselves called Dreamings. Each person and group has associations with particular Dreamings. The work of the Dreamings is narrated in myths and enacted in rituals that transmit their power to the landscape and to the community. Australian indigenous religion is more concerned with place than with time. Within their own "country" (territory, land) people are aware of Dreaming tracks, paths along which the Dreaming figures traveled, and Dreaming places where the powerful beings rested or engaged in creative actions. In the Dreaming perspective people belong to their country and share life with all the other species that inhabit it. It is the responsibility of the people to tell the stories and to perform the rituals so that the community of land, animals, plants, and people will flourish. People understand themselves as belonging to the land and bearing a responsibility to sustain it through carrying out the rituals given to them in the Dreaming.

Through the work of Émile Durkheim (1858–1917) and others the terms *mana* and *tapu* have entered the lexicon of religious studies and taken on a wider significance. (Durkheim 2008 [1912], 140–152, 221–242). In the Pacific *mana* is a quality of being in which a person or an object is, temporarily or permanently, under the influence of gods, spirits, or other powers. The Anglican missionary R. H. Codrington (1830–1922) characterized Melanesian religion as a process of acquiring *mana* (Codrington 1891, 118–121, 191–193). Whereas *mana* suggests a manifestation of power and is often glossed as "supernatural power," *tapu* implies a restriction or curbing of power. *Tapu* is usually rendered in English as "taboo" and glossed as "forbidden." Objects, persons, and behaviors that are seen as dangerous to ordinary people are said to be *tapu* (taboo). Thus, places where spirits dwell are potentially dangerous and are usually *tapu*. When it is necessary to venture there, for instance to harvest fruit or nuts or to hunt, people carry out protective rituals. The historian and linguist Anne Salmond observes that Polynesian words like *mana* and *tapu* and *atua* (god) are "highly theory-dependent, and correspondingly difficult to interpret and translate." She points out that they arise "from an explanatory project which in this case takes the physical experience of mating, reproduction, and growth, and from that base develops a genealogical description language to account for the relations among entities of all kind (e.g., people; their ancestors and ancestor-gods; plants and animal species; and phenomena such as the stars, sky, earth, the sea, land, the mountains and the wind) and the emergence of the cosmos itself" (Salmond 1989, 57).

Symbolic Words and Works

In Oceania most indigenous people either live in rural areas or retain links with rural communities. Many sustain themselves, as their ancestors did, by gardening, hunting, and fishing. In daily life people communicate in "ordinary" language and perform "ordinary" labor to provide food. But in rituals to sustain the land (and sea) they use multivalent words and actions to forge fruitful connections across the many domains of experience and particularly with the spirit beings. Everyone uses symbolic words and symbolic works, and some societies entrust their most significant myths and rituals to specialists such as healers and priests. For example, as Michael Young discusses in *Magicians of Manumanua*, in the Massim society of Kalauna in Papua New Guinea the "guardians" of the community are hereditary ritual specialists who know the myths concerning food and who conduct rituals to banish famine and to promote the supply of food. In symbolic words, such as spells for gardens and prayers for the growth of children, and in symbolic works for healing and renewal, ritual specialists and their clients work to achieve balance and prosperity.

In adopting Christianity, peoples of the Pacific accommodated traditional rituals, such as the Hawaiian hula, to changing circumstances. Prior to the arrival of missionaries in 1820, the hula, a combination of dance and chant, which according to one legend was instituted by the goddess Laka, was performed to honor the gods, to pay tribute to chiefs, and to celebrate nature and the community. Hula chants and dance movements evoke the natural environment with its valleys and forests and rivers, its ferns and flowers and fruits. Missionaries were offended by the sexual imagery of the hula, which depicted both human love and the fruitfulness of nature, and denounced it as heathen. Traditional forms of hula declined, but there was a resurgence during the reign of King David Kalākaua (1874–1891) in which a form of hula, the *hula ku'i*, combined traditional and new elements. To appeal to tourists in the twentieth century hula was presented as an entertainment with a focus on the exotic charms of the dancers. Since the 1960s with the Hawaiian Cultural Renaissance there has been renewed interest in the study and practice of ancient hula that have accompanied a struggle for land, a reclamation of traditional forestry and farming practices, and a return to Polynesian voyaging.

Environmental Ethics

Religions provide guidance on how to live in the natural world that may be couched in a Pacific ethic of reciprocity, or in a Christian ethic of stewardship of the Earth, or in other terms. Pacific and Christian ways are not without common ground, and both are tested by contemporary realities. Traditional communities used both manual labor and symbolic processes to maintain balance in their environment but sometimes, as on Rapa Nui, they failed in their efforts. Polynesians, who settled on Rapa Nui perhaps as late as 1200 CE, felled trees to create fields for agriculture and to use in the transport of huge stone statues called *moai*, which represented their sacred chiefs and gods and the unity of their community. Over time destruction of forests led to erosion of topsoil and a decline in agricultural productivity. By the 1830s competition for resources and loss of confidence in the chiefs had led to internecine wars and the collapse of the society. In most parts of Oceania, however, people were able to adjust to the constraints of their environment. From the chiefly societies of Polynesia to the more egalitarian societies of highland New Guinea an ethic of reciprocity prevailed, but not everyone was equal in the social network. In the chiefly societies lower status people lacked the privileges of the higher status people, and in most societies women were considered inferior to men. The networks of relationships making up the worlds of meaning of Pacific peoples were not static. They constantly needed adjustments and corrections that rituals of healing and reconciliation provided.

In the more than two centuries of Western presence in the Pacific the traditional ethic and Christian assertions about social justice and ecological responsibility have been severely challenged by labor recruiters, whalers, miners, loggers, and bio-prospectors. The Western incursion into the Pacific has seen profound transformations and severe dislocations of traditional community life. For example, in Fiji there are difficulties in the relationship between indigenous Fijians and Indo-Fijians, the descendants of the Indians brought in the nineteenth century to work in the sugarcane plantations established by the British. Indo-Fijians are either Muslim or Hindu while indigenous Fijians follow both Christianity and traditional ways. Meanwhile, in New Guinea many people who once made gardens and kept pigs now earn wages by working for mines and logging companies. In most Pacific states there is a tendency to rely on economic opportunities afforded by resource exploitation. Some leaders resist the multinational companies, railing at their desecration of sacred places and exploitation of native labor. Others urge accommodation and cooperation in order to negotiate deals that are beneficial to both sides. International resource-extracting companies have been concerned primarily with returns to their shareholders and not with benefits to local communities or protection of the environment.

Nuclear testing in Oceania was part and parcel of colonialism, a matter of outsiders using and abusing the region in their Cold War strategies. The sponsors of nuclear testing in the region (Great Britain, the United States, and France) had little regard for the health of indigenous peoples living in remote areas or for the likelihood of environmental damage. The United States exploded bombs over Bikini and Enewek atolls in the Marshall Islands from 1946 to 1958 and over Johnston Atoll and Kirimati (Christmas Island) in 1962. Great Britain carried out testing between 1952 and 1958 at Maralinga and Emu Field in south Australia and in the Monte Bello Islands and Kirimati off the west Australian coast. France, having been forced out of the Sahara by Algeria, carried out testing in French Polynesia from 1966 to 1996. At the beginning of nuclear testing the two major powers in the region, Australia and New Zealand, were allied with Great Britain in the enterprise. But from the 1970s an antinuclear sentiment developed in the Pacific island nations, and in Australia and New Zealand, leading to the signing in 1985 by member states of the South Pacific Forum of the Rarotonga Treaty for a South Pacific Nuclear Free Zone. The treaty bans the use, testing, and possession of nuclear weapons within the zone. It was signed, and subsequently ratified, by Australia, the Cook Islands, Fiji, Kiribati, Nauru, New Zealand, Niue, Papua New Guinea, the Solomon Islands, Tonga, Tuvalu, Vanuatu, and Western Samoa. The Pacific Council of Churches was a strong advocate for the nuclear-free zone. Although nuclear testing in the Pacific ended in 1996 there are still people and places suffering its aftereffects. Nuclear threats, such as shipment of nuclear wastes through the Pacific, proposals to dump nuclear waste on Pacific atolls, and uranium mining in Australia continue. Commenting on the campaigns seeking redress for nuclear testing, the journalist and researcher Nic Maclellan observes that they "have common demands, calling on the nuclear weapons states: to acknowledge their responsibility for the health and environmental impacts of past nuclear tests; to introduce or extend programs for monitoring, cleanup, and rehabilitation of former nuclear test sites; to open up their archives to allow independent researchers access to documentation and studies on the health and environmental impacts of testing; to compensate former test-site workers, and civilian and military personnel at the sites, and neighboring local communities; to continue long-term funding for the necessary programs of monitoring, cleanup, rehabilitation, compensation, and reparations" (Maclellan 2005, 368–369). Opposition to nuclear testing has been an important element in the forging of common identity among the indigenous peoples of Oceania and settler peoples who today call the region home (Mara 1997).

Oceania and the Global Community

Oceania now consists of independent nations as well as of states and territories that are part of external countries such as the United States and France. Within Oceania there is a marked contrast in economic opportunity between those who live in the Pacific islands and those who live in the more prosperous nations of Australia and Aotearoa / New Zealand or in the state of Hawaii. Yet even in those places the indigenous citizens have less opportunity than the settler citizens. The indigenous peoples are caught, as it is often put, "between the local and the global." Both their cultural survival and the survival of their habitats are at stake. Rising sea levels resulting from global warming will almost certainly submerge the low-lying homelands of some island dwellers. In August of 2008, religious leaders from various faith groups within Australia united with their counterparts from the Pacific islands to challenge the Australian government to take immediate action on climate change to assist the Pacific's small island nations. In an open letter to the Australian government they stated that Australia has a moral obligation since it has an historical responsibility for this serious situation.

Like the peoples of Oceania, indigenous people in many parts of the world have seen their resources seized and their ways of life changed by colonial intrusion. The Declaration of the Rights of Indigenous Peoples, adopted by the United Nations in September of 2007, addresses some of the issues that arise from the colonial experience. The declaration sets out the individual and collective rights of indigenous peoples including their rights to culture, identity, language, employment, health, and education. It asserts the right of indigenous peoples to maintain and strengthen their own cultures and religions and prohibits discrimination against them. The declaration is nonbinding but, nevertheless, it represents an important step in the formulation of relationships between indigenous peoples and the global community. Religion, an integral part of traditional culture in the Pacific, and, in the form of Christianity, an integral part of Pacific life today, offers perspective on the local/global relationship. The indigenous ethic of reciprocity and contemporary Christian understandings of social justice and ecojustice provide frames within which to discuss the environmental violations of the mining and logging companies and the matter of biopiracy. It is the hope of many of the religious bodies within Oceania that their cooperation within the region and their engagement with the global community can contribute to sustaining the lands and cultures of the Pacific.

Mary N. MacDONALD
Le Moyne College

FURTHER READING

ABC Radio Australia. (2008, August 18). Faith groups in Pacific climate change appeal. *Pacific Beat.* Retrieved June 5, 2009, from http://www.radioaustralia.net.au/programguide/stories/200808/s2334303.htm

Barker, John. (Ed.). (1990). *Christianity in Oceania: Ethnographic perspectives.* Lanham, MD: University Press of America.

Boutilier, James A.; Hughes, Daniel T.; & Tiffany, Sharon W. (1978). *Mission, church, and sect in Oceania.* ASAO Monograph No. 6. Ann Arbor: University of Michigan Press.

Connell, John, & Waddell, Eric. (Eds.). (2007). *Environment, development and change in rural Asia-Pacific: Between local and global.* London and New York: Routledge.

Codrington, Robert Henry. (1891). *The Melanesians: Studies in their anthropology and folk-lore.* Oxford, U.K.: Oxford University Press.

Durkheim, Émile. (2008 [1912]). *The elementary forms of religious life.* Carol Cosman (Trans.), Mark S. Cladis (Ed.). Oxford, U.K.: Oxford University Press.

Emerson, Nathaniel Bright. (1965). *Unwritten literature of Hawaii: The sacred songs of the hula.* Collected and translated, with notes and an account of the hula (rev. ed.). Rutland, VT: Tuttle.

Feld, Steven. (1990). *Sound and sentiment: Birds, weeping, poetics, and song in Kaluli expression* (2nd ed.). Philadelphia: University of Pennsylvania Press.

Grim, John A. (Ed.). (2001). *Indigenous traditions and ecology: The interbeing of cosmology and community.* The Center for the Study of World Religions' Religions of the World Series. Cambridge, MA: Harvard University Press.

Herda, Phyllis; Reilly, Michael; & Hilliard, David. (Eds.). (2005). *Vision and reality in Pacific religion.* Canberra, Australia: Pandanus Books.

Maclellan, Nic. (2005) The nuclear age in the Pacific Islands. *The Contemporary Pacific, 17*(2), 363–372.

Mageo, Jeannette Marie, & Howard, Alan. (Eds.). (1996). *Spirits in culture, history, and mind.* New York: Routledge.

Mara, Ratu Sir Kamisese. (1997). *The pacific way: A memoir.* Honolulu: University of Hawaii Center for Pacific Islands Studies, East-West Center Pacific Islands Development Program.

Meigs, Anna S. (1984). *Food, sex, and pollution: A New Guinea religion.* New Brunswick, NJ: Rutgers University Press.

Overton, John, & Scheyvens, Regina. (1999). *Strategies for sustainable development: Experiences from the Pacific.* Sydney: University of New South Wales Press.

Rappaport, Roy A. (1984). *Pigs for the ancestors: Ritual in the ecology of a New Guinea people* (2nd ed). New Haven, CT: Yale University Press.

Salmond, Anne. (1989). Tribal words, tribal worlds: The translatability of *tapu* and *mana.* In Mac Marshall & John L. Caughey (Eds.), *Culture, kin, and cognition in Oceania: Essays in honor of Ward H. Goodenough* (pp. 55–78). Washington, DC: American Anthropological Association.

Strathern, Andrew; Stewart, Pamela J.; Carucci, Lawrence M; Poyer, Lin; Feinberg, Richard; & Macpherson, Cluny. (2002). *Oceania: An introduction to the cultures and identities of Pacific Islanders.* Durham, NC: Carolina Academic Press.

Swain, Tony, & Trompf, Garry. (1995). *The religions of Oceania.* London and New York: Routledge.

Young, Michael W. (1983). *Magicians of Manumanua: Living myth in Kalauna.* Berkeley: University of California Press.

Young Leslie, Heather E. (2007). A fishy romance: Chiefly power and the geopolitics of desire. *The Contemporary Pacific, 19*(2), 365–408.

United Nations. (2007). Declaration on the rights of indigenous peoples. Retrieved April 29, 2009, from http://www.un.org/esa/socdev/unpfii/en/drip.html

Indigenous Traditions—
South America

South America is among the richest continents in terms of biodiversity. Its spirit of sustainability lies in the sustainability of spirit generated by indigenous peoples who resisted colonial and neocolonial powers that threatened not only their environment but their cultures. These people, with a worldview based on the cyclical process of cultivation nurtured and encouraged by pachamama *(Mother Earth), have thus become some of the most important actors in promoting sustainability.*

In South America, particularly the Andean region, spirituality and sustainability have been inextricably interwoven within the land-culture of its indigenous peoples. The term *land-culture* refers to the way in which indigenous peoples' histories and lives are tied to specific landscapes. Because indigenous peoples have defined themselves as descendants of those who inhabited the land before colonial societies conquered and appropriated it, the destruction of their landscapes, or their resettlement on reservations away from their native landscape, is to them quite literally an obliteration of their culture. Thus for many indigenous peoples of South America, environmental preservation is considered cultural preservation.

The Andean region as discussed here is not the one mapped by the north-south longitudes of the Western-colonial intellectual tradition. The Andean region from a precolonial view and practice is transregional, comprising western coastal lowlands, the highlands, and the eastern tropical lowlands of the Amazon—regions whose ecological niches interact within the cyclical process of *pachamama* (Mother Earth). The spirituality and sustainability expressed in this region are intrinsic to a particular way of knowing, being, and being related to the world that has existed for the last 10,000 years. This indigenous worldview embodies the system of cultivation that the

peoples' land-cultures have sustained spiritually for millennia; it is fundamentally different from the dominant Euro-American worldview.

Land-Culture versus Colonization

South America's indigenous population, whose lands (and thus land-cultures) have been appropriated and exploited, view the past and current Euro-American world as a mechanistic, positivistic, homogenizing, unsustainable way of knowing and being. That the concept of sustainability has been foreign to such a dominant, colonial worldview for the last five hundred years suggests why we are facing a global environmental, ecological, spiritual, moral, and ethical crisis for the first time in human history. For South America the spirit of sustainability and the sustainability of the spirit are deeply rooted in the perdurability of indigenous peoples, their worldview, and their land-cultures. The sustainability blueprint for today's Latin America is present, alive, and regenerating within the various strongholds of these land-cultures, languages, and *cosmovisions* (worldviews), a situation that may not be visible to the world's population at large.

The past and current colonization process has had a significant negative impact upon the lives, cultures, lands, territories, and natural resources of Latin America, whose total population of around 580 million individuals live mostly in urban areas, detached from nature, land-culture, and a holistic sense of place. According to conservative estimates, 40 million people (or less than 10 percent of the total population) are indigenous. The total surface area controlled by indigenous peoples throughout the Americas has shrunk significantly due to nation-state building. Indigenous peoples were removed from their lands in order to make room for the emerging national citizens and their descendants, who inherited the colonial mentality reflected at the hemispheric level. We thus must attend to the outgrowth of a space-based (as opposed to place-based) mentality, which creates monocultures of the mind-spirit-land. This spatial, detached view of land and nature challenges the spirit of sustainability and the sustainability of the spirit of indigenous peoples rooted in specific places. In contrast to space-based, nonsustainable monocultures, indigenous regions in South America continue to nurture cultural places through the spiritual values of the *ayllu*, a word of the Quechua and Aymara (the two most populous indigenous peoples of the Andean region), which literally means "extended family / community," but embodies the meaning that all living beings take shelter in, and value, their communal place. Here, at the core of Andean collective life, all visible and nonvisible living beings—such as plants, animals, deities, rocks, mountains, rivers, and humans—are nurtured and sustained by *pachamama*.

Cultural Diversity / Biodiversity

South America is among the richest continents in terms of biodiversity. Its spirit of sustainability lies in the sustainability of spirit generated by indigenous peoples who resisted colonial and neocolonial powers. The indigenous people of South America have thus become some of the most important actors in promoting sustainability.

For South America, and particularly for the Andean-Amazonian region, indigenous places are the crux of biological and cultural diversity. This region is populated by more than four hundred ethic groups of indigenous peoples, each with its own distinct language, social organization, and *cosmovision*. For these peoples, who live in 80 percent of the ecologically protected areas in Latin America, cultural diversity is highly correlated with both biological and agricultural diversity. From a Westernized perspective, most of these Latin American groups are considered "peasants" or subsistence farmers, a Western term suppressing the fact that such "peasants," the ones who foster the region's biological and agricultural diversity, are the sources of information the agriculture industry relies on for monetary profit. For hundreds of years, Western economies have expropriated and exploited the food security generated by the indigenous peoples, a process known as "biopiracy."

Preserving the Spirit of Sustainability

Indigenous movements of political autonomy and cultural affirmation are part of the political and intellectual labor necessary for protecting this spirit of sustainability. Movements and organizations aligned with the interests of indigenous communities in a process of *acompañamiento* (simplistically and roughly translated, a method of apprenticeship), such as the Andean Project of Peasant

Technologies (PRATEC), walk side by side with and facilitate the collection and systematization of indigenous knowledge grounded on an understanding of sustaining the resources of *pacha* (the Earth). PRATEC, a nongovernmental organization established in 1987, supports the resurgence of indigenous Andean "ritual agriculture" practices that have been challenged by anthropocentric-based methods of Western industrialism, and thus helps preserve this spirit, which is itself sustained by *pachamama*.

While Western epistemologies consider economy, society, and politics to be discrete concepts, the traditional forms of communal and collective existence that persist today for indigenous peoples, such as the *ayllu*, integrate these concepts into what could aptly be called *the sustainability of spirit* or *the spirit of sustainability*. For the vast majority of indigenous peoples this integrative worldview emerges from a ritual cycle of cultivating the land. It has now been extended into urban sectors through an indigenous ethnic diaspora. The designation *campesino* (or "peasant" farmers) has for several decades been used to characterize these displaced indigenous peoples as powerless. More problematically, the term "peasant" has further limited and confined the Andean cultivator of Andean land to a paradigm of feudal organization that is European and colonial, and which denigrates the activity of the human person who cultivates (*runa*) by reducing it to techno-bureaucratic, class-based, political analyses. The Andean *runa* lives in equity with all other living members (and persons) of the other collectivities, procuring harmony with them through continual, daily, and sometimes ritualized conversation. But indigenous peoples have been active participants in their own history (outside of the Western class and gender structures imposed on them), and there is no evidence that a derogatory or demeaning characterization will damper their spirits as they engage in the active process of recovery and affirmation. All Andean indigenous life centers on the regeneration of life as a whole; in Andean cultures nature is very distinctly lived rather than analyzed.

Quechua Natural Order

The Andean/Amazonian region's *ayllu*-cultural practices could be said to center on a Quechua "natural order" from which the Quechua people gather their language, traditional knowledge, or spiritual practices within specific landscapes. This Quechua Andean/Amazonian natural order, still accessible today, is shared with Aymara and many other native peoples. Its path—its life-way—traverses the coastal region, the Andean highland region, and the Amazonian region. Those who cultivate the land in these places are not "farmers" according to the contemporary definition, practice, and understanding of the way in which Western farmers often farm: Quechua and other indigenous peoples do not lease or own land or property and therefore do not remain tethered to the same plot of land or the same crop. The Quechua/Aymara cultivators conceive of their labor as cyclical and in a state of permanent motion—as transterritorial and transregional. The Quechua and Aymara person (*runa* and *haqi*, respectively) walks with *kawsay mama*—the living mother, the living seed—in its multiple paths, through which diversity as a spiritual practice of sustainability is cultivated.

The paradigm for this world order is a cycle of conviviality—of all beings sustained by spirit in an elliptical transverse motion, tilted in accord to the movements of all living beings (on *pacha* and in place and time) dwelling with and protected and harbored by *pachamama*, or the spirit of sustainability. This natural order renders the world both in whole and in distinction, in unity and diversity. It does not do this by dividing beings from Being (or Essence), as in many Western understandings of unity and diversity, but rather as an integrated whole whose plenitude is manifest as the conviviality of all beings, at the same time both distinct and in communion. Nor is the Essence or Being of any being considered dualistically. In terms of the division of the animate in contrast to the inanimate, for instance, all beings are animate and within spirit—*ayllu, kawsay mama, pachamama,* and *pacha.*

The Spanish word *mestizo* comes from a Latin root word (*miscere*) meaning *mixed*. Its common usage refers to a person as being of mixed, or "part" Spanish and "part" indigenous, descent and implies a sense of dismembering that does not reflect the essence of identity in the Quechua natural world order. For the Quechua/Aymara, identity involves the "re-membering" that takes place in a cycle of movement sustained by and in spirit. The identity of all beings in spirit is determined rather by the confluence of distinct beings of undifferentiated value, in equity, in a sustainable movement of harmony and balance. *Allin kawsay,* well-being, is the way that the *ayllu* welfare of all beings may be practiced through cultivation and nurturance, in an endless cycle meant to achieve balance. This integrative spirit can be seen as far back as the Inca, whose personage is the cultivator, as is any person (*runa/haqi*), in place and time on *pacha.* Neither the republican *criollo,* as a liberated colonial subject, nor the *mestizo,* as a split identity, are at play in the Andean world; Andean languages respond to the need to regenerate the whole. The *mallku* (an Andean human of authority charged with overseeing the *ayllu*) *is* the *ayllu* in the sense that he protects the *ayllu* and the *ayllu* protects *him*; the *mallku* performs *mullu,* the act of walking from household to household in the *ayllu* to converse with mothers and fathers and children about their welfare—and is said to be following the path of the seed, which is also called *mullu*—in order to achieve *ayllu* welfare, *allin kawsay.* The *mallku* follows the path of *kawsay mama* (living mother, living seed). This Quechu/Aymara way is the spirit of sustainability of *pachamama* as much as it is the sustainability of spirit of *kawsay mama.*

Tirso GONZALES
University of British Columbia Okanagan

Maria E. GONZALEZ
University of Michigan

FURTHER READING

Andean Project of Peasant Technologies (PRATEC). (2001). *Comunidad y biodiversidad. El ayllu y su organicidad en la crianza de la diversidad en la chacra.* Lima, Peru: PRATEC.

Choque, M. E., & Mamani, C. (2001). Reconstitucion del Ayllu y derechos de los pueblos indigenas: El movimiento indio en los andes de Bolivia. *Journal of Latin American Anthropology, 6*(1), 202–224.

Deruyttere, Anne. (1997, October). *Indigenous Peoples and sustainable development: The role of the Inter-American Development Bank* (No. IND97-101). Washington, DC: Inter-American Development Bank.

Escobar, Arturo. (1995). *Encountering development: The making and unmaking of the third world.* Princeton, NJ: Princeton University Press.

Escobar, Arturo. (2001). Culture sits in places: Reflections on globalism and subaltern strategies of localization. *Political Geography, 20*(2), 139–174.

Gonzales, Tirso A. (1999). The cultures of the seed in the Peruvian Andes. In S. B. Brush (Ed.), *Genes in the field: On-farm conservation of crop diversity* (pp. 193–216). International Plant Genetic Resources Institute. International Development Research Centre, Ottawa, Canada: Lewis Publishers. (Also retrieved May 26, 2009, from http://www.idrc.ca/en/ev-98735-201-1-DO_TOPIC.html)

Gonzales, Tirso A. (2008). Renativization in North and South America. In Melissa Nelson (Ed.), *Original instructions:Indigenous teachings for a sustainable future* (pp. 298–303). Rochester, VT: Bear & Company.

Grillo, Eduardo. (1998). Cultural Affirmation: Digestion of imperialism in the Andes. In Frédérique Apffel-Marglin with PRATEC (Eds.), *The spirit of regeneration: Andean culture confronting western notions of development.* London: Zed Books.

Grim, John A. (Ed.). (2000). *Indigenous traditions and ecology: The interbeing of cosmology and community.* Cambridge, MA: Harvard University Press.

Gutiérrez Leguía, Benjamín. (2007). La formalización de la propiedad rural en el Perú. Período 1996–2006, lecciones aprendidas. Retrieved June 20, 2008, from http://www.catastro.meh.es/esp/publicaciones/ct/ct60/60_5.pdf

IAASTD LAC Sub-global SDM. (2008). Retrieved May 26, 2009, from http://www.agassessment.org/

Ishizawa, Jorge and Grillo Fernández, Eduardo. (2002). Loving the world as it is: Western abstraction and Andean nurturance. *Revision, 24*(4), 21–26. Washington, DC: Heldref Publications.

IUCN. (1997). Chapter 2: What is Sustainability? In *Inter-Commission Task Force on Indigenous Peoples. Indigenous peoples and sustainability: Cases and actions.* Indigenous Peoples and Conservation Initiative. Utrecht, The Netherlands: International Books.

Kloppenburg, Jack Ralph. (1988). *First the seed: The political economy of plant biotechnology, 1492–2000.* New York: Cambridge University Press.

Lizarralde, M. (2001). Biodiversity and loss of indigenous languages and knowledge in South America. In Luisa Maffi (Ed.), *On biocultural diversity: Linking language, knowledge, and the environment.* Washington, DC: Smithsonian Institution Press.

MacCormack, Sabine. (1991). *Religion in the Andes.* Princeton, NJ: Princeton University Press.

Valladolid, J. (2001). Andean cosmovision and the nurturing of biodiversity in the peasant chacra. In John A. Grim (Ed.), *Indigenous traditions and ecology. The interbeing of cosmology and community.* Cambridge, MA: Harvard University Press.

Individualism

Individualism appears in different forms, but all variations focus on the value of the individual and the importance of individual autonomy. Individualism's emphasis on private ownership and free-market capitalism may benefit sustainability because individuals have a stake in resources. This same emphasis may also result in the exploitation of natural resources and ecosystems for individual interests.

Individualism refers to various theories and practices that affirm the value of individuals and avoid reducing individuals to a larger whole or collective, as in forms of holism, collectivism, communism, socialism, and fascism. Individualism appears in many forms, including ethical, political, ontological, and methodological variations. In its ethico-political variations, individualism can appear as an egoism (as opposed to altruism) that centers value on the individual self; a libertarianism or anarchism that limits or rejects government regulation; a social contract theory that views society as the product of decisions made by autonomous individuals; or a path of self-reliance that does not conform to conventional standards. In its ontological variations, individualism asserts the irreducible reality of the individual, which is sometimes defined according to the autonomous rationality, free will, or existential situation of humans. Ethico-political and ontological variations of individualism can be seen in religious worldviews that put more emphasis on exemplary individuals (e.g., the Buddha, Confucius, Laozi, Jesus, and Muhammad) than on ethnic identity or social class. Methodological variations of individualism appear in social science discourses that attend to individual attitudes and actions instead of explaining social phenomena in terms of overarching schemas (e.g., statistical analysis, macroeconomics, and cultural evolution). The various forms of individualism often overlap and combine ethico-political, ontological, and methodological positions.

Individualism harbors promises and problems for sustainability. Individualism can promote private property and free-market capitalism as ways to avoid what the ecologist Garrett Hardin calls the "commons effect," wherein common or collectively owned resources are overused and exploited because people lack individual stakes in them. However, privatization and deregulated markets threaten to distribute vital resources to the wealthy and exploit ecosystems for private economic interests. Also, individualism guards against patterns of "environmental fascism" or "ecofascism" implicit in holistic environmental ethics. But individualism can foster neglect for the ethical value of whole ecosystems, whether by centering value exclusively on humans, as in anthropocentrism, or on individual living beings, as in the biocentrism of the environmental philosopher Paul Taylor. Although individualism can be criticized by holistic or collectivist perspectives for reducing wholes to their constituent parts, it can also promote self-reliance and respect for individual organisms, thus balancing the tendency of holistic and collectivist orientations to ignore or exploit individuals.

Sam MICKEY
California Institute of Integral Studies

FURTHER READING

Callicott, J. B. (1999). *Beyond the land ethic: More essays in environmental philosophy.* Albany: State University of New York Press.

Daly, H. E., & Townsend, K. N. (Eds.). (1993). *Valuing the Earth: Economics, ecology, ethics.* Cambridge: Massachusetts Institute of Technology Press.

Dawkins, R. (2006). *The selfish gene.* 30th anniversary edition. New York and London: Oxford University Press.

Hardin, Garrett. (1968). The tragedy of the commons. *Science,* 162, 1243–1248.

Heller, Thomas C.; Sosna, Morton; Brooke-Rose, Christine; & Wellbery, David E. (Eds.). (1986). *Reconstructing individualism: Autonomy, individuality, and the self in Western thought.* Stanford, CA: Stanford University Press.

Taylor, Paul. (1986). *Respect for nature.* Princeton, NJ: Princeton University Press.

THE TRAGEDY OF THE COMMONS

The idea of individualism and its relation to sustainability is a complex one that has its detractors and its proponents. The ecologist Garrett Hardin wrote in his famous 1968 article "The Tragedy of the Commons" in the journal Science: *"We want the maximum good per person; but what is good? To one person it is wilderness, to another it is ski lodges for thousands." Hardin, whose primary concern was human population growth and its consequences, explains the issues of what he considered a problem without a "technical" solution.*

The tragedy of the commons develops in this way. Picture a pasture open to all. It is to be expected that each herdsman will try to keep as many cattle as possible on the commons. Such an arrangement may work reasonably satisfactorily for centuries because tribal wars, poaching, and disease keep the numbers of both man and beast well below the carrying capacity of the land. Finally, however, comes the day of reckoning, that is, the day when the long-desired goal of social stability becomes a reality. At this point, the inherent logic of the commons remorselessly generates tragedy.

As a rational being, each herdsman seeks to maximize his gain. Explicitly or implicitly, more or less consciously, he asks, "What is the utility to me of adding one more animal to my herd?" This utility has one negative and one positive component.

1) The positive component is a function of the increment of one animal. Since the herdsman receives all the proceeds from the sale of the additional animal, the positive utility is nearly +1.

2) The negative component is a function of the additional overgrazing created by one more animal. Since, however, the effects of overgrazing are shared by all the herdsmen, the negative utility for any particular decision-making herdsman is only a fraction of 1.

Adding together the component partial utilities, the rational herdsman concludes that the only sensible course for him to pursue is to add another animal to his herd. And another; and another. . . . But this is the conclusion reached by each and every rational herdsman sharing a commons. Therein is the tragedy. Each man is locked into a system that compels him to increase his herd without limit—in a world that is limited. Ruin is the destination toward which all men rush, each pursuing his own best interest in a society that believes in the freedom of the commons. Freedom in a commons brings ruin to all.

Source: Garrett Hardin. (1968). The Tragedy of the Commons. *Science,* 162, 1243 and 1244.

International Commissions and Summits

Since the 1960s, various types of international commissions and summits have met throughout the world to address sustainability. Although initially based in the global North (the socioeconomic and political division of wealthier developed nations) and facilitated by their politicians, attention increasingly shifted with the influence of religious groups to the less-developed global South and the indigenous peoples affected by the environmental crisis.

International commissions and summits have been central in articulating the standards of sustainability. The contested terrain of sustainability has been debated perhaps most heatedly in these international venues where nation-states, international political bodies, nongovernmental organizations, multilateral development organizations, and grassroots social and ecological activists meet. For many in the global North (a term used to designate wealthier developed nations, most of which are located in the Northern Hemisphere) and the industrial sector, these events have resulted in important steps toward a global ethic of sustainability. According to many marginalized peoples in the developing world, however, these meetings have provided a cover for the continued legitimization of existing power inequalities. In both cases, religious groups and representatives have played influential roles at and around important international commissions and summits.

Early Articulations of Sustainability

In 1966 the World Council of Churches (WCC) launched a five-year program devoted to studying the impacts of technology, including its environmental effects, on society. The report resulting from that study was accepted by the WCC in Bucharest in 1974, and "accepted the thesis

of nature's limits and called for a society that is both just and sustainable" (Chapman 2000, 12). In 1967 Pope Paul VI voiced support for equitable development, stating that "the new name for peace [is] development" (quoted in Therien 2005, 29).

As the 1960s drew to a close—the then-U.S. president John F. Kennedy proclaimed them as the "decade of development"—environmental concerns arose first in the cities of the industrialized world. Scientists began to better understand the impacts of large-scale agriculture and fishing, the disappearance of flora and fauna, and the limits of industrial exploitation of nonrenewable fuels. The United Nations for the first time addressed environmental issues directly in a 1969 publication entitled *Problems of the Human Environment*, which noted a "crisis of world-wide proportions . . . the crisis of the human environment" (Jolly et al. 2004, 125).

Stockholm: Growth as the Solution

This tone of crisis set the stage for the 1972 United Nations Conference on the Human Environment in Stockholm, which for the first time brought the idea of an environmental crisis to the global community by suggesting that it was correlated directly with poverty in the developing world. The conclusion drawn by the small number of political representatives and scientists was that development through economic growth was the only salve for the poverty that both made humans vulnerable to environmental fluctuations and encouraged over-exploitation of the local resource base. The most important outcome of this meeting was the birth of the United Nations Environment Programme (UNEP), headed by its conference chairman Maurice Strong and based in Nairobi, Kenya.

Barbados Declarations and the NIEO

Particularly in the poorer global South, a growing emphasis was placed on the social aspects of development. While the Stockholm gathering highlighted poverty as the primary cause of conflict and inequity, it also prescribed a somewhat invasive idea of growth, facilitated by external development bodies and governments, as its cure. In 1971, just prior to Stockholm, the WCC convened a long-term Program to Combat Racism in Barbados. The group of several social scientists took it as their task to criticize three of the primary focal points of social science:

> 1) *Scientism* "which negates any relationship between academic research and the future of these people who form the object of such investigation, thus eschewing political responsibility which the relation contains and implies; 2) an *Hypocrisy* manifest in rhetorical protests based on first principles which skillfully avoids any commitment in a concrete situation; and 3) an *Opportunism* that, although it may recognize the present painful situation of the Indians, at the same time it rejects any possibility of transforming action by proposing the need 'to do something' within the established order." (Wright 1988, 373)

These social scientists were calling attention to the "Fourth World" peoples in already so-called underdeveloped nations who were disenfranchised not only by the prevailing international economic and political powers, but also by the governments of their own nations.

In the early 1970s, several nations in the developing world proposed a Declaration on the Establishment of the New International Economic Order (NIEO). According to members of a team of U.N. analysts, "the historic importance of this proposal derives from the fact that it was an authentic third world initiative, launched at a time of probably the peak bargaining power of the poor countries in the entire postwar period" (Jolly et al. 2004, 121). However, "on the most important proposals made by the developing countries, almost nothing was done" (Jolly et al. 2004, 23).

A second Barbados conference was held in 1977, its goal to combine the concerns of the first Barbados conference, or Barbados I, with the increasing advocacy around indigenous causes. While the participants in Barbados I were mostly social scientists, many of the participants in this second conference were indigenous activists, marking the extension of their influence into international policy regimes. Like Barbados I, however, little or no action was taken on the declarations that derived from this conference. The Barbados declarations were ultimately disappointing for both indigenous peoples and the social scientists that supported their cause.

The Brandt Commission

Concern about the relationships between the developed and developing world also came from the global North. In 1977, Robert McNamara, chair of the World Bank, asked the former chancellor of the Federal Republic of Germany, Willy Brandt, to head a commission to systematically analyze the main obstacles to development, aware that the increasing dialog between the global North and South had failed to generate concrete outcomes. According to U.N. collaborators, the Brandt Commission's recommendations, presented under the title *North-South: A Program for Survival*, were "ultimately anchored in 'the great moral imperatives that . . . are as valid internationally as they were and are nationally,'" and appealed "to values more than to rational calculations" (Therien 2005, 33). The commission proposed a four-pronged solution to development problems that included: (1) the transfer of resources from North to South, (2) a global energy policy, (3) international food initiative, and (4) reform of international institutions.

While the ideas may have been somewhat innovative, the payoff was less than hoped for, as the Commission's findings were released into a Cold War world ripe with political strife. Third and Fourth World activists and the Brandt Commission repeatedly made the case that the prevailing brand of development was not environmentally and socially sustainable in most cases. But these concerns were transposed into the language of increasing economic globalization and integration into global markets.

Security and Sustainability

In 1982, former Swedish prime minister Olof Palme, chair of the Independent Commission on Disarmament and Security Issues, formed a commission modeled after the Brandt Commission, which focused on charting a long-term course toward nuclear disarmament, focusing attention on short-term arms control and stimulating public debate over security issues.

Palme and his fellow commission members suggested that the buildup of long-range Soviet missiles in Eastern Europe, far from ensuring security, was compromising not only the security of the Cold War states but of the global community. They challenged the long-revered language of nuclear deterrence with a doctrine of common security, which avoided all such competitive representations of nuclear conflict (Wiseman 2005, 46). Although largely overlooked by top leaders from the two primary Cold War nations, it was adopted and adapted undercover by various high-ranking officials, making its way across the Atlantic to the United States and through the Iron Curtain, by the end of the 1980s. In retrospect, the recommendations of the Palme Commission were adopted—at least in piecemeal form—by both sides of the Cold War, but the credit for the recognition of common security concerns fell to the nation-states and their midlevel leaders, not to the foresight of the commission or its advocates.

The Palme Commission is particularly important to sustainability for three reasons. First, security and peace are often touted as prerequisites for achieving sustainability. Wars and other armed conflicts, it should be remembered, are some of the most ecologically devastating activities in which humans engage. Second, the Commission framed such common security as pivotal for the global community, noting our interdependence, particularly in matters of nuclear warfare. Third, it demonstrated the potentially widespread political impacts of such commissions.

WCED and the Road to Rio

In the midst of these global concerns about thermonuclear warfare and unpleasant encounters with Earth's limits, the World Commission on Environment and Development (WCED) was convened in 1983 by the U.N. secretary-general. Chairperson Gro Brundtland, former prime minister of Norway, stated in the foreword of *Our Common Future* (1987), the publication of the Commission's recommendations (also known as the Brundtland Report), that the WCED was to be a "third and compelling call for political action: After Brandt's *Programme for Survival* and *Common Crisis*, and after Palme's *Common Security*, would come *Our Common Future*" (quoted in Smith 2005, 85). The Brundtland Commission's report preserved the idea put forth in Stockholm fifteen years earlier that raising standards of living in the developing world could only be achieved through economic growth facilitated by expanding technology to stretch carrying capacity (the maximum number of a particular organism that can survive indefinitely within a given resource base). The central feature of this "compelling call for political action" was the phrase *sustainable development*, broadly defined in *Our Common Future* as "the ability to meet the needs of the present without compromising the ability of future generations to meet their own needs" (WCED 1987, 8). The Commission explicitly connected this mandate to the spiritual dimension of sustainability: "We have the power to reconcile human affairs with natural laws and to thrive in the process. In this our cultural and spiritual heritages can reinforce our economic interests and survival imperatives" (WCED 1987, 1).

In 1986, the same year that the Brundtland Commission completed *Our Common Future*, His Royal Highness Prince Philip and the World Wildlife Fund (WWF) invited six of the world's religious leaders to Assisi, Italy, to discuss several points:

- how the environmental crisis is a mental and ethical crisis due . . . in part . . . to Western and Christian worldviews that encourage materialistic, dualistic, anthropocentric, and utilitarian concepts of nature
- that environmental organizations and politicians are victims of the same economic and technological thinking that provoked the crisis
- that alternative worldviews and ethics must be respected to counter current dominant thinking
- that the world's religions constitute enormous human and spiritual potentials. (Golliher 1999, 494)

This early meeting of environmental and religious minds had two important offspring. First, according to the cultural anthropologist Jeff Golliher (1999, 446), it inspired the 1993 Parliament of Religions, under the leadership of the Swiss theologian Hans Kung, to propose the Declaration Toward a Global Ethic. Second, in 1995 (nine years following the first meeting) HRH Prince Philip, the WWF, and a larger number of religious leaders (representing nine world faiths this time) met in the United Kingdom to revisit their commitments. At that meeting, the Alliance of Religions and Conservation (ARC) was formed under the leadership of the scholar Martin Palmer (Golliher 1999, 494). The ARC has maintained important working relationships with the WWF, the World Bank, and the United Nations, all of which have their own working definitions of sustainability.

The importance of global interconnectedness and moral values to the sustainability ferment was important in these northern, institutionalized venues (that is, within the established world religions, international conservation groups, and development organizations). Such optimistic assessments about the global future helped to support and preserve the idea of sustainable development.

The Rio and Johannesburg Earth Summits

The Brundlandt Report concluded by suggesting that the United Nations sponsor "an international Conference . . . to review progress and promote follow-up arrangements that will be needed . . . to set benchmarks and to maintain human progress" (WCED 1987, 343). The 1992 United Nations Conference on Environment and Development in Rio de Janeiro, which drew together over one hundred heads of state and thousands of other delegates from all over the world (Rist 1997, 188), was the largest such gathering of heads of state and government to that time (Baker 2006, 55).

In preparation for the upcoming United Nations–sponsored conference, a World Conference of Indigenous Peoples on Territory, Environment, and Development was held the week prior at Kari Oca, a site on the outskirts of Rio (perhaps symbolically highlighting the marginalization of indigenous voices in the development dialog). Invoking the metaphor of "Mother Earth" or *pachamama*, many indigenous leaders claimed that they were "knowers of nature" and that their "resistance, [their] strength comes from a spiritual relationship with nature" (Hart 2005a, 1764). One indigenous activist from Ecuador named Valerio Grefa noted that they had "come to share with the world and the United Nations our way of thinking, our visions, our way of life, an alternative. We do not speak of the 'environment'; we speak of the spiritual and physical world in which we live" (quoted in Hart 2005b, 1763). As Onondaga (of the Six Nations of the Northeastern United States) faithkeeper Oren Lyons reminded the gathered peoples, 'Life is community'" (quoted in Hart 2005b, 1763). This alternative summit drew some 20,000 additional people to Rio. This group, philosophically, politically, and geographically separated from the U.N.-sponsored Earth Summit, highlighted a different set of issues, including food production and alternative economic and environmental positions (Rist 1997, 188, 191). Thus, the idea of sustainability, and its major benchmarks, have been attended to and promoted by both institutional and elite sectors of society as well as subcultures of resistance. The values and practices that these constituencies imagine as central to achieving sustainability, however, differ greatly.

Though its overall contribution to the quest for sustainability is still contested, the Rio Summit did have five important outcomes:

1. the approval of the Rio Declaration, which included twenty-seven principles of sustainable development;
2. the approval of Agenda 21, a document of over 800 pages, that provided sets of guidelines for implementing sustainable development;
3. the formation of the United Nations Framework Convention on Climate Change (UNFCCC);
4. the approval of the Convention on Biodiversity (CBD), which endorsed the value of indigenous ecological knowledge and stated that sovereign nations should have rights to the biological resources of their territory (not approved by the United States);
5. a Declaration on Forest Principles, which created broad frameworks and recommendations for sustainable use of forest resources.

The eventual outcomes, in most cases, were more modest than hoped for by many participants. One of the reasons is that the above resolutions are nonbinding, so countries that sign on cannot be held legally responsible for noncompliance. Moreover, negotiations at the international level have typically honored the principle of subsidiarity, where decision making and binding laws are, to the extent possible, left to the smallest (most local) legislative bodies.

Although the outcomes of the Summit have been criticized, since then sustainability has been taken for granted

as a part of global governance, and an environmentally grounded spirituality is an increasingly frequent complement to the evocation of the need for sustainable development. For example, the 2002 Earth Summit in Johannesburg, South Africa (sometimes called Rio +10) saw the emergence of what environment and religion scholar Bron Taylor has called a global civic earth religion. During the opening ceremony, participants were treated to a performance that depicted the common emergence of humanity in Africa and suggested that humanity's past, and also its future, must be bounded by the limits of a finite world (Taylor 2004, 1003). As Taylor argues: "It may be that such a religion, in which the evolutionary story, embedded in the broader Universe Story, fosters a reverence for life and diverse practices to protect and restore its diverse forms, will play a major role in the religious future of humanity" (2004, 1004). In the end, however, the Johannesburg Summit is described as making "at best modest" contributions to making sustainability a cultural reality (Kates and Parris 2003, 8066).

Implications and Future Research

When participants in the sustainability movement express their goals as alternatives to the prevailing political and economic powers or invoke the outlines of a global ethic based on human worth and dignity, they often tap into religious and spiritual narratives, metaphors, and language. The emotional power of such rhetorical devices helps to reveal the values implicated in the reports from these international commissions and summits and provides the substance of various emerging sustainability ethics. While the effectiveness of these commissions and summits has been questioned, what is clear is that, since sustainability has grown into an international concern, religious institutions and groups have played an important role in generating affective and values-based narratives to promote the sustainability transition. In many cases, the most effective sustainable development programs have succeeded in large part because they were able to motivate local religious authorities to connect the goals of sustainability to local religious narratives. Moreover, when sustainability is discussed in a variety of venues, from subcultural gatherings to international political arenas, it is frequently couched in language that is explicitly religious or that promotes a naturalistic reverence for the nonhuman world, or even the entire cosmos. In such cases, normative sustainability narratives do religious work (drawing on the definition of religious work offered by Chidester 2005) by fostering community, focusing desire, and facilitating exchange. These trends deserve more focused research in coming decades.

Lucas F. JOHNSTON
Wake Forest University

FURTHER READING

Baker, Susan. (2006). *Sustainable development*. London: Routledge.

Berkes, Fikret; Folke, Carl; & Colding, Johan. (Eds). (1998). *Linking social and ecological systems: Management practices and social mechanisms for building resilience*. Cambridge, U.K.: Cambridge University Press.

Brandt, Willy. (1980). *North–South: A program for survival*. Cambridge, MA: The MIT Press.

Chapman, Audrey; Peterson, Rodney L.; & Smith-Moran, Barbara (Eds.). (2000). *Consumption, population, and sustainability: Perspectives from science and religion*. Washington, DC: Island Press.

Chidester, David. (2005). *Authentic fakes: Religion and American popular culture*. Berkeley: University of California Press.

Davison, Aidan. (2000). *Technology and the contested meanings of sustainability*. Albany: State University of New York Press.

Edwards, Anders. (2005). *The sustainability revolution: Portrait of a paradigm shift*. Gabriola Island, Canada: New Society Publishers.

Gardner, Gary. (2002, December). Invoking the spirit: Religion and spirituality in the quest for a sustainable world (Worldwatch Paper #164). Washington, DC: Worldwatch Institute.

Ghai, Dharam, & Vivian, Jessica M. (Eds.). (1992). *Grassroots environmental action: People's participation in sustainable development*. London: Routledge.

Golliher, Jeff. (1999). Ethical, Moral, and Religious Concerns. In Darrell Posey (Ed.), *Cultural and spiritual values of biodiversity* (pp. 492–495). London/Nairobi, Kenya: Intermediate Technology Publications/United Nations Environment Programme.

Gottlieb, Roger S. (2006). *A greener faith: Religious environmentalism and our planet's future*. Oxford, U.K.: Oxford University Press.

Hart, John. (2005a). World conference on indigenous people. In Bron Taylor (Ed.), *Encyclopedia of religion and nature* (pp. 1763–1765). London: Continuum.

Hart, John. (2005b). Indigenous voices from Kari Oca. In Bron Taylor (Ed.), *Encyclopedia of religion and nature* (p. 1763). London: Continuum.

International Union for the Conservation of Nature, United Nations Environment Programme, & World Wide Fund for Nature. (1991). *Caring for the Earth: A strategy for sustainable living*. Gland, Switzerland: International Union for the Conservation of Nature.

Jolly, Richard; Emmerij, Louis; Ghai, Dharam; & Lapeyre, Frédéric. (Eds.). (2004). *UN contributions to development thinking and practice* (United Nations Intellectual History Project). Bloomington: Indiana University Press.

Kates, Robert W., & Parris, Thomas M. (2003). Long-term trends and a sustainability transition. *Proceedings of the National Academy of Sciences of the United States of America, 100*(14), 8062–8067.

Meadows, Donella. (1972). *Limits to growth*. Seattle: Signet Press.

Norton, Bryan G. (2003*). Searching for sustainability: Interdisciplinary essays in the philosophy of conservation biology*. Cambridge, U.K.: Cambridge University Press.

Norton, Bryan G. (2005). *Sustainability: A philosophy of adaptive ecosystem management*. Chicago: University of Chicago Press.

Peterson, Tarla Rai. (1997). *Sharing the Earth: The rhetoric of sustainable development*. Columbia: University of South Carolina Press.

Posey, Darrell (Ed.). (1999). *Cultural and spiritual values of biodiversity*. London/Nairobi, Kenya: Intermediate Technology Publications/United Nations Environment Programme.

Prugh, Thomas; Costanza, Robert; & Daly, Herman E. (Eds.). (2000). *The local politics of global sustainability* . Washington, DC: Island Press.

Rist, Gilbert. (1997). *The history of development: From Western origins to global faith*. London: Zed Books.

Sumner, Jennifer. (2005). *Sustainability and the civil commons: Rural communities in the age of globalization*. Toronto: University of Toronto Press.

Taylor, Bron R. (2004). A green future for religion? *Futures, 36*, 991–1008.

Thakur, Ramesh; Cooper, Andrew; & English, John. (Eds.). (2005). *International commissions and the power of ideas*. New York: United Nations University Press.

World Bank. (2001). *Making sustainable commitments: An environment strategy for the World Bank*. Washington, DC: Author.

World Commission on Environment and Development (WCED). (1987). *Our Common Future*. Oxford, U.K.: Oxford University Press.

Wright, Robin. (1988). Anthropological presuppositions of indigenous advocacy. *Annual Review of Anthropology, 17*, 365–390.

Islam

The Quran teaches that humankind's stewardship of Earth is a privilege requiring profound responsibility, thus there is much in Islamic tradition to uphold an authentic environmental ethic that protects all of God's creation. Since the founding of Islam in the arid Arabian Peninsula in the seventh century CE, the Muslim world has paid close attention to water management from legal, economic, and ethical perspectives.

The Quran, Islam's primary authority in all matters of individual and communal life, as well as theology and worship, tells of an offer of global trusteeship that was presented by God to the Heavens, the Earth, and the Mountains (Sura 33:72), but they refused to shoulder the responsibility out of fear. Humankind seized the opportunity and bore the "trust" (*amāna*), but they were "unjust and very ignorant." Even so, God through mercy has guided and enabled humankind in bearing the responsibility of the *amāna*, although they have in the process also been subjected to punishment for their hypocrisy and unbelief. The Quran, however, is clear that God is the ultimate holder of dominion over the creation (e.g., Sura 2:107, 5:120), and that all things return to Him (Sura 24:42) and are thus accountable each in their own ways. In the Quran—and in the teachings and example of the Prophet Muhammad (570–632 CE), preserved in a literary form known as hadith—there is much with which to construct an authentic Islamic environmental ethic that both sustains what Muslims have achieved traditionally in this direction and leaves open a wide avenue for creative and innovative solutions in the contemporary context.

With respect to humankind's stewardship of the Earth, the privilege entails a profound responsibility. Other living species are also considered by the Quran to be "peoples or communities" (known as *ummas*; Sura 6:38). The creation itself, in all its myriad diversity and complexity, may be thought of as a vast universe of "signs" of God's power, wisdom, beneficence, and majesty. The whole creation praises God by its very being (Sura 59:24; compare with 64:1). With Him are the keys (to the treasures) of the Unseen that no one knows but He. He knows whatever there is on the Earth and in the sea. Not a leaf falls but with His knowledge: there is not a grain in the Earth's shadows, not a thing, freshly green or withered, but it is (inscribed) in a clear record (Sura 6:59).

According to the Quran, the creation of the cosmos is a greater reality than the creation of humankind (Sura 40:57), but human beings have been privileged to occupy a position even higher than the angels as "caliphs," or vicegerents (deputies) of God on the Earth. Even so, they share with all animals an origin in the common substance, water (Sura 24:45), and they will return to the Earth from which they came. The idea of human vicegerency on Earth has drawn much criticism in environmental ethics, principally since the publication in 1967 of an influential article, "The Historical Roots of Our Ecological Crisis," by the historian Lynn White Jr.; White argued that Judeo-Christian tradition encouraged exploitation of the natural world because the Bible declares human dominion over the Earth, and thus establishes anthropomorphism, and that Christianity's distinction between humankind made in God's image and the rest of a "soulless" nature make humans superior to other life forms. Muslims, as well as Jews and Christians, have had to face the intrinsic problems of such a position, historically as well as in contemporary global economic, political, and social life. But Muslims are reflecting on their fundamental and enduring religious teachings and discovering theological and moral bases for an environmental ethics that have been present, whether explicitly or implicitly, both in their sacred textual traditions and in their habits of heart, thinking, public administration, and daily life since Islam's founding. A common conviction among Muslims in this discourse is that nature is not independently worthwhile but derives its value from God. Put another way, nature is indeed incalculably worthwhile and wondrous, although according to Islam it did not self-generate but was produced in a grand divine scheme.

Heaven and Earth

The Earth is mentioned some 453 times in the Quran, whereas sky and the heavens are mentioned only about 320 times. Islam does understand the Earth to be subservient to humankind, but it should not be administered and exploited irresponsibly. There is a strong sense in Islamic teachings of the goodness and purity of the Earth. For example, clean dust or sand may be used for ablutions before prayer if clean water is not available. The Prophet Muhammad said that the Earth had been created for him [and for all Muslims, by implication] as a mosque and as a means of purification. So there is a sacrality to the Earth; it is a fit place for humankinds' service of God, whether in formal ceremonies or in daily life. In an oft-repeated statement based a worldview very much different than that of Islam, James Watt, Ronald Reagan's first secretary of the interior, said that stewardship of the environment was not really such an urgent matter in light of the prophesied destruction of the natural order on doomsday. Those in the Muslim world would thus have recalled words the Prophet Muhammad is reported to have said, "When doomsday comes, if someone has a palm shoot in his hand he should plant it."

Muslims envision heaven as a beautiful garden, which the Quran describes in many places. Among the numerous descriptions is heaven as a garden under which streams (*anhār*) of pure water flow. That image is repeated some thirty-eight times and is mostly of Medinan provenance. If life on Earth is deemed the preparation for eternal life in heaven, then the loving care of the natural environment would seem to be appropriate training for the afterlife in the company of God and the angels in an environment that is perfectly balanced, peaceful, and verdant. Muslims believe that all generations will be gathered together at the Last Judgment and that in heaven the saved will enjoy the company of generations of faithful Muslims who have been rewarded with a blessed afterlife. Whether one plants a palm shoot as the end is closing in or invests in an environmentally sound way of life for the sake of posterity, it comes to the same thing: serving God through a stewardship that reflects what the Quran throughout sets forth as God's generosity, mercy, and guidance in the first place. Concerning God's reason for creating the universe, the Divine Saying so beloved by Muslim mystics, known as Sufis, declares: "I was a Hidden Treasure and I wanted to be known, so I created creatures in order to be known by them." (A "Divine Saying" is an utterance inspired by God but expressed verbally by the Prophet Muhammad.) Community between God and His creatures does not end with death; rather, it truly begins with the afterlife, according to Islamic belief. In a stirring passage describing the end of the world, the Quran details the destruction of the natural and familiar world and then declares: "When Hell shall be set blazing; and when the Garden is brought near—then shall each soul know what it has produced" (Sura 81:12–13).

"Do you not observe that God sends down rain from the sky, so that in the morning the Earth becomes green?" (Sura 22:63). The color green is the most blessed of all colors for Muslims and, together with a profound sense of the value of nature as God's perfect and most fruitful plan, provides a charter for a green movement that could become the greatest exertion yet known in Islamic history, a "green jihad appropriate for addressing the global environmental crisis." ("Jihad" means "exertion, struggle" and only by extension includes holy warfare of a military type.)

The Power of Water

Water has the highest meaning and value in the Quranic worldview, as indicated in the frequently quoted verse: "We made from water every living thing" (21:30; cf. 25:54; 24:45). References to water in its various forms and sources under the term *mā'* occur some sixty-three times in the Quran. Although that is not nearly as high a total of occurrences as Earth (or as the sky and the heavens), the occurrences often possess significant agency, whereas Earth and sky—as wonderful as they are—are often the loci and channels for the passage of power rather than power itself. Water is power; indeed, it is the sine qua non of protoplasm. It is also important to note that significant references to water as the enabler of all life occur consistently throughout the chronological trajectory of Quranic revelation of some thirty-plus years—from early Meccan suras, when Muhammad was launching his prophetic career, to late Medinan times, when a stable theocratic system of faith and order had been established throughout the Arabian Peninsula.

God made all living creatures from water and He sustains them over time and from generation to generation with that essential liquid. "And We send down pure water from the sky, thereby to bring life to a dead land and slake the thirst of that which We have created—cattle and people (*'anāsi*) in multitudes" (25:48–49). "Have you seen the water which you drink? Was it you who sent it down from the raincloud or did We send it? Were it our will, We could have made it bitter; why then do you not give thanks?" (56:68–70). God reminds us in the Quran: "Say: Have you considered, if your water were one morning to have seeped away, who then could bring you clear-flowing water?" (67:30).

The Quran principally provides a discourse on water in terms of its significance for life and as a major resource of divine providence. The treasury of prophetic statements that have been preserved in the hadith literature includes many references to water in human life in its personal, communal, civic, agricultural, legal, and commercial dimensions. An example of the first—the personal—dimension is the hadith wherein Muhammad declares: "He who serves drinks to others should be the last to drink himself" (Nawawi, reported by Tirmidhi). An example of the civic/communal dimension of water discourse in the hadith is: "All Muslims are partners in three things—in water, herbage and fire" (reported by Ibn Majah and Abu Daud). "Fire" in this hadith is usually understood to mean wood as the bearer of flame for practical uses. Another hadith adumbrates an ethic of conservation that Muslims often repeat (as translated in a contemporary Saudi Arabian source):

> It is related that the Prophet, upon him be blessings and peace, passed by his companion Sa'd, who was washing for prayer, and said, "What is this wastage, O Sa'd?" "Is there a wastage even in washing for prayer?" asked Sa'd.; and he said, "yes, even if you are by a flowing river."(*Environmental Protection in Islam* 1994, 7)

With respect to Prophet Muhammad's own ablutions—whether they are made to remove a minor impurity (by means of basic ritual washing, *wudū'*) or a major impurity (by a full ritual bath, *ghusl*)—before Salat-prayer, the Quran states: "But waste not by excess: for Allah loveth not the wasters" (6:141). Ayesha, the Prophet's young wife, reported that Muhammad used a very small quantity of water for simple ablution and a bit more for a full ritual bathing.

The Muslim world has throughout history paid close attention to water management from legal, economic, and ethical perspectives. Water in the Islamic vision is also of fundamental importance for sustaining basic human life, whether in the production of food and drink or in personal and communal piety in the purification rites that all Muslims perform on a daily basis, from cleansing one's surroundings to washing and bathing after experiencing impurity and before worship. The standard for ablution water to be used before formal worship is quite high and the law books thoroughly treat the matter in a way that compares with extended halachic discussions of Jewish legal scholars.

The water that Muslims must use for purification, as one widely used worship guide expresses it, should be "fresh and clean like water from a tap or from a well or from the sea or from a river. Rainwater also will do." Sometimes it may take a fair amount of water to clean clothing or articles, as well as a person, from major impurity (such as contact with a pig or a dog). If one is made impure in a major way, through contact with blood and urine, for example, one must wash with water until the color, taste, and smell are removed. If a dog licks a hand or a cooking pot, as can happen, the hand or pot must be cleaned with water six times, at least, mixed with some dust. After that series of washings, the object must be washed an additional six times with fresh water without added dust. This rigorous requirement helps us to appreciate the old Persian tale of a person in the crowded bazaar who felt a moist tongue lick her bare hand as she wended her way among the other shoppers. If one cannot determine the source of the licking, one may simply declare: "Allah willing, it was a goat." Goats, like cats, are not sources of major impurity. The subject of water use in Islamic purification rituals is long and minutely detailed, but a sense of their importance has been seen from the examples given here.

Water Management in Islam

An excellent collection of essays has been published under the title *Water Management in Islam*. It is primarily based on the findings of the Workshop on Water Resources

Management in the Islamic World, held in Amman, Jordan, in December 1998. (Although the Amman conference organizers sent invitations all over the world, most of the respondents were from the Middle East.) That workshop was in response to the United Nations Environment Programme (UNEP) 1992 Water Conference held in Dublin, Ireland, called Water and the Environment: Development Issues for the 21st Century; it outlined four general objectives, the "Dublin Principles" (Faruqui et al. 2001, xvi):

- Water is a social good.
- Water is an economic good.
- Water management ought to be participatory and integrated.
- Women play a central role in water management.

Some of the general, agreed-on principles of Islamic water management set forth in the book are included here appropriate categories (Faruqui et al. 2001, 1, 22, 23, 24, 25, 27, 52, 53, 87).

Water as a Social Good

Water is a gift from God and necessary for sustaining all life. Water belongs to the community as a whole—no individual literally owns water (except in containers and set apart from its natural source). The first priority for water use is access to drinking water of acceptable quantity and quality to sustain human life, and every human being has the right to this basic water requirement. The second and third priorities are for domestic animals and for irrigation.

Humankind is the steward of water on Earth. The environment (flora and fauna) has a very strong and legitimate right to water; we must minimize pollution and hold managers, individuals, organizations, and states accountable. Water resources must be managed and used in a sustainable way. Sustainable and equitable management ultimately depends upon following universal values such as fairness, equity, and concern for others.

Water Demand Management

Water conservation is central to Islam. Mosques, religious institutes, and religious schools should be used to disseminate this principle so as to complement other religious and secular efforts. Wastewater reuse is permissible in Islam, provided that treatment is appropriate for the intended purpose and not hazardous to health. This topic has generated considerable debate, and not all Muslims agree on the matter.

Recovering costs of water management is permissible for supplying, treating, storing, and distributing water, as well as for wastewater collection, treatment, and disposal. But water pricing must be equitable as well as efficient.

Islam permits privatization of water service delivery, but government must ensure equity in pricing and service. This is extremely difficult to ensure and an ongoing struggle (e.g., in Jakarta, Indonesia's capital, 20 percent of the population has access to piped, treated water, whereas the rest—approximately 80 percent—pay about 25 percent of their income for water from private vendors).

Integrate Water Resources Management

Water management requires *shura* (mutual consultation) with all stakeholders. All nation-states are obliged to share water fairly with other nation states. (There are some very difficult issues regarding water sharing today; Turkey's damming of the Tigris and Euphrates rivers, for example, threatens to cause grave shortfalls for Iraq and Syria. Iraq, especially, has been severely affected by this.)

Water management should be integrated across sectors and regions, whether among Muslim states or between Muslim and non-Muslim nations. The former should agree on basic Islamic principles, whereas the latter should seek agreements that comply with fair and just rulings by appropriate international organizations.

A major emphasis of *Water Management in Islam* is on the importance of educating the Muslim public at the most basic levels of community life in the homes, schools, and mosques and by mothers, teachers, and imams. In Jordan, the head mufti "delivered a special fatwa (expert legal opinion) that environmental education is *wājeb*, or an obligation: under such a fatwa, all Muslims are responsible for participation in environmental education. Therefore, Islam provides a dynamic forum that is capable of reaching the entire Muslim population—in the house, street, school, and mosque" (Faruqui et al. 2001, 52–53).

Water Management in Islam describes other initiatives and acknowledges that the role of women is particularly important at all levels. The editors and contributors of the book consider such initiatives to be in their infancy at present.

Facing the Future

One of the biggest problems that Muslims face, across the Afro-Eurasian world particularly, is overpopulation and mass migration from traditional rural and agricultural areas to overstressed and rundown, often squalid and neglected urban areas. And so much of the motivation and content of usually very conservative Muslim revival movements in recent decades has focused on anti-Western and anti-secular political and social matters with little if any attention paid to Islamic teachings about the natural environment. Ironically, fundamentalist types of Muslim movements readily accept modern technologies but too often without considering their effects on the natural environment.

Water stewardship in Muslim contexts has a powerful historical foundation because of the nature of the arid zone in which so many Muslims have lived since the founding of Islam in the Arabian peninsula in the seventh century CE. But thoughtful Muslims everywhere are increasingly also feeling an urgent need for developing proper stewardship of air, land, soil, plants, and animals. There is promising thinking and activism happening in some Muslim civic contexts today. Muslims realize that Allah is not interested in treating His human adult creatures like helpless children. As the Quran declares (13:11): "God does not change what is in a people until they exercise initiative in changing what is in themselves."

Frederick Mathewson DENNY
University of Colorado at Boulder, emeritus

A section of this article was adapted from "Islam and Ecology: A Bestowed Trust Inviting Balanced Stewardship" by Frederick M. Denny, as part of the Forum on Religion and Ecology (FORE) series initiated at Harvard University's Center for the Study of World Religions; the original article can be found at http://fore.research.yale.edu/religion/islam/index.html

FURTHER READINGS

Bagader, Abubakr Ahmed; El-Chirazi El-Sabbagh, Abdullatif Tawfik; As-Sayyid Al-Glayand, Mohamad; & Izzi Deen Samarrai, Mawil Yousuf. (1994). *Environmental protection in Islam*, 2nd rev. ed. IUCN-World Conservation Union, Meteorology and Environmental Protection Administration (MEPA) of the Kingdom of Saudi Arabia, Policy and Law Paper No. 20, Rev. 1994.

Izzi Deen Samarrai, Mawil Yousuf. (1990). Islamic environmental ethics, law, and society. In J. Ronald Engel & Joan Gibb Engel (Eds.), *Ethics of environment and development: Global challenge, international response* (pp. 189–198). Tucson, AZ: University of Arizona Press.

Dobell, Patrick. (12 October 1977). The Judaeo-Christian stewardship attitude to nature. *Christian Century*, pp. 295–296.

Faruqui, Naser I.; Biswas, Asit K.; & Bino, Murad J. (Eds.). (2001). *Water management in Islam*. Tokyo, New York, and Paris: United Nations University Press.

Foltz, Richard C.; Denny, Frederick M.; & Baharuddin, Azizan. (Vol. Eds.). (2003). Islam and ecology: A bestowed trust. In Mary Evelyn Tucker & John Grim (Series Eds.), *Religions of the world and ecology* (pp. xliv, 584). Cambridge, MA: Harvard University Press for the Center for the Study of World Religions, Harvard Divinity School.

Nasr, Seyyed Hossein. (1992). Islam and the environmental crisis. In Stephen C. Rockefeller & John C. Elder (Eds.), *Spirit and nature: Why the environment is a religious issue* (pp. 85–107). Boston: Beacon Press.

White, Lynn, Jr. (1967). The historical roots of our ecological crisis. *Science 155*, 1203–1207.

If biologists believe that humans are the greatest agents of ecological change on the surface of the earth, is it not humans who, drawn from the brink, will—for their own good—abandon Mammon and listen to the prescriptions of God on the conservation of their environment and the environment of all the creatures on earth? The Islamic answer to this question is decisively in the affirmative.

MUHAMMAD HYDER IHSAN MAHASNEH

Source: Muhammed Hyder Ihsan Mahasneh. (2003). Islamic Faith Statement. Retrieved October 2, 2009, from http://www.arcworld.org/faiths.asp?pageID=75

J

Jainism

Some core values of Jainism, which originated in India as early as the sixth century BCE, lend themselves to sustainability, especially the focus on a living and eternal universe, the minimal use of natural resources, and ahimsa (nonviolence). The Jaina in India today, despite their small number, have the potential to advocate for change in environmental practices and policies.

The Jaina religion originated in India more than 2,500 years ago. It has survived as a minority faith and is currently practiced by approximately 4 million persons in India and several hundred thousand others scattered across the globe. Jainism espouses a philosophy that demonstrates some core teachings that accord nicely with sustainability principles. It teaches the pervasive and eternality of life forms and advocates a religious practice rooted in a nonviolent ethic. Jainism posits a living universe, uncreated and eternal. It emphasizes personal responsibility as well as an intimate, ongoing awareness of one's environment. It also advocates a parsimonious, minimalist use of resources, particularly for members of its monastic orders, who are deemed to live the ideal life.

Jaina Beliefs

Mahavira, the great Jaina leader to whom many Jaina teachings are attributed, lived during the same period as the Buddha, around the fourth century BCE. Mahavira taught close and careful observation of life: "Thoroughly knowing the earth-bodies and water-bodies, and fire-bodies and wind-bodies, the lichens, seeds, and sprouts, he comprehended that they are, if narrowly inspected, imbued with life" (Acaranga Sutra I:8.I, 11–12).

The Acaranga Sutra, the earliest known Jaina text, lists in detail different forms of life and advocates various techniques for their protection. It states, "All breathing, existing, living, sentient creatures should not be slain, nor treated with violence, nor abused, nor tormented, nor driven away. This is the pure, unchangeable, eternal law" (I:4.1). The Acaranga Sutra mentions how to avoid harm not only to animals but also to plants (by not touching them), and to the bodies that dwell in the earth, the water, the fire, and the air. For instance, Jaina monks and nuns must not stamp upon the earth or swim in water or light or extinguish fires or thrash their arms in the air.

The later philosophical tradition—as articulated in the Tattvartha Sutra written by Umasvati, a Jaina philosopher thought to have lived in the fifth century CE—states that the universe is brimming with souls weighted by karmic material (*dravya*). Many of these souls hold the potential for freeing themselves from all karmic residue and attaining spiritual liberation (*kevala*); they constantly change and take new shape due to the fettering presence of karma, described as sticky and colorful. These life forms can never be created, nor can they be destroyed. In a sense, by their very nature, they are not only sustainable but also indestructible. But they are constantly in a process of motion and change, moving from one birth to the next. To ensure their well-being, and to move toward spiritual liberation, Umasvati advocates carefully abiding by the five major vows: nonviolence, truthfulness, not stealing, sexual restraint, and nonpossession. Ultimately, if one perfects the practice of nonviolence, all karmas disperse and the perfected one (*siddha*) dwells eternally in omniscient (*sarvajna*) solitude (*kevala*).

According to Umasvati, 8,400,000 different species of life forms exist. These beings are part of a beginningless round of birth, life, death, and rebirth. Each living being houses a life force, or *jiva*, that occupies and enlivens the host environment. When the body dies, the *jiva* seeks out a new site based on the nature of karma generated and accrued during the previous lifetime. Depending upon one's actions, one can ascend to a heavenly realm and take rebirth as a human or animal or elemental or microbial form, or descend into one of the hells as a suffering human being or a particular animal.

The Jainas were careful to observe and describe the many life forms that they hoped to spare. They cataloged them according to the number of senses they possess. Earth bodies, plants, and microorganisms (*nigodha*), at the lowest level, are said to possess only the sense of touch. Earthworms and mollusks have the senses of taste and touch. Crawling insects add the sense of smell. Moths, bees, and flies add sight. At the highest realm, Jainas place animals that can hear and those that can hear and think, including reptiles, birds, and mammals. The detailed lists of life forms provided by Jaina scholars present a comprehensive overview of life forms as seen through the prism of Jainism. As such they have presented a view of life that presages later environmental theory, resonating in its attention to detail with such writers as the U.S. environmentalist Aldo Leopold (1887–1948).

Jainism's Sustainable Worldview

The connection between Jainism and sustainability might not be obvious at first because Jainism seems most concerned with rising above karma and not with living beings—except in regard to how one's benevolence will advance one's own spiritual trajectory. Both Hindus and Buddhists have criticized Jainism as self-absorbed and even irrelevant. But the Jaina worldview powerfully evokes an emotional landscape. It states that the material world itself contains feelings and that the Earth feels and responds in kind to human presence. Animals possess cognitive faculties, including memories and emotions, and the very world that surrounds all living things feels their presence. All entities—from the water we humans drink, to the air we inhale, to the chair that supports us, to the light that illumines our studies—feel us through the sense of touch, though we might often take for granted their caress and support and sustenance. According to the Jaina tradition, humans, as living, sensate, thinking beings, have been given the special task and opportunity to cultivate increasingly rarefied states of awareness and ethical behavior to acknowledge that the universe is suffused with living, breathing, conscious beings that warrant recognition and respect. In this regard Jaina sensibilities accord well with an ethic of sustainability.

The Jainas were quite assertive in making their minority religious views known in areas of India where they gained ascendancy. To sustain their identity required great strategic thinking and action. Many of the southern kingdoms of Karnataka offered protection and patronage to the Jainas, who won several concessions regarding public laws designed to encourage vegetarianism and discourage hunting (*saletore*). Jainism exerted profound influence throughout this region from 100 CE to 1300. In the northern kingdoms of Gujarat, they experienced a golden era when Kumarapala (reigned 1143–1175) converted to Jainism. He encouraged the extensive building of temples, and under the tutelage of the Jaina teacher Hemacandra (1089–1172) became a vegetarian. He enacted legislation that reflected Jaina religious precepts regarding the sanctity of all life. In the north-central area of India, Jincandrasuri II (1541–1613), the fourth and last of the Dadagurus of the Svetamabara Khartar Gacch of Jaina monks, traveled to Lahore in 1591 where he greatly influenced the Mughal Emperor Akbar the Great (1542–1605). Akbar protected Jaina places of pilgrimage and ordered noninterference with Jaina ceremonies. Most remarkably, he forbade the slaughter of animals for one week each year. The Jainas tirelessly campaigned against animal sacrifice, which is now illegal in most states of India. Mohandas Gandhi (1869–1948), the most well-known leader of modern India, was deeply influenced by the Jaina commitment to nonviolence and adapted it in his campaign for India's political independence from Great Britain.

The Jainas have been great protectors of life within India. They have inspired legislation to protect animals over the course of centuries and have been influential in the modern government of India. Though the great struggles to ban ritual slaughter of animals and to free India from colonial rule have largely been won, Jainism appears to be well equipped to face the new challenges in regard to sustainability faced by India as it continues to pursue a course of rapid industrialization.

Jaina Environmentalism

The Jaina community has undertaken some steps toward including environmental issues within their religious discourse. L. M. Singhvi (1931–2007), a noted jurist and member of India's Parliament, published *Jain Declaration on Nature* in 1990. It quotes Mahavira's warning that observant Jainas must be respectful of the elements and vegetation: "One who neglects or disregards the existence of earth, air, fire, water, and vegetation disregards his own existence which is entwined with them" (Singhvi 1990, 7). Singhvi himself writes, "Life is viewed as a gift of togetherness, accommodation, and assistance in a universe teeming with interdependent constituents," and, stating that there are countless souls constantly changing and interchanging life forms, he goes on to note, "Even metals and stones . . . should not be dealt with recklessly" (1990, 7, 11).

Several Jaina organizations have taken up the cause of environmentalism, regarding it as a logical extension of their personal observance of nonviolence (*ahimsa*). Reforestation projects have been underway at various Jaina pilgrimage sites, such as Palitana in Gujarat, Ellora in Maharashtra, and Sametshirkhar and Pavapuri in Bihar. At Jain Vishva Bharati University in Rajasthan, a fully accredited university, the Department of Non-Violence and Peace offers a specialization in ecology. In December 1995 the department cosponsored a conference titled "Living in Harmony with Nature: Survival into the Third Millennium." Topics included the environmental crisis, ecological degradation, and unrestrained consumerism. A conference held at Harvard University in 1998 examined the topic of Jainism and ecology, and included representatives and scholars of various sects of Jainism. These activities reflect some ways in which the tradition has been refocused and newly interpreted to reflect ecological concerns: It values all forms of life in their immense diversity, not merely in the abstract but in minute detail. It requires its adherents to engage only in certain types of livelihood, presumably based on the principle of *ahimsa*.

It must be noted, however, that the observance of *ahimsa* is secondary to the goal of final liberation, *kevala*. Looking at both the ultimate intention of the Jaina faith and the actual consequences of some Jaina businesses, then, might require some critical analysis and reflection. Although the resultant lifestyle for monks and nuns resembles an environmentally friendly ideal, its pursuit focuses on personal spiritual advancement. In a sense the holistic vision of the interrelated life is no more than an ecofriendly byproduct.

In terms of the lifestyle of the Jaina layperson, certain practices—such as vegetarianism, periodic fasting, and eschewal of militarism—might also be seen as friendly to the environment and to contribute to global sustainability. But some professions adopted by the Jainas due to their religious commitment to harm only one-sensed beings might, in fact, be environmentally disastrous. The Jainas are involved with strip mining for granite and marble throughout India. Unless habitat restoration accompanies the mining, this is neither ecofriendly nor sustainable. Other industries controlled by Jainas may contribute to air pollution, forest destruction, and water pollution. In light of new evidence by the ecological sciences, the interconnection between industry, commerce, and the environment must be reevaluated. The development of a Jaina ecological business ethic would require extensive reflection and restructuring, a tradition well known within the Jaina community. The Jaina community, despite its relatively small numbers, is extremely influential in the world of Indian business, law, and politics. If Jainas were to speak with a united voice on environmental issues, their impact could be quite profound.

Due to their perception of the "livingness" of the world, Jainas hold an affinity for the ideals of the environmental movement and are well poised to be advocates of sustainability. The Jaina observance of nonviolence has provided a model for a way of life that respects all living beings, including ecosystems. Because of their successful advocacy against meat eating and animal sacrifice, as well as their success at developing businesses that avoid overt violence, many Jainas identify themselves as environmentalists. Through a rethinking of contemporary industrial practices, and concerted advocacy of environmental awareness through religious teachings and the secular media, the Jaina tradition might help bolster a sustainable economic model.

Christopher Key CHAPPLE
Loyola Marymount University

FURTHER READING

Babb, Lawrence. (1996). *Absent lord: Ascetics and kings in a Jain ritual culture.* Berkeley: University of California Press.

Chapple, Christopher K. (1993). *Nonviolence to animals, Earth, and self in Asian traditions.* Albany: State University of New York Press.

Chapple, Christopher K. (1998). Toward an indigenous Indian environmentalism. In Lance Nelson (Ed.), *Purifying the earthly body of God: Religion and ecology in Hindu India* (pp. 13–38). Albany: State University of New York Press.

Chapple, Christopher K. (Fall 2001). The living cosmos of Jainism: A traditional science grounded in environmental ethics. *Daedalus: Journal of the American Academy of Arts and Sciences, 130*(4), 207–224.

Chapple, Christopher K. (Ed.). (2002). *Jainism and ecology: Nonviolence in the web of life.* Cambridge, MA: Center for the Study of World Religions, Harvard Divinity School, Harvard University Press.

Cort, John E. (1998). Who is a king? Jain narratives of kingship in medieval western India. In John E. Cort (Ed.), *Open boundaries: Jain communities and cultures in Indian history* (pp. 85–110). Albany: State University of New York Press.

Jacobi, Hermann. (Trans.). (1968[1884]). *Jaina Sutras: Part I. The Akaranga Sutra & the Kalpa Sutra.* New York: Dover.

Saletore, Bhasker Anand. (1938). *Medieval Jainism with special reference to the Vijayangara Empire.* Bombay, India: Karnatak Publishing House.

Singhvi, L. M. (1990). *The Jain declaration on nature.* London: The Jain Sacred Literature Trust.

Suri, Santi. (1950). *Jiva Vicara Prakaranam along with Pathaka Ratnakara's commentary* (Muni Ratna-Prabha Vijaya, Ed.; Jaynat P. Thaker, Trans.). Madras, India: Jain Mission Society.

Umasvati, Tatia. (1994). *That which is (Tattvartha Sutra): A classic Jain manual for understanding the true nature of reality* (Nathmal Tatia, Trans.). San Francisco: HarperCollins.

Jordan River Project

The Jordan River is one of the world's most sacred rivers—important to Judaism, Christianity, and Islam—but today it is also one of the most endangered ecological areas in the world, plagued by contamination and pollution, drained and diverted for agriculture. Since 1994 efforts by local NGOs, led by EcoPeace / Friends of the Earth Middle East, have raised awareness about the river's demise.

The Jordan River is spiritually important to millions of people worldwide: crossing the River Jordan marks the Israelites' entrance into the Holy Land in the Hebrew Bible; Jesus Christ was baptized in the Jordan, which makes its waters holy for Christianity; and many of the venerable companions of the Prophet Muhammad are buried near its banks. The Jordan River valley is also a lush, wetland ecosystem. Over 500 million birds migrating from Europe to Africa twice a year depend on the Jordan River valley as a vital stopover on their long journey.

Sadly, today the lower Jordan River is almost dry. The river has seen over 90 percent of its water sources diverted by Israel, Syria, and Jordan. Since the 1950s the waters of the Jordan River have been substantially rerouted to support large-scale irrigated agriculture. Competition for scarce water resources in the midst of conflict allowed little room to think about the needs of the river and its ecosystem; because so much fresh water has been diverted, Israeli, Jordanian, and Palestinian sewage, rerouted saline springs, and agricultural runoff are about the only "waters" left to flow. Since 1948 the river valley has been a military / border zone, off-limits to the public; few people even knew that a problem existed.

Over the last decade awareness of the river's demise has slowly grown, with loud calls for its restoration made in recent years. Founded in 1994 with a central focus on the Jordan, EcoPeace / Friends of the Earth Middle East (www.foeme.org) has since 2001 begun been working, through their Good Water Neighbors programs, at the community level with youth, adult residents, and mayors of nine of the most important Jordanian, Palestinian, and Israeli communities along the valley. In each community, the project has helped create recognition of their own and their neighboring community's water situation and fostered a communal sense of purpose among many residents of the valley. In each community, water-saving devices were installed and schools transformed into models of water efficiency. With the cooperation of the Israeli and Jordanian militaries, regular tours to the river took place, raising awareness about the condition of the river, which led to petitions with thousands of signatures and stories written by journalists. Having gained the trust of residents, the project focused on policy-level changes by involving municipal leaders. Mayors saw that local residents were outraged and, with the new media interest, local mayors became vocal and visible, even jumping into the river together—Jordanian, Palestinian, and Israeli—in a common call for its rehabilitation on 15 July 2007. The mayors from both banks of the river have signed "memorandums of understanding," committing themselves to advancing shared solutions to cross border problems.

But the fact that sewage still flows in the river is evidence of how much work still needs to be done. The incremental policy measures of demand management, water conservation, pricing reform, and removal of subsidies do

not attract media attention and therefore do not gain high-level political support. Conflict, competition, and cultural arrogance have been responsible for the demise of the Jordan to date. To coincide with the NGO-sponsored "International Day of Action for Rivers" on 14 March 2009, Friends of the Earth Middle East called for the governments of Israel, Jordan, and Palestine to honor their commitment to rehabilitate the lower Jordan. Cooperation based on the spirit of sustainability is necessary if the Jordan is to be revived, a feat that would bring at least some sense of peace to Jordan valley residents in the midst of the troubled Middle East.

Gidon BROMBERG
EcoPeace / Friends of the Earth Middle East

FURTHER READING

Bromberg, Gidon. (2008, October 12). Let common sense flow. Haaretz. com. Retrieved May 28, 2009, from http://www.haaretz.com/hasen/ spages/1027753.html

Bromberg, Gidon. (2008, September 18). Will the Jordan keep on flowing? *Yale Environment* 360. Retrieved May 28, 2009, from http:// e360.yale.edu/content/feature.msp?id=2064

Chabin, Michele. (2007, September). Weeping for the Jordan. *Christianity Today*. Retrieved May 28, 2009, from http://www.christianity today.com/ct/2007/september/12.17.html

Clark, Mandy. (2009, May 11). The Jordan river is dying. *Voice of America*. Retrieved May 28, 2009, from, http://www.voanews.com/ english/2009-05-11-voa20.cfm

Friends of the Earth Middle East. (2005, March). Crossing the Jordan: Concept document to rehabilitate, promote prosperity and help bring peace to the lower Jordan River valley. Retrieved March 23, 2009, from http://www.foeme.org/index_images/dinamicas/publications/ publ21_1.pdf

Tate, Paul. (2007, June 18). Jordan river among world's 100 most endangered sites. *Jordan Times*. Retrieved May 28, 2009, from, http://www. jordanembassyus.org/06182007005.htm

Walsh, Brian. (2008). Heroes of the environment. *Time*. Retrieved May 28, 2009, from, http://www.time.com/time/specials/packages/ article/0,28804,1841778_1841816,00.html

In the summer, the Lower Jordan River—the river below the Galilee—is dry in certain places, and this is a totally man-made problem. The Lower River is an open sewage canal, and the sad irony is that the sewage water is keeping the river flowing. Being baptized in the water below the dam cannot be too spiritually uplifting.

GIDON BROMBERG

Source: Quoted by Hannah Lodwick. (15 December, 2005). Makers of Jordan River body lotions not deterred by river's pollution. *Associated Baptist Press*. Retrieved October 2, 2009, from http://www.abpnews.com/index.php?option=com_content&task=view&id=843&Itemid=118

Judaism

Ideas embedded in the rich theological and legal litera-ture of Judaism have informed and influenced modern Jewish environmental ideas of sustainability: the belief that humans are temporary inhabitants of what God has created, and the inherent values of humility, moder-ation, and responsibility. Many old and new traditions—Tu b'Shvat, the Sabbath, and Sabbatical Year—celebrate care and concern for the environment.

Judaism has, throughout its history, developed a theo-centric theology while focusing much of its ethical and legal literature on the good governance of human soci-ety, which was seen at the same time as the fulfillment of God's will. In the earliest stages of Jewish history, found in the Hebrew Bible, the relationship between the people, the land, and God was conceptualized as a covenant. This was a conditional contract in which the people had obligations to be loyal to God alone and to follow God's command-ments in return for peace and fertility on the land. Failure to follow the contract meant exile from the land. Thus the land-based covenant contained several important laws that emphasized proper stewardship of the land and gratitude to God for the bounty that the land produced under His blessings. In later Jewish history, when many Jews lived outside of the land of Israel, these concepts were incor-porated into practices and rituals meant to remind Jews of their ancestral connection to the land, but they could also be applied in some part to the lands they now lived in. It was this rich theological and legal literature that has informed and influenced modern Jewish environmental ideas of sustainability.

While the language of sustainability was not used directly in Jewish environmental writing until the early 1990s, several concepts emerged in the first responses and have continued to be the major values with which Jewish

environmentalists have found connections with the classic elements of sustainability: God's ownership of Creation, human stewardship of Creation, intergenerational respon-sibility, modesty in consumption, the common good, and gratitude. These theological ethical concepts became part of the organizing discourse of the Jewish environmental movement as it began to mobilize.

Early Environmental Writings and Organizations

Jewish environmental writing began in the early 1970s as responses to three events: the famous article in the journal *Science* by Lynn White Jr., the creation of Earth Day, and the advent of major environmental legislation. These all occurred in North America, as Israeli environmentalism began in the 1950s, not as a religious movement, but as part of a secular response to development (Tal 2002). This article will therefore focus on the Jewish religious concepts of sustainability that were primarily developed in North America.

The first major Jewish environmental organization was Shomrei Adamah (Hebrew for "Guardians of the Earth," a reference to Genesis 2:15 in the New Jewish Publica-tion Society's Hebrew Bible), which was founded in 1988. Shomrei Adamah published a number of books and edu-cational materials devoted to increasing environmental awareness among Jews. One of its most successful activ-ities was the popularization of the Tu B'Shvat seder. Tu B'Shvat is the New Year for the trees, a minor event in the Jewish calendar originally used to designate the date when a tree's fruit became subject to tithing. In the six-teenth century, Jewish mystics created a seder or ritual meal to mark this event, which was reinterpreted with their elaborate cosmological system. In the twentieth century,

Tu B'Shvat was reintroduced as a kind of Jewish Arbor Day by Zionist settlers in the land of Israel. The seder was then rewritten to promote this event for Jews in the Diaspora. It was Ellen Bernstein, the founder of Shomrei Adamah, who reintroduced the mystical version of the seder within an environmental context. This ritual has spread to many Jewish communities, and Tu B'Shvat has become the de facto Jewish Earth Day. While the term *sustainability* was not originally used in the seder, the themes and practices of sustainability are now central to the seder's rituals and liturgy.

In 1992, as part of the National Religious Partnership for the Environment, the Coalition on the Environment and Jewish Life (COEJL) was founded in the United States. COEJL became a nationwide organization with many local affiliates usually connected to the organized Jewish community structures. In its founding statement, COEJL (2007) called for "mobilizing our community towards energy efficiency, the reduction and recycling of wastes, and other practices which promote environmental sustainability."

COEJL's mission statement also connected sustainability with environmental justice and the "Jewish values of environmental stewardship." The major Jewish religious denominations and rabbinical organizations in the United States have all passed numerous environmental resolutions since the early 1990s in which the language of sustainability is utilized. It is always assumed in these statements that sustainability is in consort with Jewish theology and ethics.

Ethical Obligations

It can be said that sustainability has two ethical obligations in time and space—one horizontal and one vertical. The horizontal obligation is to all humans and to all life living in the present: we must live equitably within the boundaries of what the Earth can sustain. The vertical obligation is to extend that process into the future, in other words, a commitment to generations of humans and nonhumans still unborn.

These ethical obligations can be found in the following Jewish theological assumptions upon which a Jewish concept of sustainability is based. First of all, Judaism holds that the Earth and all it contains is a creation of God. This world was not brought into being by human endeavor, nor does it exist only for human beings. For whatever reason, God created Earth and the life upon it; it all belongs to God, and human beings are temporary dwellers or tenants upon the earth (compare I Chronicles 29:11–15). This temporary tenant status also implies that humanity must leave the Earth in the same state as they entered it.

These ideas are best seen in the laws of the Sabbatical Year and the Jubilee. In Leviticus 25 (compare also Exodus 23:10), the Israelites were commanded to let the land lie fallow every seventh year. During that year—the Sabbatical Year—whatever grew on the land without human cultivation was allowed to be eaten but with the stipulation that the poor should have access to this produce as well. In a law called the Jubilee, Leviticus 25 also mandated that every fifty years, all land sold during that time was to be returned to its original owners. At the end of the stipulations of these laws it says: "But the land must not be sold beyond reclaim, for the land is Mine; you are but resident aliens with Me" (Leviticus 25:23 HB). In Deuteronomy 15:1–15, further stipulations are added to the Sabbatical Year: All debts must be cancelled and all indentured servants released. The rationale given in this source is that since the Israelites were redeemed by God from slavery in Egypt, they should imitate God and not enslave their fellow Israelites through debt. In the Torah there is also the idea of cross-generational responsibility in which the sins of one generation can end up hurting future generations (compare Exodus 20:5).

Creation is also deemed by God to be "good," which suggests a positive view of the material world. If all things created are good, then God has equal concern and delight in both human life and nonhuman life. This dual concern is found in texts such as Psalms 104 and 148. Human life, nonhuman life, and even the landscape itself form a single community in Creation. The speeches of God to Job out of the whirlwind (Job 38–41) suggest the more radical idea that humans are not the primary objects of God's concern.

Secondly, Creation has an order, (in Hebrew: *seder b'reshit*.) This order is, according to classical texts such as Psalm 148, hierarchically structured with its focus toward God. But it is also horizontally structured to remind us of the interdependence of all life. Embedded in both ethical and ritual laws in the Torah is the warning against the disruption of this order (compare Genesis 4, Leviticus 18:27–30).

Thirdly, human beings have a special place and role in the order of Creation. Of all Creation, only human beings have the power to disrupt Creation. This power, which gives them a kind of control over Creation, comes from special characteristics that no other creature possesses (compare Psalm 8). This idea is expressed in the concept that humans were created in the image of God (in Hebrew: *tzelem Elohim*). In its original sense, *tzelem Elohim* means that humans were put on the Earth to act as God's agents and to actualize God's presence in Creation. But the concept also has ethical implications, which means that human beings have certain intrinsic dignities such as infinite value, equality and uniqueness, and that human beings possess God-like capacities such as power, consciousness, relationship, will, freedom, and life. Human beings are supposed to exercise their power, consciousness, and free will to be wise stewards of Creation. They should be maintaining the order of Creation even while they are allowed to use it for their own benefit within certain limits established by God (Genesis 2:14). This ethical imperative of responsibility applies to human society as well to the natural world.

These theological concepts give rise to two ethical values in Judaism: humility and moderation. Humility calls upon human beings to recognize their place in the order of Creation. "Why were human beings created last in the order of Creation? . . . So they should not grow proud, for one can say to them, 'the gnat came before you in the Creation!'" (Babylonian Talmud, Sanhedrin 38a). While human beings do have the power to manipulate Creation, that power must be exercised carefully since humanity is dependant upon and interconnected to the rest of Creation. The second century CE Rabbi Simeon bar Yohai said: "Three things are equal in importance: earth, humans and rain." The early fourth century CE Rabbi Levi ben Hiyyata said: "And these three each consist of three letters [in Hebrew] to teach that without Earth, there is no rain and without rain earth cannot endure; while without either, humans cannot exist" (Midrash Genesis Rabbah 13:3). Humility calls humanity to understand that all actions have long-term consequences upon the Earth, that it is necessary to "tread lightly upon the Earth," and not to act out of the arrogance of power.

Moderation is a self-imposed limitation to unnecessary consumption. Moderation is a positive value that can enhance the appreciation of life. "Who is rich? One who is happy with his portion" (Mishnah Avot 4:1). One of the great Jewish texts on moderation is the *Eight Chapters* of Moses Maimonides (1135–1204), an introduction to his commentary to Mishnah Avot. Chapter Four describes the path of moderation between two extremes as the definition of virtue. And while Maimonides was especially concerned with showing how extreme asceticism is not a virtue in itself but only as a means to an end, his basic principle of understanding how destructive extreme behavior can be to the human psyche is quite relevant today in discussions about sustainability and countering the modern culture of consumerism. The Jewish tradition has never exalted poverty and has always seen material welfare as a blessing and a reward from God, but it also saw the unlimited acquisition of wealth as a danger to true spiritual and ethical values. For example, the medieval French rabbinical authority Rashi (1040–1105), in his commentary to Numbers 32:16, speaks disapprovingly of how the tribes of Gad and Reuben had more concern for their cattle and wealth than for their children. During the Middle Ages, many Jewish communities had sumptuary laws that included limitations upon extravagance in dress and as well as limitations on the amount of spending at life-cycle celebrations. One is also

not supposed to be excessive in eating and drinking or in the kind of clothes that one wears (Maimonides Mishneh Torah, Laws of Discernment, chapter 5).

It is thus easy to understand how modern Jewish environmentalism embraced the concept of sustainability within traditional theology. But Judaism has always sought to concretize its theology and ethical values within a discrete system of legal actions (in Hebrew: *halakhah*). One particular law has been part of Jewish environmentalism since its start: the mitzvah (meaning "commandment") of *Bal Tashchit* ("Do not destroy"). This law, one of the 613 commandments that Rabbinic Judaism has traditionally found in the Torah, is based on Deuteronomy 20:19–20:

> When in your war against a city you have to besiege it a long time in order to capture it, you must not destroy its trees, wielding the ax against them. You may eat of them, but you must not cut them down. Are trees of the field human to withdraw before you into the besieged city? Only trees that you know do no yield food may be destroyed; you may cut them down for constructing siege works against the city that is waging war on you, until it has been reduced.

This law was expanded in later Jewish legal sources to include the prohibition of the wanton destruction of household goods, clothes, buildings, springs, food, or the wasteful consumption of anything (see Maimonides, Mishneh Torah, Laws of Kings, and Wars 6:8, 10; Hirsch 2002, 279–280). In modern Jewish environmentalism, *Bal Tashchit* is considered the primary call to sustainable living. Thus Jews are obligated to consider carefully their real needs whenever purchasing anything. There is an obligation when having a celebration to consider whether it is necessary to elaborate meals and wasteful decorations. There is also an obligation to consider energy use and the sources from which it comes.

In classic rabbinic sources there is also a strong commitment to the common good. For example:

> Rabbi Shimon Ben Yochai taught: It can be compared to people who were in a boat and one of them took a drill and began to drill under his seat. His fellow passengers said to him: "Why are you doing this?!" He said to them: "What do you care? Am I not drilling under me?!" They replied: "Because you are sinking the boat with us in it!" (Midrash Leviticus Rabbah 4:6)

There is also the Talmudic legal principle of *geirey diley* (Aramaic for "his arrows"). In this principle, it is forbidden for a person to stand in his own property and to shoot arrows randomly while claiming that there was no intent to cause damage (Talmud Bava Batra 22b). Thus people are forbidden to establish polluting workshops in a courtyard where other people are living. This principle can also be applied to sustainability in that we cannot claim that our unsustainable consumption is morally neutral. We know that it is causing harm to other human beings in the resources extracted to create the things we consume and in the waste it produces when we throw it away. "His arrows" creates a principle of responsibility even when there is no intention of harm and even at great distances from the original act of consumption.

Lastly, Jewish environmentalism has tried to create better awareness of sustainability in Jewish liturgy and ritual practice. For example, Jewish liturgy has a large number of blessings for many different occasions: eating, celebrating, and experiencing the wonder of Creation, to name a few. Blessings and other prayers also help to create an understanding of God's ownership of Creation. When a blessing is said, a moment of holiness is created, a sacred pause. Prayer also creates an awareness of the sacred by taking people out of themselves and their artificial environments to truly encounter natural phenomenon. Prayer creates a loss of control, allowing people to "see the world in the mirror of the holy," according to the twentieth-century theologian and philosopher Abraham Joshua Heschel (Tirosh-Samuelson 2002, 409). It is then possible to see the world as an object of divine concern, placing people beyond self and more deeply within Creation. Prayer also engenders a sense of gratitude for what we have and allows people to better value the things of this world.

Another important ritual aspect of Judaism that has been utilized by modern Jewish environmentalism is the Sabbath. By its restrictions of everyday work and activity and by its positive elements of prayer, rest, and celebration, the Sabbath can engender a sense of love and humility before Creation and help to foster a way to live a sustainable life. For one day out of seven, people must limit their use of resources. Traditionally people walk to attend synagogue and drive only when walking is not possible. One does not cook or shop; the day is used for relaxation and spiritual contemplation. As Rabbi Ismar Schorsch (b. 1935) once wrote, "To rest is to acknowledge our limitations. Willful inactivity is a statement of subservience to a power greater than our own" (COEJL 1994, 20).

Thus Judaism holds many traditional theological concepts, values, and actions that the modern Jewish environmental movement has connected with the value of sustainability. More and more Jewish communities and congregations are integrating these ideas into every day life and into the ritual rhythm cycle of the Jewish year and the imperatives of Jewish ethics.

Lawrence TROSTER
GreenFaith

FURTHER READING

Bernstein, Ellen. (Ed.). (1998). *Ecology & the Jewish spirit: Where nature and the sacred meet*. Woodstock, VT: Jewish Lights Publishing.

Bernstein, Ellen. (2005). Shomrei Adamah. Retrieved June 30, 2009, from http://ellenbernstein.org/about_ellen.htm#shomrei_adamah

Benstein, Jeremy. (2006). *The way into Judaism and the environment*. Woodstock, VT: Jewish Lights Publishing.

Coalition on the Environment and Jewish Life (COEJL). (1994). *To till and to tend: A guide to Jewish environmental study and action*. New York: Author.

Coalition on the Environment and Jewish Life (COEJL). (2007). Retrieved June 30, 2009, from http://www.coejl.org/~coejlor/about/history.php

Hirsch, Samson Raphael. (2002). *Horeb: A philosophy of Jewish laws and observances* (Isidore Grunfeld, Trans.) (7th ed.). London: Soncino Press.

Tal, Alon. (2002). *Pollution in a promised land: An environmental history of Israel*. Berkeley: University of California Press.

Tirosh-Samuelson, Hava. (Ed.). (2002). *Judaism and ecology: Created world and revealed word*. Cambridge, MA: Center for the Study of World Religions, Harvard Divinity School, Harvard University Press.

Yaffe, Martin D. (Ed.). (2001). *Judaism and environmental ethics: A reader*. Lanham, MD: Lexington Books.

Justice

Philosophical and religious texts traditionally consider humans, their societies, and their institutions to be the main agents involved in the appropriate relationships that define justice. Sustainability and the environment are often implicitly suggested, rather than clearly articulated, as important contributing factors to justice. Broader accounts of justice require establishing the moral status of nonhuman animals, the environment, and future generations intrinsic to human concerns.

The concept of justice concerns the appropriateness of relationships between parties. For this reason, justice involves primarily questions of fair distribution, but it is also relevant to issues of retribution and correction. The allocation of material goods and opportunities, negotiations of rights and duties, and determinations of crime and punishment all fall under traditional notions of justice. Although human beings, communities, and institutions historically have been considered the main agents of justice, others' accounts extend the reach of justice to include nonhuman animals, the natural environment, and future generations. In religious and theological discourse, God or representations of the divine are also considered sources or instruments of justice.

Philosophical Approaches to Justice

Justice can be understood as a virtue as well as a central concept within utilitarian frameworks (in which the morality of an action is judged by its consequences or usefulness) and deontological frameworks (in which the moral content of an action is judged primarily by rules or laws). A person who displays the virtue of justice possesses characteristics that suggest a life of habits in conformity with some overarching vision of the good. For Plato, who attempts to define justice in *The Republic*, the notion of the good, from which the ideal of justice is extracted, is both related to and independent of the laws of a state. A just person is therefore not necessarily one who only obeys laws, but rather one who is also attuned to a higher, perfected conception of the good. Formulations of the good and of justice, however, can be ambiguous and do not help in determining the good of obeying civil laws relative to justice. Obeying civil laws, even when perceived as unjust, may nonetheless promote peace and stability, both of which may also be considered societal goods. Judging the importance of peace and stability compared to justice, when all three qualities may be understood as components of the good, presents an intractable conundrum for Platonic ideals of justice.

Aristotle describes the virtue of justice with greater contextual specificity than Plato and often with reference to the norms of a particular state. Justice is a characteristic that can be applied to both persons and state laws; justice is also a norm that governs distributive, retributive, and remedial aspects of governance. Like other virtues, justice is described as a kind of mean, that is, a balance between extremes. In contrast to other virtues such as courageousness or generosity, however, there can never be an excessive amount of justice. For the individual, justice is a characteristic habit of a citizen whose thought and behavior exhibit both respect for the law and the recognition that laws are subject to review and improvement. Like a just state, a just person responds to relevant situations by distributing appropriate rewards for merit and punishment for offenses. The difficulty with the Aristotelian view of justice as a virtue lies in the inability to discern fairness in the distribution of reward and punishment. Unless all persons have equal opportunities to obtain merit and avoid offenses—which is not the case in most societies—then rewards distributed on the basis of merit or offense may compound existing inequalities. In other words, until all persons are born into situations of equality or receive compensatory opportunities to achieve merit and avoid offenses, the distribution of reward and punishment by the state may further exacerbate inequities.

Justice from a utilitarian perspective would require the maximization of goodness and minimization of negative consequences. A utilitarian law or policy, for example, may attempt to provide as many benefits to as many persons as possible. Similarly, a state might employ utilitarian approaches to punishment in order to achieve goals of rehabilitation or deterrence. Utilitarian approaches to justice, however, are difficult to defend against the intuitional belief that every person ought to be given equal treatment concerning the distribution of goods and ought only to be punished (and only fairly) if culpable. Also, because the good can be defined in a variety of ways, utilitarian approaches to justice are fraught with problems. The good can be defined as the ability to satisfy one's desires, sensations of pleasure, or happiness. Determining which definition of the good ought to guide laws or policies may require the rejection of other definitions of the good. The process of determining utility becomes more complex as one considers the good of nonrational parties. Questions arise concerning not only the relevance or inclusion of parties determining the good (plants, nonhuman animals, air, water, future generations, etc.), but also, if they are included, their relative value compared to the interests of humans, and definitions of the good according to each of these parties. Finally, because utilitarianism relies on the ability to predict the outcome of an act, the possibility of unintended consequences may prove more harmful than beneficial.

Deontological accounts of justice typically emphasize rules, duties, or rights rather than consequences. Justice is defined primarily in terms of process rather than as end result. Heavily influenced by deontology as characterized by the eighteenth-century philosopher Immanuel Kant, John Rawls (1921–2002) in *A Theory of Justice* (1999, originally published in 1971) defines justice as fairness. Rawls elaborates on Kant's notion of the categorical imperative, which in various formulations argues that just laws are those which would be universally acceptable to rational persons. Rawls argues that if rational persons were to assume the original position cloaked by a "veil of ignorance," that is, unaware of their own biases and those of others, then they would rationally formulate the following two principles of justice. The first principle is that "each person is to have an equal right to the most extensive basic liberty compatible with a similar liberty for others." The second principle is that "social and economic inequalities are to be arranged so that they are both (a) reasonably expected to be to everyone's advantage, and (b) attached to positions and offices open to all" (Rawls 1999, 60). According to the difference principle, inequalities can be just so long as they improve the lives of the least advantaged. The most prominent critiques of *A Theory of Justice* question the assumed moral anthropology necessary for determinations of justice. The original position and the veil of ignorance, for example, require that persons separate political understandings of justice from comprehensive world views, including their religious beliefs. Robert Nozick (1938–2002), an influential thinker of the twentieth century, argues that Rawls's principles violate notions of liberty when rational persons intentionally create inequalities within society. The political philosopher Susan Moller Okin (1946–2004) critiques Rawls's theory (and Western philosophy in general) for its assumption of selfish individual concern as the basis of rational thinking and for its failure to consider the complexities of relationships of care, such as the inequalities found within families, in formulating notions of social justice.

Religious Views of Justice

Religious accounts of justice, particularly within the Abrahamic traditions of Judaism, Christianity, and Islam, vary depending on depictions of the divine and the utilization of religious scripture for legal and administrative purposes. The God of the Hebrew scriptures is described alternatively as jealous or vengeful and as loving. In the Decalogue (Exodus 20:1–17, NRSV), God states, "I the Lord your God am a jealous God, punishing children for the iniquity of parents, to the third and the fourth generation of those who reject me, but showing steadfast love to the thousandth generation of those who love me and keep my commandments." The divine justice meted out by the God described in the Ten Commandments differs qualitatively from social and institutional approaches to justice in large due to the disparity of power between God and humans. Humans owe God their obedience; if they stray from God's commands, God may punish not only those culpable but future generations as well.

God in the New Testament in the person of Jesus is described in sacrificial terms, as loving and merciful, but also as angry, contemplative, and sorrowful. The accounts of Matthew, Mark, Luke, and John describe the character of Jesus through his teaching, healing, and suffering. Although he is capable of performing acts beyond the ability of mere humans, Jesus submits to the punishment of the Roman state in a symbolic display of mercy toward humankind. The problem that the Jesus narrative presents for formulations of justice lies in his glorified submission to a seemingly unjust state.

In the Quran, God is described before each Sura (chapter of the Quran) as "the Compassionate, the Caring." The

Quran, which according to Islamic tradition contains the words of God, describes divine reward and punishment for human behavior, and offers guidance for the administration of mundane legal affairs. Accepted as divine commands, the Quranic instructions for legal and administrative rule display characteristics of justice and mercy. For many modern day Muslims, however, these verses dating to the seventh century CE are no longer applicable. Texts regarding the treatment of slaves and women, for example, are not relevant given the abolition of slavery and the emancipation of women in the modern era. This concern over the status of divine text over time applies also to sections of the Hebrew scriptures and the New Testament.

In each of the three Abrahamic traditions, the existence of a God that allows for gross human injustices presents profound problems of theodicy. The realities of suffering, injustice, and evil contradict the understanding of God as beneficent, omniscient, and omnipotent. When innocent humans (such as young children) and nonhuman forms of life (such as animals and trees) suffer, the task of reconciling God with common understandings of justice and goodness requires either the acceptance of universal guilt and punishment or the surrender of human logic to divine will.

In Buddhism, justice can be understood implicitly within the context of concepts such as the first noble truth of suffering. Suffering caused by injustice would be associated with ignorance or desire, both of which result from the faulty perception of the human condition. Buddhist practice, while not directly addressing acts of justice, emphasizes the performance of specific virtuous deeds and the avoidance of activities such as killing, stealing, and improper sexual conduct. Monastic training in ethics requires correct action, speech, and livelihood, all of which suggest justice in action and require proper perception and wisdom.

The notion of justice within Hindu practice is best determined by context. The diversity of the tradition, in part a result of the role of castes, the importance of numerous texts, narratives, and the panoply of gods and goddesses, defies any fixed definition of justice. Although the notion of *ahimsa*, or noninjury, is often associated with justice within Hinduism, exceptions are granted for members of the warrior caste, for the performance of Vedic rituals involving animal sacrifice, and for any number of reasons. The code of practice referred to as *dharma*, based on the Vedas or on culturally specific traditions, stresses the accumulation of merit, which, again, depends largely on one's situation. Consistent within the tradition, however, is the necessity understanding correctly one's place within the larger cosmos. Hence, acting justly depends on fulfilling one's responsibilities appropriate to one's caste, sex, and age, for example.

Justice and Sustainability

Philosophical and religious texts traditionally assume human beings, societies, and institutions as the primary agents of justice. Sustainability and the environment are, however, often implicitly suggested, rather than clearly articulated, as important contributing factors to justice. Fuller accounts of justice require establishing the moral status of nonhuman animals, the environment, and future generations as intrinsic to anthropocentric concerns.

Notions of the ethical life, human societies, and the future existence of communities are implied in philosophical and religious sources. Discussions concerning the education of younger generations, such as those found in Plato's *Republic* and Aristotle's *Nicomachean Ethics*, indicate that the continued existence of societies rests on the education of future generations for both knowledge and training in virtues, including justice. In religious texts, such as the creation stories found in Genesis, the Earth, plant life, animals, and humans are folded into narrative accounts that establish God as creator and as the source of moral knowledge. The creation accounts in Genesis 1 and 2 imply both directly and indirectly the appropriate relationship among humans (including between the sexes), animals, and plants. Genesis 1 states that God allows humankind to "have dominion over" animals and that humans ought to "fill the Earth and subdue it." The creation account in Genesis 2 sets a different template for appropriate relationships among men, women, and the environment. In this account, God creates man first and then woman as "a helper." As a result of eating from the tree in the middle of the Garden of Eden, God curses the serpent, the woman, and the man such that they and their offspring will suffer and toil the earth into perpetuity. Women will suffer pain in childbirth; men will have to labor in the fields to obtain food to eat; in death, humans will return to the earth from which they were made.

The anthropocentric quality of philosophical texts and Judeo-Christian creation accounts validates hierarchical relationships but also provides resources for responsible stewardship. In philosophical accounts of justice from Plato to Rawls, rational persons are the primary agents in determining, dispensing, and demanding justice. This standard often excluded nonhuman animals and the environment, as well as women, slaves, and other marginalized groups, who were until the modern era deemed irrational or otherwise expendable members of society. Accounts of environmental justice movements demonstrate the connection between social injustice and environmental degradation. Warren County, North Carolina, for example, became a focal point for environmental justice movements when the state chose it as the site for a toxic landfill. A series of highly publicized, but ultimately unsuccessful, protests resulted from the decision to burden a poor, largely African American community with wastes that wealthier, white counties refused. Reaffirming the connection between marginalized status and environmental harm, the 1984 Cerrell Report, issued by a public relations firm for the state of California, identified poor, uneducated Catholic communities as ideal for toxic waste sites because of their presumed inability to sponsor resistance movements. Noting how environmental degradation impacts the quality of women's lives directly, the 2004 recipient of the Nobel Peace Prize, Wangari Maathai, initiated the Green Belt Movement to empower women to plant trees in Kenya.

The expansion of frameworks of justice also extends to nonhuman animals and the environment. The animal rights activist Peter Singer has argued from a utilitarian perspective that the capacity to feel pain ought to serve as the criteria for moral status. Thus animals that have nervous systems fall under considerations of justice and ought not to be treated in a way that would cause them pain. This perspective has practical implications in that it demands increased consideration for the quality of life for nonhuman animals relative to human pleasure (such as the consumption of meat, destruction of animal habitats for construction, etc.). Singer's utilitarianism, however, would not accord any moral status for severely mentally incapacitated persons or other forms of life in the natural world that have no ability to feel pain.

Formulations of justice may extend moral status to nonliving aspects of the environment, including future generations. Nonliving objects generally have been understood as extensions of human owners, and not as having moral worth in and of themselves. Children, while understood as objects in the sense that they belong to parents, are also of interest to institutions of justice (such as state governments) because of their expected participation in society as adults. Future generations, referring to age groups who are not yet born, but anticipated, tend to have lesser or no standing in discussions of justice.

If sustainability is to be a factor in justice, then future generations and nonliving entities (such as water, air, and minerals) need to be recognized as inseparable from traditional anthropocentric interests. Philosophical approaches that articulate such syncretic and diachronic conditions of justice are more likely to consider sustainability as an indispensable quality of justice. Religious scriptures contain sources that encourage the stewardship of the Earth as a whole, but they require reinterpretation beyond traditional concerns of justice. The evolution of the concept of justice thus requires the broadening of categories beyond the traditional ones of distribution, retribution, and correction.

Irene OH
George Washington University

FURTHER READING

Bullard, Robert. (2000). *Dumping in Dixie: Race, class, and environmental quality.* Boulder, CO: Westview Press.

Gottlieb, Roger. (Ed.). (1995). *This sacred Earth: Religion, nature, and environment.* New York: Routledge.

Nozick, Robert. (1974). *Anarchy, state, and utopia.* New York: Basic Books.

Okin, Susan Moller. (1991). *Justice, gender, and the family.* New York: Basic Books.

Rawls, John. (1999). *A theory of justice.* Cambridge, MA: Harvard University Press. (Original published in 1971)

Ruether, Rosemary R. (1996). *Third world women on ecology, feminism, and religion.* Maryknoll, NY: Orbis Books.

Singer, Peter. (2002). *Animal liberation.* New York: HarperCollins.

Language

Although some earlier cultures equated spoken language with the superiority of humans over the nonhuman world, more recent fields of study—including ecolinguistics, ecosemiotics, and ecocriticism—explore the relationships between human language and the natural world.

The English word *language* is derived from the Old French for "tongue," *langue*, which by metonymic association came to refer initially to speech and subsequently, by extension, to communication more generally. Communication in this wider sense is intrinsic to all life, and verbal language in particular profoundly informs human self-understandings, social relations, economic activity, and treatment of nonhuman others and the environment. The importance of language with respect to sustainability is currently being addressed within three main areas of inquiry: how human verbal language is related to other forms of communication within the biophysical world at large; how the diversity of human languages is connected with biological diversity; and how particular usages of language inform the assumptions, attitudes, and values undergirding our relationship with others—human and nonhuman—and with our shared environment.

Historical Background

Various philosophies of language have arisen within different cultures at different times, some emphasizing continuities between human and nonhuman forms of communication and acknowledging the communicative agency of plants and animals or earth and sky, while others have stressed the singularity and superiority of human speech. In many cultures, the power of speech is held to be of divine origin and invested with mystical or magical powers. In the biblical Creation narrative, for example, the world is said

to have been called into being by a divine speech act, while the privilege of naming the other creatures was accorded exclusively to the first man, Adam, by Yahweh. Medieval Europeans perceived the physical world to be pervaded by signs, but, at least as far as the church was concerned, the Book of Nature, one of two texts that early Christian doctrine considered to be written God, could only be decoded with reference to the biblical revelation in the Book of Books (i.e., the Bible, the other text attributed to God). While animist cultures, such as that of indigenous Australians, assume that all things are capable of communicating in their own right, the premodern Christian view tends to construe nonhuman entities primarily as vehicles for messages hailing from a divine, or potentially demonic, source. From the seventeenth century, with the rise of rationalism and humanism, communicative agency was increasingly restricted to humans, whose command of verbal language was presumed to be a function of the unique mental capacities that raised us above the mute realm of merely material existence. This view was challenged by European writers and philosophers of the Romantic era (c. 1770–1830), such as the German philosopher F. W. J. Schelling (1775–1854), who posited that human language had emerged from, and remained indebted to, the self-organizing, self-transforming, and self-expressive capacity inherent in nature as a whole: Nature, for the Romantics, was the first poet (Rigby 2004, 38–45, 102–103).

It was not until the twentieth century that the systematic study of communication as an inherent feature of all living systems began to be undertaken. Building upon the pioneering work in evolutionary biology and ecology of Jakob von Uexküll (1864–1944) and in semiotics (the study of signs as a function of communication) of Charles Sanders Peirce (1839–1914), current research into what has become known as *biosemiotics* (Sebeok and Umiker-Sebeok 1991) demonstrates definitively the continuity between human verbal language and other forms of communication (chemical, genetic, kinetic, facial, tonal, etc.), in which we also participate, albeit largely unconsciously. At the same time, biosemiotics shows how increasing levels of creative freedom in both the production and interpretation of signs have accrued to humans especially, but not exclusively, in the course of evolution. Some of the major implications of biosemiotics with regard to human flourishing, social justice, and environmental sustainability are explored in Wendy Wheeler's *The Whole Creature: Complexity, Biosemiotics, and the Evolution of Culture* (2006).

Linguistics and Ecology

The German philosopher J. G. Herder (1744–1803) was the first to postulate the connection between linguistic and environmental diversity; he argued that different peoples' national languages and oral literatures were informed by the physical characteristics of the natural environments that they had inhabited, and thereby also altered, over time (Rigby 2004, 72–75). More recently, some linguists, such as Einar Haugen (1906–1994), have pointed to the importance of protecting minority languages and regional dialects as a crucial source of local ecological knowledge. This has led to development of another new field of research known as *ecolinguistics*. Much work in this area concerns the negative consequences of colonization, whereby the destruction of indigenous economies and cultures leading to the loss of local languages is coordinate with the disruption of ecosystems and consequent disappearance of species.

A further area of ecolinguistic research investigates the ways in which particular usages of language, or discourses, construct the assumptions, attitudes, and values that we bring to our interactions with others, human and nonhuman, and the environment. For example, the discourse of "resource management" reinforces two questionable assumptions regarding human relations with the nonhuman world: the latter only has meaning insofar as it is of use to humans, and it is or should be at our command. While this is a modern, secular discourse, it could be argued that it is heir to the earlier Christian view of man as appointed by God to "subdue" the Earth (Genesis 1:28, NRSV) and "have dominion" over all other creatures (Genesis 1:26, NRSV).

Ecolinguistic discourse analysis overlaps with two further fields of research into language and sustainability: *ecosemiotics* and *ecocriticism*. Ecosemiotics, drawing in part on the semiological theory of the Swiss linguist Ferdinand de Saussure (1857–1913), differs from biosemiotics in focusing specifically on human communication with and about the natural world. Similarly, ecocriticism, which emerged initially in the area of literary studies, is concerned with human representations of nature, place, animals, and the environment in a wide range of texts and media, from Shakespeare to science fiction, romantic poetry to wildlife documentaries, the Bible to *Bambi* (Garrard 2004). Literary ecocritics approach the subject from various angles: Lawrence Buell (1995), for example, has sought to demonstrate the potential of certain kinds of writing to reorient our concern toward the more-than-human world. Others such as Leonard Skigaj (1999) have drawn on the phenomenology of the French philosopher Maurice Merleau-Ponty (1908–1961) or, like Jonathan Bate (2000), the German philosopher Martin Heidegger (1889–1976) to articulate a theory of *ecopoetics*. The deconstructive philosophy of Jacques Derrida (1930–2004) has also begun to be incorporated into the ecocritical thinking of writers such as Timothy Morton (2007).

The kinds of language that we use to communicate with and about others, human and otherwise, and our shared environment clearly holds great significance with regard to sustainability. Moreover, our ability to become better listeners to what the more-than-human world has to tell us might well prove pivotal to the future of life on this planet.

Kate RIGBY
Monash University

FURTHER READING

Bate, Jonathan. (2000). *The song of the Earth*. Cambridge, MA: Harvard University Press.

Buell, Lawrence. (1995). *The environmental imagination: Thoreau, nature writing, and the formation of American culture*. Cambridge, MA: Harvard University Press.

Fill, Alwin; & Mühlhäusler, Peter. (2001). *The ecolinguistics reader*. London: Continuum.

Garrard, Greg. (2004). *Ecocriticism*. London: Routledge.

Hoffmeyer, Jesper. (2008). *Biosemiotics: An investigation into the signs of life and the life of signs*. Chicago: Scranton University Press, distributed by University of Chicago Press.

Kull, Kalevi. (1998). Semiotic ecology: Different natures in the semiosphere. *Sign Systems Studies, 26,* 344–371. Retrieved May 15, 2009, from http://www.zbi.ee/~kalevi/ecosem.htm

Morton, Timothy. (2006). *Ecology without nature: Rethinking environmental aesthetics*. Cambridge, MA: Harvard University Press.

Rigby, Catherine. (2004). *Topographies of the sacred: The poetics of place in European romanticism*. Charlottesville: University of Virginia Press.

Sebeok, Thomas. A. & Umiker-Sebeok, Jean. (Eds.). (1991). *Biosemiotics: The semiotic web*. The Hague: The Netherlands: Mouton de Gruyter.

Skigaj, Leonard. (1999). *Sustainable poetry: Four American ecopoets*. Lexington: University Press of Kentucky.

Wheeler, Wendy. (2006). *The whole creature: Complexity, biosemiotics and the evolution of culture*. London: Lawrence & Wishart.

Law

Many nations have enacted and strengthened regulations to protect the environment since the 1960s, and numerous international environmental treaties have also been adopted. The realities of economics are often part of these laws; many are subject to cost-benefit analysis and enforced with financial programs (such as cap and trade) and taxes.

While sustainability has been criticized as vague or ambiguous, it has nevertheless become "an established principle of international law" and is on the verge of "general acceptance as a norm of customary international law" (Gillroy 2006, 13). The concept of sustainability is also widely invoked as a touchstone of environmental laws adopted by individual nations.

Interpretations of Sustainability Affecting Law and Policy

The classic articulation of sustainable development appears in the 1987 Report of the World Commission on Environment and Development (commonly referred to as the Brundtland Report): "meeting the needs of the present without compromising the ability of future generations to meet their own needs." In June 1992, international negotiations through the United Nations Environment Programme (UNEP) resulted in the Rio Declaration and elaborated on this definition. The Rio Declaration recognized the "integral and interdependent nature of the Earth, our home" and articulated twenty-seven principles to advance economic development, environmental protection, and respect for human rights, all under the rubric of sustainable development. At the core of sustainability is the principle of intergenerational equity, a duty to preserve or enhance resources that may be necessary for future

generations of humans while providing adequately for those living in the present. Also of central importance is the principle of intragenerational equity, a duty to ensure justice among communities and nations in the present generation. The Rio Declaration interpreted this duty to include special solicitude for the economic needs and environmental concerns of developing nations (UNEP 1992, Principle 6) and recognition of the environmental and cultural claims of indigenous peoples (Principle 22). Ecocentrists, who believe species or ecosystems have value in their own right, have also argued for recognition of interspecies equity as a principle of sustainability, but that principle has found limited acceptance in public debate and legislation (Bosselman 2006). Other Rio Declaration principles of special relevance to environmental law include: citizen participation, including "access to judicial and administrative proceedings" (Principle 10); the "precautionary approach" (Principle 15); the use of economic instruments in environmental protection (Principle 16); and the "polluter-pays" principle (Principle 16).

There remain basic disagreements about the obligations associated with sustainability as affecting environmental law and policy (Revesz and Livermore 2008). The international-law scholar Edith Brown Weiss argues that the present generation has a duty to pass along the natural (and cultural) environment in as good condition as we found it (Weiss 1989). We also have a duty to preserve the diversity of the resource base. Renewable resources—plants, animals, soil, water and air—should be used sustainably; nonrenewable resources should be conserved by using them more efficiently and, where they are depleted or destroyed, by providing substitutes for them for use by future generations.

The economist Robert Solow argues for a less restrictive interpretation: our obligation is only "to conduct ourselves so that we leave to the future the option or the capacity to be as well off as we are" (2000, 132). This obligation is measured in terms "generalized capacity to create well-being, not any particular thing or any particular natural resource" (Solow 2000, 133). Solow acknowledges that we might choose to preserve certain resources—for example, a species or a landscape—because of their intrinsic value to us, but generally we are free to consume natural resources as long as we replace them with resources of equal or greater value, such as manufacturing capacity or technological knowledge. Solow endorses environmental protection as one way to advance this notion of sustainability, but not at the expense of other forms of investment that would offer greater capacity for future well-being. Contemporary environmental law embodies elements of both these constructions of sustainability.

Modern Environmental and Natural Resource Law

From the late 1960s and on into the twenty-first century, the United States and other nations have enacted or strengthened regulatory laws to assess the environmental impacts of government decisions, control air and water pollution, address sites contaminated by toxic waste, and manage introduction of toxic substances and materials into the environment from pesticides and other products. During this same period, many nations also enacted or strengthened laws to protect natural resources such as species, wetlands, forests, and fisheries. Important international treaties addressing transnational or global environmental issues were concluded during the same period, including the Montreal Protocol (depletion of the ozone layer), the Basel Convention (transboundary movement of hazardous waste), the Ramsar Convention (wetlands and waterfowl), CITES (Convention on International Trade in Endangered Species of Wild Fauna and Flora), the Biodiversity Convention (biodiversity conservation and sustainable use), and UNCLOS (United Nations Convention on the Law of the Sea). In the last two decades, the international community has taken initial steps to deal with global climate change with the U.N. Framework Convention on Climate Change and the Kyoto Protocol, which entered into force in 2005 and includes the first binding commitments for reduction of greenhouse gas emissions by developed nations.

Much of the national and international environmental law of the last four decades embodies the polluter-pays principle, the idea, as the Rio Declaration states, that "the polluter should, in principle, bear the cost of pollution" (UNEP 1992, Principle 16).

Most environmental laws impose restrictions on emissions, discharges, or other environmental intrusions by actors such as corporations, government entities, or individuals, which must shoulder the cost of meeting those restrictions. Some impose liability for damages on agents of environmental harm; an example is the United States' Comprehensive Environmental Response, Compensation, and Liability Act, which makes parties liable for the costs of cleaning up environmental contamination attributable to them. Pollution taxes are another form of polluter-pays provision to the extent that the tax reflects the costs of pollution imposed on others. These polluter-pays provisions advance the Rio principles by forcing firms and individuals to internalize the costs of environmental damage. But some governmental programs use subsidies to advance environmental goals, effectively paying the polluter not to pollute. An example is provisions of the U.S. Farm Bill that pay farmers to reduce polluted runoff into lakes and rivers.

In the first wave of environmental law in the 1960s and 1970s, the favored approach was prescriptive: regulators specified a control technology or assigned a permissible level of pollution for each source. The level of pollution permitted might be based on the expected performance of an available control technology or on a desired environmental outcome, such as avoiding harm to fish habitat. This approach is often characterized as "command and control," because it includes both a prescriptive "command" to each source and the threat of civil or criminal enforcement ("control") if the command is not met. In part because of the limited compliance options it offers sources, commentators have criticized command-and-control regulation as inefficient and have advanced market-based alternatives such as "cap and trade" or pollution taxes (Ackerman and Stewart 1985).

Cap and trade has recently gained prominence in environmental law as an alternative approach to command and control and appears to be emerging as the instrument of choice to address global climate change. Under cap-and-trade programs, lawmakers set a cap on permissible emissions for a region or nation (or the globe in the case of climate change). Emission allowances are issued in the amount of the cap and may be freely traded among regulated sources; all sources must hold allowances at least equal to their emissions. Emitters for whom emissions reductions are relatively cheap can be expected to undertake reductions rather than buy allowances, and emitters for whom the reverse is true can be expected to buy allowances rather than make reductions. The predicted result is that the trading of allowances will produce the most cost-effective allocation of reductions consistent with achieving the desired emission reduction goal. The Rio Declaration endorses the use of economic instruments of this sort, although some commentators have criticized cap and trade as undermining the polluter-pays principle by allowing polluters to purchase allowances (sometimes pejoratively referred to as "licenses to pollute") to meet their obligations (Kelman 1981b).

In the United States, the first national scale application of environmental cap and trade was the regime for reduction of sulfur dioxide emissions from power plants under the 1990 Clean Air Act Amendments; it is widely considered to have been successful in substantially reducing sulfur dioxide emissions at much lower cost than initially projected. The U.S. Environmental Protection Agency (EPA) has extended the cap-and-trade approach to other air pollutants, such as nitrogen oxide and fine particulate matter, as well as to water discharges. Cap and trade is emerging as the instrument of choice to address global climate change both at the national and international level, although the alternative of emission taxes continues to have advocates. The Kyoto Protocol allows trading of greenhouse gas emissions allowances among the developed nations that are parties to the agreement (Article 17) and also provides for the creation of marketable emissions allowances by developing nations that are not parties (Article 12). The European Union Emissions Trading Scheme (EU ETS), established under the Kyoto Protocol, is the world's largest cap-and-trade system (Stavins 2007). Domestic legislation on climate change in the United States also appears likely to adopt a cap-and-trade approach.

There is vigorous dispute over the role of cost-benefit analysis in setting environmental law goals. Economists such as Solow argue that the policy touchstone should be welfare maximization with no special preference for the preservation of existing natural resources or levels of environmental quality. Resources are presumed to be fungible (Solow 1993). In making policy choices, the costs and benefits of options for government regulation or other protective measures are quantified and monetized to the extent possible, and this analysis is used to determine an optimal level of environmental protection where the marginal benefits of protection equal or exceed the marginal costs. Although few U.S. environmental laws expressly base their regulatory goals on cost-benefit justification, a long-standing executive order requires that all major regulatory actions by federal agencies be accompanied by cost-benefit analyses reviewable by the Office of Management and Budget (OMB 2007). The European Union, according to Article 174(3) of the European Community Treaty, also requires consideration of benefits and costs in adopting

new regulations, although it has placed less institutional emphasis on such analyses

There are numerous criticisms of cost-benefit analysis as a method for setting environmental and other public law goals, including the argument that placing prices on nonmarket goods, such as a human life or a wilderness, is immoral commodification. Critics also argue that features of cost-benefit analysis as it has been practiced in the United States result in systematic under-regulation. But in their book *Retaking Rationality* Richard Revesz and Michael Livermore (2008) contend that by correcting eight fallacies in current practice, the cost-benefit approach can provide a neutral way of systematically assessing alternative environmental goals.

Another approach to setting environmental goals is the precautionary principle, recognized by the international community in the Rio Declaration and also by Europe in the European Community Treaty. It is far less prominent in U.S. policy deliberations. The Rio Declaration states a version of the principle: in the face of potentially serious or irreversible environmental harms, "lack of full scientific certainty shall not be used as a reason for postponing cost-effective measures to prevent environmental degradation" (UNEP 1992, Principle 15). Although the precautionary principle is not exclusive of other principles, such as consideration of costs and benefits, it is generally understood to give more weight to avoiding environmental risks than cost-benefit analysis (Fogel 2003). A recent comparative study of U.S. and European environmental regulations, however, indicates that European regulations (presumably more influenced by the precautionary principle) and U.S. regulations do not differ significantly in their stringency and show signs of convergence over time (Wiener 2003).

Citizen participation is a procedural principle often associated with sustainable practice. The Rio Declaration defines it to include access to information held by public authorities and also "access to judicial and administrative proceedings, including redress and remedy" (UNEP 1992, Principle 10). The 1996 United Nations Convention to Combat Desertification was the first global environmental legal instrument to require that decisions be made with the participation of those affected. (Holtz 1996, Article 3). The transnational North American Agreement on Environmental Cooperation allows citizens to file submissions claiming that a party nation is failing to enforce its environmental law (NAAEC 1993, Article 14). In the United States, major environmental laws authorize "any person" to pursue a judicial action against the government for failing to carry out its mandates under the laws or against others for violating restrictions imposed by the laws.

Jonathan Z. CANNON
University of Virginia School of Law

FURTHER READING

Ackerman, Bruce A., & Stewart, Richard B. (1985, May). Reforming environmental law. *Stanford Law Review, 37*(5), 1333–1365.

Ackerman, Frank, & Heinzerling, Lisa. (2004). *Priceless: On knowing the price of everything and the value of nothing.* New York: The New Press.

Bosselman, Klaus. (2006). Ecological justice and law. In Benjamin J. Richardson & Stepan Wood (Eds.), *Environmental law for sustainability* (pp. 129–164). Oxford, U.K.: Hart Publishing.

Consolidated Version of the Treaty Establishing the European Community. (2006). *Official Journal of the European Union.* (C321E) 37. Retrieved August 6, 2009 from http://eur-lex.europa.eu/LexUriServ/LexUriServ.do?uri=OJ:C:2006:321E:0001:0331:EN:PDF

Gillroy, John Martin. (2006). Adjudication norms, dispute settlement regimes and international tribunals: The status of environmental sustainability in international jurisprudence. *Stanford Journal of International Law, 42*(1), 1–52.

Holtz, Uwe. (1996). *United Nations Convention to Combat Desertification (UNCCD) and its political dimension.* Retrieved September 24, 2008, from http://www.unccd.int/parliament/data/bginfo/PDUNCCD(eng).pdf

Kelman, Steven. (1981a, January-February). Cost-benefit analysis: An ethical critique. *Journal on Government and Society Regulation, 5*, 33–40.

Kelman, Steven. (1981b). *What price incentives?: Economists and the environment.* Boston: Auburn House.

Kyoto Protocol to the United Nations Framework Convention on Climate Change. (1998). Retrieved September 24, 2008, from http://unfccc.int/kyoto_protocol/items/2830.php

North American Agreement on Environmental Cooperation (NAAEC). (1993). Retrieved April 20, 2009, from http://www.cec.org/pubs_info_resources/law_treat_agree/naaec/index.cfm?varlan=english

Office of Management and Budget (OMB). (2007, January 18). Executive Order 12866 of September 30, 1993, as amended by E.O. 13258 of February 26, 2002 and E.O. 13422 of January 18, 2007: Regulatory planning and review. Retrieved September 24, 2008, from http://64.233.169.104/search?q=cache:XPW6yuHjeocJ:www.whitehouse.gov/omb/inforeg/eo12866/eo12866_amended_01-

Report of the World Commission on Environment and Development. (1987, December 11). Retrieved September 24, 2008, from http://www.un.org/documents/ga/res/42/ares42-187.htm

Revesz, Richard L., & Livermore, Michael. (2008). *Retaking rationality: How cost-benefit can better protect the environment and our health.* New York: Oxford University Press.

Richardson, Benjamin J., & Wood, Stepan. (2006). Environmental law for sustainability. In Benjamin J. Richardson & Stepan Wood (Eds.), *Environmental law for sustainability* (pp. 1–18). Oxford, U.K.: Hart Publishing.

Solow, Robert M. (2000). Sustainability: An economist's perspective. In Robert N. Stavins (Ed.), *Economics of the environment: Selected readings* (4th ed., pp.131–138). New York: Norton.

Stavins, Robert. (2007, October). *A U.S. cap-and-trade system to address climate change* (Discussion paper 2007-13). Washington, DC: The Brookings Institution. Retrieved September 24, 2008, from http://belfercenter.ksg.harvard.edu/files/rwp_07_052_stavins.pdf

United Nations Environment Programme (UNEP). (1992). *Rio declaration on environment and development.* Retrieved September 24, 2008, from http://www.unep.org/Documents.Multilingual/Default.asp?DocumentID=78&ArticleID=1163

Weiss, Edith Brown. (1989). *In fairness to future generations: International law, common patrimony, and intergenerational equity.* Ardsley, NY: Transnational Publishers.

Wiener, Jonathan B. (2003). Whose precaution after all? A comment on the comparison and evolution of risk regulatory systems. *Duke Journal of Comparative and International Law, 13*, 207–262. Retrieved April 20, 2009, from http://www.nicholas.duke.edu/solutions/documents/whose_precaution_after_all.pdf

> Though barely out of its infancy, the science of conservation biology is taking its first steps toward a comprehension of biodiversity. It is able to identify species that are indicators or keystones for an entire ecosystem. . . . It can offer a crude measure for the overall health of the earth. For when the natural variety of species in a habitat declines, it is highly likely that the associated condition of the land, air, water, and food chain in that location is also declining. The necessity of a healthy environment, therefore, is helplessly intertwined with the importance of natural species diversity. Only life possesses both the ability and the liability to reflect fundamental environmental change. This is why biodiversity law will inevitably become the central tenet of environmental law.
>
> WILLIAM J. SNAPE
>
> *Source*: William J. Snape. (Ed.). (1996). *Biodiversity and the Law*, p. xxi. Washington, DC: Island Press.

Liberationist Thought

Liberationist thought, developed by many theologians and philosophers since the 1960s, seeks liberation for the poor and oppressed. Several religious traditions— including Christianity and Buddhism—see a correlation between the oppression of both people and animals and the destruction of the natural world: in their view, environmental injustice cannot be separated from other types of discrimination.

Liberationist thought describes a range of religious and philosophical positions from all over the world whose goal is liberation from oppression. Three kinds of liberationist thought—Christian liberation theologies, Buddhist liberation movements, and animal liberation—each identify a lack of environmental and economic sustainability as a source of oppression.

Christian liberation theology emerged in Latin American in the late 1960s when theologians realized that European theology did not address the conditions and needs of the vast majority of Latin American people who are poor. In his groundbreaking work, *A Theology of Liberation*, the Peruvian theologian Gustavo Gutierrez argued that the Christian Gospel demands that the Church concentrate its efforts on liberating people from poverty and oppression. A revolutionary feature of liberation theology is that it employs analysis from other disciplines, including economics, political science, and sociology, to make sense of social reality from the vantage point of the marginalized. Liberation theologians emphasize God's "preferential option for the poor" (a tenet of Catholic social teaching that calls on people to prioritize the needs of the poor and marginalized), pointing out that the Christian Gospels and the Hebrew Bible depict God showing special concern for them. Since the 1990s Brazilian liberation theologians have argued that poverty is also an environmental

issue: Leonardo Boff wants to expand the option for the poor to include an option for the most threatened and vulnerable of all species to show how God is committed to the survival of all creatures, while Ivone Gebara connects "the oppression of the poor with the broader issue of the destruction of earth-systems" (Gebara 1999, 8). The liberationist paradigm has been adopted by theologians in a number of different contexts, and a global family of distinct yet related liberation theologies has grown up to include black theology, feminist theology, womanist (African American feminist) theology, and theologies from the global South (or the developing countries of the third world) that identify as liberationist.

Feminist theologians were among the earliest liberation theologians to reflect on the importance of sustainability to liberation. In *New Woman New Earth* (1975), Rosemary Radford Ruether argues that there is a relationship between the oppression of women and the destruction of the natural world. Women's liberation is necessarily connected, therefore, to living in a sustainable society. More recently, the womanist Karen Baker-Fletcher appeals to principles of sustainability when she asserts the interrelatedness of all our lives. She insists that environmental injustice cannot be separated from socioeconomic and racial discrimination, which can result in environmental racism. Coined in the 1980s, the term *environmental racism* describes the fact that poor people, particularly people of color, live in areas that are disproportionately affected by pollution, resource depletion, and waste disposal. For example, the rate of asthma among school-age children in a twenty-four-block area of Harlem is nearly 26 percent, more than six times the U.S. national average of 4 percent (Pérez-Peña 2003). While the causes of asthma are not completely known, doctors have found that environmental factors, such as pollution and fumes from diesel trucks, can trigger attacks. Baker-Fletcher argues that environmental racism can be challenged by a sustainable vision that recognizes the sacredness of life and God's presence in creation.

Buddhist liberation movements share with Christian liberation theology a commitment to liberate people from conditions of social and economic oppression. One example is the Sarvodaya Shramadana movement in Sri Lanka. Begun by A.T. Ariyaratne in the late 1950s, the movement combines two ideas—Sarvodaya, a term coined by Mohandas Gandhi to mean "the well-being of all," and Shramadana, which means "the gift of sharing one's time and labor." In order to respond to poverty in Sri Lankan villages, Ariyaratne realized that compassionate thought, a cornerstone of Buddhism, was not enough to liberate people from oppression. Ariyaratne began community projects that mobilized people toward charitable action. Projects begin with the needs of a particular community, whether it is for clean water, waste management, or new public buildings. Sarvodaya Shramadana projects emphasize the importance of meeting the economic and social needs of the present, while ensuring that future generations will have sufficient resources.

A third kind of liberationist thought is the philosophical position in favor of animal liberation. The Australian philosopher Peter Singer, its best-known proponent, argues that people who are concerned with the liberation of socially and economically marginalized human beings should also be concerned with the liberation of animals. Since human animals and nonhuman animals share the capacity for suffering, there is no morally relevant distinction between the groups to justify the mistreatment of animals. Singer argues that we need to think about practices that inflict suffering, particularly in food production and medical research, from the point of view of those who suffer. In this way Singer shares with other liberationist thinkers an emphasis on transforming practices through solidarity with others, including nonhuman animals. The most straightforward way to demonstrate such solidarity, argues Singer, is to adopt a vegetarian or vegan diet. Coincidentally, a vegetarian diet promotes sustainability because plant foods yield on average ten times as much protein per acre as meat does.

Sarah AZARANSKY
University of San Diego

FURTHER READING

Baker-Fletcher, Karen. (1999). *Sisters of dust, sisters of spirit: Womanist wordings on God and creation.* Minneapolis, MN: Fortress Press.

Boff, Leonardo. (1995). *Ecology and liberation: A new paradigm* (John Cumming, Trans.). Maryknoll, NY: Orbis Books. (Original work published 1993)

Gebara, Ivone. (1999). *Longing for running water: Ecofeminism and liberation* (David Molineaux, Trans.). Minneapolis, MN: Fortress Press.

Gutierrez, Gustavo. (1973). *A theology of liberation: History, politics, and salvation* (Caridad Inda & John Eagleson, Trans.). Maryknoll, NY: Orbis Books.

Pérez-Peña, Richard. (2003, April 19). Study finds asthma in 25% of children in Central Harlem. *The New York Times.* Retrieved May 28, 2009, from, http://www.nytimes.com/2003/04/19/nyregion/19ASTH.html

Queen, Christopher S., & King, Sallie B. (Eds.). (1996). *Engaged Buddhism: Buddhist liberation movements in Asia.* Albany: State University of New York Press.

Radford Ruether, Rosemary. (1975). *New woman new Earth: Sexist ideologies and human liberation.* New York: Seabury Press.

Singer, Peter. (1975). *Animal liberation: A new ethics for our treatment of animals.* New York: Random House.

Libertarianism

Libertarianism is characterized by the absolute priority of the individual's sovereignty, liberty, and inviolable rights. A comprehensive libertarian perspective on sustainability has yet to be developed. Libertarians are more likely to support a view of the sustainable society the less it infringes on the rights of others.

Libertarianism refers to a group of political theories or ideologies characterized by the absolute priority of the individual's sovereignty, liberty, and inviolable rights. Left libertarianism combines this with a commitment to economic equality; mainstream libertarianism rejects all intrusion on economic liberty.

Modern mainstream libertarianism is an offspring of liberalism. Its most famous representatives are Murray Rothbard (1926–1995) and Robert Nozick (1938–2002). Nozick, who deeply influenced political philosophy in general, took his inspiration from the classical liberalism of the British philosopher John Locke (1632–1704). For most mainstream libertarians, the absolute priority of individual liberty from external obstructions (negative liberty) is implied by the sovereignty of the individual over his own body and mind. They reject the promotion of positive liberty (having the means to realize aims in life) as a political goal, because it would invite the patronizing imposition of a view of the good life (cf. Berlin 1958). In principle, the only limits to liberty compatible with libertarianism are the rights of other individuals, and voluntary agreements based on informed consent of all involved.

The sovereignty of the individual also implies self-ownership, which—in John Locke's view—in turn implies legitimate ownership of the fruits of one's labor. This puts libertarians on a crash course with the welfare state and with social liberals such as John Rawls (1921–2002), who argued that the individual's natural endowments (talents and capacities) are undeserved, and that therefore any social and economic differences resulting from the use of those endowments are equally unfair and undeserved. On the libertarian view, the sovereign choice to use talents and endowments creatively in the pursuit of an individual ideal of a good life, no matter how undeserved these endowments may themselves be, makes the individual responsible for his or her economic and social success or failure. This makes "corrective" taxation and society-wide redistribution illegitimate.

Libertarianism is highly suspicious of claims to authority. Unlike anarchism, it does not necessarily reject the state: there is room for organized protection of individual rights.

Unlike liberalism, however, libertarianism does reject virtually all state interference beyond the protection of life and good. The relatively young school of left libertarianism, represented by, among others, Hillel Steiner and Peter Vallentyne, is an exception to this rule. It stresses the so-called Lockean Proviso set forth in the late seventeenth century: because no one owns nature, private appropriation of natural resources is only legitimate if "enough and as good" is left for others (Locke 2003). Inequality resulting from use of (and trade in) illegitimately acquired or produced goods demands correction. Left libertarians see room here for a degree of redistribution and for a more active state.

Although libertarianism can provide very strong support for sustainability, it also demands a thorough

271

reconsideration of the concept itself. A comprehensive libertarian perspective on sustainability has yet to be developed (Wissenburg 1998); only fragmented expositions on animal rights, pollution (Nozick 1974) and free-market environmentalism (Anderson and Leal 1991) exist. On the basis of their political views, one may expect their assessment of sustainability to reject it as a social goal while paradoxically welcoming it as a result. Insofar as sustainability is a social goal, it promotes an ideal state of affairs, prescribed and imposed without consent, violating individual sovereignty. Many definitions of sustainability also refer to ideas distrusted by libertarians, for example, the distinction between basic needs and further wants, viewing animals as natural resources only, and moral claims on behalf of nonexistent future generations where only individuals can be responsible for (the choice to create) offspring. Libertarians are more likely to support a view of the sustainable society as a social and natural environment in which the individual can provide for her needs and possibly satisfy her desires, including a desire to warrant possible children a similar chance in life—provided none of this infringes on the rights of others.

By the same token, libertarians will reject any hierarchically imposed sustainability policy, but they can and will support policies based on informed individual preferences, and on legitimate limits to individual property rights. Thus, libertarianism seems to reject pollution, unjustifiable acquisition and inefficient use of natural resources (possibly including the potential of renewable resources to renew themselves) as infringements on individual rights. In line with this support for free trade, it supports privatization of resources and the creation of markets for tradable emission rights. Also, defenders of fair trade will find their strongest supporters among libertarians. Finally, in particular, left libertarians will support a degree of redistribution of (the benefits of) access to natural resources to rectify past injustice.

Marcel WISSENBURG
Radboud University Nijmegen

FURTHER READING

Anderson, Terry L., & Leal, Donald R. (2001). *Free market environmentalism*. New York: Palgrave.

Berlin, Isaiah. (1958). *Two concepts of liberty*. Oxford, U.K.: Clarendon Press.

Boaz, David. (1997). *Libertarianism: A primer*. New York: Free Press.

Duncan, Craig, & Machan, Tibor R. (2005). *Libertarianism: For and against*. Lanham, MD: Rowman & Littlefield.

Locke, John. (2003). *Two treatises of government* and *A letter concerning toleration* (Ian Shapiro, Ed.). New Haven, CT: Yale University Press.

Nozick, Robert. (1974). *Anarchy, state, and utopia*. New York: Basic Books.

Rothbard, Murray N. (1998). *The ethics of liberty*. New York: New York University Press.

Steiner, Hillel. (1994). *An essay on rights*. Oxford, U.K.: Blackwell.

Vallentyne, Peter. (2007). Libertarianism and the state. *Social Philosophy and Policy, 24*, 187–205.

Vallentyne, Peter, & Steiner, Hillel. (2000). *Left-libertarianism and its critics: The contemporary debate*. Basingstoke, U.K.: Palgrave.

Wissenburg, Marcel. (1998). *Green liberalism*. London: Routledge UCL Press.

M

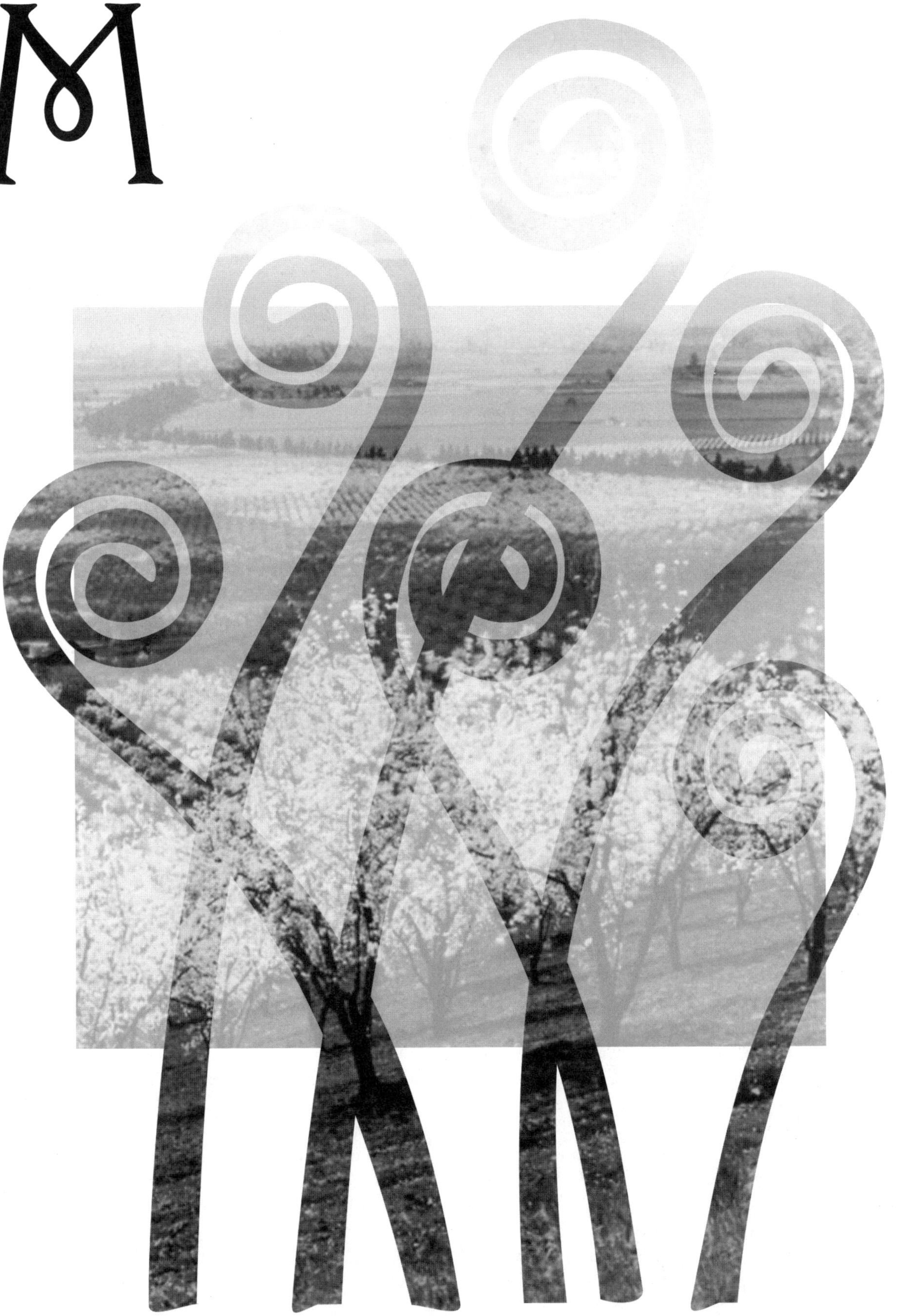

Meditation and Prayer

Spirituality is important to the concept of sustainability; it allows humans to observe and embrace the important things in life (as opposed to the material ones). Too often this journey is impeded by inattention; religions can help remove these distractions through prayer and meditation. These acts become forms of listening—ideally, wise and compassionate listening that is essential for sustainability.

The spiritual side of sustainable living is nourished with a sense of being animated and engraced (to be receptive to, and energized by) a healing power greater than oneself: strangers and friends, hills and rivers, stars and galaxies, gods and goddesses. It begins with joy, not anger. In human life, one of the deepest obstacles to receiving such joy is inattention.

The religions of the world offer various correctives to this distractedness. Buddhists typically approach it directly and in psychological terms. They compare our minds to drunken monkeys that are flitting from one branch of a tree to another, such that, for most of us, having a calm and undistracted mind—a mind of presence—is very difficult. We think that we control our thoughts, they say, but in fact our thoughts control us. Accordingly, many Buddhists recommend a daily practice of meditation as one way of developing a calm mind so that we can then bring into our daily activities a less distracted presence. With practice, they say, we can gradually find ourselves more centered and more available to the call of each present moment.

Similarly, some Christians who are influenced by the contemplative traditions within Christianity recommend a daily practice of centering prayer. If we learn to "center down" even for a brief time every morning, say these Christians, we slowly understand that we can live from the immediacy of God's presence in our daily lives. We realize that each present moment is a sacrament of sorts, and that the very light of God shines through the face of the other people who need our listening ear. Some, such as the Benedictines, go further and say that we meet Christ in the other person, whether stranger or friend, attractive or frightening. The Benedictines are a religious group within Catholic Christianity who highlight listening as a key aspect of the life of discipleship. "When I was hungry you gave me food, and when I was in prison you visited me," says Jesus in the Gospel of Matthew (25:34–36, RSV). "And when I needed someone to talk to," the Benedictines seem to add, "you listened to me."

Here listening refers to the act of being present, of being aware, of being open and available to what is given for experience. Of course there are many reasons a person might seek to listen. The kind of listening at issue here, the kind that is conducive to sustainability, is best illustrated in what a Buddhist might call wise and compassionate listening. When this listening is directed toward another human being, it is guided not by the aim of conquering or controlling but by the aim of being with that person in a sensitive way, and of responding wisely and compassionately. We might call it attunement or deep listening. It can be the spirit in which people feel attuned not only to one another, but also to plants, animals, and minerals. We might call it ecolistening.

Attunement is not simply a matter of the ears. It can also occur through touch, sight, smell, and sound; it can be guided by intuition, imagination, and reason. When a nurse gently binds the wound of a person who is injured, she is listening with her hands; when a businessman calculates the possible outcomes of a business decision with an eye to helping build a green community, he is listening with his reason. There are many ways to listen and there are many kinds of listeners.

Who is it, then, who should be listened to in an age needful of sustainability. The answer is whoever addresses us. Some people in the modern West would have said that it is humans and only humans who can address us. But most advocates of sustainability recognize that we can be addressed by hills and rivers, trees and stars, cats and dogs. They may not speak to us in languages we learn from childhood or formal schooling, but they present themselves to us to be heard, to be listened to. A primary value of prayer and meditation is to learn to listen and then respond to them.

Of course in many cultural traditions there is another kind of prayer that is important: namely, prayers in which we ourselves address something greater than ourselves. We may name this something God or the Universe or Ancestors or Amithaba Buddha or Krishna. We may address it with words, our feelings, our rituals, or our dancing. We may seek an active response from this something, or we may be content with the companionship of having been listened to. We may conceive it monotheistically (with a belief in one God), polytheistically (with a belief in many gods), monistically (believing that reality is a unified whole, in which all parts are ascribed to single system, or panentheistically (seeing the whole in God, as opposed to pantheistically, believing that God is the whole). In any instance the very act of addressing can play an important role in sustainable living. It externalizes the depths of human feeling, turning our inner lives inside out, so that we can see who we are and who we seek to become.

Of course the content of the prayer matters, too. If we pray that our enemies be massacred, that the Earth be destroyed, or that people who are "different" be eliminated, our hopes are not consistent with the ethical norms of sustainable living. The better hope is that the content of

prayers can contribute to the hope that communities can emerge on Earth in which the will of the Spirit is done on Earth as it is in heaven (to adapt the most remembered prayer of Jesus).

Advocates of sustainability recognize that the Spirit can be conceived in many different ways. Indeed people may not believe in the Spirit and yet still have a sense of spirituality if they have a sense of connection with the Earth and an appreciation of the beauty of life. Healthy agnosticism is among the living options within ecospirituality. But even agnostics can pray. Even agnostics can address the universe in praise, lamentation, and wonder. Their prayers are completed, along with those of monotheists and polytheists, monists and panentheists, when they act on those prayers, helping to add beauty to the world.

Jay McDANIEL
Hendrix College

FURTHER READING

Kaza, Stephanie (Ed.). (2000). *Dharma rain: Sources of Buddhist environmentalism.* Boston: Shambhala.
May, Gerald. (1982). *Will and spirit: A contemplative psychology.* San Francisco: Harper & Row.
McDaniel, Jay B. (2000). *Living from the center: Spirituality in an age of consumerism.* St. Louis, MO: Chalice Press.
Randour, Mary Lou. (2000). *Animal grace: Entering a spiritual relationship with our fellow creatures.* Novato, CA: New World Library.
Thurman, Howard. (2006). *Howard Thurman: Essential writings.* Maryknoll, NY: Orbis Books.
Ware, Kallistos. (1979). *The orthodox way.* Crestwood, NY: St. Vladmir's Seminary Press.

Millennium Development Goals

Millennium Development Goals were established by the United Nations in 2000 to combat poverty, inequality, and disease, and to promote a global partnership toward sustainable development. Although some progress has been made, meeting the target date of 2015 for these eight specific goals provides an ongoing challenge.

In September of 2000, world leaders met at the United Nations Millennium Summit to envision a way to simultaneously support growth, reduce poverty, and achieve sustainable development. The product of this meeting, The Millennium Declaration, was adopted by 189 nations. Over the next year, experts articulated eight Millennium Development Goals (MDGs) with quantifiable targets based on the Declaration to be achieved by 2015. The U.N. Millennium Development Goals (2008) aim to:

- eradicate extreme poverty and hunger;
- achieve universal primary education;
- promote greater equality and empower women;
- reduce child mortality;
- improve maternal health;
- combat HIV/AIDS, malaria, and other diseases;
- ensure environmental sustainability;
- develop a global partnership for development.

In addition, in partnership with the United Nations Developmental Programme, separate targets specify what each goal entails (UNDP 2008). For example, the seventh goal (ensure environmental sustainability) has four targets:

1. integrate the principles of sustainable development into country policies and programmes and reverse the loss of environmental resources;
2. reduce biodiversity loss, achieving, by 2010, a significant reduction in the rate of loss;
3. halve, by 2015, the proportion of the population without sustainable access to safe drinking water and basic sanitation;
4. by 2020, to have achieved a significant improvement in the lives of at least 100 million slum dwellers.

In turn, using measurable indicators will enable nations to assess progress toward a target. For instance, reducing biodiversity loss (the second target) is measured by monitoring the "proportion of terrestrial and marine areas protected" and the "proportion of species threatened with extinction" (UNDP 2008).

The specificity of the MDG targets and indicators attracts supporters but draws criticism. Of course, the targets enable nations to track progress and help identify where more work is needed. Articulating specific targets can also encourage policy formation. When countries making progress are identified, their policies can serve as examples for other nations; however data is not available for many of the indicators. Indeed, some indicators (such as the number of people who contract malaria each year, information needed to monitor the sixth goal, eradicating illness) will be incredibly difficult, if not impossible, to track due in part to the difficulty in collecting data in places with poor access to medical care. Data collection on the MDG indicators has increased since 2000, but the money and expertise necessary to do so is in short supply, particularly in countries furthest from reaching the goals.

Though the MDGs' reliance on hard-to-find data draws criticism, especially from experts, many applaud setting ambitious goals as the moral thing to do. The ethical foundation of the MDGs almost certainly rests on the varied religious beliefs of its signatories since so many traditions emphasize helping the disadvantaged, and religion is a major motivating force in many lives. Yet the Millennium Declaration does not directly discuss religion, rather it identifies shared values that were deemed relevant for development by its signatories. These values include freedom, equality, solidarity, tolerance, respect for nature, and shared responsibility. With these values as a stated foundation of the MDGs, nations maintain that helping people out of poverty, promoting economic growth, and achieving sustainable development are moral imperatives. This explicitly ethical stand separates the Millennium Declaration from previous international development plans such as Agenda 21, the U.N. action plan for sustainable development approved in 1992. While Agenda 21 sought to combat conditions including disparities between nations, worsening poverty, health, and illiteracy based on ethical ideals such as responsibility and equity, its prescription for sustainability focused on economic development, research, and governmental and nongovernmental actions through which basic needs could be met, living standards improved, and ecosystems protected without articulating or developing its ethical foundations.

Grassroots movements also support the MDGs for ethical reasons. One of the largest of such groups is the One campaign (one.org), which is comprised of more than 2.4 million Americans and allied with over a hundred major nonprofit organizations. The One campaign aims to educate Americans about poverty, health, education, and HIV/AIDS and to remind elected officials of their promises about foreign aid. It recognizes ways in which problems of sustainability, such as impacts of global warming, and lack of clean water supplies and sanitation disproportionately affect the world's poorest people. This nonpartisan group includes Americans of all belief systems—Buddhists, Christians, Hindus, Jews, and Muslims—as well as many secular organizations. Members of the One campaign e-mail elected officials about pending legislation, encourage people to consider poverty and HIV/AIDS when voting, and run educational programs. One-campaign groups and individual members are often aligned with religious organizations, therefore the MDGs have been promoted through sermons, religious education, and prayer gatherings in recent years.

As of 2008, considerable progress had been made toward some of the goals, including decreasing the proportion of people in extreme poverty, raising primary school enrollment rates, and increasing the gender parity of primary education. Yet many regions of the world are not on track to meet a number of the goals, including reversing the rates of deforestation, improving sanitation, and decreasing the rate of climate change. Achieving the MDGs by 2015 will require increased moral, political, financial, and scientific support. Partnerships such as the one between the Global Environment Facility—the largest fund established to protect the environment—and the United Nations Developmental Programme, which has financed more than 8,400 sustainability projects sponsored by nongovernmental and community organizations, can function as models for other agencies and organizations determined to help facilitate MDGs.

Sarah E. FREDERICKS
University of North Texas

FURTHER READING

About UNDP-GEF. (n.d.). Retrieved May 25, 2009 from http://www.undp.org/gef/05/about/index.html

Aspirations and obligations: The UN's Millennium Development Goals. (2005, September). *Economist, 376*(8443), 67–68.

The issues affecting global poverty. (n.d.). Retrieved May 6, 2009, from http://www.one.org/us/issues

Millennium Declaration. (2000, September 8). Retrieved August 12, 2008, from http://www.un.org/millennium/declaration/ares552e.pdf

The millennium development goals report 2008. (2008). Retrieved March 30, 2009, from http://www.un.org/millenniumgoals/2008highlevel/pdf/newsroom/mdg%20reports/MDG_Report_2008_ENGLISH.pdf

Moldan, Bedrich; Billharz, Suzanne; & Matravers, Robyn. (Eds.). (1997). *Sustainability indicators: A report on the projection indicators of sustainable development.* New York: John Wiley & Sons.

One Campaign. (2008). One sabbath. Retrieved May 25, 2009 from http://www.one.org/us/onesabbath/

One Campaign. (2009). Issue brief: The millennium development goals. Retrieved May 25, 2009 from http://www.one.org/c/us/issuebrief/762/

U.N. Millennium Development Goals. (2008). Retrieved August 12, 2008, from http://www.un.org/millenniumgoals/

United Nations Development Programme (UNDP). (n.d.). About the MDGs: Basics. Retrieved August 12, 2008, from http://www.undp.org/mdg/basics.shtml

Mormonism

Although the Church of Jesus Christ of Latter-day Saints (the Mormon Church) has not issued any official statement regarding sustainability, its sacred texts and recent institutional developments indicate a belief in divine principles that are consistent with the highest standards of sustainable living.

The Church of Jesus Christ of Latter-day Saints (also known as the Mormon or LDS Church) is a modern-revealed religion that admits the paradox of inherent, eternal value in the temporal, the corporeal, and all forms of more-than-human life. In the book of Moses, believed to be a prophetically restored account of the creation that supplements the Genesis story, the world is created spiritually before it is created physically. All things, as the LDS Church founder Joseph Smith taught, contain both spiritual and physical matter; plants and animals are "living souls" (Moses 3:9). (All scriptures cited in the article come from a three-volume set that includes *The Book of Mormon*, *Doctrine and Covenants*, and *Pearl of Great Price* [LDS 1983].) A belief that Earth will become heaven and that the bodies of all living things will become immortal suggests the immanence of the spiritual, not transcendence of the physical; it is a tenet that sees as holy the earthly task of sustaining all forms of life. The fall is thus fortuitous: "Adam fell that men might be; and men are, that they might have joy" (2 Nephi 2:25). Seeing the postlapsarian conditions—bringing children into the world and providing sustenance through physical suffering and labor—as blessings, not curses, has inspired Mormon economic drive and has led in the past to an assumed obligation to have large families. Adam and Eve are told, however, that their stewardship is to work to ensure that all humankind and all of creation alike enjoy the privilege of posterity. Today, members are encouraged to plan families prayerfully, according to individual needs and inspiration.

Believers are also expected to take aesthetic pleasure in God's creations. Before Adam learns that fruits of the tree could be used for food, God intends the tree to be "pleasant to the sight of man; and man could behold it" (Moses 3:9). In a revelation to Joseph Smith, all things of the earth are given "both to please the eye and gladden the heart" (Doctrine and Covenants [D&C] 59:18). God provides for human sustenance, but human greed is kept in check by the capacity to take pleasure in natural beauty as a witness of Christ's love.

The Lord promises that there is "enough and to spare" (D&C 104:17) to feed the human family, but He is clear that it "must be done in mine own way" (D&C 104:16). This "law of consecration" involves a radical redistribution of resources so that "the poor will be exalted" and the "rich will be made low" (D&C 104:17). Key to this social aim is awareness that ownership is a merely human and secular convention. Property is made sacred by using only what is necessary for oneself and one's family and donating excess to the church welfare system (which operates without overhead costs) for redistribution to the poor in local communities and throughout the world. The sustainability of this practice, of course, would depend upon truly global and strict obedience to more modest consumption so as to lessen the ecological footprint and free up more resources for others. In the revelations of Joseph Smith, as long as natural resources are disproportionately used "the world lieth in sin. And wo[e] be unto man that sheddeth blood or that wasteth flesh and hath no need" (D&C 49:20–21).

One particularly untapped potential in Mormon practice is Joseph Smith's 1833 revelation known as the Word of Wisdom (D&C 89). Although best known for its prohibition of drugs and alcohol and strictly obeyed as such by the faithful, this dietary law instructs believers to eat a moderate and balanced diet of fruits, grains, and vegetables in season and to eat meat sparingly and to remember that God's provisions are not for man alone. With current understanding of the damaging effects of eating mass-produced meat, on both the environment and on animal life itself, and the costs of transporting food across greater distances, the need for deeper compliance to this law is becoming obvious to many believers.

Although it has made no official statement about the importance of sustainable living, the LDS Church was lauded in 2008 by the Sierra Club for its faith-based effort to create a mixed-use area, City Creek Center, as a LEED for Neighborhood Development project. (LEED is an internationally recognized green building certification system developed by the U.S. Green Building Council.) The new Church History Library meets silver LEED qualifications, and future church meetinghouses will be LEED certified. A Global Energy Management Committee also monitors and evaluates church facilities and activities worldwide. Because these efforts are not broadcast in official statements urging members to live more sustainably, they are not well known among the general membership, and the potential of LDS beliefs to promote greater sustainability is often diminished by the historically anti-environmentalist sentiment in the Intermountain West (the area in North America lying between the Rocky Mountains to the east and the Sierra Nevadas and Cascades to the west). LDS doctrines, however, are inspiring an increasing number of church members concerned about the global environmental crisis. Ad hoc developments, including the website LDS Earth Stewardship, and several recent publications, most notably *New Genesis: A Mormon Reader on Land and Community* and *Stewardship and the Creation: LDS Perspectives on Nature*, bear witness to a spirit of deeper creation care.

George B. HANDLEY
Brigham Young University

FURTHER READING

Ball, Terry B.; Peck, Steven L.; & Handley, George B. (2006). *Stewardship and the creation: LDS perspectives on nature.* Provo, UT: Religious Studies Center.

Church of Jesus Christ of Latter-day Saints. (LDS). (1983). *The Book of Mormon / The Doctrine and Covenants / The Pearl of Great Price.* (3 vols.). Provo, UT: Author.

LDS Earth Stewardship. (2008, July 12). Retrieved March 21, 2009, from http://lds.earth.stewardship.googlepages.com/home

Williams, Terry Tempest; Smart, William B.; & Smith, Gibbs M. (Eds.). (1998). *New Genesis. A Mormon reader on land and community.* Layton, UT: Gibbs Smith.

19 For, behold, the beasts of the field and the fowls of the air, and that which cometh of the earth, is ordained for the use of man for food and for raiment, and that he might have in abundance.

20 But it is not given that one man should possess that which is above another, wherefore the world lieth in sin.

21 And wo[e] be unto man that sheddeth blood or that wasteth flesh and hath no need.

THE DOCTRINE AND COVENANTS 49

Source: Church of Jesus Christ of Latter-day Saints. (LDS). (1983). *The Book of Mormon / The Doctrine and Covenants / The Pearl of Great Price.* (3 vols.). Provo, UT: Author.

National Religious Partnership for the Environment

An association of four independent U.S. faith groups, the National Religious Partnership for the Environment (NRPE) seeks to educate and advocate on matters relating to sustainability and ecojustice. In addition to educating about religious concern and responsibility for the Earth as God's creation, global climate change has been a major focus of the group.

The National Religious Partnership for the Environment is a coalition of four religious umbrella groups: the Eco-Justice Program of the National Council of Churches of Christ (NCC), which represents a number of Protestant, Anglican, Orthodox, Evangelical, historic African American and Living Peace churches; the Environmental Justice Program of the United States Catholic Conference of Bishops (USCCB); the Evangelical Environmental Network (EEN); and the Coalition on the Environment and Jewish Life (COEJL). The latter three were all established concurrently with the NRPE. The partnership came out of the 1990 Joint Appeal of Religion and Science for the Environment, issued by Carl Sagan, Al Gore, James Morton (dean of the Cathedral of St. John the Divine in New York City), and a host of other scientists, religious leaders, and politicians. Out of this effort, the NRPE was born in 1993, under the directorship of Paul Gorman, then assistant to Morton. Well-supported by grants, each group was given $250,000 per year for three years to reach out to congregations across the country—by producing and mailing 135,000 educational "creation care kits" per year, for example, each tailored to the different faith traditions. This was an important jump-start to the emerging religious environmental movement in the United States. Over the years, the NRPE groups have held conferences and trainings, fostered advocacy, written statements, and produced educational materials, videos, books, and worship resources on a variety of issues. The NRPE was initially housed at the Cathedral of St. John Divine, but eventually moved to Amherst, Massachusetts. As of 2009, Gorman was still the executive director.

In addition to educating about religious respect and care for the Earth as God's creation, global climate change has been a major focus of the organization, in part because of the urgency of the situation, and in part because the issue was firmly grounded in justice concerns that all four groups shared. The various members of the NRPE ran media ads on the crisis of global warming, collected petitions in reference to the 1997 U.N. Kyoto Protocol talks, and arrived on the Detroit doorsteps of U.S automakers in hybrid cars driven by Catholic nuns in 2003. The EEN particularly focused on this campaign by asking "What Would Jesus Drive?" and ran ads that questioned "If God is with Me All the Time, Does That Include the Auto Dealership?" Starting in 1999, COEJL and the NCC's Eco-Justice Working Group collaborated on establishing the Interfaith Climate Change Network (ICCN) and interfaith climate and energy campaigns in over twenty states; this type of state-based organizing on energy and climate change is now done by Interfaith Power and Light groups. Although seemingly not as active amidst the thriving number of religious environmental organizations that it helped stimulate, the NRPE remains a center for the coordination of the efforts of its constituent members and is recognized for the key role it played in helping to launch the interfaith environmental movement through its leadership training, advocacy, and wide-ranging educational efforts.

Laurel D. KEARNS
Drew Theological School and University

FURTHER READING

Christiansen, Drew, & Grazer, Walter E. (Eds.). (1996). *And God saw that it was good: Catholic theology & the environment.* United States Council of Catholic Bishops.

Gottlieb, Roger S. (2006). *A Greener faith: Religious environmentalism and our planet's future.* New York: Oxford University Press.

Gould, Rebecca. (2007). Binding life to values. In Jonathan Isham & Sissel Waage, (Eds.), *Ignition: What you can do to fight global warming and spark a movement* (pp. 119–134). Washington, DC: Island Press.

Lerner, Steve. (1998). *Eco-pioneers: Practical visionaries solving today's environmental problems.* Boston: The MIT Press.

Morton, James Parks. (1997). Religion and sustainability. In Peter H. Raven (Ed.), *Nature and human society* (pp. 443–454). Washington, DC: National Academy Press.

The National Religious Partnership for the Environment. (2009). Retrieved April 6, 2009, from http://www.nrpe.org

Nature

Concepts of "nature" are critical to discussions about sustainability. The term's many meanings, images, and uses shape various senses of humanity's moral place in the world. Imagining sustainability may require new ways of looking at nature, including non-Western models that do not separate humanity from the rest of nature.

Nature is an encompassing, elusive, and malleable concept, bearing various meanings across and within cultures. Indeed, it bears so many linguistic uses and such interpretive complexity that defining nature seems impossible—certainly so within an encyclopedia article. But that very complexity makes "nature" an unavoidable dimension of the moral imagination and an important concept of analysis for understanding the discourses of sustainability.

Especially in Western cultures, nature often serves to identify and separate the categories of human, cultural, artificial, and technological. In Western religious worldviews, the natural may stand in contrast to the spiritual, supernatural, or transcendent. In ethics, nature has sometimes denoted a premoral realm of existence, which human agents then overlay with value or invest with purpose. In each of these cases, nature has often been defined or used as that which stands other to humanity and its projects.

Some critics have therefore argued that the concept of nature stands as an accomplice to dualisms that separate humanity from Earth, and cultural from ecological systems. When used as a contrastive concept, it allows persons and cultures to individuate themselves from the surrounding living world and often to hold themselves superior to it. So the very concept of nature, or at least the way it has been typically deployed in the Western world, may create attitudes that allow the degradation of the Earth and the alienation of humanity.

Many critics have therefore argued that the path to sustainability must include different ways of perceiving nature, alternative metaphors of the natural, and more apt uses for its interpretive function. Some propose to re-enchant nature, finding value, authenticity, or sacredness in the living world. Others wish to subvert nature/culture binaries by including social and religious worlds within an ecological context or by tracing the pervasive presence of natural forces or ecological agencies though every human system. Still others would keep nature as a contrastive concept precisely in order to underscore human responsibility for natural systems and the nonhuman world. For insofar as it is a ward of human powers, societies have stewardship obligations for nature.

These alternative proposals have drawn increased attention to conceptual uses of nature that do not produce so sharp a contrast with the human, cultural, or spiritual. Nature might be, for example, the encompassing world within which humans and other animals or spirits appear. It might name the divine, or the generative ground of life, or the structure of existence. In some non-Western, indigenous, and traditional worldviews, nature concepts appear in stories that privilege a reflexive, inextricable relation among humans and the nonhuman, divine, or extrahuman.

Within ethics, some concept of nature often functions normatively to support a framework of moral agency. Nature might provide grounding principles and values, or, on the other hand, it might be that which moral agency must control, transform, and overcome. It is sometimes used synonymously with "human nature," and then alternatively referring to embodiment, rationality, or will. It may refer to conative goods of any living being, as well as ambivalent desires and tendencies to evil. Despite the variety, in each case the concept of nature supports and helps regulate a moral framework that orients an agent's decisions and actions.

Nature's normative function within a system of ethics therefore corresponds to background worldviews, practical projects, and discursive systems. Those worldviews and the everyday uses of the concept define what nature means for humanity's self-understanding; they orient humanity to its own embodied existence and to Earth as a moral field. They also regulate the way nature matters for ethics by establishing nature's relative priority over other normative criteria (for example, reason, law, scriptures, tradition, and common good).

Views of sustainability usually include some implicit notion of nature and how it matters for moral agency. Describing and evaluating those notions presents a central interpretive task for cultural critics. Simply illuminating the many meanings, metaphors, and uses of nature at work in public discussion might do much for clarifying debates over sustainability.

Willis JENKINS
Yale Divinity School

FURTHER READING

Cronon, William. (Ed.). (1996). *Uncommon ground: Rethinking the human place in nature*. New York: W. W. Norton.

Evernden, Neil. (1992). *The social creation of nature*. Baltimore: Johns Hopkins University Press.

Rolston, Holmes, III. (1994). *Conserving natural value*. New York: Columbia University Press.

Worster, Donald. (1994). *Nature's economy: A history of ecological ideas*. Cambridge, U.K.: Cambridge University Press.

ON NEEDING NATURE

In the following passage from Conserving Natural Value, *philosopher and environmental ethicist Holmes Rolston III writes of the importance and meaning of nature in our modern lives.*

Americans sing "America the Beautiful," glad for purple mountains' majesties and the fruited plains stretching from sea to shining sea. People on the frontier found that they had no sooner conquered a wilderness than they had come to love the land on which they settled. As sung in the musical *Oklahoma[!]*, "We know we belong to the land, and the land we belong to is grand." Of those drawn to the city for livelihood or commodities, many really prefer to live in the "suburbs," so as to remain also near the country, in some place not consummately urban but where there is more green than anything else, where, with the neighbors, there are fencerows and cardinals, dogwoods and rabbits. We cherish our hills of home, our rivers, our bays, our country drives. Real estate agents term these "amenities" with our "commodities," but this is really nature mixed in with our culture. We want greenbelts in cities, mountains on the skyline, parks, seashores and lakeshores, spits, headlands, islands, forests, even wildernesses, including deserts, tundra, and swamps to visit. Most people identify with some countryside; indeed, our affections toward the city are often exceeded by those we have toward the landscapes on which we were reared.

Source: Holmes Rolston III. (1994). *Conserving Natural Value*, pp. 9–10. New York: Columbia University Press.

Nature Religions and Animism

Nature religions see the cosmos as a set of interrelationships among beings, human and other-than-human. The Ojibwa worldview, which accepts that even stones can enter into relationships and are thus beings, is an example of animism. Interpretations of nature religion, by observers and participants, lead to differing views of the extent to which humans must change if the world is to be sustained.

The term "nature religions" attempts to categorize an amorphous array of religious movements in which the core or focus is the celebration of nature or which consider nature sacred. Highlighting this concern with nature is useful only in the context of identifying other religions as deity-focused or self-focused. For example, the participants in monotheistic religions typically attempt to adjust their lifestyles, desires, hopes, and antipathies to those associated with their deity. Teachings derived from the deity are fundamental. What is important in self-religions, such as New Age, is the progressive enhancement of self-knowledge and personal well-being. Everything can be a tool to enable practitioners to realize their true potential. By contrast with these trends, the term "nature religions" identifies a shared perception that humans (groups or individuals) are bound up in the wider context of the living world or cosmos. This context is often defined as a communal or relational one: the world is alive with beings that call upon one another to live harmoniously. People are invited to adjust their lives to engage respectfully. Nature religions implicitly and sometimes explicitly challenge any notion that humans are separate from, let alone better than, any other beings. Some nature religions might encourage a reversal of the prevalent modern privileging of humanity over all other existences, suggesting and even insisting that the diminishment of human presence or activity would benefit the rest of life. Most commonly, nature religions are about participation and entail quests for locally meaningful forms of belonging, engagement, relationship, and harmony.

It is vital to note that "nature" in this term is a multivalent and resonant word. It can refer to a notion that authenticity, beauty, and truth are best, or only, found "out there" beyond the cities, in rural or even wilderness domains. This is usually romantic, even when it results in radical activism, because it requires a dualistic separation between human culture and other-than-human nature, and imagines "wilderness" as pristine ecosystems (unaffected by humanity) rather than as the result of human activities as diverse as hunter-gathering and genocidal clearance of previous human populations. "Nature" can also act as a reference to the entire larger living world or cosmos, usually stressing the value of all beings and communities. This "nature" is inclusive of humanity and its varied habitats, urban, rural, permanent, transient and so on. One element of the "religious" contribution to "nature religion," however, is indicated by a call to treat the world as sacred—as worthy of veneration, respect, care, responsible and sustainable relationality—in its own right. Nature religions' ethical imperative involves limiting human rights to treat the world as a resource or utility principally for human benefit. The sanctity of the world in nature religions is not best seen in the setting apart of some places, persons, or acts as being more-than or separable from others. Rather, sacrality is observable in the deliberate setting of limits on human acts, constructions, desires, and expansionism.

Some nature religionists may equally indicate that there are, or should be, limits on the activities and expansive presence of other species or individuals. But the recognition that humanity is almost uniquely capable and responsible for such massive changes in the dynamic ecosystems that together form the world reinforces the invitation to self-limitation in human ambitions or possibilities.

"Nature religions" is an umbrella term—expansive and deserving of considerable contest or debate. It can embrace the various new, self-identified Pagan traditions of Druidry, Wicca, and Heathenry; various "ethnic" reconstructions (Norse, Lithuanian, Hellenic and other traditions); and various other eclectic variations on the theme of developing contemporary Earth-respecting spiritual practices. It can also embrace many if not all indigenous religious traditions. The term is heuristically useful as it points to a difference from religions that privilege transcendent realities but should not be taken to mean that those so labeled have a Western-style notion of "nature" or a culture/nature dualism.

Should Human Behavior Change?

It is also noteworthy that both "nature" and "nature religion" have been valued in dramatically differing ways among observers and participants. In recent decades both terms have been increasingly positively evaluated, but they can be contrasted negatively both with divine and human authority and centrality. These shifting evaluations are admirably surveyed and discussed by the historian of religion Catherine Albanese and the environmental and social ethicist Bron Taylor. In brief, those committed to the (distinct) views that humans are the pinnacle of evolution or the stewards of God's creation often hold that removing humanity from the center of attention is naïve or wrong, and that the world will not benefit from radical changes in human usage. Nature religionists usually disagree and insist that there is an urgent need to alter human behaviors for the benefit both of humans and the world.

Exactly how much change is required, how change might be achieved, and whose benefit takes priority, are among the issues that divide nature religionists (and others) along allegedly "deep green" and "light (or shallow) green" lines. The darkest green elements (as Taylor discusses) evidence what some perceive to be a sinister, anti-human tendency and frequently insist that for life to flourish human well-being must be treated as irrelevant. For some (extreme) eco-activists, such as some Earth First!

activists, any thoughts about what should be sustained must focus on the nonhuman majority of the world. Self-identified "deep green" nature religion is manifest in ritual and meditative attempts by humans to "think like" and act on behalf of other-than-human beings. Usually this results in efforts to mitigate the worst effects of human separatism while seeking the well-being of other species whose lives might, after all, enrich those of humanity. Meanwhile, "light/shallow green" ecology (usually a label applied by others) involves environmentalism on behalf of species or ecosystems that are or may be necessary for human sustenance. Rainforests, for example, are to be saved in the hope that cancer cures will be found or because of their role as carbon sinks and oxygen producers. Dark, deep, and shallow green movements and individuals share similar religious acts, especially in ritual and meditation, even as they are differentiated along activist or putatively political lines.

Animism

Within these broader trends, the term "animism" has been gaining ground both among academic observers and among nature religion practitioners. It was once associated mainly with the theory of religion proposed by Edward Tylor (1832–1917), the first professor of anthropology at Oxford University. In his two-volume *Primitive Culture* (1871) he argued that religion is "a belief in souls and spirits," explaining that this was an ancient but still prevalent mistake that falsely appears to explain some common experiences. If someone dreams of meeting a deceased relative, or has a feverish vision of distant places, they may think that this means that people possess spirits that survive death and souls that can separate from bodies to gain knowledge unobtainable by the normal senses. Tylor was certain that religion—this mistaken animation of the world by souls and spirits—would fade away in the face of modern science as it demonstrated the superiority of human rationality and technology. This understanding of animism was rapidly challenged and is now largely cited only as an example of early anthropological theorizing. It can only contribute to nature religions and debates about sustainability by suggesting that some people value elements of the world for nonempirical or spiritual reasons rather than valuing physical existences (matter of any kind) for any intrinsic reason.

Animism is of far more importance when the term is used in a quite different way. Firstly, the word began to be used by those who wanted a term to encapsulate their sense that the world is a community of living beings, only some of whom are human. The world is animated, hence "animism" might usefully label varieties of nature-centered worldviews and lifeways. Secondly, scholars studying among various indigenous peoples and among contemporary, self-identified eco-activist Pagans have also found the term to be valuable. They frequently cite the work of Irving Hallowell and what he learned among the Ojibwa of Berens River in southern central Canada.

Animism and the Ojibwa

Animism is intrinsic to Ojibwa grammar, casual and deliberate discourse, and relationality as people seek to learn and perform appropriate and sustainable ways of behaving in the larger-than-human community. In the Ojibwa language (and that of all Algonkian nations) a grammatical distinction is made between animate and inanimate genders but not among masculine, feminine, and neuter genders. A suffix is added to nouns that refer to animate persons rather than inanimate objects. Verbs indicating the actions of animate persons differ from those referring to acts done to inanimate objects. For example, the researchers John Nichols and Earl Nyholm report that in the Minnesota Ojibwa dialect the plural form of the word *asin* (stone) is *asiniig*, identifying stones as grammatically animate. The question arises, is this *just* a grammatical oddity (somewhat like the French reference to tables *as if* they were female)? Do the Ojibwa treat grammatically animate stones as animate persons? Do they speak with stones or act in other ways that reveal intentions to build or maintain relationships? Irving Hallowell asked an old Ojibwa man, "Are *all* the stones we see about us here alive?" The old man answered, "No! but *some* are" (1960, 24). He had witnessed a particular stone following the leader of a shamanic ceremony around a tent as he sang. Another powerful leader is said to have had a large stone that would open when he tapped it three times, allowing him to remove a small bag of herbs when he needed it in ceremonies. Hallowell was told that when a white trader was digging his potato patch he found a stone that looked like it might have been important. He called for the leader of another ceremony who knelt down to talk to the stone, asking if it had come from someone's ceremonial tent. The stone is said to have denied this. Movement, gift-giving, and conversation are three indicators of the animate nature of relational beings, or persons.

Hallowell makes it clear that the key point is not that stones do things of their own volition (however remarkable this claim might seem) but that they engage in relationships. For the Ojibwa the interesting question is not, in fact, "how do we know stones are alive?" but "what is the appropriate way for people (of whatever species) to relate?" This is as true for humans as it is for stones, trees, animals, birds, fish, and all other beings that might be recognized as persons. Persons are known to be persons when they relate to other persons in particular ways. They might act more or less intimately, willingly, or respectfully. Since enmity is also a relationship, they might act aggressively. The "person" category is only applicable when beings are relating with others. This is quite different from the understanding of ontology in most European-derived cultures, in which personhood is an interior quality, a fact about the self-consciousness of individual humans. It offers a challenge to dominant notions of humanity and the world in modernist thought and practice. If animists are people who seek to act respectfully as participants in the myriad relationships that form their local, regional, and global environments ("nature" in its several senses), then they are required to attend to the needs of human and other-than-human neighbors.

Animism embraces the notion that the world is constituted differently from that theorized by monotheistic religions. It might also contest the failure of modern science to take seriously its own insight and evidence of human interrelationship and interdependence with all other beings. In religious language, humans are co-creators of the world. In more scientific language, we are integral participants in the current stage of the world's evolution. In both domains, a far from cozy or romantic vision of the world is required. Humans and all other species are required to attend to the needs of others and cannot, without impunity or systemic penalty, commit the hubris of acting alone to be the sole beneficiary of any act. Kinship and co-evolution requires that we cease conducting experiments (in laboratories or in the wider world) that are only for the benefit of humans—let alone only for some humans. Just as it must be immoral to expect every person in the next half million years to perfectly protect the world from our radioactive waste, so it cannot be moral to harm individuals or communities for the negligible benefit of a generation seeking to continue to live by extreme patterns of consumption.

In many indigenous animist communities (which we must perceive to be formed of many mutual and competing, specific and diverse inter-species relationships of varying degrees of closeness), there are experts who deal with the difficulties that necessarily arise. Humans cannot survive, let alone thrive, without taking the lives of other animals or of plants. If such beings are treated as persons deserving of respect, the violence conducted towards them must be (a) treated personally and (b) mitigated carefully. The name applied to people who have the job of negotiating between humans and those beings that humans necessarily harm and sometimes insult (e.g., by treating such harm casually or carelessly) is "shamans." This term is derived from Siberian cultural groups and is applicable to many similar religious experts in mediation worldwide (though this too requires some care).

Nature Religion and Sustainability

Nature religionists, animists in particular, are likely to insist that present levels of human consumerism are unsustainable. They might go further and encourage a view that any form of consumption must take into account the value and needs of others, human and other-than-human, in this and future generations. Sustainability, for such people, is a matter of appropriate relationships conducted with respect and responsibility. Although some nature religionists believe that humans are expendable, indeed that the world might be better off without humans, the majority hold that humans are integral participants in the community of life. A post-human world is likely to be the result of a devastation badly affecting all other life rather than one that benefits from human extinction. A swift cessation of human hubris and pretended separation, and their consequent hyper-consumption and pollution, may just follow from a radical adjustment to the animistic perception that humans are full participants in a fully relational world. A

number of environmental educators and activists are finding the rituals and mediation strategies of shamans invaluable in redirecting people toward life in a sacred material world in which a gift economy (replete with everyday and extraordinary ritual acts of reciprocity, as invitingly incited by Ronald L. Grimes) may prove truly sustainable for all life.

Graham HARVEY
The Open University

FURTHER READING

Albanese, Catherine L. (1990). *Nature religion in America: From the Algonkian Indians to the New Age.* Chicago: University of Chicago Press.

Grimes, Ronald L. (2002). Performance as currency in the deep world's gift economy: An incantatory riff for a global medicine show. *ISLE: Interdisciplinary Studies in Literature and Environment, 9*(1), 149–64.

Hallowell, A. Irving. (1960). Ojibwa ontology, behavior, and world view. In S. Diamond (Ed.), *Culture in history: Essays in honor of Paul Radin* (pp. 19–52). New York: Columbia University Press. Reprinted in Harvey, Graham. (Ed.). (2002). *Readings in indigenous religions* (pp. 18–49). London: Continuum.

Harvey, Graham. (Ed.). (2003). *Shamanism: A reader.* London: Routledge.

Harvey, Graham. (2005). *Animism: Respecting the living world.* New York: Columbia University Press.

Nichols, John D., & Nyholm, Earl. (1995). *A concise dictionary of Minnesota Ojibwe.* Minneapolis: University of Minnesota Press.

Plumwood, Val. (2002). *Environmental culture: The ecological crisis of reason.* London: Routledge.

Taylor, Bron. (Forthcoming). *Dark green religion.* Berkeley: University of California Press.

Tylor, Edward B. (1871, 1913). *Primitive culture* (Vols. 1–2). London: John Murray.

WHAT IS RELIGIOUS NATURALISM?

Religious naturalism, unlike a nature religion, develops spirituality—as well as a core understanding of nature—out of modern scientific understandings of the world. Thus they are not reclaiming old traditions (like some neopagan traditions), but are new understandings of spirituality emerging from things like

cosmology, evolution, and even neuroscience. See, for example, Donald A. Crosby, *A Religion of Nature* (SUNY 2002) or Ursula Goodenough, *The Sacred Depths of Nature* (Oxford, 1998).

WHITNEY BAUMAN

New Age Spirituality

Although the New Age and sustainability movements are distinct, there is significant overlap between the two. Both are strongly oriented toward the future and have generally positive assessments of human nature and potential, but not all New Agers are concerned with environmental sustainability, and some of their beliefs may work against efforts towards social and economic sustainability.

The New Age movement is a loosely connected set of practices, values, and beliefs that began to coalesce in Great Britain and the United States in the 1960s and 1970s, and has continued to spread in subsequent decades. The term itself refers to many adherents' belief that a new age of human evolution is either approaching or has begun. Although there is little that is common to every practitioner, most share an interest in health, spirituality, and self-exploration, and many value knowledge and practices derived from "traditional" (usually non-Western) religions or personal intuition rather than from religious authorities. Certain strands have also developed a keen interest in science, particularly quantum mechanics. Many authors who have been influential in New Age circles—including especially Fritjof Capra, Ken Wilber, and David Bohm—write extensively on the relationship between science and spirituality.

Although the New Age and sustainability movements are distinct, there is significant overlap in both personnel and ideas. In addition to Capra, for example, notables such as David Suzuki, Eckhart Tolle, Brian Swimme, Paul Hawken, and Thomas Berry have all been influential to individuals in both circles. Still, given the broad range of behaviors, ideas, and practices designated "New Age," there is no simple, direct correlation with sustainability. Rather, there are points of both continuity and discontinuity, revealing a promising yet decidedly ambiguous legacy.

Regarding environmental sustainability, some strands of New Age encourage environmental activism, emphasizing holistic thinking, harmony with nature, and the spiritual importance of "power spots," such as Glastonbury in the United Kingdom or Sedona and Mt. Shasta in the United States. Along with the assertion that the Earth is a living organism (known as the Gaia Hypothesis), such interests have given certain segments of the movement a decidedly "earthy" tone. Indeed, New Age sentiments have motivated activist organizations such as Greenpeace and several overtly Earth-friendly farming or gardening communities, including The Farm in Tennessee, Findhorn in Scotland, and Perelandra in Virginia. But other less socially active strands are more interested in gurus, channeling, and healing than in environmental problems, and may not embrace environmental sustainability at all in their behaviors and ethics. Some strands of New Age thus take environmental sustainability quite seriously, whereas others choose to focus their spiritual energy elsewhere.

The New Age movement is ambivalent regarding social sustainability as well. The overall ethos tends to be individualistic, advocating the exploration of personal truths rather than communal values. Moreover, the movement, which is predominantly white and middle class, has focused little energy on addressing problems such as race and class inequality. Popular New Age ideas such as the "Law of Attraction," which asserts that people's thoughts control their reality, detract attention from systemic and structural forces contributing to inequitable circumstances, tending instead to blame troubles on the victims themselves. The movement's tendency to deny the reality of the negative (except to the extent that it is considered an opportunity for spiritual growth) would thus seem to make it ill equipped to deal seriously with the world's social problems. Despite these seeming weaknesses, a substantial portion of the movement's rhetoric has focused on promoting positive societal change. For example, a central message of *The Aquarian Conspiracy* (1980), a book often considered to be the quintessential statement of New Age beliefs, was that an expanded view of human potential could lead to a radical, beneficial transformation of society. The New Age focus on the power of positive thinking can thus contribute to efforts to move toward social sustainability, while also having the potential to be a significant stumbling block.

The New Age movement is equally ambivalent about economic sustainability. Many of its critics have condemned it as a superficial consumer phenomenon, arguing that its individualism and willingness to appropriate spiritual resources from other cultures make it an emissary (albeit karma-coated) of destructive capitalism. By contrast, the movement's marketability—it forms the core of the marketing segment known as "Lifestyles of Health and Sustainability"—gives it at least some economic clout. Considering that many New Agers prefer environmentally

friendly products, they may be well positioned to promote sustainability through the power of the pocketbook.

A number of the New Age movement's ideas thus overlap with and contribute to ongoing conversations about sustainability. Given that both are strongly oriented toward the future and have generally positive assessments of human nature and potential, such affinity is not surprising. That the overlap is not complete is no less surprising: like most social movements, New Age is heterogeneous and moves in many different directions simultaneously, sometimes toward and sometimes away from the equally meandering path of sustainability.

Robin GLOBUS
University of Florida

FURTHER READING

Bloom, William. (Ed.). (2000). *Holistic revolution: The essential New Age reader.* London: Allen Lane.

Ferguson, Marilyn. (1980). *The Aquarian conspiracy: Personal and social transformation in our time.* New York: G. P. Putnam's Sons.

Heelas, Paul. (1996). *The New Age movement: The celebration of the self and the sacralization of modernity.* Oxford, U.K.: Blackwell.

Pike, Sarah M. (2004). *New Age and neopagan religions in America.* New York: Columbia University Press.

York, Michael. (2005). New Age. In B. R. Taylor (Ed.), *The encyclopedia of religion and nature* (pp. 1193–1197). London & New York: Thoemmes Continuum.

The crises of our time, it becomes increasingly clear, are the necessary impetus for the revolution now under way. And once we understand nature's transformative powers, we see that it is our powerful ally, not a force to be feared or subdued. Our pathology is our opportunity.

MARILYN FERGUSON

Source: Marilyn Ferguson. (1980). *The Aquarian Conspiracy: Personal and Social Transformation in Our Time*, p. 25. New York: G. P. Putnam's Sons.

Nonprofit Organizations, Environmental

Most environmental nonprofit organizations developed during the 1960s. Today the number has grown to tens of thousands—maybe more—and includes nonprofits that focus not only on ecology but also health, religion, and social justice. Their goals largely remain the same: to increase awareness of environmental conditions; and/or to lobby governments for change; and/or to work to preserve the environment.

Prior to the 1960s, only larger nonprofits such as the Sierra Club (founded in 1892) existed. Since the environmental movement of the 1960s, both individuals and groups have formed thousands of tax-exempt, not-for-profit organizations from mainly grassroots groups. These groups take the form of nonprofits that create conferences on specific topics (e.g., water pollution), lobby government bodies, or work directly on preserving the environment itself (e.g., cleaning up creeks and rivers).

U.S.-based nonprofits that take on the national protection of the environment include such powerhouses as the National Resources Defense Council, the Humane Society of the United States, the Sierra Club, and the National Wildlife Federation. There are also regional environmental nonprofits; there are coalitions of nonprofits focused on specific targets such as health as found in the Environmental Health Coalition. There are also state- and city-based environmental nonprofits. In other words, environmental nonprofits have made it into all levels of civic life.

Newest on the environmental nonprofit scene are those organizations that deal with the oppression of specific groups based on gender, race, and/or economics, such as the Women's Earth Alliance, the Center for Diversity and the Environment, and the Green Belt Movement. In addition, there are new nonprofits working on the creation of green jobs in response to both environmental concerns and a desire to help the poor and low-income groups. These hybrid nonprofits combine social-justice issues with environmental issues. They are sometimes referred to as ecojustice organizations. One such organization, Green for All, works on the national level to advocate for green training programs and jobs for the poor that are intended to help with the switch to alternative energy resources.

The number of nonprofits around the world today, according to Paul Hawken, founder of the nonprofit Natural Capital Institute, is upwards of 30,000 and growing. If you add in the indigenous and social-justice organizations that take on environmental issues, then it numbers 100,000-plus nonprofits. Natural Capital Institute decided to track these organizations and their growth by creating an open-source software database that offers the world community the opportunity to search for and communicate with environmental nonprofits and their supporters. It is completely community driven (much like Wikipedia) and is called WISEREarth; the name comes from the acronym for World Index of Social and Environmental Responsibility. WISEREarth is the first database of its kind created with a taxonomy of environmental nonprofits that includes forty-four large categories and hundreds of smaller ones. A few of the forty-four major categories include Agriculture and Farming, Business and Economics, Global Climate Change, and Sustainable Development and Water. The opportunity to actually track all of the environmental nonprofits in the world as they have originated and developed is the partial goal of this database. The other goal is to allow all nonprofits the ability to share best practices and concerns and to work together through the communication platform that the software provides.

Environmental religious nonprofits are the newest bodies in the environmental movement. They are, however, expanding in number rapidly. While many individuals were writing and teaching about the need for religions to take on environmental concerns beginning in the 1970s, it wasn't until after the 1980s that significant progress in the formation of religious environmental nonprofits occurred. The 1990s saw the birth of a substantial number of nonprofits in the U.S. including the Forum on Religion and Ecology, the Evangelical Environmental Movement, Floresta, the National Religious Partnership for the Environment, the Religious Campaign for Forest Conservation, Episcopal Power and Light, the Coalition on the Environment and Jewish Life, and Earth Ministry. Many nonprofits also emerged globally, such as Green An Hui in China, Compassion in World Farming in Great Britain, and Navdanya in India.

In the following decade, many more religious environmental nonprofit groups have formed, such as the Green Muslims, the National Council of Churches Ecojustice Group, and The Green Yoga Association. An example of how quickly religious groups have taken to the environmental message and practice is the huge success of The

Regeneration Project. Based in San Francisco, and originally developed as Episcopal Power and Light, it has transformed into Interfaith Power and Light, which currently works with over twenty-eight statewide programs representing over two thousand congregations, temples, synagogues, and mosques throughout the United States, Canada, and Europe. The environmental nonprofits that are religiously based are sure to grow in the coming years as we begin to grapple with the meaning of global climate change.

Eileen M. HARRINGTON
University of San Francisco

FURTHER READING

Bingham, Sally G. (Ed.). (2009). *Love God, heal Earth: 21 leading religious voices speak out on our sacred duty to protect the environment.* Pittsburgh, PA: St. Lynn's Press.

Hawken, Paul. (2007). *Blessed unrest: How the largest movement in the world came into being and why no one saw it coming.* New York: Viking Penguin.

Jones, Van. (2008). *The green collar economy: How one solution can fix our two biggest problems.* New York: Harper Collins.

Lorentzen, Lois. (2000, November-December). Paradise Paved. *Sojourners, 29*(6), 28. Retrieved April 9, 2009, from http://www.sojo.net/index.cfm?action=magazine.article&issue=soj0011&article=001121

Nonviolence

The concepts of sustainability and nonviolence are connected in many philosophies and cultural traditions; in fact, nonviolence can be practiced as a pathway to sustainability. Although the origins of this interrelationship often are attributed to India's political and spiritual leader Mohandas Gandhi, there are examples from centuries earlier.

The Indian social activist Mohandas Gandhi (1869–1948) is often cited as a historical precedent for insisting that sustainability must be approached through nonviolence. Gandhi espoused active, nonviolent resistance to colonial oppression, which he called *satyagraha*. The word is often translated as "the power of nonviolence," signifying that nonviolent resistance is active. Literally, he said, "The word *satya* [truth] comes from *sat*, which means 'to be,' 'to exist'" (Gandhi 1996, 36). A *satyagrahi*, one who trains to practice active, nonviolent resistance, acts with the power of "Truth-force" or "soul-force" *because* ". . . man is not capable of knowing the absolute truth and, therefore, not competent to punish." (Gandhi, 1996, 50–51) Since human understanding is always fragmentary, we must act nonviolently. We are seekers of truth, not omnisciently aware, so human beings can never be in a position to know that violence is justifiable. *Ahimsa*, for Gandhi, is complete nonviolence of both mind and body toward all beings, even—as he emphasized—insects.

As a model for what might now be called a sustainable lifestyle, Gandhi established a spiritual community, the Sabarmati Ashram, on 17 June 1917 near the Indian city of Ahmedabad. One of the principles he taught there was the importance of avoiding waste. Gandhi once chastised a disciple for breaking off an entire twig of a neem tree when he needed only three or four leaves. Gandhi commented, "This is violence. We should pluck the required number of leaves after offering an apology to the tree for doing so. But you broke off the whole twig, which is wasteful and wrong" (Lal 2000, 204).

Gandhi was influenced by many traditions, including Hinduism. One Hindu sect based in the Rajasthan desert of northwest India, the Bishnois, is often recognized for practicing sustainable lifestyles. The guru Maharaj Jambaji founded the sect in the late fifteenth century. He advocated twenty-nine principles (*bishnois* means "twenty-nine"), including a complete ban on felling green trees. These precepts reflect not only religious aspirations but very practical principles for maintaining the health of a fragile ecosystem.

There are many other historical inspirations for connecting sustainability with nonviolence—Buddhism (as practiced most notably today by the Dalai Lama), the Chipko (or tree hugger) movement in north India, the Indian-based Self Employed Women's Association (SEWA), and the Sarvodaya comprehensive development organization based in Sri Lanka, are a few examples.

Partly inspired by these historical precedents, but also by urgent contemporary issues such as global warming and species extinction, many contemporary green organizations connect the goal of sustainability with the practice of nonviolence. Notably, at a Global Greens Conference held in Canberra, Australia, in April 2001, green movements from around the world committed to a charter that includes six basic principles: ecological wisdom, social justice, participatory democracy, nonviolence, sustainability, and respect for diversity. The commitment to sustainability includes

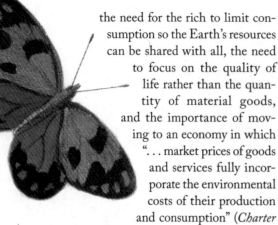

the need for the rich to limit consumption so the Earth's resources can be shared with all, the need to focus on the quality of life rather than the quantity of material goods, and the importance of moving to an economy in which ". . . market prices of goods and services fully incorporate the environmental costs of their production and consumption" (*Charter of the Global Greens* 2001).

One of the important themes that runs from Gandhi through the contemporary greens, as well as through many of the diverse organizations around the world that work toward a more sustainable world, is the need to understand sustainability in a diverse, but integrated, way. Sustainability includes scientific and ecological wisdom, economics mediated by a vision of the quality of life, and the dimensions of gender, race, and indigenous issues. Just as Gandhi argued for the necessity of nonviolence because we are not gods, so contemporary green activists often believe that the diversity of groups working for a common purpose requires more horizontal power structures based on intentional nonviolent collaboration to replace the current vertical power structures that too often are founded on violence.

Deane CURTIN
Gustavus Adolphus College

Further Reading

Charter of the Global Greens Canberra 2001. (2001). Retrieved March 2, 2009, from http://www.global.greens.org.au/Charter2001.pdf

Curtin, Deane. (1999). *Chinnagounder's challenge: The questions of ecological citizenship.* Bloomington: Indiana University Press.

Gaard, G. (1998). *Ecological politics.* Philadelphia: Temple University Press.

Gandhi, Mohandas. (1996). *Selected political writings* (D. Dalton, Ed.). Indianapolis, IN: Hackett Publishing.

Lal, Vinay. (2000). Too deep for deep ecology: Gandhi and the ecological vision of life. In Christopher. K. Chapple & Mary Evelyn Tucker (Eds.), *Hinduism and ecology: The intersection of earth, sky, and water* (pp. 183–212). Cambridge, MA: Harvard University Press.

We should deal with nature the way we should deal with ourselves. We should not harm ourselves; we should not harm nature. Harming nature is harming ourselves, and vice versa.

Thich Nhat Hanh

Source: Thich Nhat Hanh. (1988). The Individual, Society, and Nature, p. 41. In Fred Eppsteiner (Ed.), *The Path of Compassion: Writings on Socially Engaged Buddhism.* Berkeley, CA: Parallax Press.

Order and Harmony

The notion of an inherent order and balance in the natural world has been an underlying assumption in Western thought throughout history. Darwin challenged this idea through his theory of evolution, leading some Darwinians to consider taming nature to be a moral imperative. More recent thought has led to the conclusion that the seemingly chaotic web of interdependent ecosystems must be preserved to ensure the well-being of the global biosphere.

The idea that an inherent order and balance exists in the natural world pervades Western philosophical and cultural traditions. The idea underlies assumptions that objects, organisms, or species have their own essential natures and exist in a harmonious and well-ordered interdependence. For the ancient Greeks and in much of classical thought, this order and balance was seen as implicit in the structure of reality itself. Later Christian theological frameworks incorporated those perceptions into their views of divine decree and providence. Central to both was the notion that in spite of its seeming randomness and disarray, the natural world exhibits an underlying immutable order and benign harmony to which humans belong and which they should respect and follow. Disruptions of this fundamental order and balance would lead to chaos, violence, disease and strife.

Darwin's theory of evolution challenged this age-old notion of an unchanging natural order and benign balance by demonstrating theoretically how one could have design without a designer. Evolution suggested that whatever balance or order we do see in nature is the result of a violent, ceaseless and chaotic struggle for survival, in which species are neither fixed nor immutable but are continually changing to evolve some new competitive advantage to aid them in the battle for existence. Thus, although previous generations had seen the natural world as exemplifying

a timeless, beneficent order with which humans should seek to act in harmony, according to its new articulation within evolutionary theory, nature was seen as ruled by a chaotic dynamic that offered no foundational grounds for the human moral order. This led many, including the eminent Darwinian T. H. Huxley, to argue that human moral action consisted not in conformity with nature but in actively fighting against it. Indeed, in *Ethics and Evolution*, Huxley sees the technological and industrial transformation, alteration, and appropriation of the natural world by humans as almost akin to a moral imperative.

In our own day, human technological success has been so great that many suggest that it threatens not only the continued well-being and existence of the nonhuman natural world but possibly the human world as well. Indeed, many ecologists and environmentalists argue that the scale and magnitude of our impact on the environment in terms of pollution and our demand for resources has become so excessive that it could push the global biosphere to the point of collapse. In contrast to the view commonly held throughout the late nineteenth to mid-twentieth century, which saw the environment as little more than a neutral playing field on which natural species and organisms battled it out for supremacy, recent theoretical and empirical insights from the science of ecology—including theories such as dynamic equilibrium and trophic dynamics—suggest that ecological relationships between various elements and factors in an ecosystem, both biotic and abiotic, are far more interdependent and interwoven than previously thought. In many cases, this web of relationships functions to ensure a certain degree of stability and equilibrium in an ecological community. Furthermore, ecosystems themselves are not self-enclosed isolated systems but are involved in a web of relations and interdependences with other ecosystems and, indeed, the global biosystem as a whole. Nevertheless, although these webs of interdependencies allow ecosystems to exhibit a certain robust stability and equilibrium, ecologists warn that these are not infinite and that the massive production of greenhouse gas and other forms of pollutants, and loss of biodiversity caused by human industrial activity together with the demand for resources, could lead to the disintegration of these systems, culminating in a severe ecological and climatic crisis that could have a very dire impact on human existence. This has prompted many to argue that human demands on the natural environment must be curtailed and balanced with a concern for the overall well-being and continuing existence of the natural world.

Recently the ecologist Daniel K. Botkin, in his books *Discordant Harmonies* and *No Man's Garden,* has critiqued the predominant paradigm in ecology, as he interprets it, which holds that ecosystems are stable, enclosed, internally regulated systems. Botkin suggests that this view, as well as the reliance of many environmentalists on it, is fundamentally inspired and based on the age-old Western "myth" of the natural order and balance. He further posits that the new paradigm emerging in ecology is that ecosystems are far more open and often in a state of dynamic disruptive change and flux. Blotkin himself, however, has been criticized by many ecologists, such as Brian Czech, for essentially straw-manning the prevailing consensus in ecology and presenting as radically new challenges to the current paradigm concepts that have been conventional wisdom since the late 1960s.

Nevertheless, for the most part, these debates within ecology appear to be more a matter of emphasis than of fundamental disagreement. If one side of the debate chooses to stress the more dynamic aspects of ecological processes while the other its more stabilizing character, neither is denying that both are fundamental features of ecosystems. Consequently, it appears that the new picture of nature is one that combines and allows for both dynamism and stability and chaos and order. This is not the timeless natural order of classic Greek and Christian thought, but neither is it the dynamic atomistic free for all of nineteenth-century evolutionary theory. Increasingly, it appears that humanity is caught up in a broader web of natural dependencies and dynamic interactions that, as the environmental crisis demonstrates to us, we ignore at our peril.

T. R. KOVER
Katholieke Universiteit Leuven

FURTHER READING

Botkin, Daniel. (1992). *Discordant harmonies: A new ecology for the twenty-first century.* New York: Oxford University Press.

Botkin, Daniel. (2001). *No man's garden: Thoreau and a new vision for civilization and nature.* Washington, DC: Island Press.

Czech, Brian. (2001). Straw men in "No Man's Garden." *BioScience,* 51(3), 250–255.

Glacken, Clarence J. (1967). *Traces on the Rhodian shore: Nature and culture in Western thought from ancient times to the end of the eighteenth century.* Berkeley: University of California Press.

Huxley, Thomas Henry. (1902). *Evolution and ethics: And other essays.* New York: D. Appleton and Company.

Irvine, William. (1963). *Apes, angels and Victorians: The story of Darwin, Huxley and evolution.* New York: McGraw-Hill.

Lovejoy, Arthur Oncken. (1964). *The great chain of being: The study of a history of an idea* (30th ed.). Cambridge, MA: Harvard University Press.

Worster, Donald. (1994). *Nature's economy: A history of ecological ideas* (2nd ed.). New York and Cambridge, U.K.: Cambridge University Press.

P

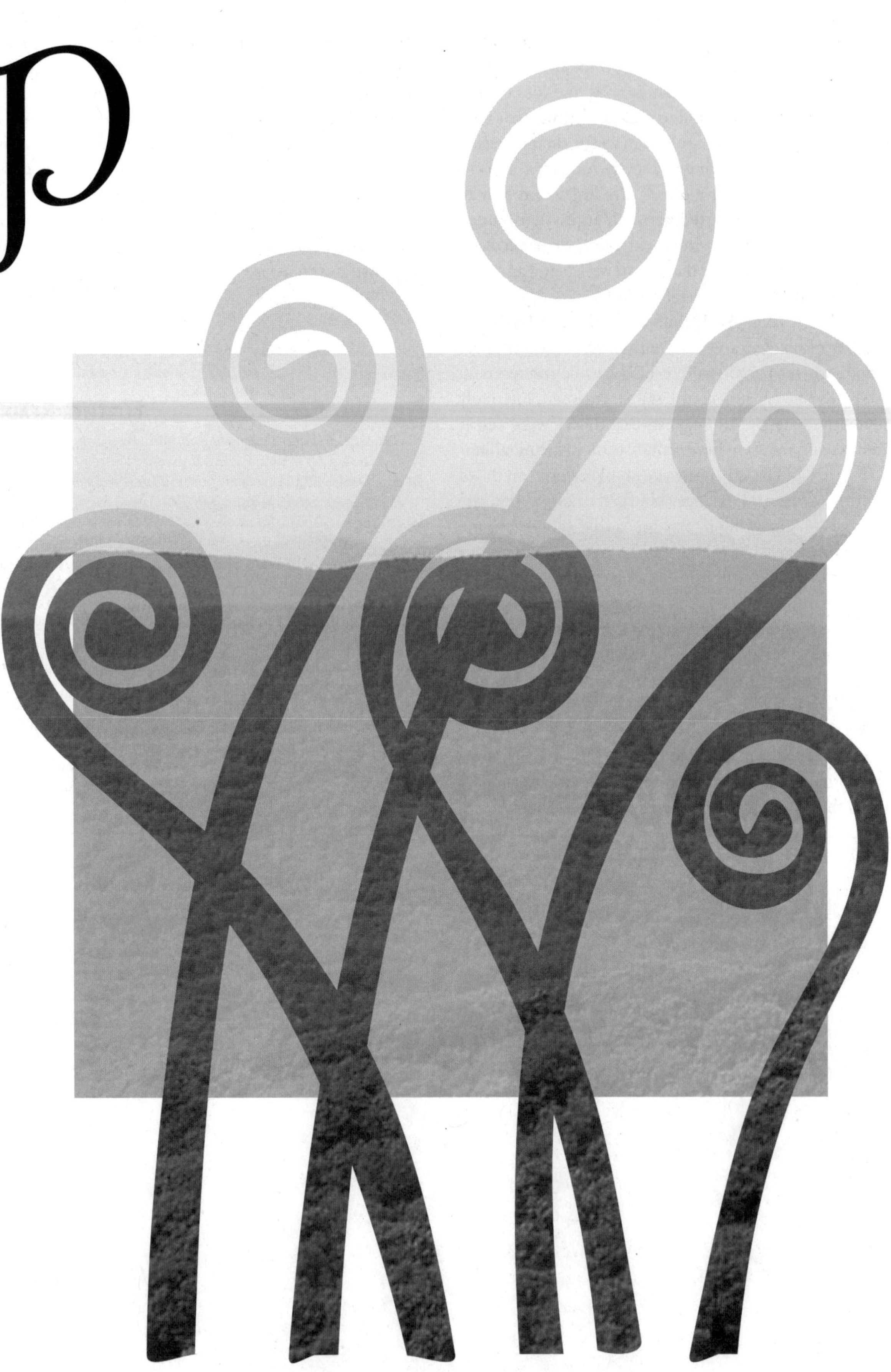

Paganism and Neopaganism

Paganism and Neopaganism include contemporary spiritual practices and religions that celebrate and revere nature. Pagans honor their sacred relationship with Earth and all that lives on Earth. The principles of their Earth-based spirituality foster sustainable lifestyles and provide the basis for the discussion and formulation of an ethics of sustainability.

Paganism or Neopaganism typically describes a collection of contemporary spiritual practices and religions that are grounded in this world and celebrate nature. Within the context of sustainability, two questions will be addressed: First, how does Paganism support sustainability? Second, to what extent do Pagans practice sustainable lifestyles?

Debate continues about how to define Paganism and the extent to which Paganism is a nature religion. This article will treat Paganism as a range of spiritual practices that celebrate nature, marking the processes of life and death, seasonal changes, and lunar cycles.

Contemporary Paganism takes many forms, the most common being witchcraft, initiatory Wiccan traditions, Druidry, and eclectic Paganism. Less prevalent forms include Goddess spirituality, Ásatrú (Norse Paganism), shamanism, and Reconstructionist traditions. Pagans are usually polytheists who honor immanent deities (deities that are inherent to or dwell within the material world), treat the Earth as sacred, and hold the animist belief that "all that exists lives."

An Ethics of Sustainability

In as much as Paganism celebrates nature, it offers an excellent grounding for an ethics of sustainability. Theoretical discussion has only begun quite recently, perhaps because Paganism is rooted in practice, not belief. However, several Pagans have offered an ethics, and while the influences and details vary, all discussions are rooted in the theme of *relationship*.

The idea that the Earth is a single organism, scientifically formalized in British scientist James Lovelock's Gaia hypothesis, was an early influence on Pagan ethics, initially through Oberon Zell-Ravenheart (1971), and later, via influential British Wiccans like Doreen Valiente and Stuart and Janet Farrar. Zell-Ravenheart co-founded the Pagan Church of All Worlds in 1962. Doreen Valiente had an early and enduring influence on British Traditional Wicca while Stuart and Janet Farrar wrote several widely read books about that same tradition. More recently, animist beliefs which require a respectful relationship with other-than-human beings have been brought to the foreground: Emma Restall-Orr's Druid ethics of connection, Douglas Ezzy's "intimate relationship" with place, Thom Van Dooren's "sacred community" (de Angeles, Restall-Orr, and Van Dooren 2005), and Starhawk's systems-based model all emphasize this principle.

While deep ecology and ecofeminism are influential, other approaches have been fruitful: the feminist theologian Carol Christ applies process philosophy, which recognizes that "all beings are connected in the web of life" (Christ 2003); Sylvie Shaw (2004) uses ecopsychology to understand the spiritual power of nature; and Starhawk increasingly draws on permaculture principles to learn how to design human systems that mimic natural systems. Bioregionalism is another significant influence: Chas Clifton emphasizes that a Pagan must "learn where you are on the earth" (1998), while bioregional animism—relating to the land or bioregion as the source of one's religion and culture—has grown from Cascadia, a bioregion in the northwestern United States and Canada, in 2000 into a global movement.

There is a coherent and commonly held Pagan ethic of sustainability grounded in sacred relationship, but the question of how that relationship can be maintained remains less clear.

Sustainable in Practice?

Research into Pagans' lifestyles is inconclusive: although Regina Smith Oboler's 2004 study found above average levels of sustainable behavior amongst U.S. Pagans, other factors made conclusions difficult. Barbara Davy suggests that only a minority of Pagans are environmentally active, but this is to be expected: Pagans, like most people, strive to live up to their ethical principles and often fall short. But certain aspects of the cultural history of Paganism may be inimical to an ethics of sustainability. Some claim that the influence of esotericism can create inconsistencies by encouraging Pagans to "understand 'nature' as a symbol" rather than the actual living environment (Davy 2007). Starhawk concludes that Paganism's potential to encourage sustainable lifestyles depends on rooting it "in the real earth, and not just in our abstract ideas" (Starhawk 2005).

Such a grounded spirituality emerges from practical embodied knowing. Genuine relationships take time and require careful observation, so Starhawk's Earth Activist Training combines a permaculture design course with Earth-based spirituality. Adrian Harris' Sacred Ecology emphasizes the embodied knowing of gut feelings, while Susan Greenwood notes that a "connected wholeness" (2005) can emerge through dancing or drumming. Harris subsequently identified more of these "processes of connection" including trance, ritual, and the wilderness effect theorized by ecopsychology (2008).

Although Paganism principles strongly support sustainable lifestyles, the rich potential inherent in those principles is not always realized in practice. Pagans are increasingly engaged in developing an ethic of sustainability, however, and exploring how their spiritual practices can best encourage sustainable behavior.

Adrian HARRIS
Faith, Spirituality and Social Change Project

FURTHER READING

Christ, Carol P. (2003). *She who changes: Re-imagining the divine in the world.* New York: Palgrave.

Clifton, Chas S. (1998). Nature religion for real. Retrieved August 5, 2008, from http://www.chasclifton.com/papers/forreal.html

Davy, Barbara J. (2007). *Introduction to Pagan studies.* Lanham, MD: AltaMira Press.

de Angeles, Ly; Restall-Orr, Emma; & Van Dooren, Thom (Eds.). (2005). *Pagan visions for a sustainable future.* Woodbury, MN: Llewellyn Publications.

Ezzy, Douglas. (2005). I am the mountain walking: wombats in the greenwood. In, Ly de Angeles, Emma Restall-Orr, and Thom Van Dooren, *Pagan visions for a sustainable future.* Woodbury, MN: Llewellyn Publications.

Greenwood, Susan. (2005). *The nature of magic: An anthropology of consciousness.* Oxford, U.K.: Berg Publishers.

Harris, Adrian P. (2008). *The wisdom of the body: Embodied knowing in eco-Paganism.* (PhD thesis). University of Winchester, U.K.

Oboler, Regina Smith. (2004). Nature religion as a cultural system? Sources of environmentalist action and rhetoric in a contemporary Pagan community. *The Pomegranate: The International Journal of Pagan Studies, 6*(1), 86–106.

Restall-Orr, Emma. (2005). The ethics of Paganism: The value and power of sacred relationship. In, Ly de Angeles, Emma Restall-Orr, and Thom Van Dooren, *Pagan visions for a sustainable future.* Woodbury, MN: Llewellyn Publications.

Shaw, Sylvie. (2004). At the water's edge. In Jenny Blain; Douglas Ezzy; & Graham Harvey (Eds.), *Researching Paganisms.* Walnut Creek, CA: AltaMira.

Starhawk. (2004). *The Earth path.* New York: HarperCollins.

Starhawk. (2005). Pagan politics, Pagan stories: An interview. In Ly de Angeles, Emma Restall-Orr, & Thom Van Dooren, *Pagan visions for a sustainable future.* Woodbury, MN: Llewellyn Publications.

Van Dooren, Thom. (2005). Dwelling in sacred community. In, Ly de Angeles, Emma Restall-Orr, and Thom Van Dooren, *Pagan visions for a sustainable future.* Woodbury, MN: Llewellyn Publications.

Zell-Ravenheart, Oberon (under the name of Otter G'Zell). (1971, July 1). Theagenesis: The birth of the goddess. *Green Egg, 4*, 40.

Peace

Scholars focus on social, economic, and environmental dimensions when analyzing how to achieve peace, and, with it, the basis for a sustainable existence. Theorists admit all three of these categories contain some valid and essential aspects that would contribute to sustainable peace in spite of their extremely different recommendations.

The sustainability of the environment and the resolution of political conflicts are integrally related. When analyzing how to achieve a sustainable peace, scholars tend to focus on three dimensions of relationships in their analysis: the social dimension, the economic dimension, and the environmental dimension. In their analyses, scholars look at the networks of relationships present in each dimension.

Three Dimensions

The social dimension pertains to our relationships with each other. The economic dimension focuses on the relationships around production. Finally, the environmental dimension examines the relationship of humans to the rest of the biosphere. A sustainable peace is considered to be one in which the configuration of relationships across these three dimensions allows all organisms to live well while not jeopardizing the quality of life of future generations. Conflict can be seen as an indication that something within these three dimensions has deviated from what is required for sustainability.

Although any final verdict on sustainability must await the test of time, we can focus on certain specific indicators that serve as litmus tests for whether a system might be sustainable into the future. These indicators are: biodiversity (environment), true-cost accounting (economic), and social capital and civil society (social).

Biodiversity is defined as the range of noninvasive biological diversity found within an ecosystem. True-cost accounting (or pricing) is when the price of a product in the market reflects the true costs to society and the environment of its production and consumption. High social capital is evidenced by dense, inclusive, and overlapping social networks that contain norms of mutual trust and generalized reciprocity.

Practitioners within the peace studies field analyze these three indicators and develop interventions around the vulnerable dimension(s) to rearrange or develop relationships such that civil society, true-cost accounting, or biodiversity are maintained. Considerable variation, however, exists among peace scholars concerning the most appropriate practices to achieve these sustainable indicators. These variations can be catalogued roughly into three general categories of perspectives: the conservative perspective, the managerial perspective, and the radical perspective (Humphrey 2002).

Three Perspectives

The conservative cluster emphasizes individual-oriented, free-market approaches as the mechanism for ensuring sustainability. Practitioners within this perspective tend to focus on individual education or awareness campaigns and letting the market decide what types of relationships should emerge. For example, contemporary theorists in this paradigm would argue that there is no environmental crisis around oil. Eventually, the high price of petroleum will force new alternatives to arise and, subsequently, new relationships will emerge.

The conservative paradigm views conflict as a temporary phase that occurs during a time of transition between sets of values, whether economic or cultural. Conflict is perceived as a clash between "appropriate" and "inappropriate" cultural values, and generally is only considered relevant when the conflict directly addresses a cause-and-effect relationship. Once citizens with inappropriate values have been reeducated, or the proponents of an inappropriate system have died out, then conflict should disappear. (Interestingly, both individual-oriented environmental education campaigns [such as a recycling campaign] and the political scientist Samuel Huntington's view of the clash of civilizations, in which he predicted that violent conflict would be caused by religious and cultural differences, not the ideological friction among nation-states, would fall within the conservative paradigm.)

The managerial cluster of social theories focuses on the importance of ensuring that individuals and corporations absorb the true consequences of their actions. This paradigm contends that free markets are going to be unsustainable in the long term because individuals and groups constantly will be seeking to capture the positive consequences of their actions while foisting the negative consequences of their actions on to others. Garrett Hardin's "The Tragedy of the Commons" is a good example of this tendency within the commons era of England. Simply put, in a system in which the community absorbs the negative consequences (long term) and the individual gains the positive outcome (in the short term), all individuals will choose short-term gain over long-term stability.

Managerial theorists see conflict emerging from groups that have crossed a tipping point in the amount of negative consequences they can absorb. To avoid this conflict, practitioners in this paradigm advocate creating mechanisms that force organizations and individuals to absorb the full consequences, both negative and positive, of their actions. These might be a set of individual-oriented rewards and punishments, forms of social pressure, or state interventions—laws of coercion, tax breaks of persuasion, or institutions such as the Environmental Protection Agency (EPA) that monitor behavior and can distribute punishments for infractions. Unfortunately, this perspective only really becomes fully engaged after the conflict has risen to the level of expressing itself toward the cause of the negative consequences. The normal cycle of conflict doesn't necessarily point to the root causes in early stages when violence and aggression are more likely pointed at members of the oppressed group or other scapegoat figures.

The social theorists that fall into the radical category are more suspicious of assumptions about the sustainability of democratic capitalism as a system. They would contend that a system that requires the treadmill of production to survive cannot be ultimately sustainable—socially or environmentally. In the social arena, these theorists contend that power inevitably will become concentrated as competition forces individuals or organizations to "cheat" and push the negative consequences on to someone else. These theorists see conflict as inevitable as the environment degrades and forces marginalized individuals to react or as the social systems become more and more power-centralized in an attempt to maintain growth in a competitive environment. Intervention strategies in this category tend to be oriented around zero-growth economics, power decentralization, and the overthrow or elimination of the entire system.

Solutions for the Future

Which cluster of theories are the most appropriate for achieving sustainability has been difficult to verify empirically. Theorists admit that as a result of the highly integrated and extremely complex nature of society and the environment, all three of these categories contain some element of truth in spite of their extremely different recommendations for achieving a sustainable peace. Pragmatic practitioners immersed in the complexity of social interventions tend to draw on a mixture of elements from each of the clusters. For example, pragmatists may recognize the radical paradigm critique concerning the dangers of a growth-orientation in the economy yet also recognize that the capitalist system has generated a level of well-being unheard of in previous epochs. Or they may recognize that free-market pressures are important solutions as advocated by the conservative theorists, yet also recognize that allowing groups and individuals to foist the negative consequences of their actions on to others or the environment is a temptation in society. As such, pragmatists tend to emphasize maintaining a balance between the paradigms of intervention by advocating sustainable growth, balancing the exploitation of resources with the preservation of future potential, and recognizing the importance of individual choice and corporate responsibility while still seeing the necessity of state or social incentives and disincentives to avoid cheating or unsustainable behaviors. Ultimately, what pragmatists focus on in any situation of conflict or social need are questions such as: Is civil society being strengthened? Is true-cost accounting in evidence? And, perhaps most important, is biodiversity being maintained?

Terrence JANTZI
Eastern Mennonite University

Aaron KISHBAUGH
Independent scholar, Singers Glen, Virginia

FURTHER READING

Hardin, Garrett. (1968). The tragedy of the commons. *Science, 162,* 1243–1248.

Humphrey, Craig R.; Lewis, Tammy L.; & Buttel, Frederick H. (2002). *Environment, energy & society: A new synthesis.* Belmont, CA: Wadsworth Books.

Huntington, Samuel. (1997). *The clash of civilizations and the remaking of world order.* London: Simon & Schuster.

Gilligan, James. (2001). *Preventing violence.* New York: Thames & Hudson.

Pilgrimage

Making a spiritual journey, or pilgrimage, has historically been a ritual for believers of many faiths who find fulfillment in the physical and emotional association with a sacred place. The ideas of connectedness between living beings, the divine, and resources of the ecosystem relate pilgrimage to sustainable ways of living; ironically many religious sites today feel the impact of our ecological footprint.

Pilgrimage is a spiritual journey or quest for fulfillment whose physical destination is often a shrine. The holy place may be a site of local deities, or a place where important events in the history of the religion, the deaths of its martyrs, or the lives of its founders occurred. The English word is derived from the Latin terms *peregrinus*, meaning "wanderer," and *per agrum*, meaning "through the fields." Reverberating through the word is an ancient echo of an intricate relationship between geography and the sacred in motion. In this sense both the concept and the practice of modern pilgrimage can draw attention to sustainable ways of living on Earth and the need to care for the ecosystem: the respect and devotion implicit in pilgrimage can enhance the connection humans feel to the lands they inhabit, the creatures they share them with, and the natural resources that make life possible.

Pilgrimage is common to many indigenous cultures, as well as to the major religions of the world. Jerusalem attracts pilgrims from all of the Abrahamic religions, while Buddhists, Hindus, Jains, and followers of Bön (Tibet's oldest indigenous religion) regard Mount Kailash in the Himalayas as a holy place. Modern Christians, who still have strong ties to the Holy Land, also flock to Roman reliquaries and to Lourdes in France. The largest annual pilgrimage in the world, the hajj, is one of the five pillars (duties) of Islam and requires every Muslim who is capable of traveling to go to Mecca at least once in a lifetime.

Cultural anthropologists in the twentieth century made several attempts to categorize pilgrimage. Victor and Edith Turner regard pilgrimage as a "liminoid" or transitional experience, in which pilgrims leave the established systems of society and form an egalitarian *communitas*, or "a social antistructure," on the road (Turner and Turner 1978, 250–251). John Eade and Michael Sallnow's *Contesting the Sacred* (1991) challenged Turner's concept of *communitas* for being (in part) too idealized and remote. Simon Coleman and John Eade, looking at the "on the road" aspect of a journey, have emphasized the movement involved in pilgrimage processes in various religious traditions, which they portray as "kinetic rituals" (Coleman and Eade 2004).

Turner and Turner (1978, 7) have noted a relationship between pilgrimage and mysticism. "If mysticism is an interior pilgrimage, pilgrimage is an exteriorized mysticism." Such links presuppose cosmologies where the divine is not considered to be distant to nature but immanent and present in landscape, movement and body. This interconnectedness in nature is an aspect of many indigenous religions whose creation myths derive from an Earth Mother and which today practice sustainable ways of living in the spirit of devotion and respect. Phil Cousineau, the author of *The Art of Pilgrimage: The Seeker's Guide to Making Travel Sacred*, suggests "that we follow our spiritual compass and put the soles of our shoes to the soul of the world. It means getting back in touch with our earth, our roots, ourselves" (O'Reilly and O'Reilly 2000, xv).

The positive impact of pilgrimage as it relates to sustainability can be seen in numerous accounts of how such spiritual journeys heighten people's sensitivity to the relation and balance among the human and nonhuman creatures, the divine, and the resources of our ecosystem. While the term *pilgrimage* has adopted an increasingly secular connotation—traveling to pay tribute to a cultural icon, for instance, or calling a popular cultural center a "tourists' Mecca"—the underlying implications of pilgrimage as a quest for fulfillment remain strong. The October 2008 Grace Pilgrimage to the Peace Village of San José de Apartadó, for instance, originated not as a religious-based journey but as a form of social activism in the civil-war-torn areas of Colombia; its focus was to help villagers work ecologically, technologically, and socially toward a dignified and sustainable future.

The negative impact of pilgrimage—the fact that many religious shrines of the world suffer from traffic, pollution, and the demands of tourism—reminds pilgrims (and enthusiastic tourists alike) that the journey "through the fields" should be made with care, and with an effort to reduce the human ecological footprint on Earth as a whole.

Sigridur GUDMARSDOTTIR
Reykjavik Academy

FURTHER READING

Coleman, Simon, & Eade, John. (Eds.). (2004). *Reframing pilgrimage: Culture in motion.* London: Routledge.

Cousineau, Philip. (2000). *The art of pilgrimage The seeker's guide to making travel sacred.* Newburyport, MA: Red Wheel.

Eade, John, & Sallnow, Michael J. (1991). *Contesting the sacred: The anthropology of pilgrimage.* London and New York: Routledge.

O'Reilly, Sean, & O'Reilly, James. (Eds.). (2000). *Pilgrimage: Adventures of the spirit.* Palo Alto, CA: Travelers' Tales.

Timothy, D. J., & Olsen, Daniel. (Eds.). (2006). *Tourism, religion and spiritual journeys.* London: Routledge.

Turner, Victor, & Turner, Edith. (1978). *Image and pilgrimage in Christian culture: Anthropological perspectives.* New York: Columbia University Press.

chat — Berkshire's authors and editors welcome questions, comments, and corrections: sustainability.updates@berkshirepublishing.com

Place

Concepts of "place" are numerous and diverse; they provide insight for discussions about what it means to live in a socially and environmentally conscious manner. Many environmental advocates insist that an understanding of place is a key component of working toward environmental sustainability—and that local, community, or place-based approaches are more effective for the negotiation of social and environmental sustainability.

The literature on "place" is diverse, extensive, and multidisciplinary. It ranges from phenomenological studies of "sense of place" to cultural analyses of "place meaning" to detailed research on the political economy of places and their position in the networks of ecological, economic, and discursive flows in national, regional, and global systems. Scholars and thinkers such as Edward S. Casey, Tim Cresswell, David A. Gruenewald, and Carla K. Trentelmans have made important contributions to the study of place, devising numerous terms and related concepts including sense of place, place attachment, and place identity. "Place" is also located in relation to other concepts such as "community," "local," "territory," and "globalization," as well as to hybrid terms such as "glocal."

The basic argument for why place may be important to sustainability is that knowing one's place is a deeply experiential process that aids the individual and social group to develop knowledge and caring appropriate for the task of living well, that is, in a socially and environmentally conscious manner. The North American farmer-philosopher-poet Wendell Berry (1972) summarizes this view: "Without a complex knowledge of one's place, and without the faithfulness to one's place on which such knowledge depends, it is inevitable that the place will be used carelessly, and eventually destroyed." In this view, place matters because knowledge, values, and behavior are assumed to be intimately linked to a context.

What Is "Place"?

Although places are spatial, place is differentiated from "space." Space is not place until someone gives it a meaning. John Agnew and J. S. Duncan (1989) identify three crucial aspects of place: location, locale, and sense of place. *Location* is the fixed geographic coordinates on a map. *Locale* is the way that the space is configured—the concrete material characteristics that shape interaction. *Sense of place* is the affective dimension of the place. Space is not place until someone gives it a meaning. These physical and emotional aspects are collectively used by persons to make space into a meaningful place. According to Robert Sack (1993), three realms influence the construction of placeness: the physical world (including built and natural objects, nonhuman and human others), the social world (including social, economic, political, race, class, gender, and bureaucracy), and the realm of meaning (the ideas, values, and beliefs that make up the forces of the mind).

Places are locations that are specific, distinct, and have a particular identity for someone. Place is a human construction of a location created through intersubjective human experience of the location itself, and not simply appropriated as if there is a singular essence of a place. Values associated with a place will be correspondingly multiple and varied in the strength with which they are assigned.

A solid body of research in the social sciences has investigated the role of meaningful locales in fostering a *sense of place*. Humanistic geographers began using this idea in the 1970s to move beyond an overemphasis on the physical traits of places (Relph 1976; Tuan 1977). The concept has gained sufficient recognition to be used by the U.S. government's Environmental Protection Agency (EPA) in a guide on community-based environmental outreach (U.S. EPA, 2002). A sense of place could be said to enhance the value of a locale in economic as well as affective terms. Architects, tourism promoters, and planners use sense of place in their work. Much of the early research emphasized "rootedness" or long residence in a place as crucial in the development of a sense of place. Such assumptions are still prevalent, although they also have been challenged by recognition that everyone has their own sense of the place; because places do not have a single identity or value, duration of inhabitation will only generate changing senses of place, but not "correct" ones.

A related concept is *placelessness*, which is said to characterize places that do not have a unique character and are relatively homogenous and undifferentiated from other places. Such places may include ubiquitous strip malls on the outskirts of major cities, or fast-food chains or new, standardized (and architecturally boring) housing developments. Arguably, such places may develop particular meanings for someone frequenting them, but an assumption of placeless space is that one such location can be substituted for another with little lost. The value of placeless places would be short-term, as long as people and production could move elsewhere if environmental degradation occurs.

Sense-of-place research is especially prevalent in cultural geography, but psychology, anthropology and, to a lesser extent, sociology have also identified sense of place or similar concepts. Social and environmental psychologists, for example, tend to focus on attachment to place or the ways that individuals incorporate "special places" into their own self-identities. Sociologists often focus social relations in social space and the negotiations over constructions of meaning about these social relations and the locales in which they occur. Whether by intention or not, we could call these projects of *place making* as the characteristics and values of a place are negotiated and manipulated.

Recent scholarship has begun to emphasize how specific places and senses of place are associated with other places and larger scales (Cresswell 2004; Escobar 2001; Massey 1997). Even though some contemporary environmental problems are global in scope, the local variability in their manifestation can be significant. Global temperature rise, for example, is greater in northern latitudes where ecosystems are also less resilient. Attention to global environmental phenomena, perhaps counterintuitively, shows the limits of universalizing tendencies within globalization discourse. That is, although places are affected by what goes on in other places and around the planet, the myriad of ways these global forces are reformulated by unique peoples, cultures, and places means that globalization might be a hybridizing process rather than leading only to placelessness. The anthropological tradition emphasizes that culture is often place-specific (Feld and Basso 1996; Escobar 2001). As the anthropologist Clifford Geertz wrote, "No one lives in the world in general" (Feld and Basso, 1996). Escobar shows that attention to local particularities (including the

way that people construct their sense of place and localized social relations) within that reconfiguration of extralocal contact opens rich possibilities for understanding human life. This global-local hybridization has been termed "glocalization" (Robertson 1992).

By this argument, an important stage in developing an ability to live in an environmentally aware manner is to rebuild ties to local places, including local culture, ecology, and economies. Critics argue that modern education has abstracted the natural world as it has decontextualized knowledge rather than being grounded in particular social and ecological circumstances; in ignoring place and direct experience, education has encouraged technological domination over the things of this world. The alternative for the environmental educator David Orr "is to rediscover and reinhabit our places and regions, finding in them sources of food, livelihood, energy, healing, recreation and celebration" (1994, 147). An alternate, place-conscious education would counteract alienation and fertilize the growth of environmental concern (Gruenewald 2003).

Nevertheless, it is crucial to assess the political, economic, and cultural forces that impact unique places. The field of political ecology examines the processes by which more and more places are pulled into production for global capitalism (Peet and Watts 2004). The "small is beautiful" school of democratic thought argues that localized civil society is an antidote to rationalized but blind political-economic forces that would erase the sustainability of particular places. Many scholars and activists insist that environmental protection begins in local places, hence the need for regionally based local economies and decentralized politics. A long-serving Montana (U.S.) state politician and city mayor, Daniel Kemmis writes of a politics and economics intentioned for local benefit. "This kind of economic development is not possible without a shift in thinking that replaces the abstract, placeless notion of the market with the localized, particularized concept of a market*place*" (Kemmis 1990, 92 [italics in original]). Such proposals are similar to the philosophy of bioregionalism (McGinnis 1999). A bioregion is an ecologically or physically determined location—such as a watershed, or an ecotone (like the Sonoran desert)—in which human culture is shaped by "living in place." Many place-based writers have unproblematically described an idealized past, or unapologetically announced their proposals for sustainability as recovering older traditions of land use and human–place relationships.

Finally, a focus on place may increase attention to ecological factors and their extralocal relations rather than an exclusive focus on human processes in a location. Environmental practice extends human relations beyond social space to include ecological processes and objects, and relations between human and other-than-human. This includes breaking down the standard dichotomies of modernity, such as culture/nature. The human realm does not exist apart from the biophysical but is integrally located within that realm while simultaneously organizing the institutional and symbolic ways by which members understand and interact with that environment. These are contributions of the concept of place for environmental sustainability.

Problems of "Place"

Contrary to the simple and at times romantic theorizing about place described earlier in this article, the notion of "place" is also problematic. A "place" is constructed within many relationships (Cresswell 2004; Massey 1997). Place meanings and place attachments will differ among individuals and social groups, sometimes dramatically. For example, logging or mining disputes often pit one local group versus another (although often with the unacknowledged entanglements of transnational capital). These are genuine conflicts over differing senses of place.

Places are historically constructed, but the past alone is not constitutive of all meanings. There is no automatic reason to privilege older ways of relating to the land, particularly in changing times; also, these traditions may be reconstructions of mythic memory rather than history. Another criticism of place-based approaches is place-boundedness. This can be expressed as parochialism—that one place is better than another—or that certain senses of a place (usually historically privileged) are more legitimate than other constructions. Also, places can be highly exclusionary, as evidenced by those who seek the anonymity of larger population centers where social censure arising from tight relations is diluted (Young 1990).

Places are "fuzzy." A bioregional emphasis can help make one aware of the characteristics of where one lives but has several problems. First, the place will have different boundaries depending on who draws them. In addition, as Doreen Massey (1997) points out, all places are dependent on other places for important items needed for sustenance of lifestyle. Reconstructing lifestyles to be solely based in a locale does not acknowledge these real connections. It is not possible to understand a particular place without placing it in its context and its relationships with other places. More so, contemporary lifestyles cannot be turned back to a bucolic and imaginary past when humans were said to "live off the land." North American culture is mobile—just as others are—and urbanization accelerates worldwide. Migrating from rural areas to find work, more than 50 percent of the world's population now lives in cities, with much social dislocation. Finally, travel, communications, and media show us places far beyond our own locale. The result is a simultaneous deplacing and expanding of awareness through experience. Places are located within larger geographies, such that localized understandings may misanalyze the causes and consequences of environmental and social problems that are more than local in character.

In her conceptualization of a *global sense of place*, Doreen Massey highlights as a problem "the persistent identification of place with 'community'" (1997, 321). The notion of community is a lengthy and complex concept, but in the context of this discussion it is sufficient to say that communities can exist without being located in a locale, and that places alone do not generate community—consider most government housing projects, for example. Similarly, it could be argued that gangs and the nationalist movements have strong senses of place or territoriality and the acceptable social structure for the community of their particular place. Massey believes that a sense of place may be mobilized as a hedge against insecurity and change in an unsettling and globalizing modern world. If so, this could reinforce a search for the essentialist or "real" meaning of place, and a reactionary response of place-boundedness or parochialism rather than a progressive and open approach. In other words, attachment to place will not automatically produce progressive values or environmental awareness.

There are genuine questions as to whether a place-based focus would help produce a more environmentally sensitive populace, environmental values, or sustainable practices. Place-based approaches can be plagued by the "not in my back yard" (NIMBY) syndrome, whereby place figures prominently in the opposition to undesirable uses, such as a hazardous industry. NIMBY opposition may lead to diverting the rejected project into another community with fewer resources to combat such siting. As a contrast to the parochial NIMBY ethic, the environmental ethicists Bryan Norton and Bruce Hannon (1997) added the more comprehensively place-conscious NIABY ("not in anyone's back yard") ethic. They argue that the accumulation of many locally based sustainable ethics result in an effective place-based approach to environmental decision making.

Conclusion

Place making is complex. Place-making projects are not free from domination, oppressions, or inequities. Place making also seeks to position the specific place in relation to larger scales (such as provinces, regions, and nations) and in relation to other places. Constructions of place remain projects, that is, ever incomplete, advancing in bursts and stalls, and with contestation, especially as varied actors employ their resources and negotiate the many values they associate with the places. Place making, then, is personal and collective, discursive and material, social and ecological. The values associated with particular constructions of a place may be as varied as the social actors themselves.

Because place meanings can be varied and actions toward places can be multifaceted, it would not seem that a consciousness of place alone would be an adequate basis on which to presume an environmental or social ethos.

Nevertheless, place remains an important concept for environmental sustainability, if for no other reason than that behavior needs specific locations in which to be performed. Places remain as the experiential ground of action, where values are performed, irrespective of the political, economic, cultural, phenomenological, and other influences.

Randolph HALUZA-DeLAY
The King's University College (Alberta)

FURTHER READING

Agnew, John. A., & J. S. Duncan. (Eds). (1989). *The power of place: Bringing together geographical and sociological imaginations.* Boston: Unwin Hyman.

Berry, Wendell. (1972). *A continuous harmony: Essays cultural and agricultural.* New York: Harcourt Brace Jovanovich, Brace Books.

Casey, Edward S. (1997). *The fate of place: A philosophical history.* Berkeley: University of California Press.

Cresswell, Tim. (2004). *Place: A short introduction.* Malden, MA: Blackwell.

Escobar, Arturo. (2001). Culture sits in places: Reflections on globalism and subaltern strategies of localization. *Political Geography, 20,* 139–174.

Feld, Steven, & Basso, Keith H. (Eds). (1996). *Senses of place.* Sante Fe, NM: School of American Research Press.

Gruenewald, David A. (2003). Foundations of place: A multidisciplinary framework for place-conscious education. *American Educational Research Journal, 40*(3), 619–654.

Kemmis, Daniel. (1990). *Community and the politics of place.* Oklahoma City: Oklahoma University Press.

Massey, Doreen. (1997). A global sense of place. In Trevor Barnes & Derek Gregory (Eds.), *Reading human geography: The poetics and politics of inquiry* (pp. 315–323). London: Arnold.

McGinnis, Michael V. (Ed.). (1999). *Bioregionalism.* New York: Routledge.

Norton, Bryan G., & Hannon, Bruce. (1997). Environmental values: A place-based theory. *Environmental Ethics, 19*(3), 227–45.

Orr, David. (1994). *Earth in mind: On education, environment, and the human prospect.* Washington, DC: Island Press.

Peet, Richard, & Watts, Michael. (Eds.). (2004). *Liberation ecologies: Environment, development, social movements,* 2nd ed. New York: Routledge.

Relph, Ernest. (1976). *Place and placelessness.* London: Pion.

Robertson, Roland. (1992). *Globalization: Social theory and global culture.* London: Sage.

Sack, Robert D. (1993). *Place, modernity and the consumer's world: A relational framework for geographical analysis.* Baltimore: John's Hopkins Press.

Trentelmans, Carla K. (2009). Place attachment and community attachment: A primer grounded in the lived experience of a community sociologist. *Society and Natural Resources, 22,* 191–210.

Tuan, Yi-Fu. (1977). *Space and place: The perspective of experience.* Minneapolis: University of Minnesota Press.

United States Environmental Protection Agency (EPA). (2002). *Community culture and the environment: A guide to understanding a sense of place.* (EPA 842-B-01-003). Washington, DC: United States Environmental Protection Agency.

Young, Iris M. (1990). *Justice and the politics of difference.* Princeton, NJ: Princeton University Press.

WHERE IS THE COUNTRY?

In The Thing Itself, *a meditation on the search for authenticity in contemporary life, Richard Todd writes about the rural landscape—"a well-ordered countryside," he goes on to say, the only place where one can "cling to the dream of a classless landscape."*

Drive with me up the main road leading into my town, my actual town, the one I live in. There's little traffic though the road is broad, and we move along at a good clip. In fact the road is too broad, if you ask me, the product of a misguided engineering project a generation ago. . . . Only the occasional house comes into view as we go by. The houses, old ones, are a pleasantly organic part of the scene, a couple of Capes on either side of the road, a nineteenth-century farmhouse . . . I live in what I am pleased to call the "country."

Where is the country? . . . In our imagination the country is a repository of purity, of tradition, of simplicity; it is the enemy of modernity. But of course modernity lurks everywhere, and in most instances it doesn't really bother us. The eighteenth-century houses hold computers—so, for that matter, do the dairy barns, and a very good thing: it helps them to stay in business. We are making our tour in a late-model truck, a marvelous piece of engineering. Somehow these inconsistencies, if that's what they are, don't affect us the way the look of the landscape does. Now we come to a house I would just as soon not see at all, a "split-level ranch" (the very name suggests that it belongs elsewhere, but of course such houses don't belong on ranches, either). It seems to have been scooped up from a suburb somewhere and dropped down here. . . .

Many rural dwellers who value their surroundings spend a lot of time fretting over issues like these, trying to reassure themselves that the country is in fact where they live. We watch like hawks for an incursion of anything that might be called suburban.

Source: Richard Todd. (2008). *The Thing Itself,* pp. 69, 70–71, and 83. New York: Riverhead Books.

Politics

Sustainability has become a topic in politics around the world. Whether through government regulations, international agreements, grassroots and direct action, or religious contexts, the current political engagement with sustainability is pervasive and acknowledges its critical importance.

At the end of the twentieth century sustainability and protecting the environment became issues of global politics—the theories and activities of local, national, and international government—but sustainability and politics were also on the minds of great thinkers in ancients times. In his *Politics*, Aristotle argues that the goal of political life should be the common good. Aristotle recognizes many challenges to shared political life, among them that when people own property it is in their interest to care for it well, but that "what is common to many is taken least care of" (Aristotle 1986, 29). This challenge has come to be known as "the tragedy of the commons."

In a renowned 1968 essay in the journal *Science*, Garrett Hardin addresses the challenge. Hardin foresaw that parasitic treatment of Earth's commons would have tragic consequences, and he argues for coercion as a possible remedy. Hardin does not endorse government coercion by local, national, or international bureaucrats; rather he advocates a kind of mutual coercion in which people reassess their needs and relationships with common resources. The "tragedy of the commons" has raised important political questions about how to care for Earth's commons, including the oceans, atmosphere, rivers, and land. Another avenue of theorizing politics and sustainability has been to reevaluate the logic of individual rights. The political scientist Robyn Eckersley argues that individual rights cannot be abstracted from their ecological and social context. Individual rights should consider also, then, the ecological welfare of citizens. An individual has not only a right to privacy and to freedom

of speech, for example, but should also have the right to a healthful environment (Eckersley 1992, 136–137).

International Politics

Perhaps the most significant political developments around questions of sustainability have come in international treaties. The U.N. General Assembly commissioned a report from an international group of political and environmental experts in order to formulate a global agenda to address the environmental crisis. In 1987, the Brundtland Commission (named after Gro Brundtland, the former prime minister of Norway and an internationally recognized leader in public health and sustainable development) developed a widely cited definition of sustainability: "Humanity has the ability to make development sustainable—to ensure that it meets the needs of the present without compromising the ability of future generations to meet their own needs" (World Commission on Environment and Development 1987, 8). In order for sustainable development to be possible, the commission argued, a new political will and vision must emerge in which the ecological dimensions of policy be considered at the same time as economic, energy, and agricultural dimensions. Just as separate policies and institutions can no longer deal effectively with questions of sustainable development, nor can governments acting unilaterally.

The Montreal Protocol on Substances that Deplete the Ozone Layer is an important example of how shared political responsibility for resources held in common is essential. The ozone layer is a layer of Earth's atmosphere that absorbs the majority of the sun's ultraviolet (UV) rays, which are potentially damaging to life on the planet. Depletion of the ozone layer results in an increase in UV rays, which scientists have identified as a contributing factor to skin cancer. In the mid-1980s, scientists began to connect the production of chlorofluorocarbons (CFCs), used in refrigeration and aerosol sprays, with depletion in the ozone layer. Signatories to the Montreal Protocol agreed to stop the production of CFCs and other ozone-depleting substances. Since the treaty entered into force in 1989, the ozone layer has begun to replenish and it is expected to recover by 2050 (U.S. Environmental Protection Agency, 2008).

The Kyoto Protocol to the U.N. Framework Convention on Climate Change is an international agreement that seeks to reduce greenhouse gases in an effort to limit human influences on climate change. Climate change describes long-term changes in average weather in a particular region. Climate change is sometimes referred to as "global warming" because these changes in average weather often have been experienced as warmer temperatures. The potential effects of climate change are catastrophic; they include rising sea levels, desertification, and species extinction. The greatest single factor believed to contribute to climate change is the increase in greenhouse gases, particularly from an increase in levels of carbon dioxide resulting from fossil fuel combustion since the beginning of the Industrial Revolution. The Kyoto Protocol calls for developed nations to curb their production of carbon dioxide and other greenhouse gases, while developing countries (including China, India, and Brazil) have no obligations beyond monitoring and reporting emission rates. While 182 nations have ratified the Protocol, the United States has signed but not ratified it. Although it is one of the world's leading greenhouse gas emitters, the United States thus far has refused to ratify the Protocol because it believes that Kyoto should also call for a decrease in carbon dioxide production in developing nations. The United States asserts that meeting the Protocol's requirements would place it in an unfavorable position to be competitive with emerging economies like India and China who are not obliged to limit emissions.

Sustainability has been an organizing principle of some political parties. The first Green Party was organized in Germany in the late 1970s in opposition to nuclear power. While environmental issues lead Green political platforms, Green parties are concerned also with contingent questions of social justice, including racial, gender, and economic justice, and promoting grassroots democratic organizations. Currently there are Green parties operating at the local and national levels throughout Europe, North America, and Oceania. Recently the Greens have organized in Kenya, Iran, and Pakistan.

Direct Political Action and Civil Disobedience

Political questions about sustainability are addressed also through direct political action, including grassroots organizing and civil disobedience. A prime example of grassroots organizing, which refers to people at the local level and not at the centers of political activity, is the Green Belt Movement in Kenya, which has planted over 30 million trees in a coordinated effort to rehabilitate the natural environment and promote peace. Begun in 1977, the movement aims to give people the means to meet basic needs and protect their local environments. Planting trees slows soil erosion and desertification, produces food for people and animals, provides people with fuel and building materials, gives shade, and improves the aesthetic environment. In 2004 the movement's founder, Wangari Maathai, was awarded the Nobel Peace Prize. In her acceptance speech, Maathai explained that at the heart of the Green Belt Movement was the close connection between good governance, sustainable management of resources, and peace. As people learn the connections between planting trees and improvement in their own quality of life, insists Maathai, they begin to understand that they have a right to a clean and healthy environment and they connect human rights with the rights of other species.

Civil disobedience is another kind of direct political action. It describes the act of breaking the law in a conscientious way in order to draw attention to laws or policies that are considered unjust. The term *civil disobedience* is often attributed to the U.S. writer and naturalist Henry David Thoreau (1817–1862), whose 1848 essay "Resistance to Civil Government" explains Thoreau's reason for refusing to pay the poll tax that was implemented to support the U.S. war against Mexico and the Fugitive Slave Law. Thoreau explains that he broke the law because "it is not desirable to cultivate a respect for the law, so much as for the right. The only obligation which I have a right to assume is to do at any time what I think right" (Thoreau 1983, 387). Herein lies a seeming contradiction of civil disobedience: a person protests an unjust law by breaking the law, but accepts the consequences of his or her actions. Central features of civil disobedience include publicity and nonviolence. Typically, dissenters publicize their plans in order to clarify that it is moral conviction that inspires the violation of the law. Civil disobedience is nonviolent, because nonviolence is seen to diminish the negative effects of breaking the law and avoids the possibility of breaching other people's liberty in the act of breaking the law.

Perhaps the largest campaign of civil disobedience in the twentieth century was the Indian independence movement led by Mohandas Gandhi (1869–1948). He developed the method of *satyagraha*, nonviolence that is persistent and firm in its quest for loving kindness and truth. While the concept of sustainability was not available to Gandhi in the way that is widely used today, he called for a community-oriented model of development in which people produce necessary goods locally and therefore are aware of and can manage local environmental impacts. Freedom and self-reliance were the hallmarks of Gandhi's vision for an independent India.

The 1930 Salt March is an example of Gandhi's insistence that Indians control production of essential goods and his commitment to *satyagraha*. In 1882 the British colonial government claimed a monopoly on the manufacture of salt and imposed a tax. Gandhi chose the salt tax as a focus of his protest because of its strategic and symbolic significance: everyone in India used salt, the tax hurt the poorest disproportionately, and making salt was easily done but had been legislated as illegal by the colonial government. Gandhi planned a twenty-three-day march from his home to the coast in order to protest British control of salt production. Before the march, Gandhi announced his plans to leading British officials and the details of the proposed march were circulated widely in the press. Although Gandhi offered to suspend the march if Indians were permitted to make their own salt, British officials ignored Gandhi's appeals and the march went forward. Thousands of people marched with Gandhi to protest the salt monopoly. Upon reaching the coast, Gandhi made salt, thereby conscientiously breaking the law. Gandhi and thousands of others were arrested following the march, but the nation had been galvanized.

Gandhi's philosophy of civil disobedience and *satyagraha* were continued in the northern Indian Chipko movement that originated in the 1970s. The movement sought to prevent the national government from felling trees in Himalayan forests. Deforestation led to environmental degradation in the form of soil erosion, landslides, and destabilized water sources. Women, who were responsible for collecting fuel and food from the forest, were most aware of and adversely affected by logging. In organized protests to prevent trees from being cut down, women surrounded the trees, sometimes hugging them, to prevent them from being felled. The name of the movement comes from a Hindi term that means "embrace" or "cling." The Chipko movement, which is often credited as being the genesis of the term *tree huggers* to describe environmental activists, was inspired by Gandhi's model of nonviolence and by his commitment to sustainability. Chipko activists wanted to protect the health of the natural world, which was also the source of their livelihood. In 1980, Chipko persuaded the national government to enact a fifteen-year ban on green felling in the Himalayan forests. Currently Chipko does not seem to be an active movement, but it continues to inspire contemporary activists.

Politics, Religion, and Sustainability

Political activists and even government agencies appeal to religious values and norms as important resources for political engagement with issues around sustainability. The Malaysian government has drawn from Islamic standards to guide its city planning and economic development. Islam is the official religion of Malaysia, a country that faces rapid urbanization and the associated deforestation of greenbelts, soil erosion, and destruction of natural water catchments. Having identified the inadequacy of current development policy as the root cause of current ecological problems, the government has turned to Islamic principles to promote a balanced relationship between human beings and their environment. The Malaysian Total Planning and Development Doctrine emphasizes the concept of *Ihsan*, a term that means "doing beautiful things" and encourages development planning to take into account not only human needs, but the needs of all creation. The Doctrine also stresses the importance of *khalifa*, which means "trustee" or "steward" and describes the duty that God has bound human beings to perform on His behalf. In the Quran, God calls on Adam to serve as His vicegerent, to look after God's creation in a way that is pleasing to Him (Quran 2:31).

In Thailand, the political activist Sulak Sivaraksa (b. 1933) appeals to Buddhist principles in his call for "alternative politics for Asia." Rapid industrialization, urbanization, and intensified agricultural production have resulted in deforestation. While in 1961 approximately 53 percent of Thailand was covered by forest, in 1998 only 25 percent was forested. During the same period the character of Thai farming changed dramatically. A transition from farming practices based on self-reliance to growing cash crops has made farmers vulnerable to market fluctuations, which can quickly drive farmers into debt. In order to reverse current trends, Sivaraksa outlines a "spiritual green agenda" based on the Four Noble Truths, a central Buddhist teaching. The Four Noble Truths hold that suffering exists, that suffering stems from greed, hatred, and delusion, and that by investigating the causes of suffering we can understand its common characteristics and work to change it. Sivaraksa argues that contemporary Thai development and environmental policies are delusional, because they presume that human beings are the highest form of life and see the world only from an anthropocentric perspective. This delusion blinds many people to the truth of another central Buddhist teaching, interdependent co-arising, which asserts the essential interdependence of all things. Sivaraksa argues that a Buddhist approach to development would recognize the profound truth of the "mutually dependent relationship between all forms of nature" (2005, 76).

Political appeals to religious norms are often controversial because political actors may disagree about whether or not religious standards are appropriate for political discussion and religious practitioners may disagree about the kind of public-policy stance a religious tradition's doctrines or principles would endorse. The U.S. context offers examples of both types of controversy. The First Amendment to the U.S. Constitution provides for a two-part protection of religious liberty, which includes the protection of religious institutions from government intrusion and prohibits the state from endorsing any particular religious belief or practice. There has been a coincident tradition in American liberal political philosophy to sanction religious reasons from public debate. The most well-known proponent of the position is John Rawls (1921–2002), who famously argued that in order to participate in political discussions, citizens should appeal to public reasons, whose "nature and content is public, being given by the ideals and principles expressed by society's conception of political justice" (Rawls 2005, 213). Rawls allows that comprehensive doctrines (designating not simply religious, but also nonreligious moral doctrines) can be introduced into political argument, but people must also present what they believe are the public reasons for their argument in terms that are equally available to every citizen. Despite general consensus about Rawls' position among many political theorists, the growing political engagement of evangelical Christians challenged Rawls's view.

In the 1980s politically conservative and predominantly white evangelical Christians became a political force in the United States. In the millennial decade they were credited with being decisive in the election and reelection of George W. Bush, who identifies himself as an evangelical Christian. Many evangelicals agree with President Bush that environmental issues are best handled by the free market and that recent claims about climate change are unsubstantiated. But in the middle of the decade some evangelicals began to rethink these positions. Chief among them is Richard Cizik, a leader of the National Association of Evangelicals (NAE), a prominent lobbying group. Cizik became convinced by scientific explanations of human influences on climate change and developed a theological position of "creation care" to advocate what he sees as a biblical imperative to protect the environment. Cizik refers to passages in which God calls on Adam to tend the Garden of Eden (Genesis 2:15, NRSV) and which promise that God will destroy those who have destroyed the Earth (Revelation 11:18). Cizik's "creation care" is controversial within the leadership of the evangelical community, however. Other prominent evangelical leaders see no clear biblical imperative to protect the environment.

While the American case demonstrates a debate about whether scriptural warrants or traditional resources can or should encourage environmental practices and sustainable development, debates about the Narmada dams project in India show how the term *sustainability* itself can be at the center of political contestation. The third longest river in India, the Narmada flows almost 1,300 kilometers through forest and agricultural land and has twenty-five million people living in its valley. Construction on the dams project began in the early 1980s. Proponents of the project argue that it will provide drinking water to millions of people upriver, provide irrigation for farmers in drought-prone areas, and provide electricity to villages that are without a reliable power source. Opponents argue that the project has ignored the protests of the rural poor who depend on the existing shape and flow of the river and will require the resettlement of more than 200,000 people. Opponents point out, furthermore, that existing dams on the river have resulted in sharp increases in the number of cases of malaria, huge 180-meter-wide deposits of silt that cut off access to the river and in which livestock get stranded and die, and the disruption of community life because people can no longer travel across the river to visit family and friends. Although each side has a different vision of the good life and of the value and goals of development, both appeal to sustainability to defend its position. The Narmada debate reveals, then, the rhetorical flexibility of the term *sustainability* and how it may be invoked to support a massive project that will disrupt ecosystems and result in the dislocation of hundreds of thousands of people.

Sarah AZARANSKY
University of San Diego

FURTHER READING

Aristotle. (1986). *The politics* William Ellis (Trans.). Buffalo, NY: Prometheus Books

Badiner, Allan Hunt. (Ed.). (1990). *Dharma gaia: A harvest of essays in Buddhism and ecology*. Berkeley, CA: Parallax Press.

Baviskar, Amita. (2004). *In the belly of the river: Tribal conflicts over development in the Narmada Valley*. New York: Oxford University Press.

Dalton, Dennis. (1993). *Mahatma Gandhi: Nonviolent power in action*. New York: Columbia University Press.

Doherty, Brian, & de Geus, Marius. (1996). *Democracy and green political thought*. New York: Routledge.

Eckersley, Robyn. (1992). *Environmentalism and political theory: Toward an ecocentric approach (Environmental Public Policy Series)*. Albany: State University of New York Press.

Foltz, Richard C. (Ed.). (2005). *Environmentalism in the Muslim world*. New York: Nova Science Publishers.

Foltz, Richard C.; Denny, Frederick M.; & Baharuddin, Azizan. (Eds.). (2003). *Islam and ecology: A bestowed trust*. Cambridge, MA: Harvard University Press.

Gottlieb, Roger S. (2006). *A greener faith: Religious environmentalism and our planet's future*. New York: Oxford University Press.

Iqbal, Munawar. (Ed.). (2005). *Islamic perspectives on sustainable development*. New York: Palgrave MacMillan.

Rawls, John. (2005). *Political liberalism. Expanded edition*. New York: Columbia University Press.

Roy, Arundhati. (1999). *The cost of living*. New York: Modern Library.

Sivaraksa, Sulak. (2005). *Conflict, culture, change: Engaged Buddhism in a globalizing world*. Boston: Wisdom Publications.

Thoreau, Henry David. (1983). *Walden* and *Civil Disobedience*. New York: Penguin Books. (Original works published 1854 and 1849)

U.S. Environmental Protection Agency. (2008, August 25). Ozone layer depletion—science: Brief question and answer on ozone depletion. Retrieved May 29, 2009, from http://www.epa.gov/ozone/science/q_a.html

World Commission on Environment and Development. (1987). *Our common future*. New York: Oxford University Press.

Population

The planet's human population has doubled since 1960, and is on track to be triple that level by the middle of the twenty-first century. At the same time, increasingly powerful technologies have magnified humanity's collective ecological impact on the planet, and this has resulted in a loss of habitat and biodiversity, the degradation of ecosystems, and global climate change. Ethicists disagree on what measures should be taken to develop a new paradigm of sustainable development.

It will not be possible to achieve a greater measure of ecological sustainability without changes in the patterns of human reproduction, production, and consumption. The planet's human population has doubled since 1960 from 3 billion to over 6 billion, and is on track to reach 9 billion by the middle of this century. At the same time, increasingly powerful technologies have magnified humanity's collective ecological impact on the planet, which has resulted in a loss of habitat and biodiversity, the degradation of ecosystems, and global climate change.

This article examines ethical dimensions of population and consumption issues by first describing the demographic situation and then illustrating the main points of debate, in part by focusing on how the discussion has taken place among North American Christian ethicists. Moral concern about these issues has been substantially rejuvenated by recent studies examining the amount of ecological degradation attributable to the affluent few and the numerous poor. Although all studies show that the vast majority of ecological degradation to date has been produced by the overconsumptive lifestyles and environmentally harmful technologies of the wealthiest citizens of the planet, a growing level of concern is being raised about the increasing level of degradation posed by the many citizens who are poor. For example, China now emits more greenhouse gases than the United States, even though the emissions per person in China are not even one-eighth those of citizens in the United States. The first section of this article provides a brief summary of important demographic information and trends shaping the rate of human reproduction and the quality of life on the planet. The second section offers a summary of key ethical issues and the related views of main figures in these debates.

The Current Demographic Situation

According to the most recent projections by the United Nations, the world's population of approximately 6.7 billion people in 2008 is expected to increase by 2.5 billion to reach 9.2 billion in 2050. Virtually all of this growth will take place in nations of the developing world. Although the population of developed countries over this period of time is expected to remain at approximately 1.2 billion people, the population of the least developed countries will more than double from 0.8 billion in 2007 to 1.7 billion in 2050, and the rest of the developing world will grow from 4.6 billion in 2007 to 6.2 billion in 2050. At current growth rates, the world adds about 78 million people per year, which is almost equivalent to adding a population the size of Ethiopia (UN 2007).

This global demographic situation is a paradox. Statistically, the situation has never looked better, yet, in terms of the lives of actual human beings, things have almost never been worse. Through international family planning and development efforts, the annual rate of global population growth has decreased from its peak of 2.06 percent (in the years 1965 to 1970) to 1.17 percent in 2007 (UN 2007). In addition, the total fertility rate (TFR) in less developed countries has declined from 6.0 children per woman in 1960 to 2.8 today, bringing fertility more than halfway toward the goal of a replacement rate of 2.1 children (PRB 2008).

Unfortunately, because the age structure of many developing nations has been substantially altered, these diminished rates of population growth and fertility still produce significant growth in human populations through a phenomenon called demographic momentum. As a result, the significant investments that have been made in social development since 1950 have been diminished by a world population that has more than doubled during this same period. The sad fact is that, although the *statistical proportions* of per capita income, food supply, access to health services, potable water, and so on have all improved, the *actual number* of people who are poor, hungry, sick, and without drinkable water has almost never been higher. In 2008, the World Bank estimated that one-fifth of the world's population, 1.4 billion people, live in conditions of absolute poverty on less than $1.25 per day.

Faced with the likelihood that global population will continue to grow beyond 9.2 billion people in 2050, experts project that the global economy will need to grow by 3 to 5 percent a year to meet the needs and aspirations of 10 billion people. The problem is that the explosion of economic growth in the twentieth century created enormous environmental degradation. Ecologists warn that the planet will not permit another five- to tenfold expansion of the global economy, and some argue that—barring some significant changes in the destructive lifestyles of the affluent—humans may have already surpassed the planet's carrying capacity.

Perhaps the most dramatic and direct evidence of this phenomenon is the loss of biodiversity through an alarming rate of global species extinction. Land degradation, deforestation, and global warming also exemplify the threat humanity poses to all forms of life on the planet. Although it is unfair and inaccurate to place the blame for these ecological problems solely on population growth, it is clear that high rates of growth have exacerbated these conditions and will play a critical role in the future. It is important to stress, however, that humanity's ecological impact is determined not only by our numbers but also by our levels of consumption and the type of technologies we use in our production of goods. Although some problems are significantly influenced by population growth, other problems are primarily a result of inefficient production technologies and irresponsible levels of consumption.

Key Figures and Main Issues

In international forums, the significant increase in global population has stimulated much concern and, occasionally, rancorous debate. At the heart of this discord is the view of many in developing countries that those in developed countries focus too much on the ecological dangers posed by population growth and not enough on the dangers posed by their own overconsumption. They have emphasized correctly that the ecological impact of human societies is measured not only in terms of the rates of reproduction but also in terms of the patterns of consumption and the means of production. For this reason, it is becoming increasingly apparent that all discussions of population growth must also include moral reflection on consumption issues.

This emphasis on the *relationship* of population and consumption issues has not been substantially emphasized in the field of religious ethics until recently. An initial generation of reflection responded to controversial proposals for "triage" or "lifeboat ethics," which were proposed as responses (Vaux 1989; Wogaman 1973). Moral reflection on consumption issues during this time ranged from a focus on simpler lifestyles to a relatively rigorous critique of capitalism, as in the U.S. Roman Catholic Bishops' pastoral letter *Economic Justice for All* (NCCB 1986). The most substantial integrated reflection on population and consumption issues was generated by those exploring the "limits to growth" debate (Stivers 1976 and 1984) and the notion of "sustainable development" or a "sustainable society" (Engel and Engel 1988; Cobb and Daly 1989).

The area of population policy underwent some significant changes during the years from 1974 to 1994. With the failure of ill-conceived and invasive policies in the 1960s, a narrow focus on population control and contraceptive technologies was increasingly rejected in favor of placing population programs within the broader context of development policies, and, to a far lesser extent, women's reproductive rights and health. These important policy changes were largely codified in the watershed Program of Action that resulted from the United Nations International Conference on Population and Development held in Cairo, Egypt, in September 1994. It called for a move away from a narrow and quantitative focus on numbers of people, demographic goals and rates of contraceptive use to a broad and qualitative emphasis on the empowerment of women, reproductive rights, and improvement in the lives of all people.

In the past, ethicists have evaluated population policies that contain various types of incentives, disincentives, and forms of coercion by considering their impact on four primary human values: freedom, justice, social welfare, and security or survival. Although responsible moral evaluation of specific population polices involves reflection on all four of these primary values, ethicists have arranged these values in different orders of priority. For example, some have made the values of social welfare and security/survival subordinate to the more fundamental values of freedom and justice. Ethicists such as Ronald Green and Daniel Callahan have argued that efforts to maximize freedom and equality are more effective means of securing the common good than coercive means that violate human dignity (Callahan 1976; Green 1976). Other ethicists have taken the opposite approach and have emphasized that without a fundamental measure of general welfare and security it is impossible to experience the values of freedom and justice. Michael Bayles and James Gustafson have argued that it may be necessary and justifiable to limit certain individual rights and regulate human fertility out of a concern for the common good of present and future generations (Bayles 1980; Gustafson 1984).

This difference in the ordering of primary moral values is reflected in more recent moral reflection on population issues as well. Following Green and Callahan, Rosemary Radford Ruether has argued that it is vital to ground population issues in a broader context of social and economic justice. Linking population and consumption issues, Ruether argues that the "high consumption of the wealthy" and the "low consumption of the many" are not separate but interdependent realities caused by global economic systems that benefit the affluent few and harm the numerous poor. Ruether also insists that another essential dimension of population policies must be the goal to improve the status of women and to empower them in terms of moral agency. Policies that do not place a priority on improving the status of women and their moral agency will be abusive to women and also will not work. Ruether argues that the best way to avoid a doubling in the world's population is by addressing the twin challenges of poverty and patriarchy (Ruether 1992).

Another important figure in more recent discussions of population and consumption issues is John Cobb Jr. On the consumption side, Cobb has worked hard to offer conceptual foundations and workable policies for a more just, peaceful, and sustainable world (Cobb 1992; Cobb and Daly 1989). One of the unique contributions Cobb has made is his bold, albeit quite biblical, claim that the Western industrial nations *worship* endless economic growth. When viewed through the prism of civil religion it is easier to understand why consumption issues are so volatile and difficult to address. Cobb argues that consumption issues involve not only habits of consumption but also rites of faith. Cobb's most important contribution, however, has been his attempt with Herman Daly in *For the Common Good* to sketch the outlines of an alternative form of development that would be just, participatory, and ecologically sustainable, which would require revolutionary changes in current patterns of human production, consumption, and reproduction.

On the population side, John Cobb sketched moral foundations for population policy in *The Liberation of Life*, a book he coauthored with Charles Birch in 1990. In league with Ruether, Cobb recommended that population growth be viewed within the larger context of the process of development and that the real key to lower fertility rates rested with improvement in the lives of women. Here Cobb emphasizes that "justice and sustainability coincide" (Birch and Cobb 1990). There is no mention in this book, however, of a controversial proposal he and Herman Daly offered in *For the Common Good*, where they consider the governmental implementation of "transferable birth quota plans," which would issue birth rights certificates to parents to sell or use as they deem fit on an open market.

Like Cobb, James Nash offered similar realistic sentiments in his book *Loving Nature*. Throughout the book, Nash consistently links his treatment of population and consumption issues, referring to both as manifestations of "anthropocentric imperialism" (Nash 1991). Nash argues that contraception must serve as the centerpiece of a morally adequate policy aimed at curbing population growth, and he emphasizes that a morally adequate population policy will need to be part of a broader goal of increasing socioeconomic justice and sustainable development. Cutting against the increasing international emphasis on reproductive rights and the United Nations Declaration of Universal Human Rights, Nash argues that humans do *not* have the right to reproduce, although they may have the right not to be *forced* to reproduce. In his discussion of the relationship of human rights to human environmental rights, Nash argues that "[s]ecurity and subsistence rights always impose limits on other citizen's freedoms of action" (Nash 1991, 50). Thus, Nash is able to support the limitation of human reproductive freedoms on the grounds of ecological security and couches such action in terms of ecological justice.

Not surprisingly, a host of Catholic leaders and theologians have played important roles in debates about population and consumption issues. The Vatican delegation played an important role at the United Nations International Conference on Population and Development in Cairo. The Vatican opposed terms such as "reproductive rights," "reproductive health," and "safe motherhood" on the grounds that these terms implied an approval of abortion. In reaction to the views of the Vatican, debate in Roman Catholic circles on population issues splits along at least two lines. Some, including Frances Kissling and Daniel Maguire, view the Vatican's views as essentially misogynistic and hopelessly patriarchal (Kissling 1994; Maguire 1993). Maguire has also worked with other scholars to explore the right to contraception and abortion in other world religions (Maguire 2001 and 2003). Other Catholic theologians, including Charles Curran and Sean McDonagh, have challenged the Vatican's opposition to artificial means of contraception and question how "pro-life" these policies are when they contribute to higher rates of infant mortality, poverty, and environmental degradation (Curran 1985; McDonagh 1990). Finally, Maura Ann Ryan and

John Schwartz have tried to frame moral reflection on population policy within the broader context of Roman Catholic social teaching (Ryan 1994; Schwartz 1998).

While many may agree with Ruether's dual emphasis on social and economic justice as well as the importance of improving the lives of women (Martin-Schramm 1997), and may as well share her confidence that development policies redesigned to serve the needs of the poor and social reforms designed to improve the status of women represent the best chance to achieve global population stabilization, others may side with Cobb, who believes that the failed paradigm of development as economic growth must be replaced with a new paradigm of sustainable development. Until it becomes clear that alternative approaches have been tried and have failed, it might be difficult to abide discussion of various forms of coercion in population programs, although there may be a place for carefully monitored incentive packages.

James B. MARTIN-SCHRAMM
Luther College

FURTHER READING

Bayles, Michael D. (1980). *Morality and population policy*. Birmingham: University of Alabama Press.

Callahan, Daniel. (1976). Ethics and population limitation. In Michael D. Bayles (Ed.), *Ethics and population*. Cambridge, MA: Schenkman.

Cobb, John B., Jr. (1992). *Sustainability: Economics, ecology, & justice*. Maryknoll, NY: Orbis Books.

Cobb, John B., Jr., & Birch, Charles. (1990). *The liberation of life*. Denton, TX: Environmental Ethics Books.

Cobb, John B., Jr., & Daly, Herman E. (1989). *For the common good: Redirecting the economy toward community, the environment, and a sustainable future*. Boston: Beacon Press.

Coward, Harold, & Maguire, Daniel C. (Eds.). (2000). *Visions of a new Earth: Religious perspectives on population, consumption, and ecology*. Albany: State University of New York Press.

Curran, Charles E. (1985). Population control: Methods and morality. In *Directions in Catholic social ethics*. Notre Dame, IN: University of Notre Dame Press.

Engel, John Robert, & Gibb Engel, Joan. (Eds.). (1988). *Ethics of environment and development: Global challenge, international response*. Tucson: University of Arizona Press.

Green, Ronald M. (1976). *Population growth and justice: An examination of moral issues raised by population growth*. Missoula, MT: Scholars Press for Harvard Theological Review.

Gustafson, James M. (1984). *Ethics from a theocentric perspective* (Vol. 2). Chicago: University of Chicago Press.

Kissling, Frances. (1994). Theo-politics: The Roman Catholic Church and population policy. In *Beyond the numbers: A reader on population, consumption, and the environment*. Washington, DC: Island Press.

Maguire, Daniel C. (Ed.). (1993). Poverty, population, and the Catholic tradition. In *Religious and ethical perspectives on population issues*. Washington, DC: The Religious Consultation on Population, Reproductive Health, and Ethics.

Maguire, Daniel C. (Ed.). (2001). *Sacred choices: The right to contraception and abortion in ten world religions*. Minneapolis, MN: Augsburg Fortress.

Maguire, Daniel C. (Ed.). (2003). *Sacred rights: The case for contraception and abortion in world religions*. New York: Oxford University Press.

Maguire, Daniel C., & Rasmussen, Larry L. (1998). *Ethics for a small planet: New horizons on population, consumption, and ecology*. Albany: State University of New York Press.

Martin-Schramm, James B. (1997). *Population perils and the churches' response*. Geneva: World Council of Churches.

McDonagh, Sean. (1990). *The greening of the Church*. Maryknoll, NY: Orbis Books.

McFague, Sallie. (2000). *Life abundant: Rethinking theology and economy for a planet in peril*. Minneapolis, MN: Fortress Press.

Nash, James A. (1991). *Loving nature: Ecological integrity and Christian responsibility*. Nashville, TN: Abingdon Press.

National Conference of Catholic Bishops (NCCB). (1986). *Economic justice for all: Pastoral letter on Catholic social teaching and the U.S. economy*. Washington, DC: United States Catholic Conference.

Population Reference Bureau (PRB). (2008). *2008 World Population Data Sheet*. Retrieved May 22, 2009, from http://www.prb.org/Publications/Datasheets/2008/2008wpds.aspx

Rasmussen, Larry L. (1996). *Earth community, Earth ethics*. Maryknoll, NY: Orbis Books.

United Nations Department of Economic and Social Affairs, Population Division. (UN). (2007). *World population prospects: The 2006 revision*, Highlights, Working Paper No. ESA/P/WP.202.

Ruether, Rosemary Radford. (1992). *Gaia & God: An ecofeminist theology of Earth healing*. San Francisco: HarperSanFrancisco.

Ryan, Maura Ann. (1994). Reflections on population policy from the Roman Catholic tradition. In Laurie A. Mazur (Ed.), *Beyond the numbers: A reader on population, consumption, and the environment* (pp. 330–340). Washington, DC: Island Press.

Schwarz, John C. (1998). *Global population from a Catholic perspective*. Mystic, CT: Twenty-Third Publications.

Stivers, Robert L. (1976). *The sustainable society: Ethics and economic growth*. Philadelphia: Westminster Press.

Stivers, Robert L. (1984). *Hunger, technology, and limits to growth*. Minneapolis, MN: Augsburg Press.

Vaux, K. (1989). *Birth ethics: Religious and cultural values in the genesis of life*. New York: Crossroad Press.

Wogaman, P. (Ed.). (1973). *The population crisis and moral responsibility*. Washington, DC: Public Affairs Press.

Poverty

Despite a high and growing global average income, billions of human beings are still condemned to lifelong severe poverty, with all its ramifications of low life expectancy, social exclusion, ill health, illiteracy, dependency, and effective enslavement. The annual death toll from poverty-related causes is around 18 million, which adds up to some 360 million deaths since the end of the Cold War.

Billions of human beings are mired in severe poverty and exposed to a variety of diseases that do little or no damage in the more affluent parts of the world. And our planet's natural diversity and beauty—its resources, eco-systems, atmosphere, and climate—are avoidably being degraded at an alarming rate. These three afflictions—poverty, disease, and environmental degradation—are related not merely through a common causal origin, some believe (that is, the globalization that often pits affluent developed nations against undeveloped nations), but also in that they aggravate one another. Severely impoverished people are especially vulnerable to diseases and to environmental degradation because their bodies and minds suffer the effects of inadequate nutrition, unclean water, insufficient clothing and shelter, poor sanitation, and unhealthy working and living conditions. Severely impoverished people are also least able to protect themselves against such hazards through medical care or relocation, or through legal processes or political mobilization. In these ways ill health and environmental degradation reinforce poverty by sapping the creative energies and earning potential of people and, all too often, even killing them in their prime while decimating their families' income.

Poverty and disease also reinforce environmental problems, because the poor typically cannot afford to take proper account of the long-term environmental impact of their conduct. Poor people cannot afford fuel-efficient and low-pollution cooking methods, and must take what combustible materials they can find regardless of cost to the environment. To be sure, poor people do far less environmental damage *per person* than is typical among the more affluent. But they do far more environmental damage *per unit of income.* And this suggests that, other things being equal, a more even distribution of income and wealth that would avoid severe poverty is environmentally preferable to the existing extremely uneven distribution. There is another aspect to this consideration of even greater long-term significance: very poor people cannot afford to limit their off-spring because they face serious uncertainly about whether any given child will reach adulthood and about whether, without surviving children, they themselves could survive beyond their prime. As is well confirmed empirically (Sen 1994), severe poverty is causally related to more rapid population growth, which in turn is one main driver of environmental degradation. Eradicating severe poverty is thus a plausible and effective strategy of working for an early leveling-off of the human population, hopefully below the 10 billion mark.

These two kinds of relationship—common causal origin and mutual reinforcement—suggest that those concerned about any one of the three afflictions should collaborate intellectually and politically in developing and implementing reform ideas that address them all. For example, consider an institutional mechanism that would provide incentives for the development of new medicines, one that would allow pharmaceutical innovators to forgo their claim to patent-protected high prices on any product in exchange for a stream of reward payments based on the product's global health impact. Making advanced medicines immediately available wherever they are needed at the lowest feasible cost, stimulating new research into diseases concentrated among the poor, and encouraging pharmaceutical innovators to pursue the actual health impact of their inventions—all goals of the Health Impact Fund, a program of the nonprofit organization Incentives for Global Health—would substantially reduce both severe poverty and the burden of global disease (Hollis and Pogge 2008). Or consider the idea of a "global resources dividend" that would put a price on resource depletion and pollution, thereby slowing down these main contributors to environmental degradation while also creating a stream of revenues that could be directed at poverty reduction—at financing the Health Impact Fund, for example (Pogge 2008, ch. 8). Reform mechanisms like these illustrate how any ethic of sustainability must centrally and collaboratively address world poverty.

World Poverty: Explanation and Responsibilities

Despite a high and growing global average income, billions of human beings are still condemned to lifelong severe poverty, with all its attendant ramifications of low life expectancy, social exclusion, ill health, illiteracy, dependency, and effective enslavement. The annual death toll from poverty-related causes is around 18 million, which adds up to some 360 million deaths since the end of the Cold War (WHO 2004, 120–125).

In spite of magnitude of this problem, many political scientists and scholars of social justice view this as solvable. The World Bank very narrowly defines the poor as those who live on less, per person per month, than could be bought for $38 in the United States in 2005. Suppose we double this to the purchasing power equivalent of $76 per person per month. We would find that in 2005, 3.14 out of 6.44 billion human beings were living in poverty (Chen and Ravallion 2008, Table 8). At market exchange rates, all these poor people taken together consumed only about 1.3 percent of the global product, and would have needed just 1.1 percent more to escape poverty so defined. The high-income countries, by contrast, with only 15.7 percent of the world's population, had 79 percent of the global product (World Bank 2006, 289). With an average per capita income 190 times greater than that of the poor, many concerned with global justice believe that affluent countries could eradicate severe poverty worldwide if they chose to try—in fact, could have eradicated it decades ago.

Some believe that citizens of the rich countries, however, are conditioned to downplay the severity and persistence of world poverty and to think of it as an occasion for minor charitable assistance. Thanks in part to the rationalizations dispensed by a number of economists, many believe that severe poverty is a minor problem or one that is rapidly disappearing or one whose persistence is due exclusively to local causes. It is worthwhile briefly to address these common prejudices.

Though the aggregate income shortfall of the global poor is small, the effects of this shortfall are unimaginably large: 963 million human beings are undernourished (FAO 2009), 884 million lack access to safe drinking water, and 2.5 billion lack adequate sanitation (WHO & UNICEF, 2008, 30 and 7). About 2 billion lack access to essential medicines, 1 billion have no adequate shelter, and 1.6 billion lack electricity (NIH 2009 and UN Habitat 2009). Some 774 million adults are illiterate and over 200 million children between the ages of five and seventeen do wage work outside their household—often under harsh or cruel conditions: as soldiers, prostitutes or domestic servants, or in agriculture, construction, or textile or carpet production (ILO 2006).

Severe poverty is not rapidly disappearing. The number of persons living on less than the purchasing power equivalent of $76 per person per month is higher than it was twenty-five years ago (Chen and Ravallion 2008, Table 8) and the number of undernourished has also been trending upward even before the recent financial crisis (FAO 2009). The persistence of such severe poverty in the face of solid increases in the global average income is due to rapidly rising global inequality. In the high-income Organisation for Economic Co-operation and Development (OECD) countries, household final consumption expenditure per capita (in constant 2000 U.S. dollars) rose by 59.4 percent over the globalization period from 1984 to 2005 (UNFPA 2006). During the same period, the poorer half of humankind fared much worse, with the real (purchasing-power adjusted) consumption expenditure of the poorest rising less than 10 percent.

Harm to the Poor

Calling attention to the harm that severe poverty inflicts on the global poor, and to the magnitude of the problem of poverty and its causes, is necessary if we are to take steps to eradicate it. The usual ethical debates surrounding poverty concern the stringency of moral duties to help the poor abroad. Some believe that these duties are feeble, meaning that it isn't very wrong to give no help at all. Against this view, some philosophers have argued that our positive duties are stringent and demanding (Singer 1972; Shue 1996; Unger 1996). Others, such as Liam Murphy (2003) have defended an intermediate view according to which our positive duties, insofar as they are stringent, are not very demanding. We do, of course, have positive duties to rescue people from life-threatening poverty. But it can be misleading to focus on them when more stringent negative duties are also in play: duties not to expose people to life-threatening poverty and duties to shield them from harms for which we might be actively responsible.

A number of social and political theorists argue that poverty is an ongoing harm affluent countries inflict on large populations of the world (the global poor), and they hold that such a charge seems completely incredible to most citizens of the affluent countries. Many, in this view, call it tragic that the basic human rights of so many others remain unfulfilled—and are willing to admit that they should do more to help—but rarely assume an active responsibility for this catastrophe. If they did, such theorists concur, then civilized and sophisticated denizens of the developed countries would be guilty of the largest crime against humanity ever committed, the death toll of which exceeds, every week, that of the 2004 Indian Ocean tsunami and, every three years, that of World War II, the concentration camps and gulags included.

Such a view raises questions and ethical dilemmas. Are there steps affluent countries could take to reduce severe poverty abroad, given the enormous inequalities in income and wealth? Can the 1 billion citizens of affluent countries be morally entitled to 79 percent of the global product in the face of three times as many people mired in severe poverty? Acknowledging such a radical inequality between affluence and dire need assumes the burden of proof: the wealthy must show why they should be morally entitled to so much while the poor have so little. There are two common ways of supporting this entitlement, both challenged by any number of thinkers who address issues of social justice, environmental policies, and globaliztion.

First Challenge: Actual History

Many believe that the existing radical inequality can be justified by reference to how it evolved, for example, through differences in diligence, culture and social institutions, soil, climate, or fortune. But this sort of justification can be said to lose its credibility in light of the violent history through which the present radical inequality in fact accumulated. Much of it was built up in the colonial era, when today's affluent countries ruled today's poor regions of the world— trading their people like cattle, destroying their political institutions and cultures, taking their lands and natural resources, and forcing products and customs upon them.

Some will respond that citizens of former colonial powers cannot be held responsible for what their ancestors did long ago. But many would argue that it does not follow that today's citizens may insist on the *fruits* of these crimes or that they are entitled to the great head start these countries enjoyed going into the postcolonial period, benefits which have allowed them to shape the world to their advantage and which continue to give them dominance over the poor from birth. The historical path from which affluence arose in fact weakens any moral claim to it—certainly in the face of those whom the same historical process has delivered into conditions of acute deprivation.

Second Challenge: Global Institutional Arrangements

A second way of thinking about the justice of a radical inequality involves reflection on the institutional rules that reproduce it. Using this approach, one can justify an economic order and the distribution it produces (irrespective of historical considerations) by comparing them to feasible alternative institutional schemes and the distributional profiles they would produce. Many broadly consequentialist and contractualist conceptions of justice exemplify this approach. They differ in how they characterize the relevant affected parties, in the metric they employ for measuring how well off such parties are, and in how they aggregate such information about wellbeing into one overall assessment. These conceptions consequently disagree about how economic institutions should be best shaped under modern conditions. But we can bypass such disagreements insofar as these conceptions agree that an economic order is unjust when it—like the systems of serfdom and forced labor prevailing in feudal Russia or France—foreseeably gives rise to massive and severe human rights deficits. This challenges the adherents of broadly consequentialist and contractualist conceptions of justice: how can it be permissible to preserve great economic advantages for some by imposing a global economic order that regularly reproduces instances of deprivation, especially when there is a feasible institutional alternative under which such severe and extensive poverty would not persist?

Because some economists are inattentive to a number of factors, they believe that the existing global institutional order plays no role in the persistence of severe poverty, that internationally diverse national factors alone can explain why poverty persists where it does. Once freed from this explanatory nationalism, many will find global factors relevant to the persistence of severe poverty. In the WTO negotiations, the affluent countries insisted on continued and asymmetrical protections of their markets through tariffs, quotas, antidumping duties, export credits, and huge subsidies to domestic producers. In the view of many theorists such protectionism provides a compelling illustration of the hypocrisy of the rich states that insist and command that their own exports be received with open markets (Pogge 2008, 18–23). And it greatly impairs export opportunities for the very poorest countries and regions. If the rich countries scrapped their protectionist barriers against imports from poor countries, the populations of the latter could benefit greatly: hundreds of millions could escape unemployment, wage levels would rise substantially, and incoming export revenues would be higher by hundreds of billions of dollars each year.

Instead, say critics of protectionism, the rich countries pay nothing for the externalities they impose through their disproportional contributions to global pollution and resource depletion while charging billions for their intellectual property. The global poor benefit least, if at all, from polluting activities, and also are least able to protect themselves from the impact such pollution has on their health and on their natural environment (such as flooding due to rising sea levels). Reform devices such as a "global resources dividend" have been proposed to create funds for protecting the poor from pollution, while also mitigating actual polluting activities by incorporating environmental externalities.

Addressing Global Poverty in the Future

The two challenges discussed here converge on the supposition that the global poor have a compelling moral claim to some of the world's affluence, and that the affluent, by denying them what they are morally entitled to and urgently need, are actively contributing to their deprivations.

This view holds that once the causal nexus between a global institutional order and the persistence of severe poverty is understood, the injustice of that order, and the continued imposition of it, becomes visible: a small global elite—the citizens of the rich countries *and* the holders of political and economic power in the resource-rich developing countries—are enforcing a global property scheme under which they claim the world's natural resources for themselves and distribute these among themselves on mutually agreeable terms. Consideration of these tenets suggests that a restructuring of the world economy that ends the exclusion of the poor and achieves ecological sustainability can be approached through careful and caring reform.

Thomas POGGE
Yale University

FURTHER READING

Anand, Sudhir; Segal, Paul; & Stiglitz, Joseph. (Eds). (forthcoming). *Debates in the measurement of global poverty.* Oxford, U.K.: Oxford University Press.

Chen, Shaohua, & Ravallion, Martin. (2008). The developing world is poorer than we thought, but no less successful in the fight against poverty. World Bank Policy Research Working Paper WPS 4703 (2008), 34. Available at econ.worldbank.org/docsearch.

Food and Agricultural Organization of the United States (FAO). (2009). Number of hungry people rises to 963 million. Retrieved Augsut 13, 2009, from www.fao.org/news/story/en/item/8836/icode/

Hollis, Aidan, & Pogge, Thomas. (2008). *The health impact fund: making new medicines accessible to all.* New Haven, CT: Incentives for Global Health.

International Labour Office (ILO). (2006). *The end of child labour: Within reach.* Geneva: ILO.

John E. Fogarty International Center: United States Institutes of Health (NIH). (2009). Summary of the NIH Representatives Meeting. Retrieved August 13, 2009, from http://www.fic.nih.gov/programs/international/forum/2009/summary_mar2009.htm

Murphy, Liam. B. (2003). *Moral demands in nonideal theory.* New York: Oxford University Press.

Pimentel, David.; Westra, Laura.; & Noss, Reed F. (Eds). (2000). *Ecological integrity: Integrating environment, conservation, and health.* Washington, DC: Island Press.

Pogge, Thomas. (2004). The first UN millennium development goal: A cause for celebration? *Journal of Human Development, 5*(3), 381–385.

Pogge, Thomas. (2008). *World poverty and human rights: Cosmopolitan responsibilities and reforms* (2nd edition). Cambridge, U.K.: Polity Press.

Sen, Amartya. (September 1994). Population: Delusion and reality. *New York Review of Books:* New York.

Shue, Henry. (1996). *Basic rights: Subsistence, affluence and US foreign policy.* Princeton, NJ: Princeton University Press.

Singer, Peter. (1972). Famine, affluence and morality. *Philosophy and Public Affairs, 1*(3), 229–243.

Unger, Peter. (1996). *Living high and letting die.* New York: Oxford University Press.

UN Habitat. (2009). Urban energy. Retrieved August 13, 2009, from www.unhabitat.org/content.asp?cid=2884&catid=356&typeid=24&subMenuId=0

UNFPA State of World Population. (2006). Indicators. Retrieved from /www.unfpa.org/swp/2006/english/notes/indicator_tech.html

World Health Organization (WHO). (2004). *World health report 2004.* Geneva: WHO.

World Health Organization (WHO) & United Nations Children's Fund (UNICEF). (2008). *Progress on drinking water and sanitation: Special focus on sanitation.* New York and Geneva: UNICEF and WHO. Available at www.wssinfo.org/en/40_MDG2008.html

World Bank. (2006). *World development report 2006.* New York: Oxford University Press.

Pragmatism

Pragmatism, a philosophical approach developed in the United States in the 1870s, postulates that knowledge and truth are attained and may be transformed as a consequence of human interaction with the environment. Pragmatism's emphasis on harmonious adaptation of individuals to surrounding natural and social environment contributes to the development of an ethic of environmental sustainability.

"**P**ragmatism" is one of those crossover philosophical terms that appears in both popular speech and academic discourse. In its everyday, nontechnical usage, being "pragmatic" typically implies that one is focused more on achieving results than on conforming to higher principles or doctrinal purity. In its least flattering articulation, pragmatism becomes synonymous with political expediency, a reading that suggests a sharp division between pragmatism and ethical integrity. While aspects of the popular meaning of pragmatism do parallel its philosophical expression, the latter is much more sophisticated (both epistemologically and ethically, that is, concerning both the nature of knowledge and a system of moral standards) than the common-sense usage might lead one to believe.

Historical Roots and Philosophical Dimensions

Historically, the pragmatist tradition in philosophy may be traced back to the "Metaphysical Club," a short-lived philosophical discussion group that met in Cambridge, Massachusetts, in the early 1870s. Its members included first-generation pragmatist philosophers such as Charles Sanders Peirce (1839–1914) and William James (1842–1910), who sought to reconstruct philosophical concepts and methods to comport with a Darwinian and post-Cartesian worldview (an outlook that entailed the rejection of fixed essences and uninvestigated truths). The classical pragmatist tradition would reach its peak with the work of the philosopher John Dewey (1859–1952) in the early decades of the twentieth century. Dewey's "instrumentalist" version of pragmatism is especially known for its attempt to make philosophical analysis relevant to pressing ethical, social, and political questions.

Pragmatism's influence in academic philosophy waned greatly by the 1940s, when it became overshadowed by the rise of logical positivism and logical empiricism, which were much more concerned with the formal study of logic and semantics. The eclipse of pragmatism in academic philosophy was not total during this period, however, since quasi-pragmatist ideas were kept alive in the work of analytic philosophers such as Willard Van Orman Quine (1908–2000) and Rudolf Carnap (1891–1970), who are sometimes considered "analytic pragmatists." Moreover, pragmatism experienced a significant resurgence in philosophy beginning in the 1970s, a rebirth largely attributable to the work of "neopragmatist" philosophers such as Richard Bernstein, Cornel West, Hilary Putnam, Jurgen Habermas, and especially Richard Rorty.

The intellectual heterogeneity of pragmatism (both past and present) makes it challenging to offer meaningful generalizations about the tradition as a whole, especially regarding the genealogical connections between the major neopragmatists and classical pragmatists. Some contemporary neopragmatists, for example, reject much of the substantive philosophical trappings of historical pragmatism; Rorty's postmodernist makeover of Dewey's pragmatism is notorious for attempting to jettison any trace of Dewey's metaphysical and epistemological commitments to science and to the logic of experimental inquiry. To make matters even more complicated to categorize, pragmatism has captured the imagination of a diverse assortment of scholars outside of philosophy, including those in law, cultural theory, history, politics, religion, and economics, to name a few. Philosophically, pragmatism is defined by a loosely connected set of theories regarding truth, meaning, inquiry, and value. The "pragmatic maxim" first stated by Peirce—the idea that a belief about an idea or object is properly fixed by inquiry into its practical consequences—provides a basic logical entrée to philosophical pragmatism, though we can recognize a number of identifying commitments and concepts that begin to flesh out the tradition in more detail.

One of the most significant philosophical moves within pragmatism is the rejection of foundationalism, that is, the denial by pragmatists of the idea (shared by both traditional rationalists and empiricists) that knowledge and belief must be grounded in a class of certain, fixed, and basic beliefs that themselves require no justification (i.e., they are self-evident or self-justifying in some manner). In questioning the existence of such foundational truths, pragmatists like Dewey rejected traditional philosophy's "quest for certainty" and embraced a more experimental and fallibilistic view of knowledge in which all beliefs—even those we have good reason to hold based on previous experience—are open to criticism, revision, and replacement. For the pragmatists the refutation of a foundational anchoring for knowledge, however, did not require a turn toward skepticism. As the philosopher Hilary Putnam has suggested, the notion that one could be both a fallibilist and an antiskeptic is perhaps the most unique epistemological insight of pragmatism.

Another hallmark commitment of pragmatism is the rejection of all manner of philosophical dualisms (e.g., mind and body, essence and appearance, etc.). Pragmatists believe it is pointless, and often intellectually disastrous, to make overly sharp, metaphysically inscribed distinctions between the elements of human existence. As philosophical naturalists, pragmatists stress the basic continuity of human experience in the physical and social world. This commitment also leads pragmatists to reject any ontological division between fact and value: pragmatists privilege an empirical view supported by facts about human experience that might provide evidence for moral claims about what is, in fact, good or right (or bad or wrong)—evidence that is always capable of being overturned in light of additional experience.

Pragmatists also place emphasis on the realm of human practice (as opposed to the sphere of the ideal). Pragmatism is a thoroughly active and reconstructive philosophy that arises from practical experience and takes shape as individuals and communities confront problematic situations and adjust and improve their relationship with their environment. Empirical beliefs and moral principles are therefore

tools for social experimentation and adaptation. Pragmatists endorse a thoroughly pluralistic view of value and the good. Given that individuals are differently situated and are shaped to a significant degree by dissimilar traditions and experiences—and that novel ethical situations and problem contexts are always emerging—adherence to any single moral principle or rule in the face of such complexity and change is viewed by pragmatists as misguided.

Finally, within pragmatism there is a high regard for the epistemic, moral, and political value of the community. Pragmatists like Charles Sanders Peirce and John Dewey embraced community as an institution capable of solving complex scientific and social problems. They believed that, working in concert, a diverse association of "inquirers" (which could include experts, citizens, or both), was better positioned to identify facts and to solve problems than were individuals operating by themselves, hampered by their idiosyncratic perspectives and biases. For Peirce, who sought to develop pragmatism as a scientific metaphysics, truth would eventually emerge from the ideal workings of organized experimental inquiry over the long run. In Dewey's understanding, this idealized view of cooperative/scientific inquiry was manifest in what he called the method of "social intelligence." In Dewey's writing this process, patterned after the style of inquiry successful in the natural and technical sciences, was linked to the political culture of democracy. A democratic social order characterized by openness, toleration, freedom of expression, and the other democratic virtues would permit social intelligence to function most effectively, that is, to facilitate free and cooperative inquiry and the collective resolution of social problems. But for Dewey community was also a core moral concept, embodying a communicative and social ideal in which individuals participated in collective experience, contributing to the development of shared values and the direction of civic affairs.

The Emergence of "Environmental Pragmatism"

Although the first generation of pragmatists did not write much about conservation or environmental protection, the human–environment continuity reinforced by their commitment to philosophical naturalism and the strong anti-dualistic orientation of pragmatists like Dewey provide what we might think of as an "ecological" view of the human self, one in which the individual is seen as thoroughly enmeshed in larger natural and cultural–historic systems. Likewise, the pragmatist emphasis on the harmonious adaptation of individuals to the surrounding natural and social environment (rather than on physical domination or technological control) suggests an orientation toward nonhuman nature very similar to what we would today call a "sustainability ethic."

Even if Peirce, James, Dewey, and their academic allies did not devote much explicit attention to the natural world as a subject of philosophical concern, a broadly pragmatist sensibility may be seen to characterize the work of key early twentieth-century progressive conservationists and planners such as Liberty Hyde Bailey, Lewis Mumford, Benton MacKaye, and Aldo Leopold. Despite their differences, these writers emphasized (as did the pragmatists) the significance of human experience in the environment and its role in shaping and transforming belief and value. Furthermore, they accepted the pluralism of environmental values (including both instrumental and intrinsic values of nature), and they made a number of important connections between the proper design and conservation of the American landscape and the affairs of the human community, especially public spiritedness and civic renewal. The pragmatic conservationists and planning reformers also stressed the imperatives of respect for and human adaptation to natural conditions, as well as a sense of ethical restraint and humility, found in the mature pragmatism of Dewey and others.

The linkages between philosophical pragmatism and contemporary environmentalism became a focal point of academic concern in the 1990s as environmental philosophers began to incorporate pragmatist ideas and methods in their arguments for a more practical and policy-oriented approach to environmental ethics. Environmental pragmatists rejected the dominant philosophical focus in environmental ethics, non-anthropocentrism. As a "nature-centered" philosophy suspicious of humanistic value systems and justifications for environmental policies and practices, non-anthropocentrism was criticized by environmental pragmatists as both metaphysically and epistemologically flawed, a philosophical posture unlikely to motivate citizens and decision makers to support a sufficiently strong environmental policy agenda. The broad humanism, the experimentalism, the pluralism, and above all, the practical temperament of the tradition of Peirce, James, and Dewey were seen by environmental pragmatists as offering a more compelling philosophical backdrop to environmental protection. Some environmental pragmatists, Ben A. Minteer and Robert E. Manning, for example, also argued that this tradition comported better with core social and political commitments such as public deliberation and the maintenance of a strong democratic culture.

In addition to its role in reshaping much of the discussion in environmental philosophy, in recent years pragmatism has also been evoked as providing a rationale for several important projects in environmental policy, politics, and science. The legal scholar Daniel A. Farber, for example, has defended a pragmatic approach to environmental law and regulation that rejects the traditional reliance on formal decision tools such as cost–benefit analysis

for a more dynamic, long-sighted, and pluralistic method of environmental decision making. Similarly, the environmental advocates Ted Nordhaus and Michael Shellenberger (authors of the controversial "Death of Environmentalism" essay and the 2007 follow-up book, *Break Through*)—have criticized American environmentalism for being too negative and beholden to a "politics of limits" that they argue should be replaced by a more progressive and ameliorative form of pragmatic environmentalism. Finally, the Ecological Society of America's 2004 "vision statement" advocates a new scientific research agenda in ecology that seeks to connect ecological research directly to the social and policy imperatives presented by increasing urbanization and the accompanying strain on ecosystems. This new "pragmatic ecological science" accepts human agency in environmental systems and seeks to manage and, in some cases, to creatively design ecological services with the goal of achieving a sustainable future.

Pragmatism, Sustainability, and Natural Piety

One of the most significant recent attempts in environmental philosophy to wed pragmatism to the sustainability idea has been made by Bryan Norton in his 2005 book, *Sustainability: A Philosophy of Adaptive Ecosystem Management*. There, Norton defends an integrated scientific and value discourse for discussions of sustainability across the fields of environmental science, policy, and management. In doing so, he reframes environmental problems as linguistic failures (rather than ethical ones) and sets a new agenda for environmental philosophy in the pragmatics of language and communication. In developing the philosophical tenets of adaptive management as a pragmatic instrument to achieve eco-social sustainability, Norton articulates an epistemology of community-level experimentation, a methodologically naturalistic approach that subjects both empirical beliefs and environmental/social values to a common process of collective inquiry and adjustment.

The religious dimension of pragmatism—often neglected in contemporary neopragmatist discussions—may also prove significant in developing a richer understanding of the moral and philosophical dimensions of sustainability. In Dewey's religious writing, for example, natural conditions are valued as a fundamental source of human ideals, and as goods for which each subsequent generation bears responsibility. Respect for the social and physical environment, called "natural piety" by Dewey in his underappreciated 1934 book, *A Common Faith*, was thus the proper attitude to take toward enabling these conditions of human value and experience, not an arrogant anthropocentrism. Dewey's notion of natural piety contributes an important idealistic dimension to the broadly instrumentalist view of nature in human experience, and as such may help bring the aesthetic and religious elements of classical pragmatism into the era of environmental sustainability.

Ben A. MINTEER

Arizona State University

FURTHER READING:

Anderson, Elizabeth. (1998). Pragmatism, science, and moral inquiry. In Richard W. Fox & Robert B. Westbrook (Eds.), *In face of the facts: Moral inquiry in American scholarship* (pp. 10–39). Washington, DC: Woodrow Wilson Center and Cambridge University Press.

Bernstein, Richard J. (1992). *The new constellation: Ethical-political horizons of modernity/postmodernity.* Cambridge, MA: MIT Press.

Brint, Michael, & Weaver, William. (Eds.). (1993). *Pragmatism in law and society.* Boulder, CO: Westview Press.

Bromley, Daniel W. (2006). *Sufficient reason: Volitional pragmatism and the meaning of economic institutions.* Princeton, NJ: Princeton University Press.

Dewey, John. (1986). *A Common Faith.* In Jo Ann Boydston (Ed.), *John Dewey: The Later Works, 1925–1953: Vol. 9. 1933–1934* (pp.1–58). Carbondale: Southern Illinois University Press.

Farber, Daniel A. (1999). *Eco-pragmatism: Making sustainable environmental decisions in an uncertain world.* Chicago: University of Chicago Press.

Feffer, Andrew. (1997). *The Chicago pragmatists and American progressivism.* Ithaca, NY: Cornell University Press.

Festenstein, Matthew. (1997). *Pragmatism and political theory: From Dewey to Rorty.* Chicago: University of Chicago Press.

Gunn, Giles B. (1992). *Thinking across the American grain: Ideology, intellect, and the new pragmatism.* Chicago: University of Chicago Press.

Haack, Susan. (2004). Pragmatism, old and new. *Contemporary Pragmatism 1,* 3–41.

Hamner, M. Gail. (2003). *American pragmatism: A religious genealogy.* Oxford, U.K.; New York: Oxford University Press.

Light, Andrew & Katz, Eric (Eds.). (1996). *Environmental Pragmatism.* London: Routledge.

Menand, Louis. (2001). *The metaphysical club: A story of ideas in America.* New York: Farrar, Straus, and Giroux.

Minteer, Ben A. (2002). Deweyan democracy and environmental ethics. In Ben A. Minteer & Bob P. Taylor (Eds.), *Democracy and the claims of nature: Critical perspectives for a new century* (pp. 33–48). Lanham, MD: Rowman & Littlefield.

Minteer, Ben A. (2005). Environmental ethics and the public interest: A pragmatic reconciliation. *Environmental Values 14,* 37–60.

Minteer, Ben A. (2006). *The landscape of reform: Civic pragmatism and environmental thought in America.* Cambridge, MA: MIT Press.

Minteer, Ben A. (2008). Pragmatism, natural piety, and environmental ethics. *World Views: Global Religions, Culture, and Ecology 12,* 179–196.

Minteer, Ben A., & Manning, Robert E. (1999). Pragmatism in environmental ethics: Democracy, pluralism, and the management of nature. *Environmental Ethics 21,* 193–209.

Nordhaus, Ted, & Shellenberger, Michael. (2007). *Break through: From the death of environmentalism to the politics of possibility.* Boston: Houghton Mifflin.

Norton, Bryan G. (1991). *Toward unity among environmentalists.* Oxford, U.K.: Oxford University Press.

Norton, Bryan G. (2005). *Sustainability: A philosophy of adaptive ecosystem management.* Chicago: University of Chicago Press.

Palmer, Margaret; Bernhardt, Emily; Chornesky, Elizabeth; Collins, Scott; Dobson, Andrew; Duke, Clifford; et al. (2004, May 28). Ecology for a crowded planet. *Science 304,* 1251–1252.

Posner, Richard A. (2003). *Law, pragmatism, and democracy.* Cambridge, MA: Harvard University Press.

Putnam, Hilary. (1994). *Words and life.* Cambridge, MA: Harvard University Press.

Schellenberger, Michael, & Nordhaus, Ted. (2004). The death of environmentalism. Retrieved March 25, 2009, from http://www.thebreakthrough.org/images/Death_of_Environmentalism.pdf

Precautionary Principle

Since the latter twentieth century, the precautionary principle has been adopted by a number of governments and organizations as a guiding structure for decision making. It states that when the health of humans and the environment is threatened, it is not necessary to receive conclusive or definitive scientific evidence of that harm before taking action. Today it is more commonly implemented in the European Union.

The origin of the precautionary principle is generally attributed to the German concept of *Vorsorgeprinzip* ("fore-caring principle"), which may be translated to signify having concern for or foresight of the possible consequences of one's action. The precautionary principle came into public discussion in the mid-1980s as European policy makers began to use it to define a meaningful regulatory framework to control the introduction of new technologies and products. This had followed the extraordinary string of legislative successes that had occurred in the United States throughout the 1970s with the enactment of major environmental laws on air and water quality, toxic substances and hazardous wastes, and the adoption of quantitative risk assessment procedures among federal and state agencies. Among these were the Resource Conservation and Recovery Act (1976), the Toxic Substances Control Act (1976), and the Clean Water Act (1977).

On the international front, the precautionary principle was initially introduced at the First International Conference on the Protection of the North Sea in 1984; it also was embedded in the Maastricht Treaty (1992), which led to the formation of the European Union, and with earlier elements present in the 1976 Barcelona Convention against Pollution in the Mediterranean Sea. Finally at the 1992 United Nations Conference on Environment and Development (UNCED), informally known as the Rio Earth Summit, the precautionary principle was adopted as Principle 15 in their conference report, the Rio Declaration on Environment and Development, which stated: "In order to protect the environment, the precautionary approach shall be widely applied by states according to their capabilities. Where there are threats of serious or irreversible damage, lack of full scientific certainty shall not be used as a reason for postponing cost-effective measures to prevent environmental degradation" (UNEP 1992).

While more widely accepted within the European Union, at present there is little acceptance of the precautionary principle in the United States, especially among private-sector companies and major trade associations, who have adamantly opposed the use of such a regulatory approach for conducting their commercial activities. What accounts for this transatlantic divide? To understand why this regulatory impasse in international trade has occurred, one must examine the differing ethical standards and philosophical worldviews of the two regulatory cultures.

Despite earlier legislative action toward environmental protection, regulatory officials in United States have less difficulty in accepting risk assessment and risk management principles for defining environmental and public health standards or, for example, for issuing effluent discharge permits to a manufacturing plant. In contrast, European officials do not view risk-assessment procedures as adequate for controlling toxic substances and hazardous products in commercial transactions, especially as they pertain to importation of manufactured goods from other regions of the globe. They more often judge that new products may come into the market without adequate knowledge or without proper assessment of their potential impact on the natural environment. The adoption of the precautionary principle as an overarching regulatory guideline has thus been more appealing to many European policy makers.

In June 2007, based on the conceptual foundation of the precautionary principle, the European Union (EU) put into force a landmark regulatory framework called REACH (Regulation, Evaluation, Authorization and Restriction of Chemical Substances). This EU directive streamlines the process by which private industries assess and manage the production, use, and marketing of chemical substances, along with providing safety information to users in their member countries. Since the *Vorsorgeprinzip* became the fundamental basis of German environmental law in the early 1970s, it has been referred to in judiciary and regulatory proceedings in other countries around the globe.

Although the basic concept of the precautionary principle still has not taken root in the United States, a few state and local governments have adopted its underlying tenet in their decision-making process. The Wingspread Statement on the Precautionary Principle was formulated in 1998 by scientists, environmentalists, policy makers, and lawyers at a conference in Racine, Wisconsin. It states that "[w]hen an activity raises threats of harm to human health or the environment, precautionary measures should be taken even if some cause and effect relationships are not fully established scientifically." As early as 1989, the Commonwealth of Massachusetts enacted the Toxic Use Reduction Act (TURA) that provided industries in the state with planning tools to voluntarily reduce their production, use, and emission of toxic substances; such an approach does not depend on establishing the scientific certainty of their harmful effects. In 2003, the City of San Francisco passed a precautionary principle ordinance, which states that ". . . lack of scientific certainty relating to cause and effect shall not be viewed as sufficient reason for the City to postpone measures to prevent the degradation of the environment or protect the health of its citizen . . . Where there are reasonable grounds for concern, the Precautionary Principle is meant to help reduce harm."

A. Karim AHMED
National Council for Science and the Environment

FURTHER READING

Massachusetts Precautionary Principle Project. (2009). Retrieved on July 12, 2009, from http://www.sehn.org/pppra.html

Montague, Peter. (2006, March 16). Getting beyond risk assessment. *Rachel's Democracy & Health News*, (846). Retrieved on July 12, 2009, from http://www.precaution.org/lib/06/prn_alternatives_to_qra.060316.htm

O'Riordan, Timothy, & Jordan, Andrew. (1995). The precautionary principle, science, politics and ethics. Retrieved on July 12, 2009, from http://www.uea.ac.uk/env/cserge/pub/wp/pa/pa_1995_02.pdf

The precautionary principle. (2005). Paris: UNESCO. Retrieved on July 12, 2009, from http://unesdoc.unesco.org/images/0013/001395/139578e.pdf

The precautionary principle and environmental policy. (2000). *International Journal of Occupational and Environmental Health*, (6). Retrieved on July 12, 2009, from http://www.sehn.org/pdf/ppep.pdf

San Francisco adopts the precautionary principle. (2003, March 19). Retrieved June 2, 2009, from http://www.rachel.org/en/node/5656

United Nations Environment Programme (UNEP). (1992). Rio declaration on environment and development. Retrieved on June 2, 2009, from http://www.unep.org/Documents.Multilingual/Default.asp?DocumentID=78&ArticleID=1163&l=en

Wingspread statement on the precautionary principle. (1998, January). Retrieved June 2, 2009, from http://www.sehn.org/wing.html

Process Thought

Process thought envisions the biosphere (and the cosmos as a whole) as a community of dynamic diverse subjects who must all be accorded some degree of intrinsic value in and for themselves, as well as instrumental value for others. Its capacity to mediate differences among disciplines—to empower a cooperative, problem-solving venture regarding the fate of our biosphere—is in itself a valuable tool for working toward sustainability.

Process thought refers to a wide-ranging set of discourses, primarily philosophical and theological but interfacing with such diverse fields as physics, biology, ecology, psychology, educational theory, gender theory, and economics. These share a common inspiration in the philosophy and speculative metaphysics of Alfred North Whitehead (1861–1947), a British mathematician and logician. As a movement process thought has exercised a disproportionate and long-term influence on the development of ecological thought and practice. Process thought asserts that at the most fundamental level of reality we find not enduring substances but processual events emerging through an internal integration of their relationships and then "perishing" into a (potential) influence on forthcoming events. Its move beyond traditional "substance metaphysics" is ground for a comprehensive critique of the mechanistic materialism upon which modern science has largely been founded. Its alternative—what Whitehead has called a philosophy of organism—attempts to balance two complementary cosmological principles: a dynamic, creative spontaneity, ensuring that the world is never the same from one moment to the next, and an intricately interrelated order, ensuring the continuity of complex structures in the world. One of process thought's primary objectives is to bridge some of the most entrenched dichotomies (or "bifurcations" in Whitehead's language) characteristic of the modern worldview,

including matter vs. mind, fact vs. value, nature vs. culture, rationality vs. aesthetics, and the hard sciences vs. the humanities. Its ecological vision of cosmic interdependence along with its philosophical capacity to facilitate constructive interdisciplinary conversations—particularly between the sciences and the humanities—make it an indispensable framework for addressing issues of sustainability, whether environmental, social, or economic.

Major Thinkers and Ideas

In the later years of his life, Alfred North Whitehead came to Harvard University to develop a unique philosophy influenced in part by American pragmatists (primarily William James and Charles S. Peirce) and Henri Bergson's philosophy of becoming. Whitehead's later works were, in large part, a constructive philosophical response to some of the most cutting-edge developments in the science of his day, including relativity theory, particularly its challenge to the idea of a purely neutral, objective framework from which to measure things; quantum mechanics, which was discovering the discontinuous and unpredictable jumps of matter's smallest structures; and evolutionary biology, which described novel, complex, "organismic" structures "emergent" from a more simple ground to which they were irreducible. For Whitehead, this combination of insights seemed to undermine the Newtonian ideal of reductionism, which held that all of reality could ultimately be broken down into independent, substantial, material particles, behaving in a law-abiding, mechanistic fashion. While Whitehead appreciated modern science's materialist empiricism as an original and useful mode of abstraction with powerful applications, he found it utterly insufficient as a comprehensive worldview within which to coordinate larger goals, values, and relationships. He was particularly concerned about its inability to explain credibly the role of mind and value.

Whitehead's alternative metaphysical schema argues that *all* of concrete, actual reality comes into being through a process of becoming ("concrescence") that includes within it both a receptive ("physical") phase and a self-creative ("mental") phase. This philosophy of events (also called "actual occasions") constitutes what could be well described as an ecological metaphysic in which no entity's existence can be thought apart from the environment through which it comes into being. What we think of as enduring entities or creatures are actually communities ("societies") of actual occasions that interlock within an infinite web of other societies throughout time and space. In a certain sense, then, what we are in the most fundamental sense *is* our relationships, although how or what we become through those relationships always includes an element of openness and freedom in which value plays some (if only a very small) role. Thus, although there are different levels of "intensity" of creative becoming, *everything* in the cosmos—organic or inorganic, conscious or unconscious—can be understood to "experience" (or "enjoy") a certain self-creative, relational becoming. It is for this reason that process thought is often identified with the doctrine of pan-psychism, though the label *pan-experientialism* may be more accurate since Whitehead and his followers firmly believe that although everything has experience (in which "mentality" in his redefined sense does play a certain role), this does not entail that everything is conscious.

Charles Hartshorne, a philosopher profoundly influenced by Whitehead at Harvard, further expanded the theistic implications of Whitehead's schema bringing process thought to the University of Chicago where it would have a number of strong proponents, both philosophical and theological, over the years. John Cobb, a student of Hartshorne's, developed process theology in greater depth and helped establish the Center for Process Studies at the Claremont School of Theology. Process theology is rooted in Whitehead's understanding of a "di-polar" God who—like the actual occasion—has both a creative and a receptive pole: God's "primordial nature" is the ground for novelty or creative advance in the universe, while God's "consequent nature" receives into itself the totality of what the universe has become. Thus the new possibilities God opens for creation are integrally connected to God's internal "feeling" of the world as it actually exists. Process theology breaks from traditional theism in explicitly disavowing the doctrine of divine omnipotence. Because God's power operates as a persuasive rather than a coercive power, creatures are endowed with real (rather than illusory) freedom, and the future is genuinely open—even for God.

Process thought has played a key role in various ecotheologies that have challenged theology's traditional anthropocentric tenets (the idea of divinely sanctioned human dominion over nature, for instance) so as to reconceptualize humanity's ethical responsibility toward the rest of creation. John Cobb's writings have brought process theology and philosophy into explicit conversation with environmental ethics, evolutionary biology (see *The Liberation of Life*, written with Charles Birch, for an exploration of both), and economics (see *For the Common Good*, written with Herman Daly). Thus, Cobb is a key figure in process thought's interdisciplinary engagement with issues of sustainability.

Process Thought and the Ethics of Sustainability

Process thought begins with the idea that relations are primary—it is only through dynamic interdependent processes that anything can even be said to exist in the first place. No simplistic, dichotomous separation between human reality and its nonhuman context is possible within this framework. In this way, the adequacy of the word "environment" as a descriptor for our nonhuman context would be held suspect by process thought insofar as it makes the latter out to be somewhat of an external backdrop to human culture. Along these same lines, process thought would critique the idea that human life should be granted some kind of special ontological, metaphysical, or theological status by virtue of our capacity for culture, language, and/or self-awareness. This is not to deny the uniqueness of humanity but rather to set the human project into a larger cosmological context within which its unique, self-creative expressions are quite at home. If *everything* in the world is capable of *some* level of value-driven, relational "experience," the emergence of life and, later, of human consciousness, no longer stand out as confounding anomalies, but can be affirmed as part of the movement of the "living" cosmos toward greater complexity and relational intensity. Although this larger movement can be described as "purposeful" in a certain qualified sense, any sense of cosmic determinism, Hegelian or otherwise, is explicitly disavowed.

In affirming a naturalistic cosmos in which human creativity is just another expression of the inherent self-creativity of all of nature, process thought moves in the direction of a kind of "partnership ethic" between humanity and the rest of the natural world.

It recognizes that modern Western civilization's recent habit of treating our nonhuman ecological context as a mere stockpile of external resources to be objectified and instrumentally exploited is not only illusory and wrong, but dangerously unsustainable. Process thought instead envisions the biosphere (and the cosmos as a whole) as a community of diverse subjects—all of whom must be accorded some degree of intrinsic value in and for themselves as well as instrumental value for others. (This is consonant with Whitehead's philosophy of events as described above, in which each actual occasion is both a unique, irreplaceable event unto itself and a potential influence for all that succeeds it).

Process thought's challenge to substance metaphysics functions as a critique of the centrality of individualism within major Western thought traditions. It is not that liberalism's valuation of the individual as an end in itself is necessarily rejected; process thought recognizes *every* creature as having intrinsic value. Rather, it recognizes that this value is meaningless without the complex matrix of relations that sustain it. Freedom (political or otherwise) can only be cultivated in a relational context in which the value and agency of the nonhuman is affirmed. In this way, process thought would supplement the liberal "rights-based" approach to ethics with a more communitarian emphasis, contending that ideals such as democracy and freedom require the cultivation of a common world shared by genuinely diverse beings. To describe responsibility to the other merely in terms of individual face-to-face interactions is inadequate. Responsibility might be better understood as a flowing network of reciprocity shared among a plurality of diverse subjects.

Debates around sustainability have often been caught between two mutually exclusive positions—an anthropocentric perspective which unabashedly embraces the priority of human life above all else and seeks to "manage" resources so as to render them sustainable for human life; and a biocentric (or ecocentric) perspective that proposes equal moral consideration for the different life-forms of this biosphere, perhaps as part of an imperative to preserve ecological health. Barbara Muraca, an Italian scholar whose work has focused on process thought's contribution to sustainability discourses, has suggested that process thought may point to a kind of "third way" between these polarized positions: while process thought would stand with biocentrism in its holistic commitment to the health of the entire biocommunity, it would also recognize the profound difficulty of applying any meaningful concept of "equality" to nature's radical diversity. Process thought, then, would assist in the development of pragmatic tools for negotiating competing claims within the co-creative process of assembling and sustaining a common world. Although process thought affirms the subjective agency and intrinsic value of every being, it is also resolutely sober about the fact that life lives off of other life in a way that is unavoidably appropriative (in Whitehead's words, "Life is robbery"). This does not lead, however, to an uncritical affirmation of the doctrine of the survival of the fittest. Whitehead, for example, explicitly criticizes the predominance of an evolutionary model privileging competition within a fixed environment, suggesting that it obscures life's more significant imperative to co-create a mutually beneficial environment through cooperative processes. Whitehead nonetheless recognizes that the sacrifice of certain living entities for the becoming of other living entities is an unavoidable part of the natural process through which the cosmos generates value and intensity.

Some process thinkers, including John Cobb, have therefore suggested that graded distinctions can be made in the relative intrinsic values of certain kinds of life-forms in relation to others. These "grades" of intrinsic value have to do with the level of relational complexity and intensity a given life form is capable of integrating into its becoming. (Few would doubt the wisdom of killing a virus in order to save the life of a human being, for example.) While process thought has at times been criticized for the seeming anti-egalitarianism of this idea, this strategy should be understood as a limited, pragmatic response to the inevitable ethical dilemmas with which life confronts us—one that is neither paralyzed by an egalitarian-inspired relativism nor seduced by an absolutist anthropocentrism. Any practical use of this ethic would have to begin holistically with the health of the larger biotic (and social/economic) community. In this way, process thought's approach would perhaps share affinities with Aldo Leopold's "land ethic" as it would strive to hold in balance the needs of a variety of beings, all considered integral to the larger health of the biosphere. Similarly, process thought would likely steer away from the ideal of total nonintervention into the Earth's processes (as articulated by some of the more radically biocentric environmental thinkers) seeking instead to build constructive alliances between human beings and their nonhuman partners in such a way as to increase the sustainability of life for as many as possible.

Process Thought and Sustainable Economics

John Cobb and Herman Daly made a groundbreaking contribution to the theory of sustainable economics with their book, *For the Common Good*. Anchored in a "process" perspective the authors contend that the central unity of economic theory should be "persons in a community" rather than "individuals in a market." Contemporary economics' focus on self-interest as the only motivational force worth considering violently "abstracts" from the social/communal dimensions of human life. Cobb and Daly suggest that smaller regions should produce more of the goods they need, closer to where they are consumed. This economic strategy is intended to cultivate the self-reliance of local communities who can then reinvest their energies in the health of the immediate bioregions to which they belong.

Because of its reliance on Whitehead's philosophical vocabulary, some of which can come across as abstruse and technical to the average reader, process thought has sometimes been pigeon-holed as an overly abstract—even arcane—field of theoretical research with little to contribute to the practical realms of ethics and politics. This image of process thought may ironically belie the area of its greatest potential contribution—namely its capacity to mediate methodological differences between disciplines so as to empower a larger, cooperative, problem-solving venture in regard to our collective fate on this biosphere. This strength is reflected in the fact that thinkers from a whole range of disciplines have incorporated process insights into their work toward a number of diverse ends. If conversations on sustainability have taught us anything, it is that we cannot address any one aspect of our world's problems—whether environmental, social, or economic—in isolation from the others. Process thought offers a conceptual framework for thinking through our various levels of relational "entanglement" (whether social, biological, political, aesthetic) in such a way that addresses the health of the whole without trying to capture or reduce it to any single, static schema. As it becomes increasingly clear that human civilization's current patterns of consumption and behavior cannot sustain life on this planet. Process thought's holistic yet open-ended strategies for thinking through and solving problems may prove to be invaluable.

Luke B. HIGGINS
Drew University

FURTHER READING

Cobb, John B. (1972). *Is it too late? A theology of ecology*. New York: Bruce Publishing Col. (Revised Edition, Denton, TX: Environmental Ethics Books, 1995)

Cobb, John B & Birch, Charles. (1990). *The liberation of life*. Denton, TX: Environmental Ethics Books.

Cobb, John B. & Daly, Herman E. (1989). *For the common good: Redirecting the economy toward community, the environment, and a sustainable future*. Boston: Beacon Press. (Updated and expanded edition, 1994)

Kearns, Laurel, & Keller, Catherine. (Eds.). (2000). *Eco-spirit: Religions and philosophies for the earth*. New York: Fordham University Press.

McDaniel, Jay Byrd. (1995). *With roots and wings: Christianity in an age of ecology and dialogue*. Maryknoll, NewYork: Orbis Books.

Muraca, B. (2005, Spring-Summer). Welt, umwelt, mitwelt: Cultural, natural, and social world as complex intertwined field of internal relations: The contribution of process thought to a general theory of sustainability. *Process Studies, 34*(1), 98–116.

Stengers, Isabelle. (2002). A 'cosmo-politics'—Risk, hope, change. In Mary Zournazi (Ed.), *Hope: New Philosophies for Change* (pp. 244–272). New York: Routledge.

Whitehead, Alfred North. (1978). *Process and reality, corrected edition*. David Ray Griffin and Donald Sherburne (Eds.). New York: The Free Press.

Whitehead, Alfred North. (1997). *Science and the modern world: Lowell lectures, 1925*. New York: Simon & Schuster.

Property and Possessions

Property and possessions have environmental and spiritual significance. Some religions emphasize living without excess possessions—while others see possessions as a divine gift to be treated with reverence—and see the link between such values as creating a lower environmental impact.

Property and possessions—the material items (including land) that are owned or used by an individual or a group—have environmental significance. The ownership and use of land has an impact on the land's ecology, particularly the decisions made by the land's owner in terms of farming, preserving, or developing it. The ownership and use of other possessions, from clothing and food to cars and furniture, also impacts the environment, as it implies use of resources to create and maintain those possessions, in addition to the environmental impact of their disposal.

Property and possessions also have spiritual significance. Many religions advise minimizing possessions and counsel against vices such as greed and gluttony. For other traditions, material riches signify divine blessing, a gift to be used reverently and gratefully. In discussing property and possessions, several related questions arise, which will be examined in each of the following sections; different religious traditions answer these questions in distinctive ways.

Is Private Property Legitimate?

Most traditions teach that the created world is a divine gift, intended for the well-being of all humans (and, for some, all nonhumans as well). Private property, with its unequal distribution of goods, is significantly different from this ideal state of universal access. Many teach that private property is not natural and was not instituted by God, but

is a necessary evil. In Judaism, the land ultimately belongs to God, but has been distributed to God's people according to God's plan. In Christianity, Thomas Aquinas (1225–1274) teaches that because private property helps imperfect humans to take responsibility for stewardship and avoid the inevitable squabbling that arises with shared goods, it is a defensible, though imperfect, system. Islam accepts private property, but teaches that private wealth should not be hoarded. Rather, wealth should be circulated, through almsgiving or economic activity, so that it may be maximally helpful to the community.

Some traditions emphasize the nonideal nature of private property, focusing on the divine ownership of the world. The Hindu Vedas urge collective ownership and equitable sharing of possessions, because humans are merely stewards and not really owners of the created world. Many indigenous peoples do not see land as something that can be owned, but rather as a home that all must share. Additionally, Islam has a concept of "public property," which applies to assets belonging to an entire community, such as rivers, roads, forests, bridges, and pasturelands. These may not be individually owned but, rather, are tended communally.

How Should Property Be Distributed?

Many religious traditions are concerned about the distribution of property, particularly the materials necessary for basic human well-being. Many avoid advocating absolute material equality for all but promote sufficiency for all and equity in fair dealings. The needy, according to most traditions, have a justified claim (simply by virtue of being human) to receive enough material assets to allow them to live in dignity and health. Many traditions assert that the creator has created the world in such a way that everyone's basic needs can and should be met. The human task is to redistribute goods to make this possible.

One popular mode for the redistribution of property is almsgiving, a nearly universal practice of voluntary donations to the poor or to a religious institution. In Judaism, 10 percent of all harvest or other income should be given to the temple priests to support temple festivals, religious workers, and the poor. The Hebrew scriptures also describe cycles of redistribution, in which the land is redistributed according to God's plan every fifty years in accordance with the laws of Jubilee. Though Jubilee land distribution no longer takes place in the Jewish community, the scriptures describing it remain part of the sacred writings, venerated as God's description of holiness (Leviticus 25, 27).

Early Christian scriptures speak of collections to support poorer congregations. Christianity teaches that the poor are blessed because Jesus identifies himself with them; the rich are obliged to help them as if they were giving to Jesus himself (Matthew 25:31–46). Some early Christians practiced a communal sharing of goods. Many foundational theologians, notably Clement of Alexandria (150–211) and John Chrysostom (347–407), teach that Christians of means must give alms to help the poor. Additionally, Aquinas teaches that in cases of dire need, the necessities of life may be stolen without blame, since the creation is intended to nourish all humans equally.

In Islam, *zakat* is one of the five pillars, or central practices: a certain percentage of wealth and produce is to be delivered to the poor, the disabled, those in crisis, and religious workers. In Islamic states, this form of almsgiving is administered by the government, as it was in some parts of Europe in the sixteenth and seventeenth centuries.

Other religions practice different forms of almsgiving and property redistribution. Buddhism encourages *dana*, generous giving, as a way of practicing nonattachment to possessions. Buddhist monks are often pictured with begging bowls, as they acquire their living through the alms they receive from lay people. Hindu practitioners may acquire merit by giving food and other donations to temples and holy practitioners.

What is the Value of Asceticism?

Some religious traditions encourage asceticism, a disciplined life that renounces sensual pleasure and luxurious living. Other traditions, however, reject strong asceticism. Judaism, for example, has a scant ascetic tradition.

Judaism's God promises the chosen people a land flowing with milk and honey, a place of ease and abundance, as a reward for their faithfulness (Exodus 3:8). Judaism's unique cycles of productive work and holy rest arise from observing the Sabbath, a weekly day of rest, when production ceases and adherents engage in spiritual activities. This tradition of periodic rest functions less as an ascetic self-denial than as a limit on productive work (and therefore on property and possessions), placing them in their proper spiritual perspective.

Christians seek to follow the example of Jesus of Nazareth (approximately 2 BCE–36 CE), who led an itinerant life with few possessions and invited his followers to give up what they own in order to follow him (Mark 10:17–31). Jesus' example is not unequivocal: he seemed to possess little but ate enthusiastically, earning him a reputation as a "glutton and a drunkard"—hardly an ascetic (Luke 7:34). In the Christian scriptures, excess property and possessions are seen as a spiritual danger, as in the parable of the rich fool, which describes the spiritual peril of those who put stock in great wealth rather than in God (Luke 12:16–34). Institutional Christianity became increasingly comfortable with riches, defending them as gifts from God. Nevertheless, reformists—from Christian monks and nuns, vowing poverty, to Anabaptists, to Christian Socialists—have called for simpler, more ascetic living. Although the ascetic strain in Christianity is strong, so is the teaching that worldly wealth indicates God's favor. Max Weber's (1864–1920) influential thesis holds that the acquisitiveness and luxury of capitalism arose in Europe largely thanks to certain characteristics of Protestant Christianity.

Islam is not strongly ascetic regarding property and possessions. The Prophet Muhammad (570–632 CE) counseled his followers against monastic austerity. He urged them, rather, to eat what is good and be moderate in their consumption (Quran 5:87–88). Muhammad himself worked as an honest businessman and became a householder, owning and leasing property. Islam holds a positive attitude toward wealth and material well-being, if it is procured in a virtuous way and is appropriately shared with others.

Siddhartha Gautama (563–483 BCE), who became known as the Buddha, lived an itinerant life with few possessions. He renounced a luxurious, royal lifestyle to begin his quest for enlightenment, but he also rejected a path of extreme austerity, seeking rather a "middle way." Buddhist monks and nuns live very simply with few possessions. They own only three robes and beg for their food, eating without complaint what they are given. For Buddhism, the essential concern is the inner attitude toward possessions: if one can practice nonattachment to one's property, one may find a path to *matannuta*, or moderation in property and possessions.

Jainism is particularly remarkable in its commitment to austerity and simplicity. Jain monks keep a strict vegetarian diet, renounce possessions and comforts, and take great care not to harm any living being, not even the smallest insect. Hinduism is also known for its holy practitioners who go to great lengths of ascetic practice and live with very few possessions. But not all Hindus are called to the ascetic life: Hinduism acknowledges the worthy goals of material goods, eros, and dharma, or law. Although spiritual practice in pursuit of liberation from the fetters of material existence is the highest goal, it is not the only one in Hinduism.

Other Eastern traditions seek a compromise between excesses of asceticism and indulgence. The Sikh gurus preferred the life of a householder to the life of a wandering sage; salvation, they taught, came from finding a balance between renunciation and indulgence. Confucianism and Daoism teach balance, in echo of nature's balance, between renunciation and pleasure seeking.

What is the Danger of Attachment to Possessions?

Most religions agree that possessions have the potential to undermine good spiritual practice. Judaism warns against idolatry—granting supreme status to "things" rather than to God. Christianity speaks of vices such as greed and gluttony as injurious to the soul, a distorted desire for the things of this world rather than spiritual values. Augustine of Hippo (354–430 CE) articulates a difference between "using" one's possessions and "enjoying" them (delighting in them for their own sake). He argues that only God may be enjoyed; all "lesser" items must only be used, as instrumental to higher goods; to do otherwise is to risk idolatry.

Buddhists hold that suffering results from inordinate desires, and that reducing those desires by practicing nonattachment will reduce suffering. From a Buddhist perspective, all grasping and greed is a futile attempt to please the ego-self, which is insatiable and is in fact a delusion. Chasing after desires, according to the Buddha, is like drinking saltwater, which only increases one's thirst. Succumbing to inordinate desire will make one resemble a "hungry ghost," a being in the Buddhist tradition who has a large, empty stomach and a pitiful pinhole mouth: always hungry, never satiated.

Other traditions also denounce greed. Confucianism sees greed as a rupture of the social fabric, a self-indulgent pursuit at the expense of others. Society must protect its poorer and less capable members: truly magnanimous leaders are those who help the lesser, rather than puffing themselves up. Hindus strive for *aparigraha*, the absence of acquisitiveness: greed denies divine ownership of the world and shows a lack of trust. As Mohandas Gandhi (1869–1948) famously said, the world contains enough resources for everyone's need, but not for everyone's greed.

How Does Power Affect Property?

For indigenous peoples, the topic of property and possessions evokes the exploitation many have endured at the hands of colonizing forces. Many indigenous peoples have had their possessions looted by imperial collectors. Many have lost their tribal lands, burial grounds, and other property, in misunderstandings or fraudulent dealings with colonizers or others in power. Indigenous peoples worldwide have been systematically removed from their land: this loss not only of property but also of communal identity has had a devastating effect on many communities. Some peoples have, themselves, been regarded as property, as they were enslaved by their conquerors and treated as chattel. Also at issue for indigenous groups is the question of intellectual property rights for medical plant knowledge and breeding. Medical researchers increasingly mine native botanical insights for "new" compounds to be used in pharmaceuticals, raising the question of permission and compensation for such knowledge.

Women have also been regarded as property: many women have, for centuries, engaged in nonvoluntary household labor. Marriages have, historically, been political, economic, and social arrangements using women's labor and reproductive potential as a possession to be traded between social groups. Some religious traditions have sought to rectify this by asserting the equality of women. Islam is significant as the foremost religious tradition to explicitly grant property and inheritance rights to women (Quran 4:11–12). Other traditions, notably Orthodox Judaism and traditional Hinduism, have significant scriptural resources that undermine women's rights to own and inherit property.

Property, Possessions, and the Environment

Land ownership and related concepts have a significant environmental impact. Islamic Public Property (a term that refers to communal resources held in trust) is often treated differently than individual, discretionary private property. Indigenous concepts of land ownership—the denial of any legitimate claim by one person to own land—offer a useful reminder of the transcendent value of land that cannot be encapsulated in any concept of property. Traditions such as Judaism, Christianity, and Hinduism, which assert divine ownership of creation, encourage stewardship. According to some Hindu writers, rather than devastating natural resources, humans must find ways to "milk" the earth's bounty sustainably.

The Buddhist precept of *ahimsa*, or causing no harm, may apply to environmental concerns as well. Buddhists assert the interdependence of all beings, recognizing that one small action may indirectly harm other beings. Therefore, many Buddhists advocate minimal meat consumption and careful awareness of the effects of other kinds of consumption, to minimize harmful environmental and social impacts. The Jewish practice of Sabbath-keeping, refraining from work one day per week in order to rest, study, and pray, also has environmental potential. Less work and more prayer can lead to simpler living and a lighter impact on the earth.

Generally, there is a strong link between living with minimal excess possessions and a lower environmental impact. But as many religious traditions assert, there is also value in embracing the bounties of the created world. Being a good steward of one's property and truly appreciating one's modest possessions may be the key to good environmental practice.

Laura M. HARTMAN
Augustana College (Illinois)

FURTHER READING

Alam, Mohammad Manzoor. (1996). *Perspectives on Islamic economics*. New Delhi: Institute of Objective Studies.

Augustine, St. (1997). On Christian doctrine (D. W. Robertson, Jr., Trans.). Upper Saddle River, NJ: Prentice Hall.

Bokare, M. G. (1993). *Hindu economics: Eternal economic order*. New Delhi: Janaki Prakashan.

Clement of Alexandria. (1980). Who is the rich man that shall be saved? In A. Roberts (Ed. & Trans.), *The Ante-Nicene fathers: Translations of the writings of the fathers down to A.D. 325*. Grand Rapids, MI: William B. Eerdmans.

David, J. E. (2003). Exploitation of indigenous knowledge. *Religion and Society, 48*(4), 79–88.

Fletcher, Joseph F. (1947). *Christianity and property*. Philadelphia: The Westminster Press.

Garnsey, Peter. (2007). *Thinking about property: From antiquity to the age of revolution*. Cambridge, U.K.: Cambridge University Press.

Kaza, Stephanie. (Ed.) (2005). *Hooked! Buddhist writings on greed, desire, and the urge to consume*. Boston: Shambhala.

Knitter, Paul, & Muzaffar, Chandra. (Eds.) (2002). *Subverting greed: Religious perspectives on the global economy*. Maryknoll, NY: Orbis Books.

Habiger, Matthew. (1990). *Papal teaching on private property, 1891–1981*. Lanham, MD: University Press of America.

Oubré, Alondra. (1996). Plants, property, and people: Should indigenous peoples be compensated for their medical plant knowledge? *Skeptic, 4*(2), 72–77.

Parel, Anthony. (1979). Aquinas' theory of property. In A. Parel, & T. Flanagan (Eds.), *Theories of property: Aristotle to the presen*, (pp. 89–111). Waterloo, Canada: Wilfrid Laurier University Press.

Schumacher, E. F. (1975). *Small is beautiful: Economics as if people mattered*. New York: Harper Colophon.

Schweiker, William, & Mathewes, Charles. (Eds.) (2004). *Having: Property and possession in religious and social life*. Grand Rapids, MI: William B. Eerdmans.

Sharif, M. R. (1996). *Guidelines to Islamic economics: Nature, concepts and principles*. Dhaka: Bangladesh Institute of Islamic Thought.

Tamari, Meir. (1987). *With all your possessions: Jewish ethics and economic life*. New York: The Free Press.

Weber, Max. (2005). *The Protestant ethic and the spirit of capitalism* (T. Parsons, Ed.). London: Routledge.

Wilson, Rodney. (1997). *Economics, ethics and religion: Jewish, Christian and Muslim economic thought*. Basingstoke, U.K.: MacMillan Press.

Wogaman, J. Philip. (1986). *Economics and ethics: A Christian enquiry*. London: SCM Press.

Wheeler, Sondra Ely. (1995). *Wealth as peril and obligation: The New Testament on possessions*. Grand Rapids, MI: William B. Eerdmans.

Racism

Indigenous ethnic groups have much to contribute to redevelopment of sustainable practices in environmental management. Yet race and ethnicity have played a part in corporate and political decisions that result in ecological degradation. From the siting of hazardous waste facilities in the United States to the building of petrochemical plants in South Africa, racial and ethnic groups have had to bear a disproportionate share of environmental burdens.

When the ability to sustain a cultural lifestyle and identity is threatened by policies and practices regarding the use of resources, or when groups of people are differently affected by the distribution of environmental burdens or are underrepresented in decision making, then ethical principles of justice, and specifically environmental justice, must be addressed. Environmental burdens of modern industrial societies have strong correlations with racial and ethnic minorities across the globe. Production processes such as refineries, assembly plants, mining operations, and manufacturing, and the waste stream of pollution, especially hazardous, toxic, and radioactive waste, disproportionately affect minorities. Environmental racism is therefore one of the key concepts addressed by environmental justice.

Since the 1980s, the correlation and causation between environmental burdens and racial and/or ethnic minorities, specifically in the United States, has been well documented in several crucial studies. In 1987, the United Church of Christ Commission on Racial Justice issued *Toxic Waste and Race in the United States*, a nationwide study of the incidence of commercial and noncommercial hazardous waste facilities. This study concluded that race was the primary indicator for situating locations for these facilities. A variety of studies issued in response to this study raised issues of demographic associations pertaining to the history of

the communities in the study, the demographic measuring tools, and the remedies for this distributive injustice. The *Toxic Waste and Race* study has been subsequently repeated with special regard for measuring techniques and historical considerations. Twenty years after the initial study, the third version of the study revealed the same results of correlation between race and the incidence of hazardous waste facilities, and the racial concentration and environmental impacts actually increased since the initial study. When burdens of other elements of unsustainable industrial practices in production and waste are added to this more specific identification of hazardous waste facilities, the discriminatory patterns against racial minorities in the United States are hardly debatable.

Environmental racism and sustainability issues are therefore intertwined. When a particular group, because of racial and/or ethnic characteristics, unfairly bears a disproportion of environmental burdens without proper social and political representation, then the situation poses an added threat to cultural sustainability and environmental sustainability. Racism and related forms of discrimination must therefore be considered a fundamental impediment to effective sustainability transformations in policy proposals, shifts in values, and behavioral changes.

Across the postcolonial political world, local cultural systems and indigenous communities suffer considerably similar to the findings of studies in the United States. In his 2002 study David A. McDonald, the Director of Developmental Studies at Queens College, Ontario, shows the extent to which environmental racism pervades South African resource and development practices. Despite the differing nation-specific notions of race between the United States and South Africa, the phenomenon of environmental racism can be seen in resource management, the unsustainable petrochemical industry, and the failure of proper environmental protection for marginalized ethnic groups, even after explicit rights to environmental justice were written into the post-Apartheid constitution. Ongoing legacies of institutional patterns of racism and habitual discrimination invade indigenous communities today through an intricate web of challenges to traditional environmental knowledge, cultural expression and identification, and environmental heritage that are critical for effective sustainable practices. For instance, Aboriginal peoples throughout Australia have been instrumental in conveying sustainable fire management to the Commonwealth ecologists.

Likewise, Figueroa reports that Hispano communities in New Mexico have recovered their heritage of grazing practices that prove far more environmentally sustainable than current corporate and government grazing practices. At a global level indigenous groups and vulnerable communities identified by racial and ethnic heritage suffer environmental burdens of climate change disproportionately to affluent global counterparts in the nations of heightened industrial development, most often in the responses to desertification, food security, and weather patterns. The emergency response at federal and regional governments to Hurricane Katrina, and the affects upon the African American population of the region, particularly New Orleans, is an instance in which legacies of environmental racism pertain to the sustainability conversation. On Hershel Island of the Yukon and on Tuvalu Island of the South Pacific, rising waters caused by global warming threaten whole indigenous ways of life. Human cultures are becoming unsustainable because these places themselves are unable to withstand climate change. Thus the number of environmental refugees is dramatically increasing, and sustainability questions will require further consideration of relocation of displaced populations that includes retention of cultural knowledge and ways of life without threatening (both environmental and cultural) sustainability for host communities.

Robert Melchior FIGUEROA
University of North Texas

FURTHER READINGS

Cole, Luke W., & Foster, Sheila R. (2001). *From the ground up: Environmental racism and the rise of the environmental justice movement.* New York: New York University Press.

Figueroa, Robert Melchior. (2001). Other faces: Latinos and environmental justice. In Laura Westra & Bill E. Lawson (Eds.), *Faces of environmental racism: Confronting issues of global justice* (2nd ed., pp. 167–184). Lanham, MD: Rowman & Littlefield.

Figueroa, Robert Melchior. (2008). Environmental justice. In J. Baird Callicott & Robert Frodeman (Eds.), *The encyclopedia of environmental ethics and philosophy, Vol. 1* (pp. 341–348). Farmington Hills, MI: Macmillan Reference.

McDonald, David A. (Ed.). (2002). *Environmental justice in South Africa.* Athens: Ohio University Press.

United Church of Christ Justice and Witness Ministries. (2007). *Toxic wastes and race at twenty: 1987–2007.* Cleveland, OH: United Church of Christ.

Westra, Laura, and Lawson, Bill E. (Eds.). (2001). *Faces of environmental racism: Confronting issues of global justice* (2nd ed.). Lanham, MD: Rowman & Littlefield.

Whelan, Robert J. (1995). *The ecology of fire.* Cambridge, U.K.: Cambridge University Press.

RACE AND THE ENVIRONMENT

Environmental justice does not apply equally to all. Many people around the globe suffer disproportionately from environmental degradation when compared to members of other races; their responses to the environmental crisis also differ, as author Greg Ruiters writes.

[The] focus on environmental racism is important for at least three reasons. First, it challenges the claim that green politics transcends race and ideology in South Africa. Not only do the majority of black people face a very different set of environmental injustices on a regular basis from those faced by whites, they also face a very different struggle in trying to combat them. On a more positive note, it can also be argued that a focus on race is itself a form of resistance, and one that is deeply felt. As Michael Dorsey (1998, 505) argues in the American context, activism around environmental racism has proved that (a) blacks are interested in environmental issues, and (b) black environmental groups have organizational skills and a capacity to mobilize that set them apart from white environmental groups. Environmental anti-racism has the potential to help people reject the "facts" of their oppressive everyday lives and emphasizes the self-confidence and dignity that can be gained from organizing against environmental and self-degradation.

Source: Greg Ruiters. (2002). Race, Place, and Environmental Rights: A Radical Critique of Environmental Justice Discourse. In David A. McDonald, (Ed.), *Environmental Justice in South Africa*, p. 116. Athens: Ohio University Press.

Also cited: Michael Dorsey. (1998). Race, Poverty and Environment. *Legal Studies Forum 22*, 1, 2, and 3.

Responsibility

The subject of human responsibility in relation to sustainability is complex, and still being debated. What is certain is that some form of responsibility must be accepted if humans are to live in a sustainable world.

Questions about sustainability are closely related to the responsibility human beings, individual and collective, bear for their actions. Without responsibility for the consumption, use, development, and exploitation of natural and social resources and both the will and the means to sustain those resources, the Earth's ecosystem will become increasingly hostile to human and nonhuman life. Lacking the responsible use of forms of human power (economic, political, technological), a sustainable future will elude us and may well lead to social collapse. What needs clarification, ethically speaking, is the idea of responsibility and its relation to sustainability.

Moral responsibility is about the exercise of power, accountability for actions, and responsiveness to situations and persons in relation to some norm of what distinguishes moral from immoral actions and relations. Each of these features of responsibility is important and disputed. Without some degree of power and thus the capacity to bring about changes in the world, there are no grounds for assignments of accountability. Yet assignments are complex since they depend on either ascribing accountability to oneself or attributing it to others. For instance, can corporations be imputed accountability for environmental damages since at most they are legal entities and not actual persons and so not personal moral agents in the same way as individual human beings? Part of what one means by the concept of an "agent" is the capacity to respond intentionally to changing situations and other living beings, human and nonhuman. It is not clear, then, that "intentionality" can be attributed to nonhumans (a corporation or nation-state, for instance). Additionally, there are debates about what norm

distinguishes moral from immoral actions and relations. Is it universal obligation, God's will, social utility, virtue, or some other norm? In short, each feature of responsibility (power, accountability, responsive agents, moral norms) is subject to dispute; little wonder that different theories of responsibility have been proposed. Some thinkers concentrate on the question of power, others on accountability, and still others on patterns of responsiveness to and with others. Likewise, there is ongoing dispute about the norm(s) for responsibility, that is, the values and rules which define responsible actions and relations. A robust ethics of responsibility must include each feature as well as provide the means to relate them to a moral norm.

Concerns about sustainability have posed a novel challenge to ideas about responsibility with respect to the features mentioned above. With the massive increase of human power to alter the world through modern technology, human action both reaches into the distant future and has current global impact. This increase of technological and other forms of power reveal that unintended consequences of actions are difficult to determine. These facts threaten ascriptions and imputations of accountability. Can an agent be held accountable for the consequences of actions that are difficult to foresee? Insofar as most environmental harms are the result of collective action (e.g., nation-states; corporations), does it make sense to speak of accountability? The power of technology to alter environmental structures and forms of life also raises with new force the problem of the values and rules for responsible action to the extent that one cannot appeal to "nature" to determine what would count as flourishing or some good for which we are responsible. That is, if human beings can now alter the natural world, then the values and rules for responsible actions and relations must be derived from the conditions of responsibility itself. Given the massive global dynamics that are changing societies and the planet's environment, who is the "we"? Finally, why should "we" be responsible for sustaining an unknown and nonexistent future?

The root question is, why responsibility? In light of the threat to a sustainable future, the answer is twofold. First, any answer implies either a commitment to or rejection of morality itself, that is, a commitment to orient individual and social actions and relations with respect for and enhancement of the integrity of life in its many forms, or conversely, to reject that moral project. Yet insofar as future life is dependent on current policies and actions, a positive commitment to responsible existence obviously seems required. The grounds for that obligation arise from the fact that previous generations bequeathed and entrusted to us the conditions necessary for our responsible use of power, and, accordingly, inheritance compels its continuance. Some thinkers conceptualize this obligation as the injunction to ensure that the conditions for responsibility will endure, and this underwrites the demand of sustainability. In order for there to be responsibility on Earth, viable natural and social environments must be sustained.

The second answer to the root question about responsibility is that, as noted, this discourse is uniquely crafted to conceptualize the moral complexity and ambiguities of power. Given that human power is increasingly shaping the structures of planetary reality, an ethics of responsibility seems necessary in order to secure a sustainable future.

William SCHWEIKER
University of Chicago Divinity School

FURTHER READING

Habermas, Jurgen. (2003). *The future of human nature.* Cambridge, U.K.: Polity Press.

Hans, Jonas. (1984). *The imperative of responsibility: In search of an ethics foe the technological age.* Chicago: University of Chicago Press.

Schweiker, William. (2004). *Theological ethics and global dynamics: In the time of many worlds.* Oxford, U.K.: Blackwell.

Restoration

Although ecological restoration draws on many disciplines in its efforts to repair damaged or degraded ecosystems, the practice is considered a significant social, ethical, and spiritual one that helps to build more cooperative, sustainable human–nature relations and values. When the public participates, restoration holds inherent democratic potential in terms of its capacity to promote "ecological citizenship."

Ecological restoration is the attempt to repair ecosystems that have been damaged or degraded, most often by past human activities. The modern science of ecological restoration (called *restoration ecology*) includes a variety of fields and disciplines: conservation biology, geography/landscape ecology, wetland management, adaptive ecosystem management, and rehabilitation of resource-extracted lands (Higgs 2003). Restoration projects are varied and wide-ranging and include the following examples: the reintroduction of tall grass prairie ecosystems in the Midwest; the replanting of native beach and sea grasses along coastal wetlands; the rehabilitation of salmon streams and rivers in the Northwest; and multimillion-dollar efforts to restore wetlands, woodlands, or soils on former industrial brownfield sites in major urban areas. Given the capacity to mitigate climate change and regenerate healthy, self-sustaining ecosystems, restoration practice is viewed as integral to the global quest for ecological sustainability.

Beyond serving as an important ecological practice, restoration is viewed as a significant social, ethical, and spiritual practice, one that helps to build more cooperative, sustainable human–nature relations and values. Through the concrete activities and experiences of restoring damaged land—reintroducing, replanting, ripping out, and recontouring, for example—people can, in important ways, become reconnected to nature, especially local nature. When the public is involved in restoration efforts, as it oftentimes is, restoration holds inherent democratic potential in terms of its capacity to promote what the environmental philosopher Andrew Light calls "ecological citizenship," or stewardship, of particular landed places. International development and environmental justice scholars, including James Boyce, stress that ecological restoration efforts build democracy through empowering persons to participate in making public environmental change that promotes human and environmental well-being. And restoration work can perform symbolic, ritual activity in society, reconnecting humans with nature through the creation of larger meaning in relation to nature and its restorative care (Van Wieren 2009).

Yet public participation is not always present in restoration efforts, and restoration is not always seen as contributing much toward sustainability efforts. Early on, for example, philosophers such as Robert Elliot and Eric Katz feared that restoration would serve as a justification for natural-resource-extracting corporations to exploit nature carte blanche (Elliot 1982), or otherwise as a thinly veiled form of human domination of nature (Katz 1992). If we strip mine it, we can put it back, recreate the mountain-top, replant the trees, reintroduce the animals, re-dig the lakes and rivers, or so skeptics such as Elliot and Katz worried the rationalizing would go. Later, some restorationists became concerned

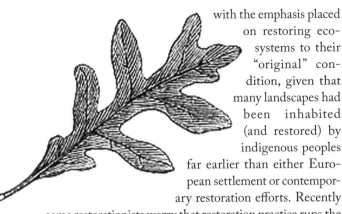

with the emphasis placed on restoring ecosystems to their "original" condition, given that many landscapes had been inhabited (and restored) by indigenous peoples far earlier than either European settlement or contemporary restoration efforts. Recently some restorationists worry that restoration practice runs the risk of "technological drift," with projects becoming dominated by scientific-technical knowledge and goals require a certain amount of scientific and technical knowledge or skilled engineering and design input (Higgs 1997, 2003).

To counter such worries, scholars have argued that "good" or "excellent" restoration will need to include consideration of factors other than scientific-technical ones. Good restoration, from this point of view, will engage the historical, social, cultural, aesthetic, and moral dimensions that are involved in restoration efforts (Higgs 1997). Furthermore, restoration practice is considered ethical where it includes volunteer practitioners, wherever possible, in all phases of a restoration project. Such involvement is seen as maximizing restoration's potential for creating social or moral value (namely, public participation in care for the environment), as well as natural value (namely, ecological health) in society (Light 2000).

Gretel VAN WIEREN
Yale University

FURTHER READING

Boyce, James K.; Narain, Sunita; & Stanton, Elizabeth A. (Eds.). (2007). *Reclaiming nature: Environmental justice and ecological restoration.* New York: Anthem Press.

Elliot, Robert. (1982). Faking nature. *Inquiry, 25,* 81–93.

Higgs, Eric S. (2003). *Nature by design: People, natural process, and ecological restoration.* Cambridge, MA: MIT Press.

Higgs, Eric S. (1997). What is good ecological restoration? *Conservation Biology, 11*(2), 338–348.

Jordan, William R., III. (2003). *The sunflower forest: Ecological restoration and the new communion with nature.* Berkeley: University of California Press.

Katz, Eric. (1992). The big lie: Human restoration of nature. *Research in Philosophy and Technology, 12,* 231–241.

Light, Andrew. (2000). Ecological restoration and the culture of nature: A pragmatic perspective. In Paul H. Gobster & R. Bruce Hull (Eds.), *Restoring nature: Perspectives from the social sciences and humanities.* Washington, DC: Island Press.

Light, Andrew. (2005). Ecological citizenship: The democratic promise of restoration. In Rutherford H. Platt (Ed.), *The humane metropolis: People and nature in the 21st century city.* Amherst: University of Massachusetts Press.

Van Wieren, Gretel. (2008). Ecological restoration as public spiritual practice. *Worldviews 12,* 237–254.

S

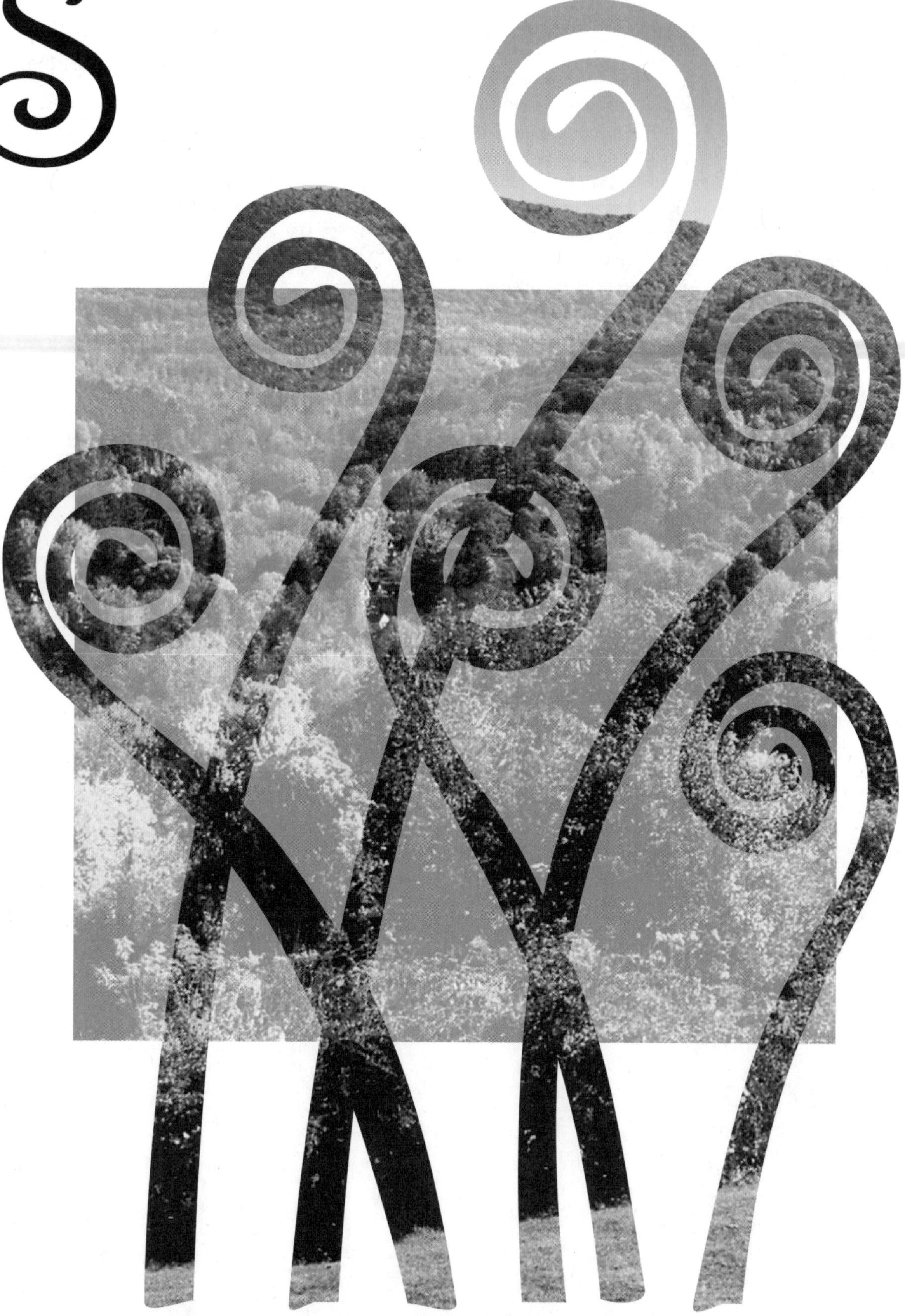

Sacrament

Early definitions of sacrament *and understandings of the immanence of the Creator expressed awareness of the presence of divinity in the natural world. Although Western Christianity later restricted the term to church-administered ritual, some Christians have returned to the view that all creation can be a natural sacrament. With traditions from other faiths and secular humanism, this spiritual consciousness promotes concrete conservation practices and Earth's sustainability.*

Sacrament, a concept with Christian origins, has broad contemporary significance for addressing issues of community well-being and environmental sustainability. In the Christian tradition, developing understandings and ritual expressions of distinct types of sacraments have had a significant impact on the ways that Christians relate to God, their Earth home, and each other. Over millennia, biblical understandings of divine encounters and of rituals that remember and renew them have led to diverse types of evolving sacramental consciousness. In the twenty-first century, sacraments have come to include, for some, not only church-based and clergy-led rituals: Earth, too is a sacrament when viewed as the original and still primary place of contact and communion with the sacred. Both natural and ecclesial sacraments then, can offer significant resources for spirituality to contribute to sustainability. This new understanding, important for Christian faith and for Earth's well-being, complements perspectives from other faith traditions and developing ideas from secular humanists. A shared ideology among these groups could catalyze collaborative conservation efforts, and significantly promote planetary sustainability.

Early Definitions

In Christian doctrine, the term *sacrament* has come, over millennia, to mean a religious ritual celebrated in a sacred structure rather than a transcendent experience in pristine nature. Theologically the earliest description of a sacrament was that of Augustine of Hippo (354–430), who had a strong sense of the presence of God in creation. Augustine defined sacraments as visible expressions of invisible grace, an understanding that allowed for a virtually limitless number and variety of mediations and experiences of the sacred in creation. The Latin Christian Church soon diminished Augustine's sacramental largesse and limited sacraments to seven church-defined and -administered rituals (baptism, confirmation, penance, holy communion, matrimony, holy orders, and anointing of the sick); Protestant reformers reduced these to baptism and communion. In Eastern Christianity, the celebration of the Divine Liturgy always retained a profound sense of the unity of religious ritual and divine creation, influenced by the thought of the monk, mystic, and martyr Maximus the Confessor (c. 580–662). Maximus described an ongoing dialogue of the divine Logos (Word) with the Logoi, the creating words of the divine that remain within each part of creation. Maximus described creation as a cloak worn by the creating Word (this imagery would be complemented in the twentieth century by Sallie McFague's metaphor of creation as the "body of God") and as the context and revelation of divine immanence.

Western Christianity's departure from Augustine's definition of sacrament stimulated a significant shift in understanding: no longer were both nature and ritual regarded as bases for experiences of God. Personal sacred moments in nature, mediated by creation, were no longer regarded as sacramental experiences. These experiences were limited to community and individual participation in rituals, usually in a church building and mediated by clergy or their representatives. "Sacred space" now ordinarily meant the area of a building that people constructed and clergy consecrated, supplanting creation as the sacred place revelatory of and consecrated by divine presence.

Western Christianity briefly recovered the idea of creation as a sacrament in the thought of Hildegard of Bingen (1098–1179) and Francis of Assisi (1181/1182–1226). In words reflective of Maximus, Hildegard, a musician, pharmacologist, poet, writer, and mystic, described God in her *Book of Divine Works* as a fiery power who kindled every spark of life and permeated everything in creation; people, through faith, can see God in creation and creatures. The itinerant monk and mystic Francis of Assisi, in his *Canticle of Creation*, celebrated inanimate creation in words and animate creation in music; he called upon all creation to praise God, in a poetic recognition of creation's sacramental revelation of God.

Creation as Sacrament

Biblical teachings and Christian theology eventually provided the bases for recovery of an earlier sacramental creation consciousness. Recognition of revelatory (but not sacramental) aspects of creation was noted in the *Catechism of the Catholic Church* (1997), which teaches that God speaks to people through visible creation. The *Catechism*, however, restricts sacraments to specific efficacious signs of grace instituted by Jesus and ritually administered by the Church. The U.S. Catholic bishops had gone further than this previously, in *Renewing the Earth* (1991), when they stated that people encounter the Creator in nature, and perceive a "sacramental universe," which presents visible signs of God's presence; this experience can stimulate people to care for their Earth home. Contemporary Catholic theologians express complementary ideas: Thomas Berry in *The Dream of the Earth* (1988) sees the natural world as a primary revelation of divine presence, and declares that species extinction is destructive of modes of that presence. Rosemary Ruether declares in *Gaia and God* (1992) that ecology informs ethics and spirituality that all things are interrelated and that species extinction is analogous to tearing out a page of the book of life. John Hart in *Sacramental Commons* (2006) states that the sacramental universe is localized in the *sacramental commons*, in which revelatory

places and moments enable people to experience the Spirit's presence, and to enhance their relationship with divine being and their concern for and commitment to conservation and community.

The renewed understanding that all creation can be a sacrament has profound theoretical and practical implications. In Earth as sacramental commons, spirituality and sustainability are integrated. As a natural sacrament, creation can be revelatory of God, a sign and symbol of divine immanence, and a visible expression of invisible divine solicitude when it is not polluted, when it is responsibly shared and used, and when it supports the evolving community of life in its Earth habitat. The elements of the ritual sacraments—bread; juice or wine—require pure, environmentally sustainable natural sacraments: organic wheat and grapes grown in clean soil with pure water. A consciousness of natural sacrament promotes sustainable conservation of sacramental Earth for present and future generations.

Biotic and abiotic sustainability in local and integrated planetary ecosystems has a greater likelihood of realization where similar perspectives are promoted by theists from diverse traditions and by secular humanists. Among theists, creation stories and other narratives about the presence of divine being or of a sacred Mother Earth contribute to planetary respect. Among secular humanists, the biologist Edward O. Wilson writes and speaks about saving "the creation," thereby sharing a term previously used primarily in biblical and other ancient religious traditions.

While "sacrament" is a specifically Christian term, then, the appreciation it expresses for creation's intrinsic value, the gratitude it implies for creation's instrumental value, and its profession of the presence of a creating Spirit are all complemented in some form by the understandings of others. The result is a shared regard for natural beauty, for all biota, and for human community; a recognition of all life's interrelated and interdependent need for Earth's natural goods ("resources"); promotion of ecojustice; and a renewed spiritual (however it is defined) sensibility. The growth of these values will promote the well-being of the human community, sustainably protect Earth's species, and conservatively use Earth's natural goods and places to create, overall, a sustainable Earth community.

John HART
Boston University

FURTHER READING

Armstrong, Regis J., OFM Cap.; Hellmann, J. A. Wayne, OFM Conv.; & Short, William J., OFM. (1999). *Francis of Assisi: The Saint.* Vol. 1 of *Francis of Assisi: Early Documents.* New York: New City Press.

Berry, Thomas M. (1988). *The dream of the earth.* San Francisco: Sierra Club Books.

Fortini, Arnaldo. (1981). *Francis of Assisi* (Helen Moak, Trans.). New York: Crossroad.

Hart, John. (2006). *Sacramental commons: Christian ecological ethics.* Lanham, MD: Rowman & Littlefield.

Hildegard of Bingen. (1987). *Hildegard of Bingen's book of divine works* (Matthew Fox, Ed.). Santa Fe, NM: Bear.

Louth, Andrew. (1996). *Maximus the Confessor.* London: Routledge.

Maximus. (1985). *Maximus confessor: Selected writings.* In George C. Berthold (Trans.), *Classics of Western Spirituality.* New York: Paulist Press.

McFague, Sallie. (1993). *The body of God: An ecological theology.* Minneapolis: Fortress Press.

Ruether, Rosemary Radford. (1992). *Gaia and God.* San Francisco: Harper.

U.S. Catholic Bishops. (1991). *Renewing the earth: An invitation to reflection and action on environment in light of Catholic social teaching.* Washington, DC: United States Catholic Conference.

U.S. Catholic Bishops. (1994). *Catechism of the Catholic Church.* Washington, DC: United States Catholic Conference.

Wilson, Edward O. (2006). *The creation: An appeal to save life on earth.* New York: Norton.

THE PATRON SAINT OF ECOLOGY'S "CANTICLE OF CREATION"

St. Francis of Assisi, born Francis Bernardone (1181/82–1226), is honored by the Catholic Church as the patron saint of animals and ecology; one of his most famous sermons was delivered to a flock of birds. A movement is afoot amongst Christians to bring back the celebration of nature as one of the sacraments. The following is St. Francis's "Canticle of Creation," sometimes referred to as the "Canticle of Brother Sun."

Most High, all-powerful, and all-good Lord,
Praise, glory, honor,
and all blessing
are yours.

To you alone, Most High, they belong,
although no one is worthy
to say your name.

Praised be my Lord with all your creatures,
especially my lord Brother Sun,
through whom you give us day and light.

Beautiful he shines with great splendor:
Most High, he bears your likeness.

Praised be my Lord, by Sister Moon and Stars:
in the heavens you made them bright
and precious and beautiful.

Praised be my Lord, by Brother Wind,
and air and cloud
and calm and all weather
through which you sustain
your creatures.

Praised be my Lord, by Sister Water,
who is so helpful and humble
and precious and pure.

Praised be my Lord, by Brother Fire,
through whom you brighten the night:
who is beautiful and playful
and sinuous and strong.

Praised be my Lord, by our Sister Mother Earth,
who sustains us and guides us,
and provides varied fruits
with colorful flowers and herbs.

Praised and
blessed be you, my Lord,
and gratitude and service be given to you
with great humility.

Source: Francis of Assisi. (2006[1225]). Canticle of creation. In John Hart, *Sacramental Commons: Christian Ecological Ethics,* pp. 28–29. Lanham, MD: Rowman & Littlefield.

Sacred Texts

The impulse toward sustainable practices sometimes arises as a reaction to sacred texts, especially in religious communities where writings are the essential guideposts for belief and action.

Sacred texts are authoritative religious writings; in some religions this might include thousands of individual texts. Writings such as the Bhagavad Gita and the Quran are called to mind when one thinks of sacred texts. Although these are paradigmatic examples, they do not show fully the diversity of what might be categorized as a "sacred text." These texts arouse devotion, aid in ritual activity, define beliefs, and enunciate moral codes. Some are assumed to be revealed by a god or divine messenger. Other texts are attributed to entirely human origins without any claim to supernatural revelation.

Interpreting Sacred Texts

When analyzing how sacred texts inform sustainability, it is important to recognize variations between and within religions. Classics of ecological literature (e.g., Gary Snyder's poetry) might serve as spiritual texts for certain new religious communities. More conservative branches of the "world religions," on the other hand, tend to look exclusively to a limited set of orthodox texts for guidance.

Once a sacred text is identified as authoritative, the question of hermeneutics (the interpretation of texts) emerges. One's hermeneutical approach helps to show how contemporary issues are related to sacred writings. "Sustainability" is a modern idea, whereas many sacred texts are hundreds or even thousands of years old. As a result, most sacred texts do not directly address the contemporary concept of sustainability. Because of this, some religious believers assert that environmentalism has no relevance to their spiritual identity, or that it must be expressed as subordinate to a traditional belief system. On the other hand, different adherents from these religions argue that scriptures strongly recommend sustainability. In each of these cases, religious communities are making significant choices on how to interpret their religious texts.

Sustainability in Sacred Texts

Assuming that sacred texts in fact are related to sustainability, what are some examples of how sacred texts can further discussions on the subject?

One way that sacred texts influence our understanding of sustainability is through the overarching worldview they present. For example, in Daoism, texts such as the *I Ching* propound a holism that emphasizes "action in inaction," or *wu wei*. Scholars see this holism and its emphasis on interdependence as similar to contemporary ecological perspectives. Hindu and Buddhist texts often stress *ahimsa*, or "non-harm" and reverence to all beings. *Ahimsa* might include the need for sustainability as essential. The theocentrism of some Christian, Islamic, and Jewish texts can be interpreted as mandating sustainable care as God's chosen stewards.

Sacred texts also present stories that enrich our understanding of the meaning of the world. For example, narratives might characterize the right relationship between creation, the sacred, and humanity. It is common for religions to emphasize the need for a cosmic harmony between humanity, the divine, and nature. The Rig Veda (one of the sacred texts of Hinduism) explores the interconnection between the divinity and the entire material world. This might imply the need to care for the divine through proper relationships with the world. Similarly, some (but not all) religions share creation stories in the pages of sacred books.

Creation narratives explain the origination, ordering, and purpose of the world. For many Jews, Christians, and Muslims, scripture argues that creation belongs to God. Narratives express the position of humans within God's ordered world, as is the case with the book of Genesis, which identifies humans as stewards of creation. Taken on the whole, religious texts might be ambivalent. Some texts show humans separated from and above nature; for example, humans are commanded to multiply and "subdue the earth" in Genesis. In contrast, groups such as the Hopi and other indigenous religions ritually pass on stories that emphasize the interconnection of the whole of creation (although this example brings up the question of whether oral narratives may be considered "texts").

Some interpret relevant metaphors and symbols as a way to show how sacred texts might promote sustainable practices. Many scriptures were written, for instance, when the vast majority of the population was involved in farming and lived "close to the land." The collapse of local stocks of resources through overuse, natural devastation, or neglect was calamitous. Therefore, religious texts sometimes use metaphors from farming, rural life, and resource gathering, and thereby point out specific responsibilities that humans have toward the land and animals in their care. For example, Jewish and Christian scriptures outline a Sabbath day for all of creation, including the land. Restrictions on harvesting and management are also aimed at just and equitable distribution of the farm fields and other lands. Similarly, some Muslims interpret the words of the Prophet Muhammad as advocating restrictions on the use of certain lands for the benefit of the whole community.

Challenges

Not all religious communities find justification for sustainable practices within their sacred texts, which leads to a problem: what is the relevance of these texts in light of contemporary environmental issues? A related question is, since many sacred texts have ritual and doctrinal uses, how might the use of sacred texts promote or hinder sustainability? The interpretation of sacred texts potentially holds great power in directing sustainability initiatives within many religious traditions, but only if guided by hermeneutical principles that focus on how sacred texts promote more or less "sustainable" attitudes and actions toward the rest of the natural world.

Forrest CLINGERMAN
Ohio Northern University

FURTHER READING

Chapple, Christopher K., & Tucker, Mary Evelyn. (Eds.). (2000). *Hinduism and ecology: The intersection of earth, sky, and water.* Cambridge, MA: Harvard University Press.

Cohen, Jeremy. (1989). *"Be fertile and increase, fill the earth and master it": The ancient and medieval career of a biblical text.* Ithaca, NY: Cornell University Press.

Habel, Norman C. (Ed.). (2000). *Readings from the perspective of the Earth (The Earth Bible Vol. 1).* Cleveland, OH: Pilgrim Press.

Kaza, Stephanie, & Kraft, Kenneth. (Eds.). (2000). *Dharma rain: Sources of Buddhist environmentalism.* Boston: Shambhala.

Miller, James; Wang, Richard G.; & Davis, Ned. (2001). What ecological themes are found in Daoist texts? In N. J. Girardot, James Miller, & Liu Xiaogan (Eds.), *Daoism and ecology: Ways within a cosmic landscape* (pp. 149–153). Cambridge, MA: Harvard University Press.

Özdemir, İbrahim. (2003). Toward an understanding of environmental ethics from a Qur'anic perspective. In Richard C. Foltz, Frederick M. Denny, & Azizan Baharuddin (Eds.), *Islam and ecology: A bestowed trust* (pp. 3–37). Cambridge, MA: Harvard University Press

Santmire, H. Paul. (1985). *The travail of nature: The ambiguous ecological promise of Christian theology.* Philadelphia: Fortress Press.

Suzuki, David, & Knudtson, Peter. (Eds.). (1993). *Wisdom of the elders: Sacred native stories of nature.* New York: Bantam Books.

Sacrifice

Traditional models of sacrifice in Western, Confucian, and dharmic religious and ethical thought served to redirect actual violence to something more positive, but postmodern consumer-oriented society has lost the sense that sacrifice can lead to greater good; the violence of selfish greed drives human action. By regaining a sense of sacrifice and consequently conscience, the greater good of environmental and cultural sustainability may be achieved.

The word *sacrifice* refers both to acts of religious ritual and an approach to human action that sets aside immediate benefit for the sake of a greater good. In the past, Jewish and Hellenistic traditions have included bloody offerings in the form of animal sacrifice. In Christianity this has been replaced with the Eucharist, which promotes human conscience and adherence to a moral code. The contemporary challenge presented by the need to develop sustainable lifestyles can draw from the traditions of sacrifice, serving as an inspiration for the development of reasonable patterns for resource management.

Sacrifice has been defined by the theologian Dennis Keenan as "a necessary passage through suffering and/or death (of either oneself or someone else) on the way to a supreme moment of transcendent truth" (2005, 11). Transcendent truth in light of global warming, resource diminishment, and species decimation has been replaced with the "inconvenient truth" that human behavior in quest of the "good life" has become rapacious and destructive. How might the practice of sacrifice move human cultures away from these behaviors and toward the actualization of a sustainable lifestyle?

The word *sacrifice* in the English language means *to make* (Latin *facere*) *sacred* (*sacre*). Throughout world history, this has often entailed killing an animal or a human in the context of religious ritual. Early anthropologists were fascinated with this process, prompting Henri Hubert and Marcel Mauss, in their seminal 1899 book *Sacrifice: Its Nature and Function*, to write that "sacrifice is a religious act which, through the consecration of a victim, modifies the condition of the moral person who accomplishes it" (1964, 13), indicating that sacrifice establishes a change in the one who performs a sacrifice and produces a larger social function. The renowned French sociologist Émile Durkheim postulated that sacrifice served an integral function in the social creation of religion, and hence in human civility.

Traditional Models of Sacrifice

The core story of sacrifice in Western civilization can be gleaned from three sources: the Hebrew Bible; Euripides's play *The Bacchae*, based on the Greek myth involving Dionysus (also called Bacchus), the god of wine and ecstatic release; and the New Testament. In the first narrative, God requests Abraham to sacrifice his first-born son. In the second story female followers of Dionysus (the Bacchae of the title), habitually driven by the god in rituals of worship to kill wild animals and livestock with their bare hands, also, in a moment of frenzy, kill Pentheus, the young king of Thebes, for denying Dionysus's divinity. The third narrative entails the Crucifixion of Jesus.

As the narratives progress, the ramifications of each sacrifice unfold. In the Hebrew Bible story, God orders Abraham to substitute an animal, sparing the life of the son. In the ancient Greek play violence spins out of control, and although the women of Dionysus's cult regret their actions—one member is Pentheus's mother—Pentheus, who has been torn apart, cannot be brought back to life. The death of Jesus gives birth to a theology of atonement, a doctrine that contemplation on the suffering and painful death of Jesus, combined with reflection on and repentance for one's own sins, results in rectification and forgiveness. The story of Abraham indicates a transition from violence to humanistic compassion; *The Bacchae* warns that humans hold the capacity to stray from the rational and fall prey to violent urges; the story of Jesus suggests a framework for learning from the mistakes of others (the Roman soldiers) and altering one's behavior. In accord with Durkheim, all three instances hold a moral imperative for the maintenance of the social order.

According to the historian and philosopher René Girard, violence has played a central role in the history of sacrifice. He suggests that sacrifice, generally of a scapegoat, "serves to protect the entire community from its *own* violence. . . . [T]he elements of dissension scattered throughout the community are drawn to the person of the sacrificial victim and eliminated" (1977, 8). In his study of world history and human civilizations, Girard detects an irrefutable link between religion and violence, stating that the sacrificial act "curtails reciprocal violence and imposes structure on the community" (1977, 317). For Girard, the Christian faith successfully defuses the power and allure of violence. Dennis Keenan comes to a similar conclusion, citing the statement of the French philosopher Emmanuel Levinas: "sacrifice requires being for the other." Keenan notes that sacrifice leads to *agape* (one of several words from ancient Greek conveying various aspects "love"), which he defines as "the sacrifice *of* the sacrifice of one's pathological sinful desire to transgress the Law" (2005, 75)—the selfless love that allows for social stability. By participating in the Christian Eucharist, a ritual that recalls the passion and love of Jesus, one is brought to atonement. By drawing the Christian lesson into oneself through the act of mimesis, seeing one's own sin in light of the larger story of Jesus, violence within oneself can be mitigated. By replacing mimetic desires of violence with imitation of Christ, one becomes rectified.

In a simpler time, this paradigm of defusing tension through religious ritual and the observance of commandments for curbing human excess prevailed throughout much of Europe and those areas of the world subjected to European colonization and Christian conversion. Persons were given a list of commandments, authorities enforced them through the rule of law, and societies were sustained. Similar social norms developed in East Asia with adherence to Confucian propriety and in South Asia with the observance of dharma (Hindu, Buddhist, Jaina, or Sikh). Islam, modeling itself on the Jewish moral code, still considers polity inseparable from religious values; for Muslims, the ultimate act of sacrifice is submitting to the will of God. Even the post-Enlightenment secular world, though proclaiming that its social norms are based solely on reason and natural law, in fact abounds with examples of sacrificial practices through which society is held in balance. One example is the insistence that one sacrifice one's own selfish needs for the sake of the common good, a foundational principle for civil society.

The birth of scientific method in the seventeenth century and its linkage first with technology, then resource exploitation, and finally with the perfection of marketing has resulted in a voracious new religion referred to by the theologian John Cobb as "economism." With advances in technology, immediate consequences of resource exploitation have become obscured and deferred. Obsession with human comfort with little or no regard for the true cost to the environment has resulted in quintessentially modern forms of idolatry. These include over-concern with one's social status and body image, excessive consumerism, and a desire to postpone one's death at all costs. Cultural cynicism and despair also may be seen as an outgrowth or byproduct of the success of the eighteenth-century European Enlightenment, as well as a breakdown of the traditional moral order. The relativism and malaise of the post-Enlightenment emphasis on the supremacy of the human combined with the use of technologically enhanced weapons such as automatic artillery, mustard gas, and nuclear weaponry resulted in great violence in the nineteenth and twentieth centuries. It also prompted a comfort-driven trivialization of human worth and meaning in the latter part of the twentieth century, extending into the twenty-first century. With the rise of individualism and a loss of a concern for the good of the group, a myopia has emerged eclipsing the efficacy of sacrifice.

In years past, the mimetic violence of ritual sacrifice helped slake blood thirst and establish a stable social order. Sacrifice helped quell hatred. Hatred boils into violent rage leading to murder; organized murder on a larger scale leads to war. The stories of Abraham, Pentheus, and Jesus helped direct human behavior away from senseless killing of other human beings. Although the efficacy of the sacrificial order went into a slow and steady decline with the birth of modernity, its enduring lessons helped prompt a turning away from the overwhelming violence that distinguished the first half of the twentieth century as the most violent period in human history. But only with radical reinterpretation can the stories of Abraham, Pentheus, and Jesus be seen as moral fables for countering human greed. Greed differs from violence. It entails a different, deferred form of destruction. This destruction can be found in exploitation of natural resources, devastation of landscapes and ecosystems, and a colonization of the mind with manufactured notions of products that must be consumed.

Today we suffer from the malaise of greed, stemming from what the Zen Buddhist philosopher David Loy has referred to as the "religion of the market" (1997, 275–290). War still simmers in various parts of the world, though the great destruction of the early to middle twentieth century will most likely (and hopefully) not be repeated. By the overly efficient exploitation of resources, however, human life has been placed in jeopardy by pollution, an autism to the natural world, a consequent lack of acknowledgment of externalities (e.g., waste disposal, deleterious carbon gases), and a lack of political will. The cautionary tales that were learned from Abraham, Pentheus, and Jesus served to provide human beings with means to develop a workable polity, a system that with a few notable exceptions helped tamp down the human tendency toward violence over the long course of history. But making infanticide, passion-driven crimes, and religious and/or political persecution aberrant rather than expected does not construct a view that reaches beyond human concerns. The story of the sacrifice in the Judeo–Greco–Christian–Islamic continuum needs to evolve in the present age into a model that allows for the protection of animals, the protection of women, and the protection of the Earth itself. We need a new model of sacrifice to counter the violence of greed.

Postmodern Thought

Postmodern thinking about sacrifice might benefit from the lessons of other cultures that have been forced to deal with abundance. The American Indians of the Northwest, particularly the Kwakiutl, enjoyed a super-abundant environment that provided untold riches of food, timber, and animal furs. The peoples of this area resolved the unavoidable tension that periodically surfaced in the drama of human life not largely through warfare, but through the potlatch, the bestowal of great riches upon neighboring tribes. Rather than hording things for themselves, the Kwakiutl gifted others, dealing in a profound way with the dark side of human inclination to compete and to provoke conflict. (In a potlatch ceremony, rather than showing one's social standing by accumulating more goods than one's neighbor, families compete to see who can bestow more wealth on others. This stands in stark contrast to the American tradition of "keeping up with the Joneses," with its ever-increasing conspicuous consumption.) For the past several decades, our merchandising machinery has enabled suburbs to sprawl further, car culture to spill over

into Asia, and food to be taken for granted, particularly in the developed world where it requires only a tiny fraction of an individual's income to procure in abundance. Rather than celebrating this surfeit of goods, the consuming public has been consistently exhorted to consume more. Patriotism in America, as some say, has been reduced to shopping.

With the limits to growth upon us, with fuller understanding of the problem of global warming, and with the inevitable adjustments to the costs of fuel and food in evidence, a shift is beginning to take place from an ideology of hording to an appreciation of sacrifice and conservationism as primary values. Sacrifice in its evolving meaning took on a negative connotation in the past thirty years, with little notion that sacrifice might result in an eventual benefit. The first part of the process—as defined in Webster's dictionary, "a giving up, destroying, foregoing of some valued thing" and "a giving up of something for less than its supposed value"—eclipsed an understanding that this process could lead to "something of greater value." The current generation has no recollection of the food rationing and other sacrifices (e.g., foregoing nylon stockings, using margarine instead of butter, etc.) made by Americans during World War II. But a change has begun. Rather than simply plucking items from the grocery store shelf or purchasing automobiles based on style and decadent or high-performance "options," individuals are reintroducing a thoughtful process into their purchases, reengaging the tools of conscience and moral judgment. By examining health effects to one's body as well as becoming cognizant of the horrors of factory farming, people are changing their food choices. By considering the social and physical effects on the human body of long commutes in oversized vehicles, as well as the impact of fossil fuels on global weather patterns, people are beginning to adjust their lifestyle expectations. Two web-based animations have been particularly effective in communicating these concerns in a graphic, easily graspable format: *The Meatrix* on factory farming and *The Story of Stuff* about the underbelly of consumer culture. Sociologists such as Robert Putnam and Juliet Schor have pointed out the loss of human connectivity that has resulted from a purchase-driven culture.

Sustainability seen through the prism of sacrifice suggests that direct human action must be taken to rectify the excesses of the modern era. The violence of Jesus' crucifixion symbolized by the Eucharist prompts the cultivation of human conscience and a move toward rectification and reconciliation.

Sacrifice and Sustainability

For the European world and North America, the killing of the goat, Pentheus, and Jesus provided a model of sacrifice that involves giving up an object for the sake of a greater good. In the case of environmental degradation, this greater good would be a cleaner environment within the context of a sustainable economic system. Just as the goat, Pentheus, and Jesus gave up their lives, modern people are being called upon to give up aspects of their lifestyles that cause harm to the environment. This can take many shapes. First, people need to be educated about the deleterious effects that energy consumption has on the planet, leading to pollution and global warming. Second, people need to feel a sense of connectedness with these problems that will spark their moral conscience. Third, the political leaders must take note and provide legislation to correct the harmful excess generated by profligate lifestyles. In the current globalized economy, changes will be required to make a shift from nonrenewable energy sources such as oil to renewable sources such as wind and solar power, from health-damaging foods to healthy, from isolating activities that promote malaise to community-building activities that promote connectivity and well-being. The giving up of bad habits will need to be accompanied with replacement strategies to avoid economic and social upheaval. Redeveloping a healthy sense of sacrifice will be essential for an effective change in energy and economic policies. This sacrificial model calls for a return to conscience, a reflection on the sin of over-consumption, and a resolve to develop a new conscience and abstemiousness.

Rethinking Sacrifice

Thomas Berry (1914–2009), a theologian also known as an "historian of the Earth," has made concrete suggestions for revising the concept of sacrifice through the principles of sustainability. His key ideas offer new approaches for constructive sacrificial action that heighten one's sense of inter-connection with the larger forces of society and the universe. Berry regards the Earth to be the primary vehicle for revelation, the context for all human flourishing, and the only path toward self-knowledge. In *The Great Work* he writes (1999, 52):

> Only Earth became a living planet filled with those innumerable forms of geological structure and biological expression that we observe throughout the natural world. Only Earth held a creative balance between the turbulence and the discipline that are necessary for creativity. . . . The universe [established on Earth] a creative disequilibrium expressed in the curvature of space that was sufficiently closed to establish and abiding order in the universe and

sufficiently open to enable the wild creative process to continue.

For Berry, all Earth expresses the sacrificial process. In order for humans to remain viable, they must go beyond themselves and return to an appreciation of the magnificence of the Earth. All encounters with nature can be seen as sacred and hence instructive, from the stark beauty of the Earth, to the realization of the harm done by human greed and exploitation. In a negative sense, the beauty of the world has been sacrificed not as a gateway toward the transcendent, but solely for the pursuit of market-driven values. In *Religion in the 21st Century* Berry (2009, 177) writes:

> Apparently, during the four centuries since Descartes, we have lost our basic sensitivity for the ever-renewing natural world with its wonder, beauty, and intimacy as well as its local and seasonal nourishment in response to our love and care of the land. We were willing to devastate all these for the illusive abundance offered by an industrial society.

Berry has made several proposals to restore balance to human–Earth relations, including foundational science education, a rejection of the idea of the Earth as primarily natural resource for the unlimited use of humans, an improved legal system that extends protection to ecosystems, and a curbing of the power of commercial-industrial corporations. By "sacrificing" the modern fetishes of technology and consumerism in favor of simpler living, we can return to a world of wonder, and recover in Berry's words, "our communication with the deeper reality of things." Our quest for transcendent truth of necessity must take us on a return journey to planet Earth.

The sacrificial model underlying Berry's approach acknowledges that the microcosm reflects the macrocosm. A small act ripples throughout the larger system, for good or ill. If one person owns a highly efficient automobile, or chooses to ride a bicycle rather than drive, it might be seen as an oddity and dismissed as eccentric. The reverse might also pertain and that person's choice might be admired and imitated by others. One person's sacrifice might be another's poison, or alternatively, a source of inspiration and change. The environmental philosopher Holmes Rolston has stated that the Earth itself is cruciform—the word literally means "arranged or shaped in a cross" but is used by Rolston to reflect that Darwinian natural history echoes classical religious themes of death and regeneration—in that the processes of evolution express a sacrificial modality.

Future Considerations

In order to foster a sustainable economic, political, psychological, and spiritual state of affairs, people need to adopt and participate in new models of sacrifice. Rather than feeling punished by high costs for goods and services, the new sacrificial order might help people return to a sense of immediacy and aliveness. As food becomes more expensive, it becomes more cherished. Similarly, travel, whether for work or pleasure, will require careful consideration not only of cost but of its wider impact on the production of carbon. Personal identity, rather than being tied to the acquisition and manipulation of things, can be measured in terms of one's connectivity with others and with the primary source of revelation, the Earth community. In conclusion, sacrificial wisdom, though differing from one cultural context to another, holds promise as a conceptual and practical resource to inspire people to take the steps necessary for personal, social, and economic sustainability.

Christopher Key CHAPPLE
Loyola Marymount University

An earlier version of portions of this entry appeared in *Worldviews: Global Religions, Culture, and Ecology*, volume 12, issue 2/3 (2008).

FURTHER READING

Bailie, Gil. (1995). *Violence unveiled: Humanity at the crossroads*. New York: Crossroad.

Bell, Catherine M. (1997). *Ritual: Perspectives and dimensions*. New York: Oxford University Press.

Berry, Thomas. (1999). *The great work*. New York: Random House.

Berry, Thomas. (2009). *Religion in the 21st century*. Introduction by Mary Evelyn Tucker. New York: Columbia University Press.

Cobb, John. (1999). *The Earthist challenge to economism: A theological critique of the World Bank*. New York: St. Martin's Press.

Durkheim, Émile. (1915 [1965]). *The elementary forms of religious life*. New York: Free Press.

Girard, Réne. (1977). *Violence and the sacred* (Patrick Gregory, Trans.). Baltimore: Johns Hopkins University Press.

Hubert, Henri, & Mauss, Marcel. (1964). *Sacrifice: Its nature and function* (W. D. Halls, Trans.). Chicago: University of Chicago Press. (Original work published 1899)

Keenan, Dennis King. (2005). *The question of sacrifice*. Bloomington: Indiana University Press.

Leonard, Annie. (n.d.). The story of stuff. Retrieved April 22, 2009, from http://www.storyofstuff.com/

Loy, David R. (1997). The religion of the market. *The Journal of the American Academy of Religion, 65*(2), 275–290.

McKenna, Andrew J. (1991). *Violence and difference: Girard, Derrida, and deconstruction*. Urbana: University of Illinois Press.

Putnam, Robert D. (2000). *Bowling alone: The collapse and revival of American community*. New York: Simon & Schuster.

Schor, Juliet. (2000). *Do Americans shop too much?* Boston: Beacon Press.

Strenski, Ivan. (1997). The social and intellectual origins of Hubert and Mauss's theology of ritual sacrifice. In Dick van der Meij, (Ed.), *India and beyond: Aspects of literature, meaning, ritual and thought* (pp. 511–537). London: Kegan Paul International.

The Meatrix. (n.d.) Retrieved April 22, 2009, from http://www.themeatrix.com/inside/

Science, Religion, and Ecology

Science, with its theories of natural selection and equilibrium, and religion, with its biblical descriptions of land forever flowing with "milk and honey," have viewed nature as ever-renewing. Both have prioritized growth and its resulting abundance. As our twenty-first-century environmental crises challenge these concepts, scientists can teach us to sustain the environment while the motivations of biblical stewardship remind us to treasure Earth's biodiversity and celebrate creation.

Life perpetually renewed in the midst of its perpetual perishing: the theme is a common one in both evolutionary natural history and Christian faith. Natural systems have evolved historically and ecosystems have been tested over thousands of years for their dynamic resilience, sometimes remaining stable and at other times undergoing change. As human life evolved, classical monotheism arose with a sense of dwelling in a promised land forever, although biblical writers acknowledged the transience of life. Concern for ecosystem health and integrity have evolved as well. Humans may now stand at a rupture point in history—facing, as some believe, the end of nature. Ecological management, with its scientific focus on preserving nature's resources and developing technologies, continues the concept of biblical stewardship. A critical question is whether to seek sustainable development or a sustainable biosphere.

A Dynamic, Enduring Earth

Both science and religion, in principle and in practice, face concerns about environmental sustainability. Both worldviews encounter an historical dynamism (i.e., forces of change) superimposed on recurring stability. Evolutionary natural history finds natural selection operating over incremental variations across enormous time spans, with the fittest selected to survive. This drives perennial change as species acquire new skills, exploit new niches, and migrate toward shifting environments.

The theory of punctuated equilibrium, in some contrast, interprets the fossil record as evidence for periods of millions of years of relative stasis, punctuated by relatively brief periods of rapid change. Biologists also speak of evolutionary-stable strategies. Natural selection drives changes, but natural selection fails without enough stability in ecosystems to make the mutations selected for dependably reliable for survival over the immediately forthcoming years. Natural systems were often "sustained" in the past for long periods of time. Critics reject such balance of nature in favor of episodic events, open ecological systems, dynamism and change. Disturbances in the orderly succession of ecosystems produce a patchwork landscape. Ecosystems have various kinds of resilience, but if the disturbances become amplified enough, the stability gets swamped by disorder. Equilibrium and non-equilibrium do represent two ends of a spectrum with real ecosystems somewhere in between, and seeing one or the other can depend on the level and scale of analysis. At the levels of population and species diversity, or community composition, ecosystems can show predictable patterns, approaching steady states on restricted ranges. When unusual disturbances come, they can be displaced beyond recovery of their former patterns. Then they settle into new equilibriums.

The processes and products originally in place will, with high probability, have been those for which organisms are naturally selected for their adaptive fits; misfits go extinct and easily disrupted ecosystems collapse and are replaced by more stable ones. Ecosystems get tested over thousands of years for their resilience. As a result, they have both stability and dynamic novelty. Many general characteristics are repeated; many local details vary. Patterns of growth and development are orderly and predictable enough to make ecological science possible. This ecosystemic nature, once flourishing independently and for millennia continuing along with humans, has in the last one hundred years come under increasing jeopardy—variously described as a threat to ecosystem health, integrity, stability, or quality.

Classical monotheism arose with a more fixed account of earth structures and processes, set in place at an initial "start-up" creation, and thereafter ongoing with little change. Facing death, as Jacob is "gathered to my people" he blesses Israel: "The blessings of your father are mighty beyond the blessings of the eternal mountains, the bounties of the everlasting hills" (Genesis 49:26, RSV). Life is an ongoing struggle, and therefore hopes arise for the advent of redemption when the Messiah comes, or, for Christians, comes again. But in the course of Earth history, if Israel keeps the commandments, God says, "then I will let you dwell in this place in the land that I gave of old to your fathers for ever" (Jeremiah 7:7).

The sages and prophets knew the transience of life. Consider "a flower of the field": "the wind passes over it, and it is gone, and its place knows it no more" (Psalm 103:15–16). But they also knew a sustainability and saw, under God, a promised land in which "it might go well with them and with their children for ever" (Deuteronomy 5:29). That certainly sounds like sustainability.

The perpetual cycle of life, which involves renewal in the midst of perishing, is a common theme in both natural evolutionary history and in Christian faith. Both science and religion agree that Earth has long sustained and renewed life, although the classical regeneration of new life out of old on the scale of millennia has expanded to that of billions of years in contemporary science.

Many scientists believe, even in a sustainability crisis, that nature cannot be abolished but nature's ability to sustain life can be irreparably damaged. Nature has not ended and never will. Humans depend on nature for their life support. Humans use nature resourcefully; they may upset and degrade natural systems. But the natural forces can and will return if humans are taken out of the equation. There is always, once, and future nature.

Other more pessimistic scientists believe that humans on Earth are at a rupture point in history. European-Western civilization is self-destructing, spreading and triggering disruptions—climate change and decreasing biodiversity—around the globe. Until now, the technosphere was contained within the biosphere. Hereafter the technosphere will explode these limits. Earth is now in a post-evolutionary phase, a post-ecological phase. The next millennium is the epoch of the "end of nature." The new epoch is the Anthropocene. That puts us indeed at a hinge point of history. What ought we to do to ensure sustainability?

Stewardship and Management

Scientists turning to environmental policy often appeal for ecosystem management. This is attractive to scientists, who see the need for understanding ecosystems objectively and for developing applied technologies, and also to humanists, who desire benefits for people. The combined ecosystem and/or management policy promises to operate at system-wide levels, presumably to manage for indefinite sustainability of ecosystems and their outputs alike.

"Sound scientific management" connects with the idea of nature as "natural resources" and at least permits a "respect nature" dimension, although the question of "manage for what" is often presumed as human benefits. Christian ethicists note that the secular word "manage" is a stand-in for the earlier theological word "steward." Adam was placed in the garden "to till and keep it" (Genesis 2:15). They may add that "trustee" is a better model than "stewardship," since stewards are managing in the interests of owners, whereas "trustees" are charged with caring for what is put into their trust.

Environmental science can inform the evaluation of nature in subtle ways. Scientists describe the *order*, *dynamic stability*, and *diversity* in biotic communities. They describe *interdependence*, or speak of *health* or *integrity*, perhaps of these communities' *resilience* or *efficiency*. Scientists describe the *adapted fit* that organisms have in their niches. They describe an ecosystem as *flourishing*, as *self-organizing*. Strictly interpreted, these are only descriptive terms; and yet often they are already quasi-evaluative terms. Ecology is rather like medical science, with therapeutic purpose, seeking such flourishing health. Theologians may remark that such terms sound like a secular celebration of the *good earth* described in the Genesis parable of creation, or the *promised land* of Israel.

Religion and science have to be carefully delineated, each in its own domain. Asking about technical ecology in the Bible is a mistake (e.g., the Lotka-Volterra equations dealing with population size and carrying capacity). But ecology is a science at native range. Residents on landscapes live immersed in their local ecology. Within the pragmatic ranges of the sower who sows, waits for the seed to grow, and reaps the harvest, the Hebrews knew their landscape. Abraham and Lot, and later Jacob and Esau, dispersed their flocks and herds because "the land could not support both of them dwelling together" (Genesis 13:2–13, 36:6–8). These nomads were exceeding the carrying capacity, ecologists now say. They knew enough to let land lie fallow in the seventh year for its regeneration.

For sustainability, one needs human ecology, humane ecology, and this requires insight into human nature more so than into wild nature. True, humans cannot know the right way to act if they are ignorant of the causal outcomes in the natural systems they modify. But there must be more. "Hear therefore, O Israel, and be careful to do [these commandments] that it may go well with you, and that you may multiply greatly, as the Lord, the God of your fathers, has promised you, in a land flowing with milk and honey" (Deuteronomy 6:3). It is not the land husbandry or the science, but rather the ethics into which the biblical seers have insight. The deeper claim is that there can be no intelligent human ecology except as people learn to use land justly and charitably. Lands do not flow with milk and honey for all unless and until "justice rolls down like waters" (Amos 5:24).

Limits to Growth

Western religion and Western science have for centuries both joined in pushing back limits. Humans have more genius at this than any other species. We have lived with a deep-seated belief that one should hope for abundance and work toward obtaining it. Christian faith brought "the abundant life"; the DuPont corporation championed "better things for better living though chemistry." One accentuates the spiritual; the other accentuates the material side of life. Still, science and religion joined to get people fed and sheltered, to keep them healthy, and to raise standards of living.

We have built the right to self-development and the right to self-realization into our concept of human rights. Religious activists and missionaries have fought for that as much as economists and development scientists. But now we have begun to realize that such an egalitarian ethic scales everybody up and drives an unsustainable world. When everybody seeks their own good, aided by applied sciences, there is escalating consumption. When everybody seeks everybody else's good, urged by gospel compassion, there is, again, escalating consumption. This brings the worry whether either such development science or such compassionate religion is well equipped to deal with the sorts of global level problems we now face. Global threats require that growth be limited in the name of sustainability.

The four main concerns on the world agenda for the new millennium are these: escalating population, escalating consumption, the increasingly horrific consequences of war, and deteriorating environment. Escalating population and consumption are enabled by science, as is the technology for war, and the spillover is a degraded environment. Religions have fostered population growth, or are ambivalent about it; they have enabled human(e) development with increased consumption; they are often ambivalent about environmental conservation. As a result, population, consumption, and environment are not sustainable on our present course. A World Council of Churches theme, "justice, peace, and the integrity of creation," has focused more attention on conserving population growth and consumption than on saving the environment.

Sustainable Development? Sustainable Biosphere?

The prime model is sustainability, but if one asks what is to be sustained, there are two foci. The favored answer is this: sustainable development. When humans face limits, they need to find growth patterns that can be sustained. Such a duty seems plain and urgent; scientists, developers, social gospel activists, and missionaries can be unanimous about it. Sustainable development is useful just because it is a wide-angle lens, an orienting concept that is at once directed and encompassing, a coalition-level policy that sets aspirations, thresholds, and allows pluralist strategies for their accomplishment. One needs the best that science can contribute (e.g., genetically modified foods, carbon dioxide monitors, and scientific models and data) and the best that religion can contribute (e.g., agricultural missions, sermons moderating escalating consumerism, etc.).

The underlying conviction is that the trajectory of development is generally right—but the developers in their enthusiasm have hitherto failed to recognize environmental constraints. Scientists can teach us how to sustain the environment, but we will need the motivations of stewardship (and, better yet, trusteeship) to succeed. Economists, who also like to think of themselves as scientists, may remark that a "growth economy" is the only economy theoretically or practically desirable, or even possible. They dislike "no-growth economies," but now accentuate "green economics."

A massive *Millennium Ecosystem Assessment*, sponsored by the United Nations, involving over thirteen hundred experts from almost one hundred nations, begins this way: "At the heart of this assessment is a stark warning. Human activity is putting such strain on the natural functions of Earth that the ability of the planet's ecosystems to sustain future generations can no longer be taken for granted" (Millennium Ecosystem Assessment 2005, 5).

But there is another possible focus: "sustainable biosphere." Ecologists want to insist that "sustainable" is not so much an economic as an environmental term. The Ecological Society of America claims the following: "Achieving a sustainable biosphere is the single most important task facing humankind today" (Risser, Lubchenco, and Levin 1991). The fundamental flaw in "sustainable development" is that it sees the Earth as a resource only.

The underlying conviction in the sustainable biosphere model is that the current "development" trajectory is generally wrong because it will inevitably overshoot, fed by the aspirations of those who always seek to push back limits. The environment is not some undesirable, unavoidable set of constraints to be subdued and conquered with clever technological fixes. Rather, nature is the matrix of multiple values; many, even most of them are not counted in economic transactions. Nature provides numerous other values (e.g., life support, biodiversity, sense of place) that we wish to sustain. The test of a good Earth is not how much milk and honey can be squeezed out of it to drip into human mouths.

A "sustainable biosphere" model demands that the economy be worked out "within" a quality of life in a quality environment—clean air, water, stable agricultural soils, attractive residential landscapes, forests, mountains, rivers, rural lands, parks, wild lands, wildlife, renewable resources. Decisions about this quality environment will need input from society at large, including its scientists and its peoples of faith. Development is desired, and society must learn to live within the carrying capacity of its landscapes. Even more humans need to treasure Earth's biodiversity, to celebrate creation. Here science and religion complement each other in teaching us how to sustain the home planet, the Earth with promise, the global promised land.

Holmes ROLSTON III
Colorado State University

FURTHER READING

Attfield, Robin. (2003). Environmental ethics: An overview for the twenty-first century. Cambridge, U.K.: Polity Press.

Burkhardt, Jeffrey. (1989). The morality behind sustainability. *Journal of Agricultural Ethics, 2*, 113–128.

Daly, Herman E., & Cobb, John B., Jr. (1999). *For the common good: Redirecting the economy toward community, the environment, and a sustainable future.* (2nd ed.). Boston: Beacon Press.

Millennium Ecosystem Assessment. (2005). Living beyond our means: Natural assets and human well-being: Statement from the board. Washington, DC: World Resources Institute.

Risser, Paul G.; Lubchenco, Jane; & Levin, Simon A. (1991). Biological research priorities—a sustainable biosphere. *BioScience, 41,* 625–627.

National Commission on the Environment. (1993). *Choosing a sustainable future: The report of the National Commission on the Environment.* Washington, DC: Island Press.

Norton, Bryan G. (2005). *Sustainability: A philosophy of adaptive ecosystem management.* Chicago: University of Chicago Press.

Rolston, Holmes, III. (1996). The Bible and ecology. *Interpretation: Journal of Bible and Theology, 50,* 16–26.

Rolston, Holmes, III. (2003). Justifying sustainable development: A continuing ethical search. *Global Dialogue, 4*(1), 103–113.

Shamanism

Although an exact definition of shamanism and shamans is difficult to arrive at, there are consistencies across cultures. Generally, shamans represent mediators between the worlds of humans and nonhumans who, in their contact with the "spirits" of nature, attempt to maintain harmony, if not "sustainable management," with the natural world.

As an academic term *shamanism* both clarifies and occludes our understanding of certain indigenous and prehistoric practices that might be termed religious. Shamans may heal the sick, cause illness, speak to spirits, or become possessed by them, journey to other worlds, seek out game by supernatural means, and alter consciousness to enter a state of ecstasy. But this list should not be seen as finite or even representative, and definition is problematic. An approach to shamans and some of the terms used to define them intellectually—such as *healing, sorcery, spirits, altered states, journeying,* and *ecstasy*—are all loaded with meanings and often tell more about the observer and what the observer wants shamans to be than about shamans themselves. While an exact definition of shamanism and shamans is difficult to arrive at, there are cross-cultural consistencies in what shamans do. Generally, shamans represent mediators between the worlds of humans and nonhumans who, in their contact with the "spirits" of nature, attempt to maintain harmony, if not "sustainable management," with the natural world.

Origins of the Term

The term *shaman* (pronounced SHAYmuhn, SHARmuhn, or SHARmahn; there is no accepted pronunciation) derives from the Tungus language group spoken by a variety of Siberian peoples, including the Evenki. The anglicized *shaman* is rendered phonetically as šaman or sama:n. The Evenki did not use written language or use the term in a general sense to encompass everything that shamans did. The term came into Western use, normalized via the Russian, as Christian missionaries began to target Siberian tribes for conversion and so needed a pagan religion against which to define themselves. By the eighteenth century, the German term *shamanen* and British *shamanism* were in widespread use, as the practices of shamans, bizarre to Western minds, became fetishized as "other." As explorers encountered new peoples across the globe, so a variety of indigenous religious practices came to be associated with shamanism.

Shamans and Shamanisms

Shamanism is now in popular use to refer to medicine men, witch doctors, healers, sorcerers, and others who engage with spirits for certain socially sanctioned tasks. The term gives a sense of coherency and specificity, and has been applied across cultures and through time. But such application risks being misleading, that the "religion" of shamanism with a discrete shamanistic worldview exists. Rather, there are shamans, and these men and women work within animistic or "animic" ontologies (ways of being) and epistemologies (ways of knowing), acting as agents who negotiate harmony between human persons and nonhuman persons, sometimes called spirits. But the term *spirit* problematically draws a spirit/matter dualism that may not be recognized by the community at issue. In addition to approaching indigenous ontologies sensitively, it is important to foreground the diversity of shamans' practices in order to embrace cultural distinctiveness. It might be better to speak of the plural, shamans and shamanisms, rather than the singular, shamanism and the shaman.

Neoshamans and Green Shamans

Shamanism has significant currency among New Age practitioners, pagans, and other alternative interest groups, perhaps best described as "neoshamanisms." For many people interested in shamanisms, shamans represent indigenous healers who, in their contact with the spirits of nature, maintain sustainable management of the natural world. Indigenous communities more generally are perceived to be harmonious in their engagements with nature, and shamans are marked out as occupying the preeminent spiritual wing of this ethos. This Western view co-opts shamans, distorting their practices away from local animic contexts in which relations between human people and nonhuman people are negotiated, toward a globalized metanarrative (a simplistic and all-encompassing explanation) in which shamans are the spiritual caretakers of the environment. Small-scale societies have a much smaller impact on the Earth's resources than Western countries have. But traditional slash-and-burn agriculture, practiced in the Amazon for instance, and evidence indicating that prehistoric peoples may have hunted a number of large animals to extinction in various parts of the world, demonstrates that humans are capable of irreparable damage to nature. This is not to dismiss, however, the significance and relevance of indigenous engagements with nature to the modern world.

Shamans and Animists

Animists, in many indigenous communities, understand the world as filled with people, only some of whom are human. There are human people, and there are other-than-human people—such as stone people, tree people, and fish people—and it is the role of shamans to maintain harmonious relations between humans and nonhumans. Animism in the Amazon, for instance, is predatory. Just as the world is filled with persons, so killing other persons is necessary to survive. It might be said that everyone is eating everyone else all of the time, in a series of cannibalist relations. Animic ontologies attempt to do violence with impunity, with shamans brokering good relations, but all too often human behavior offends nonhumans. It is then the task of shamans to engage with nonhumans via "adjusted styles of communication," which enables them to "see as others do," or meet the communicative level of others persons, to restore harmony.

Shamans and Sustainability

While indigenous and prehistoric lifeways may not necessarily be "green," their respectful, relational approach to the world, and understanding of community as not restricted to humanity, offers a practical guideline to Western people as to how living can attempt to be respectful, relational, and sustainable. Living sustainably requires humans to engage with the natural world respectfully, rather than regard it as a resource for exploitation. Humans are not "king of the hill", but simply one form of life in a diversely living world.

Robert J. WALLIS
Richmond the American International University in London

FURTHER READING

Atkinson, Jane Monnig. (1992). Shamanisms today. *Annual Review of Anthropology, 21,* 307–330.

Harvey, Graham. (2005). *Animism: Respecting the living world.* London: Hurst; New York: Columbia University Press; Adelaide, Australia: Wakefield Press.

Harvey, Graham. (Ed.). (2002). *Shamanism: A reader.* London: Routledge.

Harvey, Graham, & Wallis, Robert J. (2007). *Historical dictionary of shamanism.* Lanham, MD: Scarecrow Press.

Humphrey, Caroline, & Onon, Urgunge. (1996). *Shamans and elders: Experience, knowledge, and power among the Daur Mongols.* Oxford, U.K.: Oxford University Press.

Hutton, Ronald. (2002). *Shamans: Siberian spirituality and the Western imagination.* London: Hambledon.

Narby, Jeremy, & Huxley, Francis. (Eds.). (2004). *Shamans through time: 500 years on the path to knowledge.* London: Thames and Hudson.

Price, Neil S. (Ed.). (2001). *The archaeology of shamanism.* London: Routledge.

Taylor, Bron R., & Kaplan, Jeffrey. (Eds.). (2005). *The encyclopedia of religion and nature.* New York and London: Continuum.

Thomas, Nicholas, & Humphrey, Caroline. (Eds.). (1994). *Shamanism, history, and the state.* Ann Arbor: University of Michigan Press.

Wallis, Robert J. (2003). *Shamans/neo-shamans: Ecstasy, alternative archaeologies and contemporary pagans.* London: Routledge.

Shinto

Shinto, a Japanese religious tradition that emerged in prehistoric times, sees human beings, spiritual beings (kami), and nature as being harmoniously interrelated. Shinto followers, who revere this innate connection, follow rituals to communicate with the kami *manifest in living beings and natural forms or phenomena. The Shinto worldview embraces attitudes that place the world's natural environment in esteem and thus reinforce sustainable ways of living to preserve and value its resources.*

Shinto, Japan's native religion, embodies a combination of Japanese ethnic beliefs and rituals. Although Shinto has been intermittently influenced by religious traditions such as Daoism (especially the yin–yang theory), Confucianism, and Buddhism, it has developed its own worldview in which human beings, *kami* (spiritual beings), and nature are so close that "mortals, gods, and nature form a triangle of harmonious interrelationships" (Earhart 2004, 8). A discussion of the Shinto worldview, with its underlying reverence for nature and harmony, can provide perspective on the moral and ethical, philosophical, and even practical discussions of sustainability at a time when the world faces the challenge of preserving, protecting, and reestablishing the value of its natural resources.

While aspects of Shinto—such as animism, polytheism, shamanism, and syncretism—have often been emphasized as being "uniquely Japanese," they are not unique to Japan or to Shinto; rather they are characteristics of East Asian folk religion and, to a certain degree, other religions of the world. Therefore it is important to be cautious in characterizing Shinto as indigenous and unique, especially in terms of its relationship to nature.

Shinto can be divided into three types: Shrine Shinto (*jinja-shinto*), Sect Shinto (*kyoha-shinto*), and Folk Shinto (*minzoku-shinto*). Shrine Shinto has its roots in the primitive era, and today more than 80,000 shrines still exist as active places of worship. Sect Shinto has thirteen sects that were formed during the nineteenth century, and each sect conducts religious activities based on its own doctrine. Folk Shinto includes various and fragmented practices such as spirit possession, shamanistic healing, and divination based on folk beliefs in deities and spirits.

Etymology

The word *Shinto* 神道 combines two Chinese characters meaning *gods* or *spirits* and *way* or *path*, respectively, so that Shinto is often translated as "the way of the gods." When the word first appeared in Japanese history, it was used to express the system of indigenous rituals offered to the heavenly and earthly deities. The notion of such deities, or *kami*, is central to Shinto worship and pervades all aspects of Japanese culture.

The eighteenth-century thinker Motoori Norinaga created the following widely accepted definition of *kami*: "In general, *kami* refers first to the manifold *kami* of heaven and earth we see in the ancient classics, and to the spirits (*mitama*) in shrines consecrated to the same. And it further refers to all other awe-inspiring things—people of course, but also birds, beasts, grass and trees, even the ocean and mountains—which possess superlative power not normally found in this world. 'Superlative' here means not only superlative in nobility, goodness, or virility, since things which are evil and weird as well, if they inspire unusual awe, are also called *kami*" (Motoori 1968, 125).

Since the preliterate period the notion of *kami* has been connected with at least two meanings: the spirits of the dead and the awe-inspiring aspects of nature. While the former meaning emphasizes the closeness of human beings and *kami*, the latter meaning indicates the interrelatedness of nature and *kami*, on the one hand, and nature and human beings, on the other.

Kami in Nature

In *An Encyclopedia of Shinto* (Havens and Inoue, 2001–2006), *kami* is classified by two main categories: culture *kami* and nature *kami*. The culture *kami* can be further divided into three subcategories: (1) community *kami* worshiped by particular social groups, (2) functional *kami* related to special aspects in human life, and (3) human *kami* for historical human beings worshiped as *kami*.

The category of nature *kami* is a recognition of the "abnormal" powers or features of nature, and it can be further divided into two subcategories: celestial *kami* and terrestrial *kami*. As deified heavenly bodies and meteorological phenomena, celestial *kami* include the sun, moon, and planets, as well as wind and thunder. Terrestrial *kami* are composed of geological forms, physical processes, and plants and animals, including earth, mountains, forests, rocks, sea, rivers, islands, pine, cedar, cypress, snakes, deer, wild boar, wolves, bears, monkeys, foxes, rabbits, crows, and doves. Animal *kami* are often associated with the *kami* of natural physical phenomena and identified as the manifestations of such *kami*, while plant *kami* are often so impressive that they are easily connected with "abnormal" power.

Dwelling within natural objects or through natural phenomena and impressing human beings with a sense of awe, *kami* make humans feel the existence of extraordinary power. In other words, *kami* remain unrevealed without manifesting themselves by dwelling in natural objects. Thus, *kami* present themselves in concrete forms but not in abstract or conceptual forms. Sonoda Minoru indicates that what evokes awe "as it is" (*onozukara*) comes to be revered as *kami* (Sonoda, 2000). For instance, the spirit of the rice grain (*kokurei*) is one of the most important *kami* because it is the source of life for both the divine and human realms. Likewise, as the prayers recorded in the *Engi shiki* (*Procedures of the Engi Era*, 927 CE) show, the ancient Yamato court executed special festivals for the *kami* protecting paddy fields, the *kami* of forests and water, and the *kami* of water sources. The *Hitachi-kuni fudoki* (*Official Report from the Government Office of Hitachi Province*, eighth century CE)

tells stories in which the people of antiquity regarded wild animals such as snakes as *kami* and worshiped them when they reclaimed rice fields.

As modern linguistics suggests, the word *kami* is related to *kuma* (corner, nook) and *kumu* (to hide) and originally referred to the spiritual quality of the mountains and valleys that were the sources of water. The people of mountainous Japan have thus revered the spirituality hiding in the forests and mountains as *kami*, and they have transformed the landscape into a living cosmos in which human beings, *kami*, and nature are interrelated harmoniously.

Plurality of *Kami*

This harmony might have originated from a Japanese cosmogony in which there is no creator god but rather a plurality of *kami* coming into existence one after another generated by other *kami*. According to Japanese mythology as narrated in two important sources of Shinto theology, the *Kojiki* (*Records of Ancient Matters*, 712 CE) and the *Nihon shoki* (also known as *Nihongi, Chronicles of Japan*, 720 CE), natural phenomena are themselves the offspring of *kami*. This is apparent especially in the myth about the divine couple Izanagi and Izanami, who came together to give birth to the eight islands of Japan and the various other *kami*. It may be worth contrasting the procreation described in this ancient Japanese myth (the cosmogony of generation) to the Judeo-Christian cosmogony of creation. The cosmogony of generation, as expressed in the *Kojiki* and *Nihon shoki*, puts special emphasis on the notion of *musuhi* (the generative force), which is innate in all beings, while the cosmogony of creation is based on the notion of God as the single Creator, the transcendent origin of creation.

The Japanese myth also illustrates the proliferation of *kami* closely related to the people and the land. The fact that *kami* are collectively called *yaoyorozu no kami* (8 million *kami*) denotes a polytheistic world of *kami*. This polytheistic character of Shinto has never been lost, although the Shinto doctrine of the *kami*'s oneness was developed through medieval and early modern times in conjunction with Buddhism and neo-Confucianism.

Shrine and Forest

Considering the intimacy between *kami* and nature (especially mountains and woods), it is not surprising that most Shinto shrines are built in forests. The ancient shrines (*jinja*) were often objects of nature such as a grove or a wooded hill (*moriyama*). The fact that the characters for *jinja* 神社 are also read as *mori* (grove) shows that Shinto shrines were originally sacred groves or forests inhabited by *kami*.

According to a myth recorded in the *Nihon shoki*, the wind god Susanowo, a violent and unpredictable deity but also a cultural hero, created trees (cedar, cypress, and camphor, for instance) from his own bodily hair and taught his children how best to use the various types of wood. In addition, he made his children sow the seeds that changed the Japanese islands into a land of green forests. This myth shows the special interest the ancient Japanese paid to the cultivation and preservation of forests. From the ancient to the early modern period, the authorities and local rulers treated Shinto shrines and their forests with respect and consequently protected them.

Shinto and Rice

Shinto has also been connected with rice. The deep ethnic significance that rice has for most Japanese makes it an indispensable element of Shinto. Rice and *sake* (rice wine) are typical offerings to a Shinto altar. The sacred rope (*shimenawa*) that marks the border of a shrine or signifies the presence of *kami* is commonly made from rice straw. Planting seedlings and eating the annual harvest are important formal rituals of the emperor. The origins of Shinto can be traced to the middle of the first millennium BCE, when hydraulic rice agriculture was first established in Japan.

The *Kojiki* and *Nihon shoki* recount myths about the killing of female Earth deities, whose dead bodies produced rice and other precious crops. These Hainuwele-type myths—referring to the Wemale (Indonesian) creation myth in which the sacrifice of the maiden Hainuwele, herself a "product" of mingling human blood and the sap of a coconut branch, resulted in the growth of tuberous plants that became a staple of the Wemale diet—indicate that agriculture allowed human beings to render their societies autonomous from the natural environment and produce new environments in which humans exercised some control. The rice rituals in Shinto show that Japanese society construes a religious cosmos through cultivating nature and transforming it into a living landscape, which symbolizes the inherent relationship between Shinto and the environments of the Japanese archipelago.

Japanese View of Nature

This inherent relationship also can be seen in the Shinto festivals (*matsuri*) such as the spring festival, in which the *yama no kami* (mountain *kami*), widely regarded as ancestral *kami*, descend to the village as the *ta no kami* (*kami* of the rice paddy) to assist people in rice cultivation and production, and the autumn festival, in which the *ta no kami* return to the mountain following the harvest and reassume the role of *yama no kami*. As seen in these examples, generation and rebirth are naturally linked with the annual cycle of planting and harvesting. This view of nature and soul easily leads to the concept of the immanent nature of human beings, who have been strengthened by their sensitivity to the transitory aspects of both nature and mortals. Thus, exorcism and purification rites to drive out "pollution (*kegare*)," which are essential to Shinto, can be considered to be the way of reestablishing order and balance among *kami*, human beings, and nature.

If an animistic view of nature can be implied in the expression "nature of life" (nature is full of life) and a pantheistic notion of nature can be implied in the expression "life of nature" (all nature can be seen as one holistic life), the worldview of Japanese people can be seen to be composed of two distinct dimensions, penetrating into each other from the ancient times to the present. The mythical and religious representations of nature in Japanese culture mentioned above have formed the Japanese concept of nature. The Japanese see nature as something that always contains harmony or order. Every natural thing—mountains and rivers, rocks and trees, thunders and flowers, winds and insects—can be seen as living *kami*, which altogether compose the harmonious cosmos.

Shinto, as well as other religious traditions in Japan, has traditionally seen nature as immanently divine and, as a result, has considered the correspondence between external beauty and internal equilibrium as self-evident. Regarding nature as divine and sacred, the Japanese people have not considered nature as inferior or in opposition to human beings. They have preferred to live embedded in nature by participating in modes of expression and ritual such as flower arrangement, the tea ceremony, literati art works, and Zen painting, all of which adapt or represent some element of the natural. Nature, then, as religiously and aesthetically signified in Japanese history, is a kind of abstraction of an idealized world including human beings as well as *kami*.

It is ironic that the Japanese people, who have long been known for their "love of nature," have had to witness (and some have been to one degree or another responsible for) the destruction of nature in modern times. After the fall of the Tokugawa shogunate (1600/1603–1868), a period in which Buddhism and neo-Confucianism were favored, the Meiji government (1868–1912) intended to use Shinto as a state-sponsored religion that would both unify the new nation-state and reestablish symbolic power of the emperor. Under the strict control of the government over a limited number of "government shrines," and many other local shrines were destroyed. More drastic were changes after the end of World War II in 1945, when the rapid industrialization and urbanization transformed the life of local communities. On the other hand, shrines were to become endangered as postwar land reform required that many shrine buildings be used for other purposes, such as schools.

After the severe environmental destruction during the rapid economic growth from the 1960s to 1980s, however, the religious cosmologies of shrine forests and *kami* mountains based on animistic world view came to be revaluated. As a result, more and more people in and out of Japan are focusing on the potentiality of Shinto as an "ecological religion."

Yotaro MIYAMOTO
Kansai University

FURTHER READING

Asquite, Pamela J., & Kalland, Arne. (Eds.). (1997). *Japanese images of nature: Cultural perspectives*. Richmond, U.K.: Curzon Press.

Breen, John, & Teeuwen, Mark. (Eds.). (2000). *Shinto in history: Ways of the kami*. Honolulu: University of Hawaii Press.

Brinkman, John T. (1996). *Simplicity: A distinctive quality of Japanese spirituality*. New York: Peter Lang.

Earhart, H. Byron. (2004*). Japanese religion: Unity and diversity*. (4th ed.). Belmont, CA: Thomson/Wadsworth.

Ellwood, Robert. (2008). *Introducing Japanese religion*. New York: Routledge.

Hartz, Paula R. (2004). *Shinto*. (Updated ed.). New York: Facts On File.

Havens, Norman, & Inoue Nobutaka. (Eds.). (2001–2006). *An encyclopedia of Shinto*. 3 Vols. Tokyo: Institute for Japanese Culture and Classics, Kokugakuin University.

Inoue Nobutaka. (Ed.). (2003). *Shinto: A short history*. New York: Routledge Curzon.

Kamata Toji. (2000). *Shinto towa nanika: Shizen no reisei wo kanjite ikiru.* [What is Shinto?: To live feeling the spirituality of nature.] Tokyo: PHP Kenkyusho.

Kasulis, Thomas. (2004). *Shinto: The way home*. Honolulu: University of Hawaii Press.

Miyake Hitoshi. (1995). Nihon no minzoku shukyo ni okeru sizen-kan. [The idea of nature in Japanese folk religion.] *Shukyo Kenkyu* [*Journal of Religious Studies*], *69*(1).

Motoori Norinaga. (1968). *Kojikiden, Vol 1*. [The complete works of Motoori Norinaga, (9 vols.)]. Tokyo: Chikuma-shobo.

Nelson, John K. (2000). *Enduring identities: The guise of Shinto in contemporary Japan*. Honolulu: University of Hawaii Press.

Sonoda Minoru. (1987). The religious situation in Japan in relation to Shinto. *Acta Asiatica, 51.*

Sonoda Minoru. (1995). Shizen fudo to shukyo bunka. [The religious nature of a social-ecological system.] *Shukyo Kenkyu* [*Journal of Religious Studies*], *69*(1).

Sonoda Minoru. (2000). Shinto and the natural environment. In John Breen & Mark Teeuwen (Eds.), *Shinto in History: Ways of the Kami*. Honolulu: University of Hawaii Press.

Sonoda Minoru. (2005). *Bunka to shiteno Shinto*. [Shinto as a culture.] Tokyo: Kobundo.

Sonoda Minoru. (Ed.). (1988). *Shinto: Nihon no minzoku shukyo*. [Shinto: Ethnic religion of Japan.] Tokyo: Kobundo.

Ueda Kenji. (1991). *Shinto shingaku ronko*. [Consideration on Shinto theology.] Tokyo: Daimeido.

Sikhism

The beliefs of Sikhism lend themselves to ecological thinking: creation is a manifestation of the divine, and humanity must learn to live in harmony with it all. Ecological awareness has intensified since the 1990s; among other efforts, Sikh environmentalists and global organizations have collaborated on faith-based plans for a Sikh response to the environmental crisis.

The word *Sikh* means something like "learner of truth." Sikhism emerged in fifteenth century Punjab with the Sikh guru Nanak; ten other gurus have followed him. Guru Nanak considered himself neither Muslim nor Hindu—though influenced by both traditions—and often preached against religious intolerance. According to Guru Granth Sahib, the Sikh scripture that contains the sayings of Guru Nanak and the other ten Sikh gurus, all of creation is a manifestation of God. Because of this belief, there are many who argue that Sikhism is inherently ecosophical, that is, divine wisdom pervades all of creation and humans ought to live in harmony with creation. Humans are the "god-conscious" beings of the Earth, and human spiritual discipline should be aimed at living in harmony with the rest of God's creation, which means following God's *hukam* (or commandments). These commandments are collected together in the Rehat Maryada, or the Sikh Code of Conduct. One such commandment with environmental implications surrounds the *langar*, a community kitchen that serves a free meal, usually vegetarian, in the *gurdwara* (house of worship) every day. This meal sharing is an opportunity not only to recognize interdependence with all other humans—no one is turned away

from the meal—but also one's nourishment from the rest of God's creation.

Contemporary Sikh environmentalism can be traced to Bhagat Puran Singh Ji (1904–1992), the "Mother Teresa" of Sikhism, who devoted his live to alleviating the suffering of humanity. In addition to his service to terminally ill and crippled peoples of Punjab, he also wrote and spoke about the dangers of soil erosion and environmental pollution, making connections between sick people and a "sick" environment.

More recently, in 1999, Sikh communities around the world gathered to celebrate the beginning of the current three-hundred-year cycle and named it the Cycle of Creation (Sikhism measures time in cycles of three hundred years). This cycle will focus upon Sikh relationships to the natural world.

As a result of this, there are now many groups of Sikhs coming together in organizations to address environmental issues. EcoSikh, one such organization, was developed through a collaboration of Sikh environmentalists, the Sikh Council on Religion and Education (SCORE), the Alliance of Religions and Conservation (ARC), and the United Nations Development Programme (UNDP) to address five key areas of Sikh environmentalism: assets, education, media and advocacy, eco-twinning, and celebration. The *Guide to Creating Your EcoSikh 5-Year Plan: Generational Changes for a Living Planet* (ARC, SCORE, & UNDP 2009), outlines actions Sikh communities can adopt to protect the environment. As well as encouraging awareness of resources and promoting environmental efforts such as the greening of the *langar*, they propose the concept of "eco-twinning." In its broadest sense, "twinning" refers to the affiliation of two groups with shared characteristics to reach a common goal; eco-twinning provides pairings of *gurdwaras* in south Asia with others around the world, especially in first world countries, with the idea that these sister communities focus on environmental problems specific to their location and support one another through financial and educational means. Because many environmental issues are global in perspective, this will help groups uncover their planetary relations.

Though scholarship on Sikhism and ecology is sparse, some writing does exist. No doubt this scholarship will grow as the global Sikh community (some 23 million strong) continues to focus on the Cycle of Creation, and as the wider Earth community recognizes the beneficial implications of a Sikh ecospirituality.

Whitney A. BAUMAN

Florida International University

FURTHER READING

Alliance of Religions and Conservation (ARC). (n.d.) ARC and the faiths. Retrieved July 7, 2009, from http://www.arcworld.org/faiths.htm

Alliance of Religions and Conservation (ARC); Sikh Council on Religion and Education (SCORE); & United Nations Development Programme (UNDP). (2009, June 22). *Guide to creating your EcoSikh 5-year plan: Generational changes for a living planet.* Retrieved July 9, 2009, from http://ecosikh.org/wp-content/uploads/2009/06/EcoSikhPlansforGenerationalChangeGuidebook.pdf

Dwivedi, O. P. (1989). *World religions and the environment.* New Delhi: Gitanjali Publishing House.

EcoSikh. (2009). Retrieved July 7, 2009, from http://ecosikh.org

Lourdunathan, S. (2002, September). Ecosophical concerns in the Sikh tradition. Retrieved July 9, 2009, from http://www.sikhspectrum.com/092002/eco.htm

Narayan, Rajdeva, & Kumar, Janardan. (Eds.). (2003). *Ecology and religion: Ecological concepts in Hinduism, Buddhism, Jainism, Islam, Christianity, and Sikhism.* New Delhi: Deep & Deep Publishers.

Singh, David Emmanuel. (Ed.). (1998). *Spiritual traditions: Essential visions for living.* Bangalore, India: United Theological College.

A NEW BATTLE FOR SIKHISM: THE ENVIRONMENT

Since the fifteenth century, and throughout Sikhism's embattled history in India, concern for the environment has been an inherent part of the Sikh belief in creation as a manifestation of the divine. In the late 1990s, Sikhs began to address contemporary environmental concerns, mobilizing to fight for the restoration of Earth's resources. Martin Palmer, the current Secretary General of the Alliance of Religions and Conservation (ARC) describes how the Sikh tradition of measuring time helped shape this turn of events.

In Sikhism, time is measured in 300-year cycles. In 1999 Sikhs moved into their third such cycle. The first two cycles had been named as they began, and although the names were inspired by events just before each new cycle, they also shaped the spirit of that cycle. For example, the years between 1699 and 1999 were called the "Cycle of the Sword," because in the late seventeenth century the Sikhs were fighting for their lives against the Mughal Emperors who had invaded India; the Sikhs decided to fight back not just for themselves, but to protect all the weak and vulnerable. The Cycle of the Sword ended with a terrible civil war in the Punjab, when Sikh militants sought to create a separate state and the Indian government crushed them.

As they approached 1999, the Sikh leaders wanted a very different theme for the next 300 years. At the time ARC [Alliance of Religion and Conservation] was working very closely with the Sikhs on developing land management and alternative energy schemes. Through our discussions, the idea arose of naming the new cycle the "Cycle of the Environment" or the "Cycle of Creation." [The Cycle of Creation] was agreed [upon] by the whole community and now the Sikhs have made a 300-year commitment to focus on the environment. What does this really mean? Well, one early benefit is that many Sikh temples now hand out tree saplings as a sign of blessing to worshippers instead of a sticky sweet. It is estimated that 10 million saplings are being distributed every year, making up the woodlands and gardens of the future. Religions can make commitments like this because they think in the long, long term and have the experience of having done so for a long, long time.

Source: Martin Palmer with Victoria Finlay. (2003). *Faith in Conservation: New Approaches to Religions and the Environment*, pp. 30–31. Washington, DC: The World Bank.

Simplicity and Asceticism

Sustainability requires that humans lead lives of simplicity without all the material extras we tend to acquire. This can result in an ascetic life, which typically involves some form of self-denial. But asceticism can help individuals reconsider the role of consumerism in their lives and instead adopt a more spiritual and compassionate life, now aware of their responsibility to Earth.

A sustainable world needs people who live in a spirit of simplicity or creative frugality. Such frugality lies in taking care of material possessions, utilizing them rather than discarding them, and appreciating them. Such frugality involves a healthy respect for material things in life; indeed we might say that it is deeply materialistic. Frugality does not mean stinginess; people who consume in creatively frugal ways are often more generous than people who are absorbed in conspicuous consumption. Creative frugality has a joyful and reverential quality to it.

Imagine a man who owns a piece of furniture that he has made with his own hands: a well-made chair. He takes care of it, repairing it and making good use of it without needing to replace it with something new and improved. Perhaps he could buy a new chair, but he likes his old one. This man has a healthy respect for materiality. Or imagine a woman who shops at a local market to buy freshly grown vegetables. She scrutinizes the vegetables to make sure that they look healthy and then pays for them. Her very scrutiny is an example of conscious consumption and creative frugality. She cares about the food she eats. Let us assume that she goes home and prepares a meal for dinner and has friends over to enjoy it. She takes her time in preparing the food, and then, when the guests arrive, they share the meal, slowly and carefully. As they eat together and enjoy the meal without hurry, they, too, exemplify healthy consumption. This is very different from the kind of consumption in a fast-food restaurant. It is not hurried and restless. It is creative rather than compulsive, deliberate rather than rushed.

In addition to creative frugality, prospects for a more sustainable world can improve if people have a daily spiritual practice, whether prayer, meditation, gardening, walking, swimming, playing music, or riding a bicycle, for example. As long as the content is nonharmful, almost any practice can be spiritual if the person undertaking it intends for it to be spiritual. Asceticism comes from the Greek word *ascesis*, which pertains to athletic training. Ascetic practices help train the body and spirit for life's fulfillment, however it is understood. Advocates of sustainability might think of them as practices that help a person transcend ego-based desires and momentary whims so that he or she can grow into a more wise and compassionate person who lives lightly on the Earth and gently with others.

Ascetic practices sometimes appear unpleasant, such as when people undertake vigils during the night or when they fast for extended periods of time. Such disciplines may be valuable for helping a person overcome sovereignty of the ego. People who fast may find that it makes them more aware of the poignancy and beauty of ordinary life and the natural world. But asceticism can also be of a gentler variety. It can undertake practices such as gardening and walking to become more centered as a human being, so that one can dwell lightly on the Earth and gently with others.

In addition to helping people become more wise and compassionate, ascetic practices can also be understood as protests against the consumerist worldview that overwhelms humanity today. Consumerism emerges when society is saturated with market-driven values such as competition and a preoccupation with status, and when other more social values such as compassion and respect for animals are neglected. Some of its tangible effects are conspicuous consumption, wasteful consumption, and overconsumption. As an ideology, consumerism tells people that they are fulfilled by purchasing more and more goods; it teaches them to measure their own worth by their attractiveness as a commodity and by how much money they have; it describes status in terms of the goods they own; it tells them that they are consumers first and citizens second. Consumerism thus makes private good more important than the public good, paid jobs more important than families, and salaried work the only work worth doing.

When market values such as these dominate a society, things fall apart. Being ambitious becomes more important than being good; being attractive becomes more important than being kind; being materially successful becomes more important than being a good parent, neighbor, and friend. The social costs of consumerism are excessive individualism, a neglect of family and community, an overemphasis on money, a compulsively busy lifestyle, and a sense of emptiness that comes when life is reduced to things. An essential value of a commitment to creative frugality and the adoption of ascetic disciplines is to help people better affirm that life is not reducible to things, because all things—even chairs and food as well as people and other living beings—are living expressions of a deeper liturgy: the universe itself. This liturgy is what is forgotten in the culture of consumerism. It is what is remembered and celebrated when people live with the deep materialism of creative frugality.

Jay McDANIEL
Hendrix College

FURTHER READING

Brinkman, John T. (1996). *Simplicity: A distinctive quality of Japanese spirituality.* New York: Peter Lang.

Edwards, Tilden. (1977). *Living simply through the day: Spiritual survival in a complex age.* New York: Paulist Press.

Flood, Gavin. (2008, Winter). Asceticism and the hopeful self: Subjectivity, reductionism, and modernity. *Cross Currents, 57.*

Kaza, Stephanie. (2005). *Hooked!: Buddhist writings on greed, desire, and the urge to consume.* Boston: Shambhala.

Kelly, Thomas R. (1996). *A testament of devotion.* New York: HarperCollins.

McDaniel, Jay. (2008, Winter). Mei's invitation: A gentle asceticism for Chinese and Americans. *Cross Currents, 57.*

Rasmussen, Larry L. (2008, Winter). Earth-honoring asceticism and consumption. *Cross Currents, 57.*

Sin and Evil

The Abrahamic religions describe deviation from God's being or will as sin. Because these religions conceive God to be morally good, sin is closely and complexly related to evil—unjustified harm to sentient beings. Given their putative impropriety and potentially deleterious effects, individual or societal practices that threaten sustainability may be sinful, evil, or both.

Since human departure from moral, ecological, or religious orders can threaten the Earth's resources and inhabitants, the vocabulary of sin and evil may help to illumine sustainability problems.

Sin

Sin is culpable unrighteousness that violates God's will or otherwise deviates from holiness. While sin is consequently a religious notion, it also damages human lives and the environment, and so overlaps with moral categories. As such, sin naturally implies a morally perfect God that humans may disobey and is thus primarily a concept of Judaism, Christianity, and Islam.

The terms "sin" and "sins" often refer to distinct phenomena. Sin describes a basic lack of trust in God, or may denote a force opposed to God with power over human nature and the world. Sins are discrete, culpable acts, thoughts, and omissions that are contrary to God's will. This distinction does not represent a difference between religion and morality, for sin and sins may equally be failures of faith or virtue, or both.

"Original sin" is a distinctly Christian doctrine asserting that human beings are now born into a state of sin as a consequence of the first human couple's disobedience to God and fall from grace. By interpreting all subsequent people to be culpable for that first sin and to have inherited

a tendency to sin because of it, the doctrine supports the Christian contention that human beings cannot extricate themselves from sin or its guilt. Nevertheless, original sin has been challenged as historically implausible (since the alleged penalty for that sin—toil, suffering, and death—is said to have always been part of human experience) and morally problematic (since it involves innate culpability).

By attributing sin to social institutions and practices, the concept of "structural sin" provides a way for Christians to maintain their insistence that human beings sin inevitably and culpably without the problems associated with the doctrine of original sin. Structural sin refers to culpably unrighteous social systems that dispose all who participate in them to further sin. Structural sin thus accounts for the inevitability of human sin since it considers people to be formed by and embedded within unjust economic, political, and cultural arrangements. Unlike original sin, however, structural sin is not innate, for people are born into it rather than with it. Similarly, individuals remain meaningfully culpable in the context of structural sin, for individuals perpetuate unrighteous social systems, and it is their character that these systems shape. Yet identification of structural sin is not a contemporary innovation prompted by recent concern with perceived inadequacies in the doctrine of original sin. Instead structural sin is repeatedly denounced in the scriptures of all three Abrahamic faiths and reflects appreciation for the relational character of human being.

Evil

Evil is serious, unjustified harm of sentient beings. A distinction is often drawn between natural evil (suffering caused by impersonal natural powers) and moral evil (wicked activities of responsible agents and the suffering they produce). This distinction should not be overdrawn: at times, humans may be merely natural agents; conversely, evil caused by natural agents may warrant moral condemnation if moral agents had an obligation to avert it.

Sin and evil are closely and complexly related. All moral evil is sinful, and both sin and evil are diametrically opposed to God and the good. Sin, however, is not always evil (consider cultic impropriety), and no exclusively natural evil is sinful.

Sin and evil pose different theological problems. Sin challenges the prospects for salvation since it ruptures appropriate relations between God and human beings, and apparently precludes the communion with a righteous God that constitutes salvation. The Abrahamic faiths respond by confessing that God both gratuitously forgives human beings—thereby annulling their guilt and rectifying their relationship with God—and also transforms them by amending their tendency to sin—thus enabling human beings to cleave to God.

Evil challenges the plausibility of belief in the Abrahamic God since God must want to eradicate evil if good and must be able to eradicate evil if almighty, yet evil exists. Although denying the existence of evil would dispel this dilemma, the Abrahamic faiths have instead sought to reconcile evil's existence with God's. Recourse to free will may be one way to do so, for if moral goodness depends upon freedom, and freedom entails the possibility of evil, then evil's existence is consistent with God's power and goodness so long as moral goodness is. Any successful theodicy—the attempt to justify the existence of evil by providing a morally sufficient reason why a perfectly good and almighty God would allow it—would also resolve the tension. Such explanations commonly contend that the best possible world includes evil, and hence reconcile evil's existence with God's, but they raise the further question of whether a world with as much evil as ours is plausibly the best possible.

Frederick SIMMONS
Yale Divinity School

FURTHER READING

Augustine. (1984). *City of God* (Henry Bettenson, Trans.). New York: Penguin Classics. (Original work published 412–418)

Farley, Edward. (1990). *Good and evil: Interpreting a human condition.* Minneapolis, MN: Fortress Press.

Gutiérrez, Gustavo. (1988). *A theology of liberation: History, politics, and salvation* (rev. ed.). (Caridad Inda & John Eagleson, Trans.). Maryknoll, NY: Orbis.

Hick, John. (2007). *Evil and the God of Love* (2nd ed.). New York: Palgrave Macmillan.

Niebuhr, Reinhold. (1996). *The nature and destiny of man: A Christian interpretation: Vol. I. Human Nature.* Louisville, KY: Westminster John Knox.

chat Berkshire's authors and editors welcome questions, comments, and corrections: sustainability.updates@berkshirepublishing.com

Spirit and Spirituality

Environmental spirituality builds on age-old traditional themes found in many world religions, but contemporary understandings of spirit and spirituality will evolve as environmental crises threaten a sustainable future. At least one longstanding facet of these terms remains: a commitment to the reality of spirit, even in the face of remorseless and unthinking political, economic, or ideological power, rests on the refusal to give up on the human capacity to transcend the past and create a fully human life.

Spirit and spirituality are concepts best understood within the context of discussing ontological (meaning the question of what aspects of human identity are essential to our being human) and psychological reality. By asserting the existential reality of spirit we deny that reality is reducible to matter, and thus declare that existence has a fundamental moral and "spiritual" meaning. We talk of "spiritual" meanings and imply, for example, that human life is not properly understood in terms of social convention, self-interest, pleasure, or power. In both cases lies the suggestion that what we've asserted is in some sense higher, more important, and more real than what we've negated. Ironically, this assertion unfolds in a cultural context in which the opposite view has extremely wide acceptance. We declare that humans have spirit because the dominant worldview treats them as consumers, members of ethnic or racial groups, citizens engaged in contracts, or products of genetic codes and biochemical structures. We emphasize the importance of spirituality because the dominant worldview takes for granted that making money, buying objects, becoming famous and powerful, or having "fun" are what life is all about.

Environmental Spirituality

In the face of the sustainability crisis, spirit and spirituality have become essential concepts because many view the crisis as fundamentally spiritual. By this they mean that the source of humanity's irrational destruction of the supporting conditions of the web of life on this planet, as well as its poisoning of countless numbers of its own species, stems from a fundamental misunderstanding of what ought to be our highest values and aspirations. Saying that this is a profound spiritual mistake, which requires a profound spiritual change, suggests two crucial points.

First we must consider the scope of our environmental crisis. No simple technological fix will do. The foundational beliefs and values that guide commerce, education, science, politics, and religion (as well as a number of other societal systems) must be questioned and altered. Second, we must examine the following premise: making the needed change does not require a set of values that is opposed to our self-interest. Spiritual values are generally understood as forms of virtue that, when practiced, actually leave us happier, more fulfilled, and at the same time more supportive of the happiness and fulfillment of those around us. To be spiritual is not to sacrifice oneself for an ideal that is at odds with what we need, but to discover the true nature of that need and, casting off illusions, attachments, and bad habits, to seek to meet it.

In many ways environmental spirituality builds on long-lived spiritual themes found in world religions. Buddhist spirituality, for example, places great emphasis on overcoming attachment to possessions. In contemporary environmental writing this has flowered into Buddhist-oriented critiques of consumerism: traditional Buddhist diagnoses of the ways in which possessions lead to dissatisfaction are combined with critiques of the environmental and physiological consequences of a social order defined by trips to the mall (Kaza 2005). Islamic ecotheologians have been critical of the creation of an "elite that overconsumes and overproduces, and hence contributes to the ecological crisis by depleting the environment." Such behavior results in injustice for the entire world, and also violates a basic Islamic virtue of *hay'a* or "dignified reserve" (Ammar 2003, 287–290). In both the Buddhist and Islamic examples a general rule is exemplified: environmental spirituality has the distinct characteristic of involving spiritual seekers in political and social concerns. Because environmental destruction is a product of a complex global social system, spiritual resistance to that destruction requires an understanding of the system and the strategic decisions aimed at opposing it. Environmental spirituality is thus the natural heir of the spiritual social activism manifested by Mohandas Gandhi and Martin Luther King Jr. (Gottlieb 2003a).

One advantage of a spiritual approach to environmental sanity and sustainability is that it offers much more than a simple rejection of destructive environmental practices like consumerism. Because spirituality is ultimately not about self-sacrifice but about long-lasting and genuine fulfillment, spiritually oriented environmentalists point out the manifold ways in which other forms of human happiness can replace the temporary and addictive nature of consumption. The Jewish spiritual thinker and committed environmentalist Rabbi Michael Lerner, for example, emphasizes the idea of a Sabbath in which the making or spending of money and the extensive use of machines have no place: "Dedicate this day to joy, celebration, humor and pleasure. Let Go of Worry. . . . For one day out of the week, don't try to change, shape or transform the world. Respond to it with joy, celebration, awe and wonder. Open yourself to the miracle and mystery of the universe" (Lerner 2002, 300–301).

Another dimension of environmental spirituality—with roots most obviously in indigenous traditions but also in Abrahamic religions and secular environmentalism—involves a sensibility in which the natural world possesses its own spiritual subjectivity. Here not only do we appreciate nature as a gift and protect it through the development of spiritual virtues such as moderating desires, we commune with it as a fellow citizen of our planet. For indigenous traditions, as one Native American environmental activist asserted, "there is a profound spiritual dimension to our natural environment and without it, the war [to protect Native American lands] would not be worth fighting" (Small 1994). In general, indigenous peoples "all over the world have viewed themselves as members of a community of beings, in coexistence with fellow creatures be they trees, birds, streams, or rocks. Many of these are revered and protected as sacred" (Gadgil and Guha 1995, 91). Just

because nature has spirit, it is appropriate to be spiritual in our relations to it. At the very least, this entails care, respect, gratitude, and moderate of use resources. It will also require extensive interactive knowledge—knowledge based not in mechanical reduction but in respectful interspecies communication (Nollman 2002).

Indigenous and Traditional Views

Although the concept of human dominion over nature, or, at best, stewardship of the Earth as a gift from God, has been the main interpretive lens for understanding the relationship between humans and nature in Western religions, there are other, albeit marginalized, perspectives within the tradition. Each species, says the Quran (6:28), is a "community like yours." Biblical psalms (for example, Psalms 19 and 96) celebrate nature not only as evidence of God's power and generosity, but as marked by the capacity to celebrate God in its own way. A midrash (Jewish interpretive fable) even states that all the parts of nature follow their own Torah as those of the Jewish faith follow theirs. This acknowledges a widespread, if often violated, sensibility in which human beings exist in a world of living, significant, fellow beings.

The vocabulary of spirit and spirituality comes naturally to members of religious traditions, and not surprisingly permeates the writings of the new ecotheology of the last two decades, but it is also widespread in the ostensibly secular environmental movement (Gottlieb 2006, Chapter 6). As a public spokesman for Greenpeace USA stated, "There is broad acceptance among Greenpeace staff that the work is quintessentially spiritual, though definitions of what is meant by the term vary" (Childs 1999, 50). A survey of key environmental thinkers and groups, from conservationists such as John Muir and Sigurd Olson to large activist movements in the twenty-first century, reveals that this "spiritual" dimension of "the work" has at least three fundamental characteristics. First, the object of concern is generally considered to be all of life, rather than the interests of some particular social group. Although opposition to destructive policies is a key part of the movement, there is also a sense that the ultimate goal is health for "everyone"—all people, all living beings, all of the Earth. Second, the motivation for the work is a celebration of existence rather than a rage at oppression or injustice. It is about devotion rather than hate, about the desire to cherish and nourish rather than to overthrow or cast down. Third, there is a noticeable use of spiritual or religious terms. People often argue for the preservation of wilderness as "a site for spiritual, mystical, or religious encounters: places to experience mystery, moral regeneration, spiritual revival, meaning, oneness, unity, wonder, awe, inspiration, or a sense of harmony with the rest of creation . . . " (Nelson 1998, 168).

Environmental organizations talk about preserving the natural world as a "sacred trust." The Sierra Club joined with the National Council of Churches in a television ad calling on Americans to defend the Arctic Natural Wildlife Refuge as part of "creation." The environmental justice movement, seemingly the most people-centered and hardcore political form of environmentalism, takes as the first of its guiding principles a commitment to "our spiritual interdependence to the sacredness of our Mother Earth."

Spiritual Practice

Finally, we must consider the dimension of spiritual practice. Virtually all forms of spirituality—whether keyed to a traditional denomination or not—recognize that cultivating the spirit, especially in the face of the social realities that are bent on the spirit's denial, requires concentration and diligence. Prayer, meditation, rituals, and the study of sacred texts have been used to focus the mind, cultivate detachment, and orient human wills toward the ultimate reality that is the foundation of any spiritual path.

In response to the spiritual meaning of the environmental crisis, a whole range of rituals—some traditional in form and some new—have been created (Gottlieb 2006, Chapter 7; Gottlieb 2003b). Hundreds of examples of both traditional and newly fashioned ritual forms have arisen. Conventional congregations are saying prayers for the Earth to express their own guilt and remorse and to ask for God's help in changing their ways. In Nigeria's oil-rich Ogoni peninsula, for example, where operations by Shell have devastated the landscape and the human communities alike, a Christian pastor led his flock in praying that "no petroleum oil will be discovered in our communities. Indeed, Lord, let the oil underneath our houses and farms drift away from us." As part of southern Zimbabwe's ecumenical tree-planting campaign, a Christian bishop leading a tree-planting Eucharist addressed a seedling with the words, "Jesus Christ has created all things to be united in him. I shall not chop down another tree. Through you, tree, I do penance for all the trees I have felled" (Daneel 2001, 185). In larger contexts, the National Council of Churches and the U.S. Council of Catholic Bishops have sent out hundreds of thousands of packets to members offering resources for Earth Day services, including prayers and rituals to reconnect parishioners to nature.

In the realms of more independent, eclectic spirituality, perhaps the best-known innovation comes from Joanna Macy, a Buddhist and deep ecologist (one who sees environmentalism as extending beyond purely human interests), and John Seed, an Australian rain forest activist. As part of their Council of All Beings workshops, attendees spend hours imagining themselves as some nonhuman member of the web of life: a river, an otter, a maple tree. In an exercise of extreme, trans-species imaginative empathy, they then form a "council," reporting to others what words of sadness, hope, or instruction they have for humans.

Because the environmental crisis so severely challenges virtually all facets of the global economy and the world's cultures, contemporary understandings of spirit and spirituality will take new and unforeseen forms. But at least one age-old facet of spirit and spirituality remains. An unyielding commitment to the reality of spirit, even in the face of remorseless and unthinking political, economic, or ideological power, rests on a stubborn refusal to give up on human freedom. To believe that we are spirit, as well as all the other things we may be, is to say that whatever we have been, we can be something else. In this sense of spirit and spirituality, then, they remain the best chance humanity has, not only for facing the truth of the past but for creating a new truth in the future. Environmental spirituality offers at least a little hope that religion can desist from being a passionate attachment to private salvation or group-specific monopolized truth; and politics can avoid the trap of being little but organized, short-sighted self-interest. Both spiritual politics and politicized spirituality can serve as visionary attempts to harmonize the personal, the global, and the cosmic.

Roger S. GOTTLIEB
Worcester Polytechnic Institute

FURTHER READING

Ammar, Nawal H. (2003). An Islamic response to the manifest ecological crisis: Issues of justice. In Roger S. Gottlieb (Ed.), *This sacred Earth: Religion, nature, environment* (2nd ed., pp. 285–289). New York. Routledge.

Childs, Christopher. (1999). *The spirit's terrain: Creativity, activism, and transformation.* Boston: Beacon Press.

Daneel, Martinus L. (2001). *African earthkeepers: Wholistic interfaith mission.* Maryknoll, NY: Orbis Books.

Gadgil, Madhav, & Guha, Ramachandra. (1995). *Ecology and equity: The use and abuse of nature in contemporary India.* London and New York: Routledge.

Gottlieb, Roger S. (2003a). *A spirituality of resistance: Finding a peaceful heart and protecting the Earth.* Lanham, MD: Rowman and Littlefield.

Gottlieb, Roger S. (2003b). *This sacred Earth: Religion, nature, environment* (2nd ed.). New York. Routledge.

Gottlieb, Roger S. (2006). *A greener faith: Religious environmentalism and our planet's future.* New York: Oxford University Press.

Kaza, Stephanie. (2005). *Hooked! Buddhist writings on greed, desire, and the urge to consume.* Boston: Shambhala.

Lerner, Michael. (2002). *Spirit matters.* New York: Walsch Books.

Nelson, Michael P. (1998). An amalgamation of wilderness preservation arguments. In Michael Nelson & J. Baird Calicott (Eds.), *The great new wilderness debate* (pp. 154–198). Athens: University of Georgia Press.

Nollman, Jim. (2002). *The man who talks to whales.* Boulder, CO: Sentient Publications.

Small, Gail. (March 22, 1994). The search for environmental justice in Indian country. *Amicus Journal.*

Stewardship

Stewardship and environmental sustainability have been linked since biblical times. Stewardship ideals are accepted and discussed by religious congregations, ecologists, environmental organizations, politicians, and corporations alike. Stewardship incorporates sustainable utilization of natural resources, thoughtful care for the environment, and appropriately sharing the Earth as household, with other humans and other species.

The word "stewardship" comes from the Old English word "stiweard," now spelled "steward," which means someone appointed to manage or supervise a house or a hall. A steward may also be responsible for an estate, land-holdings, royal household, or guild. The steward serves someone else: a king, a property owner, an organization, or a community. "Stewardship" can have an explicitly religious context, such as administering or distributing wealth provided by God (Trumble 2002, 3026). Used in a modern environmental context, the term stewardship carries many of its original implications, including service in the interest of others, careful management of natural and fiscal resources, and providing for the safety and comfort of both residents and guests. Stewardship invokes images of the Earth as a household, which we share, not just with other humans but with all living organisms, including wildlife, trees, and even microorganisms.

The connection between stewardship and environmental sustainability is of biblical origin, although the concept has spread widely to the general public and even among politicians. Ironically, the King James Bible or "authorized" version

utilizes the word "steward" in the parables of Jesus, but not in any biblical passages describing the creation of the Earth, the Garden of Eden, or direct human care for plants or animals (Staff of Thomas Nelson Bibles, 2002). Environmental stewardship is a modern construction on ancient foundations. In Genesis 43, the Torah describes Joseph's brothers coming to Egypt in the time of famine. Joseph instructs his steward to provide food and to place money in their sacks. The household steward also gives them water, washes their feet, and feeds their donkeys. In the Gospel of Mathew 20, the owner of a vineyard, as a metaphor for God, instructs his steward to pay the faithful laborers. Luke 12:42 distinguishes the faithful and wise steward who provides food for his slaves, whereas Luke 16 commends the shrewd steward who ingratiates himself to his master's debtors by forgiving what they owe. Perhaps most directly applicable to the contemporary Christian context is the Letter of Paul to Titus 1:7, which declares a Christian bishop must be a steward of God, blameless and moderate in behavior, avoiding the temptation of "filthy lucre." Christians apply the concept of stewardship specifically to handling congregational finances, or managing personal finances in a responsible way, which sets aside money for charity or for religious purposes (Staff of Thomas Nelson Bibles, 2002; Coogan, Brettler, Newsom, and Perkins 2007).

Christians have combined the role of a steward as a servant of God with the Genesis passages that describe humans as created in the image of God (1:26), and God placing Adam in the garden "to till and to keep it" (2:15) (Coogan, Brettler, Newsom, and Perkins 2007). These passages imply humans should be stewards of the Earth, using what God has provided, while serving God's interests. Sound stewardship incorporates care of one's neighbors, preserving the beauty of the Creation, protecting the poor and needy, and treating the Earth as if it belongs to God.

The words "ecology" and "economics" are derived from the Greek word *oikos*, which means "house" or "household." The New Testament makes frequent use of *oikos* to identify families, lineage, ethnicities, or homes, including those that are pious or well managed. Both religious and non-religious environmentalists have reasoned that the stewardship model suggests astute management of the *oikos*, or the Earth's household, as well as of the resource economics of the Earth (Morrison 1979, 283–284). The ideal steward combines thoughtful decision making, accountability, measured administration, a heart for the common good, and a balanced concern for the ecological, family, and national spheres of interest.

Stewardship and Sustainability

Environmental stewardship is often linked to the concept of sustainability. Although sustainability is discussed in diverse arenas—from the United Nations to the U.S. Congress to businesses to high schools—a universally accepted definition of the word has, thus far, proven elusive. The environmentalist Sharad LèLè (1991, 608) notes "the concept of sustainability originated in the context of renewable resources such as forests or fisheries, and has subsequently been adopted as a broad slogan by the environmental movement." Initially, professional resources managers sought "sustainable" means for harvesting resources that could replenish themselves through regrowth, recharge, or reproduction (such as rangelands, tree plantations, or groundwater), or that, like sunlight or geothermal energy, would outlast the human race. Sustainable environmental management practices should provide food, water, energy, or building materials over not just years but centuries. Ideally, sustainable policies and strategies leave productive farms, fisheries, and aquifers for the use and enjoyment of future generations. The concept of sustainability spread easily to environmentally focused awareness organizations such as Greenpeace and Sierra Club, because the public accepts the importance of maintaining the economic viability of natural resource extraction.

Nonprofit organizations, however, are apparently not the only proponents of sustainability. Although multibillion dollar corporations such as the major oil companies have come under fire from environmental groups, they have responded with their own definitions of sustainability. In the company's 2007 Corporate Citizenship Report, ExxonMobil articulated their policy of striving to "conduct business throughout the world in a manner that is protective of the environment and compatible with the environmental and economic needs of the communities in which we operate." The report described of the corporation's commitment to "improving our environmental performance through scientifically sound and practical solutions with the goal of driving incidents with real environmental impact to zero." Although one might question if ExxonMobil's goal of reducing anthropogenic levels of environmental influences to zero is actually possible, ExxonMobil is one of many resource-based corporations considering whether their current production strategies are sustainable over decades or centuries. The U.S. National Science Foundation (2009) supports research into sustainable engineered systems "that support human well-being and that are also compatible with sustaining natural (environmental) systems. These systems provide ecological services vital for human survival. The long-term viability of natural capital is critical for many areas of human endeavor."

Stewardship is compatible with sustainability, as both call for long-term and well-planned economic administration, and both share the goal of continued provision for the entire Earth household or community. The two concepts are often combined to make a more robust model for environmental action or policy. International Business Machine Corporation (2008) released a "white paper" calling for both sustainable energy production business strategies and corporate commitment to "environmental stewardship," in the belief sustainable growth is consistent with corporate social responsibility. To promote environmental sustainability in the twenty-first century, environmental ethicists have proposed a holistic ecological approach based on three of the main facets of our society and implemented through policy initiatives and environmental legislation that foster economic, social, and environmental stewardship. Thus the success in fostering stewardship and implementing environmental sustainability policy at the national level hinges on the reconciliation of different communities' interests concerning resource use, economic growth, and societal wellbeing (Barrett and Grizzle 1998). It is only by defining environmental sustainability as a conscious synthesis of various parties' desires that the health of the Earth will be able to flourish along with economically motivated interests, and all facets of our society will be able to truly thrive.

Religion and Environmental Stewardship

Evangelical theologians began to publish entire volumes on the general topic of stewardship in the 1950s (Sheldon 1992). In the early 1960s, Arthur Peacocke introduced the term into discussions of the relationship between religion and science, and by the 1970s stewardship had "become the environmentalist path most often proposed by Protestant Christians seeking to serve God and God's creation" (Fowler 1995, 76). In 1980, the Fellows of Calvin Center for Christian Scholarship published *Earthkeeping: Christian Stewardship of Natural Resources,* edited by the theologian Loren Wilkinson. The volume and its revised edition helped to convey the idea of stewardship as "the exercise of delegated dominion in the service of creation" to students at faith-based colleges and to evangelical congregations (Wilkinson 1980, 308). Douglas John Hall culminated a series of theological projects projecting the steward as an ideal Christian caring for life in a world dominated by death and sin (Hall 1986). Jews, including David Ehrenfeld, a founder of the Society for Conservation Biology, entered the dialogue about the biblical basis for environmental care, as did Roman Catholics, who emphasized the critical link between stewardship and social justice (Ehrenfeld and Bentley 1998; Jegen and Mano 1978).

A key religious theme has been that humans do not own the Earth as property, but the planet belonged to God in perpetuity, and therefore should be managed to reflect God's interests, including care for the poor and sharing with others. Stewardship assumes care and provision for future generations, and for all God's creatures. A proper application of stewardship corrects misinterpretation of biblical passages such as Genesis 1:26, which in some translations instructs humans to "take dominion over the Earth." Both secular and religious stewardship advocates believe stewardship is a duty of all humans, which we have often failed to fulfill. Stewardship celebrates the beauty and wonder in nature, as well as the human dependence on a well-cared-for environment (Fowler 1995; Berry 2006).

Criticisms and Successes

Some environmentalists have criticized the stewardship position as too oriented toward resource use and too complacent concerning current economic strategies for environmental exploitation. As such, it can seem to be a compromise with middle-class values. Christian views of stewardship may also view humanity in separation from their environments by holding that humans play a special role in creation or have a divine call to stewardship, whereas some environmentalists reject the concept that humans are unique, or attempt to overcome dualist views that emphasize human uniqueness (Fowler 1995, 78).

A success of the stewardship model, however, is it widely accepted by moderate to conservative members of biblically based faiths, including Evangelical Christians. It incorporates the issues of family care and economic security, which are of high concern to religious practitioners with a commitment to biblical ethics. Stewardship also can provide an attractive basis for religious environmental ethics that emphasize the ultimate authority of God.

Although stewardship has been a widespread model for environmental care, for more than half a century, sophisticated discourse continues. Robert J. Berry (2006), a geneticist, has assembled an entire volume on the topic of Christian environmental stewardship with commentaries on a variety of environmental issues. Berry's collection covers both the weaknesses of the stewardship model, and provides potential new applications, including sea Sabbaths for stressed fisheries and purification for chemically overloaded agricultural soils. The theologian Michael Northcott (2007) has invoked historic Christian commitment to "careful stewardship," including sharing resources with the poor, simultaneously with sustainable dwellings, food production, and energy economics, as a route to resolving a very current issue: the excessive contribution of wealthy nations to the increasing level of green house gases in the atmosphere. Northcott (2007) presents both concepts as encouraging common citizen to pursue actions likely to curtail impending global climate change.

Stewardship has become an important model for appropriate attitudes toward long-term environmental use, care, and respect. Today, it is often in combination with advocacy for sustainability. Stewardship ideals are accepted and discussed by religious congregations, ecologists, environmental organizations, politicians, and corporations alike.

Susan Power BRATTON
Austin COOK-LINDSAY
Baylor University

FURTHER READING

Barrett, Christopher B., & Grizzle, Raymond E. (1999). A holistic approach to sustainability based on pluralistic stewardship. *Environmental Ethics, 21*(1), 23–42.

Berry, Robert J. (2006). *Environmental stewardship: Critical perspectives, past and present*. London: Continuum Publishing.

Coogan, Michael D.; Brettler, Mark Z.; Newsom, Carol A.; & Perkins, Pheme. (Eds.). (2007). *New Oxford annotated Bible with the Apocrypha, augmented third edition, New Revised Standard Version*. Oxford, U.K.: Oxford University Press.

Ehrenfeld, David, & Bentley, P. J. (1985). Judaism and the practice of stewardship. *Judaism: A Quarterly Journal of Jewish Life and Thought, 34*, 301–311.

ExxonMobil Corporation. (2007). Corporate citizenship report. (Brochure). Retrieved April 19, 2009, from http://www.exxonmobil.com/Corporate/files/Corporate/community_ccr_2007.pdf

Fowler, Robert Booth. (1995). *The greening of Protestant thought*. Chapel Hill: University of North Carolina Press.

Hall, John Douglas. (1986). *Imaging God: Dominion as stewardship*. New York: Eerdmans/Friendship Press.

International Business Machine Corporation (IBM). (2008). Improving business responsibility through smart energy and environmental policy. Retrieved April 18, 2009, from http://www.935.ibm.com/services/us/cio/energy/assets/ee_feature_offer_wp.pdf

Jegen, M. E., & Manno, B. V. (Eds.). (1978). *The Earth is the Lord's: Essays on stewardship*. New York: Paulist Press.

LèLè, Sharad. (1991). Sustainable development: A critical review. *World Development, 19*(6), 607–621.

Morrison, Clinton. (1979). *An analytical concordance to the Revised Standard Version of the New Testament*. Philadelphia: Westminster Press.

Northcott, Michael. (2007). *A moral climate: The ethics of global warming*. Maryknoll, NY: Orbis Books.

Sheldon, Joseph. (1992). *Rediscovery of Creation: A bibliographic study of the Church's response to the environmental crisis*. American Theological Library Association Bibliography Series, No. 29. Metuchen, NJ: Scarecrow Press.

Staff of Thomas Nelson Bibles. (2002). *Compact Holy Bible King James Version (KJV), containing the Old and New Testaments*. Nashville, TN: Thomas Nelson Publishers.

Trumble, William R. (Ed.). (2002). "Steward" and "Stewardship." *Shorter Oxford English Dictionary, Vol. 2, N–Z, 5th edition*. Oxford, U.K.: Oxford University Press.

U.S. National Science Foundation. (2009). Environmental sustainability (program page). Retrieved April 18, 2009 from http://www.nsf.gov/

Wilkinson, Loren, (Ed.). (1980). *Earthkeeping: Christian stewardship of natural resources*. Grand Rapids, MI: William B. Eerdmans.

Wilkinson, Loren, (Ed.). (1991). *Earthkeeping in the '90s: Stewardship of Creation*. Grand Rapids, MI: William B. Eerdmans.

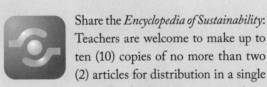

Subsistence

Subsistence, the traditional worldview of indigenous peoples, involves a spiritual, respectful relationship to the land and all living beings. Anthropological and sociological definitions of subsistence feed a "developed nation" sense of superiority over subsistence life; they do not recognize that all cultures are subsistence cultures. The subsistence worldview has important implications for sustainability and the future of humanity.

Sustainability has its roots in the much more ancient concept of subsistence, and that concept can help place contemporary discussions of sustainability in context with contemporary ways of life and worldviews. Subsistence involves more than practical strategies for using basic resources; it evokes rich intellectual and spiritual patterns. To understand this fully, a common definition of the term *subsistence* must be recognized and rejected.

Subsistence in Anthropology and Sociology

Anthropology generally defines subsistence as the means by which a society comes by its food. This definition narrows subsistence to an economic term, and indeed, many anthropologists speak of a "subsistence economy." Defining subsistence in this way may seem appropriate to observers who see village people on the land, pursuing the most easily visible portion of a subsistence life. In Alaska, for instance, where many people still pursue a subsistence life, nonnative lay people and academics may speak of subsistence as "hunting, fishing, and berry-picking." (This article provides specific examples from indigenous Alaskan groups to make points about subsistence life in general.)

Sociology frequently ties subsistence to the technology used to carry out subsistence activities, and some sociologists tie a culture's entire social structure to its use of technology. Sociology, especially ecological-evolutionary theory (EET), classifies a culture according to the "level" of its technology. Subsistence technology in this context refers to the tools necessary to obtain food and the basic necessities of life.

The earliest cultures are identified as "hunters and gatherers." A second level that uses a higher level of technology is comprised of "simple horticulturalists." At a level above them are the "complex horticulturalists." A still higher level of culture is identified as "agrarian." The contemporary (tenth) level is termed "industrial." These levels represent a hierarchy of ascendance that developed as societies moved away from hunter-gatherer subsistence. Some scholars use other terms for these stratifications, but the highest, most complex, and most evolved culture always seems to be the Western market culture, as if this culture has severed its subsistence roots in favor of a "cash economy" or an "industrial economy." Contemporary nonnative cultures, and Western dictionaries, sometimes refer to subsistence people as living at a "*mere* subsistence level."

One value of such hierarchical lists is that they do not explicitly deny the subsistence life that is the foundation of every culture from ancient to modern. Their liability is that they fail to mention explicitly that all cultures everywhere are still subsistence cultures. Such lists, wittingly or unwittingly, feed a Western sense of superiority and result in the condescension that Western "developed" cultures exhibit toward those still living the subsistence life. The lists enable societies to forget they are all still hunters and gatherers, and not much more evolved or sophisticated than, say, Inupiat and Yup'ik Eskimo cultures or Aboriginal cultures. Rather than hunting, fishing, and berry picking, many members of "developed" cultures obtain food by driving to the nearest supermarket. Purchasing food allows the illusion that indigenous peoples' subsistence is tied to the land, while contemporary market cultures are not. While many people in "developed" cultures no longer gather food directly and may have no idea of its production and provenance, their dependence on the land is no less strong, only less visible and direct.

Subsistence and Indigenous Peoples

Indigenous peoples start with a different definition of subsistence, and they use a more revealing and comprehensive vocabulary when talking about it. Most indigenous people give themselves a name that means "the people," "the real people," or "the people of this place." An example of a traditional name for a Yup'ik Eskimo group would be "Kuskokwagmiut." The suffix *miut* means "people," and combined with the stem *Kuskokwag*, the whole word means "people of the Kuskokwim River." The people and place are bonded together in their sense of themselves and their land, and the bond is deeply embedded in their language. Until recently, indigenous tribes did not think of themselves as a "culture," but as a "people." "I never heard the word *culture* used in southwestern Alaska thirty years ago," writes the anthropologist Ann Fienup-Riordan. "Today it is on everyone's lips." It came into use as Yup'iks were forced "to preserve and reproduce past practices and defend them against assimilationist pressures" (Fienup-Riordan 2005, xiii).

Culture is a word that may be appropriate for nonindigenous life; it has roots deep in the language of Western culture, and it is related to many contemporary words including *cult, agriculture, cultivated,* and *cultured.* The latter two terms have come to mean *educated* and *sophisticated,* and they have lost the descriptive indication that has to do with agriculture, the land, religion, and the sacred.

Village people in Alaska describe subsistence as "our way of life," or they say, "Subsistence is our life." Subsistence for them includes more than hunting, fishing, and berry picking. It is more than a set of strategies, practices, or technologies for gathering food, which are but parts of a worldview much larger in scope. Philosophy, theology, history, literature, biology, hydrology, geology, ethics, mores, relationships, kinship patterns, and the arts of music,

dance, sculpture, drawing, and storytelling are all part of what village people mean when they talk about subsistence. Subsistence involves a highly intellectual and richly spiritual life that ramifies through every act. Modern cultures break these into different disciplines and give them separate roles. In the indigenous subsistence life, everything is connected, and each relationship, whether with other humans or with all the other manifestations of the natural world, is one of relative to relative. Fienup-Riordan (2005, 235) writes of "the ideology of subsistence":

> In contrast to the modern separation between society and nature, at the core of Yup'ik views of non-Natives is their belief that all persons—including animals and *ircenrraat* [spirits, whether animal or human]—are essentially related. Among the most profound expressions of this view is the well-known adage, *Ella-ggug allamek yuituq,* translated variously as "Humankind populates the world, and all peoples are one" and, more literally, "The world contains no others, only persons."

Since in Yup'ik tradition all peoples, fish, birds, animals, plants, and landforms have personhood, relationships with them are nourished and maintained by respect. Respect becomes the key for traditional people created by Raven or any other mythical creature.

"They were created by Raven," writes the cultural anthropologist A. Oscar Kawagley (1995, 31) speaking of his own Yup'ik Eskimo heritage, "so how could they be better than or superior to other animals, plants, and the earth?"

That respect, engendered by the worldview, ramifies throughout the whole concept of subsistence. It is outwardly demonstrated in making tools; in dance; in the ritual handling of fish, game, and birds; in the telling of stories; in the education of the young; and even in the naming of children.

Links between Subsistence and Sustainability

For modern, industrialized Western culture, sustainability has become an important word, especially in the last two decades. There have been calls for a sustainable environment, sustainable yields of fish and timber, sustainable communities, and sustainable economies. Not many are calling for a sustainable culture yet, although it is becoming increasingly clear that we do not have a sustainable culture, and fear seems to be growing that we may not even be a sustainable species. We are witness to the end point of Earth's fossil fuels, increasingly polluted rivers and lakes, and aquifers that are being drained faster than they can replenish themselves. The toxic burden carried in our bodies has increased dramatically, and children's bodies are carrying a heavier toxic burden than their parents' bodies.

The picture is further complicated as we recognize that Earth's topsoil has been either sterilized by our use of toxic chemicals or lost to erosion; climate change has disturbed weather patterns; food no longer contains the nutritional value it had a generation ago, and what some call the sixth great species die-out is accelerating. Even the rain we once prayed, danced, and gave reverent thanks for has become an acidic enemy because we've not done enough to control the emissions of our industrial smokestacks and automobile tailpipes. The necessity for creating a sustainable culture has become an urgent reality.

This dilemma has grown from modern culture, not from indigenous people of the land. We are just dimly beginning to realize that our culture is not as distant from our land, or immune to the implications of its misuse, as we once thought. The technologies we've created haven't bent nature to our will, as it seems we intended them to do since the time of Sir Isaac Newton (1643–1727), and they have apparently fostered the problems we now face. On the other hand, indigenous peoples have sustained themselves for thousands of years longer than Western civilization. If time is stretched a bit, our Western heritage can be traced back about 3,000 years. Archaeology can trace Aleut, Eskimo, and Athapaskan peoples back 14,000 years. What has allowed them to persist while more knowledgeable societies with more sophisticated science and technology are failing and endangering us all? These indigenous populations must know something we Westerners have not yet learned.

Mary Evelyn Tucker, a scholar of religion and ecology at Yale University, was not writing about subsistence in *Confucianism and Ecology*, but her comment describes perfectly the way in which modern "developed" cultures consider the natural world: "Nature is seen as a 'resource' to be used rather than a 'source' of all life to be respected" (Tucker and Berthrong 1998, 189). Rather than denigrate those who live at a "mere subsistence level," we might learn that in order to become a sustainable culture, we may have to change our worldview to align it more closely to the view that traditional people have held for millennia.

Our first steps toward sustainability begin with our recognition that all cultures are subsistence cultures, although not all cultures are sustainable. Our modern culture is as dependent on the land and all its "ten thousand things," as the ancient Chinese spoke of it, as any subsistence people

ever were, although we seem to have become blind to this fact. Roaming oil geologists are as much hunter-gatherers as are indigenous caribou hunters. When those modern geologic hunters fail, jobs are lost, food becomes scarce, and hunger stalks the land. Our industrialized cultures have not dealt with the land with respect; instead, we have used the land for our advantage. We have seen nature as a resource, and we have abused it to the point that it is refusing to support us any longer. How do we now deal with this?

When successful, the indigenous subsistence hunter does not assume it was his skill that brought the deer down; instead, he gives thanks to the deer for giving itself up to him. When the deer does not come down, the hunter assumes that he has failed to be faithful to the deer, and he examines himself to discover how he had offended the animal he depends on for survival. In our more modern culture we take nature's resources, leave the wreckage of "development" behind, and congratulate ourselves on our prowess. To shift Western developed culture toward sustainability, nature asks us to acknowledge that our contemporary culture is also a subsistence culture; it asks us to forsake our arrogance, examine our own behavior, and learn from the wisdom of traditional people about how we can relate to nature in a way that gives us a future.

Subsistence is never achieved once and for all. We create it daily as we choose how we will relate to other humans, other species, the land and all its attributes, and the air and waters that surround us all. If we decide to treat each element of nature with the respect it deserves, we may yet create a sustainable culture. If we continue to view nature as ours to exploit, we erect a discernable limit to the time we can subsist and survive. Sustainability has its roots deep in the concept of subsistence, a concept more ancient than Western civilization. It depends on worldview as much as it does on technology. The common task of all people is to create a sustainable culture by preserving our subsistence, each day, every day.

Gary HOLTHAUS
Island Institute; The Atheneum School

FURTHER READING

Bernard, Ted, & Young, Jora. (1997). *The ecology of hope: Communities collaborate for sustainability.* Gabriola Island, Canada: New Society.

Berry, Thomas. (1990). *The dream of the Earth.* San Francisco: Sierra Club Books.

Cajete, Gregory. (1994). *Look to the mountain: An ecology of indigenous education.* Asheville, NC: Kivaki Press.

Chamberlin, J. Edward. (2003). *If this is your land, where are your stories? Finding common ground.* Toronto: Alfred A. Knopf Canada.

Colburn, Theo; Dumanoski, Dianne; & Myers, John Peterson. (1997). *Our stolen future: Are we threatening our fertility, intelligence, and survival? A scientific detective story.* New York: Plume Books.

Fienup-Riordan, Ann. (1990). *Eskimo essays: Yup'ik lives and how we see them.* New Brunswick, NJ: Rutgers University Press.

Fienup-Riodan, Ann. (Ed.). (1996). *Agayuliyararput: Kegginaqut, Kangiit-llu* [*Our way of making prayer: Yup'ik masks and the stories they tell*]. (Marie Meade, Trans.) Seattle: University of Washington Press.

Fienup-Riordan, Ann. (2005). *Wise words of the Yup'ik people: We talk to you because we love you.* Lincoln: University of Nebraska Press.

Holthaus, Gary. (2006). *From the farm to the table: What all Americans need to know about agriculture.* Lexington: University Press of Kentucky.

Holthaus, Gary. (2008). *Learning native wisdom: What traditional cultures teach us about subsistence, sustainability, and spirituality.* Lexington: University Press of Kentucky.

Jackson, Wes. (1994). *Becoming native to this place.* Lexington: University Press of Kentucky.

Kawagley, A. Oscar. (1995). *A Yupiaq worldview: A pathway to ecology and spirit.* Prospect Heights, N J: Waveland Press.

McKibben, Bill. (2006). *The end of nature.* New York: Random House.

Morrow, Phyllis, & Schneider, William. (Eds.). (1995). *When our words return: Writing, hearing, and remembering oral traditions of Alaska and the Yukon.* Logan: Utah State University Press.

Nasr, Seyyed Hossein. (1996). *Religion and the order of nature.* New York: Oxford University Press.

Nelson, Richard K. (1983). *Make prayers to the raven: A Koyukon view of the northern forest.* Chicago: University of Chicago Press.

Schweitzer, Albert. (1953). *Out of my life and thought: An autobiography.* (C.T. Campion, Trans.). New York: New American Library.

Snyder, Gary. (1974). *Turtle Island.* New York: New Directions.

Tucker, Mary Evelyn, & Berthrong, John. (Eds.). (1998). *Confucianism and ecology: The interrelation of heaven, Earth, and humans.* Cambridge, MA: Harvard University Center for the Study of World Religions.

World Commission on Environment and Development. (1987). *Our common future.* Oxford: Oxford University Press.

PRODUCTION FOR USE VS. PRODUCTION FOR EXCHANGE

Subsistence economies often welcome the chance to learn from Western societies and their cash economies. But by adopting Western agricultural practices, small rural villages must abandon more than farming methods, often to their disadvantage. The social anthropologist Stephen Gudeman explores this situation in Panama in his book The Demise of a Rural Economy: From Subsistence to Capitalism in a Latin American Village.

I have a story to relate about a rural economy in Latin America. At its simplest the plot concerns the way in which the people of a small Panamanian village began to leave aside planting rice and maize in order to accommodate a new crop, sugar cane. But this crop change entailed more than a reorganization of agricultural practices: the introduction of sugar cane represented a transition from subsistence farming to cash cropping, and this agricultural reorientation itself presaged a total transformation of the people's economy. Thus, more broadly, my narrative is about a rural economy caught in the moment of transition between two competitive forms of organization, production for use and production for exchange. . . . An account of the local economy must stretch in time and space beyond the geographic borders of its ostensible subject. My story, then, revolves about a subsistence economy: to inquire into its essence is also to ask how it was generated by and maintained on the margins of a different economy, eventually to be absorbed by that larger system.

Source: Stephen Gudeman. (2004). *The Demise of a Rural Economy: From Subsistence to Capitalism in a Latin American Village*, p. 1. From the series *Routledge Library Editions: Anthropology and Ethnography, Volume 1 of South America.* London: Routledge. (Originally published 1978)

Sustainability Theory

Theories of sustainability attempt to prioritize and integrate social responses to environmental and cultural problems. An economic model looks to sustain natural and financial capital; an ecological model looks to biological diversity and ecological integrity; a political model looks to social systems that realize human dignity. Religion has entered the debate with symbolic, critical, and motivational resources for cultural change.

In its literal rudiments, sustainability means a capacity to maintain some entity, outcome, or process over time. Agriculture, forest management, or financial investment might be deemed sustainable, meaning that the activity does not exhaust the material resources on which it depends. An analogous use of the term "sustainability" refers to dependent social conditions; for example, a peace treaty, an economic policy, or a cultural practice may be called sustainable if it will not exhaust the support of a political community. In its increasingly common use, the concept of sustainability frames the ways in which environmental problems jeopardize the conditions of healthy economic, ecological, and social systems.

On a global scale the political challenge of sustainability raises a set of basic problems and comprehensive goals. By focusing on the ecological dependency of economic and social systems, sustainability illuminates the mutual effects between environmental degradation caused by human activities and the perils to human systems presented by global environmental problems. The concept of sustainability thus raises a starkly basic question: can human activity successfully maintain itself and its goals without exhausting the resources on which it depends?

Asking that question directs attention toward the planetary impact of human activity and its durability over time. It therefore provokes reflection on the manner and

purposes of global human society. Problems like biodiversity loss and climate change point to the global reach of humanity's powers and the scale of its risk. Mitigating their impact and risk seems to require reform across many human systems—financial, political, production, energy, transportation, and even communication and education. Yet those reforms could complicate other goals of the international community, such as overcoming extreme poverty and protecting human rights. How can these overlapping interests be prioritized?

Of course the mutual relations that sustainability brings into view illuminate the dependency of those goals on ecological conditions; overcoming poverty cannot, over the long run, stand in competition with protecting sufficient biodiversity. The practical challenge of sustainability is to find specific ways to pursue those distinct goals that conform to their mutual relation. Therein lies the possibility of maintaining (or developing) over time a decent quality of human life for all. Sustainability concepts thus confront societies with a new kind of moral question: What must be sustained? What goods may be imperiled by the dramatic expansion of human systems? Which goods must be protected? Which goals must be pursued? And what is the shared foundation for doing so?

Within particular institutions, those practical questions can be put into context by the group's purpose and its relation to ecological and social systems. For a university, sustainability may primarily be an aspect of how it manages its energy and food systems in relation not only to its budget, but also to its sense of civic leadership and educational mission. For a corporation, sustainability may mean anticipating how the reflexivity of ecological, economic, and social systems will determine market conditions over longer periods of time than those covered by quarterly or annual reports.

At local and global levels, then, sustainability directs practical attention to the complex mutuality of human and ecological systems. Economic health, ecological integrity, social justice, and responsibility to the future must be integrated to address multiple global problems within a coherent, durable, and moral social vision. That inclusive scope and prospective vision makes sustainability ideologically absorptive and politically popular. Sustainability is used to argue for and against climate treaties, for and against free markets, for and against social spending, and for and against environmental preservation. Finding a standard definition seems elusive.

Some critics have therefore dismissed sustainability as conceptually meaningless, or at least too susceptible to competing ideas to be politically useful. But as long as the disagreements generally recognize mutual feedback between human and ecological systems, they reflect substantive differences about what to sustain over time. So sustainability produces a significant discursive arena for a new kind of moral and political debate. Precisely because those considerations are so urgent and important, we should expect diversity of opinion and conceptual disagreement.

The very fact that debate about what should be sustained occurs as a practical political question indicates new dimensions of human responsibility and reflects new conditions of jeopardy. Humanity's technological and economic powers expanded so dramatically in the twentieth century that the fate of future generations and the survival of many other forms of life have now became subject to political decisions. Previously unthinkable impacts like a mass extinction caused by humanity or significant anthropogenic changes to the planet's biosphere indicate a major shift in humanity's relation to the rest of nature and its own future. Yet the twentieth century also witnessed the formation of an international community whose institutions pursued real expectations of lifting the poor from destitution and securing basic human rights in every country. Recognition of human responsibility has also expanded in temporal scope (i.e., obligations to future generations), spatial scale (i.e., consideration of planetary processes), and cultural reach (i.e., a shared ethic for all nations and peoples). Sustainability names a major way to invoke and organize these new responsibilities.

Brundtland and Beyond

The idea of sustainability came to public attention after a 1972 report, "Limits to Growth," issued by the international think tank Club of Rome. In 1980 the World Conservation Strategy developed by the International Union for Conservation of Nature, in collaboration with the U.N. Environment Programme and World Wildlife Foundation, worked to make sustainability a benchmark of international action. Then the term "sustainable development" achieved international public prominence through the 1987 report of the World Commission on Environment and Development, *Our Common Future*, often called the "Brundtland Report" after the name of its chair, former Norwegian prime minister Gro Harlem Brundtland. It presented the famous definition: "Sustainable development is development that meets the needs of the present without compromising the ability of future generations to meet their own needs" (WCED 1987, 43).

For many organizations and agencies, that formula or something close to it remains a working definition. Some have criticized the Brundtland definition for binding sustainability too closely to development and for focusing on human needs to the exclusion of other life. But the Brundtland Report has helped initiate an international public debate on sustainability that has since generated numerous alternative formulations.

This article focuses on the concept of "sustainability" as it stands apart from "sustainable development" and other related but distinct terms like "sustainable communities," "sustainable resource management," "sustainable livelihoods," or "sustainable societies." By first considering sustainability on its own, we can better understand how it has been adopted to define and modify other concepts and endeavors.

We have seen that sustainability is an inclusive and ambiguous concept precisely because it brings society's ecological dependency into moral relation with its economic and political systems. In an early expression of what that relation implies, the 1974 Cocoyoc Declaration (the result of a U.N.-sponsored symposium in Mexico) stated that sustainability relates "inner limits" of human needs to the "outer limits" of Earth's resources. Among the first uses of sustainability as a concept to help integrate response to related environmental and social problems was the 1975 program of the World Council of Churches (WCC) for a "just, participatory, and sustainable society." For the WCC, sustainability might well contradict existing development processes as well as reshape economic and political priorities.

Any appeal to sustainability proposes to somehow integrate responses to social and ecological problems, taking account of feedback between human and biophysical systems and assuming that there are limiting conditions to those systems. By focusing on the ecological embeddedness of human social systems, concepts of sustainability mitigate perceived tensions between humanist and environmental goals. Some, in fact, insist that properly conceived, the interests of human systems and ecological systems harmonize. Noting that global environmental problems threaten prospects for the human future, some suggest that the question of sustainability essentially amounts to a question about future generations: what do we owe the future? We should sustain, this approach implies, at least that which future generations will need to sustain themselves.

But settling what we owe to the future involves moral challenges of priority: Does the future need capital more than community, beauty more than opportunity? Whose future—that of humans? Of all species? Of the Earth? More importantly, reducing sustainability to an obligation to future generations ignores the relation of these obligations to the needs of the present. Certainly in its search for durable responses to global problems sustainability is a temporally prospective concept, but it does not reduce considerations of the future because it includes contemporary problems (like overcoming extreme poverty). As the Brundtland definition indicates, sustainability must seek a way to balance obligations to the present and the future.

So discourses and debates of sustainability aspire to sort out connections and priorities among an ecologically connected series of global responsibilities. By focusing ethical debate on the multiple goods at stake and the shared perils faced by the communities of Earth, sustainability forces consideration of what we must sustain by identifying what the Earth community stands to lose.

Models of Sustainability

What must we sustain? Answers to that question are sometimes divided into "strong" and "weak" approaches. "Strong sustainability" gives priority to the preservation of ecological goods, like the existence of species or the functioning of particular ecosystems. A "weak sustainability" disregards specific obligations to sustain any particular good, espousing only a general principle to leave future generations no worse off than we are. In terms of protecting old-growth forests, for example, a strong view might argue for protection, even if it requires foregoing development that would increase opportunities for future generations. A weak view would take into account the various benefits old-growth forests provide, and would then attempt to measure the future value of those benefits against the values created by development.

The two views loosely correspond to ecocentric (ecologically centered) and anthropocentric (human-centered) positions in environmental ethics, but not perfectly. The ecocentric view requires that moral decisions take into account the good of ecological integrity for its own sake, as opposed to exclusively considering human interests. But a strong sustainability view could be held from an anthropocentric perspective by arguing that human systems depend on rich biodiversity or that human dignity requires access to natural beauty.

Note also that a weak view would not necessarily approve the expiration of natural resources, even with the prospect of lucrative profit. For insofar as opportunities for future generations depend on certain ecological processes (e.g., breathable atmosphere), some ecological goods will always be more valuable than the economic development they make possible.

There is a third approach: A pragmatic middle view holds that, while we may not have obligations to sustain any particular nonhuman form of life or ecological process (the strong view), neither should we assume that all future opportunities can be measured against one another (the weak view). The moral and political philosopher Brian Barry (1997) argues that preservation of some opportunities for future generations requires the enduring existence of particular ecological goods. For example, the opportunity to decide whether or not old-growth forests are required for a decent human life depends on their preserved existence. This approach effectively proposes that we must sustain conditions for the ongoing debate over sustainability.

In another pragmatic approach, the philosopher Hans Jonas has proposed that new powers of human agency, able to comprehensively threaten their own conditions, require a new moral imperative to act responsibly for the sake of human survival. Perhaps sustainability is neither a strong question about nature's intrinsic value nor a weak one about producing opportunities but rather a pragmatic question about keeping our species in existence (Jonas 1984). Sustainability is then a question about maintaining a decent survival.

Critics will object to such pragmatic approaches from two angles. On one hand they look too humanistic: Neither old-growth forests nor threats to the survival of polar bears are priorities of the pragmatic view. On the other hand, they look insufficiently humanistic: reducing sustainability to survival of the species may multiply inequality and ongoing poverty. A pragmatist could respond that, if the priorities of sustainability depend on a debate over what sustains us, then the argument could certainly be made that old-growth forests and the existence of polar bears sustain the human spirit, as do socially just societies and flourishing neighbors. Perhaps, rightly conceived, a decent human survival simply includes biodiversity and the end of extreme poverty. Allowing the massive loss of species would close down that option for humanity, effectively ending the debate.

By now it is evident that theories of sustainability have become too complex to organize with dualistic terms like "strong" and "weak" or "ecocentric" and "anthropocentric." We might instead think in terms of models for sustainability, each prioritizing its own component of what must be sustained. These models—economic, ecological, and political—are not mutually exclusive and often integrate complementary strengths of the others. Distinguishing them, however, helps make sense of alternative concepts of sustainability.

Economic Models

Economic models propose to sustain opportunity, usually in the form of capital. According to the classic definition formulated by the economist Robert Solow, we should think of sustainability as an investment problem, in which we must use returns from the use of natural resources to create new opportunities of equal or greater value. Social spending on the poor or on environmental protection, while perhaps justifiable on other grounds, takes away from this investment and so competes with a commitment to sustainability.

With another view of capital, however, the economic model might look different. If we do not assume that "natural capital" is always interchangeable with financial capital, argue Herman Daly (1996) and other proponents of ecological economics, then sustaining opportunity for the future requires strong conservation measures to preserve ecological goods and to keep economies operating in respect of natural limits. These considerations complement an ecological model.

From a different perspective of the relation between opportunity and capital, spending on the poor might be regarded as a kind of investment in the future. According to the economist Amartya Sen's "development as freedom" dictum (1999), we create options for the future by creating options for today's poor because more options will drive greater development. In this political model of sustainability, sustaining opportunity for the future requires investing in individual dignity today. This approach complements the political model.

Ecological Models

Ecological models propose to sustain biological diversity and ecological integrity. That is, rather than focusing on opportunity or capital as the key unit of sustainability, they focus directly on the health of the living world (see Rolson 1994). Within this model, there are two major ways of deciding which ecological goods to sustain. From an anthropocentric point of view essential natural resources should be sustained, as should those ecological systems and regenerative processes on which human systems rely. From an ecocentric point of view species should be sustained for their intrinsic value, as should ecological systems as generators of creatures with intrinsic value. In policy, as noted above, strong and weak views may converge.

Political Models

Political models propose to sustain social systems that realize human dignity. Concerned with the way in which local and global environmental problems jeopardize human dignity, these models focus on sustaining the environmental conditions of a fully human life. Environmental justice and civic environmentalism represent one strategy of this model; by focusing on environmentally mediated threats to human life they point to necessary ecological goods or sustainable environmental management schemes (see Ageyman 2005). Other strategies within this model, such as agrarianism or deep ecology, involve more substantive visions of the human good. Ultimately, these models recommend sustaining the cultural conditions needed to realize ecological personhood, civic identity, or even personal faith through ecological membership (see Plumwood 2002, Wirzba 2003).

One subset of the political model takes a pragmatist's approach and suggests that we must maintain conditions for keeping open the debate about sustainability. In this view sustaining a political system of deliberative democracy effectively requires sustaining ecological and economic goods along with political goods like procedural rights. Note, however, that both the quality and quantity of those goods is regulated by the needs of the political system, which thereby constrains sustainability commitments.

Roles for Religious Views

Many twenty- and twenty-first-century thinkers in diverse fields include discussions of religious traditions, theological concepts, and spiritual practices in debates about sustainability. If sustainability already seems a complicated and pluralist moral concept, why involve religion?

Perhaps spiritual commitments motivate change, or religious communities wield powerful authority for cultural transformation. Perhaps the roots of globalizing economic and technological systems lie in a moral consciousness profoundly shaped by religion. In that view, meaningful cultural change depends on reconsidering those religious roots and criticizing certain religious attitudes in order to renew the sustaining power of cultural worldviews.

Another view on the role of religion in sustainability debates holds that religious metaphors and spiritual practices have unique capacities for interpreting life's complexity and generating holistic responses. If part of the challenge of sustainability is to understand the mutual relations of humanity and nature within a wider worldview, then religions may have useful resources. If widespread environmental degradation indicates an alienation of human personhood from the rest of the living Earth, then spiritual practices may help heal this division and reconcile humans to their ecological web.

For some communities, the crisis of sustainability presents an opportunity for religious renewal or spiritual renaissance. Certainly the world has witnessed, in all lands and from many cultures and traditions, new forms of religious change and spiritually motivated activism as communities attempt to comprehend and respond to ecological challenges. The Earth Charter, the definitive document (finalized in 2000) of the organization Earth Charter Initiative, represents a comprehensive plan to draw from many traditions and movements in order to invoke shared sacred values and to call humans into intimacy with the community of Earth.

Religious thought enters public sustainability debates as societies are increasingly challenged to make decisions about what is worth sustaining and to formulate questions about what sustains them. There is a paradoxical depth to such questions; although they inquire about the moral minimum of a decent survival, answering them invites reflection on the totality of what sustains us. For many, a good answer must reach toward the religious—toward spirit, the sacred, God, love, faith, or grace.

Because sustainability requires humans to recognize the simple facts of ecological dependency, it can provoke reflection on our dearest values and most fundamental beliefs, our intimate habits, and our overarching worldviews. To meet the challenges of sustainability in the twenty-first century individuals and communities alike are seeking ways in which to explore the *spirit* of sustainability—from creating new rituals, such as the Council of All Beings (workshops aimed at alleviating the alienation many people feel from the living Earth) to reviving ancient values, such as respect for God's creation.

Willis JENKINS
Yale Divinity School

FURTHER READING

Agyeman, Julian. (2005). *Sustainable communities and the challenge of environmental justice.* New York: New York University Press.

Barry, Brian. (1997). Sustainability and intergenerational justice. *Theoria, 45,* 43–65.

Daly, Herman E. (1996). *Beyond growth: The economics of sustainable development.* Boston: Beacon Press.

Daly, Herman E.; Cobb, John B.; & Cobb, Clifford W. (1994). *For the common good: Redirecting the economy toward community, the environment, and a sustainable future* (2nd ed.). Boston: Beacon Press.

Jenkins, Willis. (2008). Global ethics, Christian theology, and sustainability. *Worldviews: Global Religions, Culture, and Ecology, 12,* 197–217.

Jonas, Hans. (1984). *The imperative of responsibility.* Chicago: University of Chicago Press.

Meadows, Donella H.; Meadows, Dennis I.; Randers, Jorgen; & Behrens, William W. (1972). *The limits to growth: A report for the Club of Rome's project on the predicament of mankind.* New York: Universe Books.

Norton, Bryan G. (2005). *Sustainability: A philosophy of adaptive ecosystem management.* Chicago: University of Chicago Press.

Plumwood, Val. (2002). *Environmental culture: The ecological crisis of reason.* New York: Routledge.

Robinson, John. (2004). Squaring the circle? Some thoughts on the idea of sustainable development. *Ecological Economics, 48,* 369–384.

Rolston, Holmes, III. (1994). *Conserving natural value.* New York: Columbia University Press.

Sen, Amartya. (1999). *Development as freedom.* New York: Random House.

Solow, Robert M. (1993). Sustainability: An economist's perspective. In Robert Dorfman and Nancy S. Dorfman (Eds.), *Economics of the Environment* (pp. 179–187). New York: Norton.

The Earth Charter. (2000). Retrieved April 30, 2009, from http://www.earthcharterinaction.org/content/pages/Read-the-Charter.html

Wirzba, Norma. (2003). *The paradise of God: Renewing religion in an ecological age.* New York: Columbia University Press.

World Commission on Environment and Development (WCED). (1987). *Our common future.* Oxford, U.K.; New York: Oxford University Press.

T

Technology

Discussions involving technology and sustainability raise *a number of questions: How is technology implicated in the causes of unsustainability? Are technologies neutral tools able to serve the goal of sustainability as easily as any other? Or are technologies out of human control, or perhaps even in control of human destiny? Or are technologies complex political arrangements able to be renegotiated in a spirit of sustainability?*

Questions of sustainability inevitably bear on questions of technology. Although concepts of sustainability are caught up in complex theoretical debate, there is general agreement that these concepts can and ought to guide societies and individuals in bringing about positive practical change. Such practical change necessarily involves technological change.

At this point, however, general agreement breaks down and questions abound. How is technology implicated in unsustainable causes? Does sustainability require a return to preindustrial tools and techniques? Or does sustainability require a postindustrial revolution, in the form, say, of biotechnology and nanotechnology? Indeed, is a distinction between old and new technology helpful in the search for sustainability? Are simplicity, smallness and localness attributes of sustainable technology? Or are science and capitalism vital to sustainable technology? Is the idea of sustainable technology in fact coherent?

Answers to these questions reveal technology, like sustainability, to be a contested concept. The disputed, value-laden nature of sustainability is much remarked upon. Yet, despite the proliferation of technologies in modern life, the concept of technology has received little critical attention. Before reviewing links between technology and sustainability, therefore, it is necessary to gain clearer focus on the various meanings invested in the idea of technology.

What Is Technology?

The political theorist Langdon Winner (1977, 10) suggests that technology has "come to mean everything and anything; it therefore threatens to mean nothing." This suggestion may seem unconvincing, for it is relatively easy to describe the physical detail of technological artifacts and processes. While a physicist and a child will likely provide different descriptions of a mobile phone, there seems little point in arguing that mobile phones are not technology. It is, however, more difficult to provide a generic or systematic definition of technology. What, exactly, unites mobile phones, cheese, contraceptive pills, temples, and cloned sheep as technology?

Instrumentalism

A common way of simplifying the task of explaining technology is to distinguish between nonmodern and modern technology. Dictionaries rely on this distinction in defining technology as "the scientific study of the practical or industrial arts" (Oxford English Dictionary 1989). The claim that technology is scientific study asserts that although technological objects and processes can be readily described, this materiality is, in effect, immaterial to the meaning of technology. From this claim derives the assumption that technologies are value-neutral; that they are tools lacking their own significance. In this instrumentalist explanation, modern technology is applied science. Nonmodern technology is seen to involve the application of partial, nonscientific forms of knowledge, resulting in rudimentary technologies.

Objections may be raised against instrumentalism. For instance, there are cases in which modern technologies have preceded scientific explanation and engineering practice. There are also cases in which scientists have only recently been able to explain the knowledge embodied in nonmodern technologies, such as Stradivarius violins or the medicine of indigenous people. Allowing that they often provide accurate descriptions of technological knowledge, however, instrumentalist explanations nonetheless disregard technological experience. Although instrumentalism dominates the understanding of technology in science, economics, and policy, the experience of technology prompts very different explanations in culture more generally.

Determinism

Many influential cultural explanations of technology can be grouped together under the heading of *determinism*. Deterministic explanations suggest that technology is, at least in part, out of human control. Some determinist explanations go further, suggesting that technology is, at least in part, in control of humanity. For some, the idea that technology is in charge of human destiny is uplifting, with technology being represented as a law of human evolution. For others, this idea is distressing, with technology being represented as dehumanizing and unnatural. Many others remain ambivalent, finding technological influence in human affairs to be both good and bad.

It defies scientific logic to claim that the things humans make have a life of their own, and may transform from servants into masters of humanity. Technological determinism, however, takes root in the tangled material relationships made possible by technology in everyday life. It takes root especially in the conflicting feelings provoked by technologies, since the first axe made easier both the chopping of kindling and the taking of revenge. In this sense, technologies are inseparable from the desires and fears that shape human values. Automobiles, for example, may be explained instrumentally as the application of the first law of thermodynamics or as the sum of parts assembled on a factory production line. But as a paraplegic's means of mobility or a code of social status or a cause of climate change, automobiles may inhabit human experience as agents as well as tools.

Technology Under Challenge

The twentieth century witnessed profound technological change and sustained emphasis on the importance of technological progress in improving human life. Yet bleak portrayals of technological futures were also a recurrent feature of this period. The technological dystopias envisioned in Aldous Huxley's (1894–1963) *Brave New World* (1932) and George Orwell's (1903–1950) *Nineteen Eighty-Four* (1949), and the portrayal of Charlie Chaplin's (1889–1977) "little tramp" caught in the cogs of industrialization in the film *Modern Times* (1936) struck a chord with many.

Equally disturbing, if more ambivalent, visions of a future ruled by technology have more recently been a favored theme of science-fiction films, such as *2001: A Space Odyssey* (1968), *Blade Runner* (1982), and *The Matrix* trilogy (1999–2003).

In parallel with the presence of determinism in popular culture and the arts, a small but growing number of scholars challenged the dominance of instrumentalism in intellectual endeavor during the first two-thirds of the twentieth century. Although engineers and scientists remained the official authorities on technology, the historian Lewis Mumford (1895–1990), the philosopher Martin Heidegger (1889–1976), the critical theorist Herbert Marcuse (1898–1979), and the lay theologian Jacques Ellul (1912–1994), among others, paved the way for technology to become an accepted subject of the social sciences and humanities in the final decades of the twentieth century. Although defending themselves against charges of determinism, these scholars drew attention to philosophical challenges posed by modern technology and were influential in later environmentalist disaffection with technology.

Development and Sustainability

From their origins in the late 1960s, contemporary concepts of sustainability have been linked to instrumentalist, determinist and philosophical explanations of technology, giving rise to many different agendas for technological change. Such concepts have important historical antecedents, such as eighteenth-century European traditions of forest and fishery management. Today's ideas about sustainability nonetheless reflect the distinctive circumstances of the mid-twentieth century. After two global wars and a decade of economic depression, the post–World War II period was characterized by unprecedented economic and population growth and by dismantling of colonial empires. Although capitalist and socialist nation-states vied for political and military supremacy, they were united in the view that industrialization was the path to social development.

Having enabled the globalization of warfare, technological innovation became central to the globalization of development. Indeed, many of the technologies that redefined domestic life in wealthy societies during the postwar period, such as television, plastics, airplanes, and computers, had military origins. During the 1960s and 1970s, however, policy and public confidence in the project of development weakened, giving rise to debate about whether this project was sustainable. This weakening had two principle causes. First, it became clear that the majority of humanity continued to live in abject poverty, despite strong economic growth in wealthy countries. Second, evidence gathered by life scientists and broadcast by environmental movements prompted widespread concern in wealthy countries that nature was being irreparably damaged by technology. Rachel Carson's (1907–1964) *Silent Spring* (1962) and the 1972 report *Limits to Growth*, issued by the international think tank Club of Rome, were particularly significant among the many publications that described a looming global environmental crisis.

Neo-Luddite Environmentalism

Loss of confidence in postwar development had as much to do with technology as with nature. Building on determinist anxieties about (and philosophical critique) of technology, many of the environmental movements that grew rapidly in North America, Western Europe, and Australasia during the 1960s and 1970s displayed antipathy toward technology. This antipathy was associated with two influential ideas. First, neo-Romantic ideas of wilderness had great appeal within the predominantly urban constituency of environmental movements. Understood as areas of nature untouched by technology, wilderness is held by many environmentalists to be sacred. Efforts to protect wilderness from technology, especially from conspicuous artifacts such as roads and buildings, led to repeated protest and conflict. Indeed, the absence of technology, rather than the presence of ecological criteria, has often defined wilderness. Second, the idea of a global biosphere reinforced claims that the Earth was small, fragile and interconnected, and that it was at risk of being overwhelmed by oversized, brutal, and insatiable forms of technology. Representations of the planet as finite and mortal, and even as an organism, did much to raise concern that technology was capable of destroying life itself.

Environmentalists displaying strong antipathy toward modern technology are often referred to as neo-Luddites, in reference to the early-nineteenth-century craft workers who attempted to halt industrialization in the English Midlands by, among other means, breaking the new machines. Among influential environmentalist authors identified with neo-Luddism are Edward Abbey (1927–1989), Wendell Berry (b. 1934), Bill McKibben (b. 1961), and Kirkpatrick Sale (b. 1937).

Although many neo-Luddites offer subtle political responses to technological change, the simple solution of destroying technologies has appealed to newsworthy minority of environmentalists, with the activist organization *Earth First!*, cofounded by Dave Foreman (b. 1947), gaining notoriety for its practice of "monkeywrenching" or sabotaging machinery. More generally, the deep ecology movement associated with radical environmental philosophers such as the Norwegian Arne Naess (1912–2009) has argued that technology alienates humanity from nature. Although asserting that "simple in means is rich in ends,"

and advocating practical strategies such as bioregionalism, self-sufficiency, and encounters with wilderness, deep ecologists rarely discuss favored practices in terms of technology. Such discussion has, however, been significant in forms of radical environmentalism more engaged with questions of development than with questions of nature. Of particular note are the appropriate technology movement associated with E. F. Schumacher (1911–1977), the eco-anarchist movements associated with Murray Bookchin (1921–2006) and Ivan Illich (1926–2002), and the anti-globalization movements associated with, among many others, Vandana Shiva (b. 1952).

A Shrinking Planet

Although many environmental movements of the 1960s and 1970s were highly critical of technology, they were also in many ways indebted to modern technologies. The new romance with wilderness, for example, relied extensively on the capacity of the automobile to bring remote areas within weekend reach of suburbs and cities, as well as on photography and ever-more sophisticated forms of wilderness equipment. The new global awareness similarly relied heavily on photography and transport, in the form of the images of the "blue planet" sent back from space in the 1960s as a byproduct of the Cold War space race. More generally, concern for a tightly knit global biosphere grew in step with the building of a tightly knit global technosphere through transportation and communication systems. Coming to terms with the prospect of nuclear annihilation, it is perhaps inevitable that the thoughts of many living in the rapidly shrinking global village of the 1970s turned to matters of sustainability.

Promethean Environmentalism

During the 1980s, environmental concerns were taken up in legal, economic, bureaucratic, and professional institutions, becoming a familiar focus of mainstream media. The publication of the 1987 report of the Brundtland Commission, *Our Common Future*, marks the coming of age of the concept of sustainable development. This report also marks the rise of forms of environmentalism offering high-tech solutions to environmental problems.

Environmentalists convinced that technological development has not yet gone far enough can be described as Promethean, in reference to the Greek myth in which the god Prometheus illicitly gave to humanity the sacred power of technology. Whereas neo-Luddite environmentalists emphasize the limits of nature, Promethean environmentalists share the Brundtland Commission's view that the idea of sustainable development implies "not absolute limits but limitations imposed by the present state of technology and social organization" (WCED 1987, 8). During the 1990s, efforts to overcome technological limits were couched in terms of eco-efficiency, a concept introduced by the newly formed World Business Council for Sustainable Development in 1992. Although gaining new influence, this concept is closely related to the principle of emphemeralization proposed by the futurist R. Buckminster Fuller (1895–1983) in the 1930s in his formula: "Efficiency = doing more with less ∴ EFFICIENCY EPHEMERALIZES" (Fuller 1973, 259).

Promethean environmentalism has helped forge stronger links between environmental movements and the business sector. Economists, engineers, and entrepreneurs took the lead in arguing that eco-innovation could decouple material wealth from resource use and waste production through strategies such as dematerialization (reduced material inputs per unit of production), decarbonization (reduced reliance on fossil fuels), and detoxification (reduced reliance on toxic materials). Environmental technologists have developed models of industrial production using metaphors drawn from biology and ecology. The study of resource metabolism and product lifecycles is now well under way, as are efforts to create industrial ecosystems by linking industrial processes through exchanges of inputs and outputs.

In the mid-1990s, the renewable energy advocate Amory Lovins (b. 1947) and colleagues spoke of the prospect of a "factor 4" increase in eco-efficiency, an increase claimed to double wealth while halving resource use. Yet in their landmark 1999 book *Natural Capitalism*, Lovins and coauthors declared that a "factor 10" increase could be achieved once business realizes that eco-efficiency is a path to sustained profitability and competitiveness. Technologists typically offer dry, instrumentalist accounts of how technology can secure sustainability by simultaneously increasing wealth and environmental quality. In the spirit of Buckminster Fuller, the authors of *Natural Capitalism* and other influential advocates of a convergence of capitalism and environmentalism, however, counter the negative determinism of neo-Luddite environmentalism with enthusiastic accounts of autonomous technological evolution. A strong version of this determinism can be seen in *Wired* magazine founder Kevin Kelly's (b. 1952) *Out of Control* (1994). Reputedly required reading for the cast of *The Matrix*, this book claims that "the realm of the born … and the realm of the made" are destined to become one (Kelly 1994, 2–3).

Biotechnology

In the early twenty-first century, questions of technology frequently polarize discussion about sustainability. Although technologists debate the finer points of science and engineering in technical language, neo-Luddite and Promethean sensibilities are influential in political and cultural struggles to define the relationship between technology and sustainability. Although there are many such struggles, conflict over biotechnology has been prominent in debate about the role of technology in sustainable futures and is thus considered here.

On the question of whether biotechnology is a sustainable technology, proponents argue that humans have been developing biotechnologies for millennia and that modern biotechnologies are, in essence, no different from ancient plant breeding or wine making. Without past biotechnologies, the argument continues, humanity would never have evolved from being hunters and gatherers, and without new biotechnologies humanity has no prospect of feeding a population destined to exceed 10 billion this century. In addition to existing improvements in agriculture and aquaculture, proponents point out that biotechnology is already making an important contribution to environmental management through the bioremediation of oil spills and other contaminated sites. Biotechnology is touted also as having a vital role in the development of renewable energy such as biofuels and hydrogen fuel. Although such pragmatic arguments are common in public debate, some proponents turn philosophical, arguing that natural evolution itself is as a form of genetic engineering. They point out that genetic material is inherently malleable and that species boundaries are inherently dynamic. Concluding that modern biotechnology is another step on nature's path to becoming more fully developed, these proponents argue that humanity is nature made self-conscious and, as such, has a moral obligation to use biotechnology to achieve sustainability.

For opponents of biotechnology, modern attempts to manipulate genetic material directly, and especially to transfer genes across species boundaries, are unnatural and without precedent. This view leads some to claim that attempts to create and redesign life transgress a fundamental moral law of existence: that they are, in effect, an attempt to "play God." Others with more pragmatic concerns argue that biotechnology is built on a reductionist form of science that offers flawed understanding of complex living systems and poses great risks, especially once genetically modified organisms enter ecological systems. Others point to political risks arising from concentrated corporate ownership of biotechnology and genetic material. These critics argue that the plight of hunger that devastated the lives of so many throughout the twentieth century, and that today cripples the lives of 800 million people, has its sources in uneven distribution of resources between rich and poor, rather than in a lack of food. Although some critics accept that biotechnology could play a role in future food security, they point out that, controlled by global capitalism, biotechnology has widened the gap between rich and poor and has been addressed to trivial rather than basic human needs.

Debating Technological Futures

Although many people hold more equivocal positions that those outlined earlier in this entry, deep philosophical divisions underlie much debate about technological solutions to environmental problems. Instrumentalist explanations of technology make little sense of these divisions, leaving many technologists confused by the fact that efforts to improve public understanding of science related to new technologies often does little to resolve public debate. At the same time, these divisions are reinforced by determinist desire for technological salvation and by determinist fears that technology offers only damnation.

Looking ahead, nanotechnology is set to join biotechnology at the centre of debates about technology and sustainability. Referring to an extraordinarily broad range of technological possibilities involving the manipulation of material at the nanoscale, the scale of billionths of a meter, nanotechnology is argued to herald a materials revolution. Many of these new materials already exist, such as nanotubes, a form of carbon fiber several times stronger than steel at a fraction of its weight. Indeed, some argue that, along with information technology and cognitive science, biotechnology and nanotechnology are "merging, step by step, and apparently at an accelerating rate . . . moving to a higher technological level [at which it] will be possible for all of the peoples of the world to achieve prosperity without depleting essential natural resources" (Bainbridge and Roco 2006, 2). While presented as offering everything from vast amounts of renewable energy to vastly extended human life spans, this latest in a long series of visions of technological evolution brings with it strong and often unexamined desires and fears. It can be expected to meet with opposition fueled by equally strong desires and fears in ongoing and vitally important debates about sustainability.

Aidan DAVISON
University of Tasmania

FURTHER READING

Allenby, Bradley R. (2005). *Reconstructing Earth: Technology and environment in an age of humans.* Washington, DC, Covelo, CA, and London: Island Press.

Bainbridge, Williams Sims, & Roco, Mihail C. (Eds.). (2006). *Managing nano-bio-info-cogno innovations: Converging technologies in society.* Dordrecht, The Netherlands: Springer.

Davison, Aidan. (2001). *Technology and the contested meanings of technology.* Albany: State University of New York Press.

Ellul, Jacques. (1964). *The technological society.* New York: Vintage Books.

Fuller, Richard Buckminster. (1973[1938]). *Nine chains to the moon.* London: Jonathan Cape.

Hawken, Paul; Lovins, Amory B.; & Lovins, L. Hunter. (1999). *Natural capitalism: The next industrial revolution.* London: Earthscan.

Heaton, George R.; Repetto, Robert C.; & Sobin, Rodney. (1991). *Transforming technology: An agenda for environmentally sustainable growth in the 21st century.* Washington, DC: World Resources Institute.

Heidegger, Martin. (1977). *The question concerning technology and other essays* (W. Lovitt, Trans. and Ed.). New York: Harper and Row.

Kearnes, Matthew; Macnaughton, Phil; & Wilsdon, James. (2006). *Governing at the nanoscale: people, policies and emerging technologies.* London: Demos. Retrieved May 22, 2009, from http://www.demos.co.uk/

Kelly, Kevin. (1994). *Out of control: The new biology of machines.* London: Fourth Estate.

McKibben, Bill. (2003). *Enough: Staying human in an engineered age.* New York: Times Books.

Mills, Stephanie. (Ed.). (1997). *Turning away from technology: A new vision for the 21st century.* San Francisco: Sierra Books.

Noble, David F. (1999). *The religion of technology: The divinity of man and the spirit of invention.* Harmondsworth, U.K.: Penguin.

Sale, Kirkpatrick. (1995). *Rebels against the future: The Luddites and their war on the industrial revolution, lessons for the computer age.* New York: Addison-Wesley.

Schumacher, Ernest Friedrich. (1973). *Small is beautiful: A study of economics as if people mattered.* London: Abacus.

Shiva, Vandana. (1993). *Monocultures of the mind: Biodiversity, biotechnology and agriculture.* New Delhi: Zed Books.

Tokar, Brian. (Ed.). (2001). *Redesigning life? The worldwide challenge to genetic engineering.* Melbourne, Australia: Scribe Publications.

White, Damien F., & Wilbert, Chris. (Eds.). (2009). *Technonatures: Environments, technologies, spaces and places in the twentieth first century.* Waterloo, Canada: Wildfrid Laurier University Press.

Winner, Langdon. (1977). *Autonomous technology: Technics out-of-control as a theme in political thought.* Cambridge, MA: MIT Press.

World Business Council for Sustainable Development. (2000). *Eco-efficiency: Creating more value with less impact.* Geneva: WBCSD.

Theocentrism

By positing that God is the center of all value, theocentrism sees the human and nonhuman equally, thus avoiding challenges to sustainability, such as anthropocentrism, arising in other approaches. But theocentrism can also be said to dismiss sustainability by asserting that God wants us to use whatever resources we find, even to the point of exhausting them, because God will provide other resources if necessary.

Theocentrism identifies God (Greek: *theos*) as the central basis for ethical value, existence, and/or knowledge. Thus, theocentric approaches to sustainability affirm that God is the foundation for any value and meaning that humans find in nature. Some advocates consider God to be the only thing to have true value, insofar as the entirety of creation belongs to God. All other entities have a relative value through their relationship to the divine.

As a concept, theocentrism often is compared with other positions that attempt to find the location of meaning or worth in nature. Some approaches define value in terms of a total system of the environment or all life (i.e., ecocentrism and biocentrism), while others concentrate on the human species or individuals (i.e., anthropocentrism and egocentrism). Although these other approaches are used in both religious and nonreligious contexts, theocentrism is explicitly religious in its outlook and often includes a critique of secular reasoning with regard to the environment. Often found in monotheistic religions (particularly within Christianity), theocentrism emphasizes theological and spiritual justifications as the basis for environmental ethics. For example, the Genesis narrative of creation repeatedly explains that "God saw that [what was created] was good." For Christians and Jews, this expression of value by God means that love for God leads to a respect for creation (humans and nonhumans alike).

One of the strengths of theocentric positions is that they offer a way beyond certain dichotomies sometimes found in discussions about sustainability. For example, by classifying all value as dependent upon theological concerns, theocentrism bypasses some controversies over the relationship between human culture and nonhuman nature. Theocentrism emphasizes the closeness of humanity with the rest of creation, rather than focusing on the differences. Likewise, theocentrism attempts to overcome the dilemma between present use and future needs. Because God is defined as both eternal and the center of value, theocentric approaches see God as an intermediary through which to balance the worth of humans and nature in the past, present, and future. Evaluations of future needs versus the current use of resources are dependent on how the divine has ordered or created the cosmos. Yet such benefits highlight the potential difficulties of theocentrism. Of greatest concern is the possibility of overemphasizing the spiritual at the expense of the physical world. Unless God somehow is anchored to the material world, theocentrism can result in a view that downplays the value of the material world in favor of the spiritual. In this case, God is conceptualized as creating the world simply for human and divine use. Sustainability can be dismissed by asserting that God wants us to use whatever resources we find, even to the point of exhausting them, because God will provide other resources if necessary.

Forrest CLINGERMAN
Ohio Northern University

FURTHER READING

Hoffman, Andrew J., & Sandelands, Lloyd E. (2005). Getting right with nature: Anthropocentrism, ecocentrism, and theocentrism. *Organization & Environment, 18,* 141–162.

Northcott, Michael S. (1996). The flowering of ecotheology. In Michael S. Northcott (Ed.), *The environment and Christian ethics* (pp. 124–163). Cambridge, U.K.: Cambridge University Press.

Time

Three natural phenomena, or gauges of irreversible time—thermodynamic, psychobiologic, and cosmologic—together help to explain the pace of evolution, emergence, and decay in the natural world. Earth's increasing isolation in the expanding universe can make humans feel insignificant in space, but our responsibility for engendering a sustainable future on Earth may make us highly significant in time.

Sustainability is a time-impregnated word. The very nature of sustainability implies temporal duration. Time is required for its realization. Time sets the pace for the balance of the forces of degeneration and regeneration that activate sustainability.

Time itself is a human abstraction or interpretation of what we perceive and understand about motion, change, and process. Aristotle capsulized these fundamental perceptions by positing that time is the measure or number of motion. These perceptions underlie what a number of scholars of time, including the physicist Stephen Hawking, have cited as three natural phenomena that most clearly manifest the irreversible nature of time and, thus, can be considered as gauges of time. These gauges are descriptors of the pace of the evolution, emergence, and decay that characterize the behavior of the natural world. Each, in its own way, affects and informs the nature of sustainability. The gauges are (1) the thermodynamic gauge based on the tendency in nature to progress to states of greater disorder as measured physically by the quantity called entropy; (2) the psychobiologic gauge based on the growth of complexity, organization, and information; and (3) the cosmologic gauge based on the expansion of the universe.

Thermodynamic Gauge

Examples of the operation of the thermodynamic gauge reflecting the progression to greater disorder, or entropy increase, are evident everywhere in everyday life. Spilt milk does not gather back into the glass. Food left too long in the refrigerator is no longer edible. Illustrative at a fundamental level is the time-honored physics classroom demonstration wherein a drop of ink is placed in a vessel of water. The ink becomes uniformly distributed throughout the glass, never to return to a concentrated drop.

The most striking example particularly relevant to the problem of earthly sustainability is the melting of ice masses in Antarctica and Greenland. The ordered geometric array of the water molecules in the ice crystals of these masses degrades to the more disordered distribution of molecules characterizing liquid water. Although at some time in the distant future this melting may cease and reverse, for people living in the present century, this process serves as a relentlessly ticking clock, indeed an alarm clock, whose ring seems too subtle to be heard. A number of other such clocks exist, including the threatened loss of polar bears.

From a physical point of view, all of the above degenerative processes are illustrative of the tendency in nature to reach for thermal equilibrium, wherein all matter is at the same temperature—a state of maximum entropy or disorder.

Psychobiologic Gauge

On the other hand, living, earthly nature is activated by "far-from-equilibrium processes" that exchange matter and energy with their environment for their sustenance and growth. Such processes are in operation throughout the whole spectrum of plant and animal species. This leads to consideration of the psychobiologic gauge of time.

This gauge has been operable since the first emergence of bacterial life some 3.5 billion years ago. Bacteria, the smallest living cells, exhibit remarkably purposeful mobility, coherent collective action, and sophistication in their growth and survival. As such, they were the beginners of a persistent trial-and-error process leading to ever greater levels of complexity. Each level, though dependent on the foundation provided by its predecessors, exhibits entirely new properties and capacities. Although it is true that cells, plants, and animals die, it is the growth of a species as a whole, and more importantly, the broad, general growth of complexity and information, that is relevant to the psychobiologic arrow.

The emergence of each new organism, more sophisticated than the last, can be thought of as a tick in a sporadically paced, evolutionary clock. Humans, thermodynamically the farthest-from-equilibrium phenomenon of all so far, can be considered the latest tick, but they may not be the last. It is not beyond the human imagination to vaguely envision a form of biota with capacities far exceeding those exhibited at the present stage of evolution.

The processes that drive the thermodynamic and psychobiologic gauges are in continual relation. It is the death and decay of some life forms that provides the energy and nutrition for succeeding life. Thus, in a real sense, the phenomena underlying the two gauges are mutually interdependent and are equally necessary for earthly sustainability.

In particular, if it were not for this sustaining interdependence, the development and maintenance of modern technology would not be possible. A specific feature of this technology of relevance is the cryogenically based atomic clock which now can measure time to better than one part in sixteen powers of ten (i.e., 10^{16}). That is, these clocks are only in error by one second in 60 million years. Such timing is vital to Earth's current sustainability. For example, this precision in clocks is absolutely necessary for the operation of the global positioning system (GPS), now vital for the maintenance of modern life. It may also be crucial in warding off an asteroid or meteorite threatening to collide with Earth.

Cosmologic Gauge

Modern technology has made possible ever increasing knowledge about the nature of the cosmologic gauge, which is based on the expansion of the universe. Although it has been known since the late 1920s that the universe is expanding, it was observed in 1998 that it is expanding at an accelerating rate. This is currently considered to be due to an as-yet-unknown property of gravity, called dark energy, which is repulsive instead of attractive. As this acceleration proceeds, more and more galaxies will recede from view, so that in billions of years, only those in the local galactic cluster will be observable. This prospect, though far in future time, is a distant harbinger of the magnitude of our cosmic aloneness, which even in the present cosmologic era, may be greater than is generally realized.

Earth's Temporal Uniqueness and Sustainability

Fully realizing the extent of Earth's isolation should engender understanding of its uniqueness and a profound appreciation of the unlimited value that must be accorded its sustainability.

That Earth may be unique is based primarily on what has been learned from the search for extraterrestrial intelligence (SETI), which, in terms of serious scientific observations, began in 1960. Despite impressive efforts involving remarkable and painstaking scientific and technological ingenuity, no such intelligence has been found.

Even if extraterrestrial intelligence does exist somewhere in the universe, humans may never really know. This is because they are fundamentally isolated by light's finite speed of 186,000 miles per second. An intelligent civilization could exist millions, even a billion, light years away that could effectively never be observable.

More importantly, there are remarkable features of Earth and its place in the solar system that are uniquely favorable to life. Its orbit is essentially circular with a diameter that allows an appropriate life-supporting temperature range. The angle of its axis with respect to the axis of the orbital plane is stabilized by the motion of a moon of the appropriate mass, thus providing the regular timing of the seasons. Jupiter's large mass keeps most destructive comets and asteroids out of Earth's path. Experts in the theory of planetary motion comment that such a remarkable combination of these characteristics is a very rare phenomenon.

The list of extraordinary circumstances fortunate for life continues from the existence and movement of tectonic plates that provide a supply of iron and other metals for human technology, to the timing of the appearance of water and oxygen, to the timing of global extinctions that make possible the incredible biological evolution of humans. After the discovery of well over one hundred extra-solar planets, none approach Earth's special properties. Although it is still very important to continue the SETI project, it appears more and more likely the results will be negative.

In any case, from what astronomical observations have revealed, planet Earth is unquestionably a singular, prototypical example of sustainability—an almost incredible sustainability that has fruitfully used the time, billions of years, that has been accorded for its realization.

Spiritual Perspectives and Future Time

Furthermore, the accumulated astrophysical evidence for Earth's isolation provides compelling testimony for the value that must be placed on this sustainability and the time that may be left for its continuance. The increasing body of scientific evidence indicating the future fragility of this sustainability clearly points to the magnitude of human responsibility necessary for its maintenance.

Indeed, this responsibility may be far more profound than generally realized. If, as far as humans know, they are alone in the universe, they are, in a real sense, effectively responsible for nothing less than the consciousness of the universe, or that part of it to which they have access, given the finiteness of their lives and the speed of light. In the words of the astronomer Edward Harrison, "We are the universe thinking about itself" (1985, 1). Therefore, although the minuteness of Earth compared to rest of the universe may seem to render humans extremely insignificant in space, they may be highly significant in time (Fagg 2003, 109).

This cosmic situation, attendant with heightening apprehension concerning Earth's future, presents a profound challenge to religious imagination and spiritual resources. Among the most affecting and relevant of such resources is the work of the Jesuit scholar Pierre Teilhard de Chardin. He formulated an imaginative integration of Christian biblical cosmology with physical cosmology, as it was known before his death in 1955. He saw the universe as evolving to progressive stages of ever greater complexity along what he termed a *favored axis*. This evolution proceeded from inanimate matter to animate matter or life, to *reflection* (humans and consciousness), to the society of humankind, followed possibly by a Christian society, and finally reaching the omega point, the goal of salvation, which may be associated with the second coming of Christ.

Thus, Teilhard de Chardin envisioned an oriented temporal process that embraced the concepts involved in all three of the gauges of time: the thermodynamic, the psychobiologic, and the cosmologic. More importantly, he provided a spiritual dimension to understanding the irreversible nature of time that these gauges portray. Activating this dimension is Teilhard de Chardin's view that all matter is vivified in a lifelike or preconscious interaction.

He said that matter is spirit moving slowly enough to be seen and saw no sharp demarcation between life and non-life. Life could not evolve unless inanimate matter possessed the potential for life—that is, if it did not already possess some form of primal, incipient life.

In a word, Teilhard de Chardin spoke of the *within of things* as an inner aspect of all elements of nature. This perception is clearly congenial with Daoist religious philosophy. The Dao is the gentle pervasive power that brings silent vitality to the natural world. It is the healing way of return to the harmony of man and woman with the vibrant serenity of enfolding nature.

This way of return that is so relevant to the problem of sustainability today can be catalyzed by enlisting faith, for faith propagates the personal experience of time. In other words, it requires faith, whether conscious or unconscious, to believe that the moment of time people are experiencing now will be followed by the next. This faith must be collectively employed in responding to the constraints of time that are becoming increasingly more apparent and that directly affect Earth's future sustainability. That is, this faith must energize the full exploitation of modern technology to effect this sustainability and, indeed, it must nurture the realization that the primary purpose of modern technology is its utilization for an open-ended future.

Lawrence W. FAGG
Catholic University of America

FURTHER READING

Coveney, Peter, & Highfield, Roger. (1990). *The arrow of time.* New York: Fawcett Columbine.
Davies, Paul. (1995). *About time.* New York: Simon and Schuster.
Drake, Frank, & Sobel, Dava. (1992). *Is anyone out there?* New York: Delacorte Press.
Fagg, Lawrence. (2001). A comparative study of physical and religious time concepts. In Marlene P. Soulsby & J. Fraser (Eds.), *Time: Perspectives at the millenium.* Westport, CT: Bergin and Garvey.
Fagg, Lawrence. (2003). *The becoming of time.* Durham, NC: Duke University Press.
Harrison, Edward Robert. (1985). *Masks of the universe.* New York: Macmillan.
Hawking, Stephen. (1988). *A brief history of time.* New York: Bantam Books.
Teilhard de Chardin, Pierre. *The phenomenon of man.* New York: Harper and Row.

Tragedy of the Commons, The

Garrett Hardin's 1968 article "The Tragedy of the Commons" argued that humans overexploit natural resources held in common ownership—such as oceans and the atmosphere—for economic gain. But Hardin's main concern was that unchecked human population growth on the ultimate commons (Earth) would lead to environmental and human tragedy.

In 1968 a biology professor named Garrett Hardin (1915–2003) from the University of California, Santa Barbara, published "The Tragedy of the Commons" in the prestigious journal *Science*. "The commons" referred to natural and environmental resources that are held in some form of group or public ownership; "the tragedy of the commons" summarized Hardin's argument that a built-in economic incentive to overexploit these resources leads to their ultimate ruin. Hardin's argument has become one of the most powerful and compelling ideas in contemporary environmental literature. His paper has been republished in over one hundred environmental and public policy-related anthologies, and a recent bibliography on papers related to managing the commons includes over 37,000 citations for it. (See the sidebar to the entry "Individualism" on page 237 for an extract of the article.)

Hardin began his paper with a very old and simple example of a commons: a pasture shared by a group of farmers. Each farmer has an incentive to let more and more cattle graze on the pasture because each receives the full benefits of this additional grazing. But the damage to the commons (in the form of degraded pasture lands caused by overgrazing), is shared by all the farmers. "Therein," wrote Hardin, "is the tragedy. Each man is locked into a system that [causes] him to increase his herd without limit—in a world that is limited" (1968, 1244).

Hardin went on in his paper to identify and explore other such examples including ocean fisheries, the atmosphere, and national parks. But his principal warning involved human population growth: the environmental capacity of the Earth to support humans was the ultimate commons, and unbridled freedom to "use" this commons as a breeding ground for unchecked population growth would inevitably result in environmental and human tragedy.

Hardin and others have noted that the issue of managing resources held in common has a long history. In fact, Aristotle expressed nascent interest in the concept of the commons when he wrote, "What is common to the greatest number gets the least amount of care." William Forster Lloyd and Thomas Malthus advanced the first "modern" expressions of concern about the commons in the nineteenth century; both directed their writings toward the issue of unfettered population growth and their associated belief that the Earth could not support very large numbers of humans. Initial "scientific" inquiries regarding the commons date to the mid-twentieth century in the context of increasing demand and exploitation of ocean fisheries and their subsequent and continuing decline. "The tragedy of the commons" continues to be applied to an increasing array of contemporary environmental issues, including global climate change, and the expression has even been extended to nonenvironmental issues such as education, health care, and cyberspace.

Scholars have defined "common property resources" as having several characteristics. First, as the term suggests, ownership of the resource is held in common, often by a large number of owners who have independent rights to use the resource. Second, control of access to the resource can be problematic for several reasons, including the large size or area of the resource, its pervasive character, its migratory nature, or its political intransigence. Third, the level of exploitation by one user adversely affects the ability of other users to exploit the resource. In addition to conventional common property resources from which tangible assets (e.g., forage, fish) and intangible benefits (e.g., enjoyment) are extracted, there are also "reverse" commons in which pollution is deposited into a resource that is owned in common, such as the oceans and the atmosphere.

Hardin argued that there are no "technical" solutions to managing the commons in a way that will ultimately avoid tragedy. More efficient technology, for example, will only postpone the need for a more permanent resolution. The only real solution to avoiding the tragedy of the commons must be found in what Hardin termed "mutual coercion mutually agreed upon," that is, social action designed to regulate and limit use of common property resources. Limits on resource use apply to all potential users and all (or at least a majority of) users agree on the limits. Examples include limits on the number of fish harvested from the oceans, the amount of pollution emitted into the atmosphere, and the number of visitors allowed in a national park. Hardin implied that the most important form of social action is a limit on family size or what he called "the freedom to breed." In rationalizing such limits, Hardin suggested, "Freedom is the recognition of necessity" (which he attributed to the German philosopher Friedrich Hegel); only by instituting the mechanisms that will ensure protection of the environment and our ultimate well-being will we be able to pursue our higher personal and societal aspirations.

Robert E. MANNING
University of Vermont

FURTHER READING

Feeny, David; Berkes, Fikret; McCay, Bonnie J.; & Acheson, James M. (1973). The tragedy of the commons: Twenty-two years later. *Human Ecology, 18,* 1–19.

Greco, Gian Maria, & Floridi, Luciano. (2004). The tragedy of the digital commons. *Ethics and information technology, 6,* 73–81.

Hardin, Garrett. (1968). The tragedy of the commons. *Science, 162,* 1243–1248.

Manning, Robert. (2007). *Parks and carrying capacity: Commons without tragedy.* Washington, DC: Island Press.

Ostrom, Elinor; Burger, Joanna; Field, Christopher; Norgaard, Richard B.; & Policansky, David. (1999). Revisiting the commons: Local lessons, global challenges. *Science, 284,* 278–282.

Ostrom, Vincent, & Ostrom, Elinor. (1977). A theory for institutional analysis of common pool problems. In Garrett Hardin (Ed.) & John Baden (Ed.), *Managing the commons* (pp.157–172). W. H. Freeman & Company.

U

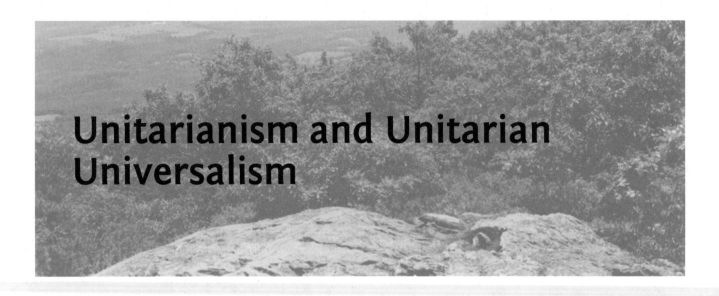

Unitarianism and Unitarian Universalism

Founded in Hungary in the sixteenth century, Unitarianism focuses on reason, rational thought, science, and philosophy. Unitarian ecological theologies have begun to develop in Europe. In the United States, Unitarianism has mostly avoided environmentalism, but Unitarian Universalists have developed a theology of humans in relation to the environment, and promote respect for the "interdependent web of all existence" in their guiding principles.

Unitarianism, founded by Ferenc Dávid in Hungary during the Protestant Reformation of the sixteenth century, spread around the world and has a small following in the United States. Its theology differs from many mainstream Protestant Christian denominations in that Unitarianism does not believe in the idea of the Trinity or the divinity of Jesus. Unitarianism professes beliefs in reason, rational thought, science, and philosophy.

Unitarianism took hold in the northeastern United States in the eighteenth century. One of the most famous and revered Unitarians is Ralph Waldo Emerson, who wrote the book *Nature* in 1836. Emerson's work places him among the distinguished group of early environmental philosophers in the United States.

The American Unitarian Church merged with the Universalist Church of America in 1961 to form the Unitarian Universalist Church, with headquarters in Boston, Massachusetts. Unitarians and Unitarian Universalists consider themselves as belonging to two different denominations, although there is an overlap in membership. Within the United States, Unitarian Universalists are greater in number.

Unitarian Universalists have developed a theology of the human in relationship to the environment conveyed by the Seven Principles of Unitarian Universalists. The seventh principle, "respect for the interdependent web of

all existence of which we are a part," embodies concern for the ecosystem; the principle has become the basis for the Unitarian Universalist (UU) environmental theology. UUs also developed a practical "green" certification program for their congregations in the United States in 2002. This accreditation process requires that congregations and sanctuaries provide ecology-based worship and religious education, and demonstrate a focus on environmental justice and sustainable living. More than fifty-nine Unitarian Universalist congregations have been accredited as "Green Sanctuaries" since the implementation of this program.

Unitarianism, on the other hand, has a lesser known environmental theology, despite Ralph Waldo Emerson's contribution. For example, ecology and the environment are not part of the American Unitarian Conference principles. In fact, in the 1990s, several Unitarian theologians expressed concern that the Unitarian Church not take on the environment as an issue for fear that it would dilute the theology into secularist beliefs.

Outside the United States, Unitarianism is a liberal religious movement with a significant presence. Members of the International Council of Unitarians and Universalists, a network of organizations joining Unitarians, Universalists, and Unitarian Universalists, can be found in many European countries including Ireland, United Kingdom, and Hungary, as well as in Australia, New Zealand, South Africa, and Canada. In Europe, Unitarians have begun to develop ecological theologies. Several theologians reflected on the human theological connection to nature

in "Unitarian Views of Earth and Nature," the 1994 publication of the Unitarian Headquarters in London. In the United Kingdom, Unitarians formed the Unitarian Earth Spirit Network in 1990 to address the need to support those who wanted to develop an ecological theology and practice. Beliefs of this network include: (1) revering the totality of the divine reality of nature that is revealed to us through the infinite multiplicity of forms and forces; (2) evolving creative ways of worship for body, mind, and spirit; (3) affirming a Pagan spiritual perspective as being fully compatible with the human quest for self-knowledge and ultimate meaning; and (4) encouraging ways of practical action on social issues which are directly related to a nature-centered faith and philosophy. Today, the Unitarian Earth Spirit Network is connected to the Unitarian Universalist Covenant of Unitarian Universalist Pagans based in the United States.

Future sustainability discussions will inevitably benefit by including the voices of Unitarians around the globe, who continue to call for development of ecological theology, and the Unitarian Universalists, whose guiding principle is to promote respect for the "interdependent web of all existence."

Eileen M. HARRINGTON
University of San Francisco

FURTHER READING

American Unitarian Conference. (2007). Retrieved May 8, 2009, from http://www.americanunitarian.org/

Dorris, Robert E. (2007). *A Unitarian perspective.* Frederick, MD: PublishAmerica.

Palmer, Joy A. (Ed.). (2001). *Fifty key thinkers on the environment.* London: Routledge.

Small, Fred. (2009). Ecology, justice, and compassion. Retrieved July 13, 2009, from http://www.uua.org/visitors/uuperspectives/59580.shtml?time010

Tomek, Vladimir. (2008). Environmental concerns: Unitarian responses. Retrieved May 8, 2009, from http://www.religioustolerance.org/tomek12.htm

Unitarian Earth Spirit Network. (2009). Retrieved May 8, 2009, from http://www.unitariansocieties.org.uk/earthspirit/index

Unitarian Universalist Association of Congregations. (2009). Retrieved May 8, 2009, from http://www.uua.org/

The Universe Story

The universe story, which seeks to describe the ever more complex transformations in our cosmos—from gaseous energy to the first life forms to human consciousness—is closely associated with a book of the same name penned by Thomas Berry and Brian Swimme. The story creates a framework in which to undertake the challenge of the twenty-first century: to reconnect our lives as human beings in a meaningful way within the context of the planet Earth and the roughly 14-billion-year process of cosmic evolution.

The term "the universe story," though commonly associated with a book of the same name written by Thomas Berry and Brian Swimme, refers broadly to current attempts to tell the story of existence from the perspective of contemporary cosmology and physics. Swimme and Berry suggest that we need a narrative that includes the whole universe, from the great "flaring forth" to the current era, in order to address problems of human alienation from "nature" and the ecological problems that result from this alienation.

However it happened in the beginning, Big Bang or by other scenarios, remnants of that originating event continue to reverberate everywhere some 14 billion years later. For eons, burning eruptions spewed gaseous, turbulent energy—fireballs, black holes, supernovas, stars, galaxies, meteorites, comets, asteroid belts, and planets—into an endless expanse. Approximately 5 billion years ago, within our universe (one of many spiraling through space and expanding in all directions) there emerged a solar system with a planet we call home.

Eventually, when conditions were favorable, some 7 million years ago, Earth came alive. The warmth of the sun, an abundance of water, and the right molecular environment gave rise to a whole new chapter in the universe story. The botanical world erupted and proliferated. Life forms evolved from single cells into a plurality of species, preparing the developmental path for humanity, female and male. All that was needed to sustain life was present in abundance.

Many place a Divine Creator at the heart of the universe story as taught by religious traditions or felt by individuals from the dawn of civilization. People of faith may not agree on the specifics of our beginnings or the origin of our species, but however we choose to explain who we are, how we came to be, and how we remain in existence, the physical aspects associated with the emergence of the cosmos and its evolutionary development cannot be ignored.

All of us on planet Earth are organically linked to the universe story and its cosmic context. Particles and waves of energy, continuously in motion, move in and out of every aspect of our physical world, including us. The universe provides for our many needs, among them, clean air and water. We no longer take this largesse for granted. Elements we thought were limitless are not. Our wasteful use of the planet's resources can no longer be sustained. Toward the end of *The Universe Story*, Berry and Swimme address a fork in the road of the future of our planetary evolution. We human beings can choose to move into the technozoic era (the era of burgeoning techology that is leading to further compromises in our Earth systems) or the "ecozoic era" (the era of ecological awareness that would essentially be a move toward sustainable living). The well-being of our planet and the welfare of our species are intimately intertwined. A mutual relationship of sustainability is essential for ensuring sufficient resources for future generations. Fundamental changes in attitudes and behavior, from unlimited consumption to careful conservation and replenishment, will be required for such a feat. We must eliminate whatever affects our environment adversely, choose to use renewable resources, and make a spirit of sustainability the hallmark of our generation and its legacy.

Miriam Therese WINTER
Hartford Seminary

FURTHER READING

Hawking, Stephen W. (2002). *The theory of everything: The origin and fate of the universe.* Beverly Hills, CA: New Millennium Press.

Steinhardt, Paul J., & Turok, Neil. (2007). *Endless universe: Beyond the Big Bang.* New York: Doubleday.

Swimme, Brian. (2001). *The universe is a green dragon.* Rochester, VT: Bear & Co.

Swimme, Brian, & Berry, Thomas. (1994). *The universe story: From the primordial flaring forth to the ecozoic era—A celebration of the unfolding of the cosmos.* New York: HarperCollins.

The renowned world religion scholar Thomas Berry, who once wrote that the "universe is a communion of objects, not a collection of things," collaborated with the mathematical cosmologist Brian Swimme to write The Universe Story. *The book takes readers from the beginning of time, the "originating reality" when "sextillion particles foamed into existence," to the dawn of human consciousness.*

Originating power brought forth a universe. All the energy that would ever exist in the entire course of time erupted as a single quantum—a singular gift—existence. If in the future, stars would blaze and lizards would blink in their light, these actions would be powered by the same numinous energy that flared forth at the dawn of time.

There was no place in the universe that was separate from the originating power of the universe. Each thing of the universe had its very roots in this realm. Even space-time itself was a tossing, churning foaming out of the originating reality, instant by instant. Each of the sextillion particles that foamed into existence had its root in this quantum vacuum, this originating reality.

The birth of the universe was not just an event in time. Time begins simultaneously with the birth of existence. The realm or power that brings forth the universe is not itself an event of time, nor a position in space, but is rather the very matrix out of which the conditions arise that enable temporal events to occur in space. Though the originating power gave birth to the universe fifteen billion years ago, this realm of power is not simply located there at that point of time, but is rather a condition of every moment of universe, past, present, and to come.

Source: Brian Swimme and Thomas Berry. (1994). *The Universe Story: From the Primordial Flaring Forth to the Ecozoic Era—A Celebration of the Unfolding of the Cosmos*, p. 7. New York: HarperCollins.

Utilitarianism

The cost-benefit analyses so integral today in making environmental regulations and decisions have roots in utilitarianism, a theory based on the principle that a moral action tends to bring the greatest good to the greatest number. Utilitarianism has also helped to shape ideas about how humans ought properly to relate to other animals.

Utilitarianism embodies a family of moral theories that are perhaps the best-known variety of teleological ethics, a discipline in which the end or purpose of an action determines whether the action is moral or immoral. Like all teleological moral theories, utilitarianism is most clearly distinguished from deontological moral theories, which differentiate between a moral and immoral action according to its conformity to a norm (e.g., respect for persons) and independently of the action's end or purpose. Unlike many other teleological theories, utilitarianism has a strong empirical (observation- or experience-related) bent. Avoiding metaphysical speculation, transcendental argumentation, and theories of natural law or natural rights, utilitarianism seeks to bridge the gap between empirical facts and prescribed standards through a calculus that weighs benefits (usually measured in terms of happiness) against costs.

Origins from Bentham to Mill

Varieties of utilitarianism have been proposed and debated since ancient times, but the British philosopher and social reformer Jeremy Bentham (1738–1842) gave utilitarianism its classic modern formulation in his *Introduction to the Principles of Morals and Legislation*. Although that formulation did not originate with Bentham, he adopted—and grounded in a systematic ethical framework—the

principle that moral action is action that tends to bring about the greatest happiness for the greatest number. Bentham equated happiness with pleasure and the absence of pain. He believed that each person's happiness was equally as important as the happiness of any other. Bentham's dictum on this matter follows: "everyone to count for one, and nobody for more than one." Bentham's articulation has shaped the outlines of subsequent utilitarian thinkers in important ways. First, utilitarianism has remained strongly egalitarian—each person counts as one and not more. Second, utilitarianism seeks to aggregate and maximize happiness. Bentham's emphasis on a hedonic calculus of pleasure versus pain has been an influential catalyst for modern cost-benefit analysis. But later utilitarians, as explained below, broadened their understanding of what constitutes pleasure, or moved away from pleasure altogether and focused instead on the satisfaction of preferences.

Like Bentham, the philosopher and economist John Stuart Mill (1806–1873)—a follower whose father was Bentham's colleague—held that "pleasure, and freedom from pain, are the only things desirable as ends" (Mill (2002 [1863]), 239). He further agreed that "[a]s between [one's] own happiness and that of others, utilitarianism requires [an individual] to be as strictly impartial as a disinterested, impartial observer" (2002 [1863], 250). Mill developed the hedonistic utilitarianism of Bentham by focusing not simply on the *quantity* but also on the *quality* of pleasure—distinguishing between different *types* of pleasure. Mill argued that pleasures of the "higher faculties," such as the intellect, imagination, and moral sentiments, were intrinsically superior to bodily pleasures. He based this conclusion on the observation that "[h]uman beings have faculties more elevated than the animal appetites," (2002 [1863], 240) and on the consensus of the only individuals capable of judging—those who have experienced both kinds of pleasure. This view of happiness and pleasure significantly expands, as well as hierarchically orders, Bentham's exposition. It also seems to bring Mill's conception of happiness close to that of at least some Greek conceptions of *eudaimonia* ("human flourishing"); Mill makes numerous references to Greek strains of thought, especially the Epicureans and the Stoics, in his discussion of the higher pleasures (2002 [1863], 240–242).

There is, however, a critical difference between Mill's conception of happiness and those Greek understandings that make virtue integral to (rather than instrumental to) *eudaimonia*. For Mill the qualitative difference between types of pleasure derived from empirical knowledge (based on observation and experience) rather than from an ideal of human nature, as *eudaimonia* did for Aristotle or the Stoics. Mill's essay *On Liberty* (2002 [1859]) is helpful in clarifying this point as well as forecasting the direction that utilitarian moral theory would take. Mill's focus was on individual spontaneity and self-direction, rather than on the conformation of the self to some ideal. As he wrote in *Utilitarianism*, "Mankind are the greater gainers by suffering each to live as seems good to themselves, than by compelling each to live as seems good to the rest" (2002 [1863], 15). Mill went on to argue (2002 [1863], 97), "[T]he individual is not accountable to society for his actions, insofar as these concern the interests of no person but himself." The only purpose for which power "can be rightfully exercised over any member of a civilized community . . . is to prevent harm to others," Mill wrote (2002 [1863], 11). Individuals should be free to live their own lives according to their own preferences, he believed, so long as they do not interfere with others' ability to do likewise. Individuals' lives are not to be shaped by an ideal of human nature, but by their own preferences. Arguably, this exposition has led utilitarian moral theory away from a focus on pleasure and toward a focus on preference satisfaction, which is a broader conception. For instance, the search for truth may be an important interest that is not transparently connected with pleasure. "Preference utilitarianism" (as opposed to "hedonistic utilitarianism") holds that the fulfillment of *any* preference of an individual, not just a preference that satisfies pleasure, constitutes a benefit for that person (and thereby adds to that person's "utility").

One of the most persistent and trenchant criticisms of utilitarian ethical theory is that the theory fails to acknowledge individual rights that cannot be violated for the sake of the greater good; the greatest good for the greatest number is described in aggregate terms, implying that good can be achieved under conditions that are harmful for some. Following his empirical bent, Bentham, for instance, argued that the word "right" has no meaning apart from utility and no existence apart from the law (2007 [1789], 7, 224). As he colorfully and famously wrote in a critique of the Declaration of Rights issued during the French Revolution: "*Natural rights* is simple nonsense; natural and imprescriptible rights, rhetorical nonsense—nonsense upon stilts," (2007 [1789], 227–228). A right, according to Bentham, is a "child of law" (2007 [1789], 731–733); it does not exist "naturally" and is not absolute or inalienable. One version of the powerful and recurring criticism of the utilitarian principle that plays on this aversion to natural rights appears in Fyodor Dostoevsky's novel *The Brothers Karamazov* (1880), which presents the moral problem of whether a perfect society would be worthwhile if it was achieved at the cost of constantly torturing a single child. Ursula Le Guin, in "The Ones Who Walk Away from Omelas," (1973) reproduces this theme in a short story in which the good fortune of a community depends on one child being kept in misery, darkness, and filth; each citizen learns of this on coming of age, and some walk away, never to return.

Mill struggles with this problem in his discussion of justice in *Utilitarianism*, which emphasizes the importance of moral rules. He states (2002 [1863], 296): "Justice is a name for certain classes of moral rules, which concern the essentials of human well-being . . . and the notion which we have found to be of the essence of the idea of justice, that of a right residing in an individual, implies and testifies to this more binding obligation." The most important of these moral rules (and their correlative individual rights) are the rules which forbid humans to harm one another and which demand that humans extend to one another what each is due. Although he agrees with Bentham that these "rights" are finally grounded in utility, Mill's emphasis on moral rules forecasts the later development of full-fledged "rule utilitarianism." While traditional "act utilitarianism" directly evaluates each *individual action* in terms of the utility (or greatest good) principle, "rule utilitarianism" evaluates behavior by *rules* that, if universally followed, would lead to the greatest good for the greatest number.

It is debatable whether Mill himself ought to be considered a "rule utilitarian." It seems likely that the idea was inchoate in his own thought. After arguing that justice and individual rights are defined in terms of moral rules, for instance, Mill casts doubt on whether his thought should be categorized as rule utilitarianism in the modern sense when he maintains, "All persons are deemed to have a right to equality to treatment, except when some recognized social expediency requires the reverse" (2002 [1863], 300). He thereby undermines the notion that he is arguing for any sort of inviolable individual rights. (For the earliest clear formulations of rule utilitarianism, see the works listed in the further reading sections below for Richard B. Brandt, John Rawls, and J. O. Umson.)

Utilitarianism and the Environment

Utilitarianism has significant resources for addressing pressing environmental issues. Because utilitarianism purports to be neutral about what counts as a benefit and merely pursues the maximization of utility or benefits through aggregation, the utilitarian calculus of cost-benefit analysis has emerged as a powerful decision-making tool. After all, at least in theory, policy makers are free to determine what will count as a cost or benefit in accord with the public good. Cost-benefit analysis, for instance, is often employed to discuss environmental regulation and how to carry out the regulation. These calculations, usually using monetarized costs and benefits, provide a relatively clear and simple algorithm aimed at aiding environmental decision making.

The roots of cost-benefit analysis in utilitarian ethical theory are clear and this analysis is often viewed as a neutral and efficient decision-making tool. But a persistent criticism of cost-benefit analysis in making decisions that affect the environment and nonhuman creatures is that, because it necessarily compares costs and benefits using a common metric (i.e., money), it cannot properly value such things as living creatures, ecosystems, or species. Because environmental concerns do not enter easily into the calculus, they are systematically devalued—at least in the view of those who believe that life has intrinsic value that cannot be captured by such cost-benefit analyses, for instance, or of those who shy away from the necessarily anthropocentric perspective that reduces "costs" and "benefits" to money. Determining what is a "benefit" or a "cost" is often not a simple matter—and how to value each is more complex still. It is difficult to attach a monetary value to many costs (loss of life, ecosystems, or vistas, for example) and benefits (preserving or improving human health, ecosystemic health, or vistas, for example), and therefore these costs and benefits may be ignored or undervalued in comparison with costs that are already monetarized (the literal cost of building or development, or compliance measures, for example) or benefits that are already monetarized (such as job creation).

Utilitarianism and Animal Rights

It is interesting to note, however, that in addition to powerful analytic tools, utilitarian theory has also helped to shape many peoples' conceptions of how human beings ought properly to relate to other animals. Bentham, for instance, was an early proponent of according ethical consideration to animals, arguing that animal suffering is similar to human suffering. He reasoned that the relevant moral question is not whether animals can reason or talk (since this would, for instance, also exclude human infants), but whether animals can suffer. Comparing the treatment of animals to slavery, Bentham maintained, "[t]he day may come, when the rest of the animal creation may acquire those rights which never could have been withholden from them but by the hand of tyranny" (2007 [1789], 311, note). Mill likewise maintained that the utilitarian standard of morality is defined as "the rules and precepts, by the observance of which" a happy life might be secured "not to [mankind] only but, so far as the nature of things admit, to the whole sentient creation" (2002 [1863], 245).

The most influential modern utilitarian voice to argue that animals' interests count ethically is the animal rights activist Peter Singer. His basic argument is simple and rests squarely on utilitarian foundations. After quoting Bentham at length, Singer argues (2002 [1975], 7): "By saying that we must consider the interests of all beings with the capacity for suffering or enjoyment Bentham does not arbitrarily exclude from consideration any interests at all. . . . The capacity for suffering and enjoyment is a *prerequisite for having interests at all*, a condition that must be satisfied before we can speak of interests in a meaningful way." Note that by arguing that the capacity to suffer is a prerequisite for having interests and that we should seek to minimize suffering or, equivalently, maximize the satisfaction of interests, Singer mixes hedonistic utilitarianism (maximize pleasure / minimize pain) and preference utilitarianism (maximize the satisfaction of preferences or interests).

If a creature can suffer, Singer continues, there is no moral justification for refusing to take its suffering into account in the moral calculus. "[T]he principle of equality requires that its suffering be counted equally with the like suffering—insofar as rough comparisons can be made—of any other being" (Singer 2002 [1975], 8). The interests of every creature with interests count and similar interests count equally. Faced with (1) this moral calculus of interests, (2) the fact that, as a practical matter, it is probably not possible to raise animals for food on a large scale without inflicting considerable suffering, and (3) the fact that we live in a densely populated world in need of large-scale food production, Singer argues on the basis of the utility principle that the most ethically justifiable route to take is to become a vegetarian.

Interests versus Individuals

Singer's view is not strictly an "animal rights" perspective. As the philosopher Tom Regan (1985) points out, the utilitarian position does not advocate rights for different individuals because of their intrinsic worth—as do most animal rights perspectives. The utilitarian is concerned with the satisfaction of an individual's *interests*, not primarily with the individuals whose interests they are. Still, what the utilitarian and animal rights perspectives share is a focus on individual creatures. Larger wholes, such as species or ecosystems, are ethically considered, if at all, through the lens of concern about the individual. To some, this is a significant weakness because so many of the environmental problems are systemic and therefore concern such "wholes" (Callicott 1980). Although utilitarians lack the resources to directly consider the moral value of "wholes" (and generally do not view individuals as constituted by their social relationships), this perspective is not without resources to address broad systemic environmental concerns. For instance, as Singer argues in his recent book, *The Ethics of What We Eat*, concern about the welfare of individual animals has ripple effects on such wide-ranging systemic issues as organic farming, free trade, eating locally, and factory farming.

The *egalitarian* (similar interests should count equally) and *aggregative* (satisfaction of interests, or happiness, should be maximized) aspects of utilitarian moral theory provide resources to influence environmental policy through cost-benefit analysis as well as to argue that the interests of animals count morally. Interestingly, however, it is difficult to see how the precision of cost-benefit analysis (in which costs and benefits are usually monetarized) can be maintained if the interests of animals, as well as other forms of life on the planet (which would be extremely difficult to measure in monetary terms) become part of the calculus.

Francisco BENZONI
U.S. Fourth Circuit Court of Appeals

FURTHER READING

Bentham, Jeremy. (2007 [1789]). *An introduction to the principles of morals and legislation*. Mineola, NY: Dover Publications, Inc.

Brandt, Richard B. (1959). *Ethical theory: The problems of normative and critical ethics*. Englewood Cliffs, NJ: Prentice-Hall.

Callicott, J. Baird. (1980). Animal liberation: A triangular affair. *Environmental Ethics 2*, 311–338. Reprinted and revised in Callicott, J. Baird. (1989). *In Defense of the Land Ethic: Essays in Environmental Philosophy* (pp. 15–38). Albany: State University of New York Press.

Mill, John Stuart. (2002 [1863]). *Utilitarianism*. In *The basic writings of John Stuart Mill*. New York: The Modern Library.

Mill, John Stuart. (2002 [1859]). *On liberty*. In *The basic writings of John Stuart Mill*. New York: The Modern Library.

Pollan, Michael. (2006). *Omnivore's dilemma: A natural history of the four meals*. New York: Penguin Books.

Rawls, John. (1955). Two concepts of rules. *Philosophical Review 64*, 3–32.

Regan, Tom. (1985). *The case for animal rights*. Berkeley: University of California Press.

Singer, Peter. (2002 [1975]). *Animal liberation*. New York: HarperCollins.

Singer, Peter, & Mason, Jim (2006). *The ethics of what we eat: Why our food choices matter*. Emmaus, PA: Rodale.

Umson, J. O. (1953). The Interpretation of the moral philosophy of J. S. Mill. *Philosophical Quarterly 10*, 33–39.

V

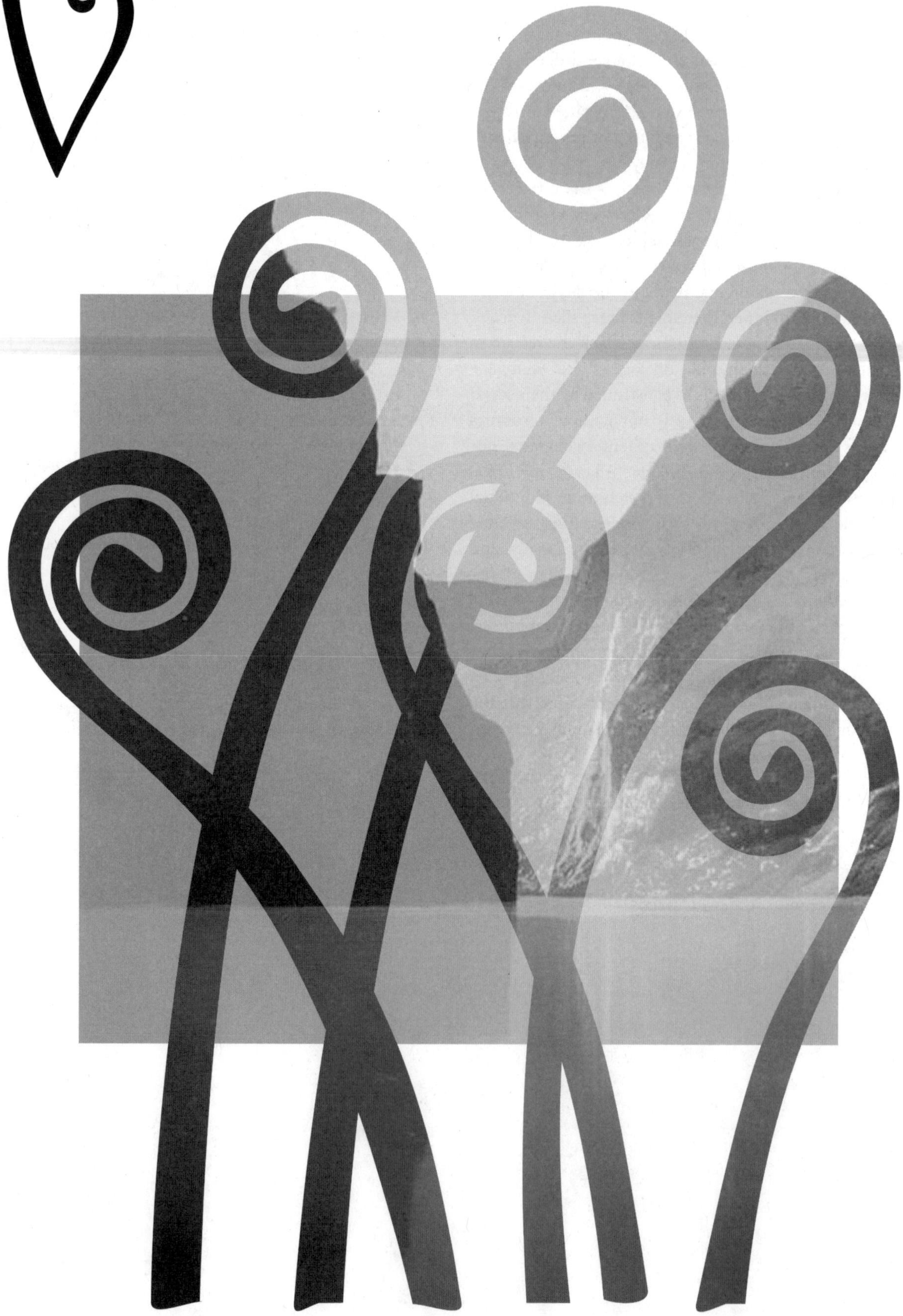

Values

Observations about what is valuable lie at the center of many current discussions of sustainability, evolving as a response to the importance attributed to nature by humans. Although there are multiple types of value involved in the debates—for example, intrinsic, extrinsic, and instrumental value—each plays a role in how sustainability is approached and addressed by society.

Value denotes the worth of a quality, a physical object, a feeling, an experience, or an idea. Our values are often related to what we believe is "good." In ethical decision making, what people value directly affects the choices they make. Yet there are different types of values, creating potential ethical dilemmas. This diversity of values is at work in many discussions about sustainability: a sustainable practice might have moral value, for instance, or it might be considered economically valuable, or both. Thus debates over value—and how to judge different claims to value—are at the heart of sustainability.

Nature's Intrinsic Value

Nearly everyone would agree that some things have more value than others. But how do we differentiate between the worth of *A* versus *B*? To answer this, some environmental ethicists investigate whether nature has intrinsic value. An intrinsic value is the worth that something has in itself, apart from any evaluator or relationship to other things.

Deep ecologists (scholars who emphasize the interconnection and fundamental relatedness of all beings in order to promote a shift in values toward a kinship with nature) and others argue that nature has intrinsic value (Rolston 1988; Naess 1973). If nature—from trees to ecosystems—has intrinsic value, then it has objective value, which is determined independently of usefulness or our perceptions. Furthermore, this position leads to a moral claim: the intrinsic value of nature necessitates our care of nature. Things such as promoting biodiversity and wilderness protection are moral duties that would be justified in terms of the intrinsic value of nature. For these ethicists, sustainability is our duty in response to nature's intrinsic value; there is intrinsic value in living sustainability.

Environmental pragmatists (those who use the insights of the pragmatist tradition to move away from theoretical debates and toward practically-oriented answers in ethics and philosophy) and others challenge the existence of intrinsic value. First, some argue that the concept of intrinsic values fails to account for the fact that all values are relational (Morito 2003); value is present only if there is someone or something that values. Intrinsic value therefore cannot be independent or inherent. Second, commentators note that environmental ethics use the term *intrinsic value* in several different ways (O'Neill 1992). As a result, theories of intrinsic value sometimes conflate or equivocate these meanings in ways that create further problems. For these positions, nature and sustainability nonetheless can have worth.

Other Types of Value in Nature

Intrinsic value is not the only type of value that influences our decision making. Extrinsic value assumes that a thing has worth only because something external to it has judged it to have value. For example, humans judge oak trees to be valuable for a number of uses: shade, lumber, fuel, and so forth. If intrinsic value is inherent to the thing, extrinsic value is worth that originates from beyond the thing itself. A related concept is instrumental value. In this case, something with instrumental value has worth as a means to an end, whereas intrinsic value is defined as the value of a thing as an end (moral or otherwise). Here we might see nature as valuable based on its utility. The ideas of extrinsic and instrumental value are sometimes associated with subjective values, which depend upon someone or something to recognize the value. Critics of intrinsic values and others have argued that the most persuasive and strongest argument for sustainability often comes from recognizing the instrumental value of protecting nature. For example, rather than arguing for the inherent worth of clean air, one might argue for the health and economic benefits of wind power for human individuals and communities.

Underlying the discussion of intrinsic, extrinsic, and instrumental values is yet another division: values can be categorized into an undefined number of realms such as aesthetic, economic, or ontological. Some actions might have different types of value than others. Some sustainable practices might be justified because they possess economic value. For example, the decision to install geothermal heating can be decided simply by weighing financial factors. Others see the value of sustainability in ethical terms, which means that decisions concerning sustainability were justified when deemed the most morally valuable choices. In this case, we might use public transportation simply because it is the right thing to do, even in cases when it is more time consuming and inconvenient. Finally, certain things might be considered to have several types of value at once. Thus the decision to landscape with native species would be justified as morally appropriate and aesthetically valuable, even if it were more expensive than other choices.

Sustainability, Values, and Axiology

Advocates of sustainability often operate under a specific system of values that are ecologically focused. These systems of value affect the way that sustainability is discussed. When nature and sustainable communities are deemed to have value, what effect does that have on our beliefs and actions? What duties and responsibilities do we have because of our values? How do we manage conflicting values?

The area of philosophy concerned with defining and differentiating categories of values is called axiology. Sustainability brings out a number of axiological questions, especially about how a given sustainable choice relates to the values we think are most important. Yet values fostered by sustainable practices sometimes come into conflict with other values held by members of the community. For example, sustainable agriculture might be valued for its positive effects on public health. But this might come into conflict with other values, such as the value of using chemical pesticides and fertilizers in order to maximize food yields in famine affected areas.

Conflicts of value can occur on at least two fronts. First, there can be a conflict between the values held by different individuals or groups. Some hold that sustainability brings greater economic, moral, and social value than nonsustainable practices. This might conflict with different, entrenched values that condone nonsustainable beliefs and practices. In some cases, it also might conflict with values that usually are not contradictory to sustainability, such as the value of human rights. Second, we might argue that nonhuman beings can value things. Ecosystems—and the Earth itself—can have relations of value. Therefore a conflict emerges between human and nonhuman systems of value, especially insofar as values are relational. If humans find the use of trees as lumber valuable but trees do not, who decides what is appropriate and on what grounds?

As we have seen, our values—what we find to be valuable—are at the center of a number of debates. Sustainability represents a shift in how and where value is identified in society, and in what responsibilities such value entails. Questions of value are also at the forefront of many practical and ethical decisions. For example, does ecological restoration provide the same values as preserved areas? What is the primary emphasis for community design? What role does "ecological literacy"—that is, our scientific, humanistic, and traditional knowledge of the natural world around us—play in our decision making? How are policy decisions informed by the values provided by sustainability? These and other questions show how the concepts of values and sustainability influence each other.

Forrest CLINGERMAN
Ohio Northern University

FURTHER READING

Lachs, John, & Kohák, Erazim. (1991). A dialogue on value. *Journal of Speculative Philosophy, 5*(1), 1–24.

Light, Andrew, & Rolston, Holmes, III. (Eds.). (2003). *Environmental ethics: An anthology.* Malden, MA: Blackwell.

McShane, Katie. (2007). Why environmental ethics shouldn't give up on intrinsic value. *Environmental Ethics, 29,* 43–61.

Morito, Bruce. (2003). Intrinsic value: A modern albatross for the ecological approach. *Environmental Values, 12,* 317–336.

Naess, Arne. (1973). The shallow and the deep, long-range ecology movement: A summary. *Inquiry, 16,* 95–100.

O'Neill, John. (1992). The varieties of intrinsic value. *The Monist, 75,* 229–237.

O'Neill, John. (2001). Meta-ethics. In Dale Jamieson (Ed.), *A companion to environmental philosophy* (pp. 163–176). Malden, MA: Blackwell.

Rolston, Holmes, III. (1988). *Environmental ethics: Duties to and values in the natural world.* Philadelphia: Temple University Press.

Vegetarianism

Vegetarianism is being increasingly practiced by many in the world for many different reasons, including religious, moral, ethical, health, and/or environmental. According to studies, meat-based diets require more land, energy, and water resources than vegetarianism, and both meat production and overfishing have been linked to environmental degradation.

Vegetarianism refers to a diet that restricts meat (including meat byproducts), fish, poultry, and, in some cases, eggs. Vegans, a subset of vegetarians, practice a stricter diet and exclude all forms of animal products, including milk products and eggs. Some vegetarians and vegans reject all use of animal products, such as leather, wool, beeswax, and lanolin. By definition, vegetarians abstain from all meat, poultry and fish, but in practice, vegetarianism is broadly interpreted. Some self-designated vegetarians abstain from meat, but eat fish and/or poultry; others, calling themselves "flexitarians," follow a primarily vegetarian diet but eat meat on some occasions. The practice and interpretation of vegetarianism tends to be linked to the individual rationale for making this dietary choice.

Individuals and groups adopt a vegetarian diet for a wide range of reasons, including morality, environment and sustainability concerns, religion, and health. Some religious traditions, notably those arising in Asia, have advocated a vegetarian diet for over two millennia; many Hindus and Buddhists, for example, do not eat meat for religious reasons. In the contemporary United States, many vegetarians have chosen this lifestyle for health or moral reasons, citing concerns for animal welfare or sustainability. Today restaurant menus and college cafeterias reflect this increasingly popular choice, and most restaurants and institutions can accommodate vegetarian requests even if they do not highlight such choices.

Until the nineteenth century vegetarianism was influential primarily in Asia or within small populations, such as the Seventh Day Adventists in the West, and various intentional communities. Some Christian monastic communities and Gnostic sects, such as the medieval French Cathars, adopted the practice, but vegetarianism was not widespread. In 1847, the Vegetarian Society was founded in England, with chapters in the Netherlands and Germany coming shortly thereafter. These groups worked actively to promote vegetarianism through public lectures and distribution of printed materials. Count Leo Tolstoy, the eminent Russian novelist and inspiration to Mohandas Gandhi, wrote: "The consumption of animal food is plainly immoral because it demands an act which does violence to our moral sentiments." (Tolstoy 1897, 20). People are increasingly adopting a vegetarian diet due to moral and environmental concerns.

Religious Dimensions

Most religious traditions address the issue of vegetarianism and incorporate some form of vegetarianism, even if only for periodic fasting. Members of some traditions, particularly those with ascetic and monastic dimensions, believe that meat inhibits one's spiritual goals and associate meat eating with impurity and aroused passions. Restrictions on meat eating also emerge from ethical standards about the appropriate treatment of animals, although in some cases, health and/or economic concerns are also contributing factors.

Asian Traditions

The Hindu, Buddhist, and Jain traditions, all originating on the Indian subcontinent, each promote some degree of vegetarianism. The basic religious and theological premise is that harming other beings, regardless of whether these beings are humans, plants, or animals, builds up one's karmic debt, despite the intentionality of those acts. (Karma refers to action and the consequences of one's actions.) One accrues karma by acting, and actions emerging from desire and passion, particularly violent actions, burden the actor with a karmic load. Karma affects the conditions of one's present life and future birth, and action, particularly violence, traps one within the circle of birth and death, or reincarnation. *Ahimsa*, the avoidance of harming living beings, is a means of reducing one's karmic load and so is one rationale for vegetarianism.

Hinduism

Hinduism has perhaps the strongest popular associations with vegetarianism, but the Hindu tradition does not require one to be vegetarian, nor are all, or even the majority of Hindus, vegetarian. Socioeconomic conditions, caste status, sectarian divisions, and personal choice affect a Hindu's choice of diet. Brahman castes (the priestly class/caste) are typically vegetarian and adhere to a strict dietary code. For the Kshatriya castes (the martial and governing classes), eating meat is beneficial to arouse the passions, anger, and strength necessary for fighting, and so these populations are less likely to be vegetarian. Vegetarianism does enjoy a high status, so often the lower castes will adopt vegetarian practices to gain caste status. Castes working with animal byproducts, such as leather tanners, typically have had low status relative to those with occupations that did not involve animal products.

Hindus avoid meat as a means to practice nonviolence, or *ahimsa*, because the violence associated with the eating and killing of meat increases one's karmic debt. For Hindus, *ahimsa* is a means of fulfilling one's dharma, or duty, to family, society, and the divine. The strongest food-related prohibition in the Hindu tradition relates to cow slaughter, and Hindus who eat fish or poultry typically abstain from beef. Hindus venerate the cow, which plays an essential role in Hindu myth, diet, ritual, and ethics. Many Hindus view the cow as a "mother" who continually gives of herself, and the cow is essential for the economic survival of many in South Asia. The cow provides substances such as ghee (clarified butter), milk, yogurt, and cow dung, which are important for ritual, food, and fuel.

For Mohandas K. Gandhi (1869–1948), cow protection was a critical element of his moral and religious philosophy. He was a devout Hindu and considered the cow holy. Gandhi viewed cows as representative of "the whole dumb creation of god," meaning that the cow represents human and nonhuman beings who cannot protect themselves and thus merits human compassion (Gandhi 1958, 65; Parel 1997, 54–5). Although he was atypical in this regard, Gandhi

himself abstained from drinking milk once he learned that even in India cows were mistreated for milk production. Gandhi, however, did not prohibit the use of leather as long as the cow was not slaughtered for this purpose.

Buddhism

Vegetarianism is an important religious and moral practice for many Buddhists. In practice, vegetarianism differs by school; for example, the Mahayana school advocates a vegetarian diet, while the Theravada and Vajrayana schools do not. Many Buddhist converts of Western heritage in Europe and the United States become vegetarian.

One of Buddhism's Five Precepts states that Buddhists should abstain from harming any life-form. This requirement does not specifically state that Buddhists should not eat meat, and the Buddha himself never required a vegetarian diet. Monks and nuns, for example, who live by begging for alms, must eat what they are given with gratitude. Compassion for all living beings is one of the two focal points of Buddhism, and so many Buddhists abstain from meat because meat consumption is seen as cruel. Mahayana Buddhists who follow the bodhisattva's path—the path to enlightenment and Buddhahood—must actively cultivate compassion for all living beings. The *Jataka Tales*, stories that depict the Buddha's previous lives as different animals and reflect the Buddha's own path to Buddhahood, teach that all life is sacred and that killing an animal is equivalent to killing a human.

Jainism

The Jain tradition originated approximately at the same time as Buddhism (sixth century BCE) and accepts similar, but more stringent, prohibitions against harming life forms. The Jain tradition is strictly vegetarian and extends restrictions to plant and insect life. Jains eat a diet based on vegetables, fruits, grains, and milk, excluding root vegetables such as onions and potatoes, which die when harvested. Many Jains take precautions, such as straining water, to ensure that they do not inadvertently kill living beings present in the water. The Jain tradition emphasizes asceticism as a path to liberation from reincarnation, and practitioners rigorously adhere to a diet and lifestyle meant to minimize violence and harm to other beings.

Abrahamic Traditions

There has been far less emphasis on vegetarianism in the biblical, or Abrahamic, traditions, although some groups within these traditions have advocated a vegetarian diet. Both the Jewish and Islamic traditions contain rigorous dietary codes regulating animal slaughter and meat eating—kosher and halal, respectively—and these codes require that animals be spared unnecessary pain and suffering when slaughtered. Followers of the Rastafarian movement, a monotheistic, Abrahamic tradition, have adopted different forms of vegetarianism. Some follow dietary restrictions of the Hebrew Bible and avoid shellfish and pork, while others avoid all meat as a form of pacifism.

Judaism

Many scholars of Judaism agree that, according to Genesis, God intended humans to be vegetarian. "And God said, 'Behold, I have given you every herb yielding seed which is on the face of all the earth, and every tree, in which is the fruit of a tree yielding seed; to you it shall be for food'" (Genesis 1:29 ASV). In an ideal state, in the Garden of Eden, Adam and Eve ate the seeds and fruits offered by God. According to the Talmud, humans were later granted permission to eat meat as a concession to lust and sin. Ancient Hebrews ate a largely vegetarian diet, however, this diet was dictated more by economic than religious reasons; for example, in an agrarian-pastoral society, animals are necessary for labor and milk.

Christianity

Most Christians have interpreted biblical passages to support meat eating. Many early Christians were vegetarian for ascetic reasons, believing that eating meat aroused the passions, but, by the time of the Roman Empire, eating meat had become the predominant lifestyle. Few Christian groups advocated vegetarianism beyond periodic fasting, although some Roman Catholic monastic orders, such as the Carthusian Order (established 1086) and the Cistercian Order (established 1140), abstained from meat as part of an ascetic lifestyle.

Clerics and laity of the Catholic and Orthodox churches avoid meat periodically for spiritual reasons. The Catholic laity is advised to abstain from meat on Fridays and during the Lenten season but otherwise do not partake in a vegetarian diet. This vegetarian diet and partial fasting is due to ascetic reasons and not ethical concerns for animal welfare.

Among Christian communities, Seventh Day Adventists have been among the strongest advocates for a vegetarian diet. One of the founders, Ellen White (1827–1915), was a vegetarian health reformer. Approximately 50 percent of Seventh Day Adventists are lacto-ovo vegetarians and eat a diet based on plants, grains and seeds, along with dairy products, including eggs and milk. The vegetarianism of the Seventh Day Adventists is based both on biblical teachings as well as human health. Seventh Day Adventists believe in the holistic nature of humankind and also that all food and drink should honor God and preserve the health of body, mind, and spirit.

Islam

Vegetarianism has not played a large role in the Islamic tradition, partly because eating meat was necessary for survival in the desert climates of the Middle East. According to Islamic tradition, Muhammad was compassionate towards animals and stated that no animals should be harmed in Mecca, however this treatment did not translate to a vegetarian diet. Today most Muslims eat meat, and some Islamic scholars state that vegetarianism is not permissible because one cannot forbid something Allah has allowed. Some members of Sufi orders are vegetarian because it promotes compassion, and abstaining from meat purifies the body for spiritual pursuits.

Religious Response to Factory Farming

Growing concern about the moral status of animals and disclosures about the conditions of factory farming has encouraged many in the United States and Europe to avoid or reduce consumption of meat, fish, and poultry. The Humane Society of the United States has highlighted the links between animal welfare and religious ethics and is working with religious traditions to codify their statements on faith and factory farming (The Humane Society of the United States, 2009). The Humane Farm Animal Care is a nonprofit organization created to improve the lives of farm animals by certifying their humane treatment. The certification requires, among other things, that the animals are raised in a cage- or crate-free environment and are both antibiotic and hormone free. Some "flexitarians" limit meat and poultry consumption to animals and birds that are humanely and sustainably raised and slaughtered.

Similar moral concerns have prompted Jewish and Islamic scholars and practitioners to reconsider animal welfare in regard to, respectively, kosher and halal codes. Today some Jewish scholars and practitioners look to the Torah to sanction a vegetarian diet. The admonition to spare animals unnecessary pain must also cover the conditions in which animals are raised, and thus meat produced in factory-farming conditions should not be considered kosher. Similarly, some Muslims abstain from meat because meat produced in factory conditions cannot be halal since animals have not been treated humanely.

Sustainability Concerns and Environmental Dimensions

Both the Jewish and Islamic responses to factory farming also cite that it is environmentally unsound and an unsustainable practice. Jewish scholars mention the principle of *bal tashchit* (you shall not waste) that admonishes humans not to waste. For Muslims, industrially produced meat can be considered *haram*, or forbidden, because its production leads to environmental degradation. Jews and Muslims cite a mandate to take care of the Earth, and factory farming violates that principle.

These responses accord with recent studies linking meat production and overfishing to accelerated environmental degradation. In 2006, the Food and Agriculture Organization of the United Nations released *Livestock's Long Shadow: Environmental Issues and Options*, a scathing indictment of the livestock industry. The report names the livestock industry as a major contributor to environmental problems such as climate change, land and water degradation, and loss of biodiversity. This study, and others, argues that a meat-based diet requires more energy, land, and water resources than a diet based on plants and dairy products. The meat-based diet of the United States and Europe and the growing desire for meat in Asian countries will place demands on the land and the earth's ecosystems that will be difficult, if not impossible, to meet. These concerns have led many to either eat little or no meat or to eat meat only from sources that are sustainable and humane. Similar concerns about sustainable fishing, including extensive overfishing of species such as swordfish and deleterious social and environmental effects of farmed seafood, have prompted many to alter consumption patterns of seafood.

A. Whitney SANFORD
University of Florida

FURTHER READING

Gandhi, Mohandas K. (1927). *Young India 1919–1922*. Ann Arbor: University of Michigan.

Gandhi, Mohandas K., & Bhave, Vinoba. (1958). *Sarvodaya [The welfare of all]*. Ahmedbad, India: Navajivan Publishing House.

The Humane Society of the United States. (2009). Animals and Religion. Retrieved June 19, 2009, from http://www.hsus.org/religion/

Iacobbo, Karen, & Iacobbo, Michael. (2006). *Vegetarians and vegans in America today*. Westport, CT: Praeger.

Marcus, Erik. (2005). *Meat market: Animals, ethics, & money*. Ithaca, NY: Brio Press.

Parel, Anthony J. (Ed.). (1997). *Gandhi Hind Swaraj and other writings*. Cambridge, U.K.: Cambridge University Press.

Rosen, Steven. (1997). *Diet for transcendence: Vegetarianism and the world religions*. Badger, CA: Torchlight.

Schwartz, Richard H. (2001). *Judaism and vegetarianism*. New York: Lantern Books.

Shabkar Tsogdruk Rangdrol. (2004). *Food of bodhisattvas: Buddhist teachings on abstaining from meat* (Padmakara Translation Group, Trans.). Boston, MA: Shambhala.

Singer, Peter. (Ed.). (2005). *In defense of animals: The second wave*. Malden, MA: Blackwell.

Steinfeld, Henning; Gerber, Pierre; Wassenaar, Tom; Castel, Vincent; Rosales, Mauricio; & de Haan, Cees. (2006). *Livestock's long shadow: Environmental issues and opinions*. Rome: Food and Agriculture Organization of the United Nations. Retrieved on April 23, 2009, from http://www.fao.org/docrep/010/a0701e/a0701e00.htm

Tolstoy, Leo. (1897). Quoted in Clubb, Henry S., (Ed.), *Food, Home and Garden*. Vol 1, New Series. Philadelphia, PA: Vegetarian Society of America.

Virtues and Vices

Virtues (such as compassion and moderation) are defined as cultivated cognitive-emotional habits that allow people to respond fittingly in diverse situations. By contrast, vices (such as wanton neglect and greed) are cultivated ways of being and acting that lead to harm, including injustice and environmental damage. The cultivation of virtues plays a role in all indigenous and world religions and is essential for a sustainable lifestyle.

As a species, human beings have evolved with a remarkable ability to live in and move between quite diverse natural and social environments. This adaptability is biologically supported by malleable patterns of cognitive and emotional processing, also called habits. Cognitive-emotional habits that allow people to respond fittingly in varying situations are commonly known as virtues (for example, respect, courage, compassion, and moderation). What counts as fitting in any particular context depends on culturally articulated visions of the good life. These normative visions usually involve a balance of personal and communal well-being. When people calibrate their cognitive-emotional habits to socially and ecologically inclusive visions of flourishing, their virtues tend to undergird sustainable lifestyles.

Still inchoate in children, virtues are perfected through experience. Once established, they produce reliable patterns of thought and action that can last a lifetime. For example, people who respect their bioregions are inclined to notice natural rhythms, other inhabitants, and their interactions. Such people are more likely than others to spot harmful changes and to take protective measures when necessary. Early warnings about climate change thus came from Inuit, whose deep respect for their Arctic regions—to them, respect for the *inuat* or spiritual owners of the universe—allowed them to notice a warming trend through changes in the ice well before mainstream climate science confirmed it.

Virtues, Religions, and Sustainability

Being group animals, people typically cultivate virtues in sociocultural contexts. There they find not only mentoring and peer feedback, but also institutionalized rules of thumb and models of personal and communal well-being that help them to fine-tune their cognitive-emotional habits. Often, such sociocultural anchors of the good life are embedded in religious myths and rituals.

Virtues play a role in all indigenous and world religions. For example, all religious traditions encourage their practitioners to cultivate compassion and moderation, but each tradition uniquely interprets what is involved in cultivating compassion and moderation through its own universe of stories, practices, and role models. Comparing virtues across religious traditions therefore involves seeing "similarities within differences and differences within similarities" (Yearley 1990, 1). Many religious beliefs and practices encourage people to cultivate virtues with alertness to the needs of the entire community of planetary life, both present and future. Typical religion-supported "sustainability virtues" are wonder, humility, sensitivity, attentiveness, caution, creativity, courage, frugality, diligence, perseverance, gratitude, generosity, respect, care, compassion, patience, justice, forgiveness, moderation, forbearance, hope, and wisdom. By encouraging people to cultivate such traditional virtues with alertness to the needs of planetary life, religions foster an indispensable aspect of sustainability: *personal* attunement to the boundary conditions of life's flourishing, which include ecological integrity, economic health, human dignity, and social justice.

Vices, Religions, and Sustainability

When people deliberately cultivate cognitive-emotional habits that prevent or undermine inclusive flourishing, their ways of being and acting are commonly referred to as vices. People tend to adopt and perfect such habits to serve limited ends, such as personal wealth. Vices often emerge from extreme behaviors that are unresponsive to feedback, such as overconsumption, excess aggression, or wanton neglect. As a result, vices typically carry harm in their wake, including social injustice and environmental damage.

Religions have a reputation for denouncing vices as personal sins. Resulting from a lack of reverence, sins represent a sickness of mind, emotion, and body that above all requires spiritual healing. Increasingly, the world's religions explicitly call for such spiritual healing as an antidote to persistent violations of the boundary conditions for complex life on Earth.

As fallible human institutions, however, religions can also reinforce the cultivation of vices among their followers. The link between religion and vice became a matter of heated debate in 1967, when the UCLA historian Lynn White Jr. published "The Historical Roots of Our Ecologic Crisis." In this article, White traces modern environmental problems to Christian support for an exploitative attitude toward nature, which replaced the humility fostered by pre-Christian pantheism. The debates stirred by White's article have encouraged many religious practitioners to engage in critical reflection on the ambiguous records of their traditions. In looking for spiritual healing and ways to cultivate sustainability virtues, religious practitioners increasingly find support in interreligious dialogue and cooperation.

At the same time, religious practitioners may also disagree on the sorts of behavior that typify vices. Consumerist behavior, for example, can be variously interpreted as an expression of vice or as justified. Many Roman Catholics view consumerist behavior as a sign of greed. According to Church tradition, greed is one of the deadly sins through which a person foregoes salvation. The Roman Catholic Church encourages its members to cultivate the opposite virtues of simplicity and generosity, which attune them to the Creator and to the needs of all created life. By contrast, many Pentecostal Christians in developing countries view consumerist behavior as an earned right. Following a so-called prosperity gospel, they believe that personal wealth is a sign of a divine reward ethic. Meanwhile, they trust divine providence to deal with its sustainability impacts.

Although religious institutions and movements historically have not always fostered sustainable personal habits, nowadays most aim to do so. The transformation of human cognitive-emotional habits from harmful to ecologically and socially fitting is a necessary, even though by itself an insufficient, condition for realizing the goals of sustainability. In most regions of the world (secularized pockets being the exception), religious involvement is also a necessary condition for such changes of deeply engrained habit.

Virtues and Sustainability in Philosophical Ethics

Virtues and vices function as key concepts in several ancient schools of philosophy, including classical Hindu, Buddhist, Confucian, Platonic, Aristotelian, Stoic, and Christian thought. During the later Middle Ages, Aristotelian virtue ethics became prominent in the Middle East and Europe through creative appropriations by Muslim, Jewish, and Christian thinkers (especially Al-Ghazali, Maimonides, and Thomas Aquinas). When eighteenth-century Enlightenment thinkers introduced the concepts of rights and utility, virtue ethics all but disappeared from Western philosophical discourse. Toward the end of the twentieth century, however, academic philosophers regained interest in the cultivation of virtues (also called *aretaic* ethics, from the ancient Greek *arete*, meaning excellence). Today much scholarly effort goes into clarifying and adjusting key concepts in virtue ethics.

Environmental ethics also became a focus of philosophical inquiry in the last quarter of the twentieth century. Discussions in the field initially unfolded along deontological (based on moral obligation) or consequentialist lines, but subsequently broadened to include the *aretaic* line. As a subfield, environmental virtue ethics (EVE) is dedicated to defining sustainable ways of flourishing and to clarifying the general and specific characteristics of matching virtues and opposing vices. While some traditional schools of virtue ethics have been narrowly anthropocentric, perspectives in environmental virtue ethics range from enlightened self-interest to biocentric egalitarianism (Sandler and Cafaro 2005).

Virtues and Social Transformation

Historically, virtue ethics has been associated more with conservatism than with social change. The stability of social systems partially depends on personal qualities like honesty, respect, cooperation, and moderation. Power elites and their intellectuals, who have an interest in the status quo, therefore tend to encourage or force citizens to cultivate such character traits. When a social system is unjust, however, mandatory cultivation of civic virtues has little to do with genuine virtue cultivation, because it will further undermine personal and communal flourishing. A scholarly interpretation of the authoritative virtue catalogues of colonialist, sexist, racist, speciesist, and otherwise elitist social systems therefore warrants a critical perspective.

In unsustainable social contexts, the personal cultivation of genuine virtues may appear radical. Virtue cultivation can play a key role in grassroots resistance. In India, for example, the Hindu virtue of respect for life, expressed in the practice of seed-keeping, has inspired the seed *satyagraha* movement, a successful resistance effort (based on Gandhi's nonviolent practice) against patented seeds, which Monsanto had genetically engineered to be sterile to protect its profits. Similarly, indigenous spiritual attitudes towards nonhuman nature inspire many participants in the so-called alternative globalization movement, which opposes the ruling neoliberal model of globalization on the ground that it is unsustainable.

In the mainstream environmental movement, virtue cultivation initially received less attention as a driver of social change than public pressure, legal reform, and fiscal measures. After several decades of effort, however, these macromeasures are showing their limits. Today mainstream environmental activists and policy makers increasingly recognize the importance of matching personal transformation. The Dalai Lama, Ecumenical Patriarch Bartholomew of the Greek Orthodox Church, Pope Benedict XVI, and other spiritual leaders who inspire the cultivation of sustainability virtues are now widely recognized as key leaders in driving the transformation towards sustainable societies.

Cultivating Virtues

From an operational perspective, the personal cultivation of virtues is a form of value-guided biological conditioning. Through practice and habituation, people are able to develop stable, situation-adjustable patterns of cognitive and emotional processing. Within a certain range of genetic, contextual and biographical possibilities, they can shape these character tools to fit their simultaneously deepening understanding of personal and communal flourishing. For example, the cultivation of generosity typically requires regular practice in giving. Through feedback from others and by observing their own reactions, people learn to adjust the timing, wording, and gestures of giving to the point where their gifts appear truly fitting.

People need social networks, such as families, friends, colleagues, or even virtual communities, in order to cultivate virtues. Although companies have a reputation for encouraging the cultivation of attitudes that support financial gain at the expense of personal and communal flourishing, they can also provide social matrices for the cultivation of virtues, including sustainability virtues. This typically happens when the pillars of corporate identity—including core values and role models, targets and metrics, rewards and incentives, office rituals and stories, site architecture, process design, and corporate branding—are streamlined to support the goals of sustainability. Like all complex social systems, business matrices for the cultivation of sustainability virtues require several years of growing time.

Practices such as cooking, horticulture, and flute playing are also cradles of character formation. People engaged in such culturally encoded productive activities must nurture and refine the requisite virtues, such as attentiveness and creativity. Musicians, for example, learn to listen closely to their own sounds and adjust them as the music requires. When playing together, musicians also learn to listen and respond to the sounds of others, moderating their personal rhythms and impulses so that they can literally go with the flow. Through regular practice, artistic traits such as attentiveness and creativity can become second nature and support the cultivation of virtues in any other life context.

With the help of the tools of neuroscience (through functional magnetic resonance imaging, for example), existing insights into ways of cultivating virtues can now be further tested, refined, and supplemented. The human ability to trust, for example, plays a key role in sustainability virtues like generosity and hope. Recent research shows that the ability to trust is supported by a rise in the level of oxytocin, a neuroactive hormone best known for its role in labor (Zak 2008). This means that people can enhance their cultivation of trust-based virtues through timely social activities that are known to raise oxytocin levels, such as touching (including massage and dancing), grooming (including hair braiding), and sharing meals. Moreover, because much of the supporting neural circuitry is laid down during early mother-and-child bonding, social structures and policies that protect this bonding process are directly relevant to the cultivation of trust-based sustainability virtues later in life.

The Spirit of Virtue Cultivation

From a spiritual perspective, the personal cultivation of virtues is often described as a process of sanctification. People who seek to perceive signs of grace in their lives tend to be struck by the many internal and external gifts that allow them to grow in virtue. At the same time, they underscore their experience that sanctification also requires purification, which may involve a lifelong struggle. This is especially true for the cultivation of virtues that mold and balance basic drives and emotions, such as courage (overcoming fear), moderation (channeling desires), and humility (inflating pride). As the gathered memory of such deeply personal journeys, most religious traditions recognize that the cultivation of virtues is a process with ups and downs, where growth ultimately occurs not as a product of human engineering but as a gift.

Monastic traditions in particular tend to retain and develop insight into the ways of virtue cultivation. For example, the three vows taken by Benedictine monks support life-long growth in virtue, each in their own way. The vow of *stabilitas* encourages the perseverance needed for dealing with the challenges of personal formation. The vow of *conversio morum* supports growing into a new lifestyle through daily, small steps. And the vow of *obedientia* supports attentively listening to what it going on and discerning how to respond. Together, these three guidelines have demonstrated their value for virtue cultivation, both inside and outside the monastery, for more than a millennium. Today, they are also showing promise as a spiritual backbone for the cultivation of sustainability virtues among Benedictines, lay Roman Catholics and other people attracted to monastic spirituality. This trend parallels the growing interest in Buddhist ways of practicing mindfulness, *ahimsa* (nonviolence), and compassion in the awareness that these habits engender sustainable ways of living (Thich Nhat Hanh 2008). The ubiquity of virtue cultivation across cultures and religions provides those who seek to develop a global sustainability ethic with a rich spiritual-ethical lingua franca. The Earth Charter—a document prepared by an independent, global commission that presents the principles required for creating a more sustainable twenty-first century—illustrates the accessible appeal of virtue cultivation with its simple yet clear call "to care for the Earth and one another" (Earth Charter 2000, Preamble).

Louke van WENSVEEN
Academia Vitae

FURTHER READING

Earth Charter. (2000). Retrieved April 28, 2009, from http://www.earth-charterinaction.org/invent/images/uploads/echarter_english.pdf

Hursthouse, Rosalind. (2002). *On virtue ethics.* Oxford, U.K.: Oxford University Press.

Newton, Lisa H. (2002). *Ethics and sustainability: Sustainable development and the moral life.* Upper Saddle River, NJ: Prentice Hall.

Sandler, Ronald, & Cafaro, Philip. (Eds.). (2005). *Environmental virtue ethics.* Lanham, MD: Rowman & Littlefield.

Thich Nhat Hanh. (2008). *The world we have. A Buddhist approach to peace and ecology.* Berkeley, CA: Parallax Press.

White, Lynn, Jr. (1967, March 10). The historical roots of our ecologic crisis. *Science, 155,* 1203–1207.

Yearley, Lee H. (1990*). Mencius and Aquinas: Theories of virtue and conceptions of courage.* Albany: State University of New York Press.

Zak, Paul J. (2008, June). The neurobiology of trust. *Scientific American,* 88–95.

chat Berkshire's authors and editors welcome questions, comments, and corrections: sustainability.updates@berkshirepublishing.com

Waste

The waste a society produces reveals much about its economic, ethical, and environmental choices. The large amount of waste from affluent, consumer-oriented, societies has adverse ecological and cultural effects worldwide. Although reduction and longer retention of consumer goods has the greatest impact on the amount of waste created, strategies to reuse waste will also have a positive effect on sustainability.

Loosely defined, waste is comprised of items no longer of purpose to the user or byproducts left over from production. It can be argued that the production of anything produces some type of waste. The European Union Environment Commission states that "any resources placed on the market are bound, sooner or later, to become waste, and any productive activity generates some form of waste" (European Union 2005). The U.S. Environmental Protection Agency (EPA) Office of Resource Conservation and Recovery likewise states that the production and consumption of anything causes waste (EPA 2009). These definitions are incomplete however, because they fail to take into account the root causes of waste and our relationship to waste culturally and ethically.

Actually, very little of what becomes entombed in landfills can be considered pure waste, that is, a completely useless material. The ways in which societies collect and process waste, in addition to the production and consumption of consumer goods, are the major cause of problems with waste. A visit to a landfill or transfer station exposes a society's underlying attitudes to the products and material no longer wanted by the producer or consumer. Witnessing the mass amounts of paper, wood, plastic, carpet, metal, and other "disposable products" being loaded into tractor-trailers destined for landfills, incinerators, or even placed on barges to be shipped somewhere else makes it easy to believe the United States produces a third of the world's waste with only 4.6 percent of the world's population.

Waste and Industrial Production

A more detailed investigation of the actual word "waste" reveals connections to our deeper cultural assumptions about it. A general review of "waste literature" yields associations with words and ideas such as *neglect, destroy, spend uselessly, useless consumption, squander, spoil,* and *fritter away.* These loaded words that address the current reality of waste and overconsumption hearken back to our past and reach into the future. The current modality of "waste" is changing due to economic and environmental conditions around the world, such as the end of monetarily inexpensive fossil fuels, global warming, and the over-extraction of natural resources.

Historically, the vast amount of waste created by nearly every member of a developed country was confined to large metropolitan areas, and the idea of waste was foreign to most people. Up to the twentieth century, literally nothing was wasted, partly due to the fact that most people could not afford to waste anything. Every item once spent for its primary use was reused for something else, mostly because the majority of goods were not industrially produced.

Also, items were made of natural products such as wood, metal, or cotton, tended to last longer and were easily fashioned into another product. In rural areas or small towns, merchants would purchase spent textiles for quilts or mattress stuffing and bones left over from cooking to be fashioned into tools. Plastic was not available until later in the

418

twentieth century, and until the end of the nineteenth and early twentieth centuries wastebaskets were not a fixture in most homes.

It was not until the early to mid-twentieth century that industrial production made it possible to create goods that were cheap to make, cheap to purchase, and cheap to replace. As the median household income began to rise, so did the desire to increase one's material goods as a sign of wealth. The creation of vast amounts of waste and its associated problems are directly related to hyper-consumerism in developed countries and economies; the disposal of waste has many connections to social and environmental justice around the world. The intensive resource extraction to support the consumption to waste modality is directly associated with habitat destruction, species extinction, climate change, and human rights. The control of these pernicious elements begins with efficiencies associated with the reduction of waste from the production, supply, and consumption of consumer goods. The production, storage, and disposal of waste results in many environmental, economic, and social negatives, but also provides many opportunities such as reuse and recycling as economic and social positives.

The Waste Hierarchy

The framework for evaluating waste streams is known as the waste hierarchy; most commonly referred to as "reduce, reuse, recycle." This hierarchy serves as a guide for making sustainable choices about the consumption and disposal of goods. The first step in the waste hierarchy is "reduce," or reducing consumption of certain items or resources. This idea is closely related to resource conservation. Preventing waste is the most effective way to conserve resources because no resources must extracted, refined, transported, or consumed and thus no energy is consumed. If for, example, consumers reduced the amount of grocery plastic bags they use, then petroleum does not have to be extracted and refined and the bag does not become waste. Next comes "reuse." By reusing items or by purchasing durable items one is able to sequester the energy placed in that item over its life cycle. Reusing the plastic grocery bag, one prevents energy being consumed to make the new bag. Lowest on the scale is "recycle." Recycling provides many benefits and is the best way to handle material that would otherwise be placed in a landfill or end up as litter. Despite the benefits of recycling, recycling material still involves many energy inputs to collect and process material. It takes much energy to collect and reprocess the plastic grocery

bag into another material. The preferred option, not to create the waste in the first place, saves the greatest amount of resources into the future.

Unregulated Waste and Environmental Justice

There are categories of waste that are, thus far, largely unregulated and until recently slipped through the cracks of diversion systems. Unregulated waste tends to follow the path of least resistance and ends up being a liability far beyond its perceived end life on the curb or in the landfill. These waste streams can be very difficult to manage and their mismanagement has consequences beyond the implications of overconsumption and overflowing landfills. The physical, ethical, and environmental dimensions of unregulated waste can best be seen in the paths of electronic waste (e-waste) and food waste. Interestingly enough, the solutions to both of these problems lie within the relative simplicity of the waste hierarchy and are likewise illustrative of how a liability can be refashioned into a benefit.

Electronic waste or e-waste comprises outdated or unserviceable electronic items such as computers, cell phones, televisions, remote controls, and music players. E-waste provides an excellent example of a stream of material that crept up on waste managers, industry, and government and ballooned into a problem that is just now being addressed.

Actual statistics about e-waste vary, but the National Safety Council estimates that 3.8 million household computers needed disposal in 2003. This is only a statistic for household computers and does not account for business and education or for the other types of e-waste. Despite landfill bans in many places, over 33 million tons of e-waste are deposited in landfills every year. Computers and other electronic material contain many materials that must first be processed, refined, created into products, and eventually disposed just like any other product we may purchase. In addition to the incredible amount of resources needed to produce modern electronics (it is estimated that production of a new computer requires 1.8 tons of total resources), they harbor many toxic materials such as lead, cadmium, mercury, polychlorinated biphenyls (PCBs), polyvinylchloride (PVC), as well as small amounts of copper, gold, and other metals that could be extracted and sold. Older-styled picture-tube monitors contain over eight pounds of lead, a neurotoxin that has been proven to cause a host of serious medical conditions.

Before e-waste became an issue for communities and waste managers, most of these items were stockpiled in closets, garages, or corners of people's homes because no one had an idea of how to handle them, aside from placing them in the municipal or commercial waste stream for disposal in the a landfill or incinerator. When these items are placed in the landfill they release the chemicals into the land and water; when they are incinerated, they release chemicals into the air. These toxic effluents then travel to the air and water of the communities that live near the landfill or incinerators. In the United States, the first move was to ban these and other toxic materials from landfills and incinerators. Some states require all electronics to be recycled when the consumer is done with them.

The response to the absolute ban of electronic material from landfills was to place electronic material on the "grey market" to be sold to scrap purchasers and shippers who would then ship it to other countries to be disposed or processed for the small amounts of copper and other metal. This "toxic trade" results in one of the most serious instances of environmental injustice in the late twentieth and early twenty-first centuries. Most of the destinations for this material lie in the lesser-developed countries in Asia, Africa, and Eastern Europe, where strict environmental regulations do not exist. Motivated by the desire for profit, brokers on this grey market sell the material to collectors who either dump the material into lakes or oceans or place them in huge piles near communities that do not have the resources to fight the dumping of toxic material. Far too often, however, poor villagers or children dismantle this material by hand by to extract the small amounts of marketable material. Dismantlers often tear apart monitors to extract copper coils and directly expose themselves to lead; large piles of copper wire insulated with vinyl are burned, resulting in a large plume of toxic smoke directly inhaled by anyone nearby. The remains of dismantled electronic material are likewise dumped in large heaps near villages or towns, where it continues to leach into the water and soil. Even with mandated recycling for electronic material in the United States and Europe, toxic trade is expected to continue because most communities and governments are not prepared to process the mass amount of electronic material expected by mandated e-waste recycling programs.

The problem of e-waste, however, produced another reaction that illuminates the value of viewing our consumption and disposal of material through the waste hierarchy. Of course, the best way to impact the problem of e-waste is to somehow convince manufacturers to increase the useable life of their products or to convince consumers to keep their devices longer. There are many nonprofit and local organizations that accept electronic material and rebuild and refurbish, most notably, computers to be reused by those who do not need the latest technology or do not have the means to purchase it themselves. In many of these cases, usable computers are sent to schools and organizations in lesser-developed countries to enable them to have access to technology. These organizations not only provide refurbished computers for sale to the public at low prices and establish onshore recycling centers for electronics, they provide jobs, skills training, and educational resources to communities.

Food Waste: Liability to Asset

Food waste provides another illustration of how our wastes can be a liability as well as a potential resource. Food waste is composed of unused raw food and uneaten food already cooked or prepared (the latter referred to as "ort"), and it is the third largest component of the overall waste stream by weight. The packaging of food and processed take-out meals also contributes to the food-waste stream, although it is not directly counted in food-waste statistics. The U.S. EPA reported in 2000 that over 96 billion pounds of food is placed in landfills and wasted every year. In addition to the massive amounts of energy and fossil fuels needed to produce and distribute food, the wasting of food contributes to climate change. When food waste enters the waste stream through a landfill it emits methane, which is twenty-three times more potent as a greenhouse gas than carbon. While there are no direct environmental justice connections to the disposal of food, wasting food by producers and consumers has its own obvious consequence as most of the food discarded by the average U.S. household could be used by someone usually locally or globally. According to the EPA, 25 percent of food purchases end up in the trash, and a University of Arizona study estimated the wasting of household food at 50 percent (Jones 2004).

When a society places food in a landfill it represents placing resources into to a sink from which they will never emerge. Food is formed from the most basic natural resources; natural decomposition returns the nutrients inherent in plants and animals to the soil. Removing these nutrients from the soil cycle and entombing them in landfills depletes soil tilth and breaks natural cycles upon which food production and all life depend. Farmers long understood the value of composting farm wastes into rich humus to augment soil, and indeed many households around the United States compost food scraps and other green wastes in backyards.

Living in a large city presents challenges to composting every food scrap produced. Population density simply does not permit everyone having a composting pile in the backyard, and a large amount of food wasted comes from the commercial sector, which is not equipped to handle large amounts of food waste. Many large cities now regularly study, collect, and compost food waste as a mechanism to reduce pressure on landfills, to meet state recycling mandates, and to create an economic and environmental resource from what was considered a stinking nuisance, rotting food.

Waste and Society

The human relationship with waste runs long and deep. It may be the least considered or studied aspect of our society, but this in itself also says a lot about a society's values and how it sees itself in the world. "Garbage anthropology" shows us that as a society increases its wealth it likewise creates more waste among the illusion of abundance; poor societies see everything as a resource, even the waste of wealthy societies. Some past cultures and societies did not even understand the concept of waste because all resources were used and reused. What a society wastes and how it handles that waste also reveals its ethical, economic, and environmental choices.

It is clear that the most effective method of impacting the waste stream is to reduce the amount of goods consumed. When goods are not unnecessarily purchased, then all the negative environmental externalities can be avoided. Purchasing durable or reused goods or keeping items a bit longer will provide a longer return on the energy needed to produce and recycle or dispose of it. As the examples in this article illustrate, any perceived waste liability may be transformed into a resource for a community or society. The key to reframing the current relationship with waste lies in the ability to extract all of the resources, raw and human energy, and untapped potential from the material we call waste.

Michael D. SIMS
Independent scholar, Eugene, Oregon

FURTHER READING

Commission of the European Communities. (2005, December 21). Taking sustainable use of resources forward: A thematic strategy on the prevention and recycling of waste. Retrieved July 28, 2009, from eur-lex.europa.eu/LexUriServ/LexUriServ.do?uri=COM:2005:0666:FIN:EN:PDF

Gerrard, Michael. (1994). *Whose backyard, whose risk? Fear and fairness in toxic and nuclear waste siting.* Cambridge, MA: MIT Press.

Hawkins, Gay. (2006). *The ethics of waste.* Lanham, MD: Rowman & Littlefield.

Jones, Timothy. (2004). Using contemporary archaeology and applied anthropology to understand food loss in the American food system. Retrieved July 28, 2009, from http://www.communitycompost.org/info/usafood.pdf

Leonard, Annie. (2005). The story of stuff. Retrieved April 20, 2009, from http://www.storyofstuff.com/

McDonough, William, & Braungart, Michael. (2002). *Cradle to cradle: Rethinking the way we make things.* New York: North Point Press.

Porter, Richard. (2002). *The economics of waste.* Washington, DC: Resources for the Future.

Rogers, Heather. (2005). *Gone tomorrow: The hidden life of garbage.* New York: New Press.

Royte, Elizabeth. (2005). *Garbage land: On the secret trail of trash.* New York: Little, Brown.

United States Environmental Protection Agency (EPA). (2009). Retrieved August 12, 2009, from http://www.epa.gov/epawaste/

Water

In many religions, water has transformative power, from concepts of sin and defilement to purity and participation in the divine. Zoroastrianism's protection of life-giving elements results in refusal to pollute holy water. In Hinduism, however, rites such as putting ashes and corpses into a river to assure salvation physically pollute holy rivers, and mechanical cleaning of rivers paradoxically renders them less holy.

From a religious or cosmological perspective there is a continuous battle between good and evil or cosmos against chaos forces. "Purity" indicates "completeness," and "impurity" may be seen as "lack of completeness." "Completeness" means godliness, and impurity is a lack of partaking in the divine or being separated from the purity of the divinities. Consequently, combating impurity, sin, and defilement represents the victory over chaos, thus the creation of the cosmos. The annihilation of impurity through the holy water's transformation of pollution to purity is a process whereby the cosmos is re-created and moral and physical evil are destroyed. Thus, the beliefs in cosmic regeneration and the capacities of holy water to annihilate all kinds of pollution may enable physical defilement of rivers because it is an aim and obligation to combat and reduce the total amount of sin, impurity, and defilement in cosmos. Holy rivers are cosmic machines transforming pollution to purity, and if they do not have this capability, they are, strictly speaking, no longer holy.

Holy Water

Holy water is unique with regards to beliefs concerning purity and pollution. Whereas most other holy objects have to be protected from physical and ritual impurity because it is a sacrilege to defile the divine, in Hinduism in particular but also in other world religions, water has precisely the function of embodying and taking on impurity before transforming it and thus remaining physically and ritually pure. The Zoroastrian veneration and protection of the water's purity is exceptional in the worlds of water, whereas in Judaism, Christianity, and Islam water is used for washing away ritual impurity whether it is in the *mikvah*, baptism, or ablutions before prayers. Thus the three latter world religions share the same underlying logic that ritual impurity and sin are washed away by consecrated water. Nevertheless, water plays a minor role in these religions compared to Hinduism. Therefore, the all-pervasive beliefs that water cleanses all types of spiritual and physical impurity have paradoxically led to a situation where the rivers and the bodies of water are deliberately polluted. This is not a sacrilege but the logical end of holy water's divine, purifying powers, and consequently beliefs in holy water may be the problem and not the solution to sustainability in a profane world.

Hindus and Zoroastrians

In all religions water is attributed with various and diverse holy qualities and spiritual properties. Hinduism, for instance, is in a unique position to be *the* "water religion." The world's largest congregation of people so far in history took place at the confluence of the Ganges, Yamuna, and the mythological, subterranean Saraswati rivers at the Kumbh Mela festival in Allahabad, India, in 2001. The Kumbh Mela is a forty-two-day pilgrimage festival that is held every twelve years, and it was estimated that all together some 50 to 70 million pilgrims came to the festival that year. On 24 January, which was the cosmologically most auspicious day, between 20 and 25 million people took a holy bath in the rivers. All the pilgrims came to

Allahabad with one single purpose: to prepare for their forthcoming death by cleansing themselves from sin in holy water.

Pollution is transferred to the holy water; this capacity to wash away sin and ritual impurity characterizes holy water. Logically and practically, as a consequence the water that cleanses the devotee becomes polluted by spiritual impurity or physical defilement. Polluting the holy is, in other contexts, a sacrilege, but not with regard to water and holy rivers. Ritual purification with water involves a process wherein an individual devotee purifies him or herself by polluting the holy both spiritually and physically. It is possible to defile holy water, and consequently religion is not only the solution but also the problem for sustainability and ecology. Some of the most holy rivers in Hinduism are also the most polluted. This seeming paradox highlights structural properties and inherent qualities of what characterizes holiness and how and why holy water can be used for particular purposes in specific ways that no other religious objects can.

Traditionally, the "holy" causes reverence, veneration, and an awe-inspiring experience of the reality and the superior power beyond the individual. In general the most eco-friendly religion regarding pollution of water and protection of the life-giving elements is Zoroastrianism. The Zoroastrians protect the life-giving elements from defilements, and it is a sacrilege to pollute the holy. Whereas most people use water for everything that is impure, the Zoroastrians protect the cleanliness of the river itself. Herodotus noted as early as the fifth century BCE that, "They never defile a river with secretions [urine or spittle] of their bodies, nor even wash their hands in one; nor will they allow others to do so, as they have a great reverence for rivers" (Herodotus I.139). Impure water could not be used for drinking or cultivation, and when water was used for purification, it was only used as a secondary purifying agent. Water could not be used as a primary cleansing agent; to use water to wash away dirt and impurities was seen as a heinous sin that exposed water to demonic impurities. Unclean objects had to be cleaned with cattle urine and dried with sand or in sunlight before water could be employed for the final washing. This extreme reverence of water has been seen as a consequence of the Zoroastrians' adaptation as nomads herding cattle on the arid Asian steppes where everything that promoted the well-being of humans and animals was venerated as precious and therefore protected from impurity and defilement. In such cases beliefs about water may promote sustainability and protection of the environment from pollution.

In Hinduism, on the other hand, holy water is attributed with other qualities and purposes. In India, the Ganges River is the holiest river, concentrating the sanctity of all rivers. The Ganges carries the "nectar of immortality"

connecting the Earth with the heavenly realms; the most auspicious place to die and to be cremated is along the banks of the Ganges River in Varanasi. Each year some forty thousand Hindus are cremated there, which enables them to cross the river of *samsara*. The associated spiritual entity Mother Ganga is so holy and powerful that even the smallest drop of water in Varanasi cleanses the devotee and liberates the dead, and the holiness of Ganges in Varanasi has since time immemorial ensured liberation from the cycle of birth and death.

The cremated remains from these tens of thousands are immersed in the river, and from all over India descendents pilgrimage with the ashes of their deceased to Varanasi. The immersion of the ashes in the holy river physically pollutes the water, but from a religious point of view this rite is necessary to ensure salvation. Water burials or immersion of corpses in the holy Ganges River have also been an intrinsic part of the funeral rites. Official reports estimated that between one thousand and two thousand corpses are immersed in the river each year, but the actual number has probably been higher. Together with domestic waste and sewage, the river has been in a horrible, polluted state. In the 1980s several hundred flesh-eating turtles were released in the river to solve the problem with decaying corpses floating in Ganges in Varanasi, and whether crocodiles should be reintroduced as a more permanent solution to the problems of floating corpses was also discussed. The opening of an electric crematorium in 1989 was therefore seen as essential to the antipollution program. Religion may thus prescribe rites that purify on an individual basis but pollute the very same river that eventually shall clean and purify others, and the holiest of the holiest river has been deteriorated physically by the ritual practices.

In Nepal, the pollution of the most holy river there became so severe that pilgrims could not use the water in their rituals and for their major festivals. Bagmati River, a tributary to the Ganges, passes by the Pashupatinath temple. It is the holiest place for Hindus in Nepal, where thousands are cremated each year, but the river has been polluted by more than just the death rituals. Prior to 2002, the holy water was sludge of domestic sewage, industrial waste, agricultural discharge, and other types of pollution. The river was only holy in its name, not in practice, and something had to be done. The solution was to cleanse the river mechanically by a sewage-treatment plant upstream of the temple, which opened in 2002 for the Shivaratri festival. With this engineering solution to physical impurity, the river changed from black sludge stream into a shiny and transparent river, but it left the devotees with a problem: was the river still holy or just pure?

Physical purity and ritual purity are related, but improving the physical quality did not necessarily enhance the spiritual quality. Although the river was too polluted to use in rituals prior to the introduction of the treatment plant, the river was still believed to be holy, but in a deteriorated state. With the mechanical cleaning the logic of the holy was challenged. The Bagmati River was perceived as the holiest river in Nepal because it had the capacity to cleanse devotees from sin and human contamination *and still remain pure*. A holy river is holy because it has the power and capacity to annihilate spiritual and physical impurity by its divine qualities. Humans *transfer* sin and pollution to the river and the river as a divine and holy body *transforms* the pollution into purity and thus the river remains pure. If the river was unable to transform impurity to purity, it was seen as a proof that the river had lost its holiness. When engineers intervened and cleansed the deteriorated river, which it should have done by itself, numerous devotees perceived the river as being physically, but not ritually, pure.

The underlying belief in the capability of holy rivers to transform impurity to purity must be understood in the flowing character of water. A river transports dirt away as water cleanses the physical body by washing. By taking a bath the body becomes clean outwardly, which is the very same process that takes place in holy bath when the soul is purified inwardly through the body. In Hinduism moral qualities are embodied, and by taking holy baths sins are washed away and transferred to the river. Thus, the logic behind holy rivers is that the water has the capability to receive and annihilate spiritual impurity by transforming it to purity, which is a process where cosmos is created out of chaos. This logic has also been extended to physical impurity that has been disposed of in rivers because the flowing water transports it away, and the river seemingly remains pure. A holy river is therefore attributed with the power to *transform* all types of pollution to purity and this has enabled humans to *transfer* all kinds of defilement in the rivers, and domestic disposals of dirt and filth are not seen as a religious sacrilege of the holy water and divine embodied substance.

Holy Water and Sustainability

In conclusion, the holiness or sacredness of water in religious traditions does not guarantee that water will not be polluted. Indeed, the spiritual "cleansing" provided by waters may be the source of further pollution. With regard to sustainability, reverence for water as sacred or holy will need to be rethought outside of the terms of mere self-purification and more in terms of purification of all life: the water, river, lake, stream or ocean then becomes a meter for how reverent humans are toward the rest of the natural water world.

Terje OESTIGAARD
University of Bergen

FURTHER READING

Boyce, Mary. (1984). *Zoroastrians: Their religious beliefs and practices.* London: Routledge & Kegan Paul.

Douglas, Mary. (1994). *Purity and danger.* London: Routledge.

Herodotus. (1996). *Histories.* (George Rawlinson, Trans.). Hertfordshire, U.K.: Wordsworth Classics of World Literature.

Oestigaard, Terje. (2005). *Death and life-giving waters: Cremation, caste, and cosmogony in karmic traditions.* Oxford, U.K.: Archaeopress.

Otto, Rudolf. (1973). *The idea of the holy: An inquiry into the non-rational factor in the idea of the divine and its relation to the rational* (John W. Harvey, Trans.). London: Oxford University Press. (Original work published 1923)

Parry, Jonathan P. (1994). *Death in Banaras.* Cambridge, U.K.: Cambridge University Press.

Tvedt, Terje, & Oestigaard, Terje. (Eds.). (2006). *A history of water: Vol. 3. The world of water.* London: I.B. Tauris.

Tvedt, Terje, & Oestigaard, Terje. (Eds.). (2009). *A history of water: Vol. 4. The ideas of water from antiquity to modern times.* London: I.B. Tauris.

White's Thesis

In 1967, the scholar Lynn White Jr. initiated the debate about Christianity's responsibility in creating and perpetuating the environmental crisis. His statements that the Bible gave humanity dominion over the natural world and set humans above the rest of Creation were interpreted as attacks on Christianity. His theories gave rise to the field of study known as Religion and Ecology.

When Lynn White Jr. wrote "The Historical Roots of Our Ecological Crisis," published in *Science* on March 10, 1967, he could not have anticipated it as the narrative starting point for the field now known as ecotheology in particular, and more broadly, "Religion and Ecology." Almost every major work on the subject references White for one reason or another, hence his inclusion in this volume. But the reception of White varies, and the methodologies and visions of the field that he has shaped are beginning to shift. In general, there are three main responses to White's thesis—what some call the apologetic, constructive/critical, and sympathetic. Many other typologies, however, are also available (e.g., Scharper 1998; Fowler 1995; Oelschaleger 1994).

Lynn White Jr. (1907–1987) was a medieval historian especially interested in the role of technology in history (Hall, 1987). His basic thesis was that "especially in its western form, Christianity is the most anthropocentric religion the world has seen" (White, 1967). He goes on to note in the *Science* article that the reason for this is that the God of Christianity is a removed, transcendent God. Since human beings are thought of as this God's representatives on Earth, they can never feel quite at home *on* the Earth.

Many scientists and scholars of religious studies have been quick to take up White's critique but fewer have taken up his further assertion that we might also find counters to the ecologically destructive ways of thinking and acting in religious traditions. For instance, he famously offers Saint Francis of Assisi as the patron saint of ecology, thereby acknowledging one, among many, ecologically sensitive traditions within Christianity.

Three Approaches

One reaction to White's thesis is the apologetic approach. In it, mostly religious (and mostly Christian) scholars set about to defend Christianity (and later other religions) from Lynn White's critique. This category of respondents notes that White caricatures Christianity; they claim that the overall message in the Bible is one of stewardship or, more recently, "creation care" (DeWitt et al. 1994). It is typical in this approach is to play down the metaphor of "dominion" in the book of Genesis and to play up the Creation narrative where Adam and Eve are caretakers or stewards of the rest of the world. Another important aspect of this response is that equal blame is usually laid on modern science and on modern capitalism/consumerism. In other words, this approach rejects White, defends Christianity, and points the finger elsewhere, primarily to science, secularism, and economics.

Second is the constructive/critical approach. In this approach—taken by religious scholars, scientists, and less by environmentalists—White's thesis is accepted; there is recognition of the culpability of Christianity in the environmental crisis, and there is recognition that religious thought and language must also be a part of the solution to the ecological crisis. The volumes in the Forum on Religion and Ecology's *World Religions and Ecology Series* fall within this approach. Former U.S. vice president Al Gore sums it up well when he suggests that the environmental crisis is, at heart, a spiritual crisis (Gore 1992). The recognition that religion does have a role to play in both the crisis and the solution is a middle ground between the apologetic and the sympathetic approaches. In other words, as many have theorized, there is the recognition that humans are religious by nature, so we can't just ignore the religious aspect of what it means to be human. On the other hand, religious traditions are not infallible; they are co-constructed by human beings and reconstructed throughout different periods of history. In this approach, then, one might rework Christian doctrines such as Creation (Moltmann 1993) or Christology (McFague 1993) in ways that help to heal human–Earth relations. Or as a scientist, one might suggest ways in which new religions emerge from looking at cosmology (Berry and Swimme 1994) or evolution and ecology (Goodenough 1998).

The third and final approach is the sympathetic approach. According to this response, religion is culpable and humans must either reject religion and move into some sort of postreligious stage, or reject environmentalism as something that religion should be concerned with. Very few religious scholars would take this approach all the way, but it has shaped the narrative of environmentalism and science in the United States especially. Similar to the combative narrative set up between Creation and evolution (a false dichotomy for sure), this approach sees the choice as one between care for the environment and religious belief. Whereas in the apologetic approach, religion is claimed to be free of blame because it has always been green (or at least the "correct" interpretation of religion will be green), in this approach religion is not green and doesn't claim to be so. A good (but extreme) example of this attitude would be Ronald Reagan's secretary of the interior, James Watt, who argued famously that national forests could be logged because it would hurry the return of Jesus. Though these direct words may be more legend than fact, a look at Watt's policies suggests that his Christian beliefs (which he drew heavily on in his judgments) boldly rejected any form of environmentalism. From the scientific/environmental perspective, this type of thinking has led to a rift between environmentalists and conservative Christians (or other religions) that is only now being bridged. Recent proponents of this approach would be those who are being referred to as the "new atheists," such as Richard Dawkins, who believe that religion is bad for the Earth (Dawkins 2006). The assumption of this either/or approach has led to misconceptions on both sides of the camp: environmentalists are seen as atheists, and Christians as fundamentalists who don't care about the Earth.

Neglected Perspectives

One of the problems with having Lynn White as the originator of the narrative of "Religion and Ecology" is that it places the origin in the Christian West and extends it to other religious traditions. This could be seen as an act of imperialism on the part of many well-intentioned scholars and religious peoples. In other words, Lynn White probably doesn't really have much to do with the Chipko tree movement in India or with Chinese Buddhist environmentalism, yet, at least in the West, he is still seen as the one who started the discussion about religion and ecology. But the narrative probably should be limited to "Christianity and Ecology" and even "Western Christianity and Ecology": The Jewish tradition, Orthodox Christianity, and Western Christianity cannot be lumped together here. Finally, beginning with Lynn White may be falsely characterizing Christianity. Hasn't all religious thought always been ecological, and doesn't it always shape our attitudes toward the land? Before Lynn White, there were other "Earth-loving" examples throughout the history of Christian thought in addition to Assisi, from tree-hugging Celtic monks to the French Jesuit Teilhard de Chardin (1881–1955), who championed for an evolutionary and cosmic understanding of God and Christ. But most importantly, starting with White and Christianity ignores the fact that our contemporary ecological crisis was not predicted by any religious tradition because no extant religious tradition began in the globalized, technological world in which we live today. In other words, Christianity—or any religion for that matter—may be culpable, but the contemporary crises we face are more about the deep realization that humans are, *indeed*, a part of the rest of the natural world. Accordingly, religious traditions will be reformed or thrown out, and new ones will be constructed in an effort to make our "religious thought" more sustainable. This is the hope, at least, of Religion and Ecology.

Whitney A. BAUMAN
Florida International University

FURTHER READING

Berry, Thomas, & Swimme, Brian. (1994). *The universe story.* San Francisco: HarperCollins.

Dawkins, Richard. (2006). *The God delusion.* New York: Houghton Mifflin.

DeWitt, Calvin B. (Ed.). (1994). *Earth-wise: A biblical response to environmental issues.* Grand Rapids, MI: CRC.

Forum on Religion and Ecology. (2004). Retrieved May 15, 2009, from http://fore.research.yale.edu/publications/books/book_series/cswr/index.html

Fowler, Robert Booth. (1995). *The greening of Protestant thought.* Chapel Hill: University of North Carolina Press.

Goodenough, Ursula. (1998). *The sacred depths of nature.* New York: Oxford University Press.

Gore, Albert. (1992). *Earth in the balance: Ecology and the human spirit.* Boston: Houghton Mifflin.

Hall, Bert S. (1989). Lynn Townsend White, Jr. (1907–1987). *Technology and Culture, 30*(1), 194–213.

Jenkins, Willis. (2009). After Lynn White: Religious ethics and environmental problems. *The Journal of Religious Ethics 37*(2): 283–309.

Lodge, David M., & Hamlin, Christopher. (2006). Beyond Lynn White: Religion, the contexts of ecology, and the flux of nature. In Peter Raven, David Lodge, & Christopher Hamlin (Eds.), *Religion and the new ecology: Environmental responsibility in a world of flux* (pp. 1–25). Notre Dame, IN: University of Notre Dame Press.

McFague, Sallie. (1993). *The body of God: An ecological theology.* Minneapolis, MN: Fortress Press.

Moltmann, Jurgen. (1993). *God in creation.* Minneapolis, MN: Fortress Press.

Oelschlaeger, Max. (1994). *Caring for creation: An ecumenical approach to the environmental crisis.* New Haven, CT: Yale University Press.

Scharper, Stephen Bede. (1998). *Redeeming the time: A political theology of the environment.* New York: Continuum.

White, Lynn, Jr. (1967). The historical roots of our ecological crisis. *Science, 155*(3767), 1203–1207. Retrieved on June 19, 2009, from http://www.uvm.edu/~jmoore/envhst/lynnwhite.html

THE WORDS OF LYNN WHITE JR.

Upon publication in Science *in 1967, White's "The Historical Roots of Our Ecological Crisis" sparked a debate regarding the relationship between Christianity and ecology.*

What did Christianity tell people about their relations with the environment?

While many of the world's mythologies provide stories of creation, Greco-Roman mythology was singularly incoherent in this respect. Like Aristotle, the intellectuals of the ancient West denied that the visible world had a beginning. Indeed, the idea of a beginning was impossible in the framework of their cyclical notion of time. In sharp contrast, Christianity inherited from Judaism not only a concept of time as nonrepetitive and linear but also a striking story of creation. By gradual stages a loving and all- powerful God had created light and darkness, the heavenly bodies, the earth and all its plants, animals, birds, and fishes. Finally, God had created Adam and, as an afterthought, Eve to keep man from being lonely. Man named all the animals, thus establishing his dominance over them. God planned all of this explicitly for man's benefit and rule: no item in the physical creation had any purpose save to serve man's purposes.

And, although man's body is made of clay, he is not simply part of nature: he is made in God's image.

Especially in its Western form, Christianity is the most anthropocentric religion the world has seen. As early as the 2nd century ... Christianity ... not only established a dualism of man and nature but also insisted that it is God's will that man exploit nature for his proper ends.

At the level of the common people this worked out in an interesting way. In Antiquity every tree, every spring, every stream, every hill had its own genius loci, its guardian spirit. These spirits were accessible to men, but were very unlike men; centaurs, fauns, and mermaids show their ambivalence. Before one cut a tree, mined a mountain, or dammed a brook, it was important to placate the spirit in charge of that particular situation, and to keep it placated. By destroying pagan animism, Christianity made it possible to exploit nature in a mood of indifference to the feelings of natural objects.

Source: Lynn Townsend White Jr. (1967). The Historical Roots of Our Ecologic Crisis. *Science 155*(3767), 1203–1207. Retrieved October 1, 2009, from http://aeoe.org/resources/spiritual/rootsofcrisis.pdf

Wilderness

Ideas about wilderness have shifted through time—from abhorrence in the premodern era to appreciation in the age of Emerson and Thoreau. Proponents of economic development in the twenty-first century argue that we must continue to develop Earth's natural resources. Proponents of ecological sustainability believe that the conservation, preservation, and restoration of the planet's wilderness are necessary actions.

The idea of wilderness challenges the dominant theory of growth-oriented sustainable development. According to that theory wilderness appears anachronistic, and the notion that large areas of the Earth should be protected from economic development seems foolish. The dominant worldview has long held that humankind is the master and possessor of nature, and thus there are no limits to growth. If progress is fueled (and identified) primarily by economic development, the appropriation of undeveloped lands is necessary.

Mainstream market economists believe that any landscape that has not been economically developed—and therefore put to its so-called highest and best use—is wasted. Wetlands must be drained; deserts made to bloom; rainforests cleared to make way for human settlement; rivers dammed to control floods and to provide water for irrigation and electrical power. Further, market use dictates that whenever possible, wild stocks of plants and animals must be replaced by genetically modified species that are resistant to disease and, most importantly, amenable to commercialization and the techniques of industrialized production. When species that require large, wild territories for survival are endangered, their limited populations can be protected in zoos. Thus the wild prolixity of life and land can be brought within the scheme of managing planet Earth for human benefit.

Since the mid-twentieth century an alternative worldview has emerged. Framed by ecologically informed considerations of sustainability, the idea of wilderness is gaining a new legitimacy. Wild and relatively wild places are now understood to provide invaluable and irreplaceable ecosystem services upon which sustainable civilization will depend. For example, rain forests such as Amazonia are (metaphorically) the lungs of the Earth, and stratospheric ozone is the shield protecting the planet's living tissue from ultraviolet sterilization. Bees pollinate vast acreages of valuable crops, and recyclers such as worms and termites process megatons of dead plant and animal materials into vital nutrients and soils. Further, wild nature is a veritable treasure trove of undiscovered plant and insect species that play vital roles in maintaining ecosystem health and harbor potential medical uses for human benefit. While the economic value of ecosystem services is difficult to calculate, ecological economists estimate that such services provide an economic value twice that of human industry alone.

And yet the present world order inexorably grinds away at the evolved, interwoven complexity of the wild Earth, propelled by the drive for progress through economic growth. While the mass media have dramatized the need for action, and while some positive steps to protect and restore wild nature have been taken, many scientists think that civilization has barely begun to take corrective action. Ecologically informed thinkers increasingly argue that sustainability can be achieved if and only if the nonlinear processes and naturally evolved complexity of the wild Earth are woven into the discourse that will determine the human trajectory over the next century. The era of human dominion is fragile, at best.

The Idea of Wilderness

Like the flora, fauna, and wild ecosystems that have evolved over millions of years, the idea of wilderness—a relatively short-term phenomenon—has itself changed. A few key moments in the history of the wilderness idea are recounted here.

A paradigmatic change in how humans conceived the Earth unquestionably came with the agricultural revolution. Permanent human settlement, the cultivation of cereal grasses, and the domestication of animal species altered a long-established relationship between humankind and nature. Paleo-anthropological studies indicate that humankind had no notion of a world apart from their home in its natural surroundings. The era that began around 250,000 BCE and lasted until the onset of the agricultural revolution (c. 15,000–12,000 BCE) is known as "The Great Hunt." Band societies (in which foraging was the primary mode of subsistence) were the rule; hunting and gathering provided the economic basis of their existence. Paleoclimatology offers the hypothesis that the agricultural revolution was engendered by the climatologically driven collapse of Pleistocene grasslands.

After the agricultural revolution, wild creatures and places were increasingly feared. Wild people (barbarians) were the scourge of villages. Wild creatures, including predators (such as wolves) and insects (such as locusts), were a constant threat to livestock and crops. Over a few thousand years villages and tribalism gave way to the rise of the first nations, Egypt and Sumeria. With these civilizations came massive changes to the landscape, such as the diversion of rivers for irrigation and the clearing of forests for fields. The natural world was no longer so much the human abode as it was a source of materials for feeding and housing growing populations.

A third phase in the history of the idea of wilderness can be marked as beginning with the Tribes of Yahweh (c. 1000 BCE), the disparate people who collectively became the nation of Israel. To these tribes, wilderness was a place of refuge from the tyranny of Sumeria and Egypt. Lingering resonances of Eden, in which humans were said to be at home in nature, can be found in the Old Testament. This period is also marked by the advent of Greek rationalism, such as the theories of Aristotle. Nature was categorized in ways suited to human utilization. However elementary and mistaken these theories seem, they were the beginnings of the continuing attempt to make humans beings the conceptual masters of nature.

The final phase occurred with the interesting fusion between Attica and Jerusalem at the advent of Christianity. The apostle Paul, for example, was conversant with the Socratic–Platonic notion of the soul as the essence of humankind. Under the impress of the New Testament—quite unlike the Old Testament—the natural world became little more than a vale of tears imposed by a supernatural creator on a sinful humanity. But the Christians taught "good news" as well: redemption and escape from the natural world of sin, pain, and suffering was at hand.

Throughout the Middle Ages in Christianized Europe wild places, such as deserts, mountains, and forests, were seen as divine punishment for original sin. Such theology played havoc with the land, as when axe-wielding monks made relentless attacks upon forested lands. These attitudes were largely transported to the New World by waves of European colonists who associated wilderness with evil and considered its inhabitants to be godless natives. Settlement therefore "redeemed" wild lands.

Modern Ideas of Wilderness

In the nineteenth century a new way of thinking about wilderness emerged. U.S. philosophers and social reformers such as Ralph Waldo Emerson, Henry David Thoreau, and John Muir were seminal influences, slowly transforming the idea from one of theological abhorrence into one of appreciation. While Christian beliefs suffuse Emerson's thinking, Thoreau famously argued that in wildness lies the preservation of the world, and Muir saw and articulated a robust sense of the intrinsic value—value in its own stead—of wild nature.

The twentieth century brought further changes to ideas about wilderness, driven in part by rapid advances in the new science of ecology. The U.S. environmentalist Aldo Leopold's *Sand County Almanac* (1949) articulated a wilderness philosophy just before mid-century that remains a cornerstone of efforts to conserve and restore wild nature. The second half of the century saw rapid developments in genetics, conservation biology, ecological restoration, and ecological economics. These sciences have radically transformed the idea of wilderness.

While neoclassical economics continue to labor under the impress of pre-ecological categories, wild nature is increasingly understood as fundamental to sustainability.

So-called ecosystem services, including the conversion of carbon dioxide to oxygen through photosynthesis, the buffering of coastal regions by marshes and wetlands, and the nitrogen cycle are now understood as not only necessary to the healthy functioning of nature's economy but as irreplaceable assets upon which the human economy is built.

The Biophysical Wilderness

Wild nature has been relentlessly humanized by such direct actions as the plowing of prairie grasslands and the channelization of rivers, and by indirect (unintended) consequences, such as the extinction of species, the melting of polar ice caps, and the collapse of coral reefs. The processes of the direct and indirect modification of the wild Earth are intensifying. The evidence is overwhelming that a sixth mass extinction of life on Earth is well underway, unlike any previous catastrophic extinction in its human (anthropogenic) origin (Wilson 1992).

George P. Marsh was among the first scientists to recognize that the long-term consequences of the modification of the Earth did not easily fit into the schemata of economic categories. He warned in the 1860s that whatever the short-term economic benefits of exploiting natural systems, these benefits would ultimately be rendered null and void by longer-term consequences. Culture continues to struggle with such issues, as is evident in the term coined for unintended consequences—"economic externalities."

The window of opportunity for meaningful changes that might conserve and/or restore wild places and processes is seen by many twenty-first-century ecologists to be considerably less than a century, perhaps less than twenty years. Nature is increasingly understood as a complex and chaotic system in which irreversible and unpredicted changes should be expected. Necessary policy changes to address this urgent situation include, as a minimum: setting aside in perpetuity a percentage of land in vital regions such as Amazonia; monitoring human activities that cause harm to ecosystem processes, including disturbance regimes such as fire and flooding; and optimizing natural subsidies to the human economy, such as solar energy.

Wilderness, Economic Development, and Social Justice

Advocates of wilderness conservation and restoration have been criticized by some writers from the global South, the area generally referred to as the third world. While the specifics of these critiques are complex, there are two essential points. First, the charge has been made that globalization has exploited the resources of undeveloped nations and created localized ecological havoc and poverty, while economic benefits flow largely to wealthy nations. Such a claim has

merit, although the criticism is more appropriately directed at globalism than conservation. Second, critics argue that there can be no justification for calls to protect wilderness in undeveloped nations without consequential changes in the lifestyles of the developed nations that combine with efforts to ameliorate global poverty.

Wilderness Conservation, Preservation, and Restoration

Driven by population growth and economic development, the rending of nature continues relentlessly. Yet there are many practical actions in progress that serve as models for a sustainable future. Conservation efforts have brought species back from the cusp of extinction to some semblance of health, the bald eagle being a case in point. The Big Thicket National Preserve in southeastern Texas was pieced together over several decades out of cut-over (often-harvested, as opposed to clear-cut) timberlands and riparian areas (lands bordering rivers and streams). Grand Canyon National Park has instituted a policy to restore fire as a natural disturbance regime in fire-adapted forests, and conservation efforts are underway to protect the springs on which the Canyon's wildlife depends. On a much larger scale, a consortium of regional conservation groups has developed plans for the "rewilding" of North America, especially but not exclusively along the spine of the Rocky Mountains.

As is the case with North American conservation endeavors, international efforts to protect wilderness have been met with mixed success. Amazonia continues to be cleared at prodigious rates. The habitat of the African gorilla continues to shrink. In India, the domain of the mighty tiger has been reduced to dangerous levels. The orangutan is in danger of becoming extinct, as the forests of Indonesia and Malaysia are being cut rapidly.

As the first decade of the twenty-first century draws to a close, a diverse scientific community has realized that civilization cannot endure without the conservation and restoration of wild nature. To proponents of economic development, such an idea seems naive, a denial of the reality (as they perceive it) that humankind has no option but to continue to develop the planet's natural resources. To the ecologically informed, a sustainable trajectory beneficial for civilization can only be realized through the conservation, preservation, and restoration of the Earth's wilderness.

Max OELSCHLAEGER
Northern Arizona University

FURTHER READING

Foreman, Dave. (2004). *Rewilding North America: A vision for conservation in the 21st century.* Washington, DC.: Island Press.

Diamond, Jared M. (2005). *Collapse: How societies choose to fail or succeed.* New York: Viking Press.

Duerr, Hans Peter. (1985). *Dreamtime: Concerning the boundary between wilderness and civilization.* F. Goodman (Trans.). New York: Basic Blackwell.

Glacken, Clarence J. (1967). *Traces on the Rhodian shore: Nature and culture in Western thought from ancient times to the end of the eighteenth century.* Berkeley, Los Angeles and London: University of California Press.

Grumbine, R. Edward. (1992). *Ghost bears: Exploring the biodiversity crisis.* Washington, DC: Island Press.

Keiter, Robert B., & Boyce, Mark S. (Eds.). (1994). *The Greater Yellowstone ecosystem: Redefining America's wilderness heritage.* London and New Haven: Yale University Press.

Lee, Richard B., & DeVore, Irven. (Eds.). (1968). *Man the hunter.* New York: Aldine de Gruyter.

Leopold, Aldo. (1949). *Sand county almanac: With other essays on conservation from Round River.* New York: Oxford University Press.

Levin, Simon A. (1999). *Fragile dominion: Complexity and the commons.* Reading, MA: Perseus Books.

Lopez, Barry Holstun. (1978). *Of wolves and men.* New York: Charles Scribners Sons.

Nash, Roderick. (1967). *Wilderness and the American mind.* New Haven, CT: Yale University Press.

Oelschlaeger, Max. (1991). *The idea of wilderness: From prehistory to the age of ecology.* London and New Haven: Yale University Press.

Sahlins, Marshall David. (1972). *Stone age economics.* New York: Aldine de Gruyter.

Shepard, Paul. (1998). *Coming home to the Pleistocene.* Washington, DC: Island Press.

Shiva, Vandana. (1989). *Staying alive: Women, ecology, and development.* London: Zed Books.

Wilkinson, Charles F. (1992). *Crossing the next meridian: Land, water, and the future of the west.* Washington, DC: Island Press.

Wilson, Edward O. (1992). *The diversity of life.* Cambridge, MA: Harvard University Press.

It may be reasonable to expect most people to dismiss the notion of a nurturing wolf as a naïve person's referent, but that doesn't seem wise to me. When, from the prisons of our cities, we look out to wilderness, when we reach intellectually for such abstractions as the privilege of leading a life free from nonsensical conventions, or one without guilt or subterfuge—in short, a life of integrity—I think we can turn to wolves.

BARRY LOPEZ

Source: Barry Holstun Lopez. (1978). *Of wolves and men*, p. 249. New York: Charles Scribners Sons.

Wisdom Traditions

Wisdom was one of Plato's four cardinal virtues; the original concept involved knowledge about the interconnectedness of life, a subject inherent in discussions about sustainability. Since Plato, wisdom has developed a religious significance that is found in many diverse traditions. Wisdom, therefore, has become a virtue of sustainability that could serve as a basis for a global religious ethic.

The notion of wisdom is connected with philosophy (from the Greek *philos-sophia*, which itself means "love of wisdom"). Yet the gradual detachment of this classical understanding of philosophy from its original sense means that philosophy today is more often than not associated with a much narrower pursuit of knowledge. In its ancient meaning, philosophy was about life and the relationship of everything with everything else. In religious terms, that relationship is necessarily inclusive of religious commitment, including (in many cases) acknowledgment of the divine. Since sustainability is about maintaining relationships between humans, other creatures, and the planet, wisdom is most properly linked with, and some might say integral to, the pursuit of sustainability.

Abrahamic Faiths

Judaism, Christianity, and Islam all draw on traditions adhered to by the biblical patriarch Abraham and, in this sense, share many of the same resources, though different emphases come to bear in the three different religions. The Hebrew tradition of wisdom develops most profoundly that corpus of books in the Hebrew Bible known as the wisdom literature: Proverbs, Job, Ecclesiastes, Psalms, Song of Songs, and the books of Wisdom and Sirach in Apocrypha, though examples of writing that show some affinity with the wisdom genre may be found throughout the

Hebrew Bible. In the Jewish tradition, wisdom was learned in the context of family life, through education, and, to a lesser extent, through observation of the natural world. Much wisdom literature seemed to support the status quo in that it affirmed royal traditions and hierarchical social arrangements. In this sense it identifies with those elements of the tradition that many believe are inimical to ecologically sensitive practice. This is particularly evident among ecofeminist interpreters of wisdom, where wisdom is portrayed as necessarily being in antithetical relationships to all hierarchical structures.

There is, however, a more subversive tradition of wisdom that points away from hierarchical arrangements. Those proverbs that encourage the reader to pay attention to non-human life encourage the kind of careful attention with which naturalists are familiar, though the writers were clearly ignorant of much of the science. An example here is Proverbs 6:6–9, where humans are exhorted to notice the "way of the ant." This seems to be more than just an implicit natural science; rather it is a promotion of a different kind of social order as epitomized in the life of ants. By recognizing wisdom in creatures that lack rulers, and even in the smallest and most insignificant of creatures—namely ants, badgers, locusts, and lizards—the royal, hierarchical wisdom tradition is challenged.

In Proverbs (Chapters 1–9) there are also references to "woman wisdom," where wisdom is celebrated not so much as the means of success in human society but as present at the primordial Creation of the world. This links Hebrew wisdom with Creation, so much so that some scholars believe that wisdom always carries an implicit theology of Creation. In Proverbs 8, wisdom is even described as a co-Creator, playfully engaged in Creation, but one who also acts as the voice of the Earth, seeing that she is aware of how the interconnectedness of the universe comes together. Such an idealized vision of wisdom, which is also associated with the Torah or "Law" in Hebrew thought, finds a counterpoint in the book of Job, which deals explicitly with the issue of unjust suffering. It is important that this strand is given due attention, as otherwise wisdom could be thought of as presenting a vision that fails to recognize sufficiently the suffering embedded in life's experiences. In such a context God is portrayed as one who speaks of the care of all creatures, not just humankind, and there are also hints that God discovers wisdom in the Earth, but this is acquired through creating, rather than akin to human searching. Such wisdom is then established and confirmed by God, and would seem to challenge more Platonic notions of wisdom being present as ideas on the divine mind. Wisdom is also associated with the spirit of God in the book of Wisdom (which was included in an ancient Greek version of the Hebrew Bible—the Septuagint—and remains in the Roman Catholic and Eastern Orthodox Old Testament); it fills the whole Earth (Wisdom 1:6) and emanates from God's glory as the breath of God (Wisdom 7:25).

Christian and Muslim Interpretations

The association of wisdom with the Torah and eventually the divine in Hebrew thought is radicalized still further in Christianity, where divine wisdom comes to be associated with the person of Christ. The earliest understanding of Christ was arguably a Wisdom Christology. Those poems associated with wisdom in the Hebrew tradition are deliberately aligned with the Christ figure. The Gospel of John mediated such a transition through a more hierarchical Logos imagery (having to do with the word in John's gospel, as in, "in the beginning was the word"), and eventually the background in *sophia*, or wisdom, traditions became suppressed. Many of the epistles associate Christ and the cross with wisdom, as in Colossians 1 or Corinthians 1. Such an understanding overturns a simple correlation between a human search for wisdom and Christian discipleship, for now more ascetic traditions come into view, where identification with Christ's cross becomes (in a paradoxical way) the mark of true wisdom. Such identification is not related to an inappropriate masochism but rather presented as a willingness to suffer for the sake of the good. In other words, it carries a sacrificial element. In addition, virtues such as wisdom are understood as not simply learned in human communities; they are also perceived as gifts given from God, through the grace of the Holy Spirit.

In Islam, wisdom in an environmental context is equated with the practice of stewardship (*khalifa*), understood as engendering a right sense of responsibility for the Earth. This is linked with two other key ideas in Islam, namely, *tawhid* (unity) and *akhirah* (accountability). The word for Earth, *arn*, occurs 485 times in the Quran. The term *masakin* describes the dwelling of all creatures, including human beings. The Earth is named as the beginning and end of human life, and the intimate relationship between humankind and the Earth sets up an appropriate response of respect and care, based on the ultimate divine ownership of the Earth. The emphasis on *taqwa* (or best provision for the Earth stemming from fear of its divine owner) during the festivals that mark the end of hajj—the annual pilgrimage to Mecca—also speaks of careful responsibility for the Earth. There are specific instructions not to be wasteful at harvest time (Quran 6:41), reminiscent of the Hebrew proverbial traditions. Some Islamic scholars are strongly critical of the global domination of the Western view of science and its materialistic forms of knowledge; they call for an Islamic science that retains a sense of nature as sacred while also insisting on a strong sense of the transcendence of God as Creator. Yet according to the Quran the main purpose of humankind is to act as a vicegerent on Earth (Quran 2:30), so that the way humans are related to the natural world is bound up with this primary sense of stewardship.

Practical Wisdom in Other Traditions

The development of practical wisdom represents another lens through which it is possible to consider the wisdom traditions. In those traditions encompassing Western values, practical wisdom can be distinguished from more theoretical wisdom that is concerned with how to think appropriately about the relationships between God, humanity, and creation, even though, as indicated above, there are strong practical implications. Practical wisdom, or *prudence* in classic traditions, is concerned with deliberation, judgment, and action, and in this sense cannot be separated from ethics. In the Aristotelian tradition, prudence or practical wisdom is the correct discernment of a particular course of action, a way of expressing a particular virtue. Practical wisdom can also be named as a virtue, or habit of mind that is oriented toward excellence. That excellence is not simply about what is good for the individual, but about the common public good or what is good for the community as a whole.

It is here that the Western traditions can find common ground with Asian traditions. For Confucius, for example, the cultivation of a moral sense has a high priority, and those that sought to acquire morality had to fit into the patterns found in the universe, leading to a peaceful, flourishing society. Confucian thinkers also affirm the role of the "heart and mind" in making decisions. The term they use for this (*in*) contained the cognitive and the emotional faculties as well as the moral sense. Christian theology has tended to separate these two functions. For example, Thomas Aquinas (c. 1225–1274) distinguished the intellectual virtues of understanding (*scientia*) and wisdom from the theological virtues of faith, hope, and charity. He strongly believed in the unity of virtues, however, so that wisdom was necessarily rooted in charity; the close connection between wisdom and compassion also resonates strongly with Buddhist wisdom.

Confucian wisdom, like that in the Abrahamic traditions, is oriented toward the good, not just of the individual but also of society as a whole. All traditions argue for a purgation of forms of selfish behavior or self-seeking as being the antithesis of wisdom. Neo-Confucian traditions also stress the importance of practice, so that knowledge without action fails to lead to progress in the moral life, including a particular emphasis on daily practice. This is an important ingredient of sustainability, for without due attention to patient implementation of good practice, all more theoretical calls for sustainability will fail to become concrete. For neo-Confucian thinkers, there was a grand design for individuals, families, and society: moral self-cultivation was the way to bring human needs into harmony with the natural world and nature's capacity for producing goods. Traditional Abrahamic faiths also adhere to belief in an ordered universe, but it was one that more often than not placed humanity as ruler of the natural world, hence the strong tradition of stewardship in Islam. There is rather less sense of finding harmony with nature than of becoming masters of it for human benefit.

Wisdom as a Virtue for Sustainable Living

The wisdom traditions remind us of the paramount importance of looking to our own human attitudes and dispositions. While for Abrahamic wisdom, the source of such insight ultimately comes from God, neo-Confucian wisdom reinforces the holistic nature of such a task. In other words, it is not just about the individual journey, but about our relationship to others and to the natural world. For those following the neo-Confucian tradition, this amounts to an expression of "the Way." For Jewish writers, such an orientation is impossible without reference to the Torah. For Christian writers, such an orientation is impossible

without reference to Christ, who is also the Way, the Truth, and the Life—and one might also say Wisdom incarnate. For Muslim writers, Muhammad provides the pattern for right human living according to wisdom.

A rather different way of perceiving wisdom takes its cues from practices that may be found in African proverbial wisdom traditions. These traditions also share some common ground with indigenous religious traditions. Arguably, those who have pressed for an ecological wisdom more often than not mean that which is, by its very nature, against any form of hierarchy or elitism that seems to persist in the Abrahamic faiths, even though there are strands within it that subvert such tendencies. The African proverbial tradition of wisdom is intuitive, relies on oral transmission, is focused on benefits for the group, and is shared in common with others through daily practices.

Wisdom may therefore be thought of as being grounded both in an understanding of the divine (for those traditions that adhere to belief in God) and as emerging from consideration of the natural world, or an ecological wisdom. In as much as wisdom connects very disparate religious traditions, it can be fruitful as a basis for discussion leading to a global religious ethic of sustainability.

Celia DEANE-DRUMMOND
University of Chester

FURTHER READING

Barton, Stephen C. (Ed.). (1999). *Where shall wisdom be found? Wisdom in the Bible, the church and the contemporary world.* Edinburgh, U.K.: T & T Clark.

Brown, Warren S. (Ed.). (2000). *Understanding wisdom: Sources, science and society.* Philadelphia: Templeton Foundation Press.

Chryssavgis, John. (2001). Sophia: The wisdom of God: Sophiology, theology and ecology. *Diakonia, 34*(1), 5–19.

Deane-Drummond, Celia. (2000). *Creation through wisdom: Theology and the new biology.* Edinburgh, U.K.: T & T Clark.

Deane-Drummond, Celia. (2006). *Wonder and wisdom: Conversations in science, spirituality and theology.* London: Darton Longman and Todd.

Deane-Drummond, Celia. (2008). *Eco-theology.* London: Darton Longman and Todd.

Habel, Norman C., & Wurst, Shirley. (Eds.). (2001). *The Earth story in wisdom traditions: The Earth Bible, Vol. 3.* Sheffield, U.K.: Sheffield Academic Press.

Wise Use Movement

The wise use movement, which began in the western United States in the 1980s, opposes restrictive environmental regulations on land use. In addition to people with economic ties to the land, this movement attracts those who support private property rights, resist government regulation, and oppose environmentalism in general. Many of this movement's goals were accomplished during the administration of former U.S. president George W. Bush.

The phrase "wise use," first attributed to Gifford Pinchot, the first chief of the U.S. Forest Service (in office 1905–1910), is currently used to describe the movement, which started in the western United States in the 1980s, of those who challenge environmental regulations as restricting the wise use of land and natural resources. "Wise use," "multiple use," or "sequential use" is the terminology in Australia, while in Canada, the term "share" is promoted. Wise use principles are also seen in those advocating sustainable development and/or free market environmentalism (Doyle 2000). The term "family values" is often invoked, linking it with other conservative movements in the U.S. This contemporary usage of the term "wise use" is attributed to Ron Arnold of the Center for the Defense of Free Enterprise (CDFE), a key figure and former Sierra Club activist, who is notorious in the environmental community for statements such as "We are sick to death of environmentalism and so we will destroy it. We will not allow our right to own property and use nature's resources for the benefit of mankind to be stripped from us by a bunch of eco-facists" (Boston Globe 1992). Despite this type of antipathy, many associated groups pose as environmental groups or advocates of sustainability, hoping to influence public opinion, as in this quote from a policy report of the Cato Institute, a major player in the movement: "Free markets have done much better than governments at providing safety, fairness, economic security, and environmental sustainability" (Henderson 2008).

Arnold is the author of several influential books such as *Trashing the Economy: How Runaway Environmentalism is Wrecking America* (1998), co-authored with Alan Gottlieb, president of the CDFE, whose 1989 book, *The Wise Use Agenda*, was an articulation of the movement's goals. Gottlieb's other publications tend to be about the rights of gun owners, which helps illustrate the range of people involved in the wise use movement: ranchers, farmers, loggers, hunters, off-road-vehicle owners and outdoor sports enthusiasts, as well as commercial interests such as land developers, chemical and agribusiness, and resource extractive industries such as mining, oil, coal and natural gas companies, all of whom oppose government regulation based on environmental concerns. Ironically, many of these same advocates benefit from U.S federal subsidies and reduced cost access to federal lands for their activities.

The movement also attracts those who have no particular ties to the lands/waters in question, but who champion private property rights, resist government regulation in general, and oppose environmentalism for a variety of ideological reasons from libertarianism and free market capitalism to claims that it is pagan and a new religion. Some opponents of the wise use movement counter by pointing out its connections with Reverend Sun Myung Moon's Unification Church (Helvarg 1994). Court suits against acts such as the Clean Air Act and the Endangered Species Act are a common tactic, and the movement is well funded by extractive industry monies. In addition to lawsuits, some in the movement have made explicit verbal and physical threats—such as leaving dead animals with notes—against park rangers, forest service employees, and environmentalists (Lunsford 1997). Another tactic is to promote round-table, consensus-based decision making to ensure that wise use interests are represented and get equal time. No consensus is then reached without major concessions toward industry interests, and often agreements are seen to be nonbinding.

Most of the twenty-five goals of the Wise Use Agenda, including opening up national parks to snowmobiles, removing species from the endangered species list, and opening up vast acres of public lands to mining, energy development, logging, and grazing, were achieved under the administration of former U.S. president George W. Bush. The Agenda was taken as a blueprint by many key agency heads, such as the former secretary of the interior Gale Norton, who all had wise use ties. Norton and others in the Bush administration began her career at the Mountain States Legal Foundation, also associated with former president Ronald Reagan's interior secretary James Watt, which described itself as the "litigation arm of Wise Use" (Helvarg 1994).

Wise use organizations often have green-sounding names to mask their industry ties: Greenspirit for a Sustainable Future (which advocates nuclear energy and clearcut logging, billing itself as "sensible environmentalism)" should not be confused with GreenSpirit, a U.K.-based creation spirituality group); and the Heartland Institute comprises climate-change skeptics. A number of groups are now seemingly defunct, such as the Environmental Conservation Organization and the National Wetlands Coalition (both founded by developers opposed to wetlands protection), as well as the Evergreen Foundation and the British Columbia Forest Alliance (both with forestry / logging industry ties). A great deal of overlap exists between wise use and groups dedicated to "free enterprise" and "liberty," such as the Cato Institute or the Acton Institute of Religion and Liberty, and with conservative religious organizations that oppose mainstream environmentalism, such as the Interfaith Council on Environmental Stewardship/Cornwall Alliance, a movement with ties to fundamentalism. The latter are illustrative of groups who do raise the need for environmental concern, but downplay or refute species loss and climate change, and who seek to promote voluntary stewardship, arguing that a free market will provide the best incentive for preserving environmental quality because it will be motivated by self-interest.

Laurel D. KEARNS
Drew Theological School and University

FURTHER READING

Arnold, Ron, & Gottlieb, Alan. (1998). *Trashing the economy: How runaway environmentalism is wrecking America.* Center for the Defense of Free Enterprise, Bellevue, WA: Free Enterprise Press.

Boston Globe. (1992, 13 January). New, militant anti-environmentalists fight to return nature to a back seat. Retrieved August 17, 2009, from http://www.exxonsecrets.org/html/orgfactsheet.php?id=23

Doyle, Timothy. (2000). *Green power: The environment movement in Australia.* Sydney: University of New South Wales Press.

Gerlach, Luther P. (1999). The structure of social movements: Environmental activism and its opponents. In Jo Freeman & Victoria Johnson Lanham (Eds.), *Waves of protest: Social movements since the sixties* (pp. 85–97). Lanham, MD: Rowman and Littlefield Publishers.

Gottlieb, Alan M. (1989). The Wise Use Agenda: The citizen's policy guide to environmental resource issues: A Task Force Report. Center for the Defense of Free Enterprise, Bellevue, WA: Free Enterprise Press.

Helvarg, David. (1994). *The war against the greens: The "wise-use" movement, the New Right, and the browning of America.* San Francisco: Sierra Club Books.

Hess, Karl, Jr. (1996). Wising up to the wise use movement. In Philip D. Brick & R. McGreggor Cawley (Eds.), *A wolf in the garden: The land rights movement and the new environmental debate* (pp. 161–184). Lanham, MD: Rowman and Littlefield Publishers.

Henderson, David R. (2008, November/December). Are we ailing from too much deregulation? Cato Policy Report. Retrieved June 16, 2009, from https://www.cato.org/pubs/policy_report/v30n6/cpr30n6-1.html

Kearns, Laurel, & Keller, Catherine. (Eds.). (2007). *EcoSpirit: Religions and philosophies for the Earth.* New York: Fordham Press.

Lunsford, Jonn. (1997). Dangerous territory: The attack on citizen participation and the environmental movement. Retrieved June 16, 2009, from http://www.westernstatescenter.org/publications/danger.html

World Bank

The World Bank is an international financial institution concerned with a host of issues at the heart of sustainable development—from environmental and agricultural concerns to the values, ethics, and faith traditions that mobilize around environmental and human development concerns. The World Bank serves as a source of financial and technical assistance to developing countries around the world. It offers loans and grants to support investment in many areas, including environmental and natural resource management.

The World Bank is an international financial institution governed by 185 member states and comprised of the International Bank for Reconstruction and Development (IBRD) and the International Development Association (IDA). The World Bank is concerned with a whole host of issues at the heart of sustainable development—from environmental and agricultural concerns to social and human development and the values, ethics, and faith traditions that mobilize around environmental and human development concerns. Current global crises, such as the energy crisis, concerns about climate change, and agricultural and food shortages, are issues of great concern for the World Bank, and the World Bank is mobilizing its resources to catalyze international cooperation on these issues.

The World Bank is a massive and complex institution, and much has been written about its history and evolution. The international community created the World Bank with the goal of rebuilding Europe after World War II. Since its inception, it has adapted and moved through many stages, with presidents of the institution and regional and country leaders guiding it through various evolutions. The mission of the World Bank—"Our Dream is a World Free of Poverty"—is displayed at its entrance, but the means and style of reaching the goal have changed. Today's World

Bank is driven by a holistic view of development, which has evolved through self-conscious reflection on the World Bank's sometimes rocky history and the critique of its critics and partners. Country-level assistance strategies are at the core of the World Bank's work, and it also serves as a think tank on development and global poverty issues.

At the Bank, development no longer means only higher gross domestic products and better economic performance; it also is concerned with the well-being of countries. Development progress is measured by a wide range of benchmarks, including the United Nations' Millennium Development Goals (MDGs), adopted in 2000 by the international community as a common framework for action and a way to track progress on fundamental development goals.

While historically perceived negatively by some for what seemed to be a "one size fits all" approach to economic development, the Bank recently has moved to better understand the "spirit" of sustainability in its work with faith leaders and institutions on development issues. In the 1990s it began to explore ways in which faith and development are connected. The Bank recognized that that some of the best experts on development and poverty eradication are religious leaders living and working in poor communities, where strong ties, local expertise and longevity, and moral authority give them special insight, understanding, and remarkable channels for social service provision. The World Bank's work with faith leaders has included sponsoring an interfaith meeting on AIDS in India in 2004; participating in a two-year structured dialogue on development and poverty issues with the International Monetary Fund (IMF) and the World Council of Churches (WCC); bringing together U.S. Evangelical Christian leaders with Moroccan Muslim leaders to talk about climate change; and working with East Asian countries on environmental and conservation concerns. The dialogue with religious leaders and institutions continues today, grounded in empirical analytical research and with efforts to include faith leaders and institutions in the work of the World Bank.

Marisa B. VAN SAANEN
Yale Law School

FURTHER READING

Marshall, Katherine, & Van Saanen, Marisa. (2007). Development and faith: Where mind, heart, and soul work together. Washington, DC: World Bank.

Marshall, Katherine. (2008). The World Bank: From reconstruction to development to equity. New York: Routledge.

The World Bank. (2009). Development dialogue on values and ethics. Retrieved March 25, 2009, from http://go.worldbank.org/HH5UDBBLZ0

THE END IS NIGH . . . PLANT A TREE

World leaders quoted by mainstream media at the September 2009 United Nations meeting on climate change used blunt and unsparing language to paint a dire picture about the fate of the Earth: "We are the very last generation that can take action," said President Nicolas Sarkozy of France. "If things go business as usual, we will not live," stated President Mohamed Nasheed of the Maldives. Oscar Arias Sánchez, president of Costa Rica, depicted the conference itself as "taking place on the brink of a precipice." Martin Palmer and Victoria Finlay, the authors of Faith in Conservation, *describe the long tradition of using scriptural language that evokes end-times or the apocalypse as a tool to foster awareness of crises such as global climate change and the destruction of tropical forests. The book, published by the World Bank in partnership with the Alliance of Religions and Conservations (ARC), challenges stereotypes about world religions and the World Bank itself.*

Imagine you are busy planting a tree, and someone rushes up to say that the Messiah has come and the end of the world is nigh. What do you do? The advice given by the rabbis in a traditional Jewish story is that you first finish planting the tree, and only then do you go and see whether the news is true. The Islamic tradition has a similar story, which reminds followers that if they happen to be carrying a palm cutting in their hand when the Day of Judgment takes place, they should not forget to plant the cutting.

There is a tension in the environmental world between those who wish to tell us that the end is nigh and those who want to encourage us to plant trees for the future. In 1992, for example, we were all told, in any number of press statements before the event, that the Earth Summit held in Rio de Janeiro was "the world's last chance to save itself." And indeed many major reports emerging from environmental bodies paint a picture of terrifying, impending destruction—in a sincere desire to shock people into action.

. . . Such groups often fall back on the vivid language of biblical or Vedic (Hindu) accounts of the end of the world—apocalyptic imagery that encapsulates our deepest terrors more graphically than any chart or statistical breakdown can ever do. Powerfully emotive language is used to make us feel that we are sitting on the edge—that in the words of the Jewish story above, the end of the world is nigh.

Source: Martin Palmer, with Victoria Finlay. (2003). *Faith in Conservation. Washington, DC: World Bank.* Retrieved October 2, 2009, from http://www.arcworld.org/news.asp?pageID=9

World Religions and Ecology

Since many values that shape attitudes toward nature come from religion, it has a unique opportunity to inspire and mobilize people to more sustainable living. Religions need to recover human–Earth relations as well as human–human and human–divine relations. World religions are now involved in shaping ecological worldviews and ethics and linking these values to policy.

The environmental crisis is one that is well documented in its various interlocking manifestations of industrial pollution, resource depletion, and population explosion. The urgency of the problems is manifold; namely, the essential ingredients for human survival, especially water supplies and agricultural land, are being threatened across the planet by population and consumption pressures. With the collapse of fishing industries and with increasing soil erosion and farmland loss, serious questions are being raised about the ability of the human community to feed its own offspring. Moreover, the widespread destruction of species and the unrelenting loss of habitat continue to accelerate. Climate change threatens to undermine efforts to reverse these trends and to move toward a sustainable future for humans and nature.

Clearly, religions need to be involved with the development of a more comprehensive worldview and ethics to ground movements toward sustainability. Whether from an anthropocentric or a biocentric perspective, more adequate environmental values need to be formulated and linked to areas of public policy. Scholars of religion, religious leaders, and laity can be key players in this articulation process. Moreover, there are calls from other concerned parties to participate in a broader alliance to halt the loss of species, topsoil, and natural resources as well as to mitigate the effects of climate change. This alliance of scholars, religious leaders, and activists is creating common ground for dialogue and creative partnership in envisioning and implementing long-range, sustainable solutions to some of our most pressing environmental problems. This is critical because the attitudes and values that shape people's concepts of nature come primarily from religious worldviews and ethical practices. The moral imperative and value systems of religions are indispensable in mobilizing the sensibilities of people toward preserving the environment for future generations.

One of the greatest challenges to contemporary religions, then, is how to respond to the environmental crisis that some believe has been perpetuated by the enormous inroads of materialism and secularization in contemporary societies, especially those societies arising in or influenced by the modern West. Others such as the medieval historian Lynn White Jr. have suggested that the emphasis in Judaism and Christianity on the transcendence of God above nature and the dominion of humans over nature has led to a devaluation of the natural world and a subsequent destruction of its resources for utilitarian ends. While the particulars of this argument have been vehemently debated, it is increasingly clear that the environmental crisis presents a serious challenge to the world's religions. This is especially true because many of these religions have traditionally been concerned with the paths of personal salvation that frequently emphasize otherworldly goals and reject this world as corrupting.

How to adapt religious teachings to this task of revaluing nature so as to prevent its destruction marks a significant new phase in religious thought. Indeed, as the historian of religions Thomas Berry has so aptly pointed out, what is necessary is a comprehensive reevaluation of human–Earth relations if the human is to continue as a viable species on an increasingly degraded planet. In addition to major economic and political changes, this will require adopting worldviews that differ from those which have captured the imagination of contemporary industrialized societies that view nature as a commodity to be exploited. How to utilize the insights of the world's religions is a task of formidable urgency. Indeed, the formulation of a new ecological theology and environmental ethics is already emerging from within several of the world's religions. Ten Harvard volumes on world religions and ecology give examples of this as does the Forum on Religion and Ecology website (www.yale.edu/religionandecology; Tucker and Grim 1997–2004). Clearly each of the world's religious traditions has something to contribute to these discussions.

Broader Ethical Contexts

The focus of ethics in the world's religions has been largely human centered. Humane treatment of humans is often seen not only as an end in itself but also as a means to eternal reward. While some have critiqued this anthropocentric perspective of world religions as rather narrow in light of environmental degradation and the loss of species, it is nonetheless important to recall that this perspective has also helped to promote major movements for social justice and human rights.

While social justice is an ongoing and unfinished effort of engagement, the challenge for the religions is also to enlarge their ethical concerns to include the more-than-human world. Social justice and environmental integrity are now being seen as part of a continuum. For some decades, environmental philosophers have been developing the field of environmental ethics that can now provide enormous resources for the world's religions in considering how to expand their ethical focus. Emerging biocentric, zoocentric, and ecocentric ethics are attentive to life forms, animal species, and ecosystems respectively within a planetary context. A new "systems ethics" of part and whole, local and global, will assist the religions in articulating a more comprehensive form of environmental ethics from within their traditions. This is a major part of the development of religions into a dialogue with the sustainability movement. Humans are seeking an ethics to respond not only to suicide and homicide but also biocide and ecocide.

Thus religions are gradually moving from exclusively anthropocentric ethics to ecocentric ethics and even to anthropocosmic ethics. The latter is a term used by Tu Weiming (1985) to describe the vibrant interaction of heaven, Earth, and humans in a Confucian worldview. In this context, humans complete the natural and cosmic world and become participants in the dynamic transformative life processes. This idea can extend ethics to apply to the land-species-human-planet-universe continuum. This is a fruitful yet still emerging path toward a comprehensive ethics for sustainability. This path has various challenges, including within the religions themselves.

Problems and Promise

It must be recognized that the world's religions, through intolerance and exclusive claims to truth, have often contributed to tensions between peoples, including wars or forced conversion. It is also the case that religions have often been at the forefront of reforms, such as in the labor movement, in immigration law, in justice for the poor and oppressed. The movements of nonviolence for freedom in India and for integration in the United States were inspired by religious principles and lead by religious leaders.

In addition, the emerging dialogue on religion and ecology also acknowledges that in seeking long-term environmental sustainability, there is clearly a disjunction between contemporary problems regarding the environment and traditional religions as resources. The religious traditions are not equipped to supply specific guidance in dealing with complex issues such as climate change, desertification, or deforestation. At the same time, one recognizes that certain orientations and values from the world's religions may not only be useful but even indispensable for a more comprehensive cosmological orientation and environmental ethics.

The disjunction of traditional religious resources and modern environmental problems in their varied cultural contexts needs to be highlighted so that new conjunctions can be identified. Scholars of religion and ecology acknowledge that religious scriptures and commentaries were written in an earlier age with a different audience in mind. Similarly, many of the myths and rituals of the world's religions were developed in earlier historical contexts, frequently agricultural, while the art and symbols were created within worldviews very different from our own. Likewise, the ethics and morality of the world's religions respond primarily to anthropocentric perspectives regarding the importance of human–human relations, and the spirituality and soteriology (a theology dealing with salvation) are formulated in relation to theological perspectives of enhancing divine–human relations.

Despite these historical and cultural contingencies, there are particular religious attitudes and practices as well as common ethical values that can be identified for broadening and deepening environmental perspectives. Thus we affirm the actual and potential contribution of religious ideas for informing and inspiring ecological theology, environmental ethics, and grassroots activism. Religions are now reclaiming and reconstructing these powerful religious attitudes, practices, and values toward re-conceiving mutually enhancing human–Earth relations. Careful methodological reflection is needed in considering how to bring forward in coherent and convincing ways the resources of religious traditions in response to particular aspects of our current environmental crisis. It entails a self-reflexive yet creative approach to retrieving and reclaiming texts and traditions, reevaluating and reexamining what will be most efficacious, and thus restoring and reconstructing religious traditions in a creative postmodern world. All of this involves a major effort to evoke the power and potential of religious traditions to function even more effectively as sources of spiritual inspiration, moral transformation, and sustainable communities in the midst of the environmental challenges faced by the Earth community.

That is because world religions are being recognized in their great variety as more than simply a belief in a transcendent deity or a means to an afterlife. Rather, religions are seen as providing a broad orientation to the cosmos and the human roles in it. Attitudes toward nature thus have been significantly, although not exclusively, shaped by religious views for millennia in cultures around the globe.

In this context then, religions can be understood in their largest sense as a means whereby humans, recognizing the limitations of phenomenal reality, undertake specific practices to effect self-transformation and community cohesion within a cosmological context. Religions thus refer to those cosmological stories, symbol systems, ritual practices, ethical norms, historical processes, and institutional structures that transmit a view of the human as embedded in a world of meaning and responsibility, transformation and celebration. Religions connect humans with a divine presence or numinous force. They bond human communities and they assist in forging intimate relations with the broader Earth community. In summary, religions link humans to the larger matrix of indeterminacy and mystery from which life arises, unfolds, and flourishes.

Certain distinctions need to be made here between the particularized expressions of religion identified with institutional or denominational forms of religion and those broader worldviews that animate such expressions. By worldviews, we mean those ways of knowing, embedded in symbols and stories, which find lived expressions consciously and unconsciously, in the life of particular cultures. In this sense, worldviews arise from and are formed by human interactions with natural systems or ecologies. Consequently, one of the principal concerns of religions in many communities is to describe in story form the emergence of the local geography as a realm of the sacred. Worldviews generate rituals and ethics, ways of acting, which guide human behavior in personal, communal, and ecological exchanges. The exploration of worldviews as they are both constructed and lived by religious communities is critical because it is here that we discover formative attitudes regarding nature, habitat, and our place in the world. In the contemporary period, to resituate human–Earth relations in a more balanced mode will require both a reevaluation of sustainable worldviews and a formulation of viable environmental ethics.

A culture's worldviews are contained in religious cosmologies and expressed through rituals and symbols. Religious cosmologies describe the experience of origination and change in relation to the natural world. Religious rituals and symbols arise out of cosmologies and are grounded in the dynamics of nature. They provide rich resources for encouraging spiritual and ethical transformation in human life. This is true for example in Buddhism, which sees change in nature and the cosmos as a potential source of suffering for the human. Confucianism and Daoism, on the other hand, affirm nature's changes as the source of the Dao. In addition, the death–rebirth cycle of nature serves as an inspiring mirror for human life, especially in the Western monotheistic traditions of Judaism, Christianity, and Islam. All religions translate natural cycles into rich tapestries of interpretive meanings that encourage humans to move beyond tragedy, suffering, and despair. Human struggles expressed in religious symbolism find their way into a culture's art, music, and literature. By linking human life and patterns of nature, religions have provided a meaningful orientation to life's continuity as well as to human diminishment and death. In addition, religions have helped to celebrate the gifts of nature that sustain life, such as air, water, and food.

In short, religions have been significant catalysts for humans in coping with change and transcending suffering while at the same time grounding humans in nature's rhythms and Earth's abundance. The creative tensions between humans seeking to transcend this world and yearning to be embedded in this world are part of the dynamics of world religions. Christianity, for example, holds the promise of salvation in the next life as well as celebration of the incarnation of Christ as a human in the world. Similarly, Hinduism holds up a goal of *moksha*—liberation from the world of samsara (repeated cycles of birth, misery, and death)—while also highlighting the ideal of Krishna acting in the world.

This realization of creative tensions leads to a more balanced understanding of the possibilities and limitations of religions regarding environmental concerns. Many religions retain otherworldly orientations toward personal salvation outside this world; at the same time they can and have fostered commitments to social justice, peace, and ecological integrity in the world. A key component that has been missing in much environmental discourse is how to identify and tap into the cosmologies, symbols, rituals, and ethics that inspire changes of attitudes and actions for creating a sustainable future within this world. Historically, religions have contributed to social change in areas such as the abolitionist and civil rights movements. There are new alliances emerging now that are joining social justice with environmental justice.

In alignment with these "ecojustice" concerns, religions can encourage values and ethics of reverence, respect, restraint, redistribution, responsibility, and renewal for formulating a broader environmental ethics that includes humans, ecosystems, and other species. With the help of religions, humans are now advocating for a reverence for the Earth and its long evolutionary unfolding, respect for the myriad species that share the planet with us, restraint in the use of natural resources on which all life depends, equitable distribution of wealth, recognition of responsibility of humans for the continuity of life into future generations, and renewal of the energies for the great work of building a sustainable Earth community. These are the virtues for sustainability, which the world's religions can contribute.

The Call and the Response

There have been various appeals from environmental groups and from scientists and parliamentarians for religious leaders to respond to the environmental crisis. In addition, there has been a striking growth in monographs and journal articles in the area of religion and ecology. Several national and international meetings have also been held on this subject. For example, environmental groups such as World Wildlife Fund (WWF) have sponsored interreligious meetings, such as the one in Assisi, Italy, in 1986. The United Nations Environment Programme (UNEP) in North America has established an annual Environmental Sabbath and distributes thousands of packets of materials for uses in congregations throughout the United States and Canada. The Parliament of World Religions, held in Chicago in 1993 and attended by some 8,000 people from all over the globe, issued a Global Ethics of Cooperation of Religions on Human and Environmental Issues statement. The subsequent Parliaments held in Capetown, South Africa, and Barcelona, Spain, had the environment as a major theme. The Parliament planned for December 2009 in Melbourne also has a major focus on the role of religions in contributing to a sustainable future. International meetings on the environment such as the Global Forum of Spiritual and Parliamentary Leaders have been held in Oxford (1988), Moscow (1990), Rio (1992), and Kyoto (1993). These included religious leaders such as the Dalai Lama as well as diplomats and heads of state, including Mikhail Gorbachev, who hosted the Moscow conference and attended the Kyoto conference to set up an International Green Cross for environmental emergencies. Moreover, the Tehran Seminar on Environment, Culture, and Religion was held in Iran in June 2001, and one on "Environment, Peace and the Dialogue of Civilizations and Cultures" was organized in May 2005. Both of these were sponsored by the Iranian government with the support of the United Nations Environment Programme. Gorbachev has held several Earth Dialogues on "Globalization: Is Ethics the Missing Link?" held in Lyon, France

(2002), in Barcelona (2004), and in Brisbane, Australia (2006). The International Union for the Conservation of Nature (IUCN), a global environmental network headquartered in Switzerland, organized the first panel on "Spirituality and Conservation" at the World Conservation Congress in Barcelona in 2009. Since 1995, the spiritual leader of Orthodox Christians, Ecumenical Patriarch Bartholomew, has convened symposia on "Religion, Science, and the Environment" that focused on water issues in Europe, the Amazon, and the Arctic. Similarly, the Alliance of Religions and Conservation (ARC) based in England has been convening conferences and activating religious communities. In the United States, the National Religious Partnership for the Environment (NRP) has organized the Jewish and Christian communities on this issue. The time is thus propitious for encouraging the contributions of particular religions to solving the ecological crisis, especially by developing a more comprehensive environmental ethics to ground movements focused on sustainability.

Harvard Conference Series

It is within this context that a series of conferences on "Religions of the World and Ecology" were held at Harvard University from 1996 to 1998. The goals of these conferences were to provide a forum for reflection on:

- reconceptualizing attitudes toward nature by examining perceptions from religions of the world with attention to the complexity of history and culture;
- contributing to the articulation of functional environmental ethics grounded in religious traditions and inspired by broad ecological perspectives;
- identifying the institutional grounds for systematic changes to be effected within religious traditions for long-term transformation regarding attitudes toward the environment;
- stimulating the interest and concern of religious leaders as well as students and professors of religion in seminaries and universities;
- linking the transformative efforts of the world's religions to larger international movements working toward global ethics for a humane and sustainable future;
- joining with those in ecological sciences, public policy, economics, business, health, education, and media who wish to reinvent industrial society.

The conferences, then, had several key objectives, namely, to stimulate original research and thinking, to encourage further educational initiatives, and to promote outreach in relation to religious institutions and policy centers with common concerns for environmental awareness and preservation. One of the primary goals of these conferences was to link scholars and theologians in the academic study of religion with the people, proposals, and institutions that are implementing ethical change with regard to the environmental crisis. More than 800 scholars and environmentalists participated in the series creating an important network for future cooperative endeavors.

Forum on Religion and Ecology

The Forum on Religion and Ecology has as a primary goal the establishment of common ground between disciplines for long-term solutions to environmental problems. Religions come as partners to these discussions, not as definitive agents of moral authority. To create a broader context for reformulating effective public policies on environmental issues it will be helpful to set in motion three ongoing strategies. The first strategy is to place disciplines in dialogue with one another, respecting the different approaches and examining the values embedded in each discipline. The second strategy is to create the grounds for disciplines to work in partnership toward common environmental concerns by recognizing the need for interdisciplinary cooperation on issues of sustainability. The third strategy is to form alliances for future collaborative projects that will mobilize both the ethical transformations and practical policies needed for reinventing industrial society on a sustainable basis.

A strong sense is emerging that religions can play a role in helping to create a sustainable future. Yet religious voices need to be thoughtfully nuanced and morally persuasive so as to be effective in further discussions with both religious adherents and policymakers. The issues facing us in this environmental crisis are too pressing and complex for mere rhetorical appeals or simplistic answers. Thus, the Forum focuses on three strategic objectives and has established a major website at Yale (www.yale.edu/religionandecology) to promote these objectives:

- research to ground a field of study in religion and ecology within the academic context, including the publication of books and articles as well as the journal, *Worldviews*, and bibliographies with annotation of all the literature in English on this topic;
- education to publish and disseminate curricular materials for classroom use and to make available information that will be useful to religious communities, seminaries, and other related institutions;
- outreach to foster the religious voice in policy issues concerning the environment and to encourage the

intersection of religion with key sectors such as science, education, economics, and public policy.

Clearly religions have a central role in the formulation of worldviews that orient us to the natural world and the articulation of ethics that guide human behavior. The size and complexity of the problems faced require collaborative efforts both among the religions and in dialogue with other key domains of human endeavor. Religions, thus, need to be in conversation with sectors—science, economics, education, and public policy—that have addressed environmental issues. Environmental changes will be motivated by these disciplines in very specific ways; namely, economic incentives will be central to adequate distribution of resources, scientific analysis will be critical to understanding nature's economy, educational awareness will be indispensable to creating modes of sustainable life, public policy recommendations will be invaluable in shaping national and international priorities, and moral and spiritual values will be crucial for the transformations required for life in an ecological age.

Thomas Berry has observed that assisting humans by degrading the natural world cannot lead to a sustainable community. The only sustainable community is one that fits the human economy into the ever-renewing economy of the planet. The human system, in its every aspect, is a subsystem of the Earth system, whether we are speaking of economics or physical well-being or rules of law. In essence, human flourishing and planetary prosperity are intimately linked.

Mary Evelyn TUCKER
Yale University

FURTHER READING

Berry, Thomas. (1999). *The great work*. New York: Random House.

Berry, Thomas (Author), & Tucker, Mary Evelyn. (Ed.). (2006). *Evening thoughts: Reflecting on Earth as sacred community*. San Francisco: Sierra Club Books.

Chapple, Christopher Key. (Ed.). (2009). *Worldviews: Global religions, culture and ecology*. Leiden, The Netherlands: Brill.

Foltz, Richard. (2000). *Worldviews, religion and the environment: A global anthology*. Florence, KY: Wadsworth.

Forum on religion and ecology. (2009, February 9). Retrieved April 27, 2009, from www.yale.edu/religionandecology

Tu Wei-ming. (1985). *Confucian thought: Selfhood as creative transformation*. Albany: State University of New York.

Tucker, Mary Evelyn, & Grim, John. (Series Eds.). (1997–2004). *World Religions and Ecology* (10 vols.): *Judaism, Christianity, Islam, Hinduism, Jainism, Buddhism, Confucianism, Daoism, Indigenous Traditions,* and *Shinto* (Shinto in Japanese). Cambridge, MA: Center for the Study of World Religions, Harvard Divinity School. (Distributed by Harvard University Press).

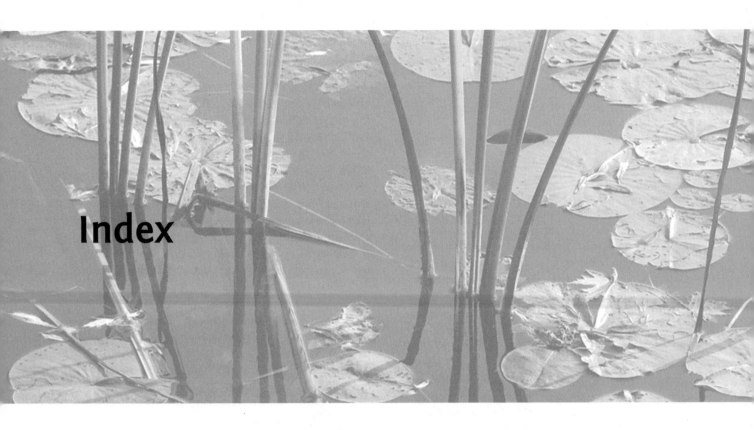

Index

Bold entries and page numbers denote encyclopedia articles.

Bold entries and page numbers denote encyclopedia articles.

Bold entries and page numbers denote encyclopedia articles.

Bold entries and page numbers denote encyclopedia articles.

Future, 182–183
imagining, 182–183
sustainable, 183
Future generations, 142, **184–185**, 255, 381

G

Gaard, Greta, 173
Gad tribes, 256
GAD. *See* Gender and development
Gaia and God: An Ecofeminist Theology of Earth Healing, 64
Gaia, 187–188, 289, 299
Gaia theory, 187, 188
See also Lovelock, James
Galileo Galilei, 83
Gandhi, Mohandas, 17, 197, 200, 250, 270, 293–294, 310–311, 333, 370, 409, 410
Ganesh(a), 17, 40
Ganges River, 199, 422–423
Gardening, 10, 34, 207, 230, 365
Gaura Devi, 52
Gautama, Siddhartha, 332
See also Buddha
Gebara, Ivone, 64, 173, 269
Geirey diley, 256
Gender, 4, 6, 40, 93, 102, 161
Gender and development (GAD), 171–172
Genesis Farm, 26
Genesis, 54, 59, 64, 87, 89, 110, 111, 154, 179, 254, 256, 260, 264, 278, 312, 347, 354, 355, 372, 374, 391, 411, 425
Genetic diversity, 37–38
Genetic engineering, 14
Genocide, 121
Geocentrism, 35
German Green Party, 195, 310
Germany, 24, 310, 409
environmental law, 326
Ghana, 40, 210–211
Global awareness, 171, 190, 388
Global citizenship, 116, 189
Global climate change, 39, 73, 266, 281,
Global communications, 190
Global Ecovillage Network, 146
Global Energy Management Committee, 279
Global Environment Facility, 277
Global ethics, 162, **164–165**
Global Ethics of Cooperation of Religions on Human and Environmental Issues statement, 442
Global Forum of Spiritual and Parliamentary Leaders, 442
Global Greens Conference, 293
Global Greens Network, 195

Global North, 238
Global South, 107, 161, 430
Global trade, 189, 325
Global warming, 68, 69, 141, 179, 180, 202, 232, 310
from fossil fuels, 152
Global Warming Petition, 180
Globalization, 4, 139, **189–190**, 215, 387, 430
Glocalization, 306
Gnostic sects, 409
God After Darwin: A Theology of Evolution, 64
God as Creator, 192, 260, 433
God, 29, 89, 166–167, **191–192**, 229, 259, 328, 433
gendered language about, xxiv
Goldschmidt, Walter, 12–13
Good Water Neighbors programs, 252
Goodall, Jane, 15
Goodness, 76, 95, 104, 260, 368
See also **Sin and Evil**
Gorbachev, Mikhail, 115, 442
Gore, Al, 123, 187, 281, 426
See also An Inconvenient Truth
Grace Pilgrimage to the Peace Village of San José de Apartadó, 304
Graham, Mary, 222
Grand Canyon National Park, 430
Grassroots movements, 277
Grassroots organizing, 310
Gray wolves, loss of protection under the Endangered Species Act, 16
See also Species, depletion and extinction; Yellowstone National Park
Grazing, and land degradation, 38
See also **Agriculture**
Great Ape Project, 16
Great Britain. *See* United Kingdom
The Great Hunt, 429
Great Learning (Daxue), 75, 77
Great Mystery, 226
Great Plains, 13, 39
Great Power, 226
The Great Work, 64, 351
Greece, 210
Greed, 200, 333, 350, 414
Greek Sophists, 166
Green An Hui, 292
Green Belt Movement, 193, 261, 291, 310
Green Cross International, 116
Green for All, 291
Green fundamentalism, 178
Green Gulch Farm, 48
Green Muslims, 292
See also **Islam**
Green parties, 194–195, 310

Bold entries and page numbers denote encyclopedia articles.

Bold entries and page numbers denote encyclopedia articles.

Bold entries and page numbers denote encyclopedia articles.

Bold entries and page numbers denote encyclopedia articles.

Bold entries and page numbers denote encyclopedia articles.